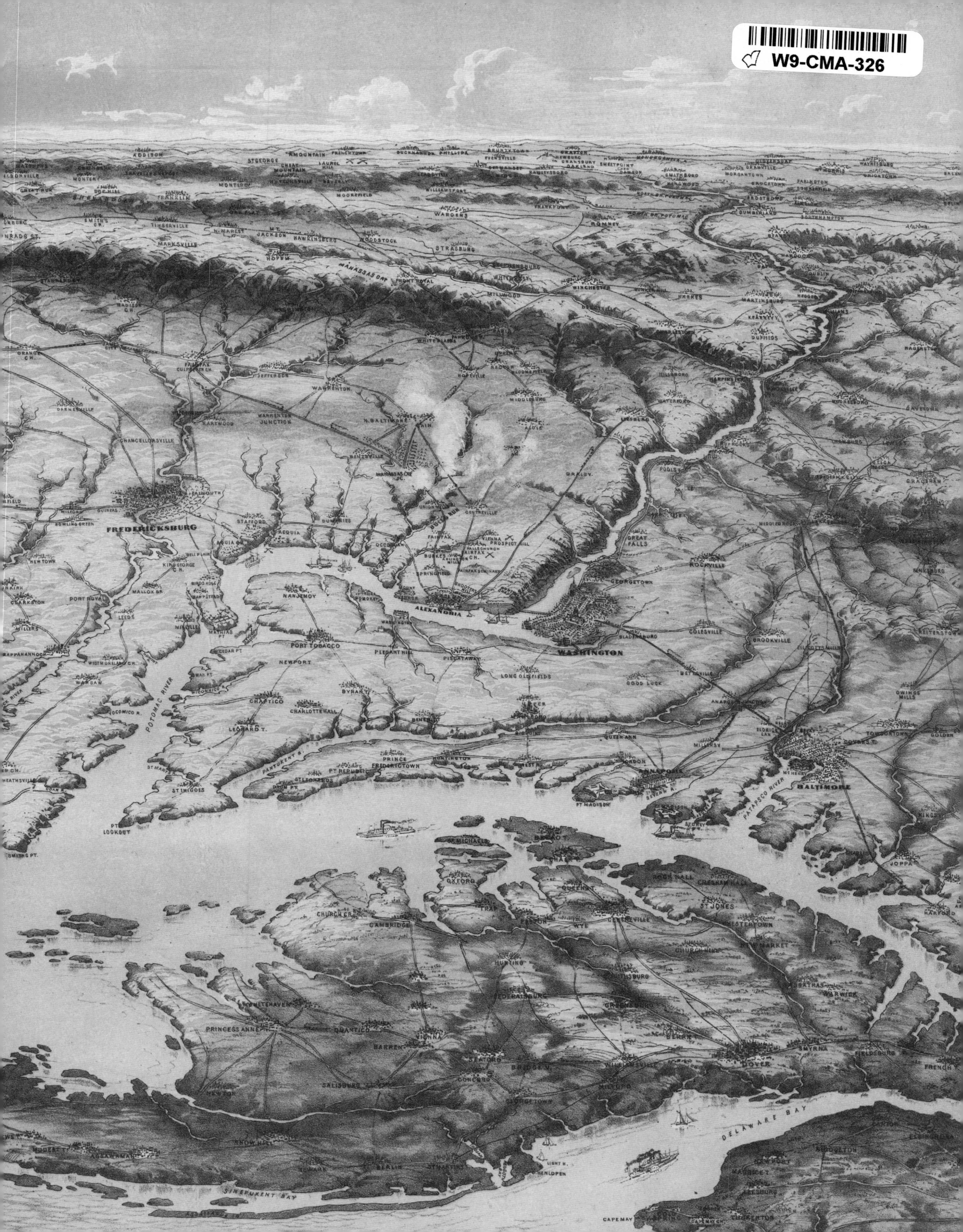
W9-CMA-326
FREDERICKSBURG
ALEXANDRIA
WASHINGTON
BALTIMORE
ANNAPOLIS
GEORGETOWN
ROCKVILLE
CHANCELLORSVILLE
WARRENTON
WARRENTON JUNCTION
MANASSAS JC.
CENTREVILLE
FAIRFAX C.H.
WINCHESTER
FRONT ROYAL
MANASSAS GAP
STRASBURG
WOODSTOCK
MARTINSBURG
CUMBERLAND
ROMNEY
GREAT FALLS
POTOMAC RIVER
PATAPSCO RIVER
PORT TOBACCO
PORT ROYAL
CHAPTICO
LEONARD T.
PRINCE FREDERICKTOWN
PT. LOOKOUT
ST. MICHAELS
OXFORD
CAMBRIDGE
EASTON
CENTREVILLE
CHESTERTOWN
DOVER
SMYRNA
MILFORD
GEORGETOWN
SALISBURY
PRINCESS ANNE
VIENNA
SNOW HILL
BERLIN
DELAWARE BAY
SINEPUXENT BAY
CAPE MAY
LONG OLD FIELDS
GOOD LUCK
COLESVILLE
BROOKVILLE
WARSAW
NEWPORT
CHARLOTTE HALL
BOWLING GREEN
KING GEORGE C.H.
STAFFORD
AQUIA
DUMFRIES
JOPPA
HARFORD
WARWICK
FREDERICK CITY
MIDDLEBURG
LEESBURG
HARPERS FERRY
HILLSBORO
MOOREFIELD
MARKSVILLE
ADDISON

ATLAS OF THE CIVIL WAR

ATLAS OF THE CIVIL WAR

A COMPREHENSIVE GUIDE TO THE TACTICS AND TERRAIN OF BATTLE

EDITED BY NEIL KAGAN TEXT BY STEPHEN G. HYSLOP
INTRODUCTION BY HARRIS J. ANDREWS

NATIONAL GEOGRAPHIC
WASHINGTON, D.C.

Contents

About This Book 6

Introduction: Mapping the War 8

Appendix:
Battles of the Civil War 246
Struggle for the Heartland 248
The Seat of War 249

Illustration Credits 250

Additional Reading 251

Contributors 251

Index 252

Acknowledgments and Staff Credits 256

Endpapers: Bird's-eye-view map of the seat of war—Virginia, Maryland, and the District of Columbia—drawn by John Bachmann, circa 1861.

Page 1: Men of the 8th Kansas Infantry strike a warlike pose in 1862.

Pages 2–3: Captain Guy V. Henry's Battery B of the 1st U.S. Artillery awaits inspection on Morris Island, South Carolina, during the siege of Charleston in 1863.

This page: Five photographs symbolize pivotal events that gripped the nation: the fall of Fort Sumter, 1861; the massive federal buildup of the Peninsula campaign, 1862; the bodies of Union dead after the Battle of Gettysburg, 1863; Fort Sedgwick during the siege of Petersburg, 1864; four condemned conspirators executed for their role in the assassination of Abraham Lincoln, 1865.

Chapter One

1861
A Change of Flags
Prelude to War
16

The War at a Glance 18

Two Americas 20
Slavery 22
Escape to Freedom 24
The Election of 1860 26
Secession 28
Fall of Fort Sumter 30
The Seat of War 32

Anaconda Plan 34
Fort Monroe 36

Bull Run 38
Showdown at Bull Run 40

Belmont 42

Port Royal 44

Chapter Two

1862
War on a Grand Scale
46

The War at a Glance 48

Shiloh 50
The Road to Fort Donelson 52
Johnston Strikes First 54
Advance and Retreat 56

Coastal War 58
Securing the Potomac 60
Burnside's Expedition in Heavy Seas 62
A Duel Between Ironclads 64
Capture of New Orleans 66

Shenandoah Valley 68
Jackson's Map of the Valley 70
Hard Lesson at Kernstown 72
Jackson Divides and Conquers at Port Republic 74

The Peninsula 76
Forward to Richmond 78
Chaos at Seven Pines 80
Lee Takes Command 82
Stuart's Ride Around McClellan 84
Decision at Gaines's Mill 86
Retreat to Malvern Hill 88

Second Bull Run 90
The Battle of Cedar Mountain 92
Jackson's Stand: The Railroad Embankment 94
Longstreet's Attack: Federal Retreat 96

Antietam 98
Battle of South Mountain 100
The Bloodiest Day 102
Hooker's Attack at Dawn 104
To Dunker Church and the Sunken Road 106
Attack at Burnside Bridge 108
Aftermath 110

Corinth 112

Perryville 114

Fredericksburg 116
Slaughter at Marye's Heights 118

CHAPTER THREE

1863 A HARVEST OF DEATH 120

THE WAR AT A GLANCE 122

STONES RIVER 124

VICKSBURG 126
GRANT'S BAYOU EXPERIMENTS 128
CLOSING THE TRAP 130
THE SIEGE OF VICKSBURG 132

CHANCELLORSVILLE 134
JACKSON STRIKES 136
A KNOCKOUT BLOW TO HOOKER 138

GETTYSBURG 140
THE BATTLE ERUPTS 142
DAY TWO: LITTLE ROUND TOP 144
WHEAT FIELD & PEACH ORCHARD 146
DAY THREE: PICKETT'S CHARGE 148
THE LAST FULL MEASURE 150

CHARLESTON 152

CHICKAMAUGA 154
CLASH AT THE RIVER OF BLOOD 156
FEDERAL FIASCO 158

CHATTANOOGA 160
LOOKOUT MOUNTAIN AND MISSIONARY RIDGE 162

KNOXVILLE 164

CHAPTER FOUR

1864 THE LANDSCAPE OF WAR 166

THE WAR AT A GLANCE 168

RED RIVER 170

INTO THE WILDERNESS 172
ACROSS THE RAPIDAN 174
THE BURNING WOODS 176
SPOTSYLVANIA 178
DESCENT TO COLD HARBOR 180
THE THRUST TO PETERSBURG 182
EXPLOSION AT PETERSBURG 184

SHENANDOAH VALLEY 186
ADVANCE ON WASHINGTON 188
THE BATTLE OF WINCHESTER 190
THE BATTLE OF CEDAR CREEK 192

SINKING THE ALABAMA 194

MOBILE BAY 196

CAMPAIGN FOR ATLANTA 198
STOPPED AT NEW HOPE CHURCH 200
KENNESAW MOUNTAIN 202
BATTLES FOR ATLANTA 204

THE ELECTION OF 1864 206

TENNESSEE CAMPAIGN 208
THE BATTLE OF NASHVILLE 210

SHERMAN'S MARCH 212
PRISONERS OF WAR 214
SURRENDER OF SAVANNAH 216

CHAPTER FIVE

1865 TIGHTENING THE NOOSE 218

THE WAR AT A GLANCE 220

FORT FISHER 222

CONQUERING THE CAROLINAS 224
THE BATTLE OF BENTONVILLE 226

THE LAST BATTLES 228
FIVE FORKS 230
THE FALL OF RICHMOND 232
PURSUIT TO APPOMATTOX 234
SURRENDER AT APPOMATTOX 236

AFTERMATH 238
ASSASSINATION OF LINCOLN 240
LINCOLN'S LONG RIDE HOME 242
RECONSTRUCTION 244

About This Book

After the battle of Antietam, the bloodiest day in American history, a topographical map was prepared by a Union officer to document one of the war's most notorious killing grounds. Immortalized in ink and paper, we see the desperate fighting at the Cornfield, Dunker Church, the Sunken Road, and Burnside Bridge. In the bottom left-hand corner of the map there is a handwritten note: *Obtained from Washington & presented to Gen. R. E. Lee by J. E. B. Stuart.*

In *Atlas of the Civil War*, this map (found on page 103) and 87 other rare period maps, together with 34 newly created maps from National Geographic's award-winning cartographers, tell the complete story of the Civil War from slavery to the assassination of Lincoln.

This project began with the goal of creating a one-of-a-kind atlas that not only traces the movement of troops and the action on the fields of battle, but also tells the human side of war. We designed *Atlas of the Civil War* with a large page format so the maps would be easy to read, and then we set out to carefully blend the maps with documentary photographs, battle sketches, and the compelling stories of soldiers and civilians.

After poring over thousands of images and artifacts including 2,840 maps and charts and 76 atlases and sketchbooks from the collections of the Library of Congress, the Virginia Historical Society, and the Library of Virginia, we selected the most informative maps, many of which are published here for the first time. We added 5 time lines, 18 biographies, and 11 orders of battle and then carefully numbered key places referenced in the text. When all of these features are viewed together, *Atlas of the Civil War* provides a surprisingly intimate view of the Civil War.

—Neil Kagan, *Editor*

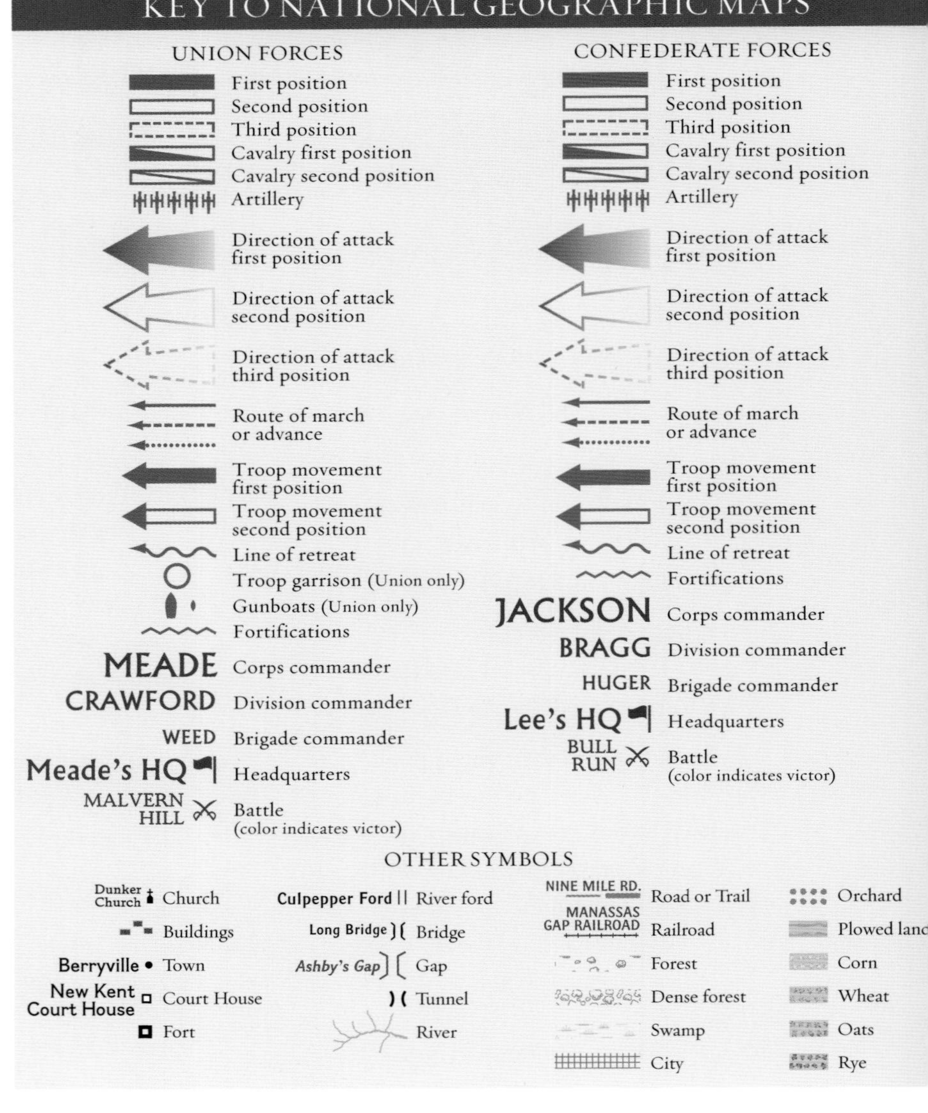

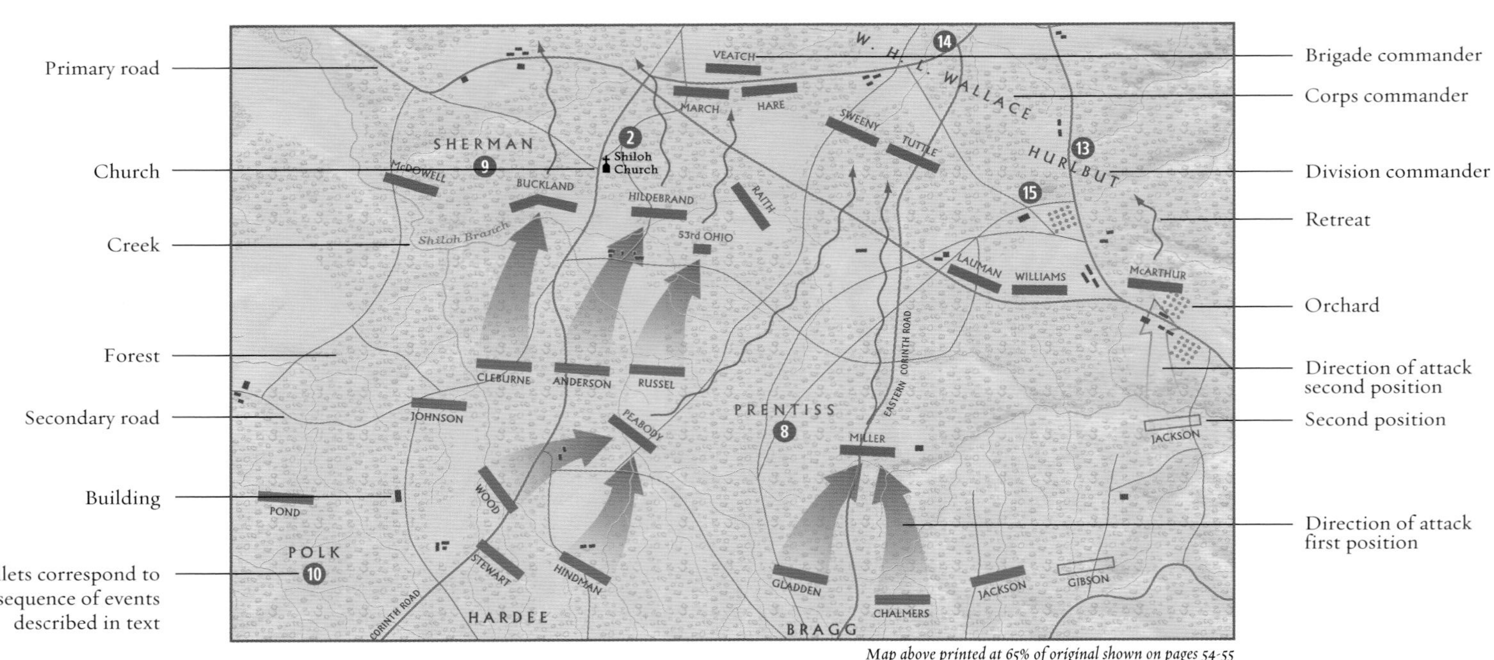

Map above printed at 65% of original shown on pages 54-55

How to Read the National Geographic Maps

This detail from the National Geographic map opposite, showing developments in the opening hours of the Battle of Shiloh, uses symbols defined in the key at top. Squiggly blue lines, for example, show Federal brigades retreating under fierce Confederate pressure. The same key applies to all National Geographic campaign and battle maps that appear in this book. The numbers on those and other maps in this volume indicate the locations of military units, ships, fortifications, rivers, towns, or other places mentioned in the accompanying text.

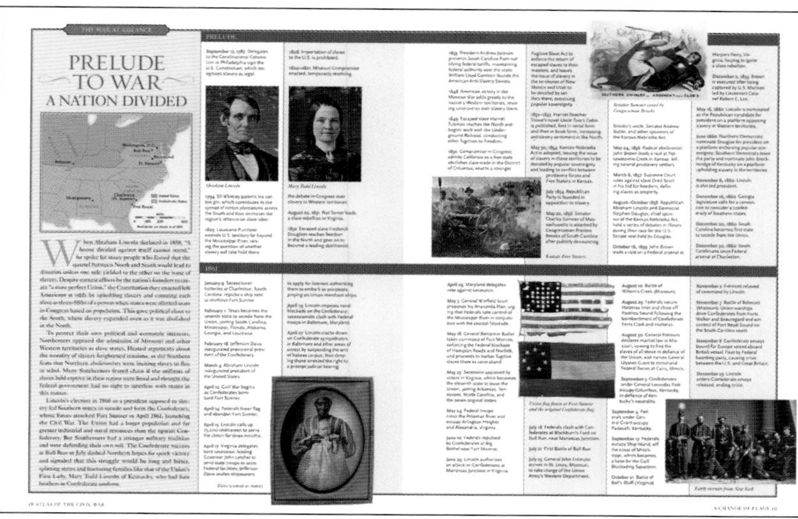

Chapter Introductions / The War at a Glance

Atlas of the Civil War is divided into five chapters, each beginning with a double-page documentary photograph followed by an illustrated time line—The War at a Glance. In the example at left, the map locates all major events, campaigns, and battles that occur during the time frame covered in chapter 1. The text offers an overview of these key events and the time line includes social, political, and military milestones. The time line illustrations, left, give us a glimpse of life during the Civil War, including rare prewar daguerreotypes of Abraham and Mary Todd Lincoln, Free Staters in Kansas, the caning of Senator Charles Sumner, a white child in the care of a slave, the torn flag that flew over Fort Sumter, the new Confederate flag, and Zouave recruits excited about the war—optimistic about a quick resolution.

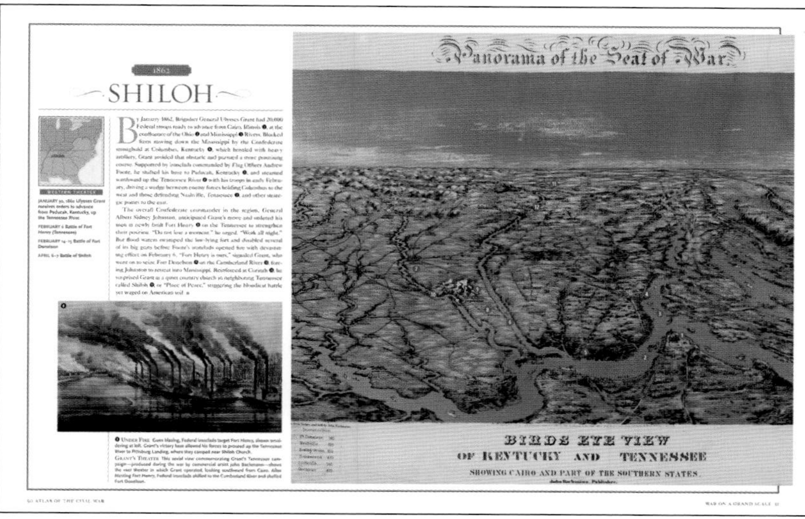

Battles and Campaigns / Bird's-Eye-View Maps

Battles and military campaigns appear chronologically within each chapter. The opening spread of each new battle or campaign (for example, the 1862 Battle of Shiloh, at left) contains a small locator map highlighting where the action takes place—in the Eastern theater of war, the Western theater of war, or as part of the blockade. Below the map a chronology lists important dates. The text provides a detailed account of events and places that are carefully numbered and keyed to the accompanying maps. Rare Civil War–era bird's-eye views, inspired by the view from hot air balloons, appear throughout the book. The panorama shown at left offers a surprisingly accurate view of the topography looking south from Cairo, Illinois, and showing parts of Illinois, Missouri, Kentucky, Tennessee, and Arkansas. Smoke over Fort Donelson, Tennessee, and the presence of gunboats on the Cumberland River depict the fort's fall to Union forces in February 1862.

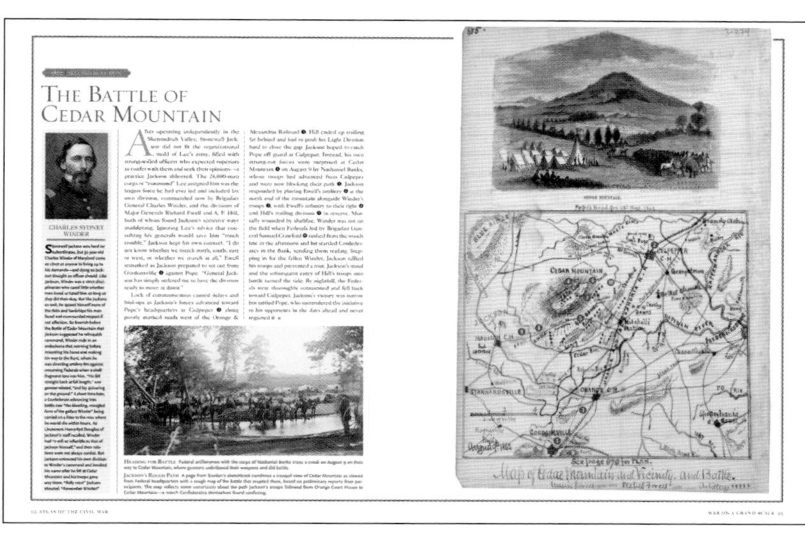

Civil War–Era Maps / Biographies

Eighty-eight archival maps—like this one of the Battle of Cedar Mountain, left, by soldier, artist, and cartographer Robert Knox Sneden, a private in the 40th New York Infantry—appear throughout the book and provide a firsthand view of how Civil War–era cartographers recorded the tactics and terrain of battle. This rare collection has been carefully selected to represent a wide range of period maps including campaign maps carried onto the field of battle, battle maps commissioned by Union and Confederate generals to record troop positions for posterity, newspaper and commercial maps created to inform the general public, bird's-eye-view maps (above), and political and cartoon maps. Eighteen biographies compliment the maps and highlight the human side of war. These biographies explore little-known facts about Civil War personalities like Charles Winder, left, one of Stonewall Jackson's most trusted subordinates killed by a shell at the Battle of Cedar Mountain.

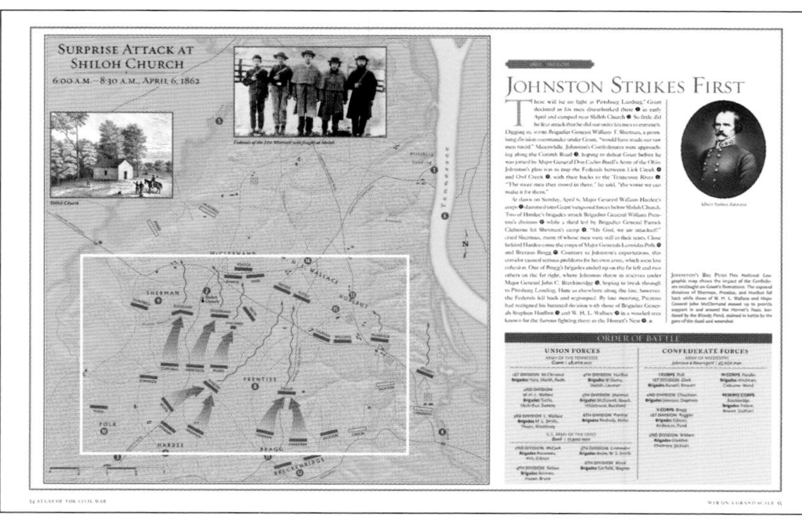

National Geographic Maps / Order of Battle Boxes

Specially created maps focus on the war's great themes, troop movements, and key moments in major battles. National Geographic cartographers utilized state-of-the-art digital mapping data to create the backgrounds for many of the new maps, resulting in a very accurate representation of Civil War terrain and topographical details. The strategic movements of troops and action sequences have been reviewed by Civil War historian Harris Andrews. In the example at left, we see the Battle of Shiloh unfolding. Period photographs and art have been embedded in the new maps to lend a sense of time and place. Use the key (opposite) to understand all 34 National Geographic maps that appear throughout this volume. Order of Battle boxes show how Federal and Confederate troops matched up during 11 major battles.

INTRODUCTION

MAPPING THE WAR

On May 20, 1863, a few weeks after the Battle of Chancellorsville, Captain Jedediah Hotchkiss, Confederate cartographer and engineer, wrote his brother from headquarters of the Army of Northern Virginia's Second Corps, near Fredericksburg. "I have been too amiss in writing to you and replying to your last letter," he began, "but I was very much engaged, as you may well suppose, during the many days of fighting that we have had." Hotchkiss was too modest to mention the part he played in the Confederate victory at Chancellorsville, where his celebrated corps commander, General Thomas "Stonewall" Jackson, used information he provided on the densely wooded Wilderness and roads traversing it to plot a daring march on May 2 around the flank of the opposing army. Jackson's surprise attack that afternoon devastated the Federals but cost him his life when he was shot accidentally by Confederates while conducting a reconnaissance late in the day. Jackson's chief engineer, Captain James Boswell, perished in that same incident.

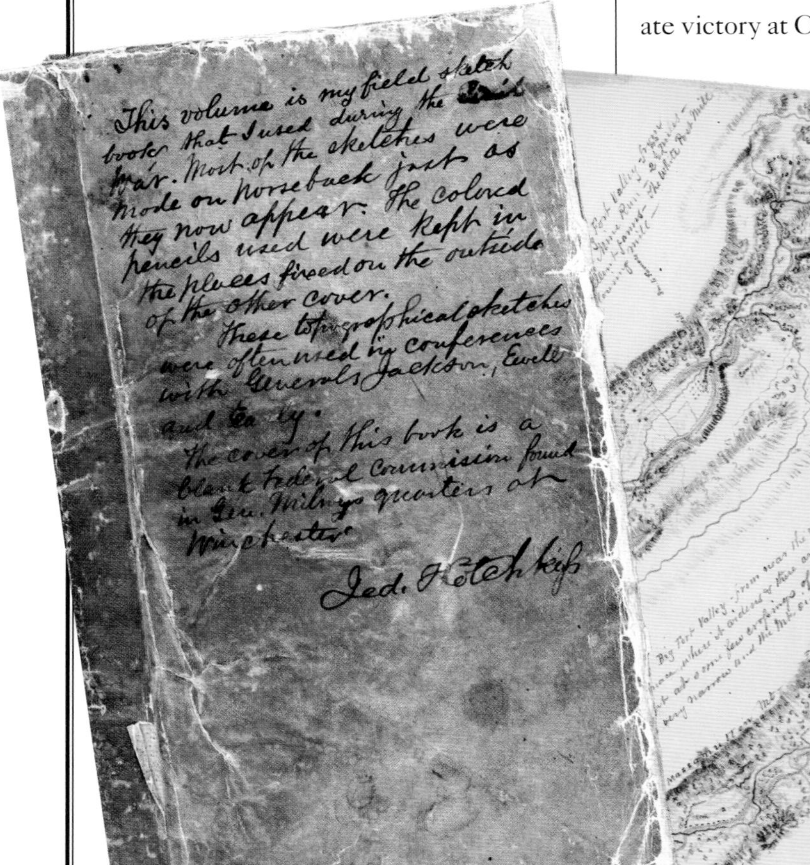

POCKET COMPANION **This field sketchbook was used by Captain Jedediah Hotchkiss during his service as a topographical engineer with the Army of Northern Virginia's Second Corps between 1862 and 1865. Hotchkiss used colored pencils to sketch roads, terrain, troop movements, and houses and later translated his field sketches into comprehensive maps.**

Hotchkiss had little time to reflect on those losses, for he received orders "the very day the fight ended to make a map of the battlefield, involving a necessity for a survey of the Wilderness, in which we fought." Returning to headquarters to complete that map—which would be of much use to Confederate officers during the Battle of the Wilderness a year later—he found the placed sadly changed. "Though spared myself it seems lonely and desolate here," he wrote; "my tent mate and well beloved friend Capt. Boswell was instantly killed and our revered and adored Commander is gone too. . . . The singular but good and great man that directed everything and stamped a peculiar character upon it is no longer at his post and everything wears an altered and lonely look, but such is earth and such are earthly things."

Hotchkiss had served as a Confederate mapmaker since the summer of 1861, but his duties had expanded dramatically when he joined Jackson's staff in Virginia's Shenandoah Valley in March 1862. The young officer was greeted by his new chief with a terse order: "I want you to make me a map of the Valley, from Harper's Ferry to Lexington, showing all the points of offense and defense in those places." The resulting map (see page 71), drawn on coated linen at the scale of 1:80,000, would be used by Jackson to plan and execute his brilliant Valley campaign in the spring and early summer of 1862. It fully displayed Hotchkiss's talent as a cartographer, a discipline that proved vital to military commanders north and south. It also showed the great value of accurate maps in the planning and conducting of military operations. As Jackson and Hotchkiss realized, maps were tools of war as assuredly as were muskets, cannon, and ironclad warships, allowing generals who would otherwise be limited to the narrow parameters of their own vision and the subjective reports of scouts, guides, and local citizens to survey and command an entire theater of operations.

The Need for Maps

When the Civil War began, commanders on both sides struggled to find maps to meet their requirements. As yet, cartographers had produced few detailed topographic maps—showing terrain, elevations, roads, and waterways—in regions where fighting might take place. No large-scale topographic maps existed, and only a handful of commercial maps showed road or rail networks accurately. Government mapping services such as the U.S. Corps of Topographical Engineers and the Treasury Department's Coast Survey produced fine maps of the nation's Western territories and coastal waters, but their prewar output was small and left large areas uncharted. Some state legislatures contracted with private cartographers to produce maps of their states. Generally drawn at a scale of five miles to the inch, they included Fielding Lucas's 1852 map of Maryland and a map of Virginia published by Ludwig von Buchholtz in Richmond in 1859. Unfortunately, the initial surveys for many of these had been conducted decades earlier and much of the information was out of date. Other state maps were commissioned by businessmen and entrepreneurs to attract investors, including Claudius Crozet's 1848 chart of Virginia showing internal improvements such as canals and railroads and the locations of coal and other mineral resources.

The decade leading up to the Civil War had witnessed an explosion of railroad construction, particularly in the North. Mapmakers created and published railroad maps (see pages 20–21) to encourage investment and advertise new rail lines to potential customers. High-quality railroad maps were issued by the New York publishing house of Joseph H. Colton. As the war progressed, Colton's "Railroad and Township Map" series proved particularly valuable to Federal military planners. Commanders on both sides also made use of county maps, marketed by subscription to local residents in some areas. Generally produced at a scale of one inch to the mile, these large maps were often displayed on walls and showed bodies of water, towns and villages, roads, railroads, mills, commercial structures, and homes, which were frequently marked with the owner's name. That was helpful

Stonewall's Mapmaker New Yorker Jedediah Hotchkiss moved to Virginia's Shenandoah Valley before the Civil War to make his living as a schoolteacher and indulge a passion for touring and mapmaking. Although he disliked the idea of secession, Hotchkiss threw in his lot with his neighbors and volunteered as a cartographer with the Army of Northern Virginia. During the war, he provided his own mapmaking instruments, including this pocket compass, altimeter, and transit (lower left), an instrument that could be used to determine distance.

to officers seeking guidance or assistance in rural areas—where most buildings and some landmarks were known only by the property owner's name—and wartime cartographers like Hotchkiss often identified houses or farms by name on their own maps (see page 75).

In the decades before the war, new printing techniques were introduced that would greatly expedite the production of wartime maps. Printers had traditionally relied on the copperplate, or intaglio, method to reproduce maps and charts. Drawings were transferred in reverse onto a copper plate using a tool that cut a V-shaped channel, which retained ink when the rest of the plate was wiped clean. The plate was then pressed onto paper, producing the image. Although the quality of reproduction was high, the process was time-consuming and costly. By the 1850s, many printers were reproducing maps and other drawings more quickly and economically using lithography, a process in which the original artwork, rendered on specially prepared paper with special ink, was transferred directly onto a plate of smooth, fine-grained limestone that underwent further preparation before it was pressed onto paper. Some printed maps were chromolithographed—a process employing a separate stone plate for each color applied to the image—but others were colored by hand. In printing as in other industries, the North was well ahead of the South by 1861, and Federals used lithography to great advantage to reproduce detailed and accurate military maps in large numbers.

The Union also had a big advantage over the Confederacy in creating maps, for it retained control of existing government mapmaking organizations like the Corps of Topographical Engineers. Established in the early 19th century, the corps's peacetime duties included charting fortifications and mapping the nation's extensive Western territories. With the outbreak of the Civil War, most of its members remained loyal to the Union and were attached to the headquarters of Federal armies, whose commanders prized their services. Some the Union's top generals were trained as topographical engineers, including George Meade and James B. McPherson, who as Ulysses Grant's chief engineer in Tennessee in 1862 oversaw production of a map detailing Grant's triumphant advance from Fort Henry to Fort Donelson (see pages 52–53). While many topographical

FIXING ON CHARLESTON General Quincy Adams Gillmore and members of his staff cluster around a large map at the Union Army's Tenth Corps headquarters on Morris Island, South Carolina, during the siege of Charleston. Federal forces besieging Charleston depended on accurate maps and nautical charts provided by the U.S. Coast Survey and Corps of Topographical Engineers.

engineers received line and staff commissions and were assigned to combat duties, sufficient numbers of trained cartographers remained in that capacity to meet Federal needs. In 1863 the Corps of Topographical Engineers was abolished and its duties were assumed by the Corps of Engineers, whose tasks also included building bridges and fortifications.

The Union also drew skilled cartographers from the U.S. Coast Survey, which produced navigational maps and charts and determined the placement of lighthouses and coastal fortifications. Coast surveyors—civilians who worked with assigned army and navy officers in peacetime—were absorbed into the military during the Civil War and served with fleets that enforced the naval blockade of the Confederacy and with armies operating along the coast or far inland, where their surveying skills proved no less useful.

The Mapmaker's Craft

Most military mapping in the field was done for reconnaissance, or providing commanders with knowledge of what lay beyond their lines. Cavalry patrols, engineers, staff officers, scouts, and topographers fanned out as armies advanced to probe the country and provide sketches and reconnaissance maps. These might be little more than hastily scrawled drawings of a road network or notes on enemy positions, with distances and bearings determined by pacing, guesswork, and a pocket compass. In other cases they might be more elaborate renderings prepared by trained engineers or topographers using more elaborate surveying gear. During William Sherman's Atlanta campaign in 1864, for example, his engineers provided him with a fairly detailed and accurate map of the area around Kennesaw Mountain as battle loomed there (see pages 202–03).

Field surveying was based on triangulation. Working from a measured baseline, surveyors made observations of a distant point at both ends of that line to measure the angle between the baseline and the line of sight. Using trigonometry, they could chart that point, located at the apex of the triangle, and determine its distance from the baseline. Typically, surveyors plotted their observations on a sheet of paper clamped onto a plane table—a small, flat table mounted on a tripod and fitted with a scope or sighting mechanism through which the observer drew a bead on the distant object. A straightedge attached to that mechanism allowed the surveyor to draw the line of sight on paper, compute its

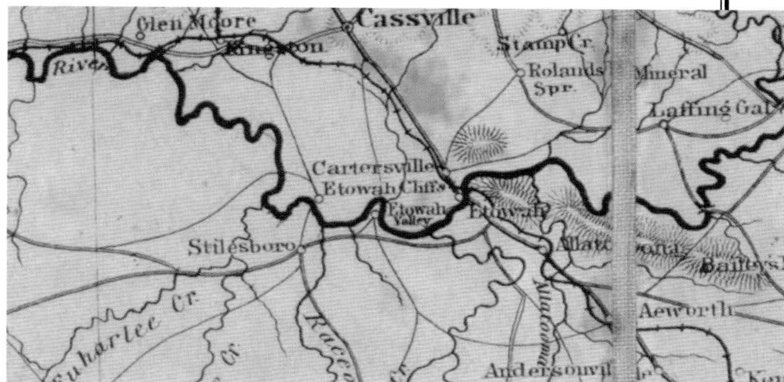

Sherman's Atlas This large, folding map of Northern Alabama and Georgia—shown front and back at top and in detail above—was printed by the Coast Survey Office in 1864 and carried through Georgia by General William T. Sherman, who inscribed his name on the back. It was compiled from various sources, including prewar maps and wartime military reconnaissance. Printed on paper backed by linen, this well-used field map was drawn on a scale of 1:633,600.

angle in relation to the baseline, and complete the triangulation. Other optical surveying instruments used where the situation permitted included transits and theodolites, often mounted on plane tables, allowing more accurate measurements of angle and distance.

Such techniques allowed surveyors to chart a large area from one position or baseline and determine the precise distance to inaccessible points such as enemy forts. Often, however, topographers mapped territory on the move, using a compass to determine direction and counting strides as they walked or rode to compute distance approximately based on the average length of a stride. To measure distance exactly, surveyors used standard 66-foot-long measuring chains made of 100 wrought-iron or steel links or recently patented retractable steel tapes. Unlike distance calculations, accurate measurement of elevation was not considered necessary on most military maps. A rough estimate of the relative elevation of hills and ridgelines and the degree of slope, depicted using parallel lines called hatching, was sufficient. When accurate elevations were necessary, topographers might use an aneroid barometer, or a less precise but less fragile mercury-filled altimeter, to measure gains in elevation as indicated by falling barometric pressure.

McClellan's Topographers **Federal topographical engineers at Yorktown, Virginia, in May 1862 stand beside their main surveying instrument—a plane table with a scope attached, set on a tripod—during General George McClellan's Peninsula campaign.**

Field mapping with cumbersome surveying gear could be a dangerous occupation. In 1862, Coast Survey assistant John W. Donn was assigned to the Army of the Potomac and tasked with mapping the formidable Confederate lines at Yorktown, Virginia. Working with fellow cartographer F. W. Dorr and others, Donn was to "direct the running of short base lines with a steel tape carried by two soldiers in a quick trot," he wrote. "Dorr with a plane table would occupy the ends of the base and rapidly sight the lines of redoubt batteries or breastworks." Knowing just how far away those enemy positions were would aid Federals in assaulting them, but the surveyors themselves became targets. "One unfortunate day," Donn related, a topographical engineer named Wagner was conferring with them around the plane table when Rebels manning a battery a thousand feet away found their range: "The first shell fired, a percussion, struck the tripod and exploding literally blew up the whole group. Dorr escaped with a scratch but Wagner and one of my chainmen were mortally wounded both dying in two days. Three men were killed outright and several slightly wounded. Nothing was left of the plane table, and the sheet was torn in half and sprinkled with Wagner's blood."

The maps military topographers made often revealed the capabilities and plans of their commanders and, if lost or seized, could be of great value to the enemy. Headquarters staffs were always on the lookout for printed maps and field sketchbooks taken from captured or killed enemy officers. And scouting parties were always on the lookout for good civilian maps, particularly when operating in enemy territory. In June 1863, Confederate forces advancing into Pennsylvania were ordered to confiscate all local maps. One Confederate staff officer recalled entering a home in Mercersburg, Pennsylvania: "I found that a citizen of the place had a county map and of course called at the house for it, as these maps had every road laid down and would be of great service to us. Only the females of the family appeared, who flatly refused to let me have the map, or to acknowledge that they had one; so I was obliged to dismount and push by the infuriated ladies." He found the map he was seeking in their sitting room, "hanging on the wall."

After battles were fought, military topographers might be asked to prepare detailed maps to illustrate official reports submitted by field commanders. Commanders at all levels in both armies—army, corps, division, brigade, and regiment—were required to file "after-action" reports, used to determine how they and their forces had performed, correct errors, grant rewards, and in some cases assign blame for defeat. Maps based on those reports delineated troop positions and were often color-coded to distinguish one side from the other or to show the positions of particular units at various times during an engagement, as in an elaborate chart produced after the Battle of Shiloh by Federal topographical engineers (see pages 56–57). The best of these battle maps are not only important historical documents but also fine examples of the mapmaker's art.

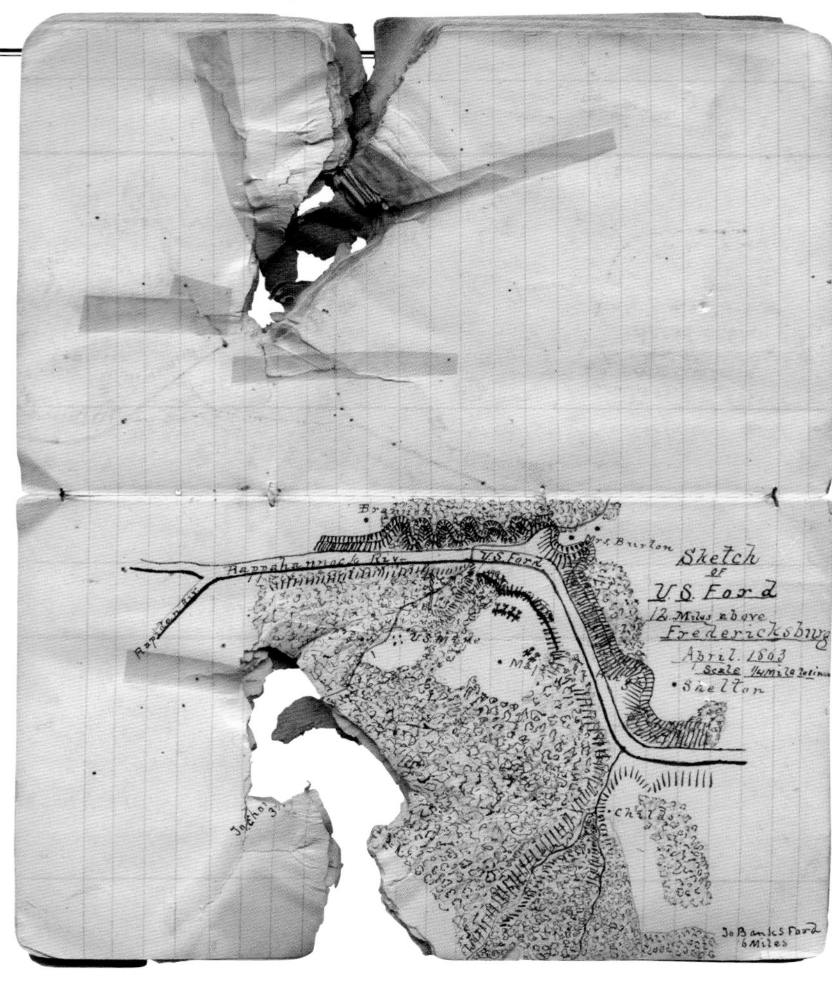

Mapmaker's Relic This bullet-pierced notebook belonging to Confederate Captain James K. Boswell bears graphic witness to the risks taken by front-line engineers and cartographers. Boswell, chief engineer on Stonewall Jackson's staff and a close friend of fellow cartographer Jedediah Hotchkiss, was struck and killed by the same volley that mortally wounded Jackson at Chancellorsville on the night of May 2, 1863.

Military Map Production

All topographers and surveyors carefully recorded their measurements and calculations in notebooks, adding sketches and notes to support their observations. These field notes and sketchbooks were the raw materials of map preparation. Hastily rendered sketch maps might be useful during the heat of battle, but the goal was to produce a finished map of an entire surveyed area. When the pace of operations permitted, cartographers assembled survey notes, sketches, and reconnaissance reports and set about making a finished map, drawn to a specific scale and often using a grid system. Once the map had been completed, it could be used by headquarters or copied for distribution to subordinate commands.

Reconnaissance maps made while an army was campaigning were often traced on fine, coated linen in India ink. Other maps, however, were printed at plants far from the battlefronts and distributed to forces in the field. Equipped with two lithographic presses purchased in 1861, the Coast Survey printed more than 65,000 maps and charts in 1864 alone. Because its wartime operations were not limited to coastal areas, the Coast Survey was able to produce a massive, ten-mile-to-the-inch base map of all the Confederate states east of the Mississippi, from which smaller section maps could easily be produced on demand. For durability and ease in transport, large-scale military maps were often cut into sections and mounted on cloth. Maps could also be lithographed on muslin, producing sturdy, washable, waterproof charts. Some armies found ways of reproducing maps mechanically in the field. The Topographical Department of the Federal Army of the Cumberland, operating in Tennessee and North Georgia, obtained two lithographic presses for map production. Those heavy presses had to remain in a central depot, however, and engineers came up with a portable alternative—a photographic printing apparatus that produced negative, white-on-black "sun prints," which could be distributed on short notice. By 1864, the Army of the Potomac in Virginia had established its own map-reproduction unit using photographic equipment.

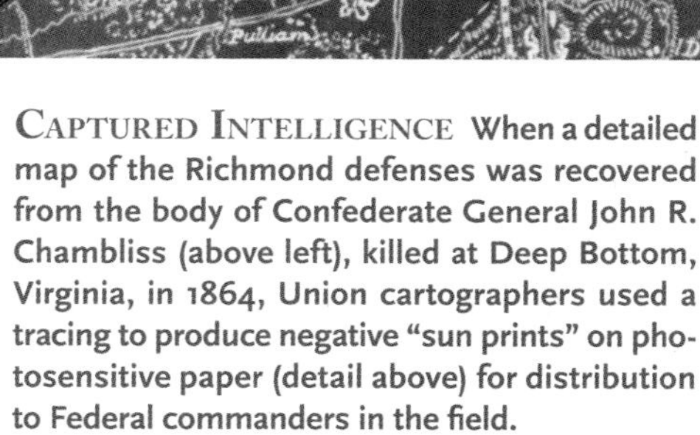

Captured Intelligence When a detailed map of the Richmond defenses was recovered from the body of Confederate General John R. Chambliss (above left), killed at Deep Bottom, Virginia, in 1864, Union cartographers used a tracing to produce negative "sun prints" on photosensitive paper (detail above) for distribution to Federal commanders in the field.

Unlike their Federal counterparts, Confederate authorities had great difficulty supplying their armies with adequate maps. The South was short of qualified mapmakers, surveying equipment, and printing facilities, making the large-scale production of maps nearly impossible. Despite these obstacles, the Confederate Topographical Department in Richmond began surveying embattled Virginia county by county in 1862. Using ink on coated linen, Confederate engineers under Major General Jeremy F. Gilmer prepared maps on a scale of 1:80,000 for most of the counties in eastern and central Virginia. When copies were required, tracings were made by hand from a master copy. Eventually the Topographical Department turned to sun prints to speed up production, but its output lagged far behind that of Federal organizations like the Coast Survey.

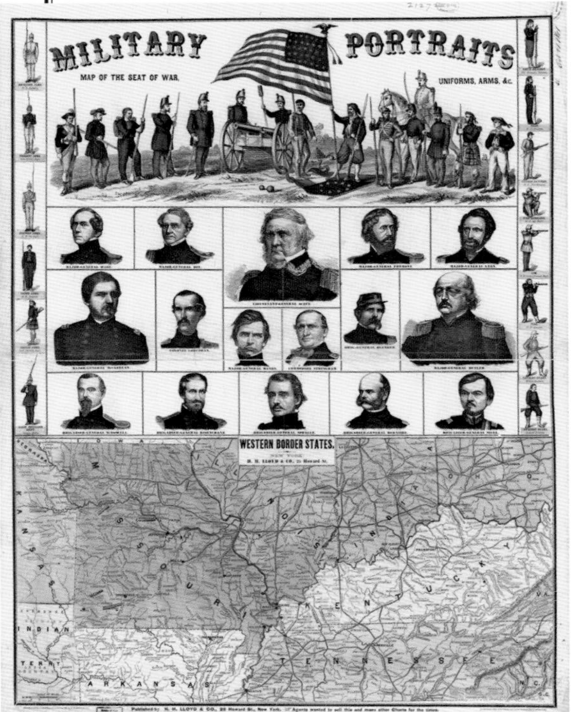

PATRIOTIC CHART This map of Western border states, produced by Edward S. Hall for a Northern audience in 1862, fanned patriotic fervor by including portraits of popular Union generals and illustrations of the uniforms of volunteer militia regiments.

MAPS FOR THE HOME FRONT

Commercial maps allowed civilians on both sides of the conflict to follow the action on far-flung battlefronts, observe changes in the political landscape, and grasp the consequences of strategic decisions. They also served as patriotic propaganda by touting triumphs and showing commanders against the backdrop of their conquests. Thematic maps published on the eve of the Civil War provided insights into the forces that were tearing the nation apart, showing the density of the slave population in the South (see pages 22–23), for example, or the ominous electoral trends in the 1860 presidential race.

During the War, commercial publishers—based largely in the North—produced some thematic or patriotic maps, but most maps were designed to meet the public demand for reliable geographical information about places that few people had ever visited but now dominated the headlines. Hundreds of maps were published portraying contested areas, including Philadelphia publisher M. H. Traubel's *Pocket Map of the Probable Theatre of the War* and James T. Lloyd's *Map of Virginia*, which appeared in several updated editions between 1861 and 1863. Panoramic perspectives, or bird's-eye views, had been produced for centuries, but the popularity of ballooning in the 1800s gave them fresh appeal. During the war, commercial artists like John Bachmann produced bird's-eye views encompassing sprawling operations like the capture of New

UNION STOREHOUSE New York publisher Charles Magnus released this bird's-eye view of Alexandria, Virginia, in 1863. The hand-colored lithograph shows the bustling river port as viewed from the Potomac River. Under Federal occupation, Alexandria became one of the world's largest military supply centers and was guarded by extensive fortifications.

Orleans (see pages 66–67). Although less accurate in scale and detail than conventional maps, these panoramas provided dramatic views of terrain and gave viewers a vivid impression of the obstacles commanders had to overcome. The public's keen geographic curiosity about the war was also met by illustrated newspapers such as the *New York Illustrated News*, *Frank Leslie's Illustrated Newspaper*, and *Harper's Weekly*, which supplemented the latest war news with specially commissioned maps and engravings based on sketches drawn in the field by battlefield artists like Alfred Waud.

Recording the War

After the Civil War, the U.S. War Department assembled a vast collection of wartime maps of all kinds, both Federal and Confederate, that served as the source for numerous published battle maps in histories and atlases. Between 1891 and 1895, the War Department published the monumental *Atlas to Accompany the Official Records of the Union and Confederate Armies*. Union and Confederate wartime maps were reproduced lithographically and issued as a series of 178 color plates. Many of the original maps that the lithographs were based on can be found throughout this volume.

In addition to using official sources, cartographers like Jedediah Hotchkiss used their wartime sketchbooks to produce up-to-date topographical maps for the civilian market. The work of one of the war's most prolific mapmakers, however, went largely unrecognized. Robert Knox Sneden, an artist and architectural draftsman who enlisted in New York in 1861 and served as a quartermaster and cartographer with the Army of the Potomac, was captured by Confederates in Virginia in 1863 and survived confinement at the notorious Andersonville Prison (see page 214). He returned home to Brooklyn in poor health but recuperated, devoting his spare hours to a massive illustrated atlas of the war, filled with hundreds of maps and drawings documenting campaigns he took part in or researched using official sources. Some of his work was published in the landmark history *Battles and Leaders of the Civil War*. But little of what he accomplished was known to the public at the time of his death in 1918 at the Soldier's and Sailor's Home in Bath, New York. "I leave no posterity, but a good war record," he remarked late in life. That remarkable record was not just one of faithful service to the Union in uniform. Throughout the war and for decades thereafter, he documented the conflict in images and words, expanding his original war diary into an epic illustrated memoir. His life's work, rediscovered by the Virginia Historical Society in 1994, ranks as one of the most compelling and comprehensive records of the war compiled by any single participant.

The Civil War had a profound impact on cartographers like Sneden and Hotchkiss, and they in turn did much to shape the conflict as it unfolded and interpret it for posterity. Southerners had the advantage of fighting this war largely on their own soil, but that was offset as the conflict progressed by the superior mapmaking resources of the North. Without the stellar services of Hotchkiss, Stonewall Jackson and Robert E. Lee would have had a harder time resisting Union might. He and other gifted mapmakers contributed substantially to the war as it was being waged, and their surviving maps provide an extraordinary cartographic record that contributes greatly to our understanding of the American Civil War today.

—Harris J. Andrews

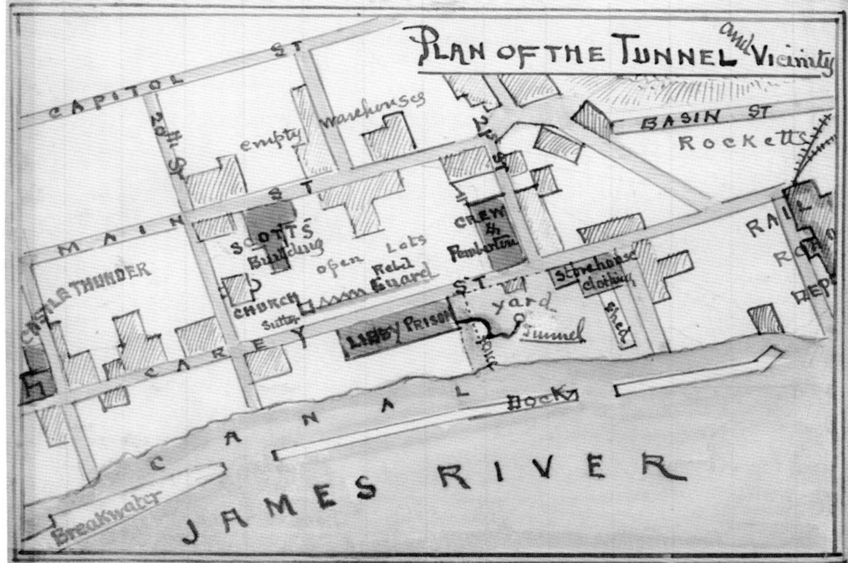
1998 The rush to escape by the Tunnel -
every one wanted to be first - In order to get down the Chimney as well as along the tunnel it was necessary to strip naked - wrap the clothes in a bundle, and push this on before them - As soon as it was seen that a few only could possibly get out before daylight, all rushed for the mouth of the tunnel who could - each man being determined to get out first - The room was now crowded to suffocation all struggling to get in the hole - The strongest men forced their way to the front while the weak ones were roughly pushed aside and jammed up against the walls -

Labor of a Lifetime The hand-drawn map and diary entry above by Robert Knox Sneden records a daring 1864 escape attempt by Federals from Libby Prison in Richmond. The map, part of an elaborate four-volume diary with a self-portrait of the author on its title page (below), was based on information Sneden gathered while being held captive in Richmond near Libby Prison when the breakout occurred. Sneden was later transferred to the infamous holding pen at Andersonville, Georgia, an ordeal he documented profusely—like the rest of his wartime experiences—in words, pictures, and maps.

CHAPTER 1

A CHANGE OF FLAGS

PRELUDE TO WAR | 1861

"The war is commenced, and we will triumph or perish."

SOUTH CAROLINA GOVERNOR FRANCIS PICKENS
FOLLOWING THE CAPTURE OF FORT SUMTER

A Confederate flag bearing seven stars for the seven states that first seceded and formed the Confederacy flies over battered Fort Sumter in Charleston Harbor after Federal forces surrendered and lowered the Stars and Stripes there on April 14, 1861.

PRELUDE TO WAR
A NATION DIVIDED

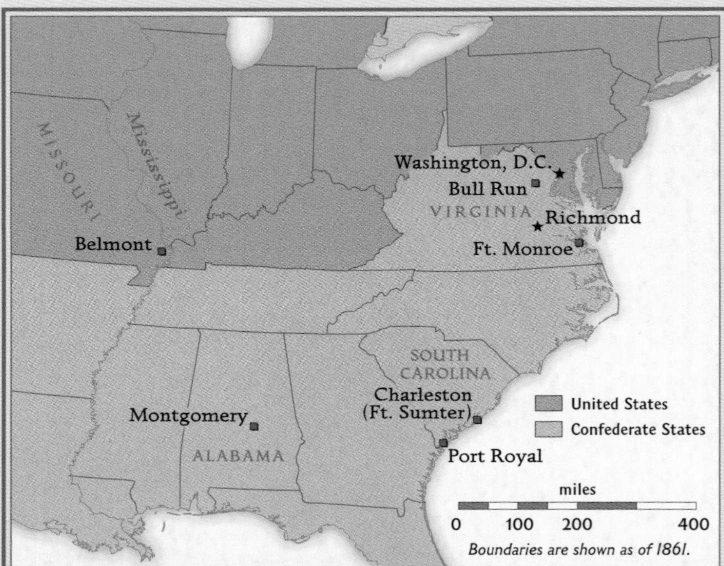

When Abraham Lincoln declared in 1858, "A house divided against itself cannot stand," he spoke for many people who feared that the quarrel between North and South would lead to disunion unless one side yielded to the other on the issue of slavery. Despite earnest efforts by the nation's founders to create "a more perfect Union," the Constitution they enacted left Americans at odds by upholding slavery and counting each slave as three-fifths of a person when states were allotted seats in Congress based on population. This gave political clout to the South, where slavery expanded even as it was abolished in the North.

To protect their own political and economic interests, Northerners opposed the admission of Missouri and other Western territories as slave states. Heated arguments about the morality of slavery heightened tensions, as did Southern fears that Northern abolitionists were inciting slaves to flee or rebel. Many Southerners feared chaos if the millions of slaves held captive in their region were freed and thought the federal government had no right to interfere with states in this matter.

Lincoln's election in 1860 as a president opposed to slavery led Southern states to secede and form the Confederacy, whose forces attacked Fort Sumter in April 1861, launching the Civil War. The Union had a larger population and far greater industrial and naval resources than the upstart Confederacy. But Southerners had a stronger military tradition and were defending their own soil. The Confederate success at Bull Run in July dashed Northern hopes for quick victory and signaled that this struggle would be long and bitter, splitting states and fracturing families like that of the Union's First Lady, Mary Todd Lincoln of Kentucky, who had four brothers in Confederate uniform.

PRELUDE

September 17, 1787 Delegates to the Constitutional Convention in Philadelphia sign the U.S. Constitution, which recognizes slavery as legal.

Abraham Lincoln

1794 Eli Whitney patents his cotton gin, which contributes to the spread of cotton plantations across the South and thus increases the region's reliance on slave labor.

1803 Louisiana Purchase extends U.S. territory far beyond the Mississippi River, raising the question of whether slavery will take hold there.

1808 Importation of slaves to the U.S. is prohibited.

1820–1821 Missouri Compromise enacted, temporarily resolving

Mary Todd Lincoln

the debate in Congress over slavery in Western territories.

August 22, 1831 Nat Turner leads a slave rebellion in Virginia.

1832 Escaped slave Frederick Douglass reaches freedom in the North and goes on to become a leading abolitionist.

1861

January 9 Secessionist batteries at Charleston, South Carolina, repulse a ship sent to reinforce Fort Sumter.

February 1 Texas becomes the seventh state to secede from the Union, joining South Carolina, Mississippi, Florida, Alabama, Georgia, and Louisiana.

February 18 Jefferson Davis inaugurated provisional president of the Confederacy.

March 4 Abraham Lincoln inaugurated president of the United States.

April 12 Civil War begins as Confederates bombard Fort Sumter.

April 14 Federals lower flag and abandon Fort Sumter.

April 15 Lincoln calls up 75,000 militiamen to serve the Union for three months.

April 17 Virginia delegates back secession, leading Governor John Letcher to send state troops to seize Federal facilities; Jefferson Davis invites shipowners to apply for licenses authorizing them to embark as privateers, preying on Union merchant ships.

April 19 Lincoln imposes naval blockade on the Confederacy; secessionists clash with Federal troops in Baltimore, Maryland.

April 27 Lincoln cracks down on Confederate sympathizers in Baltimore and other areas of unrest by suspending the writ of habeas corpus, thus denying those arrested the right to a prompt judicial hearing.

Slave woman as nanny

1833 President Andrew Jackson prevents South Carolina from nullifying federal tariffs, maintaining federal authority over the state; William Lloyd Garrison founds the American Anti-Slavery Society.

1848 American victory in the Mexican War adds greatly to the nation's Western territories, reviving controversy over slavery there.

1849 Escaped slave Harriet Tubman reaches the North and begins work with the Underground Railroad, conducting other fugitives to freedom.

1850 Compromise in Congress admits California as a free state, abolishes slave trade in the District of Columbia, enacts a stronger Fugitive Slave Act to enforce the return of escaped slaves to their masters, and leaves the issue of slavery in the territories of New Mexico and Utah to be decided by settlers there, exercising popular sovereignty.

1851–1852 Harriet Beecher Stowe's novel *Uncle Tom's Cabin* is published, first in serial form and then in book form, increasing antislavery sentiment in the North.

May 30, 1854 Kansas-Nebraska Act is adopted, leaving the issue of slavery in those territories to be decided by popular sovereignty and leading to conflict between proslavery forces and Free Staters in Kansas.

Kansas Free Staters

July 1854 Republican Party is founded in opposition to slavery.

May 22, 1856 Senator Charles Sumner of Massachusetts is attacked by Congressman Preston Brooks of South Carolina after publicly denouncing Brooks's uncle, Senator Andrew Butler, and other sponsors of the Kansas-Nebraska Act.

Senator Sumner caned by Congressman Brooks

May 24, 1856 Radical abolitionist John Brown leads a raid at Pottawatomie Creek in Kansas, killing several proslavery settlers.

March 6, 1857 Supreme Court rules against slave Dred Scott in his bid for freedom, defining slaves as property.

August–October 1858 Republican Abraham Lincoln and Democrat Stephen Douglas, chief sponsor of the Kansas-Nebraska Act, hold a series of debates in Illinois during their race for the U.S. Senate seat held by Douglas.

October 16, 1859 John Brown leads a raid on a Federal arsenal at Harpers Ferry, Virginia, hoping to ignite a slave rebellion.

December 2, 1859 Brown is executed after being captured by U.S. Marines led by Lieutenant Colonel Robert E. Lee.

May 18, 1860 Lincoln is nominated as the Republican candidate for president on a platform opposing slavery in Western territories.

June 1860 Northern Democrats nominate Douglas for president on a platform endorsing popular sovereignty; Southern Democrats leave the party and nominate John Breckinridge of Kentucky on a platform upholding slavery in the territories.

November 6, 1860 Lincoln is elected president.

December 16, 1860 Georgia legislature calls for a convention to consider a confederacy of Southern states.

December 20, 1860 South Carolina becomes first state to secede from the Union.

December 30, 1860 South Carolinians seize Federal arsenal at Charleston.

April 29 Maryland delegates vote against secession.

May 3 General Winfield Scott proposes his Anaconda Plan, urging that Federals take control of the Mississippi River in conjunction with the coastal blockade.

May 18 General Benjamin Butler takes command of Fort Monroe, enforcing the Federal blockade of Hampton Roads and Norfolk, and proceeds to harbor fugitive slaves there as contraband.

May 23 Secession approved by voters in Virginia, which becomes the eleventh state to leave the Union, joining Arkansas, Tennessee, North Carolina, and the seven original states.

May 24 Federal troops cross the Potomac River and occupy Arlington Heights and Alexandria, Virginia.

June 10 Federals repulsed by Confederates at Big Bethel near Fort Monroe.

June 29 Lincoln authorizes an attack on Confederates at Manassas Junction in Virginia.

Union flag flown at Fort Sumter and the original Confederate flag

July 18 Federals clash with Confederates at Blackburn's Ford on Bull Run, near Manassas Junction.

July 21 First Battle of Bull Run

July 25 General John Frémont arrives in St. Louis, Missouri, to take charge of the Union Army's Western Department.

August 10 Battle of Wilson's Creek (Missouri)

August 29 Federals secure Hatteras Inlet and close off Pamlico Sound following the bombardment of Confederate Forts Clark and Hatteras.

August 30 General Frémont declares martial law in Missouri, vowing to free the slaves of all those in defiance of the Union, and names General Ulysses Grant to command Federal forces at Cairo, Illinois.

September 3 Confederates under General Leonidas Polk occupy Columbus, Kentucky, in defiance of Kentucky's neutrality.

September 4 Federals under General Grant occupy Paducah, Kentucky.

September 17 Federals occupy Ship Island, off the coast of Mississippi, which becomes a base for the Gulf Blockading Squadron.

October 21 Battle of Ball's Bluff (Virginia)

November 2 Frémont relieved of command by Lincoln.

November 7 Battle of Belmont (Missouri); Union warships drive Confederates from Forts Walker and Beauregard and win control of Port Royal Sound on the South Carolina coast.

November 8 Confederate envoys bound for Europe seized aboard British vessel *Trent* by Federal boarding party, causing crisis between the U.S. and Great Britain.

December 25 Lincoln orders Confederate envoys released, ending crisis.

Early recruits from New York

PRELUDE TO WAR

TWO AMERICAS

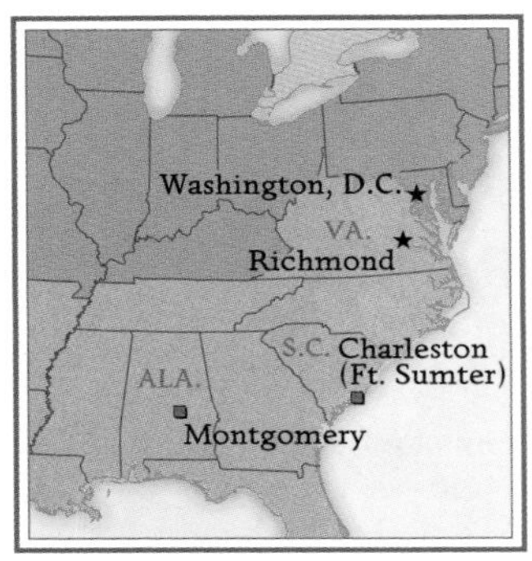

POLITICS & POWER

1820–1821 Missouri Compromise is enacted.

SEPTEMBER 1850 Fugitive Slave Act adopted.

OCTOBER 16, 1859 John Brown raids Harpers Ferry, Virginia.

NOVEMBER 6, 1860 Abraham Lincoln is elected president on an antislavery platform.

DECEMBER 20, 1860 South Carolina secedes from the Union.

FEBRUARY 18, 1861 Jefferson Davis is inaugurated provisional president of the Confederacy.

MARCH 4 Abraham Lincoln is inaugurated president of the United States.

APRIL 12, Civil War begins as Confederates attack Fort Sumter.

The United States of America grew dramatically in the first half of the 19th century. Its population increased more than fourfold and its territory nearly tripled as it acquired vast areas west of the Mississippi River by purchase, treaty, or conquest. Roads, canals, and railroads were built at a feverish pace. By 1860, the nation's rail network, shown here, would cover more than 30,000 miles, equaling the amount of track laid in all other countries combined.

This was not one nation indivisible, however, but two Americas—North and South—torn by the issue of slavery and whether blacks held captive in the South were entitled to liberty. Thomas Jefferson, the founder who declared that "all men are created equal," was a slave owner himself and lived long enough to see his fellow Southerners clash with Northerners in Congress in 1819 over admitting Missouri as a slave state. "This momentous question, like a fire bell in the night, awakened and filled me with terror," he wrote. He feared the dispute might shatter the Union, but Congress compromised and defused the situation by allowing slavery in Missouri and banning it from all other territories north of 36° 30', the line formed by Missouri's southern border.

That pact lasted until the late 1840s, when war with Mexico brought California, New Mexico, and other territories into the Union and reopened the debate. Further deals in Congress in years to come only deepened the rift between those seeking to contain or abolish slavery and those advocating its expansion. Some Southerners saw any attempt to restrict slavery as an assault on their way of life. Dependent on cotton and other crops produced by slave labor, the South remained largely rural and agricultural, while the North grew increasingly urban and industrial. New York City ❶ alone had more than twice the population of New Orleans ❷, Charleston ❸, Richmond ❹, Mobile ❺, Savannah ❻, Petersburg ❼, Memphis ❽, Nashville ❾, and Atlanta ❿ put together.

Southerners feared that the booming North would dominate them economically and dictate to them politically. The North's rail network was twice as large as the South's and served as a crucial link between New England and the Midwest, which were uniting in opposition to any further territorial advances for slavery. The North "will ride over us rough shod" and free the slaves, warned Senator James Hammond of South Carolina—a state where slaves made up more than half the population and where many whites were prepared to leave the Union if antislavery forces took charge in Washington. ■

IRON HIGHWAYS This 1860 map shows the North's extensive railroad network and the South's less-comprehensive system, containing many gaps where passengers and freight had to be hauled or shipped between railheads. Strategically significant cities are numbered in order of their population in 1860, from largest to smallest.

❶ BUSTLE ON BROADWAY People throng Broadway in New York City, home to nearly a million people by the 1860s.

❷ TRAFFIC AT NEW ORLEANS Mississippi riverboats sustained a lucrative traffic in cotton (foreground) and helped make New Orleans one of the South's busiest ports and its largest city—the only place in the Confederacy with a population exceeding 100,000.

PRELUDE TO WAR

SLAVERY

Slavery did not just persist in the South before the Civil War. It proliferated, reaching far inland from the coastal areas where it was introduced. Beginning in the 1820s, cotton plantations spread westward across the Lower South from South Carolina ❶, Georgia ❷, and northern Florida ❸ to Alabama ❹, Mississippi ❺, Louisiana ❻, and Texas ❼. As shown, slaves made up much of the Cotton Belt's population, and whites here feared disaster if they were freed, making these states the first to secede. Virginia ❽ and other states of the Upper South also had large slave populations and would join the rebellion, but many people with small farms in Appalachia ❾ had no slaves and little sympathy for secession.

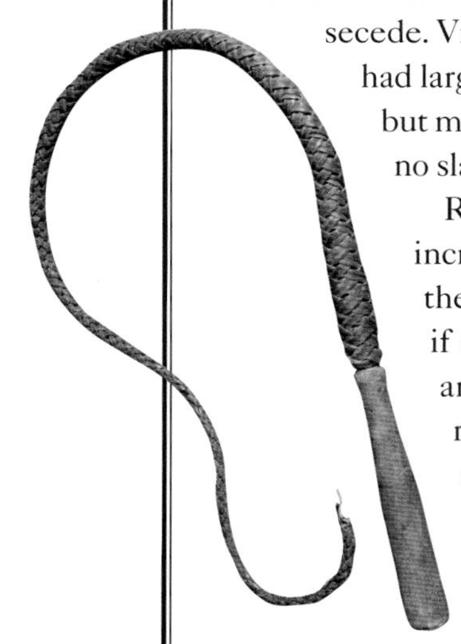

Rising demand for labor in the Cotton Belt increased the value of slaves but failed to improve their lot. Some masters fed their slaves adequately, if only to ensure that they would bear hard work and bring a high price if sold. One former slave recalled how his owner used to show off well-fed slave children as if they were "young mules," referring to one child as "a whopper" and boasting that another was worth a thousand dollars. Being sold on the auction block was one of many cruelties visited by masters on slaves, who often felt the whip (inset). Despite the risk of being hunted down by slave catchers, thousands fled their masters and headed north in search of freedom. ■

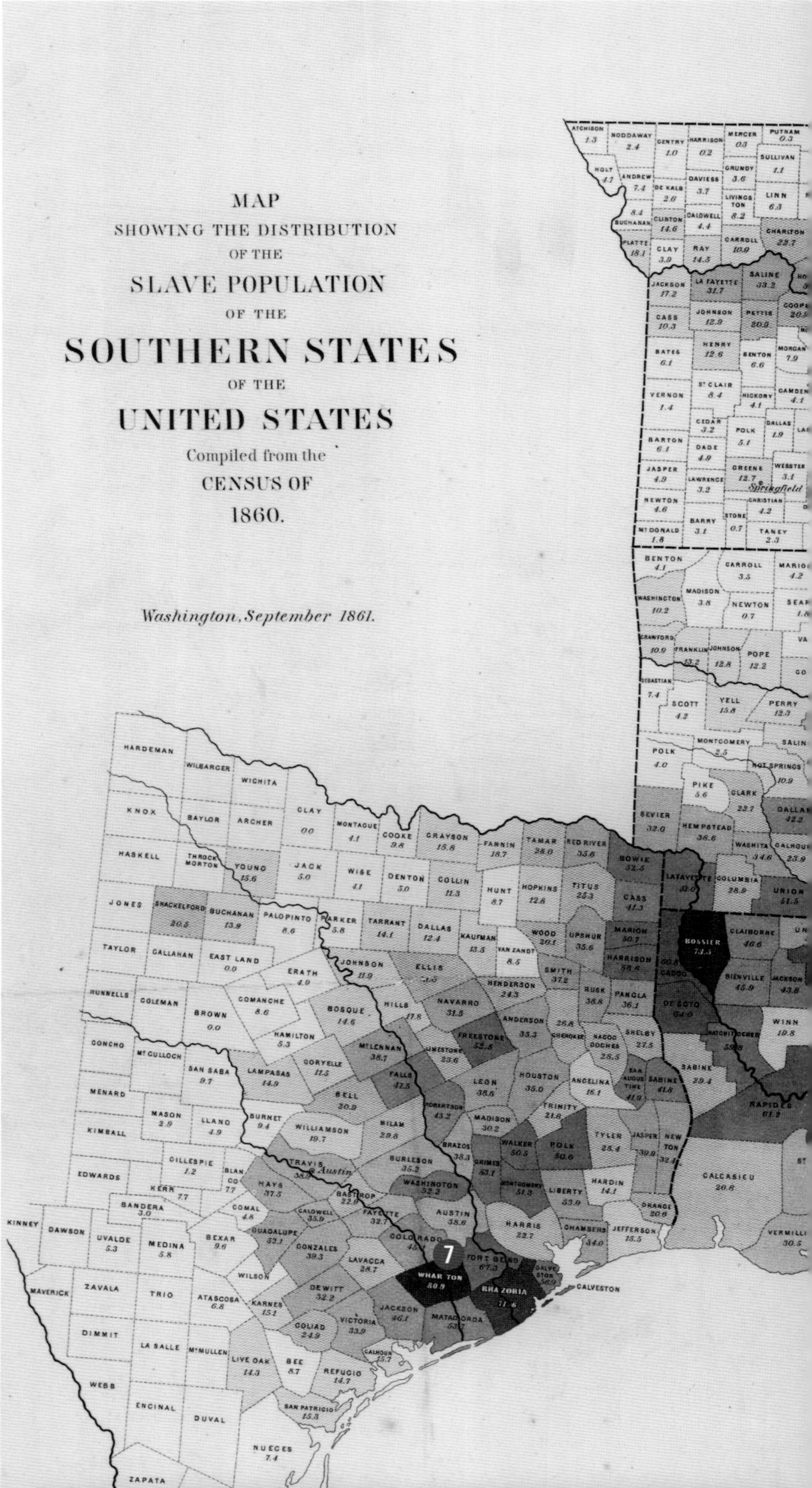

MAP SHOWING THE DISTRIBUTION OF THE SLAVE POPULATION OF THE SOUTHERN STATES OF THE UNITED STATES Compiled from the CENSUS OF 1860.

Washington, September 1861.

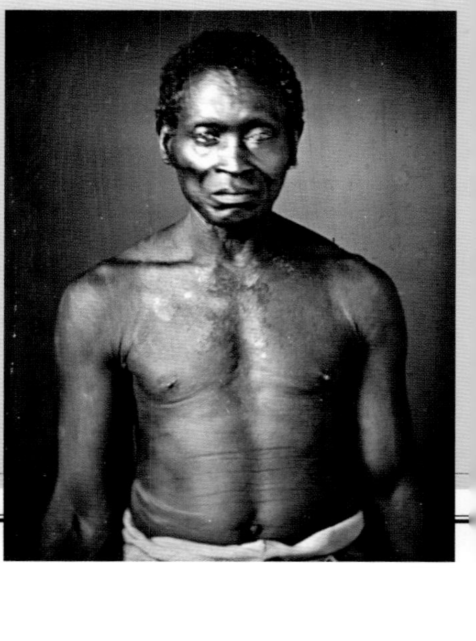

❶ SLAVE QUARTERS Shown on a plantation near Beaufort, South Carolina, these slaves were freed once Union troops occupied the area.

WHERE SLAVERY PREVAILED This revealing demographic map, based on the findings of the 1860 U.S. census, uses dark shading to show where slaves were concentrated. As the key (lower right) indicates, slaves made up more than 80 percent of the population in some parts of the South.

UNWILLING SUBJECTS Photographed in South Carolina in 1850 as part of a study of racial traits conducted by Louis Agassiz of Harvard University, these slaves show the grim resignation of people who had to do as told.

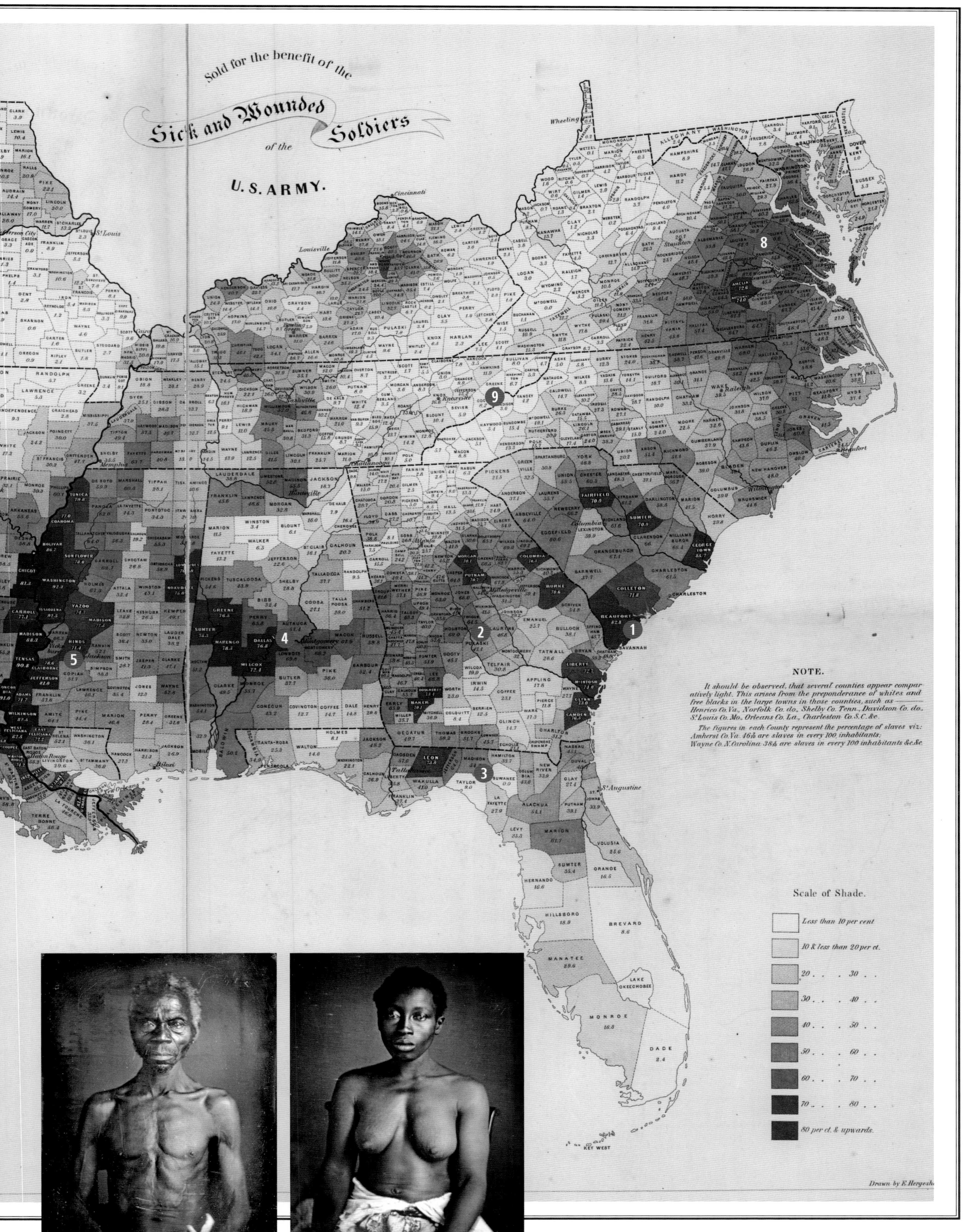
Sold for the benefit of the
Sick and Wounded Soldiers
of the
U.S. ARMY.
NOTE.
It should be observed, that several counties appear comparatively light. This arises from the preponderance of whites and free blacks in the large towns in those counties, such as ——— Henrico Co. Va., Norfolk Co. do., Shelby Co. Tenn., Davidson Co. do., St. Louis Co. Mo., Orleans Co. La., Charleston Co. S.C. &c.
The figures in each County represent the percentage of slaves viz: Amherst Co. Va. 46 1/10 are slaves in every 100 inhabitants; Wayne Co. N. Carolina 38 1/10 are slaves in every 100 inhabitants &c. &c.
Scale of Shade.
Less than 10 per cent
10 & less than 20 per ct.
20 . . 30 . .
30 . . 40 . .
40 . . 50 . .
50 . . 60 . .
60 . . 70 . .
70 . . 80 . .
80 per ct. & upwards.
Drawn by E. Hergesh

Escape to Freedom

FREDERICK DOUGLASS

Born a slave in Maryland in 1818, Frederick Douglass found his way to freedom as a young man and became a hero of the abolitionist cause, offering living proof that the degradations of slavery could be overcome. The son of a slave woman and a white man he never knew, he learned to read and write as a child but was considered unruly by his owner and placed under a "slave-breaker," who tried to beat him into submission. Finally, Douglass struck back at his tormentor, risking severe punishment. His overseer was too proud of his reputation as a slave-breaker to admit that a mere boy had defied him, however, and let him off. This triumph freed Douglass in spirit. Submissiveness gave way to "bold defiance," he recalled, "and I now resolved that, however long I might remain a slave in form, the day had passed forever when I could be a slave in fact."

When Douglass was around 20, he escaped to Philadelphia by ship. Like other fugitives, he was aided by agents with the Underground Railroad and began a new life under a new name. He soon became an outspoken abolitionist, denouncing the system that allowed slave owners to claim human beings as their legal property and treated both escaped slaves and those who aided them as criminals. "I appear this evening as a thief and robber," he told audiences. "I stole this head, these limbs, this body from my master, and ran off with them."

Fugitive slaves seeking freedom in the North followed various paths, aided by networks of sympathizers who formed branches on the so-called Underground Railroad. Not many fugitives actually traveled by rail—most fled on foot, some traveled in wagons or boats—but those assisting them likened their operations to a railroad. Safe places where freedom seekers found shelter were called stations and were run by station masters. Guides who led fugitives from one station to another were known as conductors. Wealthy abolitionists whose contributions helped fund such efforts were called stockholders. These were underground operations, cloaked in secrecy. People organizing them risked punishment in both the South and the North, where federal law called for fugitives to be arrested and returned to their masters and imposed fines or jail sentences on those who obstructed that process.

Many fugitives reached the North on their own, traveling at night to avoid detection and following the "Drinking Gourd," or Big Dipper, and the North Star to which it pointed. One branch of the Underground Railroad brought them through Maryland ❶ to Pennsylvania, New York, and New England; another line ran up the Mississippi Valley ❷ to Midwestern states. Helping them along were free blacks and white abolitionists, including Quakers like Levi Coffin, who harbored more than 3,000 freedom seekers over the years. Most agents with the Underground Railroad remained in the North and helped slaves evade arrest, sometimes guiding them to Canada. But some brave souls went south and brought fugitives back. Harriet Tubman, an escaped slave from Maryland, earned the title "Moses" for making 19 such journeys and delivering hundreds of people from bondage.

Only about a thousand fugitives successfully reached the free states each year, but efforts to liberate slaves had a huge effect on public opinion and set North against South. Passage of the Fugitive Slave Act of 1850, which authorized federal commissioners to require citizens in free states to serve on slave-hunting posses and to track down fugitives, outraged many Northerners and left militant abolitionists like John Brown, a station master with the Underground Railroad in Ohio, determined to defy their government if it continued to protect the interests of slave owners. Brown wrote that the Fugitive Slave Act made more people into "abolitionists than all the lectures we have had for years." In 1851, Brown organized the League of Gileadites, a group that included fugitive slaves, and urged members to use armed force against slave catchers. "Let the first blow be the signal for all to engage," he told them, "and when engaged do not do your work by halves, but make clean work with your enemies." Brown's notorious raid in October 1859 on the U.S. arsenal at Harpers Ferry, Virginia, funded by the abolitionist movement, failed to ignite a slave rebellion, as he had hoped, but it signaled that compromise over slavery was no longer possible. Reacting to the raid, a newspaper in Charleston, South Carolina, issued an editorial stating that the "time has arrived for a separation from the North." And Brown spoke for a growing number of Northerners who were no longer willing to tolerate slavery within the nation's borders when he declared shortly before his execution that "the crimes of this guilty land will never be purged away but with blood." ■

$100 REWARD!

RANAWAY

From the undersigned, living on Current River, about twelve miles above Doniphan, in Ripley County, Mo., on 2nd of March, 1860, A NE GRO MAN, about 30 years old, weighs about 160 pounds; high forehead, with a scar on it; had on brown pants and coat very much worn, and an old black wool hat; shoes size No. 11.

The above reward will be given to any person who may apprehend this said negro out of the State; and fifty dollars if apprehended in this State outside of Ripley county, or $25 if taken in Ripley county.

APOS TUCKER.

Reward Offered Posters like this one offering bounties for the return of fugitives were common in Missouri and other border states, where slaves did not have to go far to reach freedom.

Slave Collar Recaptured fugitives might be fitted with heavy metal collars like this one, from South Carolina, whose bells kept slaves within earshot if they tried to escape again.

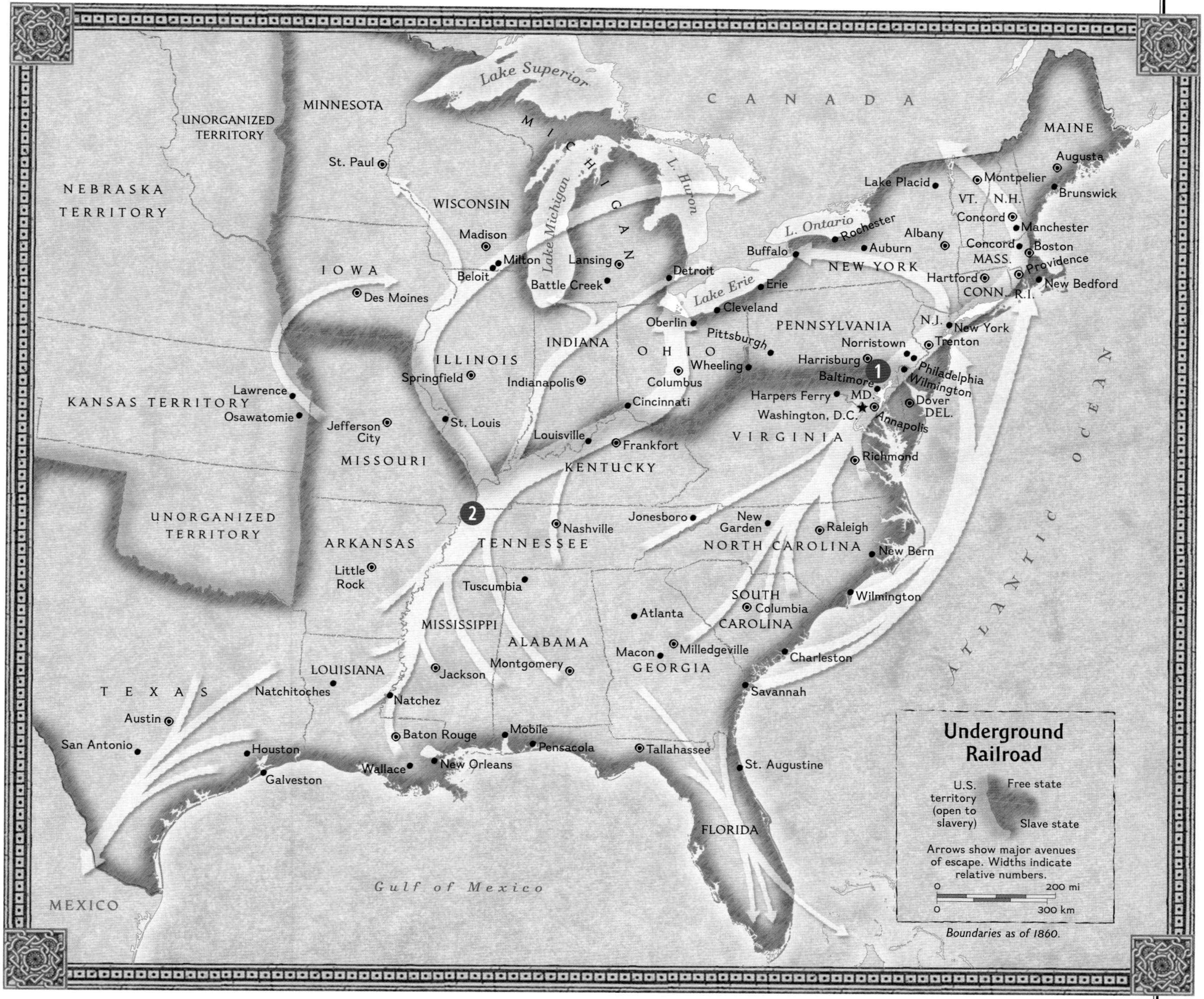

Underground Railroad

U.S. territory (open to slavery)

Free state

Slave state

Arrows show major avenues of escape. Widths indicate relative numbers.

0 200 mi
0 300 km

Boundaries as of 1860.

Paths to Freedom As shown on this National Geographic map, escaped slaves took many routes to freedom—traveling by land, by river, and by sea. Some fugitives in the Southwest set out for Mexico, but most sought refuge in Canada or in Northern states where they might settle among free blacks and elude detection.

Moses and Her People Harriet Tubman, standing at far left beside family members she led to freedom, said of her years with the Underground Railroad, "I never ran my train off the track and I never lost a passenger."

PRELUDE TO WAR

The Election of 1860

ABRAHAM LINCOLN

Critics were quick to dismiss Abraham Lincoln as a presidential contender. Born in a log cabin in Kentucky in 1809, he was largely self-taught. Derided as a "third-rate country lawyer," he was in fact a first-rate attorney in Springfield, Illinois, but his national political experience was limited to a single term in Congress. One foe who did not underestimate him was Democratic Senator Stephen Douglas, who was nearly unseated by Lincoln in 1858 and called him "the best stump speaker in the West." In highly publicized debates that year, Lincoln assailed Douglas's argument that settlers had a sovereign right to extend slavery and deflected charges that he favored the complete abolition of slavery and "Negro equality." The debates helped Lincoln win the Republican nomination for president in 1860 by defining him as a pragmatist, opposed to slavery in the West but willing to tolerate it in the South. Fire-eaters in Dixie branded him an abolitionist, however, citing his statement that the nation could not endure "permanently half slave and half free. . . . It will become all one thing, or all the other." Ultimately, Fire-eaters helped transform Lincoln into the Great Emancipator—first by splitting the Democratic Party in 1860 and easing his victory, and then by launching a rebellion that led him to conclude that slavery would have to be destroyed along with the Confederacy.

The presidential race in 1860 fractured the nation politically and led to secession. The wedge that split the electorate was popular sovereignty, or allowing settlers in Western territories to decide for themselves whether to organize as free states or slave states. Illinois Senator Stephen Douglas had championed that idea and incorporated it in the Kansas-Nebraska Act of 1854, which caused conflict between proslavery and antislavery forces in Kansas. Northerners who opposed popular sovereignty and wanted to keep the West free of slavery formed the Republican Party in 1854 and nominated Abraham Lincoln for president in May 1860. Having nearly defeated Douglas when he ran for reelection to the Senate in 1858, Lincoln appeared headed for another tight race with the "Little Giant," who was closing in on the Democratic nomination.

At the party's convention in Charleston, however, Southern Democrats bolted, unwilling to accept popular sovereignty, which Douglas saw as a compromise between North and South. Buoyed by a recent U.S. Supreme Court decision involving the slave Dred Scott, which defined slaves as property that their owners could legally introduce to any U.S. territory, Southern Democrats refused to compromise and chose their own candidate, John Breckinridge of Kentucky.

Douglas was nominated by Northern Democrats at a second convention, held in Baltimore, but finished far behind in November as Breckinridge carried most of the South and Lincoln swept the Northeast and the Midwest as well as California and Oregon. A fourth candidate, John Bell of the newly formed Constitutional Union Party, which took no position on slavery, won Virginia, Kentucky, and Tennessee. With less than 40 percent of the popular vote, Lincoln faced violent opposition in the South, where ardent secessionists called Fire-eaters welcomed his victory because it strengthened their cause. "The revolution of 1860 has been initiated," proclaimed the *Charleston Mercury*. Sure enough, on December 20, South Carolina became the first state to leave the Union. ■

LINCOLN'S LEAP An 1860 political cartoon shows Lincoln—the "rail-splitter"—leaping a fence of his own making to reach Washington ahead of Stephen Douglas. The figure caught in the rails represents the slavery issue, which Douglas could not get beyond.

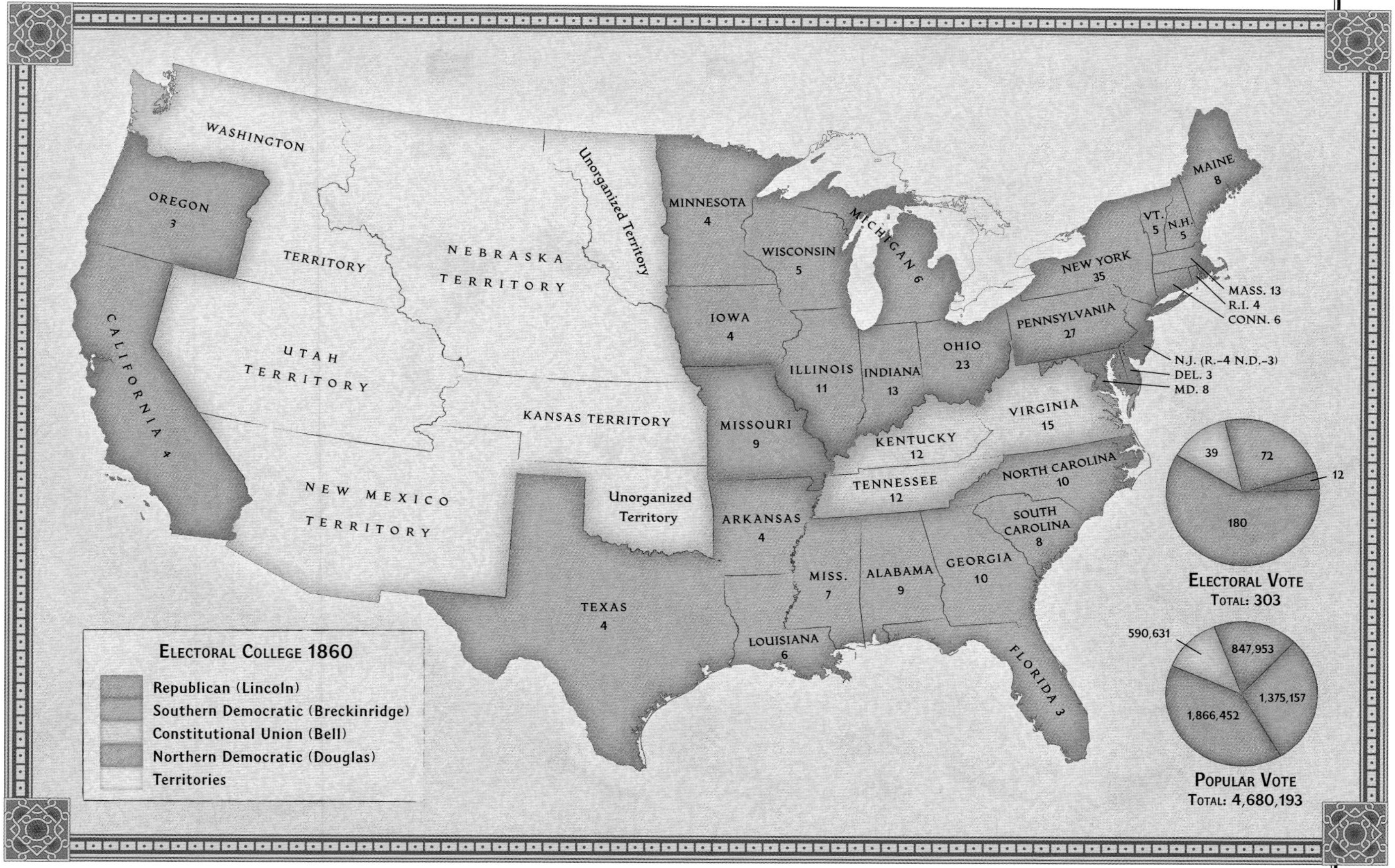

Electoral College 1860

- Republican (Lincoln)
- Southern Democratic (Breckinridge)
- Constitutional Union (Bell)
- Northern Democratic (Douglas)
- Territories

Washington Territory; Oregon 3; California 4; Utah Territory; Nebraska Territory; Unorganized Territory; Kansas Territory; New Mexico Territory; Unorganized Territory; Minnesota 4; Wisconsin 5; Michigan 6; Iowa 4; Illinois 11; Indiana 13; Ohio 23; Missouri 9; Kentucky 12; Tennessee 12; Arkansas 4; Texas 4; Louisiana 6; Miss. 7; Alabama 9; Georgia 10; Florida 3; South Carolina 8; North Carolina 10; Virginia 15; Pennsylvania 27; New York 35; Vt. 5; N.H. 5; Maine 8; Mass. 13; R.I. 4; Conn. 6; N.J. (R.–4 N.D.–3); Del. 3; Md. 8

Electoral Vote Total: 303 — 180; 72; 39; 12

Popular Vote Total: 4,680,193 — 1,866,452; 1,375,157; 847,953; 590,631

A DIVIDED ELECTORATE This electoral map for 1860 shows how the slavery issue polarized the nation politically, with the North and West backing Abraham Lincoln, the Lower South backing John Breckinridge, and some states in between supporting two less-successful candidates who hoped to avoid conflict over slavery—John Bell and Stephen Douglas. With four candidates in the race, Lincoln was able to win a substantial majority of electoral votes while receiving a much smaller share of the popular vote. He was the first president elected without any help from the Southern states.

THE RAIL-SPLITTER AT HOME A bareheaded Lincoln, standing at his doorstep in Springfield, Illinois, towers over supporters at a rally held in August 1860 during his run for president. Aside from making such local appearances, Lincoln followed the custom of earlier candidates and did not campaign actively.

PRELUDE TO WAR

SECESSION

Americans who hoped to avoid disunion and civil strife had little to celebrate as 1861 began. South Carolina ❶ had already seceded, and Mississippi ❷, Florida ❸, Alabama ❹, Georgia ❺, Louisiana ❻, and Texas ❼ would soon follow suit in that order. Fueling this secessionist movement in the Lower South were fears that Lincoln and his fellow Republicans in Congress would not only prohibit slavery in Western territories but also repeal the Fugitive Slave Act, giving free rein to radical abolitionists like the late John Brown and triggering slave rebellions—dreaded in areas where blacks greatly outnumbered whites. If left unchecked, secessionists claimed, Lincoln's policies would dispossess and demean white Southerners. "You can never convert the free sons of the soil into vassals, paying tribute to your power," Louisiana Senator Judah P. Benjamin told Republicans, "and you never, never can degrade them to the level of an inferior and servile race."

Seeking to avoid conflict and keep states of the Upper South from seceding, Lincoln pledged to enforce the Fugitive Slave Act and back a constitutional amendment guaranteeing slavery in those places where it already existed. But he would not support a proposed deal in the Senate allowing slavery in Western territories south of the old Missouri Compromise line. Even if he had been inclined to make that concession, it would not have satisfied defiant secessionists like Jefferson Davis of Mississippi. "No human power can save the Union," declared Davis, a former U.S. senator and secretary of war. Chosen in February as provisional president of the Confederate States of America, Davis announced that the time for compromise was past and vowed that the Confederacy would "make all who oppose her smell Southern powder and feel Southern steel."

Although war now appeared likely, Lincoln continued to offer conciliatory words to Southerners, declaring at his inauguration on March 4, "We must not be enemies. Though passion may have strained, it must not break our bonds of affection." To placate uncommitted Southerners, he would avoid firing the first shot in the coming conflict, and he would ultimately succeed in keeping the slaveholding border states of Missouri, Kentucky, Maryland, and Delaware from leaving the Union. Davis did not want to be seen as an aggressor either, but he felt he must act decisively to bolster his cause. For several months, tensions had been rising in Charleston Harbor, where U.S. troops holding Fort Sumter were surrounded by rebellious South Carolinians. On April 9, Davis and his cabinet, determined to strike a blow before a relief expedition sent by Lincoln arrived, ordered Fort Sumter attacked if its defenders did not surrender immediately. The ensuing hostilities would draw four more Southern states—North Carolina ❽, Arkansas ❾, Tennessee ❿, and Virginia ⓫—into the Confederacy. ■

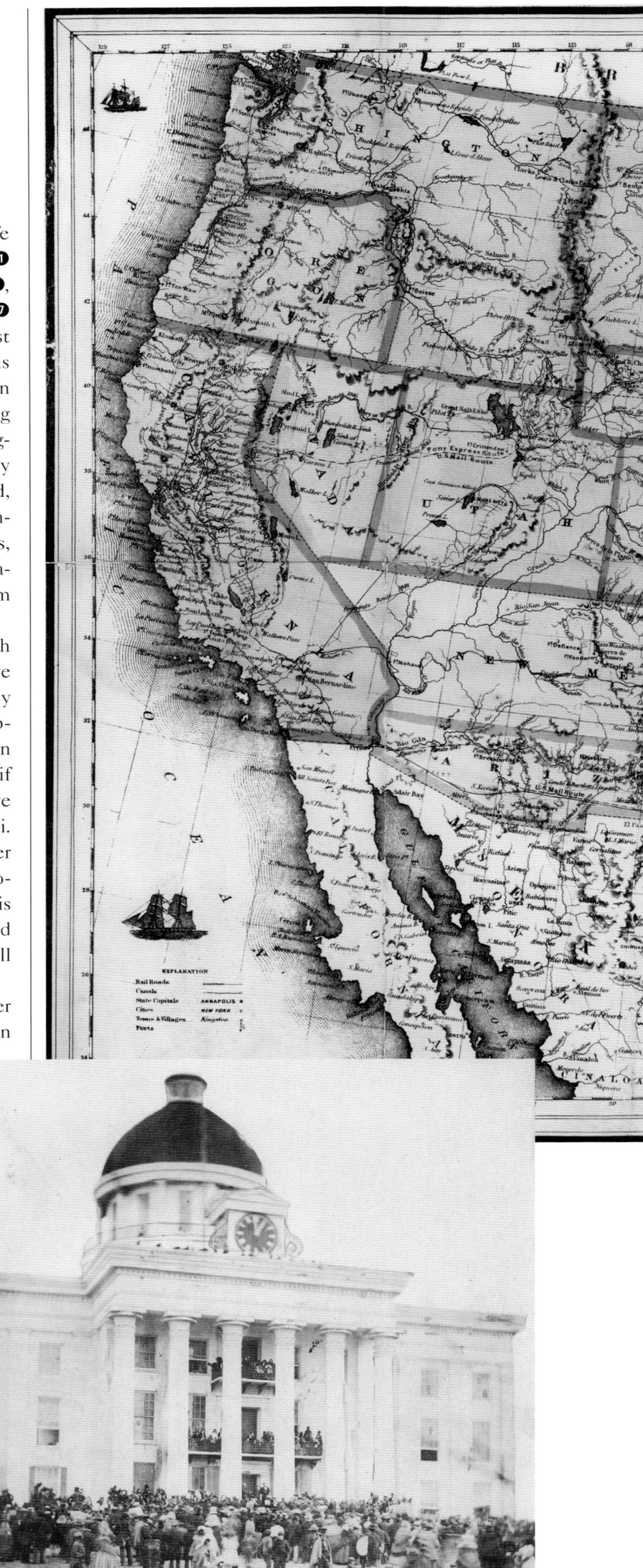
❹

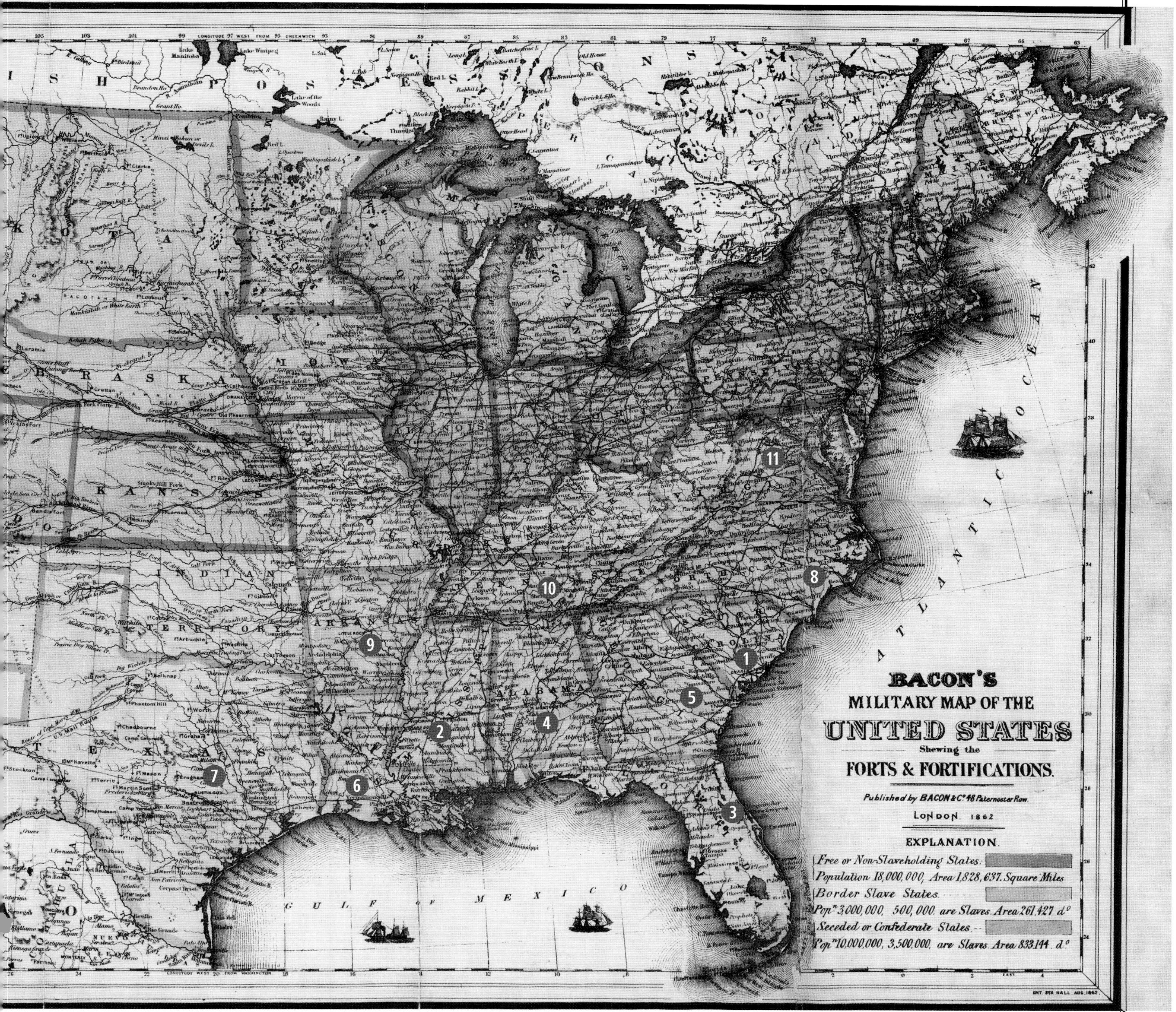

BACON'S
MILITARY MAP OF THE
UNITED STATES
Shewing the
FORTS & FORTIFICATIONS.

Published by BACON & Co. 48 Paternoster Row.
LONDON. 1862

EXPLANATION.

Free or Non-Slaveholding States.
Population 18,000,000, Area 1,828,637. Square Miles
Border Slave States.
Popn. 3,000,000, 500,000 are Slaves Area 261,427 do
Seceded or Confederate States.
Popn. 10,000,000, 3,500,000, are Slaves. Area 833,144. do

WHERE LINES WERE DRAWN Although labeled "military," this 1862 map shows political boundaries between the United States (green) and the Confederate States (pink), numbered here in the order in which they seceded. Among the territories designated as "Border Slave States" (yellow) are the Union-controlled area that separated from Virginia and became the state of West Virginia in 1863; the Indian Territory, where Cherokees and other Indians split into Union and Confederate factions; and New Mexico, where slavery was allowed briefly before the war but never took hold. Confederates advancing westward from Texas claimed Arizona as their territory but had no real control there.

❹ CONFEDERATE INAUGURAL A crowd gathers at the state house in Montgomery, Alabama, the first Confederate capital, on February 18, 1861, for the inauguration of Jefferson Davis as provisional Confederate president—an appointment later ratified by general election.

PRESIDENT AND FIRST LADY Jefferson and Varina Davis accepted as his due the honor bestowed on him at Montgomery, but both felt he was better suited to be the Confederacy's military chief than its political leader.

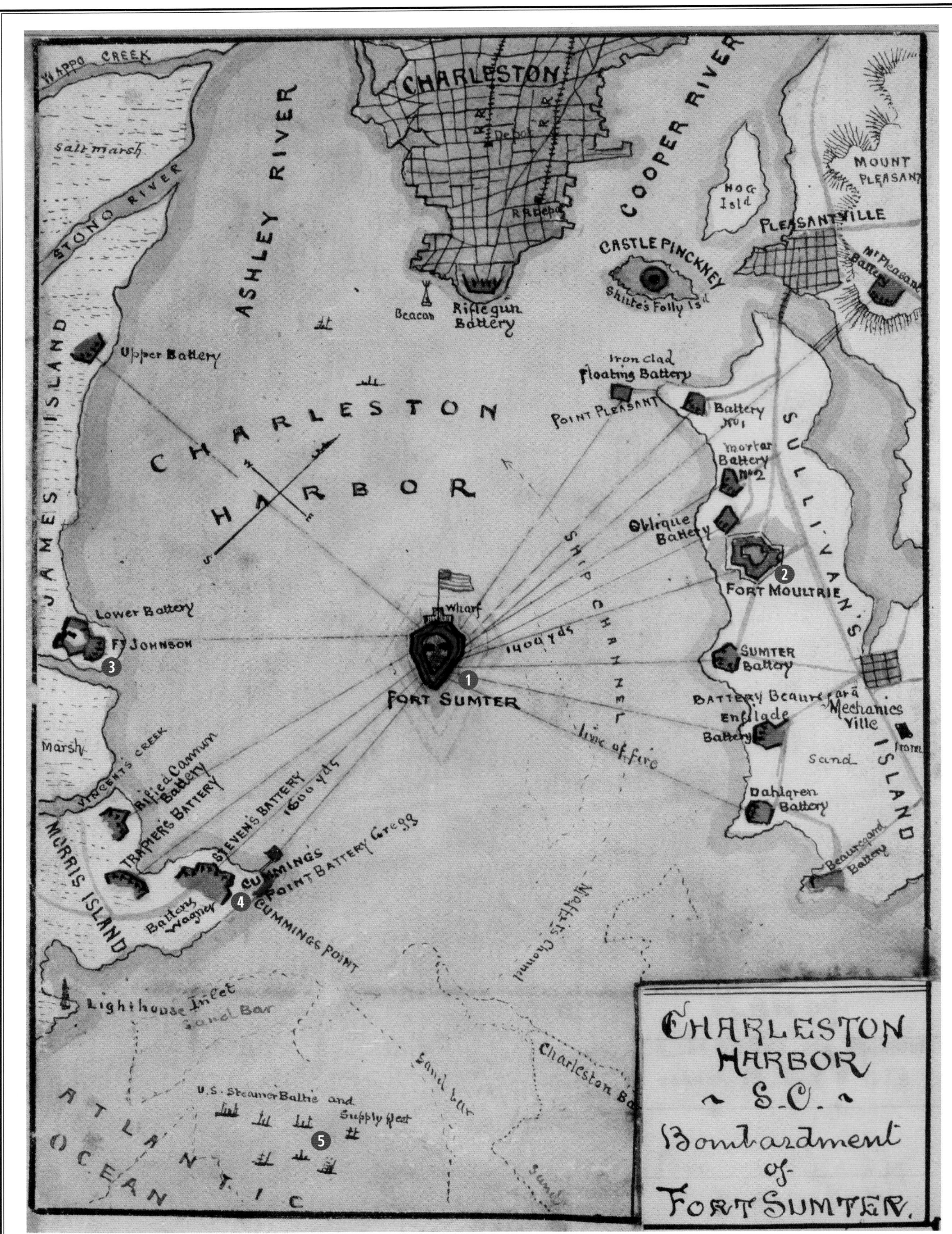
WAPPO CREEK
Salt marsh
STONO RIVER
ASHLEY RIVER
CHARLESTON
Depot
RR Depot
COOPER RIVER
HOG Isld
MOUNT PLEASANT
PLEASANTVILLE
CASTLE PINCKNEY
Shute's Folly Isd
Beacon
Rifle gun Battery
JAMES ISLAND
Upper Battery
Iron Clad Floating Battery
POINT PLEASANT
Battery No 1
Mortar Battery No 2
Oblique Battery
SULLIVAN'S ISLAND
CHARLESTON HARBOR
SHIP CHANNEL
Wharf
Lower Battery
Ft JOHNSON
FORT SUMTER
1400 yds
FORT MOULTRIE
SUMTER Battery
BATTERY Beauregard
Enfilade Battery
Mechanics Ville
line of fire
Sand
Dahlgren Battery
Beauregard Battery
Marsh
VINCENT'S CREEK
Rified Cannon Battery
TRAPIER'S BATTERY
STEVEN'S BATTERY
1600 yds
CUMMING'S POINT BATTERY Gregg
MORRIS ISLAND
Battery Wagner
CUMMINGS POINT
Maffit's Channel
Lighthouse Inlet
Sand Bar
Charleston Bar
Sand bar
U.S. Steamer Baltic and Supply fleet
ATLANTIC OCEAN
Sand
1
2
3
4
5
CHARLESTON HARBOR S.C. Bombardment of FORT SUMTER.

1861

Fall of Fort Sumter

On April 11, Confederates demanded that Major Robert Anderson and his men evacuate Fort Sumter ❶. Charleston had been seething since South Carolina seceded in December and Anderson moved his Federal garrison from vulnerable Fort Moultrie ❷ to the more defensible Fort Sumter, where he raised a huge American flag. Confederates had then fortified their batteries around the harbor and prevented Anderson from receiving reinforcements or supplies, leading President Abraham Lincoln to send a fleet to reprovision the post, where food was running out. Anderson countered the Confederate demand by offering to withdraw on April 15 if he did not receive supplies or orders to hold the fort at all cost by then. Determined to take Sumter before the fleet arrived, Confederates prepared to open fire on signal from Fort Johnson ❸.

Eagerly awaiting that moment was Edmund Ruffin, a Fire-eater from Virginia who had come here to incite war. "The shedding of blood," he said, would make Southerners not yet committed to the Confederacy "zealous for immediate secession." At 4:30 A.M. on April 12, as a mortar shell lobbed from Fort Johnson burst over the harbor, signaling the attack, Ruffin fired one of the first shots from Cummings Point ❹. Other batteries joined in the bombardment, setting Sumter aflame. That afternoon, Federal supply ships approached the entrance to the harbor ❺, but they lacked firepower and did not risk battle. With many of its guns disabled, Sumter was doomed. On April 13, Anderson yielded, evacuating the post with his men the next day after lowering the Stars and Stripes. "The war is commenced," wrote Governor Francis Pickens of South Carolina, "and we will triumph or perish." ■

Fire-Eater in Uniform At 66, pioneering agricultural chemist and ardent secessionist Edmund Ruffin helped launch the attack on Sumter.

A Dangerous Harbor As shown in one of many revealing battle maps produced by the prolific soldier-artist Robert Knox Sneden, Fort Sumter was surrounded by more than a dozen Confederate batteries and was thoroughly outgunned.

❶ Fort Sumter in Flames Federal gunners gamely return fire from the burning Fort Sumter under a barrage that ultimately led them to surrender.

1861

THE SEAT OF WAR

ELMER ELLSWORTH

Few Union officers had a more devoted following when the war began than 24-year-old Colonel Elmer Ellsworth, commander of a regiment from New York City called the Fire Zouaves. Drawn from volunteer fire departments there and clad in baggy pants and short jackets of the sort worn by French North African troops during the Crimean War, Ellsworth's recruits were caught up in a craze that he helped create by touring in 1860 with his champion drill team, the U.S. Zouave Cadets. Close to President Abraham Lincoln, who called him "the greatest little man I ever met," Ellsworth had the honor of occupying Alexandria, Virginia, a busy port on the Potomac that would serve as a Federal staging ground for campaigns against Richmond. All went smoothly until Ellsworth entered the Marshall House, a hotel in Alexandria, on May 24 to remove a Confederate flag flying from the roof. As he descended the stairs with flag in hand, he was met by innkeeper James Jackson, a dedicated secessionist, who killed him instantly with a shotgun blast. Jackson, who had vowed that the flag would never be taken down but over his dead body, became a martyr for his own cause when a Zouave corporal took his life moments after Ellsworth fell. Ellsworth's body was carried to the White House, where Lincoln mourned him like a lost son, and later taken to New York, where thousands honored the Union's first fallen hero.

Confederates who hoped that seizing Fort Sumter would encourage wavering Southerners to join their ranks were not disappointed. On April 15, as Northerners protested the attack in Charleston, Abraham Lincoln asked for 75,000 volunteers to put down the rebellion. Two days later, Virginia's delegates passed an ordinance of secession. Virginia would not secede until the act was approved by voters in May, but Governor John Letcher did not wait to send state militia against the Federal arsenal at Harpers Ferry ❶—site of John Brown's raid—and Gosport Navy Yard ❷, where Union ships were burned or scuttled to keep them out of enemy hands.

Confederate leaders saw Virginia, the South's most populous and prosperous state, as the jewel in their crown and shifted their capital to Richmond ❸, the Confederacy's second largest city and home to the vital Tredegar Iron Works, which would turn out more than a thousand cannon during the war. This move placed Jefferson Davis's presidential mansion barely 100 miles from the White House ❹ and transformed the land between into the war's bloodiest theater. This terrain presented numerous obstacles to armies moving north or south, including tangled woodlands like the Wilderness ❺, near Fredericksburg, and swirling rivers like the Rappahannock ❻ and Rapidan, flowing from west to east and not easily crossed except at bridges that were subject to destruction.

Before Lincoln could challenge Confederates in Virginia, he had to secure Maryland, a slave state where secessionists were raising Cain. In late April, they attacked troops from Massachusetts passing through Baltimore ❼ on their way to Washington and cut communications between the Federal capital and cities to the north. Washington was all but defenseless until Union volunteers arrived by ship in Annapolis ❽, home to the U.S. Naval Academy, and reached the capital by rail. As more troops poured in, Lincoln imposed martial law in Maryland, arrested defiant state officials and legislators, and stemmed the secessionist tide there. Then on May 24, after Virginia formally seceded, Federals crossed the Potomac and occupied lightly defended Arlington Heights ❾ and Alexandria ❿, where Colonel Elmer Ellsworth was slain after cutting down a Rebel flag and became a martyr for the Union. Federals also advanced from Fort Monroe ⓫, a coastal stronghold that remained in their hands. But Confederates went unchallenged elsewhere in Virginia until July, when Union forces approached Manassas Junction ⓬ and entered into battle along a stream called Bull Run. ■

FROM WASHINGTON TO RICHMOND A map published in Boston early in the war offers a bird's-eye view of the hotly contested territory between the Union and Confederate capitals, looking southward from Maryland. Federal troops advancing overland toward Richmond faced difficult terrain and fierce resistance, but naval superiority gave Union forces another route south from Washington by way of the Potomac River and Chesapeake Bay.

VOLUNTEERS FOR VIRGINIA Fresh recruits of the 1st Virginia Infantry show their steel in a photograph taken soon after their state seceded. Like other Confederates, they saw themselves as patriots, fighting for independence like the American colonists who defied the British.

❹ GUARDING THE WHITE HOUSE Local volunteers stand guard in front of the White House in April 1861. Lincoln anxiously awaited the arrival of additional regiments from the North to shield the vulnerable capital.

1861

ANACONDA PLAN

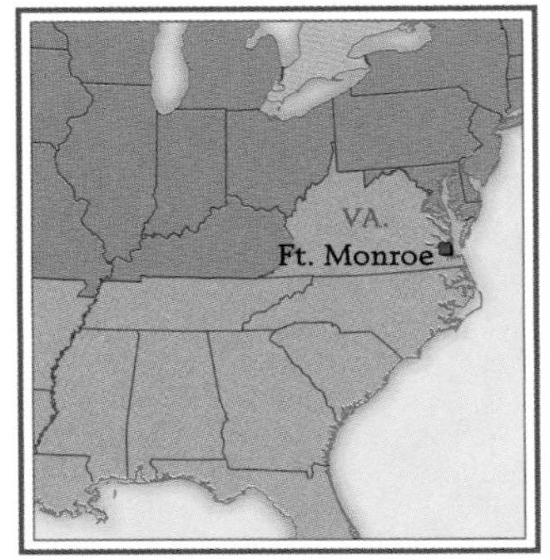

THE BLOCKADE

APRIL 17, 1861 Jefferson Davis invites shipowners to apply for Confederate licenses authorizing them to embark as privateers.

APRIL 19 Lincoln imposes a naval blockade on the Confederacy.

MAY 3 General Winfield Scott proposes his Anaconda Plan, urging that Federals take control of the Mississippi River in conjunction with the coastal blockade.

MAY 18 General Benjamin Butler takes command of Fort Monroe, enforcing the Federal blockade of Norfolk and Hampton Roads.

The Union war effort broadened considerably on April 19 when Abraham Lincoln declared a blockade of the Confederate coastline, extending nearly 3,500 miles from the mouth of the Rio Grande ❶ to the Chesapeake Bay ❷ once Virginia and North Carolina seceded. Lincoln took this action—which defined the Confederacy as a belligerent nation and undermined his argument that the Rebels had no claim to independence—after Jefferson Davis invited Southern privateers (privately run warships) to seize Union merchant ships. Imposing a blockade allowed Federal warships to intercept privateers as well as vessels involved in the lucrative overseas cotton trade that brought the South weapons and other strategic assets in return.

The blockade did not promise quick victory. It would take years for the Union to translate naval superiority into naval supremacy and seal off the many coastal inlets used by blockade-runners. Most Northerners hoped for victory within months, but some in Washington foresaw a prolonged conflict in which gradual measures like the blockade might prove decisive. Among them was General-in-Chief Winfield Scott, a venerable Mexican War hero from Virginia who remained loyal to the Union. Scott doubted that the raw volunteers flocking to Washington would soon be ready for battle and worried that Lincoln might heed calls for "instant and vigorous action, regardless, I fear, of the consequences." Instead of a hasty advance into Virginia, where Confederate forces were concentrated, Scott proposed a carefully prepared "movement down the Mississippi to the ocean," involving 60,000 well-trained troops supported by gunboats. That thrust would isolate the heart of the South from rebellious states west of the Mississippi, he argued, and in conjunction with the blockade would place mounting pressure on Confederate leaders, bringing them "to terms with less bloodshed than any other plan."

Scott's proposal, labeled the Anaconda Plan because it involved squeezing the Confederacy until it yielded or expired, was derided in the press. Critics considered the scheme far too slow and cumbersome at a time when editor Horace Greeley was raising the cry "Forward to Richmond!" and urging capture of that city before the Confederate Congress convened there on July 20. Only after hopes of quick victory were dashed would the public recognize the grim necessity of slowly throttling the Confederacy. Ideas that once seemed far-fetched—such as wrecking the Southern economy by preventing cotton from reaching market ❸ and causing slaves to rebel ❹ or flee their cruel overseers ❺—began to make sense as Northerners realized that their foes would not yield until deprived of the means to wage war. ■

DRAGON-SLAYER Despite his heroic reputation, Winfield Scott—shown here as Hercules slaying a Hydra representing various Confederate leaders—faced public criticism for his Anaconda Plan, whose merits were not widely recognized until after he retired in late 1861.

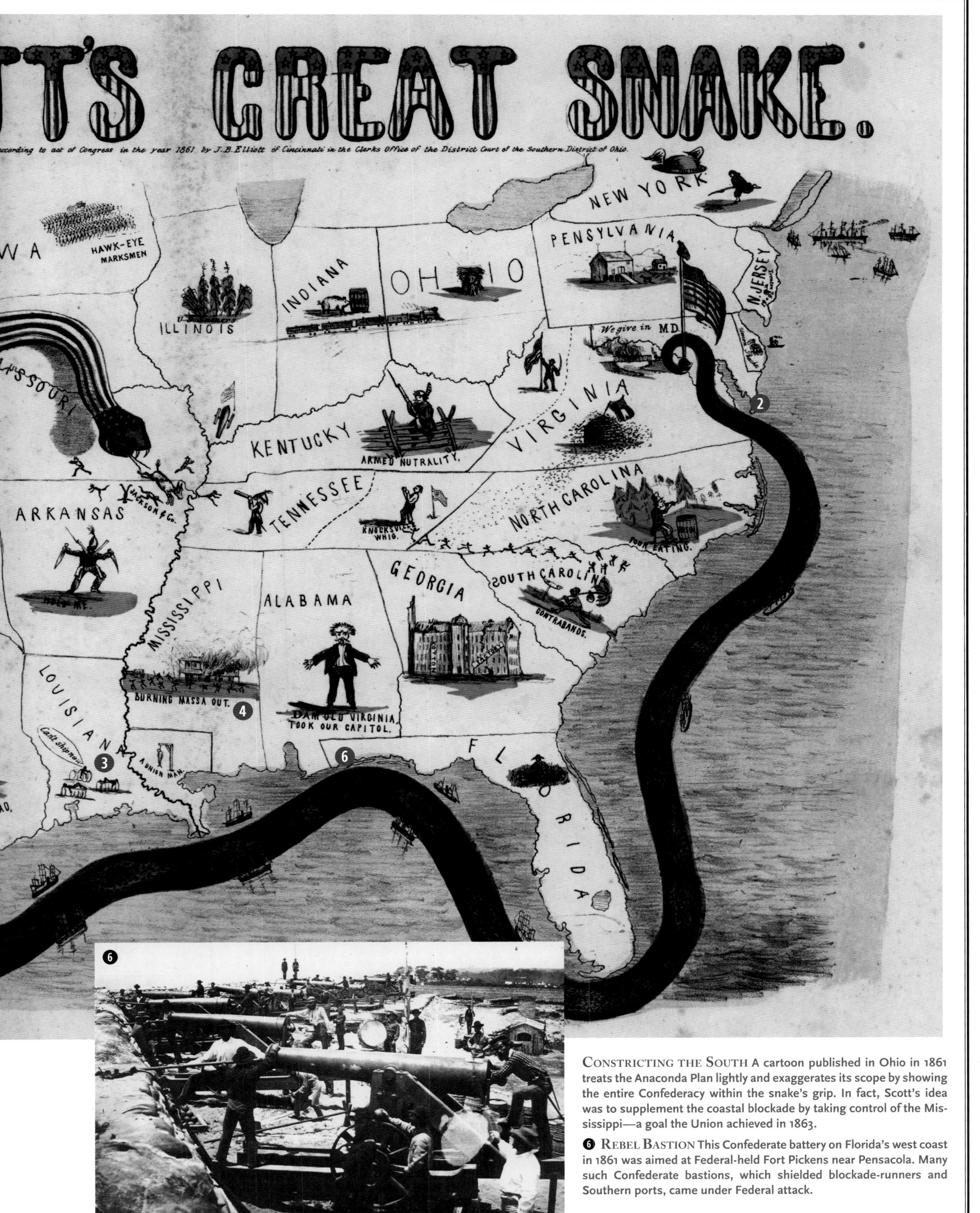

Constricting the South A cartoon published in Ohio in 1861 treats the Anaconda Plan lightly and exaggerates its scope by showing the entire Confederacy within the snake's grip. In fact, Scott's idea was to supplement the coastal blockade by taking control of the Mississippi—a goal the Union achieved in 1863.

❻ Rebel Bastion This Confederate battery on Florida's west coast in 1861 was aimed at Federal-held Fort Pickens near Pensacola. Many such Confederate bastions, which shielded blockade-runners and Southern ports, came under Federal attack.

FORTRESS MONROE, OLD POINT COMFORT AND HYGEIA HOTEL, Va.

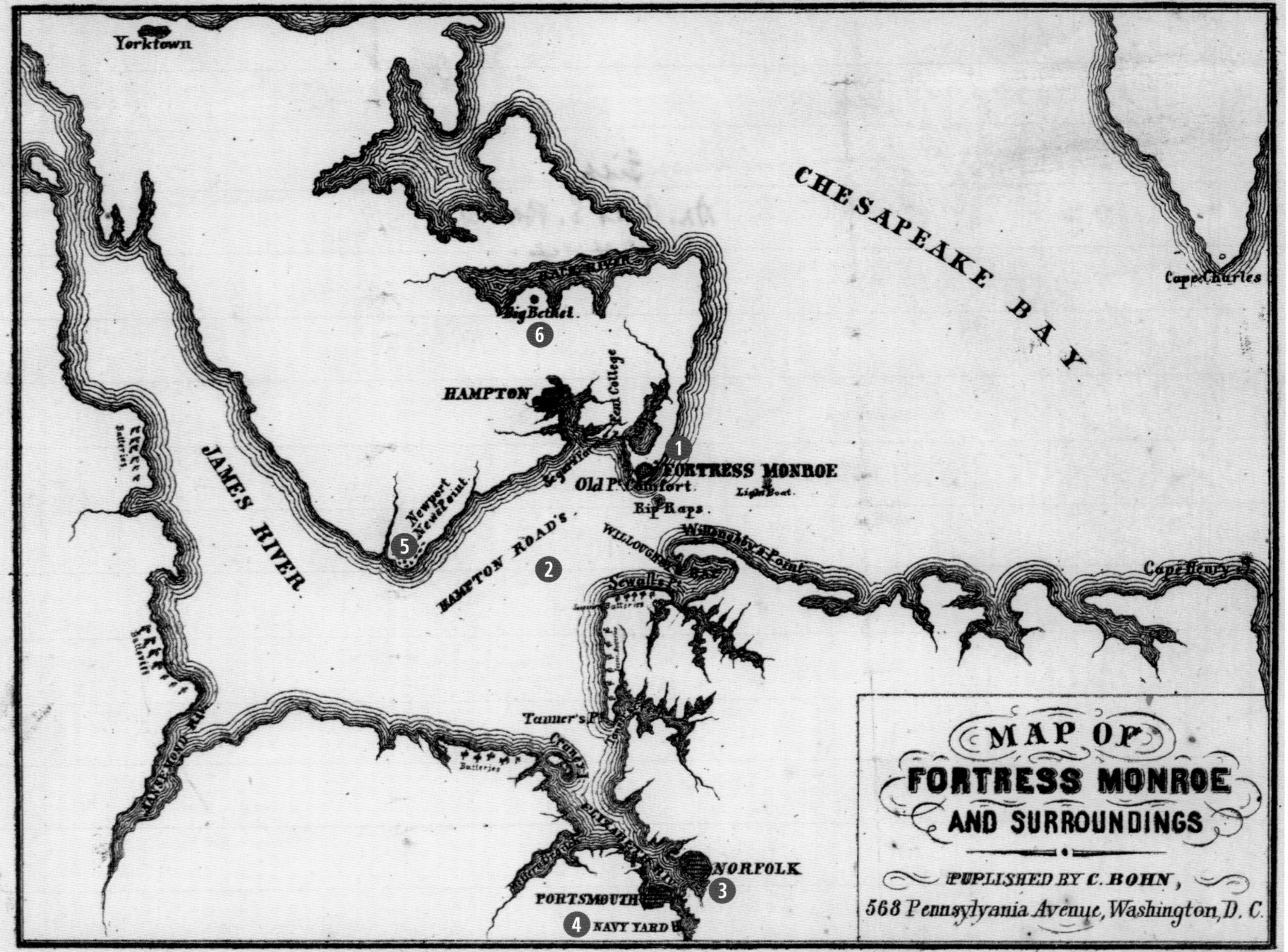

Yorktown
CHESAPEAKE BAY
Cape Charles
Big Bethel
6
HAMPTON
1
FORTRESS MONROE
Old Pt. Comfort
Light Boat
Rip Raps
JAMES RIVER
Batteries
Newport News Point
5
HAMPTON ROADS
2
Willoughby's Point
Cape Henry
Sewall's Pt.
Batteries
Tanner's Pt.
Batteries
NORFOLK
3
PORTSMOUTH
4
NAVY YARD

MAP OF
FORTRESS MONROE
AND SURROUNDINGS

PUPLISHED BY C. BOHN,
568 Pennsylvania Avenue, Washington, D. C.

1861 ANACONDA PLAN

Fort Monroe

Crucial to Federal hopes of sealing off the Confederacy and hampering its economy and war-making capacity was control of Fort Monroe ❶, overlooking Hampton Roads ❷, a channel at the mouth of the James River that linked Richmond, Norfolk ❸, and Confederate-held Gosport Navy Yard ❹ to the outside world. Often referred to as a fortress, Monroe—one of the few Federal strongholds in the South not seized by secessionists—helped enforce the naval blockade with its heavy artillery, including a 52,000-pound blockbuster called the Union Gun, which could hit targets up to four miles away.

Fort Monroe also served as a springboard for Federal occupation forces, who advanced toward Newport News Point ❺ in May. When asked by a Virginian what right they had to invade the state's "sacred soil," their commander replied, "By God, sir, might makes right." By June, there were nearly 5,000 Federals in the area, led by newly arrived Major General Benjamin Butler. A former state senator from Massachusetts, Butler lacked military experience but demonstrated his political acumen when escaped slaves sought refuge at Fort Monroe. Some of them had been employed erecting Confederate batteries, and he felt compelled "to deprive their masters of their services." Freeing them was sure to antagonize slave owners in border states vital to the Union, however, so Butler held them as "contraband of war," or enemy property subject to confiscation. The slaves he harbored worked for the Union and received food and, eventually, wages in return. Soon nearly a thousand fugitives, including entire families, were living here at the place they called "fort freedom."

Alarmed by recent Federal advances, Confederates dug in at Big Bethel ❻, about eight miles from Fort Monroe. Seeking to dislodge them, Butler launched an ill-conceived attack on June 10 in which two Federal columns following separate paths converged there before dawn and accidentally exchanged fire, killing or wounding a number of men and alerting Confederates to their presence. "The enemy were not in line of battle on the open field as we expected," wrote one Federal, "but entrenched behind a thicket of brush and woods." After charging those works to no avail, Butler's troops retreated, having "fought both friend and foe alike with equal resolution," as one Northern newspaper reported. This was a mere skirmish compared to later battles in Virginia, but it signaled how hard it would be for Federals unfamiliar with this country to defeat Confederates on their own ground. ■

STRONGHOLD AT HAMPTON ROADS Shown at left in 1861, Fort Monroe was built on a spit of land separating Hampton Roads from the Chesapeake Bay and was too strong for Confederates intent on breaking the Federal blockade to challenge. As Winfield Scott remarked, "Fort Monroe is by far the most secure post now in possession of the U.S."

❺ ❻ **WAR AND PEACE** Two sketches by artist Alfred Waud, who followed Union troops and portrayed the conflict firsthand, show a family of fugitive slaves called contrabands gathered quietly outside their hut at Newport News and Zouaves of the 5th New York Infantry mounting a promising attack at Big Bethel that was ultimately repulsed.

❺

"I shall hold these Negroes as contraband of war."

FEDERAL MAJOR GENERAL BENJAMIN F. BUTLER
AT FORT MONROE

❻

1861

BULL RUN

EASTERN THEATER

JUNE 29, 1861 Lincoln authorizes an attack on Confederates at Manassas Junction in Virginia.

JULY 16 Federal forces under General Irvin McDowell advance from the Potomac, prompting General P. G. T. Beauregard to withdraw Confederate troops from outposts at Fairfax Court House and Centreville and take up a defensive position below Bull Run.

JULY 18 Federals clash with Confederates at Blackburn's Ford on Bull Run near Manassas Junction.

JULY 19 Confederates under General Joseph Johnston begin arriving from the Shenandoah Valley at Manassas Junction to support Beauregard's forces.

JULY 21 First Battle of Bull Run (Virginia)

Against the advice of generals who said Union forces were not ready for battle, Abraham Lincoln authorized an attack on Confederates at Manassas Junction ❶ in late June. The 75,000 troops he had summoned in April were three-month volunteers, and they were expected to fight before their terms expired. Congress had recently called for 500,000 three-year volunteers, but the patriotic fervor that drew recruits to Washington after Fort Sumter fell would fade if Lincoln did not strike back soon. Major General Irvin McDowell wanted more time to train his raw troops before challenging the enemy in Virginia, but Lincoln was firm. "You are green, it is true," he told McDowell, "but they are green also."

The task of defending vital Manassas Junction—where the Manassas Gap Railroad ❷ from the Shenandoah Valley joined the Orange & Alexandria Railroad ❸, which connected with a line to Richmond—fell to Brigadier General P. G. T. Beauregard, who had led Confederates at Charleston. Unlike McDowell, Beauregard had orders to remain on the defensive, which could be advantageous in an era when increasingly lethal artillery and small arms placed attackers at greater risk than well-prepared defenders. Beauregard had around 20,000 troops at Manassas to hold off McDowell's 36,000-man army, and other Confederates were prepared to come to his aid, including reserves under Brigadier General Theophilus Holmes at Aquia Landing ❹. Beauregard's force would nearly equal McDowell's if Brigadier General Joseph Johnston's Confederate Army of the Shenandoah, holding Winchester ❺, shifted to Manassas. To prevent that, Major General Robert Patterson was sent to reclaim Harpers Ferry for the Union and menace Winchester. But Patterson faltered, allowing Johnston to embark for Manassas Junction, where his forces began arriving by train as battle loomed.

Informed of McDowell's movements by cavalry scouts and by Confederate spy Rose O'Neal Greenhow, Beauregard withdrew from advance outposts at Fairfax Court House ❻ and Centreville ❼ in mid-July and awaited attack behind Bull Run ❽. A sluggish stream that could be crossed by a stone bridge on the Warrenton Turnpike ❾ or at one of several fords, Bull Run had steep banks and made a good defensive barrier. But Beauregard was not thinking strictly defensively. He placed most of his troops east of the bridge near the Orange & Alexandria Railroad, expecting McDowell to seek the shortest path to Manassas Junction and focus his attack there. This lopsided deployment gave Beauregard the opportunity to counterattack once he had deflected the expected Federal thrust along the railroad, but it left an opening for McDowell west of the Stone Bridge, where he would attempt to outflank the Confederates. ■

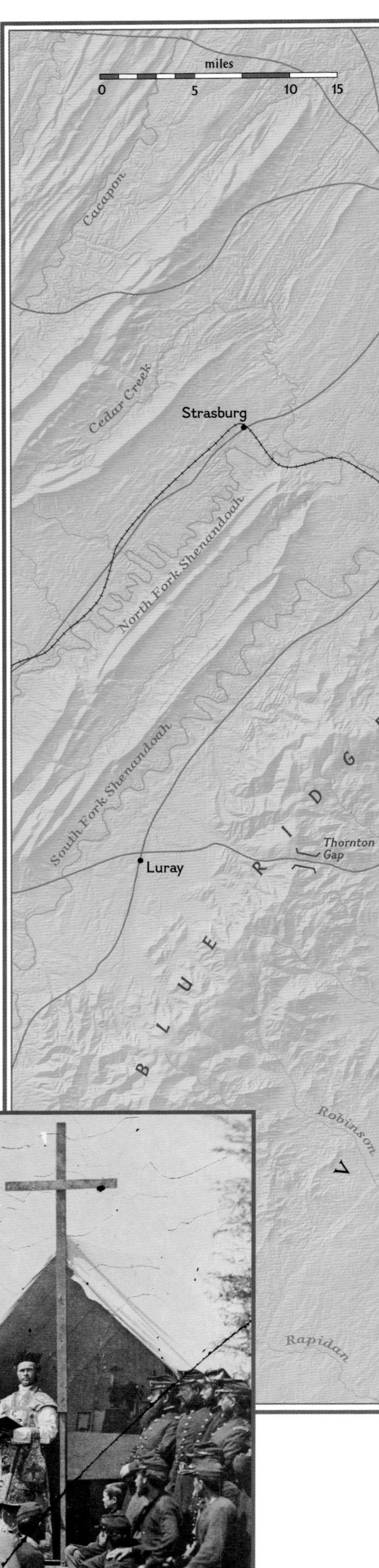

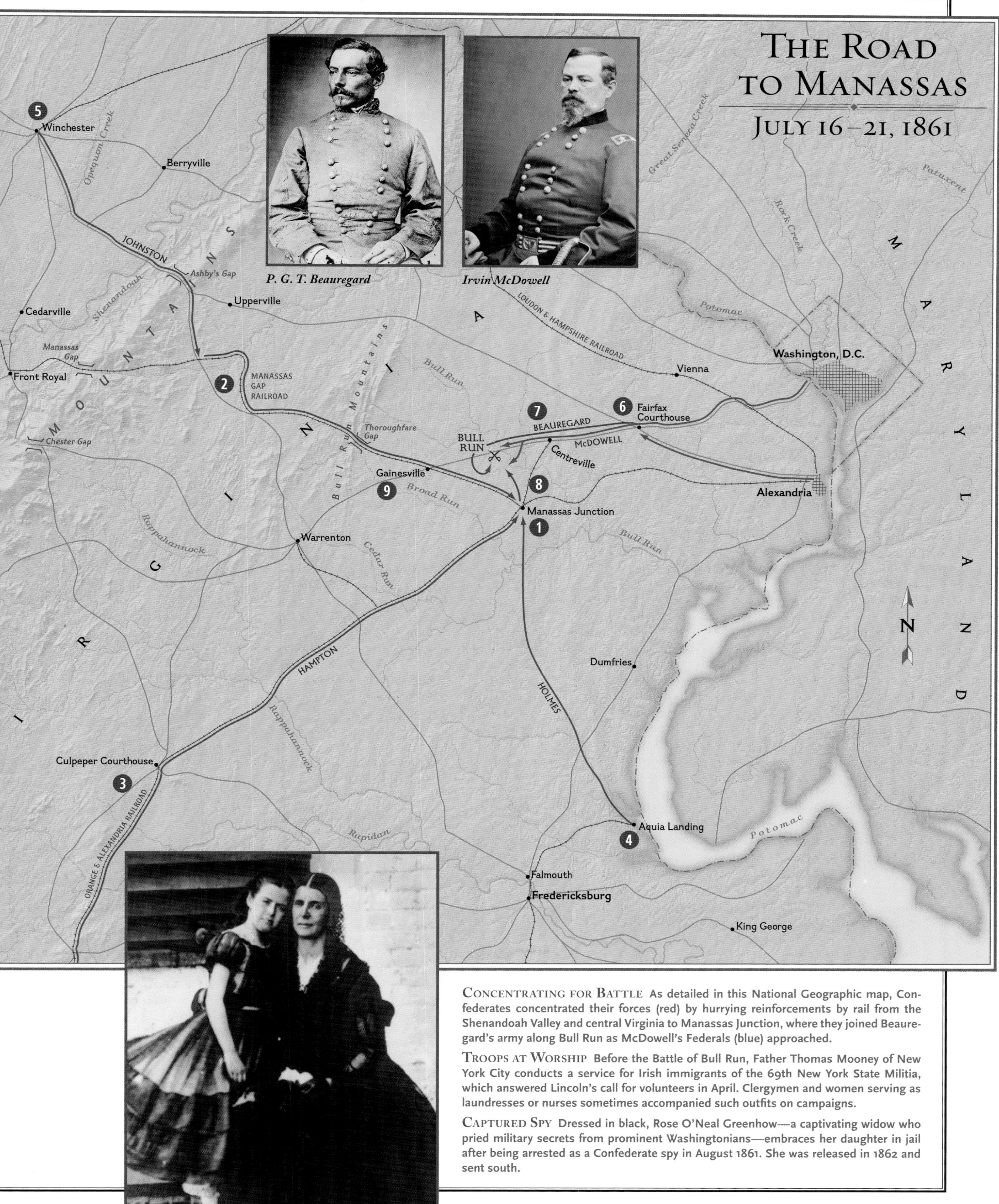

CONCENTRATING FOR BATTLE As detailed in this National Geographic map, Confederates concentrated their forces (red) by hurrying reinforcements by rail from the Shenandoah Valley and central Virginia to Manassas Junction, where they joined Beauregard's army along Bull Run as McDowell's Federals (blue) approached.

TROOPS AT WORSHIP Before the Battle of Bull Run, Father Thomas Mooney of New York City conducts a service for Irish immigrants of the 69th New York State Militia, which answered Lincoln's call for volunteers in April. Clergymen and women serving as laundresses or nurses sometimes accompanied such outfits on campaigns.

CAPTURED SPY Dressed in black, Rose O'Neal Greenhow—a captivating widow who pried military secrets from prominent Washingtonians—embraces her daughter in jail after being arrested as a Confederate spy in August 1861. She was released in 1862 and sent south.

1861 | BULL RUN

SHOWDOWN AT BULL RUN

Sent ahead by Major General Irvin McDowell on July 18 to probe enemy defenses along Bull Run, Federal troops under Brigadier General Daniel Tyler advanced along Centreville Road ❶ and clashed with Virginians led by Brigadier General James Longstreet at Blackburn's Ford ❷. As this contest indicated, Brigadier General P. G. T. Beauregard was ready for an attack there and at other crossings near the Orange & Alexandria Railroad ❸ and had strengthened that sector at the expense of his left flank, west of the Stone Bridge ❹. McDowell made plans to turn that flank by sending nearly half his troops toward Sudley Ford ❺ while the rest of his army kept Beauregard's main force pinned down to the east. While McDowell prepared this attack, thousands of enemy reinforcements reached Manassas Junction ❻.

Around 9 A.M. on July 21, Federals of Brigadier General David Hunter's division ❼ emerged from the woods, crossed Sudley Ford, and slammed into Confederates led by Colonel Nathan Evans and Major Roberdeau Wheat ❽. Their exposed forces held out long enough for Brigadier General Barnard Bee and Colonel Francis Bartow—both of whom later fell mortally wounded here—to reinforce them near the Stone House ❾. Around noon, however, Colonel William T. Sherman's brigade crossed near the Stone Bridge and helped dislodge those Confederates, who retreated in disarray toward Manassas Junction. Only quick action by Brigadier General Joseph Johnston and his keen subordinate, Brigadier General Thomas J. Jackson, saved Beauregard from disaster.

While Johnston hurried the last of his forces to reach Manassas Junction into action, led by Brigadier General Edmund Kirby Smith ❿, Jackson earned the name "Stonewall" by standing firm under fire with his Virginians ⓫, who then overran the Union battery commanded by Captain James Ricketts ⓬. Rallying, Confederates drove their foes back from the Henry House ⓭ and across Bull Run in a rout that did not end until the demoralized Yankees reached Washington. The battle "was lost to us," Sherman concluded, "because our army was as green as grass." ■

Thomas J. Jackson in 1857

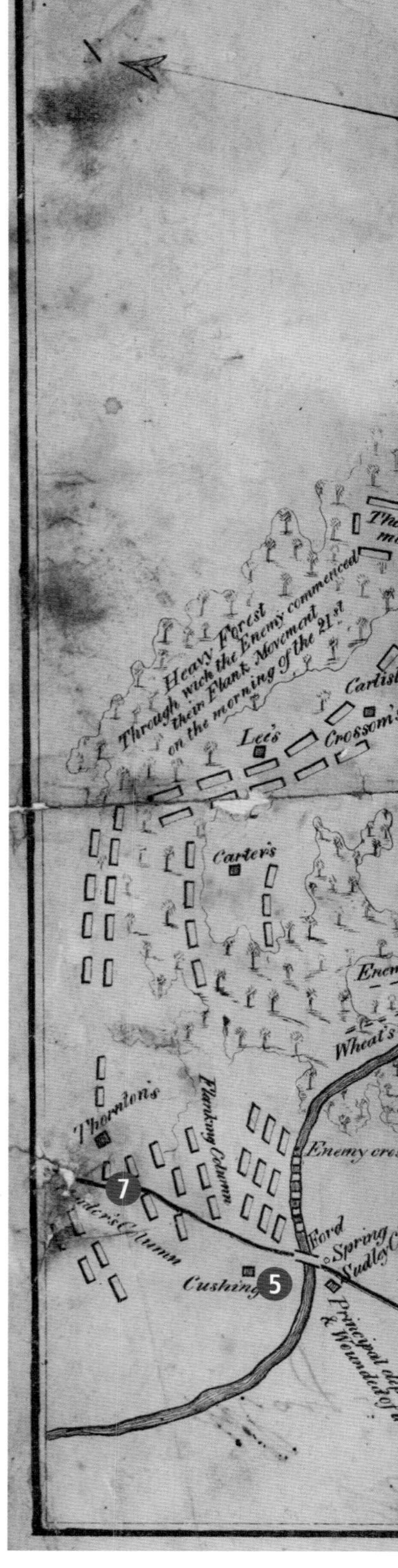

THE FIRST GREAT BATTLE Brimming with eyewitness details, this map was prepared by Captain Samuel Mitchell of the 1st Virginia Infantry, which fought at Blackburn's Ford and came under artillery fire during the Battle of Bull Run. As revealed by the key and notes showing where Confederate officers such as Colonel Bartow and General Bee fell, Mitchell knew the Rebels' situation well but identified few opposing units and overstated the number of Union troops and losses. Around 2,600 Federals and 2,000 Confederates were reported killed, wounded, or missing.

❾ **STONE HOUSE** This residence at the intersection of the Warrenton Turnpike and Sudley Road fared far better than the Henry House nearby, where a shell tore through the wall on July 21, killing bedridden widow Judith Henry.

❹ **STONE BRIDGE** During the battle, Federal troops crossed this span, later destroyed by Confederates when they withdrew from here in 1862.

ORDER OF BATTLE

UNION FORCES

McDowell | 36,000 men

1ST DIVISION *Tyler*
Keyes, Schenck, Sherman, Richardson
2ND DIVISION *Hunter*
Porter, Burnside
3RD DIVISION *Heintzelman*
Franklin, Willcox, Howard
RESERVE DIVISION *Runyon*
5TH DIVISION *Miles*
Blenker, Davies

CONFEDERATE FORCES

ARMY OF THE POTOMAC
Beauregard | 22,000 men

Brigades Bonham, Ewell, D. R. Jones, Longstreet, Cocke, Early, Evans, Holmes
Unbrigaded Regiments (Infantry, Cavalry & Artillery)
Hampton, Stuart, Radford

ARMY OF THE SHENANDOAH
Johnston | 10,000 men

Brigades Jackson, Bartow, Bee, Elzey

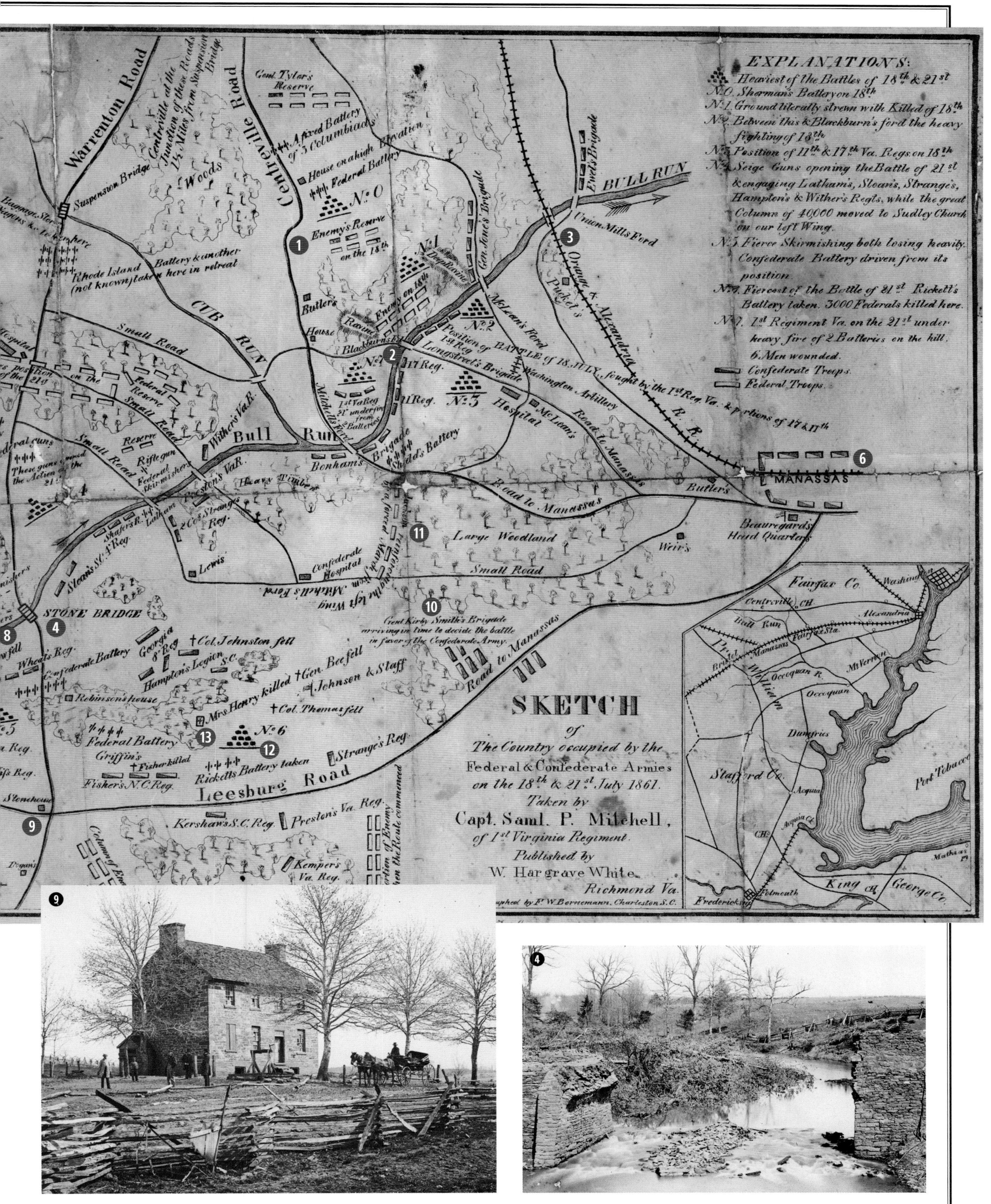

EXPLANATIONS:
Heaviest of the Battles of 18th & 21st
No. 0. Sherman's Battery on 18th
No. 1. Ground literally strewn with Killed of 18th
No. 2. Between this & Blackburn's ford the heavy fighting of 18th
No. 3. Position of 11th & 17th Va. Regs. on 18th
No. 4. Seige Guns opening the Battle of 21st & engaging Latham's, Sloan's, Strange's, Hampton's & Wither's Regts. while the great Column of 40,000 moved to Sudley Church on our left Wing.
No. 5. Fierce Skirmishing both losing heavily. Confederate Battery driven from its position.
No. 6. Fiercest of the Battle of 21st. Rickett's Battery taken. 3000 Federals killed here.
No. 7. 1st Regiment Va. on the 21st under heavy fire of 2 Batteries on the hill. 6 Men wounded.
Confederate Troops.
Federal Troops.
SKETCH
of
The Country occupied by the Federal & Confederate Armies on the 18th & 21st July 1861.
Taken by
Capt. Saml. P. Mitchell,
of 1st Virginia Regiment.
Published by
W. Hargrave White.
Richmond Va.
Warrenton Road
Centreville Road
Suspension Bridge
Woods
Gent. Tyler's Reserve
A fixed Battery of 3 Columbiads
House on a high Elevation
Federal Battery
Enemy's Reserve on the 18th
Rhode Island Battery & another (not known) taken here in retreat
BULL RUN
Union Mills Ford
Ewel's Brigade
Gen. Jones's Brigade
CUB RUN
Small Road
Butler's House
Blackburn's Ford
McLean's Ford
Orange & Alexandria R. R.
Pucket's
Longstreet's Brigade
Washington Artillery
Hospital
McLean's
Road to Manassas
BATTLE of 18 JULY, fought by the 1st Reg. Va. & portions of 17 & 11th
Withers Va. R.
Bull Run
Bonham's
Shield's Battery
Preston's Va. R.
Heavy Timber
MANASSAS
Butler's
Beauregard's Head Quarters
Large Woodland
Weir's
Small Road
Confederate Hospital
Lewis'
STONE BRIDGE
Gent. Kirby Smith's Brigade arriving in time to decide the battle in favor of the Confederate Army.
Road to Manassas
Wheat's Reg.
Confederate Battery
Georgia 8th Reg.
Hampton's Legion S.C.
Col. Johnston fell
Gen. Bee fell
Johnsen & Staff
Robinson's house
Mrs Henry killed
Col. Thomas fell
Federal Battery
No. 6
Griffin's
Fisher killed
Ricketts Battery taken
Strange's Reg.
Fisher's N.C. Reg.
Leesburg Road
Stonehouse
Kershaw's S.C. Reg.
Preston's Va. Reg.
Kemper's Va. Reg.
Fairfax Co.
Washington
Centreville
Bull Run
Alexandria
Manassas
Mt. Vernon
Occoquan
Dumfries
Stafford Co.
Port Tobacco
King George Co.
Fredericksburg
1
2
3
4
6
8
9
10
11
12
13

1861

BELMONT

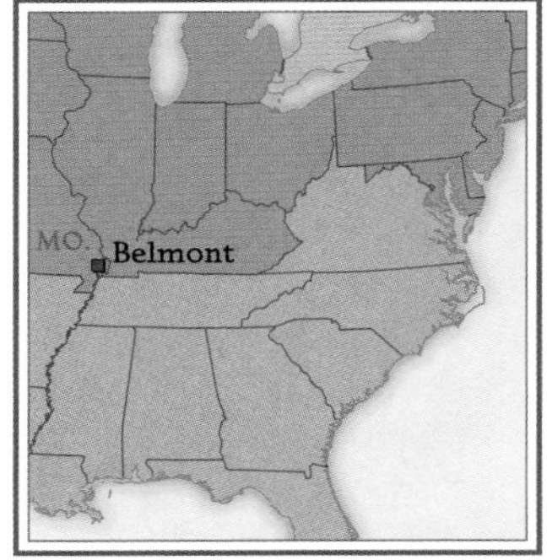

WESTERN THEATER

JULY 25, 1861 General John Frémont arrives in St. Louis, Missouri, to take charge of the Union Army's Western Department.

AUGUST 10 Battle of Wilson's Creek (Missouri)

AUGUST 30 Frémont declares martial law in Missouri and names General Ulysses Grant to command Federal forces at Cairo, Illinois.

SEPTEMBER 3 Confederates under General Leonidas Polk occupy Columbus, Kentucky.

NOVEMBER 7 Battle of Belmont (Missouri)

Following the debacle at Bull Run, McDowell was replaced by Major General George McClellan, a perfectionist who put off campaigning until his men were fully trained. But the Union commander in the West, Major General John Frémont, could not avoid battle in Missouri, where Federals were defeated at Wilson's Creek on August 10. To punish those who aided Confederates or proslavery Border Ruffians haunting the Missouri-Kansas line, Frémont announced his intention to free all slaves belonging to disloyal citizens, causing Lincoln to remove him. Frémont's parting gift to his department was the officer he chose and left in charge at strategically situated Cairo, Illinois, where the Ohio River meets the Mississippi—Brigadier General Ulysses S. Grant.

On November 7, Grant attacked Belmont, Missouri, a weak Confederate outpost across from heavily fortified Columbus, Kentucky, where Rebel batteries ❶ brooded over the Mississippi. After steaming downriver from Cairo in transports ❷, led by the river gunboats *Tyler* and *Lexington* ❸, Grant landed with 3,000 men north of Belmont and seized the enemy camp ❹, igniting a wild celebration by his men, raw recruits from Illinois and Iowa. Euphoria gave way to panic when the "Fighting Bishop," Major General Leonidas Polk, ferried Confederate reinforcements over from Columbus and bombarded Grant's troops and gunboats ❺. Some Union officers wanted to surrender, but Grant would have none of it. "We cut our way in and can cut our way out," he said. By extricating his forces from Belmont, the resolute Grant averted disaster and earned a reputation as one who would never give up. ■

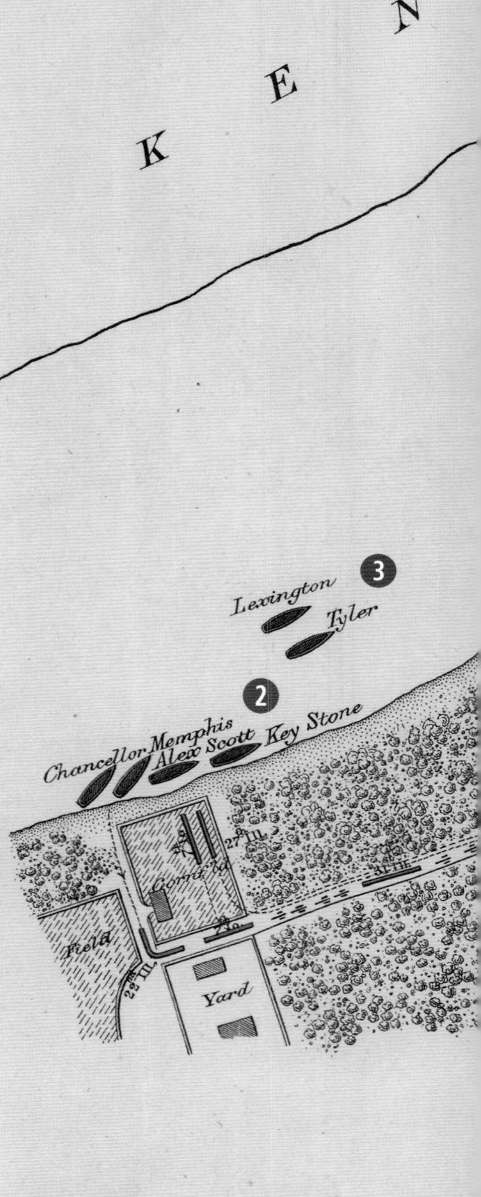

FAST TRANSPORT Grant, who considered swift movement the key to victory, used the steamboat *Aleck Scott*, photographed in early 1862, and other transports to carry troops to Belmont from his base here in Cairo.

GRANT'S DEBUT A postwar U.S. Army map shows the path Grant's forces followed at Belmont. Grant, shown in 1861, was obscure compared with his opponent, Polk, a West Point–trained Episcopalian bishop from Louisiana.

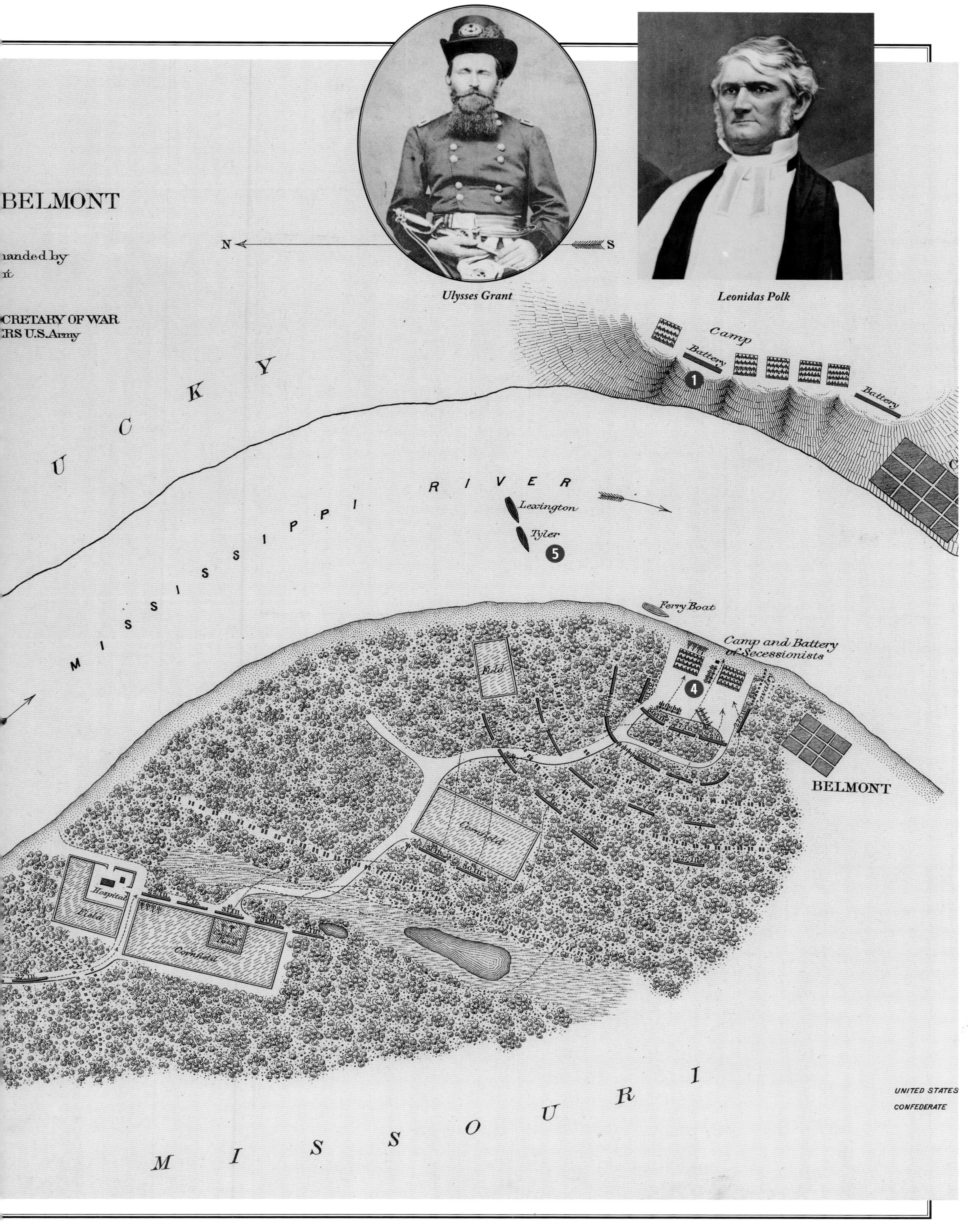

Ulysses Grant

Leonidas Polk

PORT ROYAL

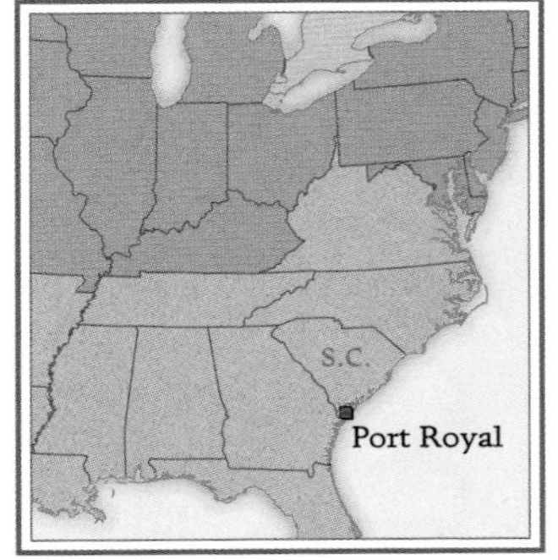

THE BLOCKADE

AUGUST 29, 1861 Federals secure Hatteras Inlet and close off Pamlico Sound following the bombardment of Confederate Forts Clark and Hatteras.

SEPTEMBER 17 Federals occupy Ship Island, off the coast of Mississippi, which becomes a base for the Gulf Blockading Squadron.

NOVEMBER 7 Union warships drive Confederates from Forts Walker and Beauregard and win control of Port Royal Sound, which becomes a base for the South Atlantic Blockading Squadron.

In a year when Confederate troops prevailed on land, the Union made significant gains in coastal waters. On August 29, a Federal fleet drove Rebels from forts guarding Hatteras Inlet and secured that objective, thus sealing off Pamlico Sound on the North Carolina coast. Later in the year, the U.S. Navy targeted Port Royal Sound ❶, a deep-water harbor on the South Carolina coast coveted as a base for ships on blockade duty, which had no coaling or supply stations between Hampton Roads and Key West. Coal was essential because increasing numbers of Union warships relied less on sails than on steam power, which allowed them to enter inlets and bombard forts without being adversely affected by wind or tide.

Assembled for the Port Royal assault was the largest U.S. armada to date, made up of 77 vessels, including transports carrying more than 12,000 troops to occupy the harbor. Early on November 7, Union warships commanded by Flag Officer Samuel Du Pont entered the mouth of the sound ❷ and cruised in an oval course while exchanging fire with Forts Beauregard ❸ and Walker ❹. Confederates there were heavily outgunned and did little damage to their moving targets. In contrast, one officer reported, the Federals poured in shots "with the precision of target practice." This thunderous battle, heard more than 50 miles away, ended that afternoon when the forts' battered defenders ran short of ammunition and withdrew. The capture of Port Royal Sound gave the Union a superb base from which to blockade Savannah ❺, Charleston ❻, and other ports vital to the Confederacy. ■

❷ FLAGSHIP TRIUMPHANT Flying the Stars and Stripes, Du Pont's flagship, U.S.S. *Wabash*, pounds a Confederate fort at the entrance to Port Royal Sound in a Currier & Ives lithograph celebrating the Union victory there.

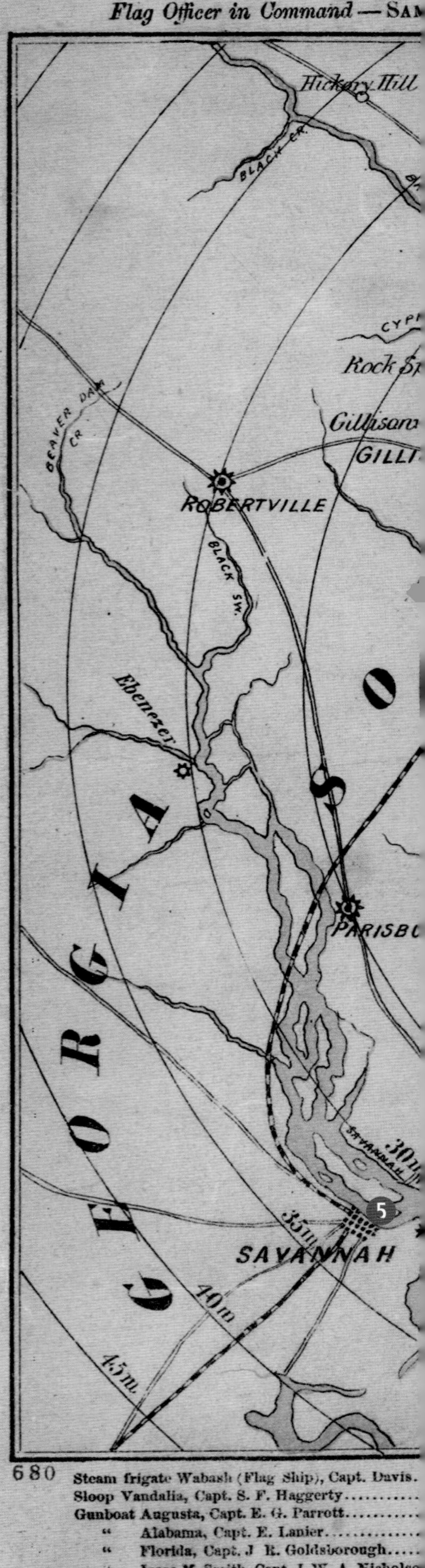

THE UNION'S NEW BASE A commemorative chart published in Boston portrays Port Royal Sound and lists ships involved in capturing it. The big Federal base established here extended from Beaufort on Port Royal Island to Hilton Head Island and sheltered many slaves seeking freedom.

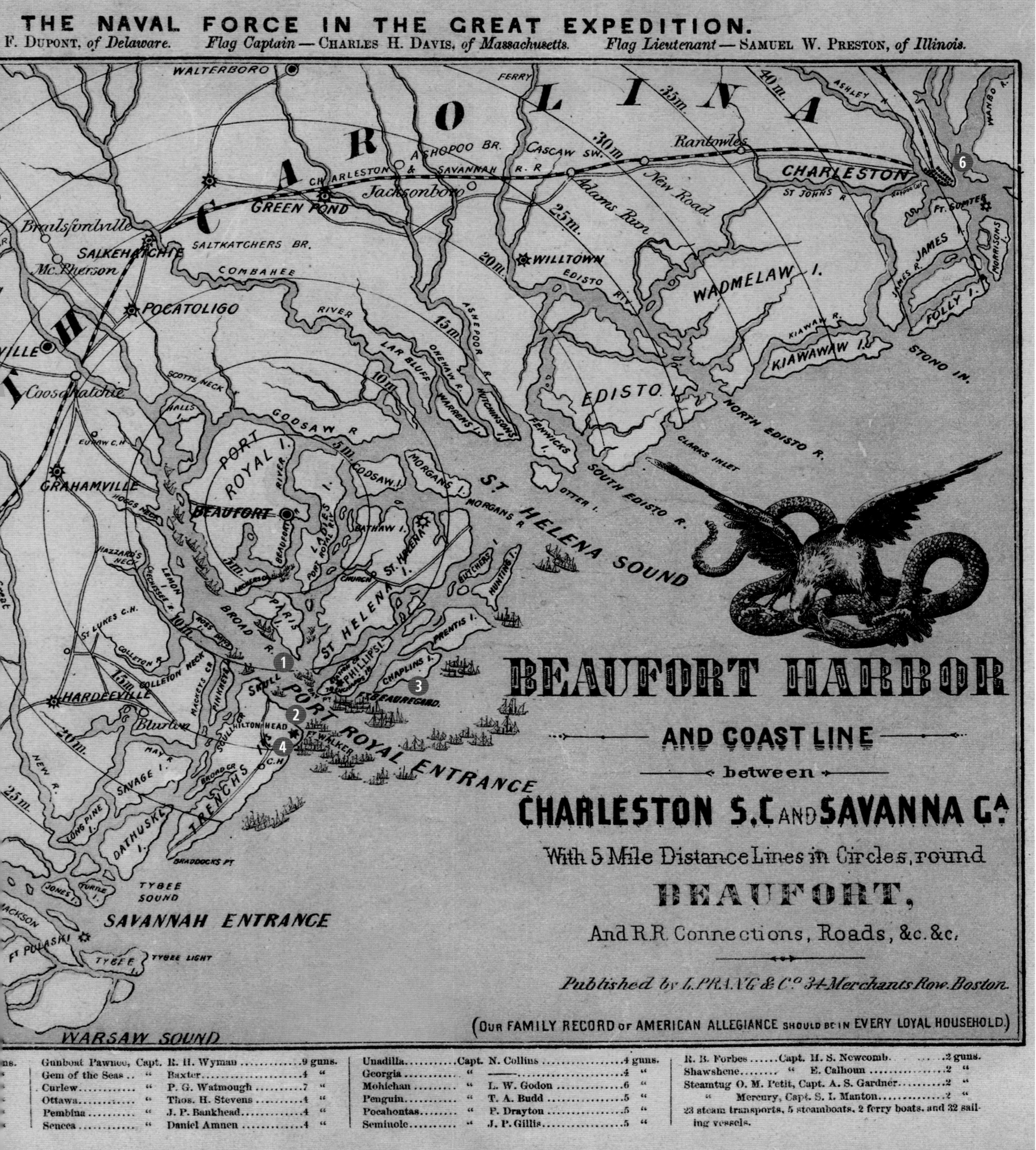

THE NAVAL FORCE IN THE GREAT EXPEDITION.
F. Dupont, of Delaware. Flag Captain — Charles H. Davis, of Massachusetts. Flag Lieutenant — Samuel W. Preston, of Illinois.
CAROLINA
WALTERBORO
CHARLESTON
Rantowles
CHARLESTON & SAVANNAH R. R
ASHEPOO BR.
CASCAW SW.
Jacksonboro
GREEN POND
Adams Run
New Road
SALKEHATCHIE
SALTKATCHERS BR.
Bralsfordville
McPherson
COMBAHEE RIVER
WILLTOWN
EDISTO RIV.
WADMELAW I.
JAMES I.
FT. SUMTER
FOLLY I.
KIAWAWAW I.
STONO IN.
POCATOLIGO
Coosawhatchie
EDISTO I.
NORTH EDISTO R.
SOUTH EDISTO R.
OTTER I.
GRAHAMVILLE
PORT ROYAL I.
BEAUFORT
ST HELENA SOUND
ST HELENA I.
BROAD R.
HARDEEVILLE
Bluffton
HILTON HEAD
FT WALKER
BEAUREGARD.
PORT ROYAL ENTRANCE
SKULL CR.
TRENCHS I.
SAVAGE I.
DATHUSKE I.
TYBEE SOUND
SAVANNAH ENTRANCE
FT PULASKI
TYBEE
TYBEE LIGHT
WARSAW SOUND
1
2
3
4
6
BEAUFORT HARBOR
AND COAST LINE
between
CHARLESTON S.C AND SAVANNA G^A.
With 5 Mile Distance Lines in Circles, round
BEAUFORT,
And R.R. Connections, Roads, &c. &c.
Published by L. Prang & Co. 34 Merchants Row. Boston.
(Our FAMILY RECORD of AMERICAN ALLEGIANCE should be in EVERY LOYAL HOUSEHOLD.)
Gunboat Pawnee, Capt. R. H. Wyman ....9 guns.
Gem of the Seas .. " Baxter....................4 "
Curlew............ " P. G. Watmough ....7 "
Ottawa............ " Thos. H. Stevens ....4 "
Pembina .... " J. P. Bankhead.............4 "
Seneca .... " Daniel Amnen ....4 "
Unadilla..........Capt. N. Collins ....4 guns.
Georgia .... " ——.......................4 "
Mohichan .... " L. W. Godon ....6 "
Penguin........... " T. A. Budd ....5 "
Pocahontas........ " P. Drayton ....5 "
Seminole.......... " J. P. Gillis..................5 "
R. B. Forbes ......Capt. H. S. Newcomb..........2 guns.
Shawshene........ " E. Calhoun ....2 "
Steamtug O. M. Petit, Capt. A. S. Gardner..........2 "
" Mercury, Capt. S. I. Manton.............2 "
23 steam transports, 5 steamboats, 2 ferry boats, and 32 sailing vessels.

CHAPTER 2

1862 | War on a Grand Scale

"All tell me that I am held responsible for the fate of the Nation & that all its resources shall be placed at my disposal."

GENERAL GEORGE McCLELLAN,
AFTER TAKING COMMAND OF FEDERAL FORCES

Union soldiers overlook a supply base at Cumberland Landing in Virginia, used to equip McClellan's army of more than 100,000 men as it approached Richmond in May 1862.

1862
NO EASY VICTORY

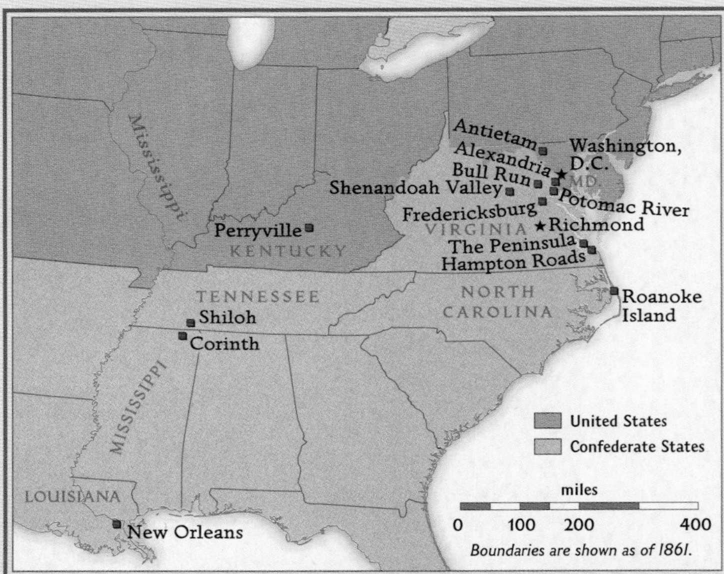

When the Civil War began, many Americans thought it would be over before the year was out. And when 1862 dawned, few suspected that what they had witnessed since April was trifling compared to the carnage that lay ahead. The prevailing sentiment on both sides was to stay the course, or the sacrifices made thus far would count for nothing. As essayist and Unionist Ralph Waldo Emerson wrote on New Year's Day, "Far better that this grinding should go on, bad and worse, than we should be driven by any impatience into a hasty peace restoring the old rottenness."

Prospects for peace receded in the year ahead as the war grew vastly in scale and scope without bringing a decision. Few areas were unaffected, as Confederates from Texas invaded New Mexico, igniting conflict that drew Union soldiers from Colorado and California. Creeks and Cherokees of the Five Civilized Tribes were divided, with Indians fighting on both sides in Arkansas. But the biggest battles were waged on land and water between the Mississippi River and the Atlantic Coast. Ulysses Grant led Union forces deep into Tennessee, clashing with Confederates at Shiloh as a Federal fleet gathered to take New Orleans. To the east, George McClellan advanced against Richmond and confronted Robert E. Lee, who returned the favor by heading north into Maryland and meeting McClellan at Antietam on September 17—the nation's bloodiest day and the event that prompted Abraham Lincoln to issue the Emancipation Proclamation. The coinciding invasions of Maryland by Lee and of Kentucky by Braxton Bragg raised Confederate hopes that were dashed when the Rebel tide receded. But Union spirits were crushed in turn by a devastating defeat at Fredericksburg. To paraphrase Emerson, the grinding went on from bad to worse, with no end in sight.

JANUARY–JUNE

January 11 Ambrose Burnside launches a Federal amphibious expedition to the North Carolina coast.

January 18 Confederates lay claim to a disputed area in southern New Mexico, calling it the Territory of Arizona.

January 19–20 Battle of Mill Springs (Kentucky)

January 27 Abraham Lincoln issues General War Order No. 1, calling for Union forces to move "against the insurgent forces" on several fronts.

January 30 Ulysses Grant receives orders to advance from Paducah, Kentucky, up the Tennessee River, supported by ironclads.

February 6 Battle of Fort Henry (Tennessee)

February 8 Battle of Roanoke Island (North Carolina)

February 10 Battle of Elizabeth City (North Carolina)

February 14–15 Battle of Fort Donelson (Tennessee)

February 22 Jefferson Davis is inaugurated in Richmond, Virginia, following a general election confirming his provisional appointment as Confederate president.

February 25 Union troops occupy Nashville, Tennessee.

March 1 Stonewall Jackson receives orders to prevent Federal forces in the Shenandoah Valley from threatening the flank of the Confederate army defending Richmond.

Ironclads in Grant's campaign

JULY–DECEMBER

July 11 Halleck appointed general-in-chief of Union forces.

July 24 Farragut withdraws with fleet down the Mississippi River from Vicksburg, Mississippi, ending the first Federal campaign there.

August 3 Lincoln recalls McClellan's army to Washington; Lee launches offensive against John Pope in northern Virginia.

August 9 Battle of Cedar Mountain (Virginia)

Confederate currency, issued July 1862

August 17 Minnesota Sioux Uprising begins, diverting Federal troops from the war against the Confederacy.

August 22 Jeb Stuart raids Pope's headquarters at Catlett's Station.

August 26 Stonewall Jackson raids Federal supply depot at Manassas Junction.

August 28 Confederate army under Bragg enters Kentucky.

August 28–30 Second Battle of Bull Run, or Manassas (Virginia)

August 30 Confederates repulse Federals near Richmond, Kentucky, and go on to occupy Lexington.

September 1 Battle of Chantilly (Virginia)

September 2 Lincoln removes Pope from command and places McClellan in charge of all Federal troops around Washington.

September 4 Lee invades Maryland.

March 7–8 Battle of Pea Ridge (Arkansas)

March 9 Ironclads *Virginia* and the *Monitor* clash at Hampton Roads (Virginia).

March 14 Battle of New Bern (North Carolina)

March 17 George McClellan's Army of the Potomac begins embarking from Alexandria, Virginia, for Fort Monroe to advance against Richmond.

March 23 Battle of Kernstown (Virginia)

March 26–28 Federals clash with Confederates in New Mexico at Apache Canyon and Glorieta Pass, forcing them to return to Texas.

April 6–7 Battle of Shiloh (Tennessee)

April 11 Henry Halleck arrives at Pittsburg Landing in Tennessee to take charge of Grant's forces following the Battle of Shiloh.

April 16 Jefferson Davis approves an act of the Confederate Congress making every white male between 18 and 35 subject to conscription for three years' service.

Benjamin "Beast" Butler, as viewed by Southerners

April 18 Federal fleet led by David Farragut launches attack on Forts Jackson and St. Philip and goes on to take New Orleans.

April 25 Federal occupation of New Orleans begins, with Benjamin Butler as military governor.

May 3 Confederates besieged by McClellan's forces withdraw from Yorktown, Virginia.

May 5 Battle of Williamsburg (Virginia)

May 8 Battle of McDowell (Virginia)

May 9 Confederates evacuate Norfolk, Virginia.

May 15 Confederate gunners at Drewry's Bluff, Virginia, repulse ironclad *Monitor* and other Union warships moving up the James River.

May 23 Stonewall Jackson takes Front Royal, Virginia, and ousts Federals from Winchester two days later.

May 31 Federals occupy Corinth, Mississippi.

May 31–June 1 Battle of Seven Pines, or Fair Oaks (Virginia)

June 2 Robert E. Lee takes command of Confederate forces defending Richmond.

June 6 Union forces seize Memphis, Tennessee.

June 8 Battle of Cross Keys (Virginia)

June 9 Battle of Port Republic (Virginia)

Federal artillerymen at Seven Pines

June 10 Halleck restores Grant as commander of the Federal Army of the Tennessee, headquartered at Memphis.

June 12 Confederate General James Ewell Brown (Jeb) Stuart launches raid in Virginia that will take his cavalry around McClellan's army.

June 25–July 1 Lee repulses McClellan in Seven Days' Battles around Richmond

June 27 Jefferson Davis relieves P. G. T. Beauregard as commander of the Army of Tennessee and replaces him with Braxton Bragg.

Lincoln at Antietam

September 13 McClellan enters Frederick, Maryland, in pursuit of Lee.

September 14 Battle of South Mountain (Maryland)

September 15 Harpers Ferry falls to Confederates.

September 17 Battle of Antietam (Maryland)

September 18–19 Lee withdraws from Maryland into Virginia.

September 19 Federals clash with Confederates at Iuka, Mississippi.

September 22 Lincoln issues Emancipation Proclamation.

October 3–4 Battle of Corinth (Mississippi)

October 4 Lincoln confers with McClellan at Antietam and urges him to advance quickly into Virginia.

October 8 Battle of Perryville (Kentucky)

October 10 Stuart raids Chambersburg, Pennsylvania.

October 26 McClellan crosses from Maryland into Virginia.

October 27 Lincoln removes Don Carlos Buell as commander of the Army of the Ohio for failing to pursue Confederate forces as they withdrew from Kentucky into Tennessee and replaces him with William Rosecrans.

November 4 Democrats make big gains in Northern congressional elections, reflecting dissatisfaction with Lincoln's war policies.

November 6–7 Lincoln removes McClellan as commander of the Army of the Potomac for moving too slowly and replaces him with Ambrose Burnside.

November 7 Battle of Prairie Grove (Arkansas)

November 15 Burnside launches his forces toward Fredericksburg.

November 17 First Federal forces reach the Rappahannock River across from Fredericksburg but are unable to cross before Lee's troops arrive to defend the town.

December 11 Federals begin laying pontoon bridges and crossing the Rappahannock.

December 13 Battle of Fredericksburg

December 20 Confederate General Earl Van Dorn raids Federal supply depot at Holly Springs, Mississippi, hampering Grant's efforts to advance overland toward Vicksburg.

December 29 Union troops led by General William T. Sherman repulsed at Chickasaw Bluffs, near Vicksburg.

French Mary, mercy worker at Fredericksburg

1862

SHILOH

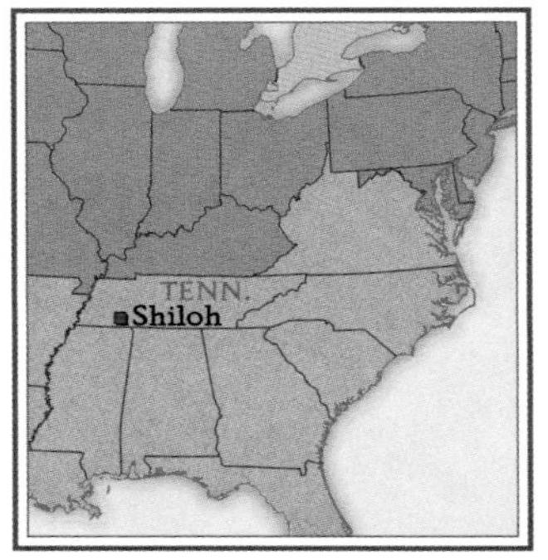

WESTERN THEATER

JANUARY 30, 1862 Ulysses Grant receives orders to advance from Paducah, Kentucky, up the Tennessee River.

FEBRUARY 6 Battle of Fort Henry (Tennessee)

FEBRUARY 14–15 Battle of Fort Donelson

APRIL 6–7 Battle of Shiloh

By January 1862, Brigadier General Ulysses Grant had 20,000 Federal troops ready to advance from Cairo, Illinois ❶, at the confluence of the Ohio ❷ and Mississippi ❸ Rivers. Blocked from moving down the Mississippi by the Confederate stronghold at Columbus, Kentucky ❹, which bristled with heavy artillery, Grant avoided that obstacle and pursued a more promising course. Supported by ironclads commanded by Flag Officer Andrew Foote, he shifted his base to Paducah, Kentucky ❺, and steamed southward up the Tennessee River ❻ with his troops in early February, driving a wedge between enemy forces holding Columbus to the west and those defending Nashville, Tennessee ❼, and other strategic points to the east.

The overall Confederate commander in the region, General Albert Sidney Johnston, anticipated Grant's move and ordered his men at newly built Fort Henry ❽ on the Tennessee to strengthen their position. "Do not lose a moment," he urged. "Work all night." But flood waters swamped the low-lying fort and disabled several of its big guns before Foote's ironclads opened fire with devastating effect on February 6. "Fort Henry is ours," signaled Grant, who went on to seize Fort Donelson ❾ on the Cumberland River ❿, forcing Johnston to retreat into Mississippi. Reinforced at Corinth ⓫, he surprised Grant at a quiet country church in neighboring Tennessee called Shiloh ⓬, or "Place of Peace," triggering the bloodiest battle yet waged on American soil. ■

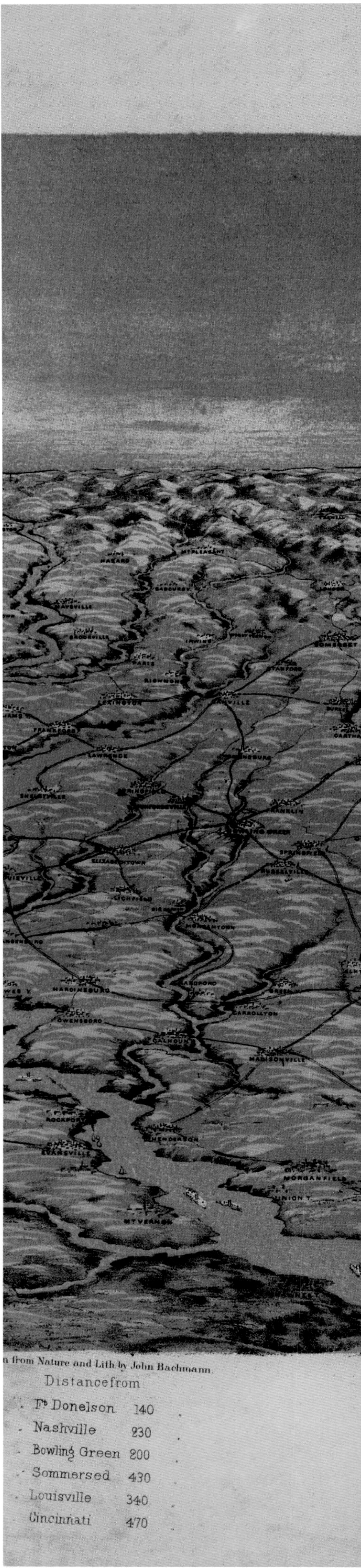

❽ **UNDER FIRE** Guns blazing, Federal ironclads target Fort Henry, shown smoldering at left. Grant's victory here allowed his forces to proceed up the Tennessee River to Pittsburg Landing, where they camped near Shiloh Church.

GRANT'S THEATER This aerial view commemorating Grant's Tennessee campaign—produced during the war by commercial artist John Bachmann—shows the vast theater in which Grant operated, looking southward from Cairo. After blasting Fort Henry, Federal ironclads shifted to the Cumberland River and shelled Fort Donelson.

Panorama of the Seat of War.

1
2
3
4
5
6
7
8
9
10
11
12
CAIRO
MOUND CITY
CALEDONIA
BIRDSPOINT
COLUMBUS
CLINTON
HICKMAN
NEW MADRID
MEMPHIS
JACKSON
TRENTON
PARIS
DRESDEN
MURRAY
LOCUST GROVE
MAYFIELD
WADESBORO
BENTON
PADUCAH
SMITHLAND
PRINCETON
EDDYVILLE
FT. DONELSON
FT. HENRY
WAVERLY
HUNTINGDON
LEXINGTON
DECATURVILLE
SAVANNA
WAYNESBORO
PURDY
BOLIVAR
POCAHONTAS
RALEIGH
RANDOLPH
FULTON
OSCEOLA
GREENOCK
MARION
MOUND CITY
NEW LIBERTY
METROPOLIS
OHIO R.
GOLCONDA
VIENNA
PULASKI
OHIO CITY
CHARLESTON
WETAUG

Entered according to act of Congress in the year 1861 by John Bachmann in the Clerk's Office of the District Court of the U.S. for the Southern District of New York.
BIRDS EYE VIEW
OF KENTUCKY AND TENNESSEE
SHOWING CAIRO AND PART OF THE SOUTHERN STATES.
John Bachmann, Publisher.

1862 | SHILOH

THE ROAD TO FORT DONELSON

CHARLES SMITH

It does not quite seem right for me to give General Smith orders," remarked Ulysses Grant. Charles Ferguson Smith had been commandant when Grant entered West Point in 1839 but fell promptly into line when his former pupil became his superior in 1861. "I am now a subordinate," he assured Grant, urging him to "feel no awkwardness about our new relations." Smith turned the tide at Fort Donelson by leading a charge that punctured enemy defenses. When Confederate commander Simon Buckner proposed a meeting the next day to discuss "terms of capitulation," Smith urged Grant to stand firm. "No terms with the damned Rebels," he insisted, setting the tone for Grant's famous reply to Buckner: "No terms except complete and unconditional surrender can be accepted."

Afterward, Grant fell out with his chief in St. Louis, Major General Henry Halleck, who ordered him to remain behind while Smith led troops up the Tennessee River. Grant said he was willing to serve "as faithfully under Smith as he had done under me," but that was not to be. Halleck soon reconciled with Grant and sent him to resume field command in relief of Smith, who was disabled by an infected wound that ultimately proved fatal. Grant would face the greatest test of his promising young career at Shiloh without the services of a subordinate he considered his equal, if not his superior.

With Fort Henry ❶ in hand, Grant moved quickly against Fort Donelson ❷, located 12 miles away on the west bank of the Cumberland River ❸. For troops used to traveling by steamboat, the march was taxing. "The roads were muddy and the country hilly," recalled one soldier under Grant, who wrote that the path his troops followed ❹ was reduced "to the consistency of soft porridge of almost immeasurable depth." Men cast aside their overcoats in the unseasonably warm weather, only to suffer sorely when snow fell a short time later. By February 13, however, Grant's forces had Donelson's defenders hemmed in. Unwilling to abandon the fort's battery ❺—which overlooked the Cumberland and shielded Nashville and other strategic targets upriver from attack—Johnston had sent reinforcements, raising the stakes in a contest he had little confidence of winning. "If you lose the fort," he wrote Donelson's commander, Brigadier General John Floyd, "bring your troops to Nashville if possible."

That message did nothing to encourage the wavering Floyd, a former U.S. secretary of war who was viewed as a traitor in the North and feared prosecution if captured. Not even the success of his gunners, who repulsed Foote's ironclads on February 14, gave Floyd hope he could hold out long against Grant, who gained strength as Federal transports landed troops north of the fort ❻. Early on February 15, Confederates attempted to break out by smashing through enemy lines below the town of Dover ❼, beyond which lay roads south to Clarksville ❽ and Nashville. The hard-pressed Yankees were giving way when Floyd and his second-in-command, Brigadier General Gideon Pillow, grew cautious and paused to regroup. That gave Grant a chance to repair the damage on his right and mount a counterattack on his left ❾, led by his trusted subordinate, Brigadier General Charles Smith, who ordered his men to fix bayonets and not fire a shot "until the enemy's works were reached and their lines broken." That daring charge demoralized Floyd, who fled with Pillow by boat that evening, leaving 13,000 men behind under Brigadier General Simon Buckner to surrender unconditionally to Grant. Shaken by the defeat, Johnston abandoned Nashville and its arsenal to the enemy and withdrew southward to the vital rail junction at Corinth, Mississippi, with Federals in pursuit. "Corinth will fall much more easily than Fort Donelson did," predicted Grant, unaware that Johnston was regaining confidence as reinforcements arrived by rail and was preparing to hit back. ■

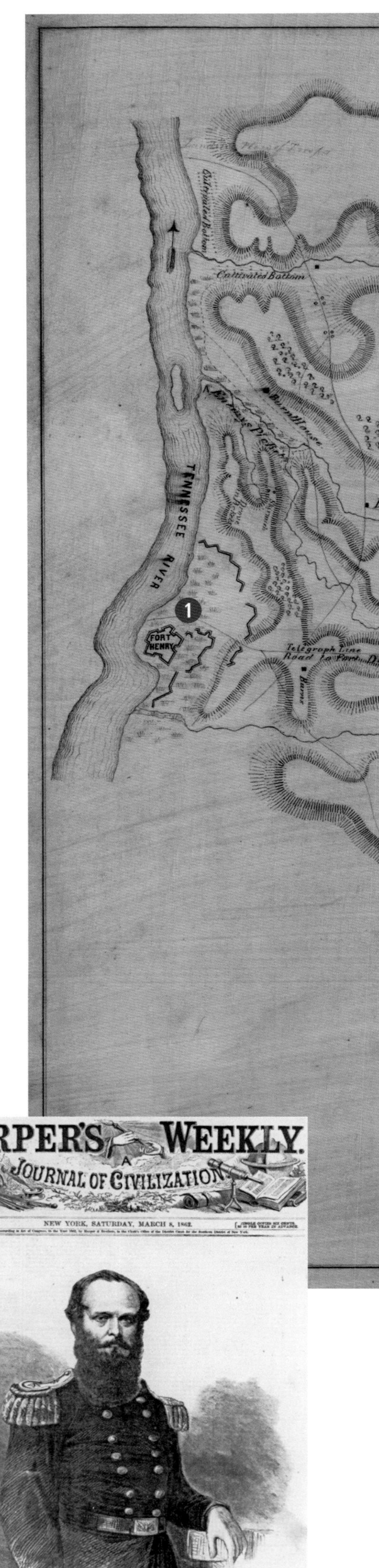

GRANT GLORIFIED Northerners knew little of Grant, shown here on the cover of *Harper's Weekly,* before he captured Fort Donelson—a victory that earned him promotion to major general—and became an overnight sensation. Admirers quipped that Grant's initials U. S. stood for "Unconditional Surrender."

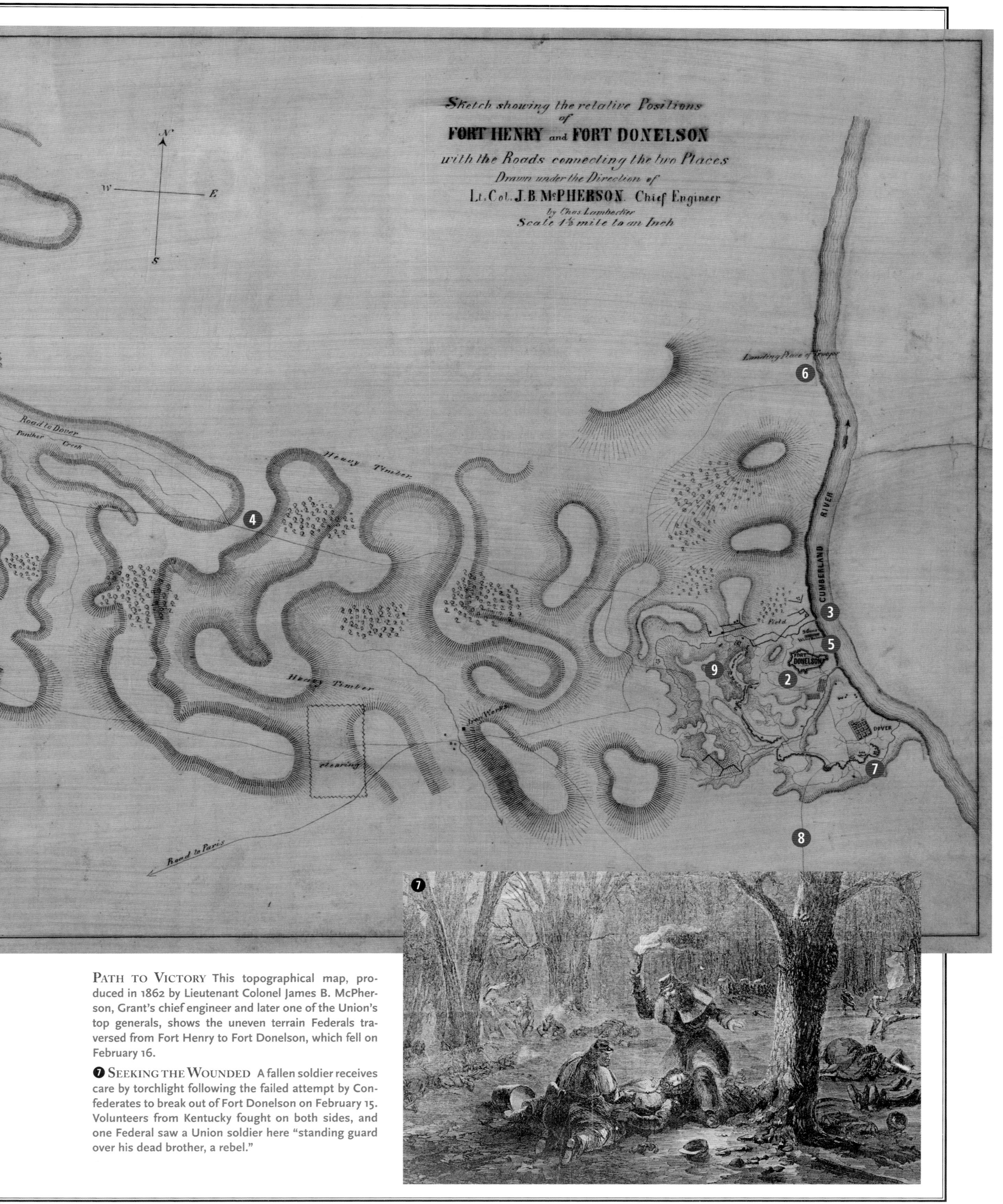

PATH TO VICTORY This topographical map, produced in 1862 by Lieutenant Colonel James B. McPherson, Grant's chief engineer and later one of the Union's top generals, shows the uneven terrain Federals traversed from Fort Henry to Fort Donelson, which fell on February 16.

❼ SEEKING THE WOUNDED A fallen soldier receives care by torchlight following the failed attempt by Confederates to break out of Fort Donelson on February 15. Volunteers from Kentucky fought on both sides, and one Federal saw a Union soldier here "standing guard over his dead brother, a rebel."

Shiloh Church

Federals of the 21st Missouri who fought at Shiloh

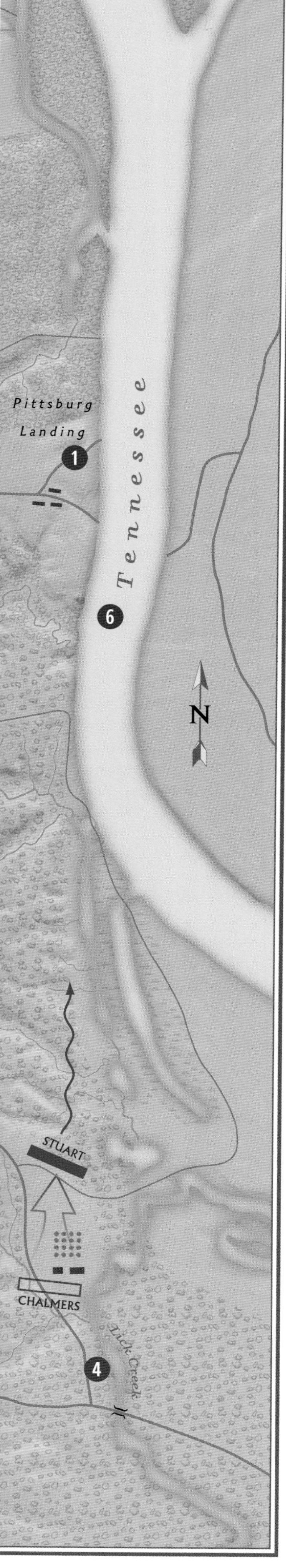

1862 | SHILOH

JOHNSTON STRIKES FIRST

"There will be no fight at Pittsburg Landing," Grant declared as his men disembarked there ❶ in early April and camped near Shiloh Church ❷. So little did he fear attack that he did not order his men to entrench. Digging in, wrote Brigadier General William T. Sherman, a promising division commander under Grant, "would have made our raw men timid." Meanwhile, Johnston's Confederates were approaching along the Corinth Road ❸, hoping to defeat Grant before he was joined by Major General Don Carlos Buell's Army of the Ohio. Johnston's plan was to trap the Federals between Lick Creek ❹ and Owl Creek ❺, with their backs to the Tennessee River ❻. "The more men they crowd in there," he said, "the worse we can make it for them."

At dawn on Sunday, April 6, Major General William Hardee's corps ❼ slammed into Grant's exposed forces below Shiloh Church. Two of Hardee's brigades struck Brigadier General William Prentiss's division ❽ while a third led by Brigadier General Patrick Cleburne hit Sherman's camp ❾. "My God, we are attacked!" cried Sherman, many of whose men were still in their tents. Close behind Hardee came the corps of Major Generals Leonidas Polk ❿ and Braxton Bragg ⓫. Contrary to Johnston's expectations, this corridor caused serious problems for his own army, which soon lost cohesion. One of Bragg's brigades ended up on the far left and two others on the far right, where Johnston threw in reserves under Major General John C. Breckinridge ⓬, hoping to break through to Pittsburg Landing. Here as elsewhere along the line, however, the Federals fell back and regrouped. By late morning, Prentiss had realigned his battered division with those of Brigadier Generals Stephen Hurlbut ⓭ and W. H. L. Wallace ⓮ in a wooded area known for the furious fighting there as the Hornet's Nest ⓯. ■

Albert Sydney Johnston

JOHNSTON'S BIG PUSH This National Geographic map shows the impact of the Confederate onslaught on Grant's formations. The exposed divisions of Sherman, Prentiss, and Hurlbut fell back while those of W. H. L. Wallace and Major General John McClernand moved up to provide support in and around the Hornet's Nest, bordered by the Bloody Pond, stained in battle by the gore of the dead and wounded.

ORDER OF BATTLE

UNION FORCES

ARMY OF THE TENNESSEE
Grant | 48,000 men

1ST DIVISION *McClernand*
Brigades Hare, Marsh, Raith

2ND DIVISION
W. H. L. Wallace
Brigades Tuttle, McArthur, Sweeny

3RD DIVISION *L. Wallace*
Brigades M. L. Smith, Thayer, Whittlesey

4TH DIVISION *Hurlbut*
Brigades Williams, Veatch, Lauman

5TH DIVISION *Sherman*
Brigades McDowell, Stuart, Hildebrand, Buckland

6TH DIVISION *Prentiss*
Brigades Peabody, Miller

U.S. ARMY OF THE OHIO
Buell | 17,900 men

2ND DIVISION *McCook*
Brigades Rousseau, Kirk, Gibson

4TH DIVISION *Nelson*
Brigades Ammen, Hazen, Bruce

5TH DIVISION *Crittenden*
Brigades Boyle, W. S. Smith

6TH DIVISION *Wood*
Brigades Garfield, Wagner

CONFEDERATE FORCES

ARMY OF MISSISSIPPI
Johnston & Beauregard | 45,000 men

I CORPS *Polk*
1ST DIVISION *Clark*
Brigades Russell, Stewart

2ND DIVISION *Cheatham*
Brigades Johnson, Stephens

II CORPS *Bragg*
1ST DIVISION *Ruggles*
Brigades Gibson, Anderson, Pond

2ND DIVISION *Withers*
Brigades Gladden, Chalmers, Jackson

III CORPS *Hardee*
Brigades Hindman, Cleburne, Wood

RESERVE CORPS
Breckinridge
Brigades Trabue, Bowen, Statham

1862 | SHILOH

ADVANCE AND RETREAT

Time was of the essence for the Confederates at Shiloh, for Buell's Federals were approaching from the northeast and would soon be ferried across the Tennessee River ❶ to Pittsburg Landing ❷. If Johnston did not win quickly, the reinforced Grant would have a huge advantage over him. At first, it seemed the Federals would be swiftly routed, as the divisions of Sherman ❸ and Prentiss ❹ fell far back from their starting positions that morning (shown here in blue). "Don't go out there, they will *give you hell!*" one demoralized Yankee warned soldiers of McClernand's division ❺ as they entered battle. Sherman and Prentiss steadied their shaken troops, however, and joined with other commanders to hold off swarming Confederates around the Hornet's Nest ❻. Around 2 P.M., Johnston rode to the front to spur his men forward but fell mortally wounded. Command passed to General P. G. T. Beauregard, who had drawn up the battle plan that stalled here. Headquartered at Shiloh Church ❼, he knew little of the situation up front and could see no way around the Hornet's Nest, throwing one brigade after another into that costly fight. Late that afternoon, Federals there gave way and fell back toward Pittsburg Landing, where they formed new lines (black), shielded by Grant's reserve artillery ❽. As daylight waned, Beauregard concluded that his victory was "sufficiently complete" and postponed any further attacks until the next day.

That evening, while the gunboats *Tyler* and *Lexington* ❾ bombarded battle-weary Confederates, Buell's troops began crossing the Tennessee River. By early morning on April 7, Federals greatly outnumbered their foes and rushed from their positions (shown in red) in a blistering counterattack that staggered the Confederates. "Our force was disorganized, demoralized, and exhausted," recalled corps commander Bragg, who faulted Beauregard for not pressing his advantage earlier. Like the Yankees the day before, however, the Rebels gave way grudgingly. The positions that Sherman and other Federal commanders occupied when the battle ended that afternoon (shown in brown) were at or near their starting point on April 6. Grant had held his ground, a technical victory overshadowed by the appalling cost: over 13,000 Union casualties and nearly 11,000 Confederate losses. Yet unlike other bloody campaigns that brought the Union no gain, Grant's deep thrust into Tennessee did lasting damage to the Confederacy. ■

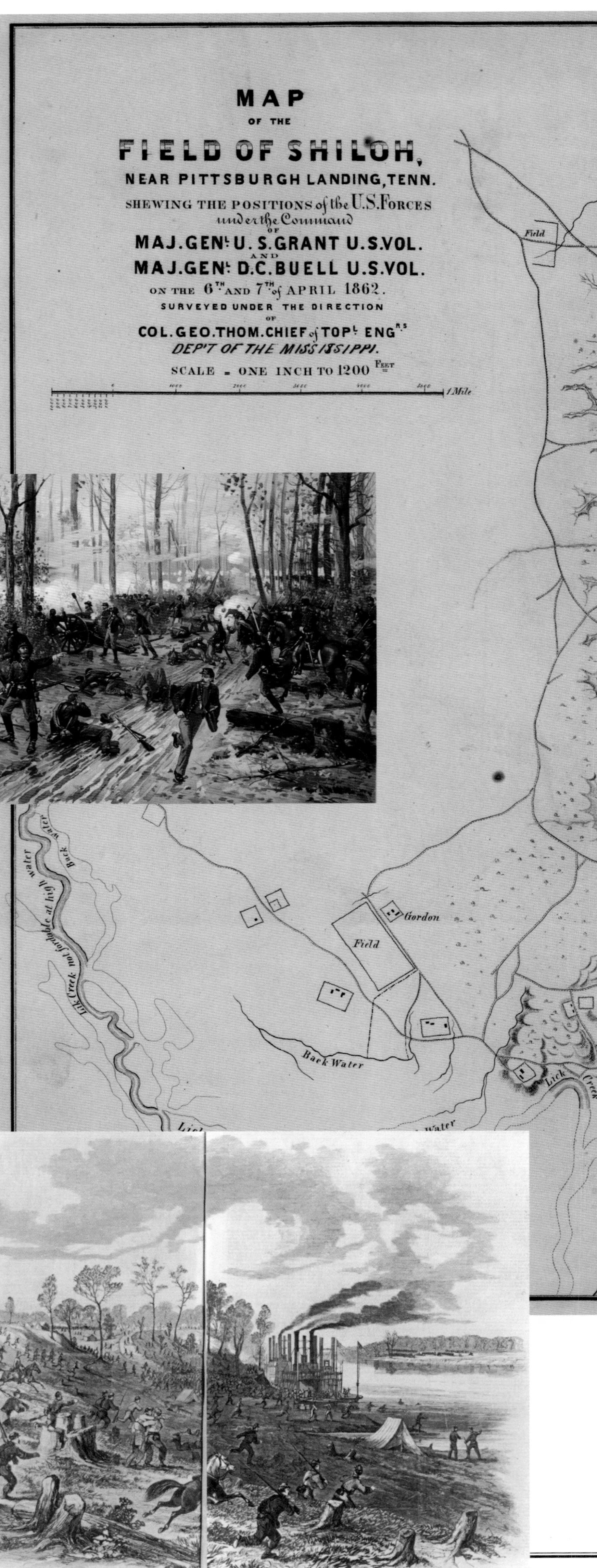

❷ PITTSBURGH LANDING Retreating in panic to the landing, Federals plunge into the Tennessee River. Grant restored order and held out here, allowing reinforcements to be ferried across the river.

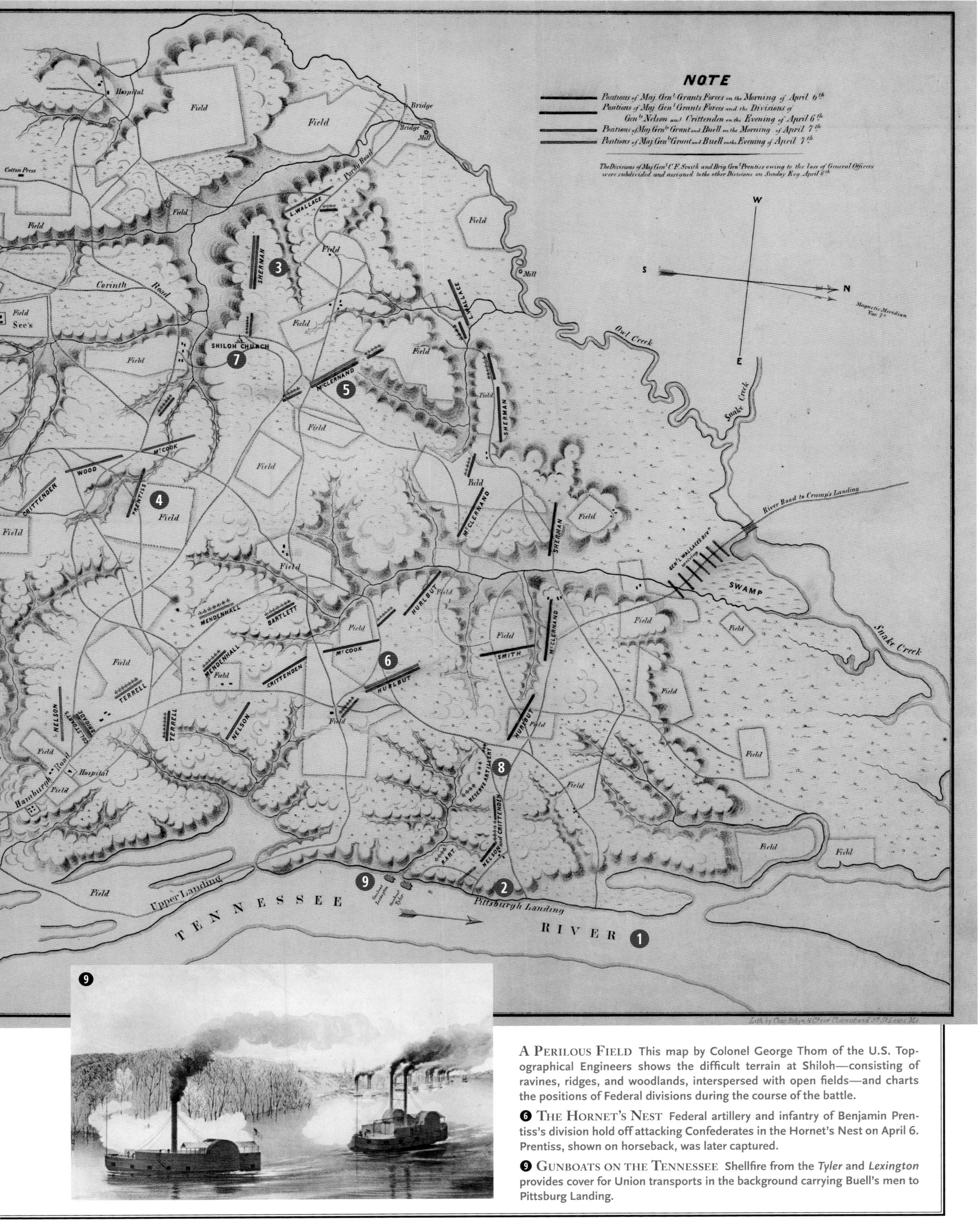

A PERILOUS FIELD This map by Colonel George Thom of the U.S. Topographical Engineers shows the difficult terrain at Shiloh—consisting of ravines, ridges, and woodlands, interspersed with open fields—and charts the positions of Federal divisions during the course of the battle.

❻ THE HORNET'S NEST Federal artillery and infantry of Benjamin Prentiss's division hold off attacking Confederates in the Hornet's Nest on April 6. Prentiss, shown on horseback, was later captured.

❾ GUNBOATS ON THE TENNESSEE Shellfire from the *Tyler* and *Lexington* provides cover for Union transports in the background carrying Buell's men to Pittsburg Landing.

1862

COASTAL WAR

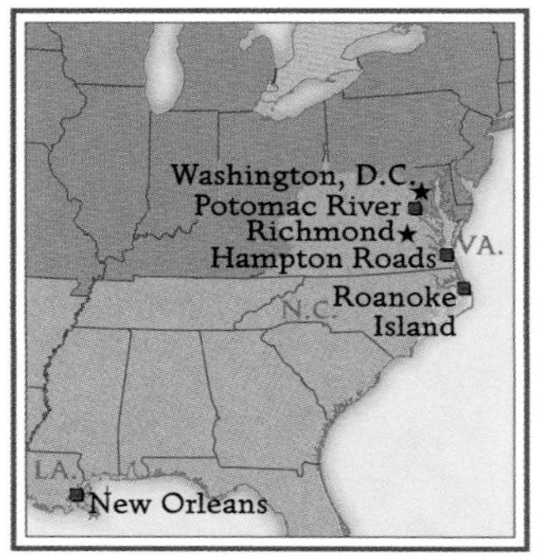

THE BLOCKADE

FEBRUARY 8, 1862 Battle of Roanoke Island (North Carolina)

MARCH 9 The *Virginia* and the *Monitor* clash at Hampton Roads (Virginia).

MARCH 14 Battle of New Bern (North Carolina)

MARCH 17 McClellan's Army of the Potomac begins embarking from Alexandria, Virginia, for Fort Monroe following the evacuation of Confederate batteries on the lower Potomac River.

APRIL 18–28 Federal forces led by David Farragut take Forts Jackson and St. Philip and go on to capture New Orleans.

Frustrated by Confederate success in eluding the blockade and importing weapons and other supplies from abroad, Federals in early 1862 stepped up efforts to seal off the South and seize enemy ports and strongholds. Much remained to be done if the North was to fulfill Winfield Scott's ambitious Anaconda Plan, which called for Union gunboats to take command of the Mississippi River while warships blockaded the Atlantic and Gulf Coasts. Federals had ousted Confederates from coastal forts at Hatteras Inlet ❶ and Port Royal Sound ❷, and the U.S. Navy had greatly enlarged its fleet by turning out new ships and converting ferryboats and other commercial vessels for military use. But Southerners had barely begun to feel the squeeze. Nine in ten ships that tried to run the Federal blockade in 1861 succeeded. And after salvaging the wooden ship U.S.S. *Merrimack* at Gosport Navy Yard near Norfolk ❸, Confederates were now converting it to an ironclad, C.S.S. *Virginia*, designed to smash enemy vessels patrolling narrow Hampton Roads ❹ and reopen the James River to maritime traffic.

To reinforce the blockade and support McClellan's upcoming campaign against Richmond ❺—which he would launch by moving his massive Army of the Potomac by boat from the Washington area to Fort Monroe ❻, just outside Hampton Roads—Federals took action on several fronts. In early February, a combined army-navy force under Brigadier General Ambrose Burnside and Flag Officer Louis Goldsborough entered Pamlico Sound through Hatteras Inlet and took Roanoke Island ❼. Its objective was to seize ports on the North Carolina coast, including Elizabeth City ❽ and New Bern ❾, and move inland, severing Richmond's supply lines to the south while McClellan closed in on the capital from the east. In early March, other Federal forces cleared the way for McClellan's advance down the Potomac by ousting Confederates from batteries on the Virginia side of that river around Cockpit Point ❿. Meanwhile, the newly built ironclad U.S.S. *Monitor* was on its way from New York City to Hampton Roads, where it clashed with the *Virginia* in a spectacular battle on March 9.

For all the attention it received, the showdown at Hampton Roads was a brief squall compared to the storm brewing in the Gulf of Mexico, where Flag Officer David Farragut was preparing to assault Forts Jackson and St. Philip ⓫—formidable Confederate bastions at the mouth of the Mississippi—and seize New Orleans ⓬, the South's largest city and leading port. "Nothing afloat could pass the forts," boasted one resident, but Farragut would prove otherwise. ■

DESTINED FOR GLORY David Farragut had been in the U.S. Navy for half a century when the Civil War erupted, having enrolled as a midshipman at the age of nine. A longtime resident of Virginia, he was regarded with some suspicion in Washington before he was named flag officer of the West Coast Blockading Squadron and assigned to take New Orleans. Sure of success, he wrote his wife, "I have now attained what I have been looking for all my life—a flag—and having attained it, all that is necessary to complete the scene is a victory."

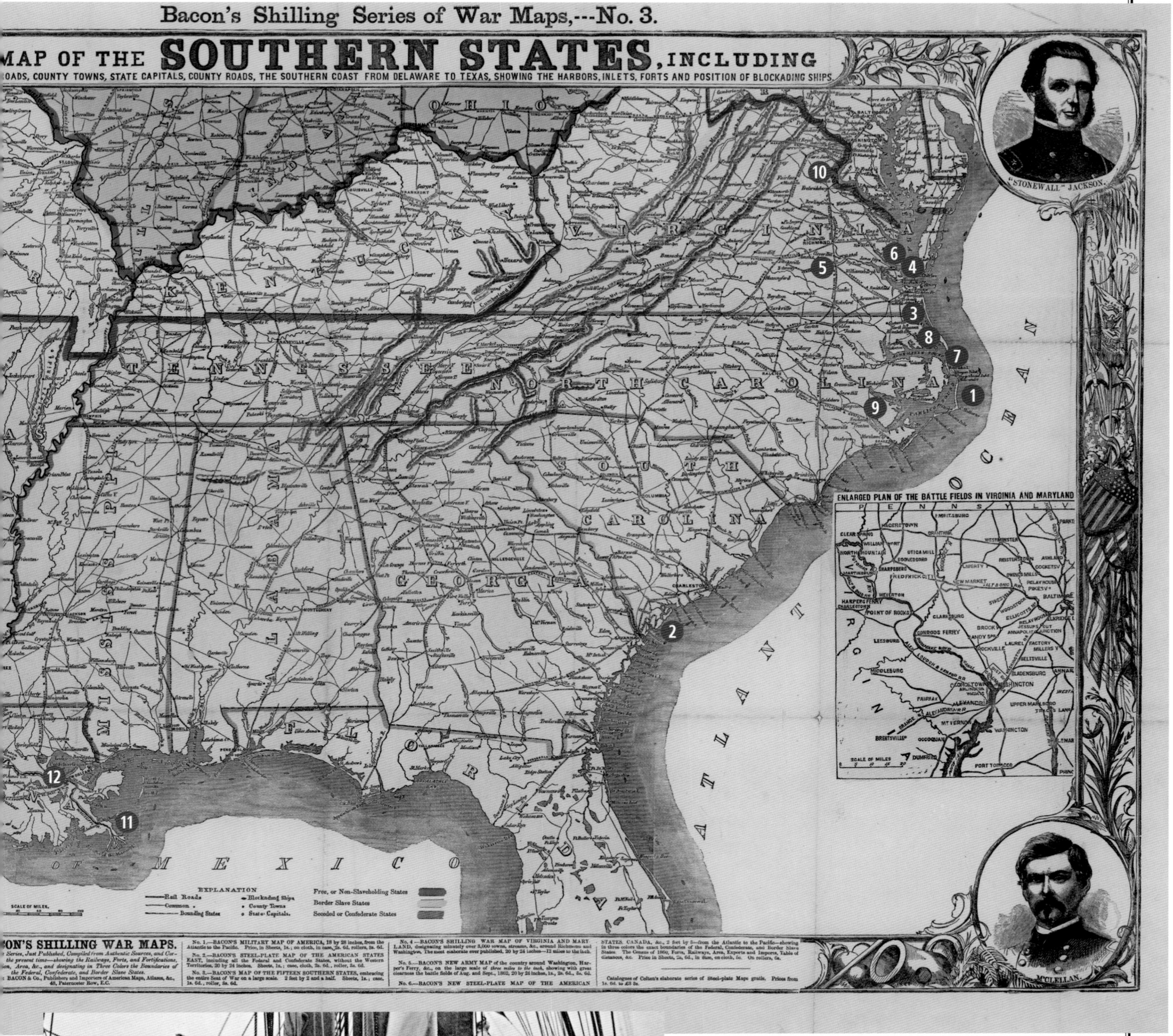
Bacon's Shilling Series of War Maps,---No. 3.
MAP OF THE SOUTHERN STATES, INCLUDING
ROADS, COUNTY TOWNS, STATE CAPITALS, COUNTY ROADS, THE SOUTHERN COAST FROM DELAWARE TO TEXAS, SHOWING THE HARBORS, INLETS, FORTS AND POSITION OF BLOCKADING SHIPS.
"STONEWALL" JACKSON.
ENLARGED PLAN OF THE BATTLE FIELDS IN VIRGINIA AND MARYLAND
EXPLANATION
ON'S SHILLING WAR MAPS.
M'CLELLAN.

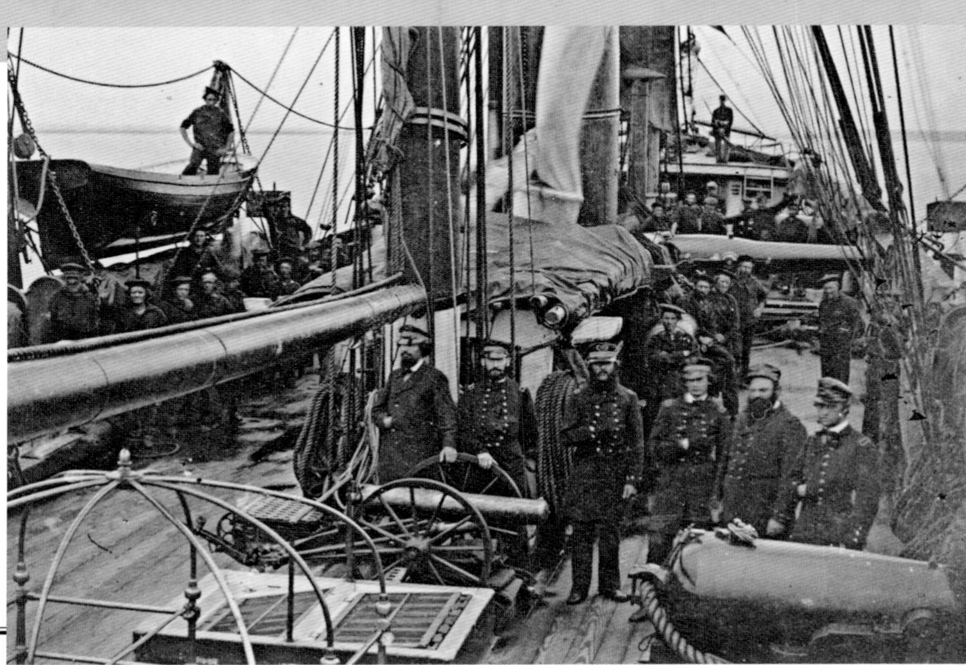

REBEL COASTLINE This detailed map of the Confederacy, showing the many inlets and rivers that Federal blockading squadrons had to seal off, appeared in *Harper's Weekly* in late 1861 and was later published in London, where firms had commercial ties to both the North and the South and interest in the Civil War ran high.

BLOCKADE DUTY Officers and crew crowd the deck of the U.S.S. *Pocahontas*, a steam-powered sloop that patrolled the Gulf Coast and captured two enemy blockade runners.

REBEL BATTERY at BUDD'S FERRY. Va POTOMAC RIVER. February 1862.

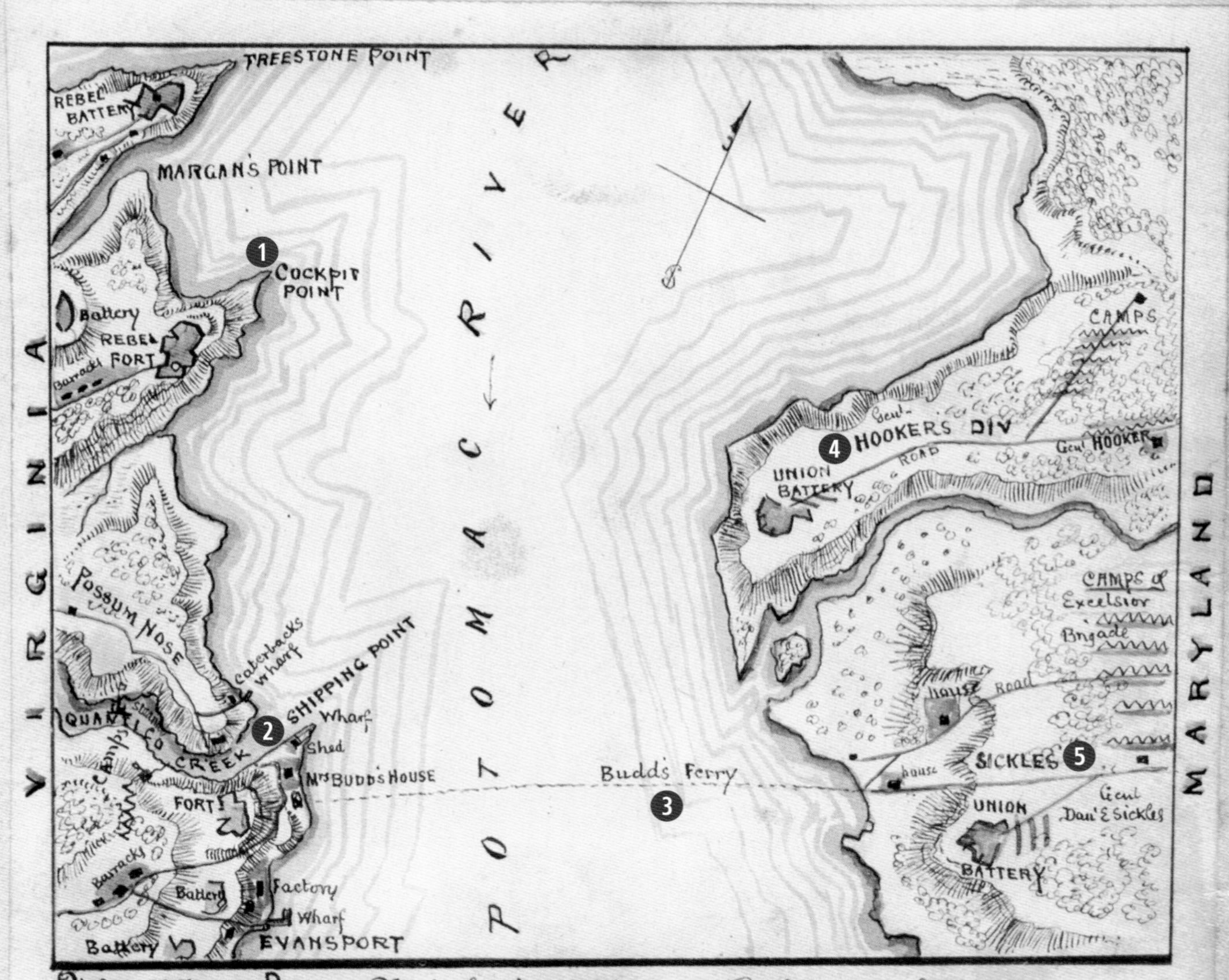

BLOCKADE OF THE POTOMAC. Map showing Union and Rebel Batteries. January 1862.
The Rebels evacuated all their Batteries night of 9th March 1862

The Rebel troops and Batteries were Commanded by Genl HOLMES. C.S.A. during the BLOCKADE which lasted from Decr 1861 to 9th March 1862.

1862 COASTAL WAR

SECURING THE POTOMAC

While Federal officials in Washington worked to tighten the blockade, they faced a nagging problem nearby. The Potomac River—a vital conduit for Union forces defending the capital or advancing against Confederates to the south—was far from secure. With the exception of Alexandria and other areas close to Washington occupied soon after the war began, the Virginia side of the Potomac remained in enemy hands. To keep the river open down to Chesapeake Bay and prevent Virginians from trafficking with sympathizers in neighboring Maryland, the U.S. Navy relied on the Potomac Flotilla, a motley assortment of converted merchant vessels weighing as little as 90 tons—pipsqueaks compared to larger warships like the *Merrimack,* which exceeded 4,000 tons.

One of the most hazardous stretches of the river for the little gunboats of the Potomac Flotilla lay south of Washington around Cockpit Point ❶ and the mouth of Quantico Creek ❷. Several enemy batteries there menaced Federal vessels and shielded Budd's Ferry ❸, one of many such links between Confederate Virginia and neutral Maryland. Cockpit Point was "made quite strong by the enemy," recalled Union Admiral David Dixon Porter, "and for a time it was considered quite a dangerous place to pass." In early 1862, with McClellan's campaign looming, the army and navy combined to eliminate that threat. Pressured by the flotilla and by the divisions of Brigadier Generals Joseph Hooker ❹ and Daniel Sickles ❺, whose troops manned Federal batteries on the Maryland side, Confederate gunners abandoned their positions. The coast was now clear for McClellan's army, which moved down the Potomac in March in an armada of several hundred transports. "As we arrived off Cockpit Point," wrote cartographer Robert Knox Sneden, who had earlier mapped the area, "the Rebel earthworks loomed up on the steep clay banks." But those batteries were now empty and the Federals passed unmolested, proceeding down the moonlit Potomac as if on a pleasure cruise. "The white sandy beach and dark black pine trees throwing deep shadows on the water made a charming picture," Sneden noted, "while the churning of wheels and screws from 330 steamers made a strange noise as the echoes reverberated from the heavily wooded shore." ■

❺ PATROLLING THE POTOMAC **Brigadier General Daniel Sickles and his staff lead a mounted reconnaissance along the Potomac River in a sketch made on the scene by artist Alfred Waud.**

BATTERIES NEAR BUDD'S FERRY **While stationed near Washington in February 1862, Robert Sneden sketched a Rebel battery overlooking Budd's Ferry on the Virginia side of the Potomac (opposite, top) and drew a map of the area, showing Federal and Confederate positions on either side of the river. Sneden returned here in March with McClellan's army as it moved down the Potomac to Fort Monroe.**

CONRAD'S FERRY **Another sketch made along the Potomac by Sneden portrays Conrad's Ferry, a contested crossing located upriver from Washington.**

BURNSIDE'S EXPEDITION IN HEAVY SEAS

AMBROSE EVERETT BURNSIDE

Renowned for his prominent sideburns—a term that originated as a play on his name—Ambrose Burnside was a meticulous New Englander better suited for overseeing slow, methodical operations like the amphibious assault on coastal North Carolina than for commanding troops in the heat of battle. He did not lack courage and demonstrated as much by taking as his headquarters the smallest of the boats bound for Hatteras Inlet. Time and again mountainous waves "would ingulf us," he wrote, "but the little vessel would ride them and stagger forward in her course." The success of his North Carolina campaign led Lincoln to view him as a likely replacement for McClellan as chief of the Army of the Potomac, but Burnside held back, insisting that he was "not competent to command such a large army as this." At the Battle of Antietam in September 1862, his corps was slow to advance across the span known thereafter as Burnside Bridge, and a golden chance to vanquish Lee's army was lost. McClellan bore most of the blame, however, and Burnside reluctantly agreed to succeed him afterward. Spurred on by Lincoln, he threw his army into a desperate battle at Fredericksburg that December and suffered terrible losses. Staggered by his failure, he had to be restrained from personally leading a potentially suicidal attack the next day.

The Union launched its largest amphibious operation to date in January 1862 when 13,000 troops under Ambrose Burnside embarked from Annapolis, Maryland, and rendezvoused at the mouth of Chesapeake Bay with a squadron of 20 gunboats commanded by Louis Goldsborough. All the vessels selected for this expedition had suitably shallow drafts in order to pass through Hatteras Inlet ❶, which was only about eight feet deep, but that made them unstable in the high seas that often battered Cape Hatteras in midwinter. "As far as the eye can see, the water is rolling, foaming and dashing over the shoals," wrote one soldier as the invasion fleet approached Hatteras Inlet. "This is no time for man to war against man."

Burnside and his men wallowed miserably in swells for nearly two weeks before the seas grew calm enough for them to approach the treacherous inlet—only to discover that the sands there had shifted and the water was just six feet deep. By emptying boats of cargo and using the keels of heavy steamships as dredges, they made it through into Pamlico Sound ❷ by early February and set their sights on Roanoke Island ❸, a Confederate bastion guarding the entrance to Albemarle Sound ❹. A pesky "mosquito fleet" of nine small Rebel gunboats lurked behind a barrier of sunken ships and pilings ❺ off the island's west coast. But Goldsborough ignored that obstacle and opened fire on nearby Fort Bartow ❻ on February 7 to screen Federal troops as they landed south of that stronghold at Ashby's Harbor ❼. The following day, Burnside's men—who greatly outnumbered the island's defenders—captured a redoubt ❽ blocking the island's main road and went on to force the surrender of Bartow and other forts at the northern end of Roanoke. Goldsborough's squadron capped the Federal victory by crushing the mosquito fleet, leaving the Union in full command of both Pamlico and Albemarle Sounds. Burnside went on to capture New Bern, North Carolina's second largest port after Wilmington, but he and most of his forces were called away to support the embattled McClellan near Richmond before they could advance inland. ■

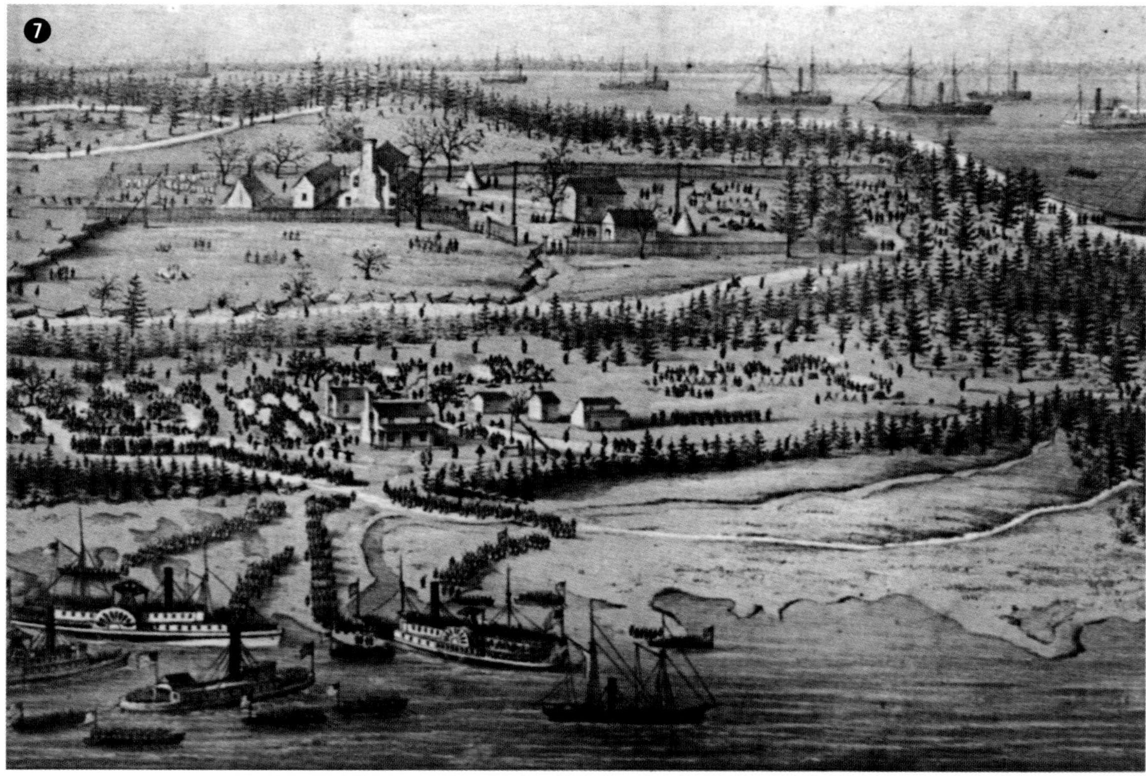

❼ LANDING AT ROANOKE **Ferryboats and other commercial vessels requisitioned as transports for Burnside's campaign disembark troops at Ashby's Harbor on February 7. Burnside chose this landing site on Roanoke Island after receiving intelligence from a slave who escaped from a plantation there.**

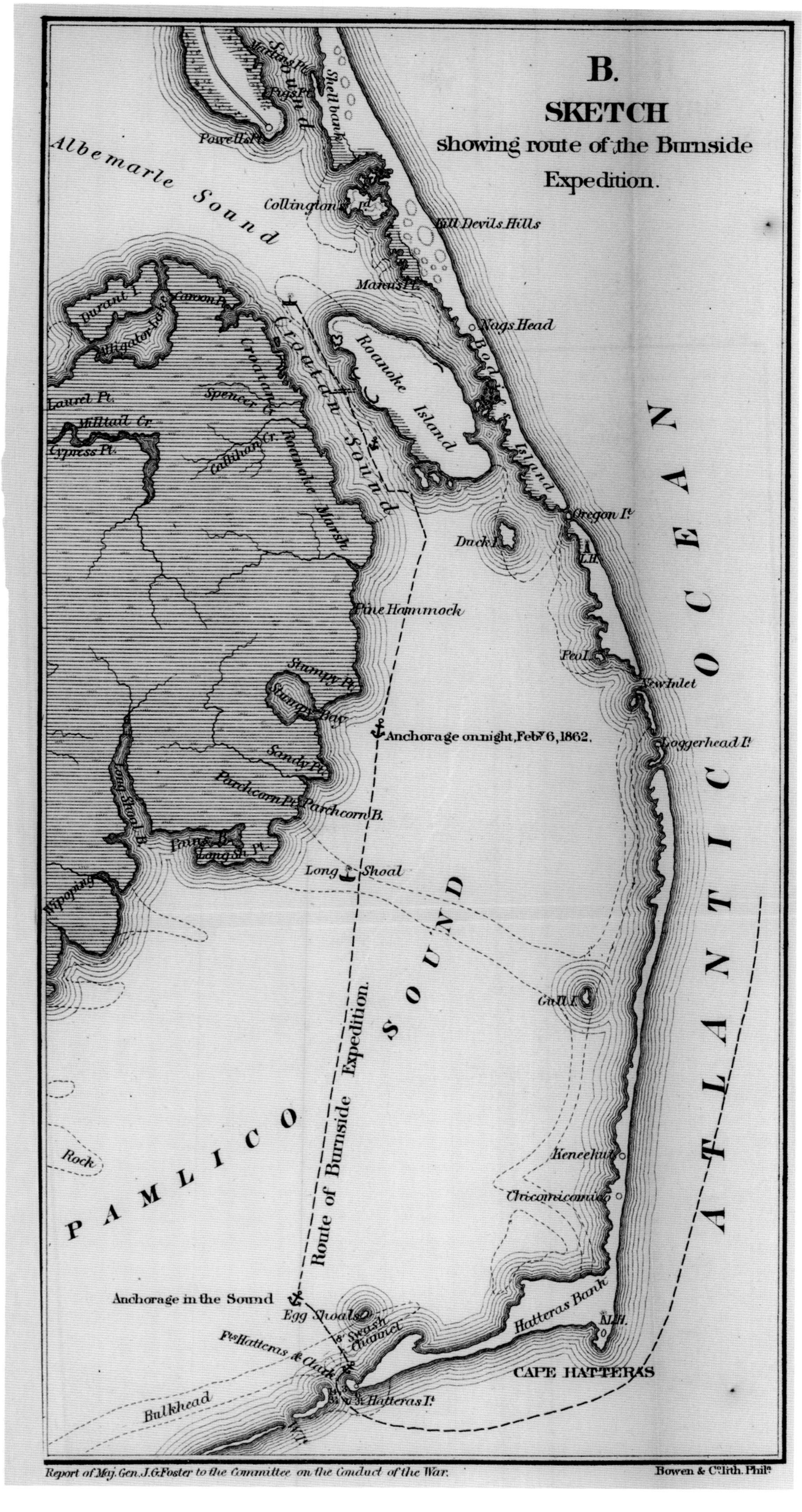

B.

SKETCH

showing route of the Burnside Expedition.

Report of Maj. Gen. J. G. Foster to the Committee on the Conduct of the War.

Bowen & Co. lith. Phil^a.

"As far as the eye can see, the water is rolling, foaming and dashing over the shoals.... This is no time for man to war against man."

SOLDIER'S DIARY

ON ROUNDING CAPE HATTERAS IN HEAVY SEAS WITH BURNSIDE'S EXPEDITION

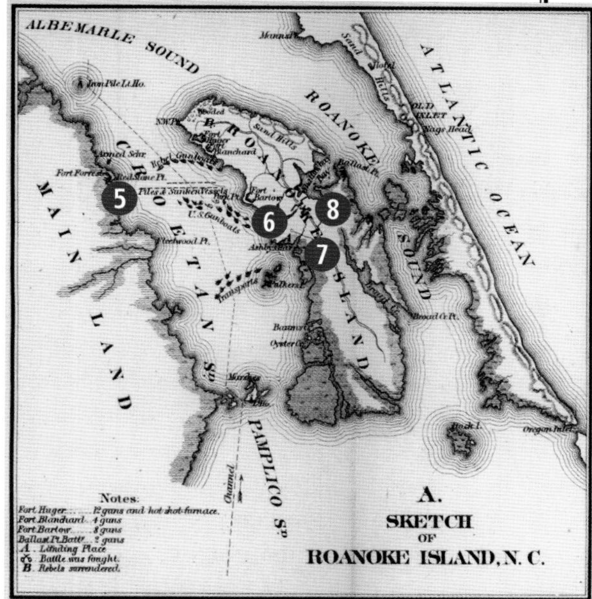

PATH TO VICTORY Two maps accompanying an official report on Burnside's campaign by Brigadier General John Foster, who led the attack on Roanoke Island, show the path the Federal fleet followed through Hatteras Inlet into Pamlico Sound (left) and the situation at Roanoke Island as Union troops prepared to land there on February 7 (above). Federal gunboats pounded Fort Bartow and kept the Confederate mosquito fleet at bay while Burnside's transports entered Ashby's Harbor unopposed.

A Duel Between Ironclads

By February 1862 the Confederate ironclad *Virginia*—built around the salvaged hulk of the Union frigate *Merrimack*—was near completion at Gosport Navy Yard ❶, below Norfolk ❷. With heavy armor, ten big guns, and an armored ram at its bow, the *Virginia* posed a huge threat to wooden ships enforcing the Union blockade of narrow Hampton Roads ❸. Aware that Federals were preparing to meet that challenge with an ironclad of their own design, the *Monitor*—which left New York for Hampton Roads on March 6—Confederates rushed the *Virginia* into service. Some workmen were still aboard when it cast off on March 8 to attack the Yankee blockading fleet. Steaming toward Newport News Point ❹, the *Virginia* rammed and sank the sloop *Cumberland* and set the 50-gun frigate *Congress* ablaze. Another frigate, the *Minnesota*, tried to aid the stricken vessels but ran aground ❺, leaving only two Union warships to contend with the dreaded ironclad.

Overnight, while Confederates dreamed of finishing off the fleet and breaking the blockade, the *Monitor* entered Hampton Roads, prompting the first-ever battle between ironclads. It looked like a mismatch, for the ugly little *Monitor*—likened by one observer to a "tin can on a shingle"—had only two guns. But those potent 11-inch Dahlgrens swiveled ingeniously in a turret, while the hulking *Virginia* had to turn laboriously to deliver broadsides and could not enter shallow waters with the *Monitor* because its draft was much deeper. In the end, this historic contest between "pygmy" and "giant," as Captain Henry Van Brunt of the *Minnesota* put it, proved agonizingly close. For four hours on the morning of March 9, the two ironclads exchanged fire near Van Brunt's stranded frigate ❻. At first, the *Virginia*'s shots had no more effect on the *Monitor* "than so many pebble stones thrown by a child," he observed. Around noon, however, the *Monitor* withdrew into the shallows after a shell hit its pilot house and temporarily blinded its captain, Lieutenant John Worden (inset). That ended the duel, with the Confederates claiming victory. But they were unable to break the blockade and, after losing Norfolk to the Federals in May, destroyed the *Virginia* to keep the ironclad out of enemy hands. ■

Captain of the Monitor Wounded in the battle, Lieutenant John Worden was visited afterward by Lincoln. "You do me great honor," Worden said. "It is not so," Lincoln replied. "It is you who honor me and your country."

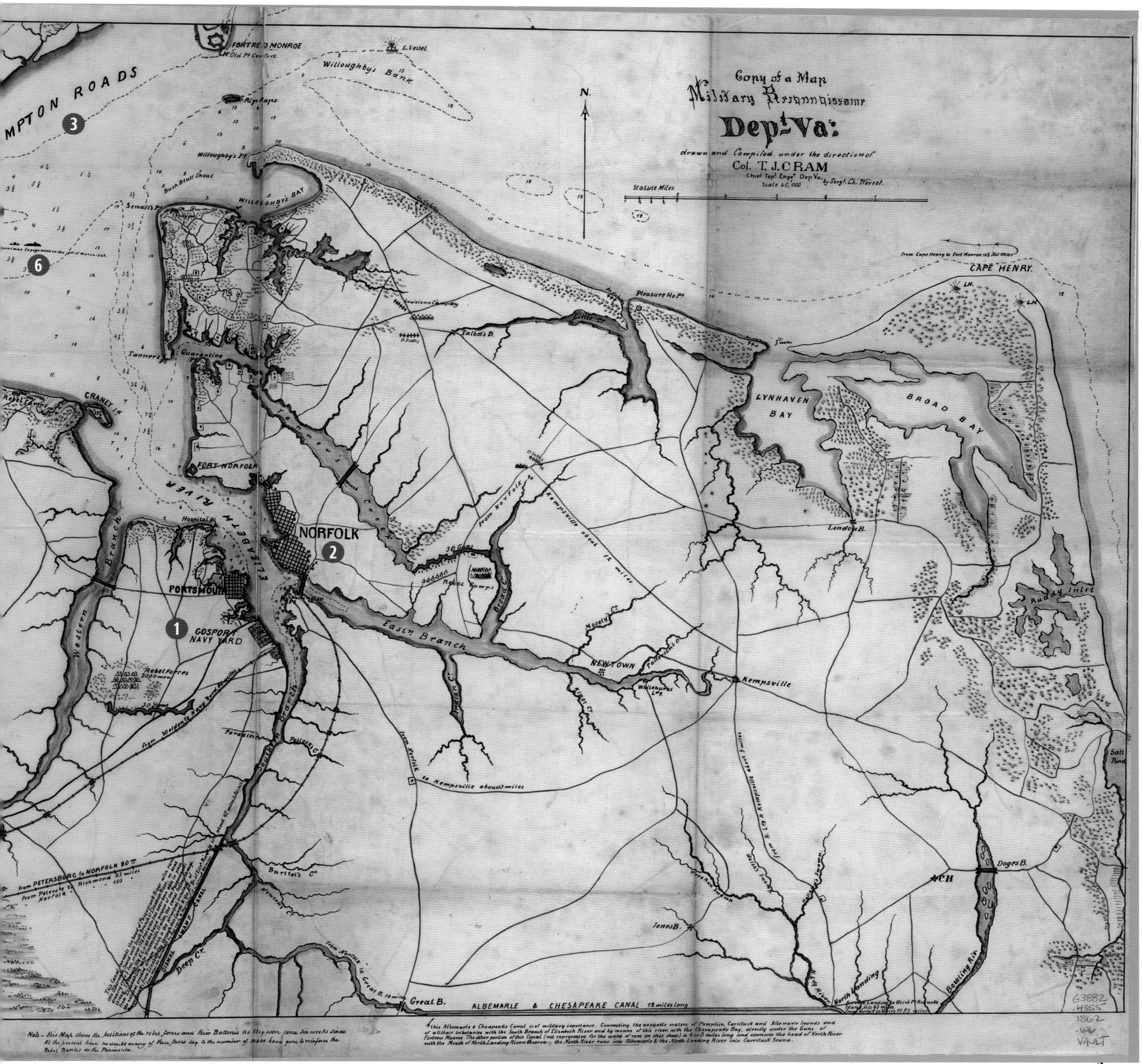

HAMPTON ROADS This map, compiled by the Virginia Department of the U.S. Topographical Corps after the battle in Hampton Roads, shows where the two ironclads met and charts the depth of the water in fathoms (red numbers) or feet (black numbers) to aid Federal ships navigating the harbor. The *Virginia*—referred to here as the *Merrimac*, a common misspelling—had a draft of 22 feet (about three and a half fathoms) and briefly ran aground during the battle.

❻ GUNS BLAZING The compact *Monitor* (foreground) and the larger *Virginia* exchanged fire at close range during their furious battle on March 9. The *Monitor*'s low profile, rotating turret, and greater maneuverability helped it contend with its heavily armed opponent.

SAILORS AT EASE Crewmen relax on the cramped deck of the *Monitor*, which remained in service after the battle in Hampton Roads and ranked first in the class of 56 such monitors produced by the Union during the Civil War.

1862 | COASTAL WAR

Capture of New Orleans

To reach New Orleans ❶, Farragut and his fleet ❷ had to run a fearsome gauntlet. Guarding the mouth of the Mississippi were Forts Jackson ❸ and St. Philip ❹, boasting 126 guns between them. Obstructing the river nearby were heavy iron chains strung between hulks, designed to snag enemy ships under the forts' guns. If Federal ships broke through, they would then have to contend with the Rebel fleet shielding New Orleans, including a dozen or so gunboats and two ironclads, the ram *Manassas* and the unfinished *Louisiana*, towed into place above the forts to serve as a floating battery.

None of this fazed Farragut, whose approach to battle was unswerving. "I will attack regardless of consequences," he vowed, "and never turn back." In April, his fleet of 18 warships and a squadron of 20 mortar schooners commanded by Commander David Porter entered the river through passes at its delta ❺. For several days, the mortar schooners lobbed 200-pound shells at the fortified Confederates in preparation for the assault. Then after sending two gunboats upriver to sever the chain barrier, Farragut attacked before dawn on April 24. Battle smoke shrouded the river, obscuring the view of the forts' gunners as Federal ships swept past them and clashed with opposing vessels. When the smoke cleared at daybreak, the Confederate fleet lay in shreds, with the *Manassas* abandoned and the *Louisiana* stranded. Farragut, having lost just one ship, had a clear run to New Orleans and captured the city on April 28. ■

❸ **Running the Gauntlet** Attacking early on April 24, Farragut's fleet steams past Fort Jackson (left) and Fort St. Philip (right) to challenge Confederate gunboats (background).

Path to New Orleans This bird's-eye view of the lower Mississippi, drawn by John Bachmann following the fall of New Orleans, shows the path Farragut's fleet followed upriver past the Confederate forts, which surrendered to the Federals soon after the battle. Major General Benjamin Butler followed in Farragut's wake with 10,000 Union troops and occupied New Orleans.

1862

SHENANDOAH VALLEY

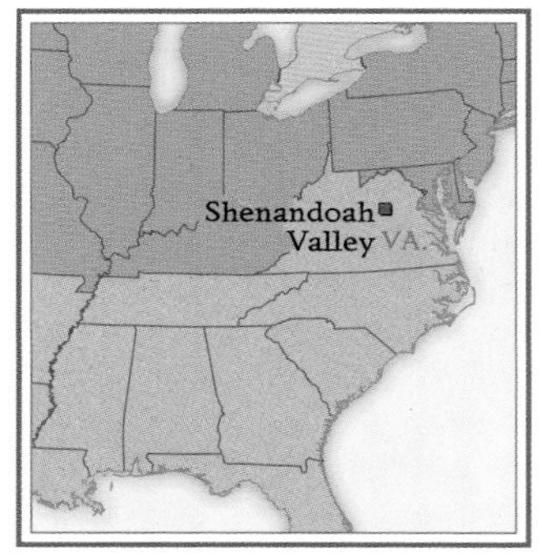

EASTERN THEATER

MARCH 1, 1862 Stonewall Jackson receives orders to prevent Federal forces in the Shenandoah Valley from advancing eastward through gaps in the Blue Ridge and threatening the flank of the Confederate army defending Richmond.

MARCH 23 Battle of Kernstown

MAY 8 Battle of McDowell

MAY 23 Jackson takes Front Royal and ousts Federals from Winchester two days later.

JUNE 8 Battle of Cross Keys

JUNE 9 Battle of Port Republic

As Confederate commander in Virginia's Shenandoah Valley, Major General Stonewall Jackson waged an ingenious campaign of maneuver and deception in the spring of 1862 and bedeviled the Yankees. "If the Valley is lost, Virginia is lost," wrote Jackson. Indeed, this was the state's breadbasket and flanked the hotly contested corridor between Washington, D.C., and Richmond. The side that had control of the Valley could launch invasions to the north or south or send troops eastward through gaps in the Blue Ridge to menace the opposing capitals. The rugged terrain of the Valley, with its forested ridges, helped Jackson conceal his movements. "Always mystify, mislead and surprise the enemy, if possible," he declared. As McClellan advanced against Richmond, Jackson stumped his numerically superior foes and tied down tens of thousands of troops here who might otherwise have descended on the Confederate capital and sealed its fate.

The fighting began in March at Kernstown ❶, where Jackson was repulsed by a larger Federal force. That setback helped his cause in the long run by fixing Federal attention on the Valley and involving Union troops in fruitless efforts to contain and pursue Jackson, who withdrew southward toward Harrisonburg ❷, enlisted fresh recruits, and gained a firm grasp of the country with the help of mapmaker Jedediah Hotchkiss. He then threw Federals off his track by departing the Valley through Brown's Gap ❸ before returning furtively with his men along the Virginia Central Railroad ❹. That ruse allowed him to surprise and defeat the vanguard of Major General John Frémont's army at McDowell ❺ in May. With scarcely a pause, Jackson's army marched north on the Valley Turnpike ❻ at a blistering pace and outflanked Major General Nathaniel Banks at Strasburg ❼ by turning east through a gap in Massanutten Mountain ❽, linking up with Major General Richard Ewell's Confederates at Luray ❾, seizing Front Royal ❿, and driving the bewildered Banks back through Winchester ⓫ into Maryland.

Fearing an attack on Washington, Lincoln withheld from the advance on Richmond 40,000 troops led by Major General Irvin McDowell, who sent a division under Brigadier General James Shields to join with Frémont in pinching off Jackson's army. Jackson got between them, however, and bested Frémont at Cross Keys ⓬ before repulsing Shields at nearby Port Republic ⓭. In McDowell's words, Jackson had managed to "paralyze a large force with a very small one," thus saving the Shenandoah Valley for the South and diverting Federals from Richmond, where Robert E. Lee's army now had a fighting chance. ■

Jackson's forage cap

A CAMPAIGN OF MOVEMENT **A National Geographic map details the fast-moving campaign of Jackson, who overcame his initial setback at Kernstown and triumphed in the Shenandoah Valley by outmaneuvering larger forces and attacking them when they were divided. His army never numbered more than 17,000 men but dominated this theater by enduring marches of up to 35 miles a day in fair weather or foul.**

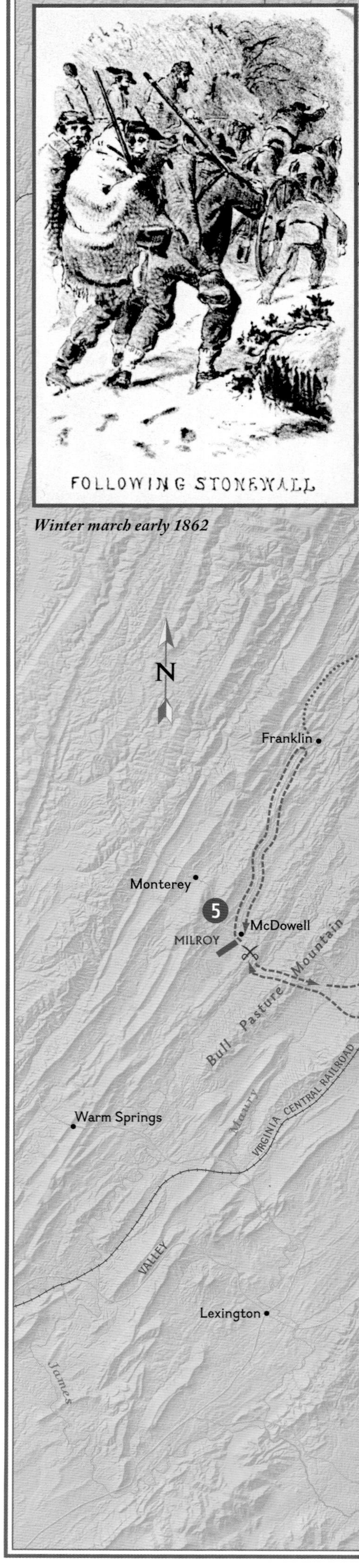

Winter march early 1862

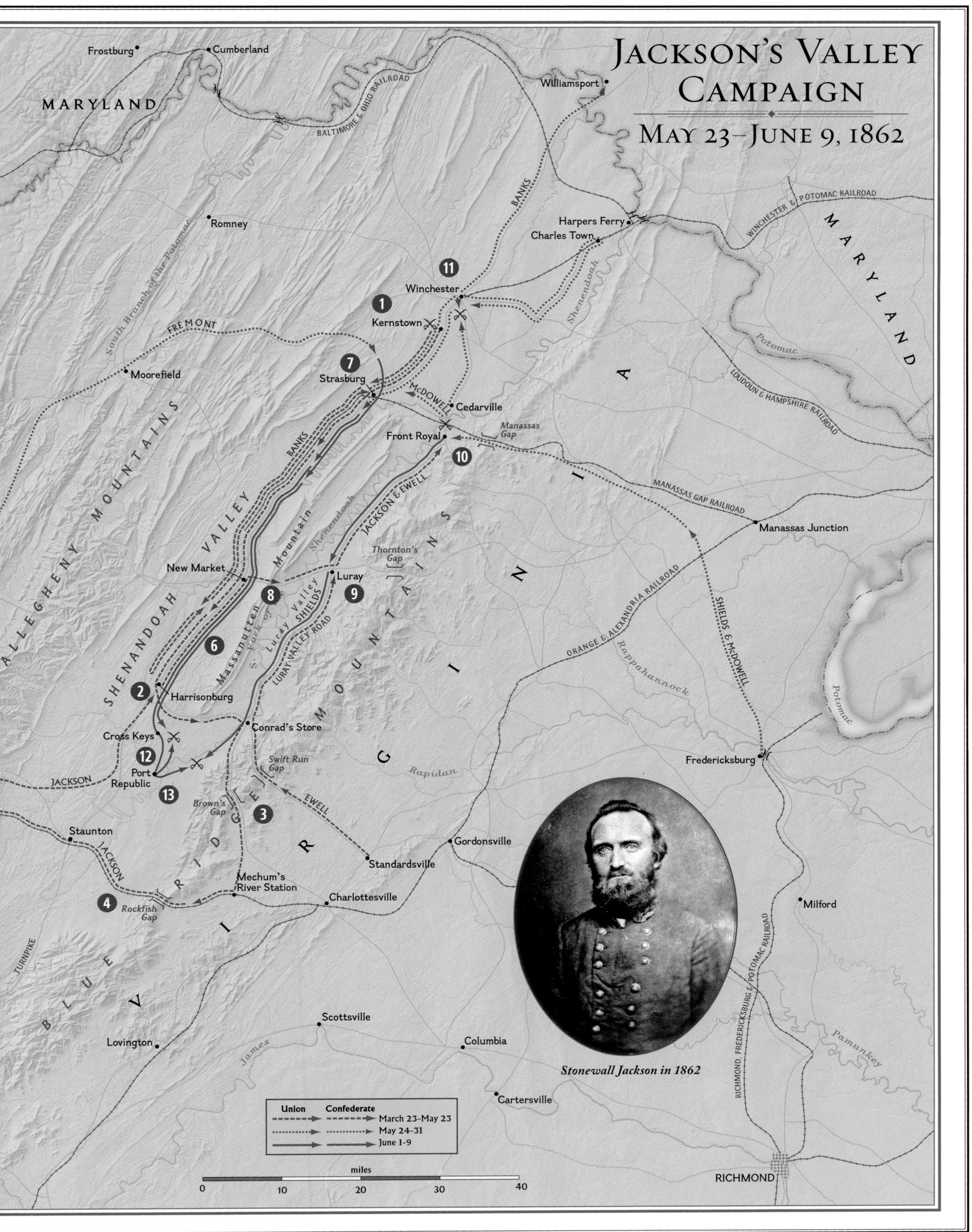

Stonewall Jackson in 1862

1862 | SHENANDOAH VALLEY

Jackson's Map of the Valley

Shortly after enlisting as a topographical engineer in March 1862, Jedediah Hotchkiss received a summons from Stonewall Jackson that altered his own destiny and the fortunes of the Confederacy. "I want you to make me a map of the Valley, from Harper's Ferry to Lexington," Jackson said. That was no small task, encompassing an area of more than 2,000 square miles over which Jackson would campaign tirelessly in months to come.

Although he had been a professor at the Virginia Military Institute (VMI) in Lexington before the war, Jackson did not know the Shenandoah Valley intimately and had no detailed map of the area. His hopes of holding the Valley and keeping Federals there from menacing Richmond hinged on the work of Hotchkiss, a self-taught cartographer from New York who had moved to Luray as a young man and sided with his adopted Virginia when it left the Union.

Furnished by Jackson with a wagon and driver and equipped with compasses, an altimeter, and other instruments, Hotchkiss scoured the Valley and drew charts, which he then translated into a comprehensive topographical map of the area (opposite) measuring eight and half feet long. This alone was a major contribution to the Confederate cause, but Hotchkiss took on other important duties as directed by Jackson, including guiding officers and troops and scouting enemy movements. "Never take counsel of your fears," Jackson told him—advice Hotchkiss did his best to heed when he came under fire. In his revealing diary, he bore witness to Jackson's ability to get the most out of his men. Early on, many considered him a heartless taskmaster, but as the campaign progressed they realized that outpacing their foes made defeating them less costly. "I am obliged to sweat them tonight," Jackson said of his troops during one long march, "that I may save their blood tomorrow." Soldiers who once cursed and grumbled now "cheered the General as we rode along," Hotchkiss noted.

Jackson, for his part, relished commanding an army whose success relied not on fortifications or defensive maneuvers but on swift movement and bold strokes. As he told Hotchkiss proudly during the Valley campaign, "Our men would rather fight and march than dig." ■

REST FOR THE WEARY Stonewall Jackson (center) and his troops pause beside a stream during a strenuous march through the undulating Shenandoah Valley in this idealized painting. To quicken the pace when battle loomed, Jackson had his men cast aside everything but their weapons and ammunition. "We knew there was some game at hand then," one soldier recalled, "for when General Jackson ordered knapsacks to be left behind he meant business."

CHARTING THE VALLEY Shown in full at left and in detail above, the campaign map of the northern Shenandoah Valley that Hotchkiss produced for Jackson in 1862 was drawn in pen and ink on drafting linen and divided into three sections. The close-ups above, covering the area outlined in white at left, show the region's main highway, the paved Valley Turnpike—along which Jackson's men made rapid progress—and the locations of individual farmhouses, where they often received aid and comfort.

"I am obliged to sweat them tonight, that I may save their blood tomorrow."

STONEWALL JACKSON
AFTER ORDERING HIS MEN TO MARCH THROUGH THE NIGHT

1862 | SHENANDOAH VALLEY

HARD LESSON AT KERNSTOWN

TURNER ASHBY

Fierce, bold, and majestically bearded, Colonel Turner Ashby was the consummate Virginia cavalier. "Riding his black stallion, he looked like a knight of the olden time," observed a fellow officer. But his freewheeling ways vexed his commander, Stonewall Jackson, a strict disciplinarian who wanted Ashby to keep his men under tighter rein. He had only about half his cavalry force at hand when fighting erupted at Kernstown on March 23 and did little to hold Federals in check there during the battle as instructed by Jackson. Jedediah Hotchkiss, who greatly admired Ashby, was dismayed one day to find many of his troopers "under the influence of apple-jack" and unfit for duty. "When Ashby's men are with him they behave gallantly," he noted, "but when they are away from him they lack the inspiration of presence and being undisciplined they often fail to do any good." In late April, an exasperated Jackson placed Ashby and his men under the command of infantry officers to keep them in line but backed down when Ashby offered his resignation. He was too valuable to let go. And despite their occasional lapses, his troopers proved indispensable to Jackson by screening his furtive movements and tracking enemy forces. Ashby's death while battling Federal cavalry at Harrisonburg on June 6 was "a loss irreparable," wrote Hotchkiss, and came as a heavy blow to Jackson, who "walked the floor of his room, for some time, in sorrow."

The Battle at Kernstown ❶ marked an unpromising start for Jackson's campaign but taught him a valuable lesson. Spoiling for a fight, he trusted in a misleading report from his cavalry commander, Colonel Turner Ashby, who was informed by civilians that Union Brigadier General James Shields, after being wounded in a skirmish with Ashby's men, had withdrawn northward from Kernstown, leaving behind only a rear guard. In fact, Shields had feigned a withdrawal and left most of his division near the town.

Approaching from the south on March 23 along the Valley Turnpike ❷, Jackson ordered Ashby's cavalry ❸ and Colonel Robert Chew's battery ❹ to tie down Federals east of the pike ❺ while he attacked what looked to be weaker forces to the west ❻. At this early stage in his campaign, Jackson had only about 4,000 men, and some of them had fallen behind during the hard march to Kernstown. He was unaware that Federals were present here in far greater numbers and were shifting regiments from east to west, where they counterattacked, pinning down Confederates led by Brigadier General Richard Garnett behind a stone wall ❼. Late that day, Garnett fell back, infuriating Jackson, who had him arrested.

In truth, the fault lay with Jackson for failing to reconnoiter and gauge enemy strength. Although the battle paid off strategically by drawing Federal attention to Jackson and diverting troops from the advance on Richmond, it violated Jackson's stated principle of never fighting "against heavy odds if by any possible maneuvering you can hurl your own force against only a part, and that the weakest part, of your enemy and crush it." In later contests, he would do just that. ■

❼ STORMING THE STONE WALL Union troops advance against Confederates crouching behind the stone wall at Kernstown in a sketch by battlefield artist Alfred Waud.

WHERE JACKSON FALTERED This map by Jedediah Hotchkiss—who joined Jackson's army shortly before the Battle of Kernstown and charted the field afterward—shows how Federals (positions shown in blue) reinforced their lines north of the stone wall before repulsing the Confederates (red), whose units are numbered here and identified in the key at lower right.

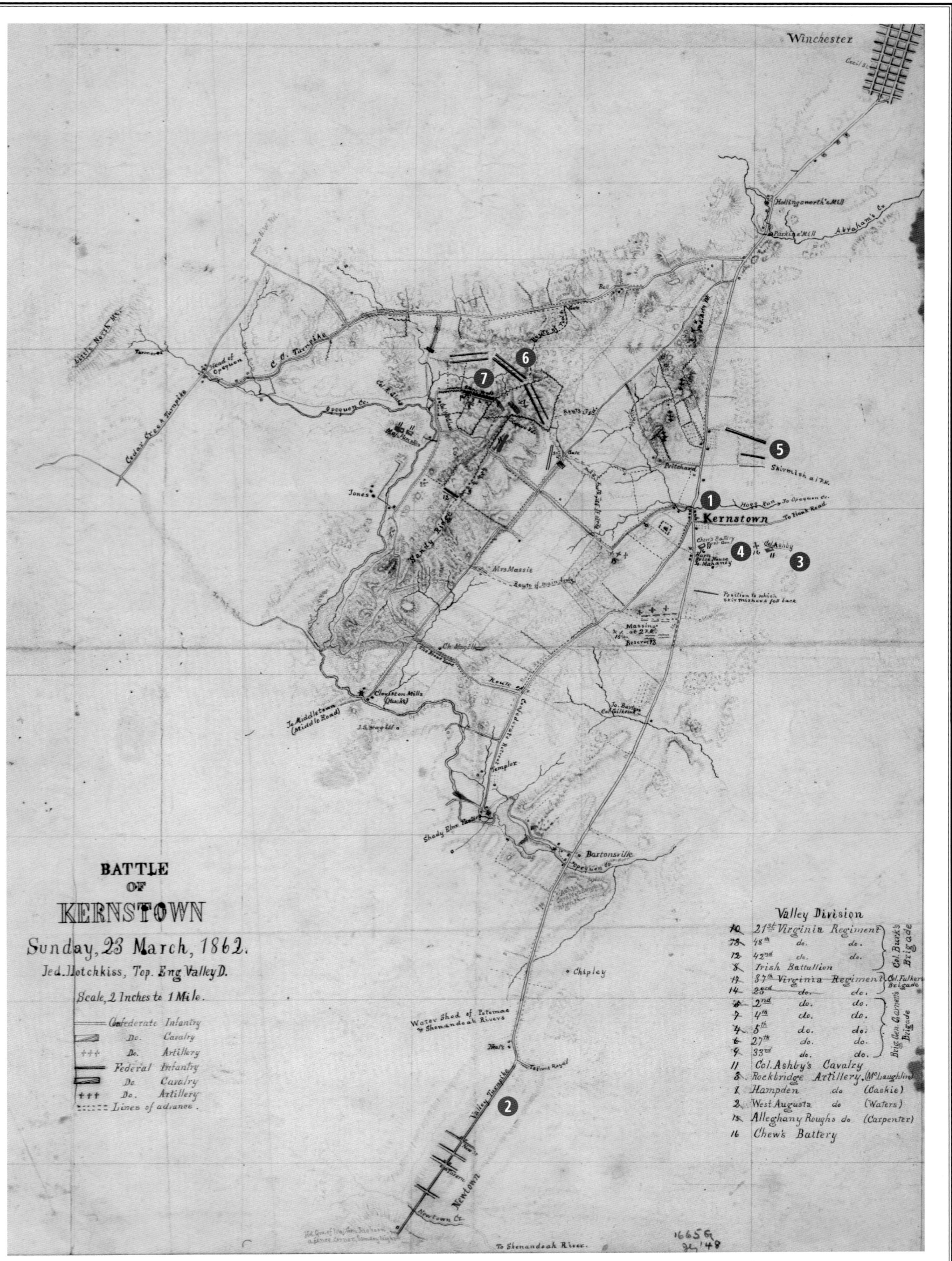

BATTLE OF KERNSTOWN
Sunday, 23 March, 1862.
Jed. Hotchkiss, Top. Eng Valley D.
Scale, 2 Inches to 1 Mile.
Confederate Infantry
Do. Cavalry
Do. Artillery
Federal Infantry
Do. Cavalry
Do. Artillery
Lines of advance.
Valley Division
10 21st Virginia Regiment
13 48th do. do.
12 42nd do. do.
8 Irish Battallion
Col. Burk's Brigade
17 37th Virginia Regiment
14 23rd do. do.
Col. Fulkerson Brigade
5 2nd do. do.
7 4th do. do.
4 5th do. do.
6 27th do. do.
9 33rd do. do.
Brig. Gen. Garnett's Brigade
11 Col. Ashby's Cavalry
3 Rockbridge Artillery. (McLaughlin)
1 Hampden do (Caskie)
2 West Augusta do (Waters)
15 Alleghany Roughs do (Carpenter)
16 Chew's Battery
Winchester
Hollingsworth's Mill
Abraham's Cr.
C. O. Turnpike
Head of Opequon
Cedar Cr. & Turnpike
Opequon Cr.
Jones
Pritchard
Kernstown
Hogg Run
To Front Road
Col. Ashby
Skirmish at 1 P.M.
Position to which skirmishers fell back
Mrs Massie
Sandy Ridge
Massing at 2 P.M.
Reserve
To Middletown (Middle Road)
Shady Elm
Bartonsville
Opequon Cr.
Chipley
Water Shed of Potomac & Shenandoah Rivers
To Front Royal
Valley Turnpike
Newtown
Newtown Cr.
To Shenandoah River.
1
2
3
4
5
6
7

Jackson Divides and Conquers at Port Republic

By early June, Stonewall Jackson had become a major concern for the Federals and their anxious commander-in-chief. Fearing for Washington's safety after Jackson took Front Royal and Winchester, Lincoln withheld Irvin McDowell's forces from McClellan's campaign against Richmond, freeing the division of James Shields—battle-tested at Kernstown—to return to the Shenandoah Valley and join John Frémont in seeking and destroying Jackson's army. "This movement must be made immediately," Lincoln wired Frémont, who was as deliberate as Jackson was quick. "Put the utmost speed into it. Do not lose a minute."

Prodded by the president, Frémont got moving but failed to intercept Jackson as he hurried south from Winchester along the Valley Turnpike to avoid being cut off. After clashing with pursuing Federals at Harrisonburg on June 6 and losing Turner Ashby, Jackson reached Port Republic ❶. That placed him between Frémont's force to the north and Shields's division to the east, allowing him to take full advantage of this strategic point where the North River ❷ and South River ❸ converge to form the South Fork of the Shenandoah River ❹. By commanding bridges and fords across those rivers with artillery and guarding the approaches to town with infantry, he could prevent Frémont and Shields from uniting and deal with them separately.

On June 8, Frémont attacked several miles north of Port Republic at Cross Keys but was rebuffed by forces led by Richard Ewell, Jackson's reliable second-in-command. That setback stalled Frémont long enough for Jackson to send most of his forces against the approaching Shields on June 9. Advancing east of Port Republic between the South Fork and River Road ❺, Confederates collided with Shields's vanguard and were raked by shellfire from a Federal battery positioned above the road at a hillside "coaling" ❻, where wood was burned to make charcoal. In heavy fighting, Confederates under Ewell—who had hurried here from Cross Keys at Jackson's bidding—overcame Federal regiments defending that battery and turned its guns on Shields's troops down below, who grudgingly withdrew. Belatedly, Frémont resumed his advance toward Port Republic, only to find that Jackson had burned the North River Bridge ❼ to deny him entry. After lobbing a few shells across the river, Frémont turned away, unwilling to prolong his efforts now that Shields had retreated.

By dividing, defeating, and demoralizing his numerically superior opponents, Jackson fulfilled his mission in the Shenandoah Valley. Soon he would move east to help Lee and his troops defend Richmond. ■

CAVALRY AT THE CROSSING Federal troopers with Frémont's army cross the North Fork of the Shenandoah River in pursuit of Jackson on June 5.

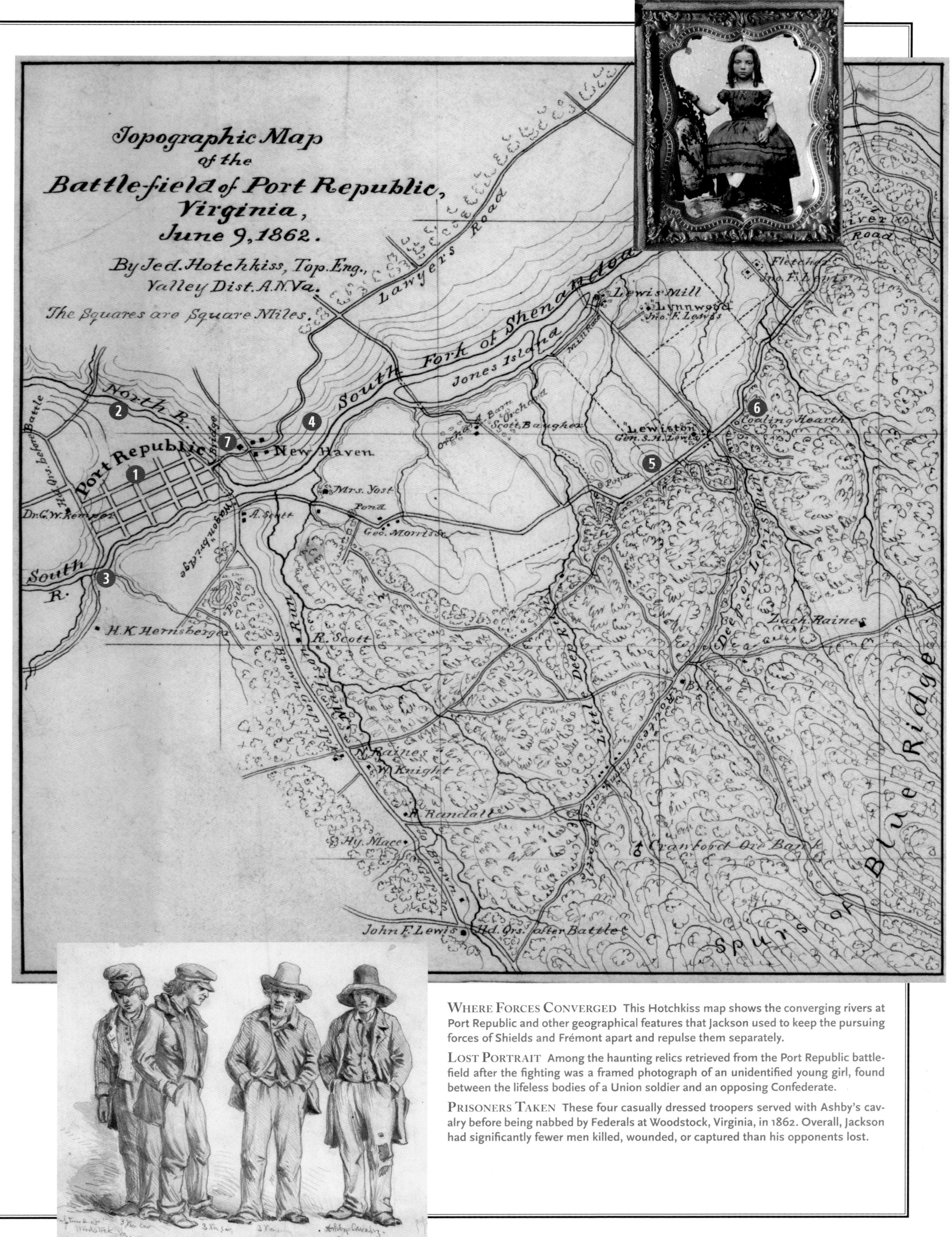

WHERE FORCES CONVERGED This Hotchkiss map shows the converging rivers at Port Republic and other geographical features that Jackson used to keep the pursuing forces of Shields and Frémont apart and repulse them separately.

LOST PORTRAIT Among the haunting relics retrieved from the Port Republic battlefield after the fighting was a framed photograph of an unidentified young girl, found between the lifeless bodies of a Union soldier and an opposing Confederate.

PRISONERS TAKEN These four casually dressed troopers served with Ashby's cavalry before being nabbed by Federals at Woodstock, Virginia, in 1862. Overall, Jackson had significantly fewer men killed, wounded, or captured than his opponents lost.

1862

THE PENINSULA

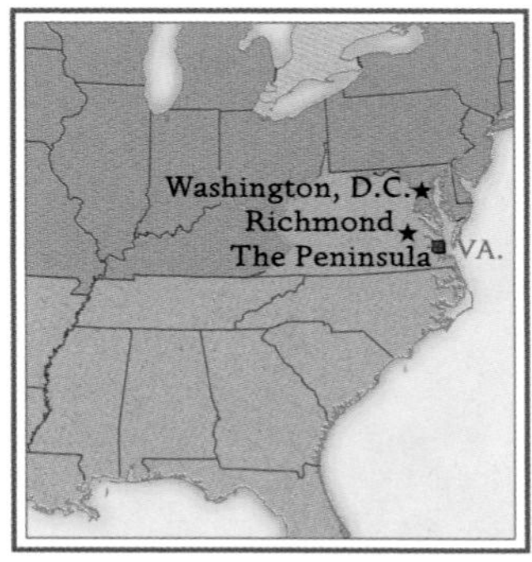

EASTERN THEATER

MARCH 17, 1862 McClellan's Army of the Potomac begins embarking from Alexandria, Virginia, for Fort Monroe to launch campaign against Richmond.

MAY 3 Besieged Confederates withdraw from Yorktown.

MAY 5 Battle of Williamsburg

MAY 31–JUNE 1 Battle of Seven Pines, near Richmond

JUNE 2 Lee takes command of forces defending Richmond.

JUNE 25–JULY 1 Seven Days' Battles around Richmond

JULY 1 McClellan withdraws to Harrison's Landing following Battle of Malvern Hill.

AUGUST 3 Lincoln recalls McClellan's army.

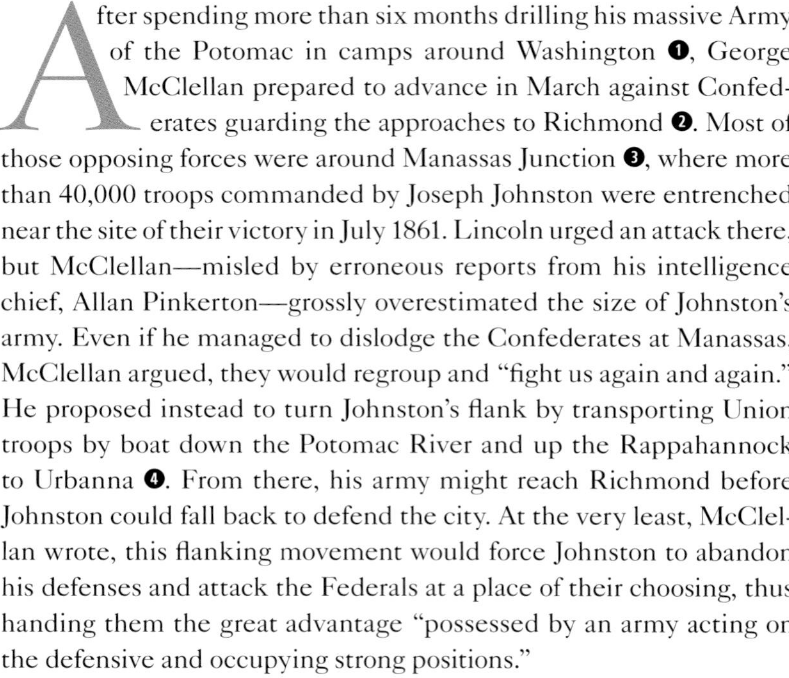

After spending more than six months drilling his massive Army of the Potomac in camps around Washington ❶, George McClellan prepared to advance in March against Confederates guarding the approaches to Richmond ❷. Most of those opposing forces were around Manassas Junction ❸, where more than 40,000 troops commanded by Joseph Johnston were entrenched near the site of their victory in July 1861. Lincoln urged an attack there, but McClellan—misled by erroneous reports from his intelligence chief, Allan Pinkerton—grossly overestimated the size of Johnston's army. Even if he managed to dislodge the Confederates at Manassas, McClellan argued, they would regroup and "fight us again and again." He proposed instead to turn Johnston's flank by transporting Union troops by boat down the Potomac River and up the Rappahannock to Urbanna ❹. From there, his army might reach Richmond before Johnston could fall back to defend the city. At the very least, McClellan wrote, this flanking movement would force Johnston to abandon his defenses and attack the Federals at a place of their choosing, thus handing them the great advantage "possessed by an army acting on the defensive and occupying strong positions."

McClellan was forced to modify his plan when Johnston anticipated the threat to his flank and withdrew southward below the Rappahannock in early March. The Army of the Potomac would disembark not at Urbanna, McClellan decided, but at Fort Monroe ❺. By landing there and advancing up the Virginia Peninsula ❻ toward Richmond, he would have to contend initially with a force of only 15,000 or so Confederates of the Army of the Peninsula commanded by Major General John B. Magruder, holding a fortified line extending southward from Yorktown ❼. If McClellan moved quickly, he might break through there before Johnston's troops arrived in sufficient numbers to impede his advance on the Confederate capital. When Lincoln decided to withhold from this Peninsula campaign nearly 40,000 Federals under Irvin McDowell in order to protect Washington, McClellan was irate, calling it "the most infamous thing that history has recorded." But the odds were still in his favor. His army, which began embarking from Alexandria ❽ on March 17, remained a prodigious force of over 100,000 men, accompanied by 1,200 wagons and ambulances and 44 artillery batteries. One British observer likened its advance to "the stride of a giant." ■

COMMANDER AND WIFE Hailed as the Young Napoleon, George McClellan, shown here with his wife, Ellen, was just 35 when he advanced against Richmond and had never known a serious setback as a commander. "The grass will not grow under my feet," he wrote Ellen confidently from Fort Monroe. "I see my way very clearly."

MCCLELLAN'S PATH Drawn by John Bachmann, this bird's eye view of Virginia and environs, looking west, shows the area McClellan traversed as his army cruised down the Potomac from Alexandria, disembarked at Fort Monroe, and marched up the Peninsula toward Richmond. As indicated by distances listed below the map, he placed his army 30 miles closer to Richmond by beginning his march at Fort Monroe rather than at Washington.

Panorama of the Seat of War.

1 2 3 4 5 6 7 8

RICHMOND
FREDERICKSBURG
WASHINGTON
ALEXANDRIA
BALTIMORE
FT MONROE
CHESAPEAKE BAY
ANTIC OCEAN

Published by J. Bachmann, 115 Nassau St., N.Y.

BIRDS EYE VIEW

IA, MARYLAND DELAWARE AND THE DISTRICT OF COLUMBIA

DISTANCES FROM

WASHINGTON TO	BALTIMORE,	30	MILES.
"	FAIRFAX,	75	"
"	RICHMOND,	105	"
"	MANASSAS JCT.,	35	"
"	HARPERS FERRY,	58	"
"	LEESBURGH,	30	"
"	MARTINSBURG,	73	"
"	CUMBERLAND,	148	"

❶ READY FOR ACTION The 96th Pennsylvania Infantry, shown parading at camp outside Washington, was one of more than 150 regiments of the Army of the Potomac that advanced on Richmond under McClellan, who assured his troops, "It shall be my care, as it has ever been, to gain success with the least possible loss."

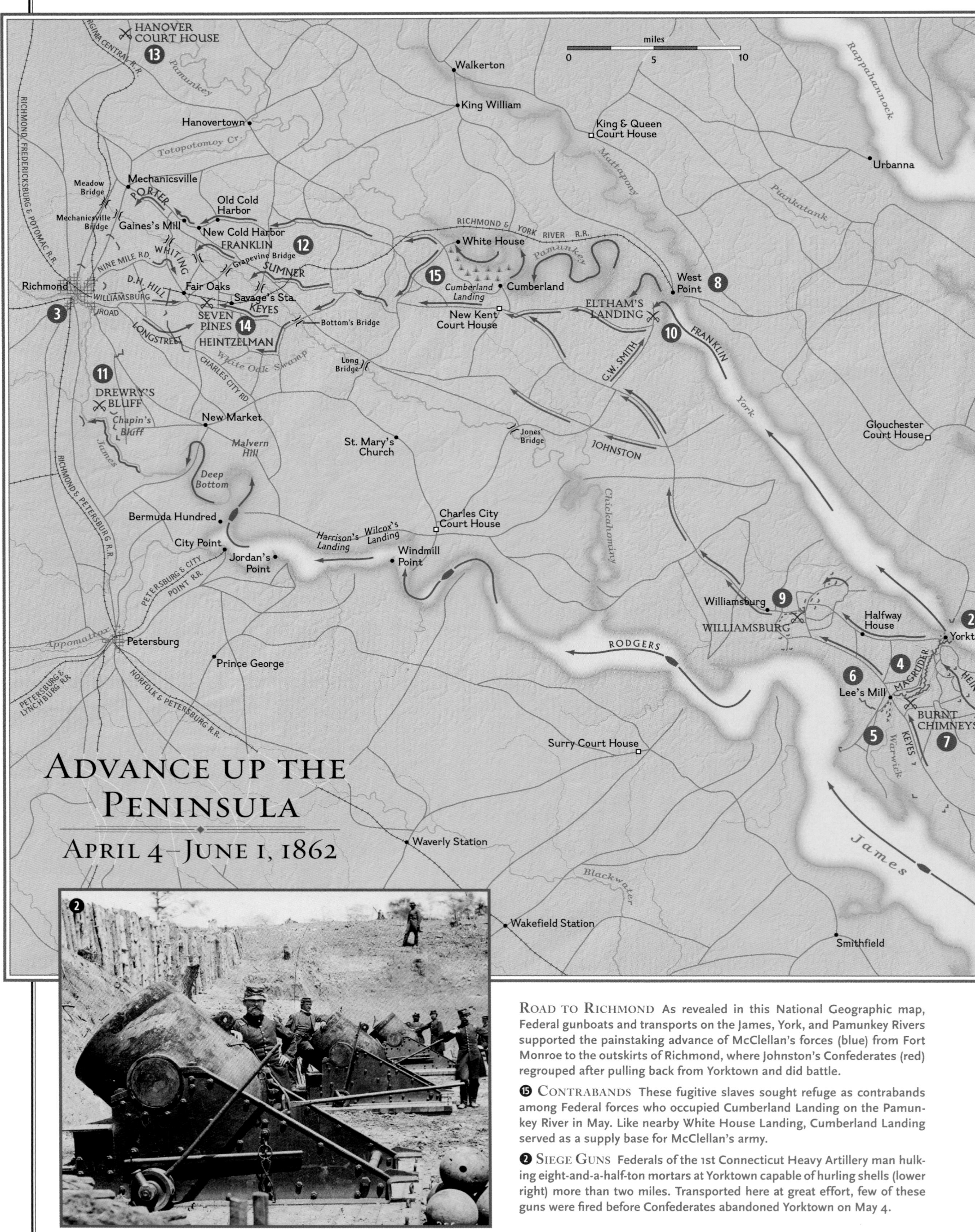

ROAD TO RICHMOND As revealed in this National Geographic map, Federal gunboats and transports on the James, York, and Pamunkey Rivers supported the painstaking advance of McClellan's forces (blue) from Fort Monroe to the outskirts of Richmond, where Johnston's Confederates (red) regrouped after pulling back from Yorktown and did battle.

⓯ CONTRABANDS These fugitive slaves sought refuge as contrabands among Federal forces who occupied Cumberland Landing on the Pamunkey River in May. Like nearby White House Landing, Cumberland Landing served as a supply base for McClellan's army.

❷ SIEGE GUNS Federals of the 1st Connecticut Heavy Artillery man hulking eight-and-a-half-ton mortars at Yorktown capable of hurling shells (lower right) more than two miles. Transported here at great effort, few of these guns were fired before Confederates abandoned Yorktown on May 4.

Federal artillery park at Yorktown

1862 | THE PENINSULA

FORWARD TO RICHMOND

When McClellan set out from Fort Monroe ❶ on April 4, he expected to take Yorktown ❷ within days and advance rapidly on Richmond ❸. His plan called for Brigadier General Samuel Heintzelman's Third Corps to approach Yorktown head on while Brigadier General Samuel Keyes's Fourth Corps skirted entrenched Confederates to the south ❹ and cut them off. Keyes found his path blocked, however, by the Warwick River ❺, which had been dammed, and by Confederates who had extended their line to cover Lee's Mill Dam ❻ and other crossings. Alarmed by demonstrations Magruder staged to make his small force look formidable, Keyes warned McClellan that no part of the enemy line thus far discovered could be "taken by assault without enormous waste of human life."

Such dire reports and tall tales by Confederate prisoners overstating Magruder's strength held McClellan back while Johnston approached Yorktown with reinforcements to take command there. He had not yet arrived when Federals tested Magruder at Burnt Chimneys ❼ on April 16 and crossed the Warwick River, threatening a breakthrough. But McClellan did not press his advantage and instead settled in for a siege, bringing up heavy guns. Not until May 4, a month into his campaign, did he take Yorktown, marching in unopposed after Johnston withdrew to spare his army.

From Yorktown, McClellan sent forces under Brigadier General William Franklin by boat up the York River to seize West Point ❽, linked by rail to Richmond. Meanwhile Brigadier General Edwin "Bull" Sumner pursued Johnston overland and clashed at Williamsburg ❾ on May 5 with his rear guard, led by Major General James Longstreet, who withdrew in good order after heavy fighting. Two days later, another keen Confederate officer, Brigadier General John Bell Hood, challenged Franklin at Eltham's Landing ❿. Hood's action shielded Johnston as he withdrew toward Richmond, but Franklin secured West Point and the navigable Pamunkey River, ensuring that McClellan would be well supplied as he approached Richmond. On May 15, an advance up the James River by the ironclad *Monitor* and other Union gunboats, launched after Norfolk fell on May 9, was rebuffed by Confederate artillery at Drewry's Bluff ⓫. Later that month, Federals drew up along the Chickahominy River ⓬, near Richmond, and began crossing. McClellan secured his right flank by routing a small force guarding the Virginia Central Railroad near Hanover Court House ⓭ on May 27. But his left flank, below the Chickahominy, was exposed and came under attack by Johnston on May 31 at Seven Pines ⓮. ■

JOSEPH JOHNSTON

At 54, General Joseph Johnston was a generation older than his opponent on the Peninsula, George McClellan, but the two men had much in common. Both were masters of logistics—moving and supplying troops—who would rather outmaneuver their foes than engage them in bloody battles of attrition. After resigning as quartermaster general of the U.S. Army in 1861 when his native Virginia seceded, Johnston hurried his troops by rail from Winchester to Manassas Junction in July and helped secure victory at Bull Run. Afterward, he became one of five Confederate commanders promoted to the rank of full general (above major general) but objected when Jefferson Davis placed him fourth on that list, below Robert E. Lee and others to whom he was senior when he left the U.S. Army. Much like McClellan, who resisted being rushed by Lincoln into battle, Johnston vexed Davis by withdrawing on the Peninsula until his troops had their backs to Richmond. Urged by Davis to attack before McClellan crossed the Chickahominy and "matured his preparations for a siege," Johnston waited until McClellan pushed two of his five corps across the river and then fell on those exposed forces at Seven Pines. His well-timed but ill-coordinated attack went awry, and he was badly wounded, leaving the defense of Richmond to Lee, whose seniority to Johnston was debatable but whose superiority in dealing with McClellan would soon become clear.

1862 | THE PENINSULA

CHAOS AT SEVEN PINES

PHILIP KEARNY

Confederates took pride in their chivalrous military tradition, exemplified by warriors like Turner Ashby who grew up on horseback in the rural South and fought with a bravado that Northern city-dwellers presumably could not match. But the Union had its own hard-charging paladins—officers like Philip Kearny who relished combat and rode up front when their troops entered battle. Born in Manhattan to a financier who denied him permission to enter West Point and insisted he study law, Kearny learned to ride on his grandfather's manor in upstate New York, where neighbors called him a "perfect horse killer." Once he came into his inheritance, he did as he pleased, entering the army and losing his left arm while leading a cavalry charge during the Mexican War. Undeterred, he went abroad as a soldier of fortune in the 1850s and earned the Legion of Honor medal serving France. As a division commander under McClellan, he boasted that he could "make men follow me to hell" and did just that in hot battles at Williamsburg and Seven Pines. Whether this "one-armed devil," as Confederates called him, could have harnessed his combativeness and risen to the challenge of commanding an army would never be known. After winning promotion to major general for his feats on the Peninsula, Kearny died in action at Chantilly, Virginia, on September 1, 1862, at the age of 46.

Seizing his chance, Johnston made plans to throw more than 50,000 Confederates against 33,000 Federals below the Chickahominy ❶ on May 31, hoping to crush them before Federal forces north of the river could come to their aid. Theoretically, he had the benefit of fighting on home ground, but inexperience, confusion, and disorientation on his own side would nullify any advantage he held.

Johnston instructed three commanders to follow separate paths and converge on Federals holding the Seven Pines crossroads ❷. Major General Daniel Harvey Hill, advancing eastward on the Williamsburg Stage Road ❸, was the only one ready to attack as planned that morning. Major General Benjamin Huger, assigned to follow the Charles City Road ❹ and come up from the south, got a late start and was further delayed when his men had to wait for Longstreet's forces to cross a bridge ahead of them. Longstreet was off track and ended up behind Hill ❺ instead of coming down from the northwest on the Nine Mile Road ❻ as planned.

Around 1 P.M., Hill attacked on his own, routing the division of Brigadier General Silas Casey ❼ and outflanking Brigadier General Darius Couch ❽, whose forces retreated with Casey's east of Seven Pines. To keep Federals to the north at bay, Johnston counted on a big push down the Nine Mile Road by Longstreet, backed by Major General Gustavus Smith. But with Longstreet sidetracked, Smith's troops were stopped short near Fair Oaks Station ❾ by Sumner's Second Corps, which crossed the Chickahominy on the rickety and flooded Grapevine Bridge ❿, slogged through swamps, and entered battle "just in time to save the day," one Yankee recalled. Sumner's advance eased pressure on Federals east of Seven Pines, where two hard-fighting brigadiers of Heintzelman's Third Corps, Philip Kearny ⓫ and Joseph Hooker ⓬, held the line with Casey and other elements of Keyes's Fourth Corps. Succeeding the wounded Johnston that evening, Smith renewed the attack on June 1 without success, bringing Confederate casualties here to over 6,000, compared to around 5,000 for the Federals. ■

AERIAL RECONNAISSANCE Aeronaut Thaddeus Lowe, who kept watch for McClellan on the Peninsula, ascends in his balloon, *Intrepid*, while men below hold mooring ropes. Strong winds on May 31 prevented Lowe from ascending until after the battle began, and once aloft the forested terrain hid enemy movements from his view.

JOHNSTON'S LOST OPPORTUNITY A detailed map of the action at Fair Oaks, or Seven Pines, on May 31 by Robert Knox Sneden, who served here with Heintzelman's corps, shows Longstreet and Huger in the "Rebel line at 9 P.M." But during the fighting that afternoon, few of Longstreet's units and none of Huger's forces entered battle, dashing Johnston's hopes for victory.

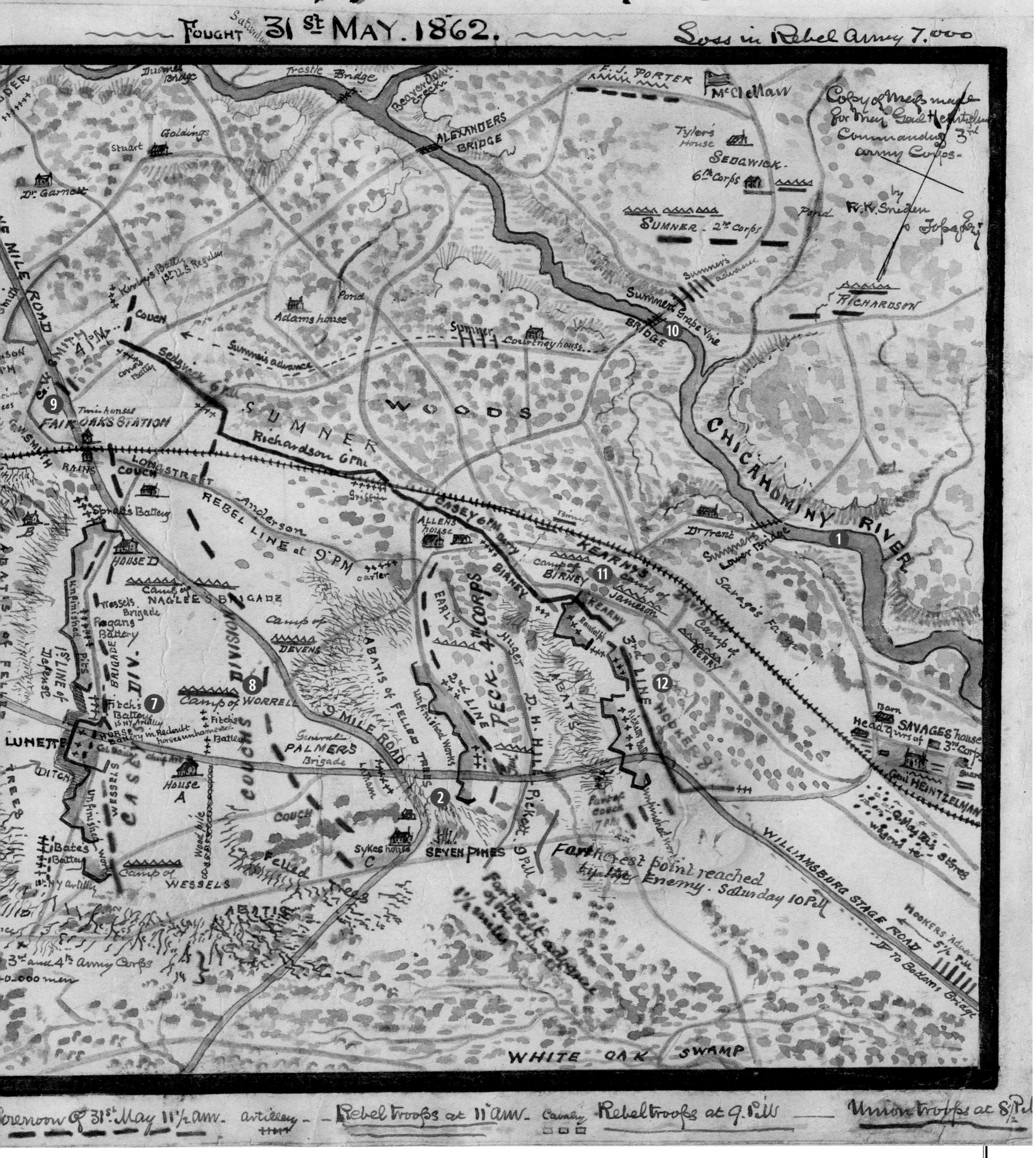
E BATTLE OF FAIR OAKS VA.
FOUGHT Saturday 31st MAY. 1862.
Loss in Rebel Army 7.000
Copy of Map made for Maj. Genl. Heintzelman Commanding 3rd Army Corps.
by R. K. Sneden Topog'r
F. J. PORTER
McClellan
Trestle Bridge
Beaverdam Creek
ALEXANDERS BRIDGE
Tyler's House
SEDGWICK 6th Corps
SUMNER - 2nd Corps
Pond
RICHARDSON
Stuart
Goldings
Dr. Garnett
Adams house
Sumner
Courtney house
Sumner's advance
Sumner's Grape Vine BRIDGE
COUCH
FAIR OAKS STATION
Twin houses
SUMNER
Richardson 6 PM
WOODS
CHICKAHOMINY RIVER
LONGSTREET
COUCH
REBEL LINE at 9 PM
Anderson
Spratt's Battery
HOUSE D
Camp of NAGLEE'S BRIGADE
Wessels Brigade
Regans Battery
CASEY 6 PM
ALLENS house
Camp of BIRNEY
KEARNY'S
Camp of Jameson
Savages Farm
Camp of BERRY
Dr. Trent
Summer's Lower Bridge
Camp of DEVENS
ABATIS of FELLED TREES
4th CORPS
PECK
D. H. HILL
EARLY
BIRNEY
3rd LINE
HOOKER'S
Camp of WORRELL
Fitch's Battery
LUNETTE
HORSE
Genl. PALMERS Brigade
9 MILE ROAD
House A
CASEY DIV.
COUCH'S DIVISION
WESSELS
DITCH
Bates Battery
Camp of WESSELS
COUCH
Sykes house
SEVEN PINES
Farthest point reached by the Enemy. Saturday 10 PM
Felled Trees
ABATIS
3rd and 4th Army Corps
WILLIAMSBURG STAGE ROAD
To Bottoms Bridge
HOOKERS advance 5 PM
SAVAGES house
Head Qrs of 3rd Corps
Genl. HEINTZELMAN
WHITE OAK SWAMP
Forenoon of 31st May 11½ am.
artillery
Rebel troops at 11 am.
Cavalry
Rebel troops at 9 PM
Union troops at 8½ PM
1
2
7
8
9
10
11
12

LEE TAKES COMMAND

When Lee took charge of Confederates defending Richmond ❶ on June 2, he was not a revered figure. Despite a stellar prewar career in the U.S. Army that led Lincoln to offer him field command of all Union forces before he sided with his native Virginia, his early service to the Confederacy brought him no accolades. Critics dubbed him the "King of Spades" for ordering soldiers to dig trenches, work some considered cowardly and suited only for slaves. Insisting that there was "nothing so important to an army as to save the lives of its soldiers," Lee defied opinion and kept his men busy after the debacle at Seven Pines fortifying their line east of Richmond. He did not mind if that made foes think he was overcautious or "timid & irresolute in action," as McClellan put it. For his plans were in fact so bold that Richmond would be at great risk if the enemy anticipated them.

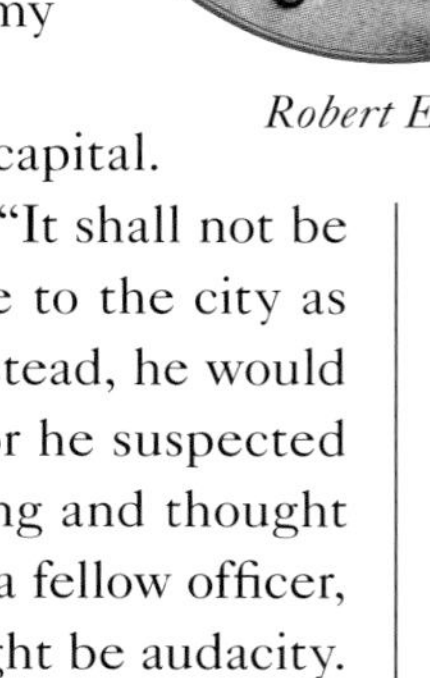
Robert E. Lee

Lee would spare no effort to protect the capital. "Richmond must not be given up," he insisted. "It shall not be given up!" If he allowed McClellan to lay siege to the city as he had to Yorktown, its fate would be sealed. Instead, he would hit his opponent hard and hit him repeatedly, for he suspected that McClellan preferred maneuvering to fighting and thought he would give way under sustained pressure. As a fellow officer, Colonel Joseph Ives, said of Lee, "His name might be audacity. He will take more desperate chances, and take them quicker, than any other general in this country, North or South."

Before setting those aggressive plans in motion, Lee sent his cavalry chief Jeb Stuart on a reconnaissance mission that became legendary and reorganized his army. He gave prominent roles to generals he thought could carry the fight to the enemy, including Longstreet, Daniel Harvey Hill, Ambrose Powell Hill—whose fast-marching Light Division would rival the exploits of Stonewall Jackson's "foot cavalry"—and Jackson himself, summoned by Lee from the Shenandoah Valley after defeating Federals diverted there from McClellan's campaign. Another commander Lee considered better suited for defensive action—John Magruder, supported by Benjamin Huger—would be left with fewer than 25,000 troops on the fortified line east of Richmond to hold off three times as many Federals while Lee threw the bulk of his forces against McClellan's right wing above the Chickahominy ❷. In a bloody ordeal called the Seven Days' Battles that began on June 25, Lee's forces would trade blows with Federals at Oak Grove ❸, Mechanicsville ❹, Gaines's Mill ❺, Savage's Station ❻, Glendale ❼, and Malvern Hill ❽. When the smoke cleared in July, McClellan would be boxed in at Harrison's Landing ❾, and no one would ever again question Lee's willingness to fight. ■

LEE'S BOLD STROKES **In the Seven Days' Battles, shown on this National Geographic map, McClellan struck first at Oak Grove, near Fair Oaks Station, on June 25, gaining little ground there. Lee then seized the initiative in a series of hammer blows that stunned his opponent and led him to retreat to Harrison's Landing.**

ORDER OF BATTLE

UNION FORCES

ARMY OF THE POTOMAC
McClellan | *100,000 men*

II CORPS
Sumner
1ST DIVISION *Richardson*
Brigades Caldwell, Meagher, French
2ND DIVISION *Sedgwick*
Brigades Sully, Burns, Dana

III CORPS
Heintzelman
2ND DIVISION *Hooker*
Brigades Grover, Sickles, Carr
3RD DIVISION *Kearny*
Brigades Robinson, Birney, Berry

IV CORPS
Keyes
1ST DIVISION *Couch*
Brigades Howe, Abercrombie, Palmer
2ND DIVISION *Peck*
Brigades Naglee, Wessells

V CORPS
Porter
1ST DIVISION *Morell*
Brigades Martindale, Griffin, Butterfield
2ND DIVISION *Sykes*
Brigades Buchanan, Lovell, Warren
3RD DIVISION *McCall*
Brigades Reynolds, Seymour, Meade

VI CORPS
Franklin
1ST DIVISION *Slocum*
Brigades Taylor, Bartlett, Newton
2ND DIVISION *Smith*
Brigades Hancock, Brooks, Davidson

CAVALRY RESERVE
Cooke

CONFEDERATE FORCES

ARMY OF NORTHERN VIRGINIA
Lee | *80,000 men*

LONGSTREET
LONGSTREET'S DIVISION
Brigades Kemper, R. H. Anderson, Pickett, Wilcox, Pryor, Featherston
D. H. HILL'S DIVISION
Brigades Rodes, G. B. Anderson, Garland, Colquitt, Ripley
A. P. HILL'S DIVISION
Brigades Field, Gregg, J. R. Anderson, Branch, Archer, Pender
HUGER'S DIVISION
Brigades Mahone, Wright, Armistead
HOLMES'S DIVISION
Brigades Ransom, Daniel, Walker, Wise

JACKSON
WHITING'S DIVISION
Brigades Hood, Law
JACKSON'S DIVISION
Brigades Winder, Cunningham, Fulkerson, Lawton
EWELL'S DIVISION
Brigades Elzey, Trimble, Seymour

MAGRUDER
D. R. JONES'S DIVISION
Brigades Toombs, G. T. Anderson
MCLAWS'S DIVISION
Brigades Semmes, Kershaw
MAGRUDER'S DIVISION
Brigades Cobb, Barksdale

CAVALRY
Stuart

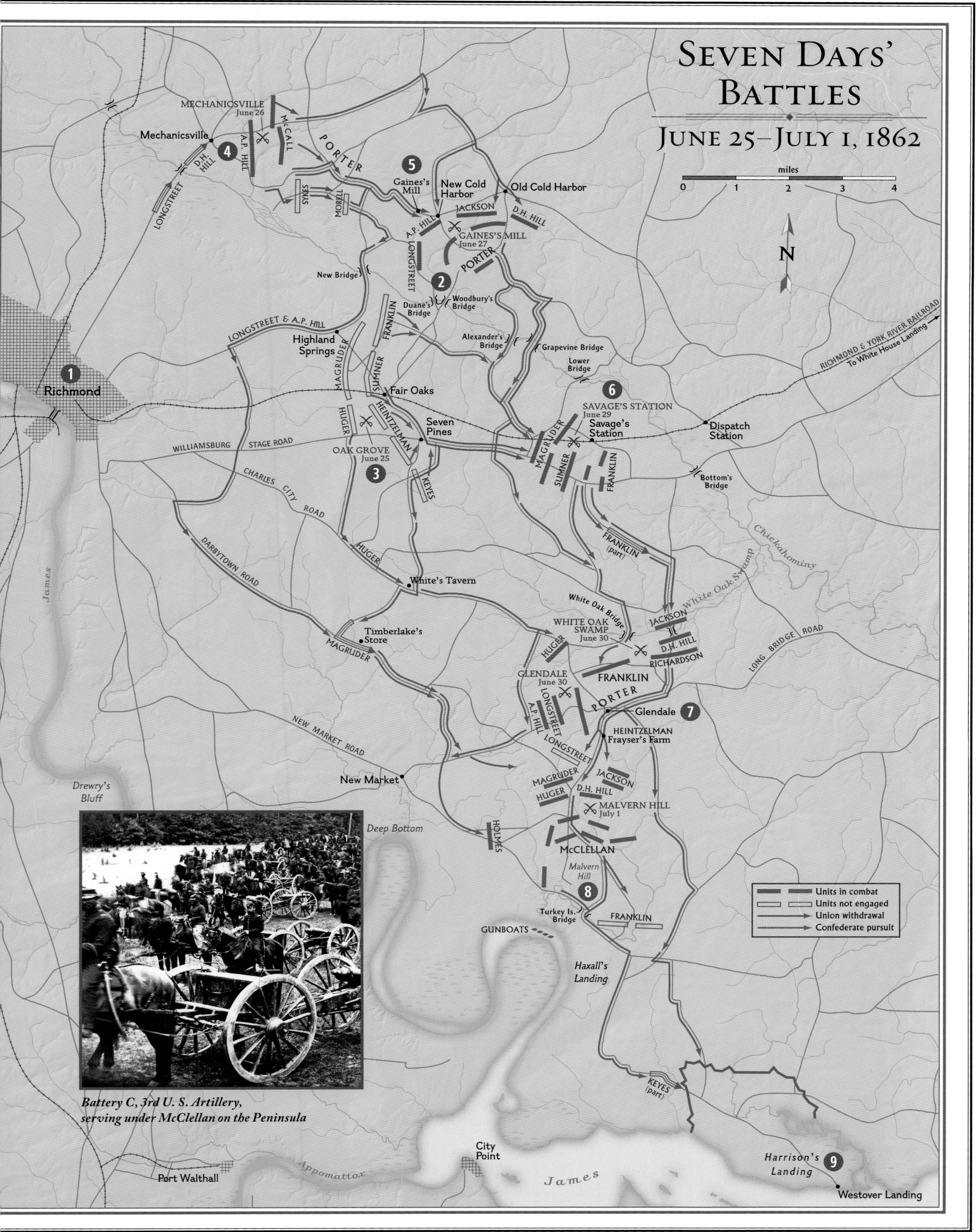

Battery C, 3rd U. S. Artillery, serving under McClellan on the Peninsula

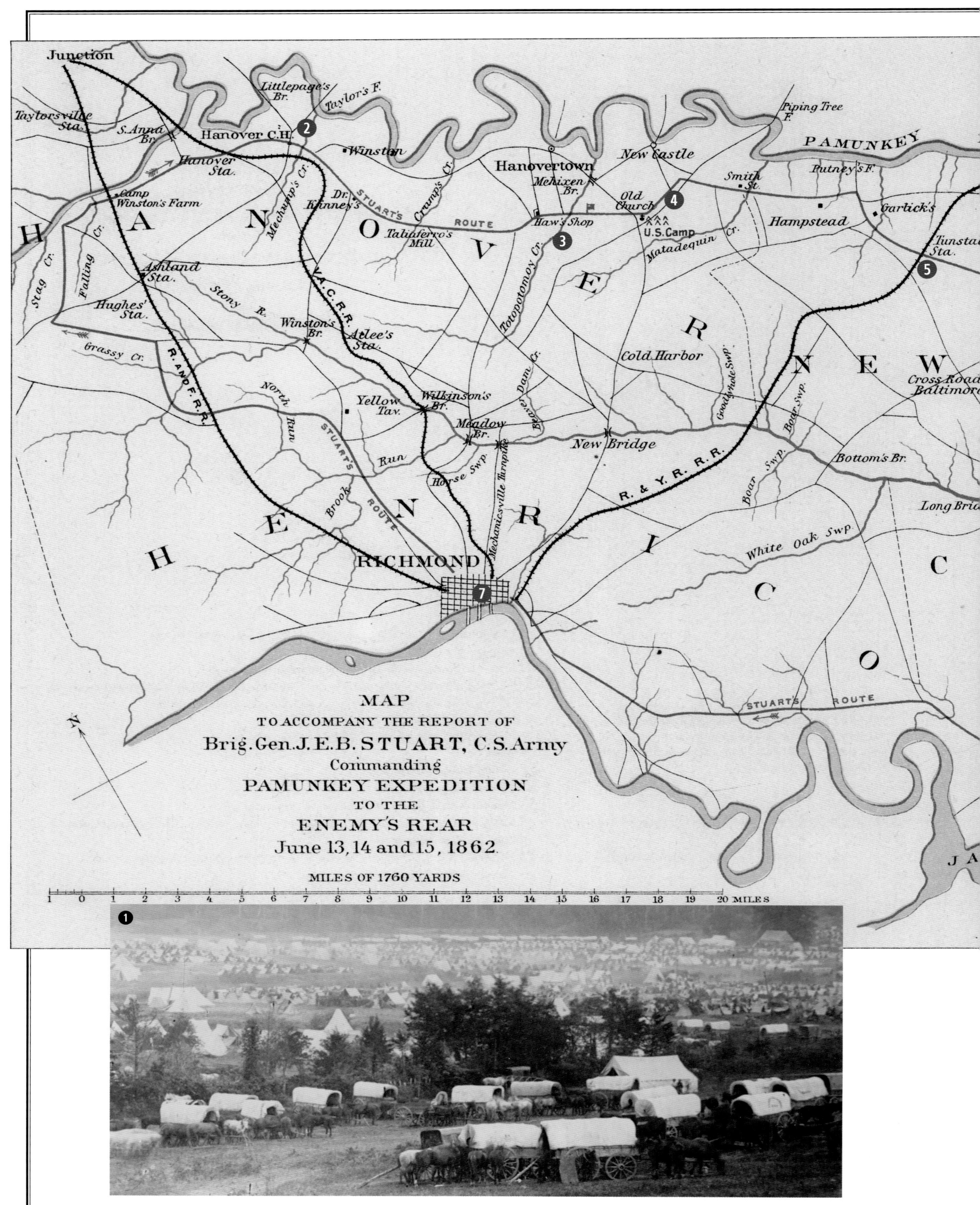
MAP
TO ACCOMPANY THE REPORT OF
Brig. Gen. J. E. B. STUART, C. S. Army
Commanding
PAMUNKEY EXPEDITION
TO THE
ENEMY'S REAR
June 13, 14 and 15, 1862
MILES OF 1760 YARDS
1 0 1 2 3 4 5 6 7 8 9 10 11 12 13 14 15 16 17 18 19 20 MILES
Junction
Littlepage's Br.
Taylor's F.
Taylorsville Sta.
S. Anna Br.
Hanover C.H.
Winston
Hanover Sta.
Camp Winston's Farm
Hanovertown
New Castle
Piping Tree F.
PAMUNKEY
Mehixen Br.
Smith St.
Putney's F.
Dr. Kinney's
STUART'S ROUTE
Cramp's Cr.
Mechump's Cr.
Old Church
U.S. Camp
Haw's Shop
Taliaferro's Mill
Hampstead
Garlick's
Matadequin Cr.
Tunstall Sta.
HANOVER
Stag Cr.
Falling Cr.
Ashland Sta.
Hughes' Sta.
Stony R.
VA. C. R. R.
Totopotomoy Cr.
Winston's Br.
Atlee's Sta.
Grassy Cr.
R. AND F. R. R.
Cold Harbor
Goodwyn's Swp.
NEW
Cross Roads
Baltimore
North Run
Yellow Tav.
Wilkinson's Br.
Beaver Dam Cr.
Boar Swp.
Meadow Br.
New Bridge
Run
Brook
Horse Swp.
Mechanicsville Turnpike
R. & Y. R. R. R.
Bottom's Br.
Long Bri
HENRICO
RICHMOND
White Oak Swp.
C
JA

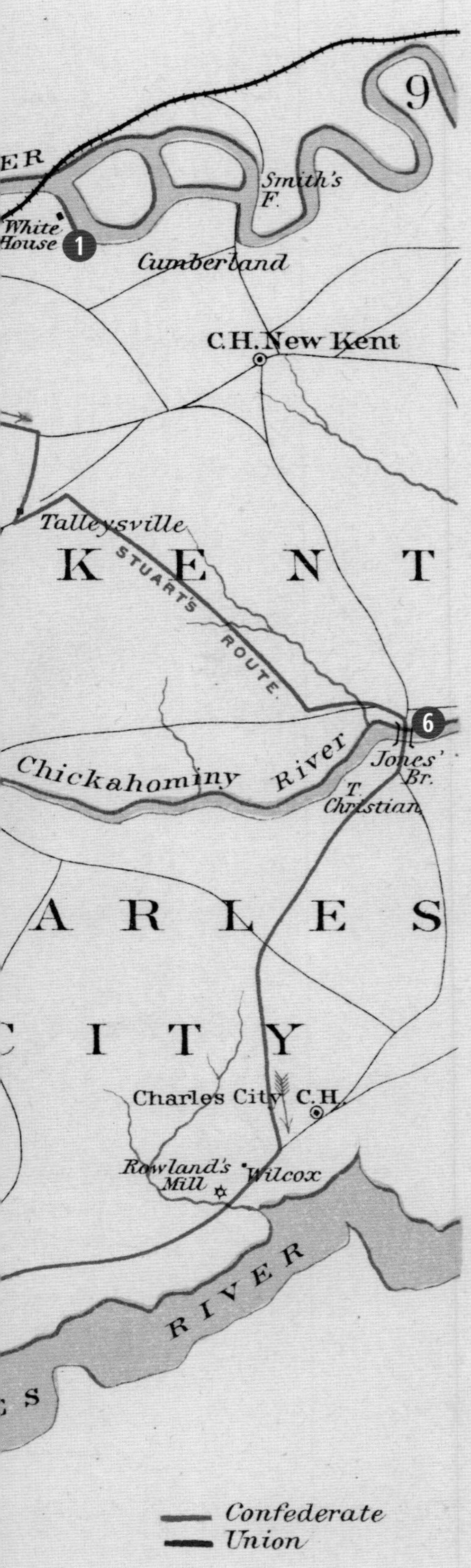

1862 | THE PENINSULA

Stuart's Ride Around McClellan

Like other dashing cavalry officers, 27-year-old Brigadier General James Ewell Brown (Jeb) Stuart was a free spirit whose forays sometimes went beyond the limits of his orders. In Lee, he had a commander who allowed trusted subordinates considerable latitude in fulfilling their instructions. That combination produced one of the war's most celebrated exploits—a reconnaissance that took Stuart clear around McClellan's army.

Lee summoned Stuart on June 10 and asked him to determine how far McClellan's right flank extended above the Chickahominy—where Stonewall Jackson would be approaching later in the month to join Lee's planned offensive—and to reconnoiter Federal supply lines from White House Landing ❶ and other depots on the Pamunkey River. Stuart thought this might be a chance for him to pursue his "favorite scheme" by encircling McClellan, and Lee did not rule that out. Setting out before dawn on June 12 with 1,200 cavalrymen, Stuart reached Hanover Court House ❷ the next day. McClellan had sent troops there in May to drive Confederates off his flank but had not secured the area, and Stuart saw nothing to prevent Jackson's troops from linking up with Lee. Proceeding eastward, the Confederates clashed with Federal troopers near Totopotomoy Creek ❸ and torched the camp of the 5th U.S. Cavalry at Old Church ❹.

Jeb Stuart

Continuing their circuit, Stuart's men drove enemy pickets from Tunstall's Station ❺ on the Richmond & York River Railroad and attacked a Federal supply train, which plowed through a barricade they erected and pulled away under a hail of bullets. As night fell, they rode southeastward toward the Chickahominy, pursued by Stuart's father-in-law, Brigadier General Philip St. George Cooke, a Unionist from Virginia whose family was torn by the war. His nephew, Confederate Lieutenant John Esten Cooke, was with Stuart as they crossed the Chickahominy River on a makeshift bridge ❻ on June 14 and destroyed the span behind them shortly before the Union troops reached the far side. "Stuart must be a great general to foil his father-in-law," wrote Lieutenant Cooke. Once across the river, Stuart rode ahead to report to Lee in Richmond ❼, where the rest of his force arrived safely on June 15, winning praise for their feat throughout the South. ■

"Stuart must be a great general to foil his father-in-law."

CONFEDERATE LIEUTENANT JOHN ESTEN COOKE

STUART'S CIRCUIT During his daring ride around McClellan's army, referred to officially on this Confederate map as the Pamunkey Expedition, Stuart crossed all three rail lines running north from the Confederate capital: the Richmond & Fredericksburg Railroad, the Virginia Central Railroad, and the Richmond & York River Railroad, which carried supplies from White House Landing to McClellan's troops near Richmond.

❶ **UNION BASE** Stuart was tempted to raid this huge Federal supply depot at White House Landing but wisely continued his ride and avoided pursuit, providing Lee with intelligence he used to cut McClellan's supply line.

1862 | THE PENINSULA

Decision at Gaines's Mill

The Seven Days' Battles opened with a bid by McClellan, whose forces advanced at Oak Grove ❶ on June 25, edging a bit closer to Richmond. Lee raised the stakes the next day at Mechanicsville ❷, seeking to shatter McClellan's right flank above the Chickahominy and sever his supply line. That attack faltered for lack of support from newly arrived Stonewall Jackson and his men, worn out by months of hard campaigning. Undeterred, Lee risked all on June 27 by leaving Richmond lightly defended by Magruder's forces—who kept up a deceptively threatening barrage ❸—and committing more than 50,000 Rebels to a desperate battle at Gaines's Mill (shown here in foreground). Opposing them were some 30,000 Federals under Major General Fitz-John Porter, holding a strong defensive position on Turkey Hill ❹ above Boatswain's Swamp ❺, with 17 batteries poised to shatter enemy lines. The ensuing battle was among the war's fiercest. As one Federal recalled, the air "was too full of lead for standing room," but men stood and fought nonetheless, falling in droves. The belated arrival of Jackson, who ordered his troops to "sweep the field with the bayonet," tipped the scale. Confederates pressed from north and west and broke through around sunset. As his forces retreated across the Chickahominy ❻, McClellan made plans to withdraw to Harrison's Landing, shielded by Federal gunboats. Before reaching that refuge on the James, however, his forces would have to contend with pursuing Confederates at Savage's Station ❼, Glendale ❽, and Malvern Hill ❾. ■

❼ LEFT BEHIND Wounded Federals, mostly casualties from the fighting at Gaines's Mill, await capture by Confederates at a field hospital near Savage's Station. More than 2,500 Federal wounded and large amounts of supplies were captured when the Confederates overran the hospital after fighting at Savage's Station and nearby Allen's Farm on June 29.

BATTLE FOR RICHMOND Artist John Bachmann's bird's-eye view of the pivotal struggle at Gaines's Mill, looking southward, shows the battle approaching its climax and the subsequent Federal retreat across the Chickahominy. Lee's attack here was slow to develop partly because he and his commanders lacked good maps of the area, delaying Jackson's arrival by several hours.

JAMES RIVER
RICHMOND
CHICKAHOMINY RIVER
2
3
4
5
6

Plan of BATTLE of MALVERN HILL. Va. Fought 1st JULY 1862.
Copy of official Map made for Maj Gen. Heintzelman 3rd Corps by RKS
RESERVES
Cartwright
A.P. HILL
JACKSON
Pollard
MAGRUDER
HUGER
HOOD
SYKES
COUCH
JULY 1st 6PM
HAMPTON
OPEN PLATEAU
31 pieces
BINFORD
HOOKER
WESTS HOUSE
SUMNER
CREW HOUSE
HOLMES
SEDGWICK
Artillery
MALVERN
RICHARDSON
WHITING
6 PM
JULY 1st
TURKEY CREEK
JUNE 30
WARREN
Bridge
MALVERN HOUSE
SMITH
PORTER
MILL POND
US Gunboat Galena
Mahaska
Turkey Pt
TURKEY BRIDGE
JAMES RIVER
THE CLIFF
CARTER'S MILL
Reference.
Union Forces
Rebel
Cavalry
Artillery
Wagon Trains
Roads
Drawn by R K Sneden
Topog Engr. 3rd Corps
A. P.
CASEY
TURKEY Bridge
RESERVES
JUNE 30th
Haxall's house
Union Hospital
Gunboat
Head Qrs 3rd Corps
1
2
3
4
5
6

RETREAT TO MALVERN HILL

The Seven Days' Battles reached a thunderous climax on July 1 at Malvern Hill, where fighting began with an artillery duel won by massed Federal batteries ❶. That left Confederates little hope of dislodging their foes, gathered on Malvern Hill in far greater strength than at Gaines's Mill and backed by the *Galena* and other gunboats on the James River ❷. "If General McClellan is there in force," D. H. Hill warned beforehand, "we had better let him alone." But Lee still hoped to destroy McClellan's army and told Brigadier General Lewis Armistead ❸ to exploit any opening that developed.

When Magruder ❹ mistakenly reported that Armistead's troops were making headway, Lee urged him to press forward and "follow up Armistead's successes." Magruder's ill-fated advance toward the Crew farmhouse ❺ triggered an even costlier assault by D. H. Hill's division ❻. "Our batteries literally cut lanes through their ranks," recalled one Federal gunner. "It was not war," concluded Hill. "It was murder." Although Lee suffered more than 5,000 casualties here to no gain, his repeated attacks staggered McClellan, who persisted in his withdrawal. Having lost Lincoln's confidence, he was later evacuated from Harrison's Landing with his battle-weary troops. ■

❷ GUNBOATS IN ACTION A sketch by Alfred Waud on July 1 shows Union cavalrymen watering their horses in the James while Federal gunboats take shots at distant Confederates, many of which fell short. "For God's sake stop your firing," a Union officer signaled. "You are killing & wounding our men."

IMPREGNABLE POSITION A map by Sneden, who witnessed the battle, shows the strong Federal lines on Malvern Hill that Confederates assaulted to no avail. When the battle began, McClellan "was not on the ground (as usual)," wrote Sneden, who added that the army's "fighting generals" viewed their distant commander with "profound contempt."

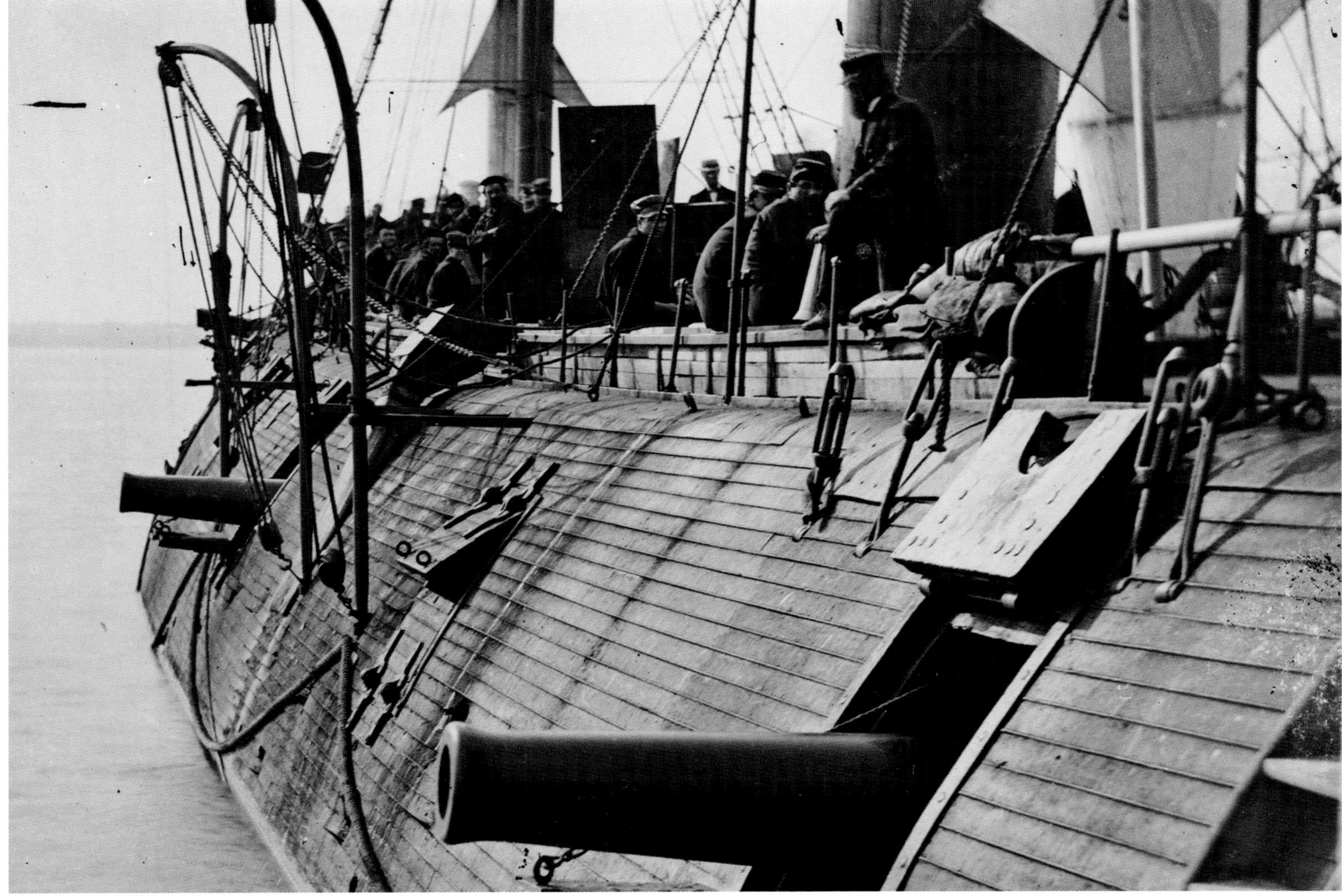

UNION IRONCLAD The *Galena* sheltered McClellan while fighting raged at Glendale on June 30. He disembarked belatedly at Malvern Hill on July 1.

1862

SECOND BULL RUN

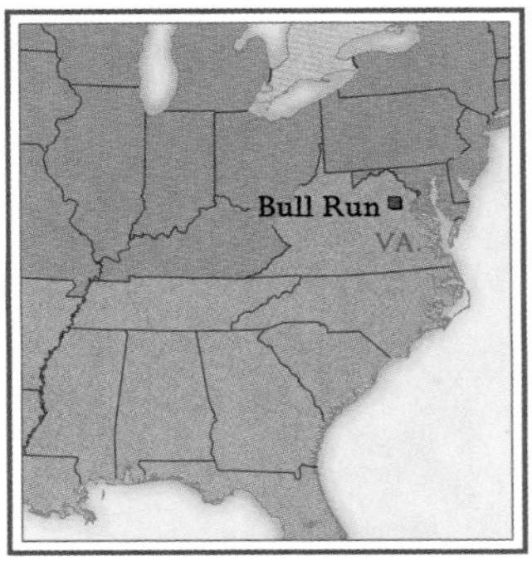

EASTERN THEATER

AUGUST 3, 1862 Robert E. Lee launches offensive against John Pope in northern Virginia.

AUGUST 9 Battle of Cedar Mountain

AUGUST 22 Jeb Stuart raids Pope's headquarters at Catlett's Station.

AUGUST 26 Stonewall Jackson raids Federal supply depot at Manassas Junction.

AUGUST 28–80 Second Battle of Bull Run (Manassas)

Contrasting himself to the cautious McClellan, Major General John Pope took charge of the Union's newly constituted Army of Virginia in late June vowing to challenge Lee head on and give no thought to retreat. "I have come to you from the West," he told his troops, "where we have always seen the backs of our enemies." A 40-year-old Kentuckian, Pope had indeed done well in the West, but he was not as capable a commander as Grant, whose abilities were called into question in Washington after he was surprised at Shiloh. Unlike Grant, Pope was stronger in words than in deeds. "Success and glory are in the advance," he declared. "Disaster and shame lurk in the rear." On July 14, he began to advance slowly toward Culpeper.

John Pope

Lee disdained his new opponent for threatening reprisals against Confederate loyalists in Virginia and told Jackson he wanted Pope "suppressed" before he received reinforcements from McClellan's army, withdrawn from Harrison's Landing in August. Advancing northward, Jackson beat back a strong challenge from Federals under Major General Nathaniel Banks at Cedar Mountain ❶ on August 9. He then linked up with Longstreet below Culpeper, threatening Pope's flank and forcing him to abandon his position ❷ and withdraw north of the Rappahannock. Late on August 22, Jeb Stuart raided Pope's new headquarters at Catlett's Station ❸ and learned he would soon be reinforced by Federals under Porter and Heintzelman ❹, formerly with McClellan. Lee then took a big gamble by dividing his army and sending first Jackson and then Longstreet on wide swings to the west ❺ that brought them to Manassas Junction ❻ before Pope could cut them off, precipitating the Second Battle of Bull Run. When Pope's elusive foes slipped behind his army, his words returned to haunt him: Disaster and shame lurked to his rear. ■

❻ MAYHEM AT MANASSAS Federal troops view wreckage strewn along the tracks after Jackson's troops surprised Pope by raiding Manassas Junction on the night of August 26.

LEE MOVES NORTH As shown in a map by Sneden, who served on Heintzelman's staff during this campaign, Lee divided his army into two commands, under Jackson and Longstreet, and traveled with Longstreet as he followed Jackson through the Bull Run Mountains toward Manassas.

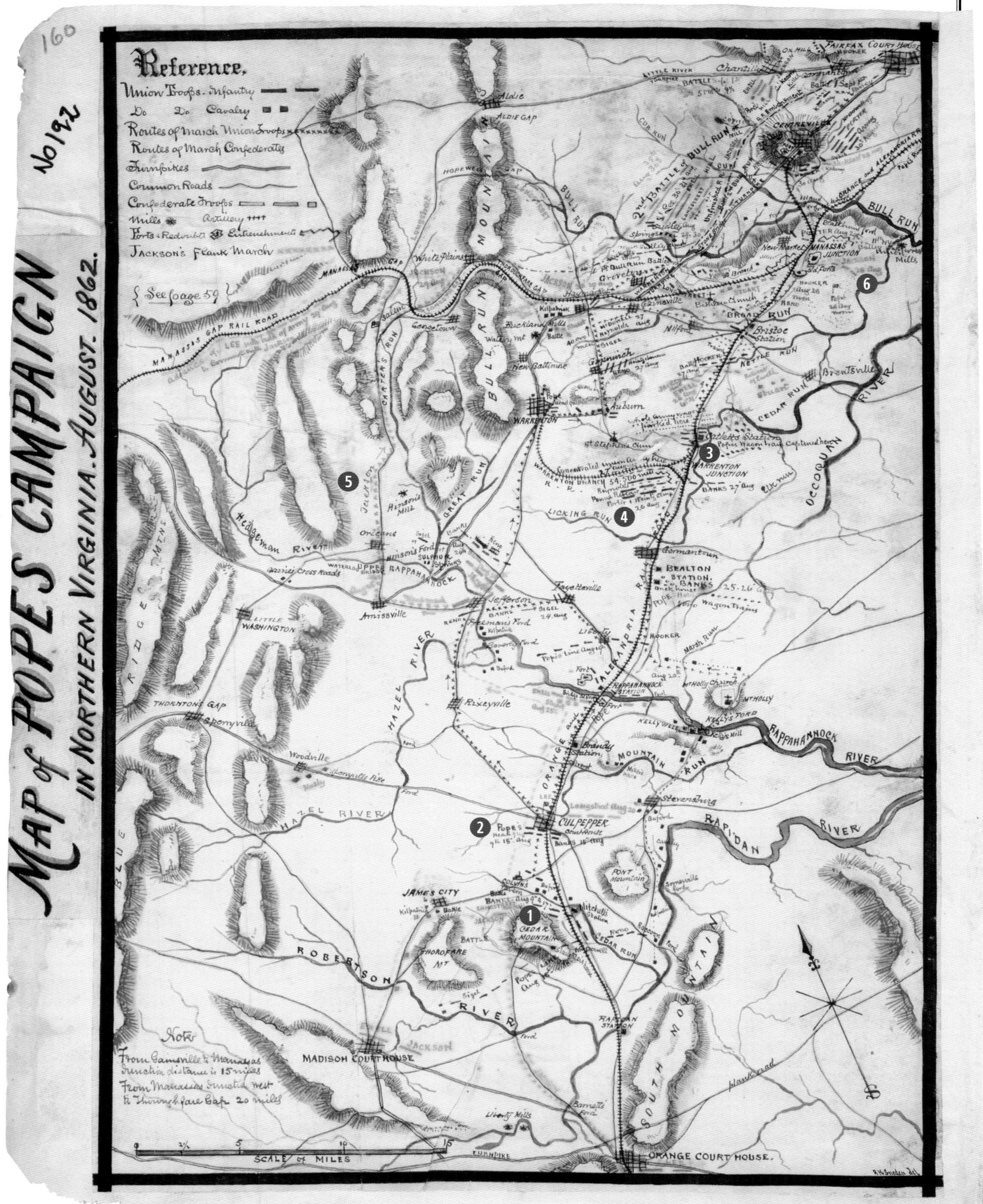

Map of Popes Campaign in Northern Virginia. August. 1862.
No 192
160
Reference.
Union Troops - Infantry
Do Do Cavalry
Routes of March Union Troops
Routes of March Confederates
Turnpikes
Common Roads
Confederate Troops
Mills
Artillery
Forts & Redoubts
Entrenchments
Jackson's Flank March
See page 59
Note
From Gainsville to Manassas Junction distance is 15 miles
From Manassas Junction west to Thoroughfare Gap 20 miles
SCALE of MILES
0
2½
5
10
15
1
2
3
4
5
6
FAIRFAX COURT HOUSE
Chantilly
Aldie
ALDIE GAP
CENTREVILLE
BULL RUN
2nd BATTLE of BULL RUN
MANASSAS JUNCTION
Bristoe Station
BROAD RUN
KETTLE RUN
Brentsville
CEDAR RUN
OCCOQUAN RIVER
Catletts Station
WARRENTON JUNCTION
WARRENTON
Auburn
New Baltimore
Buckland Mills
Gainsville
Haymarket
Thoroughfare Gap
White Plains
MANASSAS GAP RAIL ROAD
Salem
Georgetown
CARTERS RUN
GREAT RUN
LICKING RUN
Orleans
Hedgeman River
Waterloo
SULPHUR SPRINGS
RAPPAHANNOCK
Amissville
LITTLE WASHINGTON
Jefferson
Freemans Ford
Fayetteville
BEALTON STATION
Germantown
HOOKER
Marsh Run
RAPPAHANNOCK STATION
Kellys Ford
RAPPAHANNOCK RIVER
Mt Holly Church
MT HOLLY
Rixeyville
HAZEL RIVER
THORNTON'S GAP
Sperryville
Woodville
Brandy Station
MOUNTAIN RUN
Stevensburg
CULPEPPER
Pope's Headqrs
RAPIDAN RIVER
POINT Mountain
JAMES CITY
Mitchell's Station
CEDAR MOUNTAIN
CEDAR RUN
THOROFARE MT
ROBERTSON RIVER
RAPIDAN STATION
SOUTH MOUNTAIN
MADISON COURT HOUSE
JACKSON
Liberty Mills
Barnetts Ford
ORANGE COURT HOUSE
TURNPIKE
BLUE RIDGE MTNS

The Battle of Cedar Mountain

CHARLES SYDNEY WINDER

Stonewall Jackson was hard on subordinates, but 32-year-old Charles Winder of Maryland came as close as anyone to living up to his demands—and dying as Jackson thought an officer should. Like Jackson, Winder was a strict disciplinarian who cared little whether men loved or hated him so long as they did their duty. But like Jackson as well, he spared himself none of the risks and hardships his men faced and commanded respect if not affection. So feverish before the Battle of Cedar Mountain that Jackson suggested he relinquish command, Winder rode in an ambulance that morning before mounting his horse and making his way to the front, where he was directing artillery fire against oncoming Federals when a shell fragment tore into him. "He fell straight back at full length," one gunner related, "and lay quivering on the ground." A short time later, a Confederate advancing into battle saw "the bleeding, mangled form of the gallant Winder" being carried on a litter to the rear, where he would die within hours. As Lieutenant Henry Kyd Douglas of Jackson's staff recalled, Winder had "a will as inflexible as that of Jackson himself," and their relations were not always cordial. But Jackson entrusted his own division to Winder's command and invoked his name after he fell at Cedar Mountain and his troops gave way there. "Rally men!" Jackson shouted. "Remember Winder!"

After operating independently in the Shenandoah Valley, Stonewall Jackson did not fit the organizational mold of Lee's army, filled with strong-willed officers who expected superiors to confer with them and seek their opinions—a practice Jackson abhorred. The 24,000-man corps or "command" Lee assigned him was the largest force he had ever led and included his own division, commanded now by Brigadier General Charles Winder, and the divisions of Major Generals Richard Ewell and A. P. Hill, both of whom found Jackson's secretive ways maddening. Ignoring Lee's advice that consulting his generals would save him "much trouble," Jackson kept his own counsel. "I do not know whether we march north, south, east or west, or whether we march at all," Ewell remarked as Jackson prepared to set out from Gordonsville ❶ against Pope. "General Jackson has simply ordered me to have the division ready to move at dawn."

Lack of communication caused delays and foul-ups as Jackson's forces advanced toward Pope's headquarters at Culpeper ❷ along poorly marked roads west of the Orange & Alexandria Railroad ❸. Hill ended up trailing far behind and had to push his Light Division hard to close the gap. Jackson hoped to catch Pope off guard at Culpeper. Instead, his own strung-out forces were surprised at Cedar Mountain ❹ on August 9 by Nathaniel Banks, whose troops had advanced from Culpeper and were now blocking their path ❺. Jackson responded by placing Ewell's artillery ❻ at the north end of the mountain alongside Winder's troops ❼, with Ewell's infantry to their right ❽ and Hill's trailing division ❾ in reserve. Mortally wounded by shellfire, Winder was not on the field when Federals led by Brigadier General Samuel Crawford ❿ rushed from the woods late in the afternoon and hit startled Confederates in the flank, sending them reeling. Stepping in for the fallen Winder, Jackson rallied his troops and prevented a rout. Jackson's stand and the subsequent entry of Hill's troops into battle turned the tide. By nightfall, the Federals were thoroughly outmanned and fell back toward Culpeper. Jackson's victory was narrow but rattled Pope, who surrendered the initiative to his opponents in the days ahead and never regained it. ■

HEADING FOR BATTLE Federal artillerymen with the corps of Nathaniel Banks cross a creek on August 9 on their way to Cedar Mountain, where gunners unlimbered their weapons and did battle.

JACKSON'S ROUGH PATH A page from Sneden's sketchbook combines a tranquil view of Cedar Mountain as viewed from Federal headquarters with a rough map of the battle that erupted there, based on preliminary reports from participants. The map reflects some uncertainty about the path Jackson's troops followed from Orange Court House to Cedar Mountain—a march Confederates themselves found confusing.

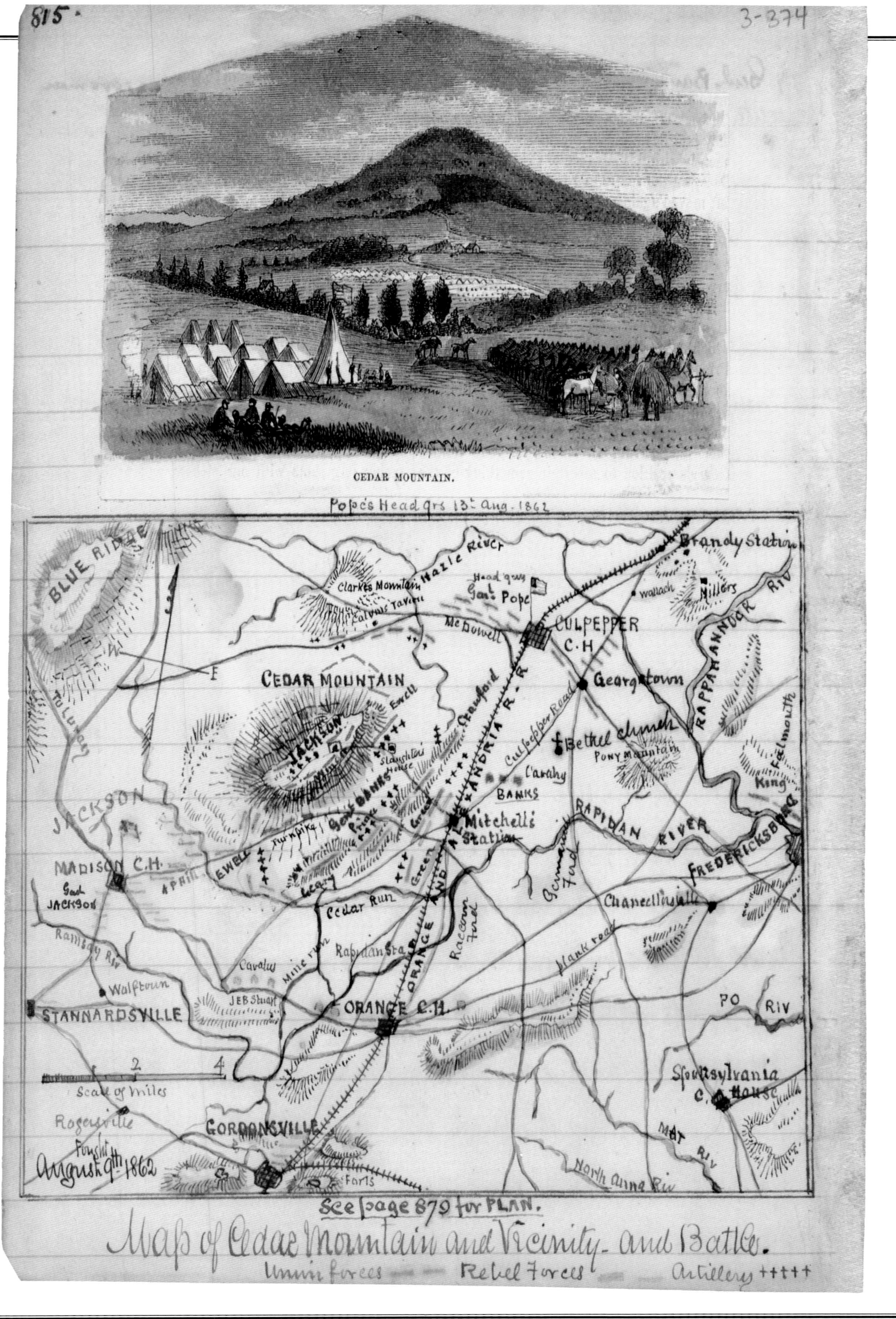
815.
3-374
CEDAR MOUNTAIN.
Pope's Head Qrs 13th Aug. 1862
BLUE RIDGE
Hazle River
Clarkes Mountain
Brandy Station
Head Qrs
Gen. Pope
Millers
CULPEPPER
C.H
McDowell
Georgetown
RAPPAHANNOCK RIV
CEDAR MOUNTAIN
Ewell
JACKSON
Crawford
Culpepper Road
Bethel Church
Pony Mountain
Falmouth
King
Cavalry
BANKS
Mitchell's Station
RAPIDAN RIVER
FREDERICKSBURG
MADISON C.H.
Gen. JACKSON
EWELL
Turnpike
Cedar Run
Green
ORANGE AND ALEXANDRIA R.R.
Raccoon Ford
Germanna Ford
Chancellorsville
plank road
Rapidan Sta.
Ramsay Riv
Cavalry
Walftown
JEB Stuart
STANNARDSVILLE
ORANGE C.H.
PO RIV
Scale of Miles
Rogersville
GORDONSVILLE
Spottsylvania
C. H. House
Fought
August 9th 1862
North Anna Riv
MAT RIV
See page 879 for PLAN.
Map of Cedar Mountain and Vicinity - and Battle.
Union forces
Rebel Forces
Artillery +++++

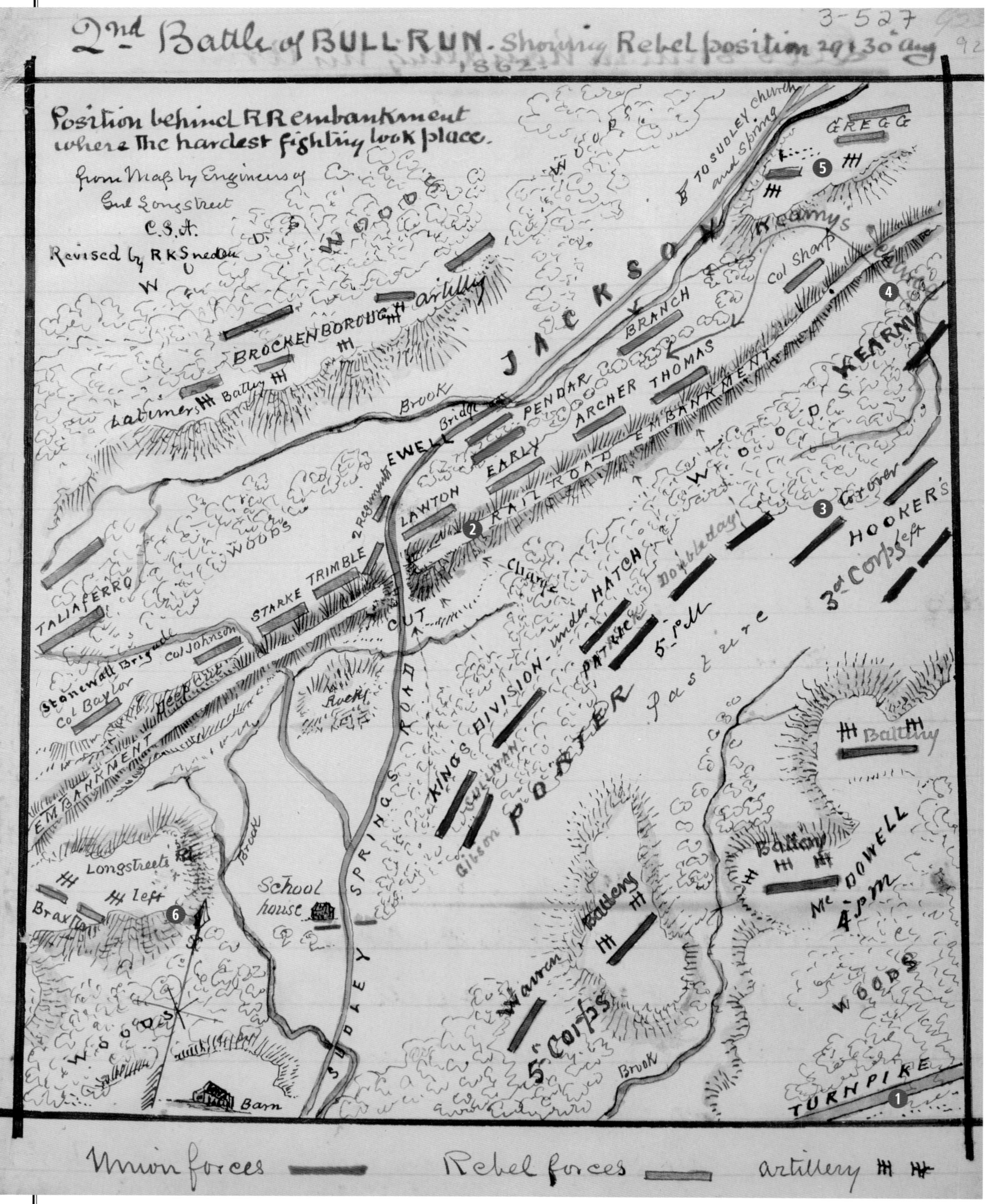

2nd Battle of BULL RUN. Showing Rebel position 29 & 30th Aug 1862.
3-527
Position behind RR embankment where the hardest fighting took place.
from Maps by Engineers of Genl Longstreet C.S.A.
Revised by R K Sneden
Union forces
Rebel forces
artillery

1862 | SECOND BULL RUN

Jackson's Stand: The Railroad Embankment

After slipping around Pope's army and raiding Manassas Junction on August 26, Jackson took a strong defensive position north of the Warrenton Turnpike ❶, behind the embankment of an unfinished railroad ❷. His task now was to preoccupy Federals while Lee and Longstreet followed in his path and moved in from the west, surprising Pope, who assumed Lee was heading for the Shenandoah Valley. Intent on crushing Jackson before he too got away, Pope ordered troops guarding Thoroughfare Gap—through which Longstreet's troops would soon file—to come to Manassas, playing into his enemy's hands.

The Second Battle of Bull Run began on August 28 when Jackson announced his presence by attacking Federals marching along the turnpike at Groveton, west of the old Bull Run battlefield. After heavy fighting near the road, he reverted to a defensive posture, knowing he would face long odds until Longstreet pitched in. On August 29, the battle reached full fury as one Federal wave after another crashed against the embankment. In mid-afternoon, troops under Brigadier General Cuvier Grover ❸ broke through with bayonets fixed, only to be beaten back. Later, Phil Kearny launched another daring charge ❹, repulsed after Brigadier General Maxcy Gregg ❺ implored his troops to give all: "Let us die here, my men, let us die here." As night fell, Pope remained obsessed with crushing the resilient Jackson, unaware that Longstreet's men were lurking in the woods to the west ❻, preparing to strike. ■

❷ Holding the Line Running short of ammunition, Mississippi Confederates hurl rocks at Union troops as they charge the railroad embankment in one of many piecemeal attacks launched on August 29 and 30 that failed to dislodge Jackson's troops.

Jackson's Defenses Sneden drew on a Confederate map to produce this detailed view of Jackson's defenses. Hooker and Kearny sent troops of Heintzelman's Third Corps against the railroad embankment on August 29. Porter's Fifth Corps and much of McDowell's Third Corps joined the Federal effort here on August 30 in a disastrous redeployment by Pope that cleared the way for Longstreet's decisive advance that afternoon.

Order of Battle

Union Forces

ARMY OF VIRGINIA
Pope | *70,000 men*

I CORPS *Sigel*
1ST DIVISION *Schenck*
Brigades Stahel, McLean
3RD DIVISION *Schurz*
Brigades Schimmelpfennig, Kryzanowski, Koltes, Milroy

II CORPS *Banks*
1ST DIVISION A. S. Williams
Brigades Crawford, Gordon
2ND DIVISION Greene
Brigades Candy, Schlaudecker, Tait

III CORPS *McDowell*
1ST DIVISION *Hatch*
Brigades Sullivan, Doubleday, Patrick, Gibbon
2ND DIVISION *Ricketts*
Brigades Duryee, Tower, Stiles, Thorburn
REYNOLDS'S DIVISION *Reynolds*
Brigades Meade, Seymour, C. F. Jackson

CAVALRY
Brigades Beardsley, Buford, Bayard

III CORPS (Army of the Potomac) *Heintzelman*
1ST DIVISION *Kearny*
Brigades Robinson, Birney, Poe
2ND DIVISION *Hooker*
Brigades Grover, Taylor, Carr

V CORPS (Army of the Potomac) *Porter*
1ST DIVISION *Morell*
Brigades Barnes, Griffin, Butterfield
2ND DIVISION *Sykes*
Brigades Buchanan, Chapman, Warren, Piatt

IX CORPS (Army of the Potomac) *Reno*
1ST DIVISION *Stevens*
Brigades Christ, Leasure, Farnsworth
2ND DIVISION
Brigades Nagle, Ferrero

Confederate Forces

ARMY OF NORTHERN VIRGINIA
Lee | *55,000 men*

I CORPS (LEFT WING) *Jackson*
TALIAFERRO'S DIVISION
Brigades Baylor, B. T. Johnson, Taliaferro, Starke
HILL'S LIGHT DIVISION
Brigades Branch, Archer, Pender, Gregg, Field, Thomas
EWELL'S DIVISION
Brigades Lawton, Early, Trimble, Strong

II CORPS (RIGHT WING) *Longstreet*
ANDERSON'S DIVISION
Brigades Armistead, Mahone, Wright
JONES'S DIVISION
Brigades Benning, Drayton, G. T. Anderson
WILCOX'S DIVISION
Brigades Wilcox, Pryor, Featherston
HOOD'S DIVISION
Brigades Hood, Law, Stevens
KEMPER'S DIVISION
Brigades Corse, Jenkins, Hutton

CAVALRY *Stuart*
Brigades Hampton, Robertson, F. Lee

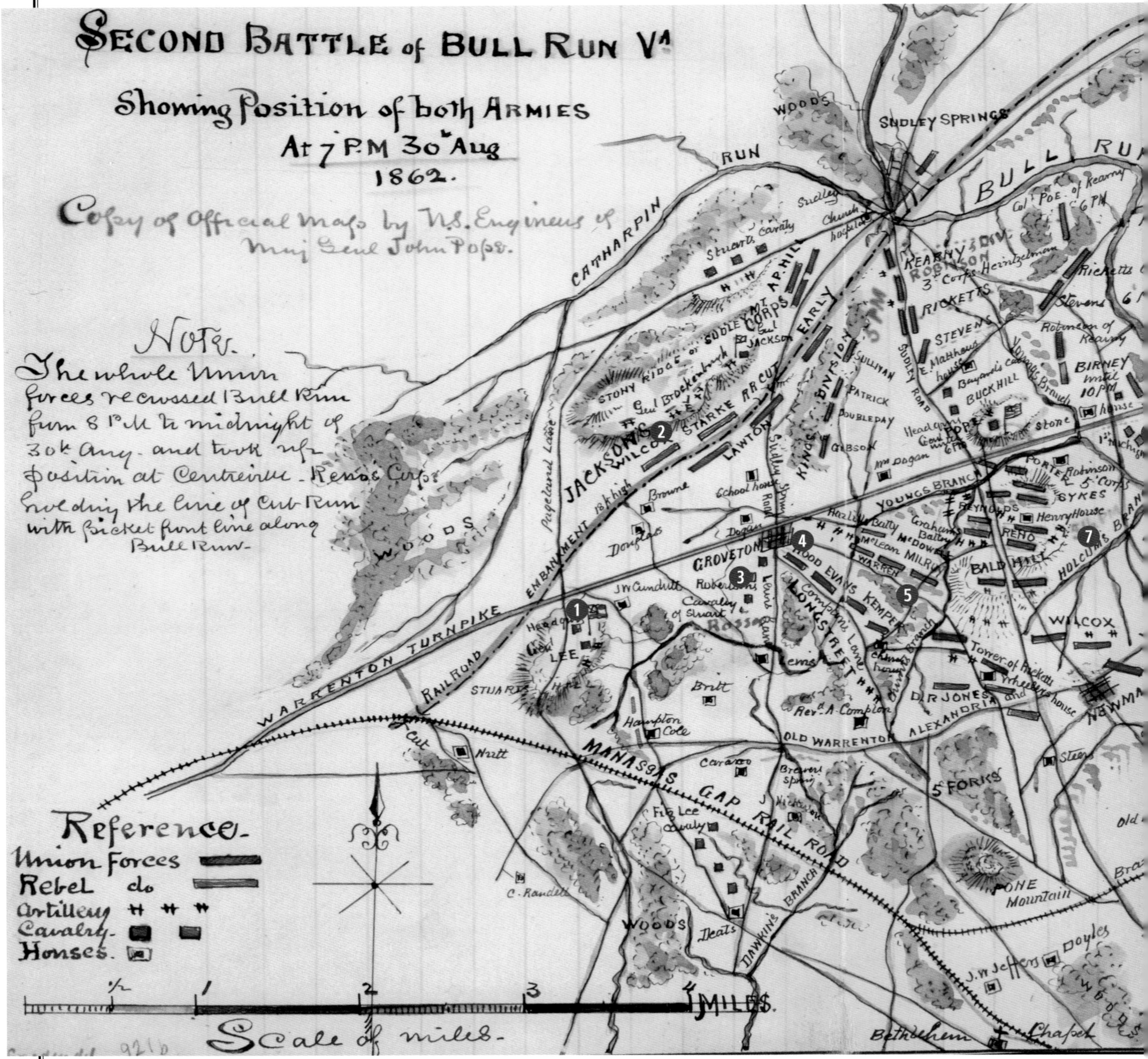

SECOND BATTLE of BULL RUN Va

Showing Position of both ARMIES At 7 P.M 30th Aug 1862.

Copy of Official maps by U.S. Engineers of Maj Genl John Pope.

Note. The whole Union forces recrossed Bull Run from 8 P.M to midnight of 30th Aug. and took up position at Centreville. Reno's Corps holding the line of Cub Run with picket front line along Bull Run.

Reference.
Union Forces
Rebel do
Artillery
Cavalry.
Houses.

Scale of miles. ½ 1 2 3 4 MILES.

Bull Run Revisited Sneden's copy of an official map of Second Bull Run by U.S. topographical engineers covers a sequence of events and is not limited to the situation at 7 p.m., by which time Warren's brigade and other Federal units shown west of Sudley Road had fallen back to the east. The second battle here was far costlier than the first, with the Confederates losing some 9,000 men and the Federals losing around 15,000, many of them captured.

❻ Avenue of Retreat Federals retreating eastward along the Warrenton Turnpike on August 30 crossed Bull Run here at the site of the original Stone Bridge, which was destroyed and rebuilt.

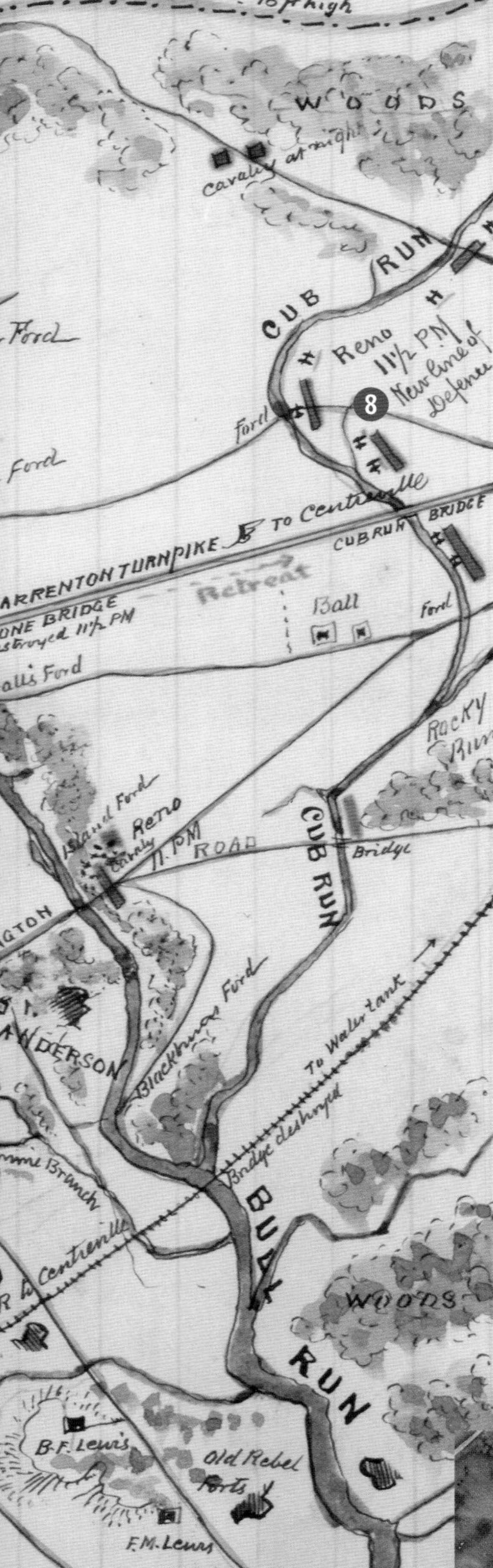

1862 | SECOND BULL RUN

Longstreet's Attack: Federal Retreat

When Lee and Longstreet successfully completed their march without alerting Pope to their presence and conferred at headquarters near the Warrenton Turnpike ❶ on August 29, Lee suggested a prompt advance to aid Jackson's embattled forces ❷. "I think not," replied Longstreet, who awaited reports from Jeb Stuart's cavalry ❸ and John Bell Hood's Texas Brigade—probing eastward toward Groveton ❹—before he committed to battle. His patience was rewarded. Hood met with strong opposition along the turnpike, and Stuart reported Federals in large numbers to the south. Overnight, however, Pope redeployed most of those forces north of the turnpike to pressure Jackson, leaving only about 8,000 men of Fitz-John Porter's corps on his left to face 25,000 troops under Longstreet, who unleashed them in mid-afternoon on August 30.

Caught in the avalanche were Zouaves of the 5th and 10th New York Infantry under Colonel Gouverneur Warren ❺, who ordered them to fall back but could not be heard above the din of battle. Nearly 300 of the 5th New York's 490 men went down as Hood's Texans hit them front and flank and chased after the survivors, clubbing men with their muskets. The hard-charging 5th Texas Infantry "slipped its bridle and went wild," Hood recalled. Had not those men later been restrained, another officer said, "they would have gone right on to the Potomac." The collapse below the turnpike forced Federals to the north to join in a wholesale retreat across Bull Run ❻ that recalled their bitter defeat here a year earlier. This time they fell back in good order, with Major General Jesse Reno holding off Confederates near the Henry House ❼ until nightfall, when his men withdrew to a new defensive line at Cub Run ❽. Such discipline and determination spared the defeated Pope the ultimate shame of losing his army. ■

James Longstreet

German Recruits These men of the all-German 41st New York Infantry fought at Second Bull Run under German-born Major General Franz Sigel, some of whose troops helped Reno hold the line at the Henry House on August 30.

1862

ANTIETAM

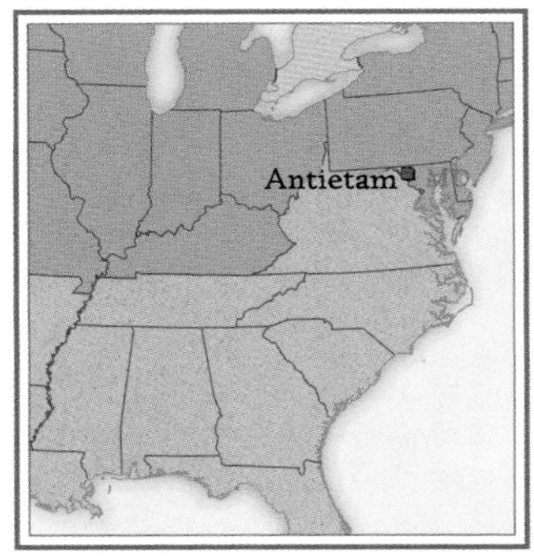

EASTERN THEATER

SEPTEMBER 1, 1862 Battle of Chantilly (Virginia)

SEPTEMBER 2 Lincoln removes Pope from command and places McClellan in charge of all Federal troops around Washington.

SEPTEMBER 4 Lee invades Maryland.

SEPTEMBER 13 McClellan enters Frederick, Maryland, in pursuit of Lee.

SEPTEMBER 14 Battle of South Mountain (Maryland)

SEPTEMBER 15 Harpers Ferry falls to Confederates.

SEPTEMBER 17 Battle of Antietam (Maryland)

SEPTEMBER 18-19 Lee withdraws from Maryland.

After clashing with Pope's rear guard at Chantilly ❶ on September 1, Lee ended his pursuit and concluded that his own forces would be at risk if they remained near heavily defended Washington with their supplies dwindling. He could refit his army by withdrawing to the Shenandoah Valley ❷ or below the Rappahannock—or he could press on by invading western Maryland, where his troops could live off the land and seek further victories. Lee chose to remain on the offensive, hoping to bring Maryland into the Confederacy and win recognition and support from European nations.

To meet this threat, Lincoln sacked Pope and folded his Army of Virginia into the Army of the Potomac under McClellan, who had been slow to send reinforcements to his detested rival Pope. "Very badly whipped he will be & ought to be," predicted McClellan, who had hindered Pope without regard for the Union, Lincoln concluded. But the Army of the Potomac was McClellan's creation, and no one else could rouse it to action as he could. He soon had his men on the move and reached Frederick ❸ on September 13, where he was hailed by Maryland Unionists and learned in an order that fell into Federal hands that Lee, after crossing the Potomac ❹, had sent many of his troops off to seize Martinsburg ❺ and Harpers Ferry ❻. McClellan had a chance to smash a divided army, but Confederates held out long enough at South Mountain ❼ for Lee to gather his forces at Sharpsburg ❽ and prepare for battle along Antietam Creek. ■

❹ CROSSING OVER In a sketch by Alfred Waud, a Federal scout takes a potshot at Lee's Confederates as they cross by moonlight from Virginia into Maryland on September 4.

PATHS TO ANTIETAM As shown in this National Geographic map, elements of the opposing armies followed various paths to Antietam. To protect his Shenandoah Valley supply line, Lee sent Jackson to drive Federals from Martinsburg before joining other Confederates in taking Harpers Ferry. That left Longstreet and D. H. Hill to hold off Federals advancing under Burnside, Sumner, and Franklin toward gaps in South Mountain, buying time for Lee to concentrate his army at Sharpsburg.

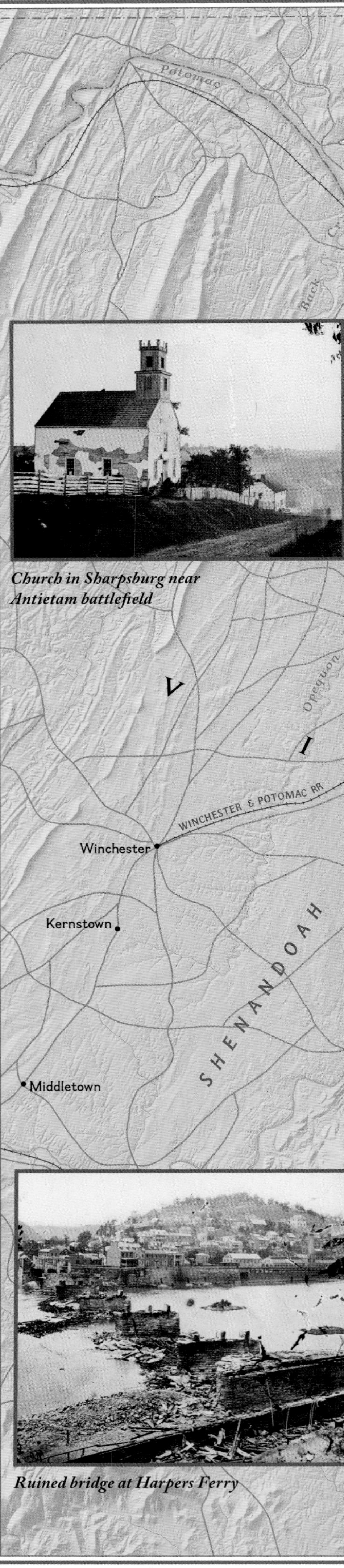

Church in Sharpsburg near Antietam battlefield

Ruined bridge at Harpers Ferry

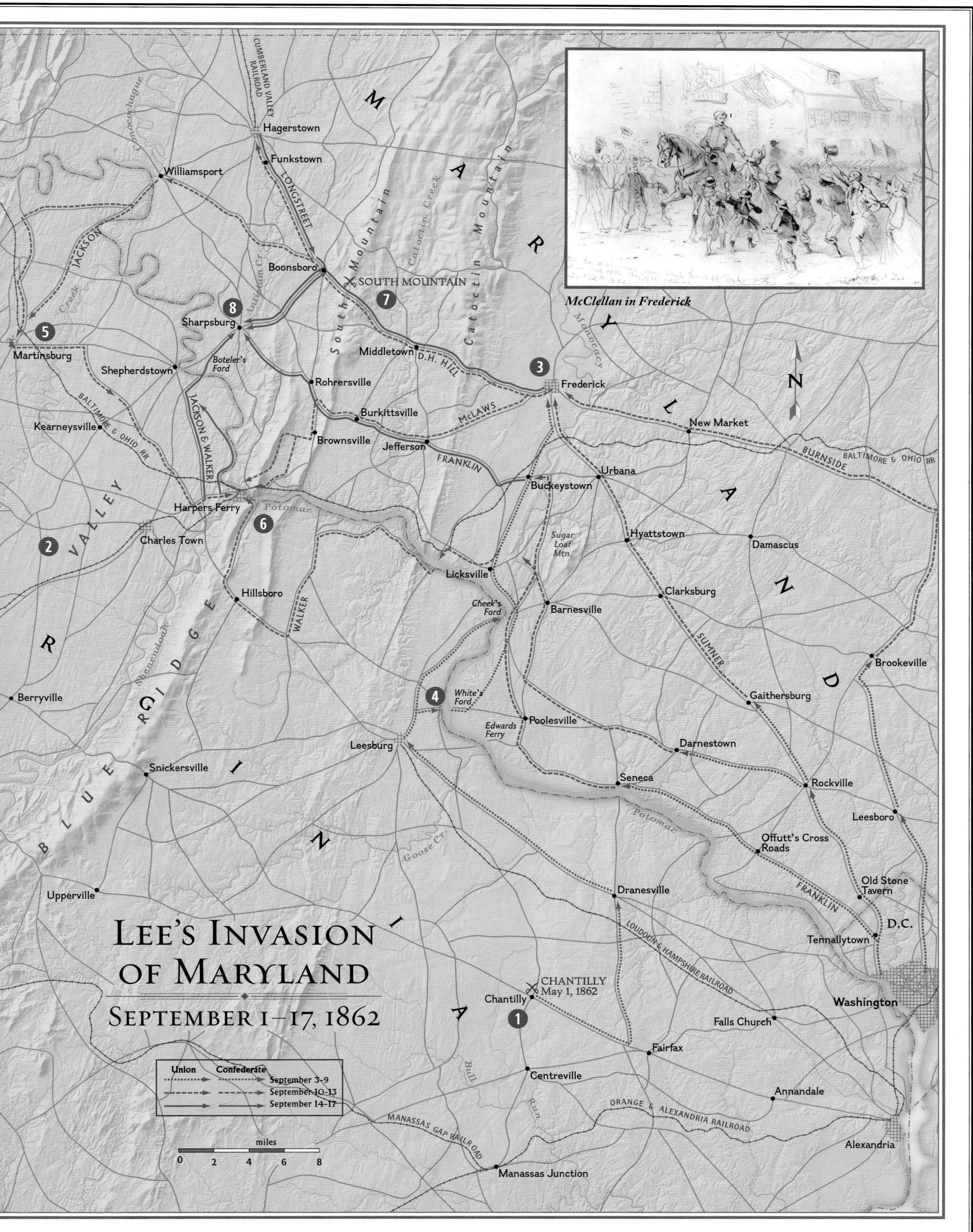
LEE'S INVASION OF MARYLAND
SEPTEMBER 1–17, 1862
McClellan in Frederick
Union
Confederate
September 3-9
September 10-13
September 14-17
miles
0 2 4 6 8
MARYLAND
VIRGINIA
BLUE RIDGE
VALLEY
D.C.
Hagerstown
Funkstown
Williamsport
Boonsboro
SOUTH MOUNTAIN
Sharpsburg
Martinsburg
Shepherdstown
Boteler's Ford
Middletown
Frederick
Rohrersville
Burkittsville
Brownsville
Jefferson
Kearneysville
New Market
Urbana
Buckeystown
Harpers Ferry
Charles Town
Hyattstown
Damascus
Licksville
Hillsboro
Clarksburg
Cheek's Ford
Barnesville
Brookeville
Berryville
White's Ford
Poolesville
Edwards Ferry
Gaithersburg
Leesburg
Darnestown
Snickersville
Seneca
Rockville
Leesboro
Offutt's Cross Roads
Upperville
Dranesville
Old Stone Tavern
Tennallytown
Washington
CHANTILLY May 1, 1862
Chantilly
Falls Church
Fairfax
Centreville
Annandale
Alexandria
Manassas Junction
CUMBERLAND VALLEY RAILROAD
BALTIMORE & OHIO RR
LOUDOUN & HAMPSHIRE RAILROAD
ORANGE & ALEXANDRIA RAILROAD
MANASSAS GAP RAILROAD
LONGSTREET
JACKSON
D.H. HILL
McLAWS
FRANKLIN
BURNSIDE
JACKSON & WALKER
WALKER
SUMNER
Potomac
Shenandoah
Conococheague
Antietam Cr.
Monocacy
Goose Cr.
Bull Run
South Mountain
Catoctin Mountain
Catoctin Creek
Sugar Loaf Mtn.
N
1
2
3
4
5
6
7
8

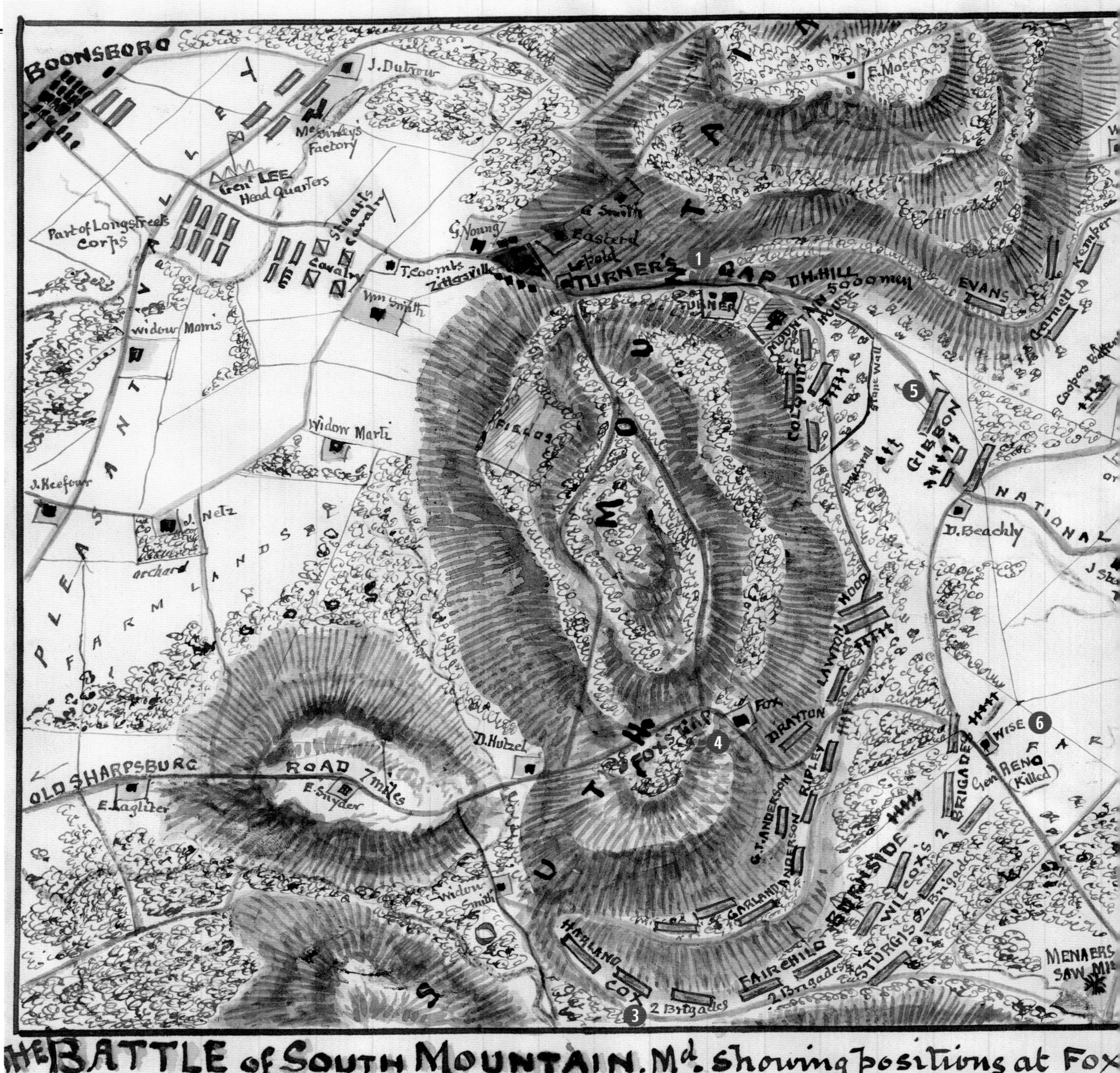

THE BATTLE of SOUTH MOUNTAIN. Md. showing positions at Fox

STORMING THE GAPS Approaching South Mountain from the east, Federals met with stiff resistance at Fox's Gap and Turner's Gap, as shown in this map by Robert Knox Sneden. Although the outnumbered Confederates were forced to withdraw that evening, their stand here prevented McClellan from catching Lee's army divided.

❹ FEDERALS ADVANCE An artist's rendering of the Union attack at Fox's Gap on the morning of September 14 shows Rutherford B. Hayes, in the foreground at left, being helped by two men after falling wounded from his horse.

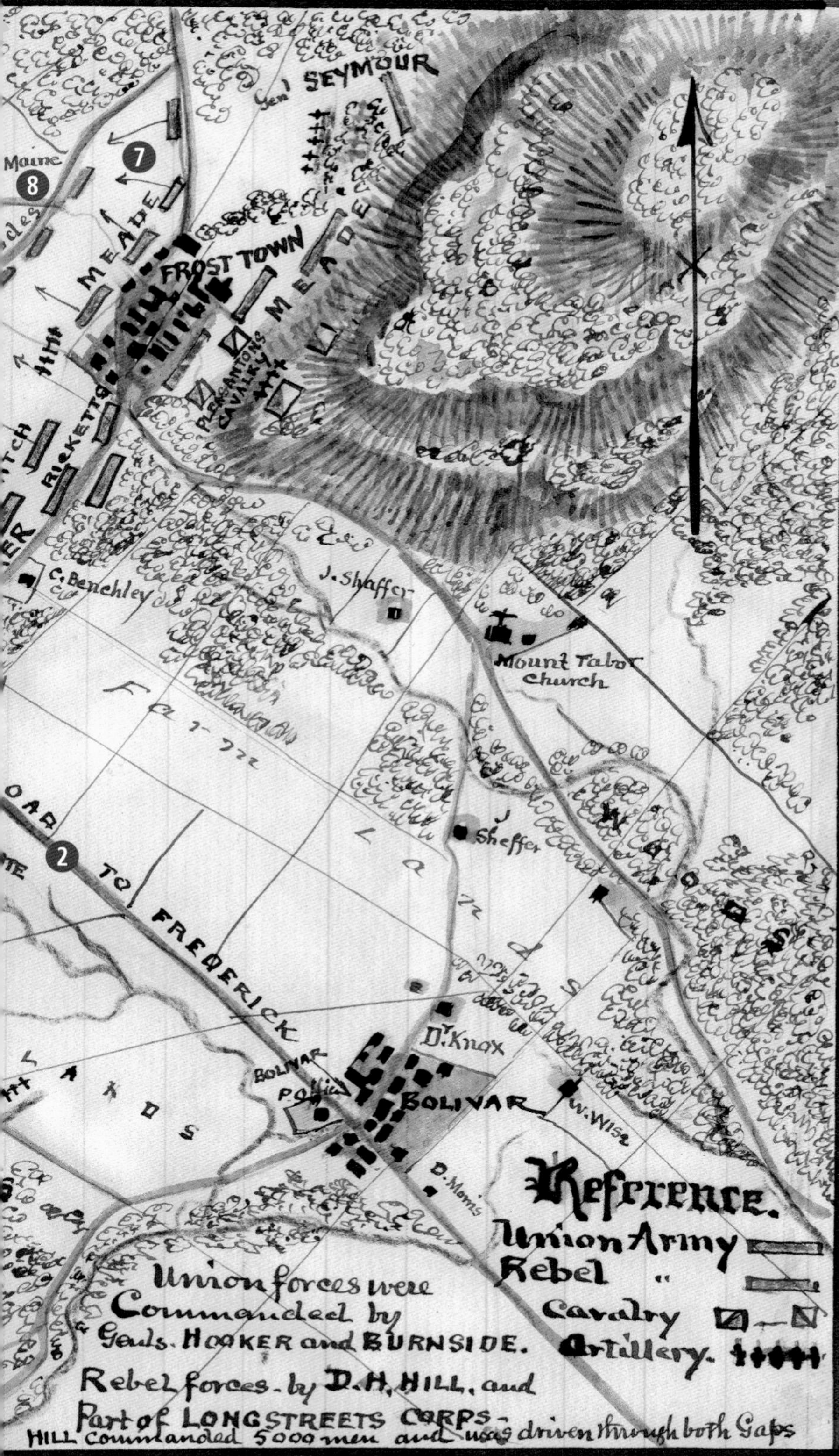

Battle of South Mountain

At daybreak on September 14, D. H. Hill, assigned by Lee to hold South Mountain with his division, rode to Turner's Gap ❶ and looked out to the east. Approaching along the National Road from Frederick ❷ were bluecoats of McClellan's army in majestic columns reaching to the horizon. "It was a grand and glorious spectacle," Hill recalled, but his admiration was mingled with alarm, for he was on his own. Lee and Longstreet were some 15 miles off to the northwest at Hagerstown, where a message had arrived the night before from a Confederate sympathizer in Frederick suggesting that McClellan had learned of Lee's plans. Anticipating that Federals would attack promptly before his scattered forces reunited, Lee sent Longstreet ahead at dawn to Turner's Gap. Until he arrived with reinforcements, however, Hill's 5,000 men would have to hold out against several times as many Federals. Hill had been in tight spots before on the Peninsula, but he could not recall ever experiencing "a feeling of greater loneliness."

The battle opened around 9 A.M. as Brigadier General Jacob Cox ❸ avoided heavily defended Turner's Gap and sent his division against Brigadier General Samuel Garland's North Carolinians holding Fox's Gap ❹ to the south. Up front was a future president, Lieutenant Colonel Rutherford B. Hayes of the 23rd Ohio. "Give the sons of bitches hell!" he shouted to his men, shortly before being shot in the arm and falling from his horse. Garland was mortally wounded in the fighting, and his men gave way, but after seizing the gap Cox's weary Federals stalled. That afternoon, McClellan increased the pressure, sending Brigadier General John Gibbon's conspicuous Black Hat Brigade ❺ up Turner's Gap while part of Major General Jesse Reno's Ninth Corps advanced near the Wise farmhouse ❻ to Gibbon's left—an attack that cost Reno his life—and Brigadier General George Meade's Pennsylvania Reserve Division ❼ swept forward to the right, overwhelming Alabamians under Brigadier General Robert Rodes ❽. The arrival of Longstreet's forces, followed by Lee himself, prevented a rout, allowing Confederates to withdraw overnight to Sharpsburg. Meanwhile, Major General William Franklin had broken through with his Sixth Corps at Crampton's Gap, south of Fox's Gap, and had a chance to relieve besieged Federals at nearby Harpers Ferry. But Franklin did not move fast enough to prevent Jackson from seizing that town on September 15 and joining Lee at Sharpsburg for the looming Battle of Antietam. ■

❻ **Embattled Homestead** Federal troops crossing the Wise farm, shown here after the battle, came under heavy Confederate artillery fire that plowed into the field "with a noise like the cutting of a melon rind," General Cox recalled.

1862 | ANTIETAM

THE BLOODIEST DAY

Approaching Sharpsburg ❶ on September 15 from the east, Lee saw high ground beyond Antietam Creek ❷ and declared, "We will make our stand on those hills." His fateful decision to stand and fight—which led to the bloodiest single day of combat in American history—came just after a bruising battle at South Mountain that nearly caused him to end his campaign. "The day has gone against us," he had concluded as his army withdrew overnight toward Sharpsburg. He saw little alternative then but to regroup by withdrawing his forces across the Potomac ❸. Around dawn, however, he learned that Jackson was about to capture Harpers Ferry, which would free Confederates there to join Lee. With his Shenandoah Valley supply line secure and help on the way, Lee decided to hold his ground, forming a defensive line west of Antietam Creek as pursuing Federals drew up along the east bank later that day.

Colors of the 34th New York carried at Antietam

Few other commanders facing such adversity would have invited battle as Lee did. Since Second Bull Run, he had lost nearly one fifth of his army to straggling as men too weary or footsore dropped out. Many who remained in his ranks were hungry, ragged, and shoeless. On September 15, Lee had fewer than 20,000 men at hand. That number would double as Confederates arrived here from Harpers Ferry over the next two days, but his army would still be outmanned nearly two to one. Lee did not have sufficient forces to stop McClellan from crossing Antietam Creek but placed troops and artillery on hills overlooking the Middle Bridge ❹ and Lower Bridge ❺ to shield the vital Harpers Ferry Road ❻, which brought Lee reinforcements from that town and would serve as his escape route, if necessary. The Upper Bridge ❼ was left unguarded, and Lee was not surprised when McClellan sent Hooker's First Corps ❽ and other forces across that span late on September 16. Hooker would lead a blistering assault on the Confederate left the next morning, while Burnside's Ninth Corps ❾ would cross the Lower Bridge (known subsequently as the Burnside Bridge) and menace Lee's avenue of retreat. McClellan's lengthy preparations allowed all of Jackson's corps except A. P. Hill's division to reach Sharpsburg before the battle and move into position near the Cornfield ❿, destined to become one of the war's most notorious killing grounds. ■

ORDER OF BATTLE

UNION FORCES

ARMY OF THE POTOMAC
McClellan | 70,000 men

I CORPS *Hooker*
1ST DIVISION *Doubleday*
Brigades Phelps, Hoffman, Patrick, Gibbon
2ND DIVISION *Ricketts*
Brigades Duryée, Christian, Hartsuff
3RD DIVISION *Meade*
Brigades Seymour, Magilton, Anderson

II CORPS *Sumner*
1ST DIVISION *Richardson*
Brigades Caldwell, Meagher, Brooke
2ND DIVISION *Sedgwick*
Brigades Gorman, Howard, Dana
3RD DIVISION *French*
Brigades Kimball, Morris, Weber

V CORPS *Porter*
1ST DIVISION *Morell*
Brigades Barnes, Griffin, Stockton
2ND DIVISION *Sykes*
Brigades Buchanan, Lovell, Warren
3RD DIVISION *Humphreys*
Brigades Tyler, Allabach

VI CORPS *Franklin*
1ST DIVISION *Slocum*
Brigades Torbert, Bartlett, Newton
2ND DIVISION *W. F. Smith*
Brigades Hancock, Brooks, Irwin
3RD DIVISION *Couch*
Brigades Devens, Howe, Cochrane

IX CORPS *Burnside*
1ST DIVISION *Willcox*
Brigades Christ, Welsh
2ND DIVISION *Sturgis*
Brigades Nagle, Ferrero
3RD DIVISION *Rodman*
Brigades Fairchild, Harland
KANAWHA DIVISION *Scammon*
Brigades Ewing, Crook

XII CORPS *Mansfield*
1ST DIVISION *Williams*
Brigades Crawford, Gordon
2ND DIVISION *Greene*
Brigades Tyndale, Stainrook, Goodrich

CAVALRY DIVISION *Pleasonton*
Brigades Whiting, Farnsworth, Rush, McReynolds, Davis

CONFEDERATE FORCES

ARMY OF NORTHERN VIRGINIA
Lee | 39,000 men

LONGSTREET'S CORPS
McLAWS'S DIVISION
Brigades Kershaw, MacRae, Semmes, Barksdale
R. H. ANDERSON'S DIVISION
Brigades Cummings, Posey, Armistead, Pryor, Parham, Wright
D. R. JONES'S DIVISION
Brigades Toombs, Drayton, Garnett, Kemper, Walker, G. T. Anderson
WALKER'S DIVISION
Brigades Manning, Ransom
HOOD'S DIVISION
Brigades Wofford, Law, Evans

JACKSON'S CORPS
LAWTON'S DIVISION
Brigades Douglass, Early, J. A. Walker, Hays
A. P. HILL'S LIGHT DIVISION
Brigades Branch, Gregg, Brockenbrough, Archer, Pender
J. R. JONES'S DIVISION
Brigades Grigsby, Warren, Jones, Starke
D. H. HILL'S DIVISION
Brigades Ripley, Rodes, MacRae, G. B. Anderson, Colquitt

CAVALRY *Stuart*
Brigades Hampton, F. Lee, Robertson

COLLISION AT SHARPSBURG A topographical map prepared by a Union officer and printed commercially shows opposing positions early in the battle on September 17 as McClellan's Federals (red) collided with Lee's Confederates (black) amid hills, fields, and woods (green). As noted here at lower left, this copy was presented to Robert E. Lee by Jeb Stuart, who obtained it from a sympathizer in Washington before he died in action in 1864.

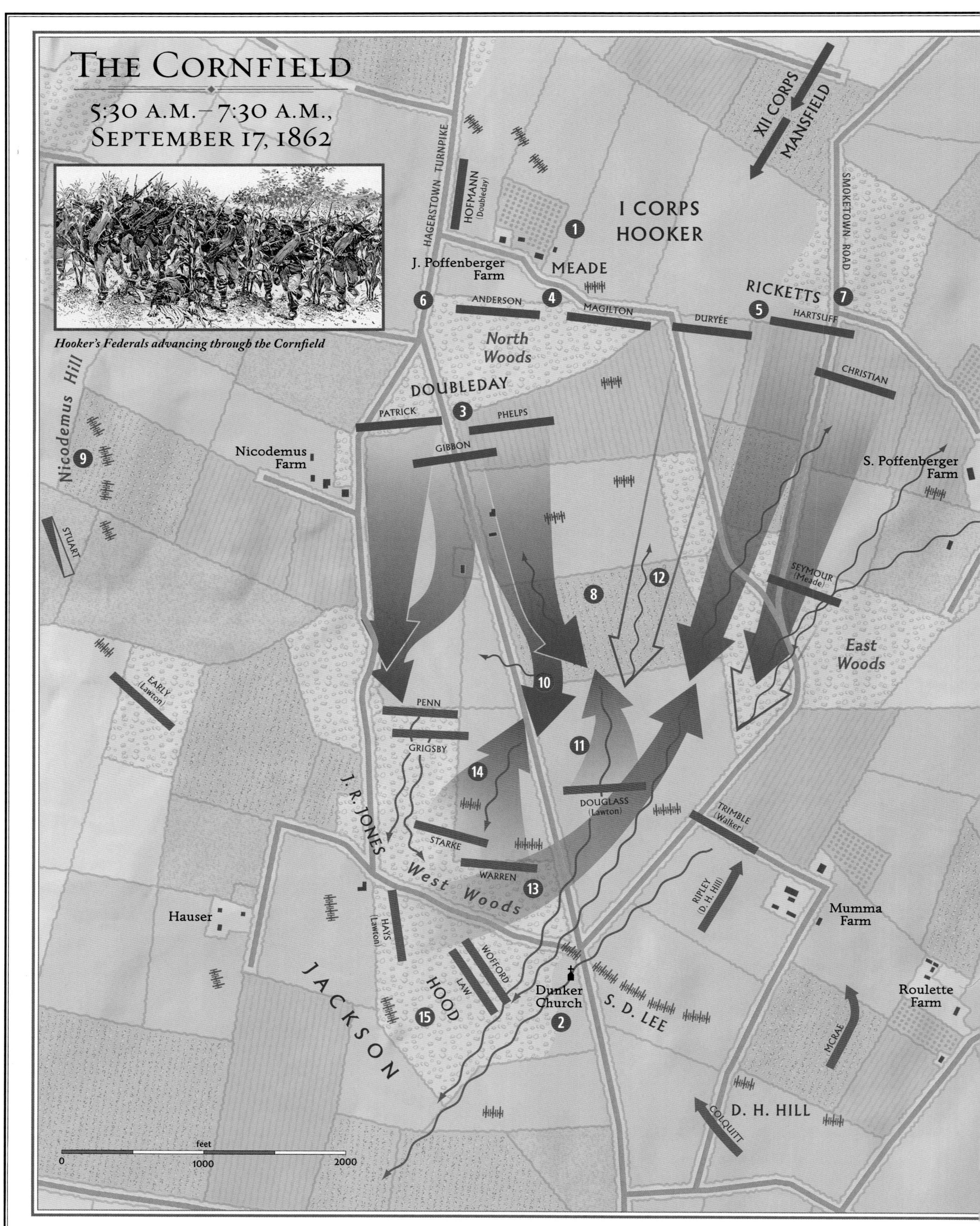

THE CORNFIELD
5:30 A.M.–7:30 A.M., SEPTEMBER 17, 1862
Hooker's Federals advancing through the Cornfield
HAGERSTOWN TURNPIKE
HOFMANN (Doubleday)
I CORPS HOOKER
XII CORPS MANSFIELD
SMOKETOWN ROAD
J. Poffenberger Farm
MEADE
RICKETTS
ANDERSON
MAGILTON
DURYÉE
HARTSUFF
North Woods
DOUBLEDAY
PATRICK
PHELPS
GIBBON
CHRISTIAN
Nicodemus Hill
Nicodemus Farm
S. Poffenberger Farm
STUART
SEYMOUR (Meade)
East Woods
EARLY (Lawton)
PENN
GRIGSBY
J. R. JONES
STARKE
WARREN
DOUGLASS (Lawton)
TRIMBLE (Walker)
RIPLEY (D. H. Hill)
West Woods
Hauser
HAYS (Lawton)
Mumma Farm
WOFFORD
LAW
HOOD
JACKSON
Dunker Church
S. D. LEE
Roulette Farm
MCRAE
D. H. HILL
COLQUITT
feet
0
1000
2000
1
2
3
4
5
6
7
8
9
10
11
12
13
14
15

1862 | ANTIETAM

Hooker's Attack at Dawn

Fighting Joe Hooker could hardly wait for the battle to begin. After passing the night at the Joseph Poffenberger Farm ❶, he had his First Corps on the move at 5:30 A.M., advancing against Stonewall Jackson's forces around Dunker Church ❷. Hooker's three divisions, under Brigadier Generals Abner Doubleday ❸, George Meade ❹, and James Ricketts ❺, pressed southward between the Hagerstown Turnpike ❻ and Smoketown Road ❼. Their paths converged on the Cornfield ❽, a 20-acre plot bordered by woods. Correspondent Frank Schell, peering through a field glass from McClellan's distant headquarters, watched in awe as they entered battle at sunrise. "Onward through the ripened corn the Yankee line pushed its way," he wrote, "its position and direction beautifully indicated by the National and regimental colors waving above the corn-stalks, and by the sparkling flashes from gun-barrels and bayonets."

Beauty and precision soon gave way to chaos and carnage. Jackson had artillery in place south of the Cornfield and on Nicodemus Hill ❾, menacing the Federal flank. Major Rufus Dawes of John Gibbon's brigade ❿, at the forefront of Doubleday's division, came under such a fierce pounding with his men in the Cornfield that he ordered them to lie low. "Shells burst around us," he recalled, "and canister whistled through the corn above us." When they dared continue their advance, they met with Georgians of Colonel Marcellus Douglass's brigade ⓫, who exchanged thunderous volleys with the Yanks that sent men on both sides down by the dozens. Those Georgians could not hold out much longer, having recently come under attack by Brigadier General Abram Duryée ⓬ of Ricketts's division, whose troops were about to break through when Brigadier General Harry Hays unleashed his Louisiana Tigers ⓭, badly mauling Duryée's men and forcing them back.

Pressing forward, Gibbon's excited Federals continued their advance along the Hagerstown Turnpike, repelling a thrust from the West Woods by Brigadier General William Starke's Confederates ⓮ in a wild scene described by Dawes: "The men are loading and firing with demoniacal fury and shouting and laughing hysterically, and the whole field before us is covered with rebels fleeing for life, into the woods." Facing disaster, Jackson committed his reserves under hard-charging John Bell Hood ⓯, who cut into the Federals along the turnpike "like a scythe," Dawes wrote. But when Hood's men advanced into the Cornfield, they were mowed down in turn by Meade's infantry and close-range Federal artillery fire that blew men apart. Several regiments lost more than half of their number on this killing ground. Hood later pronounced his division "dead on the field." ■

Fighting Joe Promoted to major general for distinguished service under McClellan on the Peninsula, Hooker was dubbed "Fighting Joe" by the press and lived up to the title at Antietam by remaining close to the action until he was shot in the foot around 9 A.M. Seeing him up front, the troops "believed in their commander," a reporter wrote, "and fought with a will."

The Battle Begins The struggle at Antietam commenced with furious fighting in the Cornfield and surrounding woods, detailed in this National Geographic map showing Hooker's initial advances and the deadly counterthrusts by Jackson's Confederates. "The slain lay in rows precisely as they had stood in their ranks a few minutes before," Hooker recalled. "It was never my fortune to witness a more dismal, bloody battlefield."

⓮ Path of Destruction Dead Confederates of Starke's brigade lie along a fence beside the Hagerstown Turnpike, where they were cut down by Doubleday's advancing Federals.

1862 | ANTIETAM

To Dunker Church & the Sunken Road

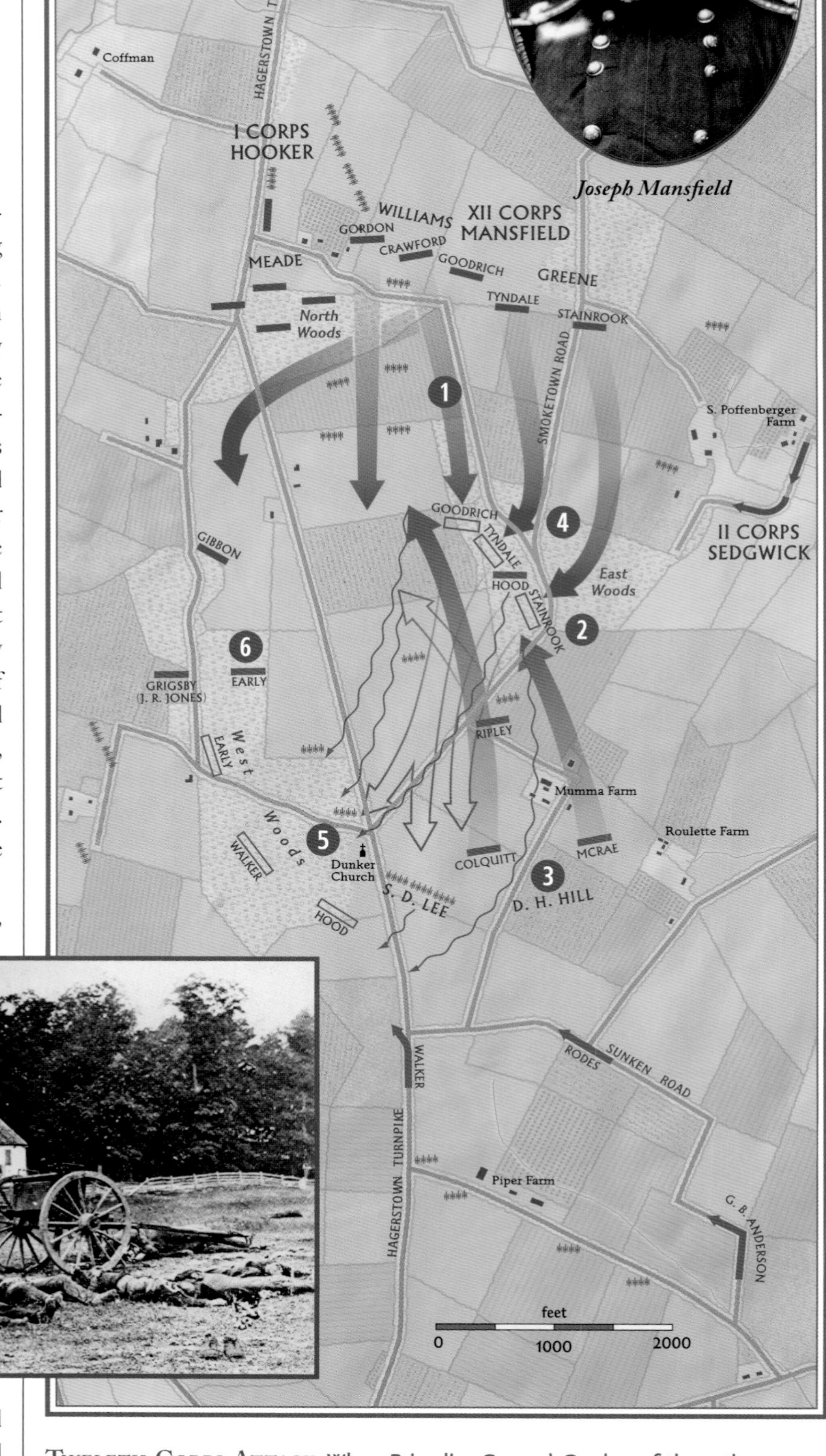

Despite his numerical advantage, McClellan committed one corps at a time against Lee's left, allowing him to shift forces and meet each challenge in turn. Not until Hooker's First Corps had lost momentum did Major General Joseph Mansfield's 12th Corps enter the fray (near right), around 7:30 A.M. Mansfield was about to advance when he saw troops of Brigadier General Samuel Crawford ❶ firing and ordered them to stop, fearing they had mistaken friends for foes. They pointed out to him riflemen of Hood's battered division lurking in the East Woods ❷, with Mansfield in their sights. "Yes, yes, you are right," Mansfield said, moments before taking a bullet to the chest that proved fatal. Brigadier General Alpheus Williams, anxiously awaiting the battle he thought might determine "the fate of our country," stepped in capably for Mansfield and led an attack that staggered Confederates of D. H. Hill's division ❸, who gave way before Brigadier General George Greene's division ❹. Approaching the Dunker Church ❺, Greene's men were pinned down by fire from Virginians in the West Woods under the command of Brigadier General Jubal Early ❻. By 9 A.M., the 12th Corps drive had stalled, and a brief lull in the fighting ensued.

This pause came as Lee was sending in reinforcements, including the divisions of Brigadier General John Walker ❼ and those of Major Generals Lafayette McLaws ❽ and Richard H. Anderson ❾. Heedless of that threat, Second Corps commander Edwin Sumner charged into the West Woods with a single division, under Major General John Sedgwick ❿, whose troops were caught in a murderous flank attack by Walker, McLaws, and Colonel George "Tige" Anderson. "My God! We must get out of this!" shouted Sumner, but 2,300 of his men fell dead or wounded before the remnant escaped those haunted woods. Left behind by Sumner when he fell into that trap were the divisions of Brigadier Generals William French ⓫ and Israel Richardson ⓬, whose men launched repeated attacks on the Sunken Road ⓭, where D. H. Hill's weary Confederates were entrenched with R. H. Anderson's reinforcements. Richardson fell mortally wounded, but his men seized a knoll flanking the Confederate position and fired down into the road, ousting the Rebels, who left their dead lying in heaps. By 1 P.M., Lee's situation here was critical, and a new threat was developing to the south at the Burnside Bridge. ■

❺

TWELFTH CORPS ATTACK When Brigadier General Gordon of the 12th Corps entered the Cornfield (above), D. H. Hill sent Brigadier General Alfred Colquitt to oppose him while Colonel D. K. McRae led his brigade into the East Woods to guard the Confederate flank. George Greene's Federal division then shattered McRae's line and advanced to Dunker Church.

❺ DUNKER CHURCH Rebel gunners lie dead near Dunker Church.

SECOND CORPS ATTACK When Sumner and Sedgwick faltered in the West Woods (opposite), Gordon and Greene of the 12th Corps were drawn into the struggle. Sumner's other divisions seized the Sunken Road, but Major General William Franklin's fresh Sixth Corps did not exploit that opening.

⓭ SUNKEN ROAD Confederate dead fill the Sunken Road after the fighting.

Israel Richardson

ATTACK AT BURNSIDE BRIDGE

CLARA BARTON

The bloody Battle of Antietam tested the courage not only of soldiers but also of civilians who came to their aid when they fell wounded. Among those who served as a nurse here as the fighting raged was Clara Barton, a 40-year-old former schoolteacher with no medical training. She began her service to the Union in 1861 as a relief worker, providing food and other supplies to soldiers recuperating in hospitals around Washington, D.C. A year later, she obtained permission from the surgeon general to go to the front, carrying supplies in a wagon and comforting those wounded in action until doctors could attend to them. At Antietam, she was offering a stricken soldier a drink when a bullet tore through her sleeve and entered his chest. "The poor fellow sprang from my hands and fell back quivering, in the agonies of death," she recalled. Later, a man with a bullet lodged in his cheekbone begged her to remove it. Having "never severed the nerves and fibers of human flesh," she urged him to wait for a doctor, but he insisted: "You cannot hurt me dear lady—I can endure any pain that your hands can create—please do it,—t'will relieve me so much." She performed the operation successfully and went on to aid so many soldiers in distress during the Civil War that she became known as "the angel of the battlefield."

Around 10 A.M., McClellan ordered the Ninth Corps to cross Burnside Bridge ❶ and attack Lee's right, below Sharpsburg ❷. Lee had shifted troops from this sector to his embattled left. If Burnside moved quickly with his corps, he could cut the Harpers Ferry Road ❸ before A. P. Hill's hard-marching Light Division arrived from the south, thus depriving Lee of support and severing his escape route. Burnside did not know that Hill's division was on the way, but he had a golden chance to deliver a staggering blow where Lee was weakest and was slow to seize it. It took hours for one of his divisions to locate lightly defended Snavely's Ford ❹ while another struggled to cross narrow Burnside Bridge under galling fire.

Opposing that crossing was Brigadier General Robert Toombs, a former Confederate secretary of state who had warned Jefferson Davis that attacking Fort Sumter would be like striking a hornet's nest, from which angry legions would "swarm out and sting us to death." Now Toombs and his sparse brigade of 550 Georgians had to keep 11,000 Yankees of Ninth Corps from swarming across the creek. Toombs placed most of his men under Colonel Henry Benning on high ground overlooking the bridge ❺ while the rest guarded the ford downstream ❻. Supported by artillery, the Georgians held out for three hours before Brigadier General Edward Ferrero's Federals ❼ took the bridge while Brigadier General Isaac Rodman pushed troops under Colonels Edward Harland and Harrison Fairchild ❽ across Snavely's Ford.

Having gained the west bank belatedly, Burnside then took his precious time bringing up fresh troops and ammunition. Around 3 P.M., his corps finally resumed its attack, with Brigadier General Orlando Willcox's division ❾ advancing toward Sharpsburg, where the depleted Confederates fell back into town under the onslaught. Meanwhile, Rodman was urging his division toward the Harpers Ferry Road when he was mortally wounded by a sharpshooter. Forging ahead, his troops collided with the vanguard of A. P. Hill's division, which had marched 18 miles since daybreak. Wearing his red flannel battle shirt, Hill threw three brigades into action under Brigadier Generals Maxcy Gregg ❿, James Archer ⓫, and Lawrence Branch ⓬ and repelled Harland and Fairchild's brigades. There was plenty of fight left in the Ninth Corps, but Hill's counterattack daunted Burnside, who pulled his troops back to the bridge after McClellan—who had promised to reinforce him—sent only a single battery. "I can do nothing more," McClellan said. "I have no infantry." In fact, he had 20,000 men in reserve, none of whom saw action before the Battle of Antietam ended that evening in stalemate. ■

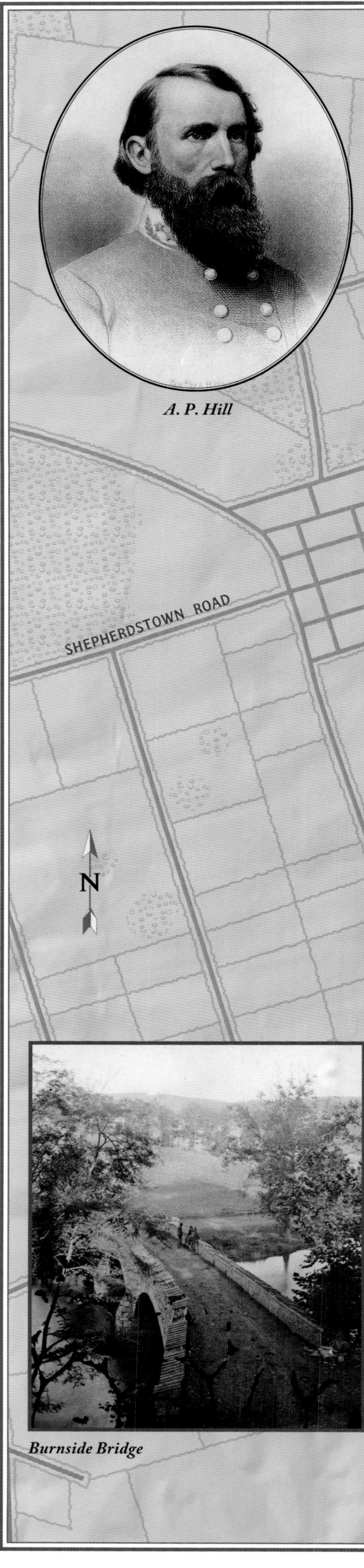

A. P. Hill

Burnside Bridge

NINTH CORPS ATTACK Burnside's push across Antietam Creek was delayed as Rodman's division searched for Snavely's Ford and the remainder were bottled up at Burnside Bridge. When the corps finally crossed over in full and began advancing in earnest, A. P. Hill's division arrived from the south and saved the day for Lee.

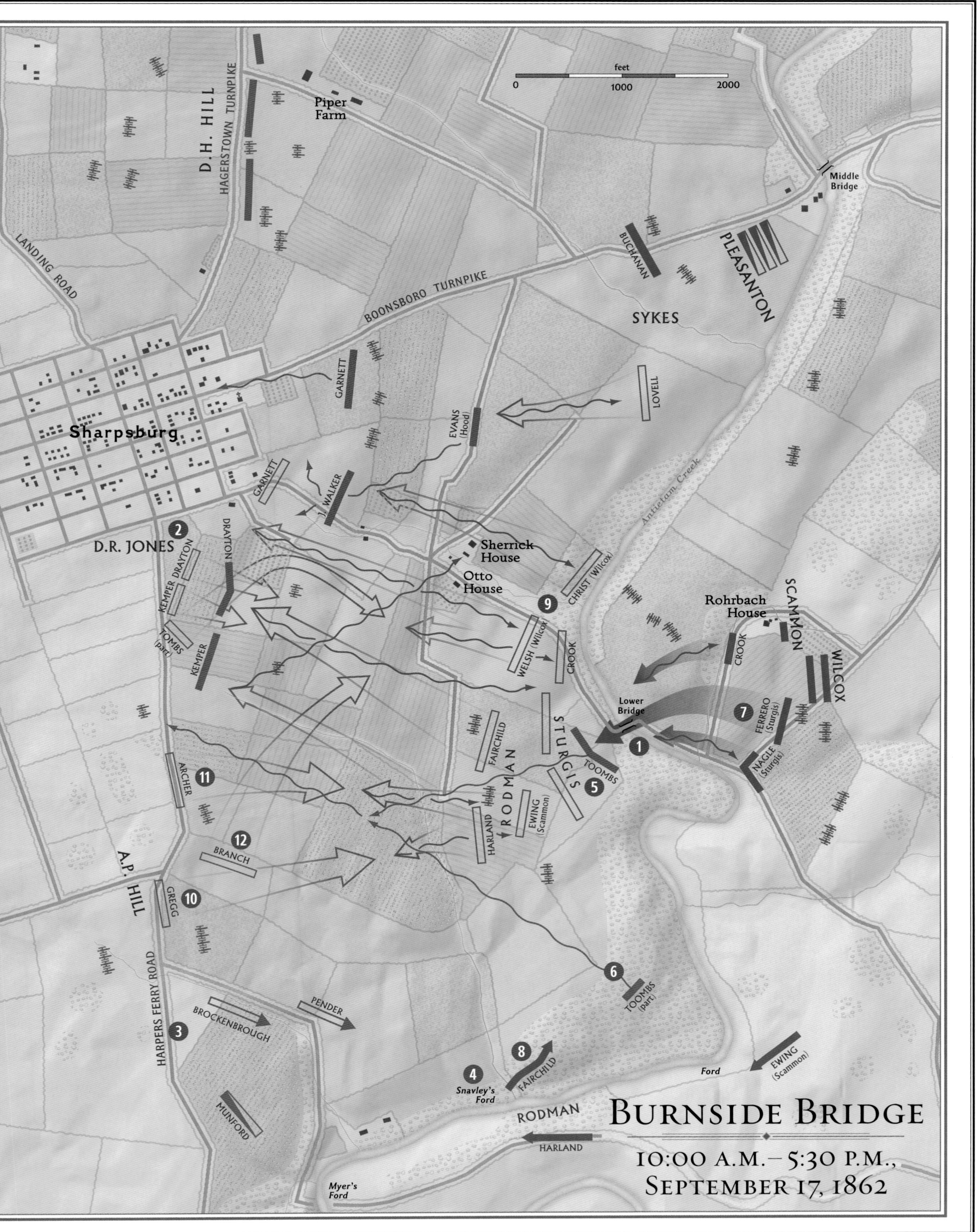
BURNSIDE BRIDGE
10:00 A.M.–5:30 P.M., SEPTEMBER 17, 1862
feet
0
1000
2000
Sharpsburg
D.H. HILL
HAGERSTOWN TURNPIKE
Piper Farm
LANDING ROAD
BOONSBORO TURNPIKE
Middle Bridge
BUCHANAN
PLEASANTON
SYKES
GARNETT
LOVELL
EVANS (Hood)
J. WALKER
GARNETT
Antietam Creek
Sherrick House
Otto House
D.R. JONES
DRAYTON
DRAYTON
KEMPER
KEMPER
TOOMBS (part)
CHRIST (Wilcox)
WELSH (Wilcox)
CROOK
Rohrbach House
SCAMMON
CROOK
WILCOX
Lower Bridge
FERRERO (Sturgis)
NAGLE (Sturgis)
STURGIS
TOOMBS
FAIRCHILD
RODMAN
HARLAND
EWING (Scammon)
ARCHER
BRANCH
A.P. HILL
GREGG
HARPERS FERRY ROAD
BROCKENBROUGH
PENDER
TOOMBS (part)
MUNFORD
Snavley's Ford
FAIRCHILD
Ford
EWING (Scammon)
RODMAN
HARLAND
Myer's Ford

AFTERMATH

Contrary to expectations, McClellan did not renew battle at Antietam ❶ on September 18. Both sides were staggered by their losses, with the Confederates reporting more than 10,000 casualties and the Federals more than 12,000. Some 6,000 men from the two armies died on the field or later from their wounds, exceeding the American toll during the entire Revolutionary War. Lee had fewer than 30,000 battle-weary troops left standing and after remaining defiantly at Antietam through the day concluded he could not risk another bloodbath. McClellan had more than 60,000 soldiers at hand, many of them still fresh. Yet he did nothing to prevent Lee from withdrawing southward across the Potomac at Boteler's Ford ❷ late on September 18. He did send forces the next day to challenge Lee's rear guard at the crossing but was not dismayed when the Confederates slipped away to Winchester ❸ to regroup in the Shenandoah Valley ❹. "Our victory was complete," he wired Washington. "The enemy is driven back into Virginia."

Lincoln dearly wished that McClellan had pressed Lee harder and crushed his army. But it was enough of a victory to give the president the boost he needed to take a fateful step. On September 22, he issued his Emancipation Proclamation, declaring that all slaves in areas still in rebellion against the Union as of January 1, 1863, "shall be then, thenceforward, and forever free." Designed to encourage slaves to leave their masters and deprive the Confederacy of their services, Lincoln's decree was opposed by many Northern Democrats, including McClellan, who did not want the war effort linked to abolitionism. Setting aside their political differences, Lincoln visited the general, still encamped at Sharpsburg in early October, and urged him to move soon against Richmond. Lee was regaining strength and in mid-October sent Jeb Stuart on another daring raid, which took him around McClellan's army to Chambersburg, Pennsylvania ❺, and back. Not until October 26 did McClellan move south across the Potomac near Harpers Ferry ❻. It took him a week to reach Warrenton ❼, by which time Lee had moved Longstreet's corps across the Blue Ridge to Culpeper Court House ❽, coming between the Federal commander and Richmond. "He's got the slows," Lincoln said of McClellan, before sacking him on November 6. His successor, Ambrose Burnside, later confronted Lee at Fredericksburg ❾. ■

Gravesite at Antietam

❶ MEETING AT SHARPSBURG Lincoln confers with General McClellan in his tent near the Antietam battlefield on October 4. McClellan wrote that Lincoln's aim was "to push me into a premature advance into Virginia," while the president complained afterward that the Army of the Potomac was doing nothing more than serving as "McClellan's bodyguard."

MCCLELLAN OUTMANEUVERED After he withdrew from Antietam into the Shenandoah Valley, Lee sent Jeb Stuart on a raid into Pennsylvania on October 10 that raised hackles in Washington. He then shifted forces eastward, between the slowly advancing Federal army and Richmond, prompting Lincoln to remove McClellan.

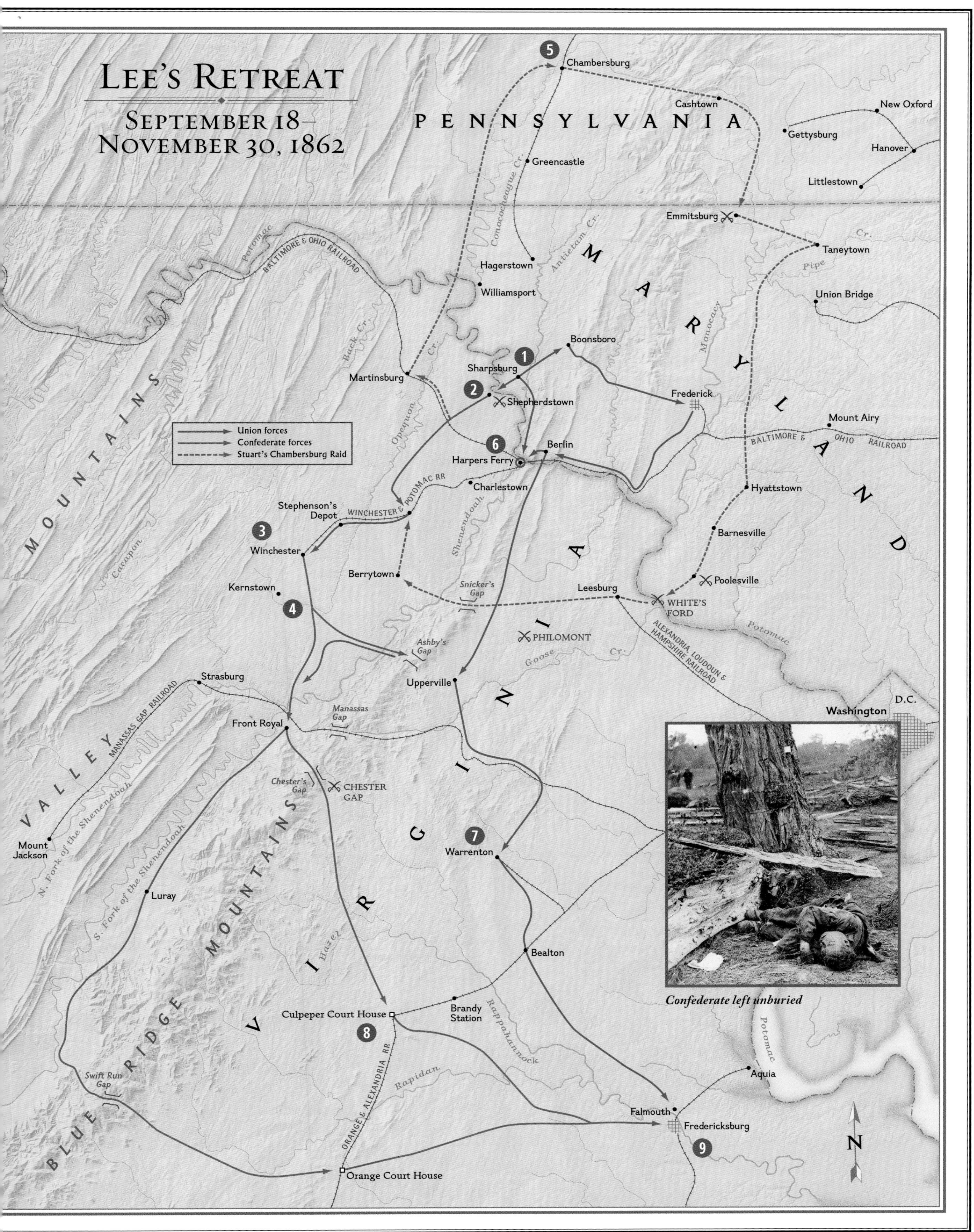

Confederate left unburied

1862

CORINTH

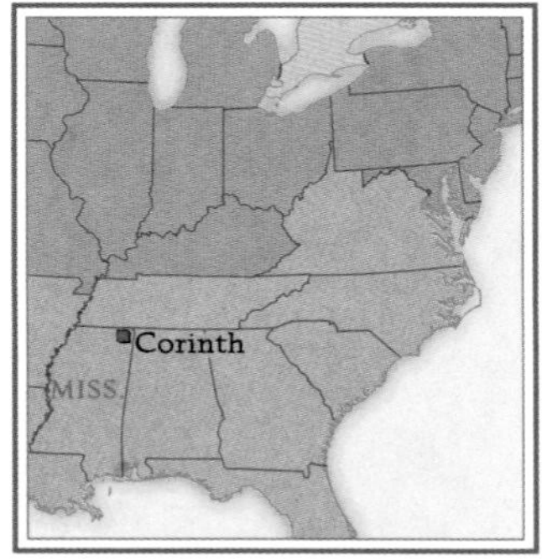

WESTERN THEATER

APRIL 11, 1862 Henry Halleck arrives at Pittsburg Landing in Tennessee to take charge of Federal forces following the Battle of Shiloh.

MAY 31 Federals under Halleck occupy Corinth, Mississippi, following withdrawal of the Confederate Army of Tennessee under P. G. T. Beauregard.

JUNE 6 Union forces occupy Memphis, Tennessee.

JUNE 10 Halleck restores Grant as commander of the Federal Army of the Tennessee, headquartered at Memphis.

SEPTEMBER 19 Federals under William Rosecrans clash at Iuka, Mississippi, with Confederates led by Sterling Price, who slips away to support Earl Van Dorn as he advances on Corinth.

OCTOBER 3–4 Battle of Corinth

While fighting in the East was largely confined to Virginia and Maryland, the war in the West was wider ranging. In campaigns covering hundreds of miles, much depended on controlling railroads and junctions like Corinth, Mississippi ❶, where the Mobile & Ohio Railroad ❷ intersected the Memphis & Charleston ❸. Following the Battle of Shiloh in April, Confederates led by P. G. T. Beauregard withdrew to Corinth behind a fortified line ❹. Federals pursued slowly under Major General Henry Halleck, who assumed command over Grant and ordered Sherman and other officers to entrench daily to guard against another surprise attack. Rejecting Grant's proposal to swing around Corinth and sever the Rebels' line of retreat, Halleck prepared to bombard the town at month's end only to find it abandoned by the enemy, who had withdrawn on the Mobile & Ohio, leaving behind a note for the Yankees: "These premises to let; inquire of P. G. T. Beauregard."

Earl Van Dorn

In June, Halleck departed for Washington to serve as general in chief and Grant resumed command, taking up headquarters in newly captured Memphis and leaving Major General William Rosecrans at Corinth with orders to construct an inner line of defense. Grant's foresight proved vital when 22,000 Confederates under Major Generals Earl Van Dorn and Sterling Price approached Corinth from the northwest on October 3 and broke through the outer line. The next morning, they attacked the inner line with a steely determination that awed the Union defenders. "They looked as if they intended to walk right over us," recalled one Federal soldier at Battery Robinett, where the fighting was fiercest. Many attackers there were cut down by artillery fire before Yankees entrenched behind the battery rose up and blasted those left upright. "It was horrible," wrote a Confederate after the defeat. "Our boys were shot down like hogs and fell back each man for himself." ■

❶ CARNAGE AT CORINTH Dead men and horses litter the field at Corinth after Confederates attacked Battery Robinett (background) on October 4. Unable to crack the inner line of defense here, Van Dorn retreated, leaving behind nearly 5,000 Confederates killed, wounded, or captured.

A CONTESTED JUNCTION This Federal map was drawn after Halleck took Corinth in May but before Van Dorn attacked in October, by which time the outer line of defense built by Confederates (red) had been reinforced by an inner line (not shown), built by Federals at the edge of town.

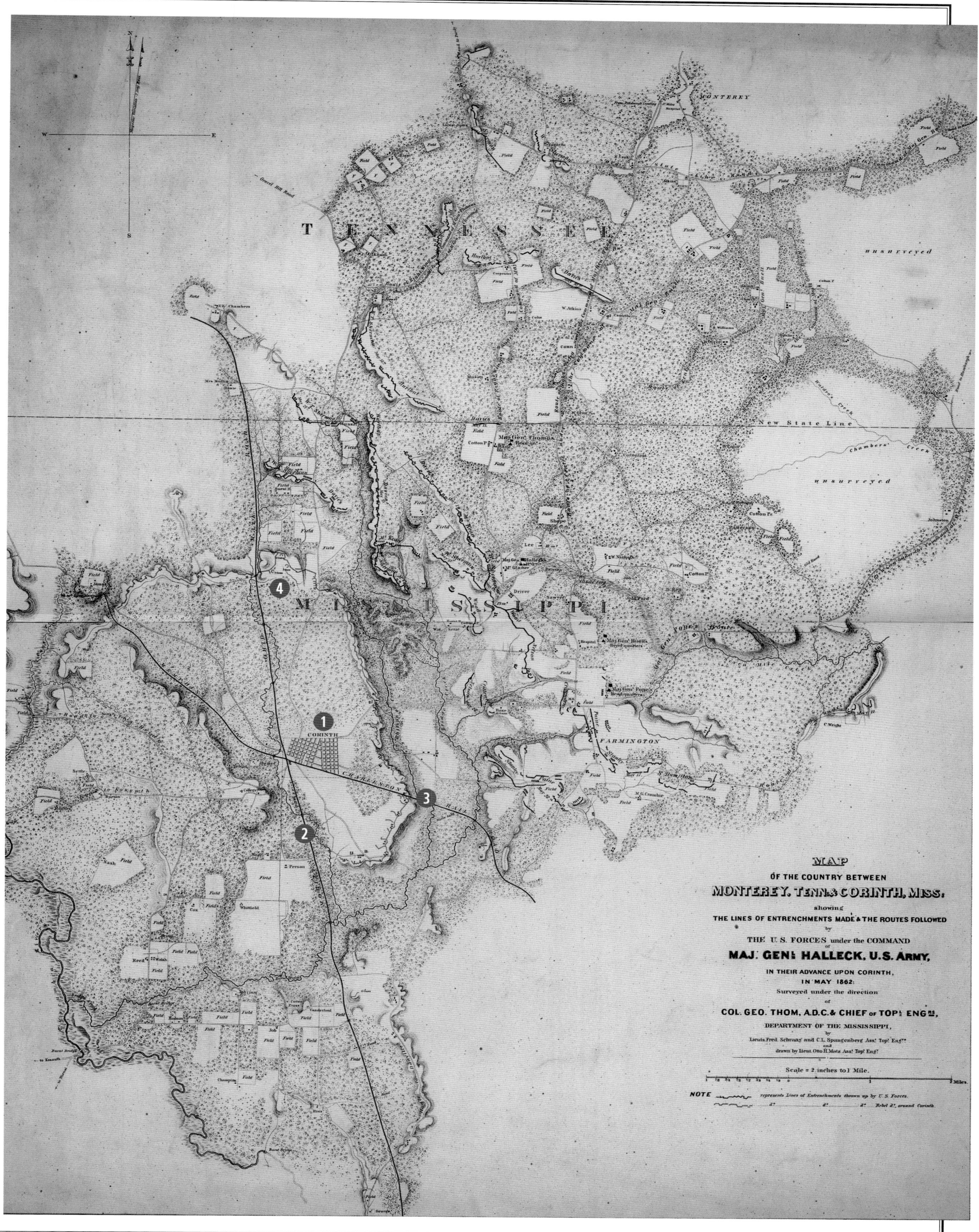
MAP
OF THE COUNTRY BETWEEN
MONTEREY, TENN. & CORINTH, MISS.
showing
THE LINES OF ENTRENCHMENTS MADE & THE ROUTES FOLLOWED
by
THE U. S. FORCES under the COMMAND
of
MAJ. GENL. HALLECK, U.S. ARMY,
IN THEIR ADVANCE UPON CORINTH,
IN MAY 1862:
Surveyed under the direction
of
COL. GEO. THOM, A.D.C. & CHIEF OF TOPL. ENGRS,
DEPARTMENT OF THE MISSISSIPPI,
by
Lieuts. Fred. Schrang and C.L. Spangenberg Asst. Topl. Engrs
and
drawn by Lieut. Otto H. Matz Asst. Topl. Engr.
Scale = 2 inches to 1 Mile.
2 Miles.
NOTE represents Lines of Entrenchments thrown up by U. S. Forces.
do. do. do. Rebel do. around Corinth.
TENNESSEE
MISSISSIPPI
MONTEREY
CORINTH
FARMINGTON
New State Line
unsurveyed
unsurveyed
1
2
3
4

1862

PERRYVILLE

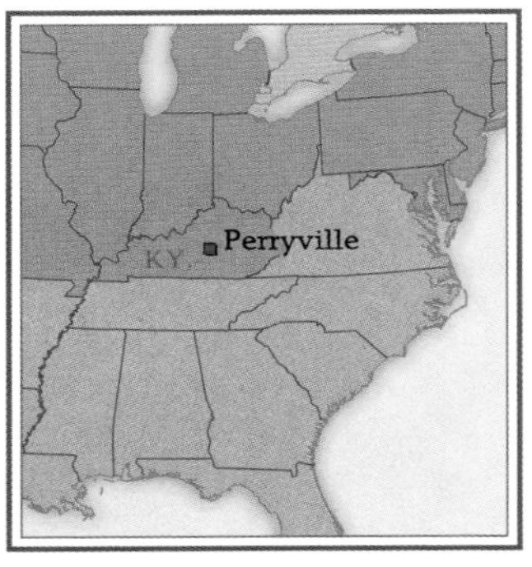

WESTERN THEATER

JUNE 27, 1862 Jefferson Davis relieves Beauregard as commander of the Army of Tennessee and replaces him with Braxton Bragg.

JULY 31 Bragg and Edmund Kirby Smith confer in Chattanooga, Tennessee, and plan a campaign that will carry them into Kentucky, pursued by Don Carlos Buell's Army of the Ohio.

AUGUST 30 Smith's Confederates repulse Federals near Richmond, Kentucky, and go on to occupy Lexington.

OCTOBER 8 Battle of Perryville (Kentucky)

OCTOBER 27 Lincoln removes Buell for failing to pursue Confederate forces withdrawing from Kentucky into Tennessee and replaces him with William Rosecrans.

Dismayed when Beauregard abandoned Corinth, Jefferson Davis relieved him in June in favor of a more aggressive commander, General Braxton Bragg. "Never, on a battlefield, lose a moment's time," wrote Bragg, but "press on with every available man, giving a panic-stricken and retreating foe no time to rally." That was a good maxim, but the temperamental Bragg was not always a good judge of when to attack and did not win the trust of his officers and men. He referred to his troops as "the mob we have miscalled soldiers" and bore down hard, commanding their obedience but not their devotion.

In July, Bragg left some of his troops in Mississippi under the command of Van Dorn and Price and took 35,000 men to Tennessee to join Major General Edmund Kirby Smith's smaller force in a campaign against the Army of the Ohio, led by Major General Don Carlos Buell (inset), who had aided Grant at Shiloh. A friend of McClellan, Buell shared his methodical approach. "The object is not to fight great battles," Buell wrote, "but by demonstrations and maneuvering to prevent the enemy from concentrating his forces." Never quick to move, Buell slowed to a crawl in Tennessee as cavalry led by Brigadier General Nathan Bedford Forrest and Colonel John Hunt Morgan cut his lines of supply and communication. Leaving their flustered opponent in the lurch, Bragg and Smith invaded Kentucky in late August, hoping to gather recruits there and draw Buell into a decisive battle. This advance coincided with Lee's invasion of Maryland, causing deep concern in the North.

In early October, Buell finally caught up with Bragg at Perryville ❶. Few Kentuckians had joined Bragg, and he had not linked up with Smith or concentrated his own army, leaving him with only 16,000 men here. "Don't scatter your forces," urged his diligent corps commander, Major General William Hardee. "Strike with your whole strength." But Bragg did not know he was facing Buell's entire 60,000-man army, and after fighting broke out along Doctor's Creek ❷ on the evening of October 7, he ordered a concerted attack the next day. Around 2 P.M. on October 8, Bragg sent Leonidas Polk's corps across the Chaplin River ❸. Federals facing this onslaught had just moved into line and were caught off balance, losing their division commander, Brigadier General James Jackson ❹, to enemy fire. Colonel John Starkweather's brigade ❺ held off the Rebels long enough to keep them from turning the Federal flank, but Buell's left wing fell back more than a mile before regrouping ❻. On his right, Major General Thomas J. Crittenden's corps remained inactive along the Lebanon Pike ❼, facing only cavalry. Crittenden did not advance until after troops of Hardee's corps on Bragg's left had been repulsed by 31-year-old Brigadier General Philip Sheridan, whose division held firm at center ❽ before mounting a late-day counterattack and driving the enemy back to the far side of town ❾. That night, Bragg realized what he was up against and withdrew before Buell could bring his full weight to bear. Buell's poor showing here against a smaller force and his failure to pursue Bragg as he retreated into Tennessee cost him his job, which Lincoln handed to William Rosecrans on October 23. ■

UNDER FIRE **After battling Confederates at Perryville, Buell came under fire for not pursuing Bragg's army. Shortly before he was sacked, Buell received a stern message from General in Chief Halleck, stating that Lincoln "does not understand why we cannot march as the enemy marches, live as he lives, and fight as he fights, unless we admit the inferiority of our troops and of our generals."**

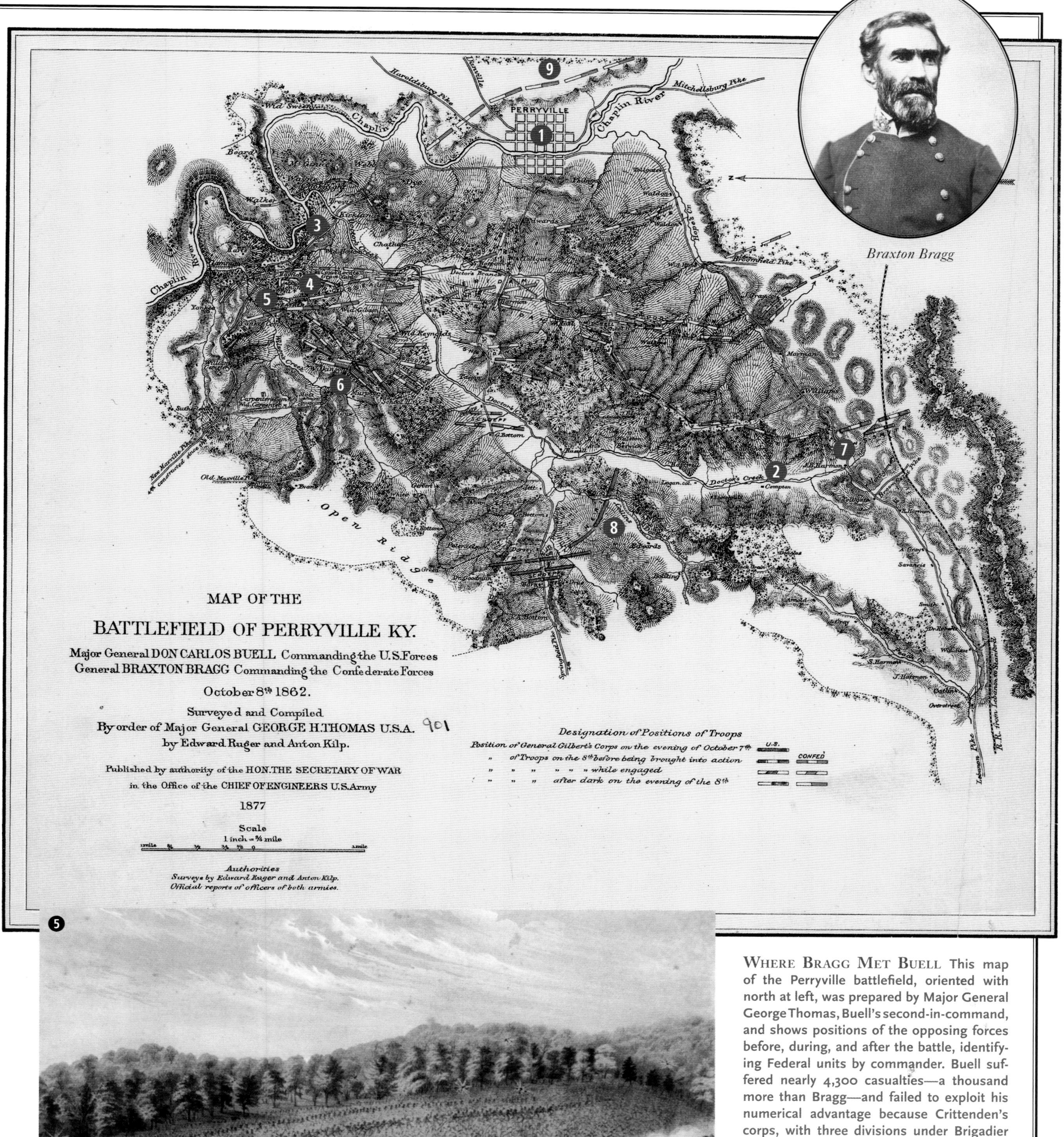

Braxton Bragg

❺

Where Bragg Met Buell This map of the Perryville battlefield, oriented with north at left, was prepared by Major General George Thomas, Buell's second-in-command, and shows positions of the opposing forces before, during, and after the battle, identifying Federal units by commander. Buell suffered nearly 4,300 casualties—a thousand more than Bragg—and failed to exploit his numerical advantage because Crittenden's corps, with three divisions under Brigadier Generals Thomas Wood, Horatio Van Cleve, and W. S. Smith, did not advance when it mattered.

❺ **Starkweather's Stand** Federals of Colonel John Starkweather's brigade fire a volley at Confederates advancing through a cornfield at the far left of the Union line. Their stand prevented Buell's beleaguered forces from being flanked and routed.

1862

FREDERICKSBURG

EASTERN THEATER

NOVEMBER 7, 1862 Burnside replaces McClellan as commander of the Army of the Potomac.

NOVEMBER 15 Burnside launches his army toward Fredericksburg.

DECEMBER 1 Stonewall Jackson's forces begin arriving at Fredericksburg to join the rest of Lee's army there.

DECEMBER 11 Federals begin laying bridges and crossing the Rappahannock.

DECEMBER 13 Battle of Fredericksburg

Chosen by Lincoln to succeed McClellan as commander of the Army of the Potomac, Ambrose Burnside accepted his promotion reluctantly. "He shrank from responsibility with sincere modesty," wrote his subordinate, Jacob Cox, "because he questioned his own capacity to deal with affairs of great magnitude." Lincoln wanted action, and Burnside obliged by marching quickly toward Fredericksburg ❶, where he hoped to cross the Rappahannock ❷ and advance on Richmond before Lee could shift eastward from Culpeper Court House to stop him. By November 18, most of Burnside's forces were at Falmouth ❸, across from Fredericksburg, where the road and rail bridges ❹ across the Rappahannock had been destroyed earlier in the year. The pontoons Burnside had ordered to construct bridges for his forces would not arrive from Washington until month's end. As he waited and agonized, Lee arrived with Longstreet's corps and took up a strong defensive position on Marye's Heights ❺. Burnside hoped to avoid a costly assault there, but his options narrowed in early December when Stonewall Jackson's corps arrived from the Shenandoah Valley and covered other likely crossings downstream. Lee grew stronger by the day as artillery and reinforcements arrived from Richmond by rail, swelling his army to 78,000 men and bringing the opposing forces assembled here to nearly 200,000. On December 10, Burnside ordered his army to advance the next day on pontoon bridges laid by engineers under Longstreet's guns at Fredericksburg and a few miles south, where Jackson waited. "Tomorrow we commence the crossing of the Rappahannock & will be sure to have a fearful fight," wrote one Federal officer, Colonel Samuel Zook. "I expect we will be licked, for we have allowed the rebs nearly four weeks to erect batteries etc. to slaughter us by thousands." ■

❷ **Bridging the Rappahannock** Advancing on December 11, Federal engineers lay planks on pontoons to form a bridge over the Rappahannock to Fredericksburg while troops ferried across by boat secure a bridgehead.

COMMANDER AND STAFF Ambrose Burnside sits facing the camera with his staff officers in camp at Warrenton, Virginia, before marching on Fredericksburg.

BURNSIDE'S OBJECTIVE An artist's rendering of Fredericksburg shortly before the battle there in December shows mounted Federals on the north bank surveying Confederate fortifications on the hills beyond Fredericksburg. One officer warned Burnside that an attack here would be "the greatest slaughter of the war; there isn't infantry enough in our whole army to carry those heights if they are well defended."

1862 | FREDERICKSBURG

Slaughter at Marye's Heights

Before dawn on December 11, Burnside's engineers began laying pontoon bridges ❶ across the Rappahannock. Dozens were hit by sniper fire, and only by sending troops across in boats that afternoon to clear the way were Federals able to complete the spans. By December 12, Burnside had possession of Fredericksburg ❷, where his troops looted homes and stores while he conferred with William Franklin, commanding the First and Sixth Corps, at his headquarters near the Bernard house ❸. Burnside asked Franklin to outflank Jackson's corps along the river ❹ while Federals advancing from Fredericksburg attacked Longstreet on Marye's Heights ❺. The next morning, the First Corps could find no way around Jackson and came up against entrenched infantry and artillery. George Meade's resilient Pennsylvania division broke through between the lines of Brigadier Generals James Lane and James Archer ❻ and killed General Maxcy Gregg of South Carolina ❼. But Jackson soon plugged that gap, and Franklin cut short the attack around 2 P.M. before committing most of his forces.

Belt buckle found at Fredericksburg with a bullet in it

The Federals storming Marye's Heights faced even bleaker prospects. Troops of the Second Corps emerged from town shortly after noon and came under heavy artillery fire before drawing within range of Confederate infantry in a sunken road behind a stone wall ❽. Admiring their heroic advance from his headquarters ❾, Lee remarked, "It is well that war is so terrible, otherwise we should become too fond of it." Beginning with the divisions of Brigadier General William French ❿ and Major General Winfield Scott Hancock ⓫, one Federal wave after another crashed against the stone wall and receded, leaving the ground "literally black with their dead and wounded," a defender wrote. Many Confederates died as well, including Brigadier General Thomas Cobb (inset) of McLaw's division ⓬. But by day's end more Federals had been lost here than at Antietam, to no gain. The bitter defeat cast a pall over the Union as a year of unfathomable suffering and sacrifice drew to a close. ■

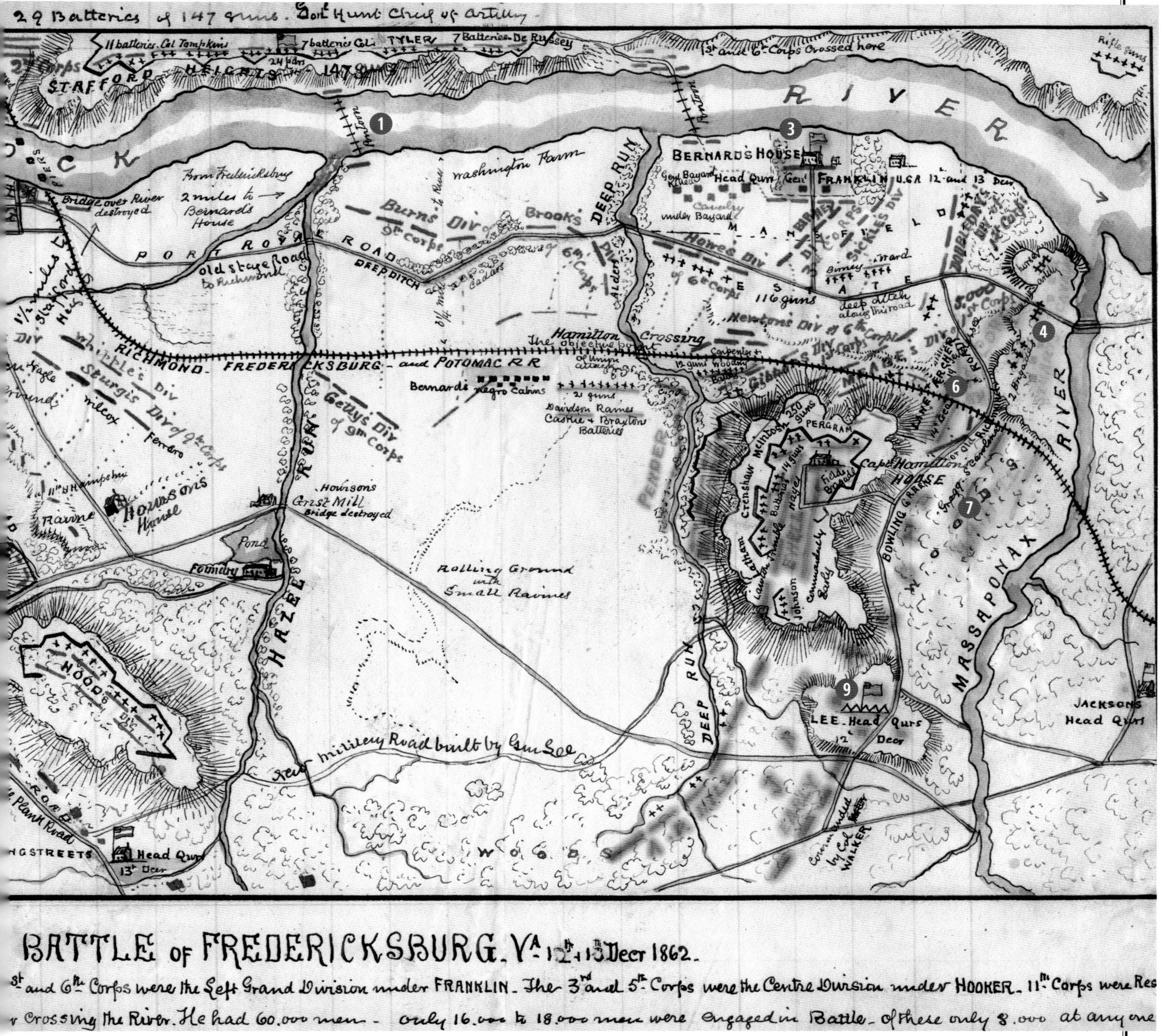

29 Batteries of 147 guns. Genl Hunt Chief of artillery

BATTLE of FREDERICKSBURG. Va. 12th + 13th Decr 1862.

st and 6th Corps were the Left Grand Division under FRANKLIN. The 3rd and 5th Corps were the Centre Division under HOOKER. 11th Corps were Res

r Crossing the River. He had 60.000 men. only 16.000 to 18.000 men were engaged in Battle. of these only 8.000 at any one

A One-Sided Battle A map drawn by Robert Knox Sneden shows the Battle of Fredericksburg as it unfolded through mid-afternoon. Burnside then prevailed on Joseph Hooker, who considered further attacks futile, to cross the river with his forces and enter battle. After losing "as many men as my orders required," Hooker desisted around dusk, ending a struggle that cost Burnside around 12,500 casualties—7,000 more than Lee sustained.

❽ The Stone Wall Confederate infantry standing in the sunken road behind this stone wall beat back doomed assaults by opposing Federals, who suffered further punishment from artillery on the heights. Among the Confederates who gave their lives holding this line was Thomas Cobb (inset), a prominent Georgia lawyer who had urged his state to secede. His brigade suffered 300 casualties here.

Burial Detail Union Troops killed at Fredericksburg—where Confederate scavengers stripped many victims of clothing before their bodies were recovered—are buried in common graves near the battlefield.

CHAPTER 3

A Harvest of Death | 1863

"Some with faces bloated and blackened beyond recognition, lay with glassy eyes staring up at the summer sun."

CORPORAL THOMAS MARBAKER, 11TH NEW JERSEY INFANTRY,
AFTER THE BATTLE OF GETTYSBURG

The bodies of Union dead, stripped of their shoes by scavengers, lie near the Peach Orchard at Gettysburg, the site of furious fighting on July 2, 1863. One survivor, Robert Carter of Massachusetts, described the battle here as "a perfect hell on earth . . . not to be surpassed, nor ever to be forgotten in a man's lifetime."

1863

ENDLESS STRUGGLE

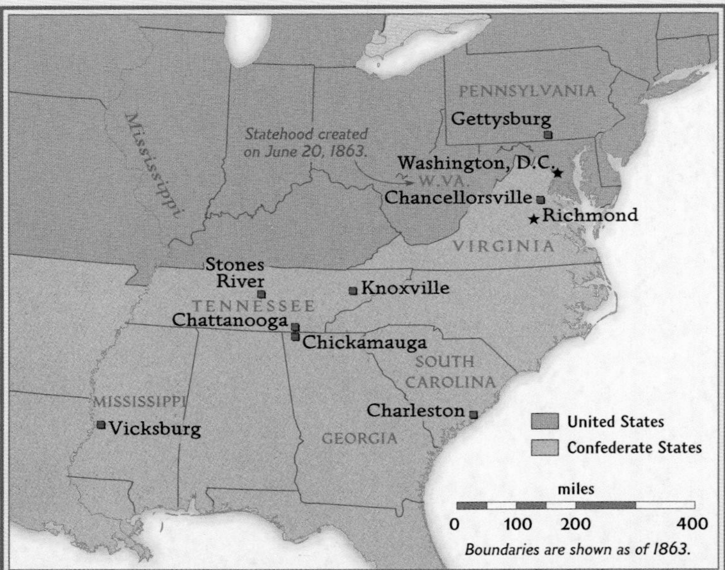

Winter was usually a time for armies to rest and recoup, but by January 1863 the Civil War had reached such a fever pitch that commanders on both sides defied the elements and campaigned without letup, hoping to shatter their opponents before their own forces lost the will or capacity to fight. In Tennessee, Braxton Bragg rang in the New Year by hurling Confederates into battle along Stones River at Murfreesboro. Near Vicksburg, Ulysses Grant kept Federal troops toiling in pestilential swamps, seeking a way around the city's forbidding batteries on the Mississippi River.

Back east in Virginia, Ambrose Burnside—whose futile assaults at Fredericksburg in December resulted in many wounded Federals dying of exposure in the cold overnight—felt compelled to return to the warpath in January with an abortive advance known as the Mud March that left him in such disrepute among his troops that Lincoln had little choice but to sack him. His successor, Joseph Hooker, revived the flagging Army of the Potomac and embarked on a promising spring offensive, only to wilt under the heat applied at Chancellorsville in May by Robert E. Lee and Stonewall Jackson, whose death did not bode well for Lee as he advanced into Pennsylvania that summer and faced the supreme test at Gettysburg.

On July 4, as Lee's battered forces withdrew from that ordeal and Grant took possession of Vicksburg, Unionists could at last glimpse on the horizon a triumphant conclusion to this fearful struggle. But grim realists like Grant and William T. Sherman knew that victory would not come easily—and might not come at all unless Northerners steeled themselves for further bloodshed and proved relentless and remorseless in fighting to the finish. To prevail in war, Sherman wrote after he helped secure Tennessee for the Union in late 1863 and prepared to invade Georgia, "we must and will harden our hearts."

JANUARY–JUNE

January 1, 1863 Lincoln's Emancipation Proclamation takes effect.

January 2 Battle of Stones River (Murfreesboro), launched on December 31, 1862, ends.

January 3 Braxton Bragg's Army of Tennessee withdraws southward from Murfreesboro, leaving William Rosecrans's Army of the Cumberland in possession of that town.

January 22 Ambrose Burnside, thwarted by bad weather in his effort to advance against Confederates around Fredericksburg, calls off his so-called Mud March.

January 26 Joseph Hooker replaces Burnside as commander of the Army of the Potomac.

January 29 Ulysses Grant moves his headquarters from Memphis,

Burnside's Mud March

Tennessee, to Young's Point, Louisiana, north of Vicksburg, and tries unsuccessfully to circumvent the city's defenses over the winter.

March 3 Lincoln signs the Conscription Act, making men between 20 and 45 eligible for the draft.

March 10 Lincoln proclaims amnesty for Union soldiers absent without leave who return to their units by April 1, after which they will be considered deserters.

JULY–DECEMBER

July 1–3 Battle of Gettysburg

July 4 Lee retreats from Gettysburg toward Virginia; Confederates surrender Vicksburg to Grant.

July 8 Confederate garrison at Port Hudson, Louisiana, surrenders after learning that Vicksburg has fallen, leaving Federals in full control of the Mississippi River.

July 10–18 Federal forces including black troops from Massachusetts land on Morris Island at the entrance to Charleston Harbor and launch unsuccessful attacks on Fort Wagner.

July 13 Draft riots erupt in New York City as officials begin drawing lots to determine who will be conscripted there.

July 26 Confederate cavalry commander John Hunt Morgan captured while conducting a raid in Ohio.

August 8 Lee offers to resign as commander of the Army of Northern Virginia following his defeat at Gettysburg, but Jefferson Davis retains him in that post.

August 21 Federals begin shelling Charleston from Morris Island; Chattanooga comes under artillery fire as Rosecrans's army attempts to dislodge Bragg's Confederates there; Confederate raider William Quantrill leads a deadly attack on Lawrence, Kansas, a Unionist stronghold.

August 25 Federals retaliate for the attack on Lawrence by ordering inhabitants to evacuate four Missouri counties along the Kansas border with large numbers of Confederate sympathizers.

Lynching during New York City draft riots

March 17 Federal troopers in Virginia clash with Confederate cavalry at Kelly's Ford.

April 2 Bread riot occurs in Richmond as women there protest food shortages and high prices.

April 7 Union ironclad fleet led by Samuel Du Pont withdraws under fire from Charleston Harbor after bombarding Fort Sumter.

April 10 Jefferson Davis urges Southern farmers to stop cultivating cotton and tobacco and devote their efforts "exclusively to the production of corn, oats, beans, peas, potatoes, and other food for man and beast."

April 16 Grant renews his campaign against Vicksburg by moving forces down the Mississippi River to Grand Gulf and then inland to Jackson to cut off Vicksburg before laying siege to it.

"Old Abe," eagle mascot for 8th Wisconsin Infantry, engaged at Vicksburg

April 27 Hooker launches campaign against Robert E. Lee's Army of Northern Virginia around Fredericksburg by sending more than 70,000 troops on a flanking movement around the Confederates.

April 29 Battle of Grand Gulf (Mississippi)

April 30 Lee learns of the threat to his flank at Chancellorsville and sends most of his forces there under Stonewall Jackson.

May 1–4 Battle of Chancellorsville

May 5 Hooker orders his troops to withdraw northward from Chancellorsville across the Rappahannock River.

May 10 Stonewall Jackson dies after being wounded accidentally by Confederate troops at Chancellorsville.

Last portrait of Stonewall Jackson

May 14 Battle of Jackson (Mississippi)

May 16 Battle of Champion's Hill (Mississippi)

May 18 Grant's forces close in on Vicksburg from the east.

May 22 Second assault by Grant in four days fails to puncture Vicksburg's defenses, compelling him to take the city slowly by siege.

June 3 Lee launches campaign that will carry his Army of Northern Virginia northward into Pennsylvania.

June 7 Hooker orders his cavalry commander, Alfred Pleasonton, to "disperse and destroy" Confederate cavalry led by Jeb Stuart, assigned to shield Lee's troops as they advance.

June 9 Battle of Brandy Station (Virginia)

June 15 Lee's troops take Winchester, Virginia, clearing the way for their advance into Maryland.

June 24 Lee's forces enter Pennsylvania; Rosecrans advances southward from Murfreesboro against Bragg around Tullahoma.

June 28 George Meade replaces Joseph Hooker as commander of the Army of the Potomac and sends John Buford's Federal cavalry division northward from Maryland into Pennsylvania in pursuit of Lee's forces.

June 30 Buford enters Gettysburg, Pennsylvania, as Confederates approach that town; Bragg withdraws from Tullahoma to Chattanooga.

Private George Murray, 114th Pennsylvania Zouaves

September 2 Federals of Ambrose Burnside's Army of the Ohio enter Knoxville, Tennessee, hailed by Unionists there.

September 6 Besieged Confederates evacuate Fort Wagner and Battery Gregg on Morris Island after Federal bombardment neutralizes Fort Sumter.

September 7 Bragg withdraws southward from Chattanooga into northern Georgia, where his forces will soon regroup below Chickamauga Creek.

September 8 Confederates repulse gunboats and transports attempting to land Federal troops at Sabine Pass in Texas.

September 10 Confederates abandon Little Rock, Arkansas.

September 19–20 Battle of Chickamauga (Georgia)

September 24 After retreating to Chattanooga, Rosecrans's army abandons nearby Lookout Mountain to Bragg's Confederates, who tighten their grip on the town.

September 30 Confederate cavalry commander Joseph Wheeler begins raiding the Federal supply line to Chattanooga.

Sergeant James Baldwin, 56th U.S. Colored Infantry

October 13 Clement Vallandigham, a prominent Peace Democrat exiled to Canada for his opposition to the Union war effort, loses his bid to be elected in absentia as governor of Ohio to War Democrat John Brough.

October 16 Grant takes charge of Federal forces between the Appalachian Mountains and the Mississippi River and replaces Rosecrans with George Thomas.

October 23 Grant arrives in Chattanooga to oversee Thomas's forces and reinforcements led by Sherman and Hooker in their forthcoming campaign against Bragg's Confederates.

October 27 Federals seize Brown's Ferry, west of Chattanooga, to open a new "Cracker Line" for hardtack and other supplies.

November 4 Bragg sends Confederates led by James Longstreet from Chattanooga to Knoxville to challenge Burnside there.

November 16 Burnside clashes with Longstreet at Campbell's Station before pulling back to Knoxville.

November 19 Lincoln delivers Gettysburg Address to dedicate the Soldiers' National Cemetery.

November 23–25 Battle of Chattanooga

November 29 Federals repulse Longstreet's attack on Fort Sanders, ending his campaign to recapture Knoxville.

November 30 Bragg's resignation as commander of the Army of Tennessee accepted by Jefferson Davis.

December 1 After failing to penetrate Lee's defenses along Mine Run in Virginia, Meade abandons his effort to force the Confederates back toward Richmond.

December 8 Lincoln issues his Proclamation of Amnesty and Reconstruction, offering pardons to most of those in rebellion willing to swear an oath of loyalty to the Union and laying out conditions for the readmission of rebellious states to the Union.

December 16 Joseph Johnston takes command of the Army of Tennessee at Dalton, Georgia.

Hardtack

1863

STONES RIVER

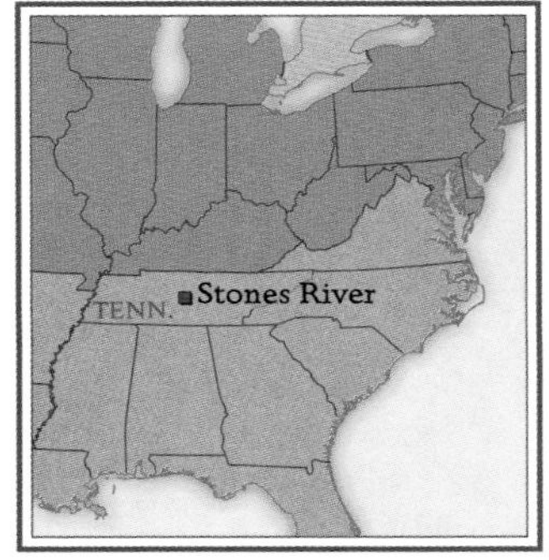

WESTERN THEATER

DECEMBER 16, 1862 William Rosecrans advances with Federal forces from Nashville, Tennessee, against Braxton Bragg's Confederates at Murfreesboro.

DECEMBER 31 Battle of Stones River (Murfreesboro) begins with a dawn attack by Bragg.

JANUARY 2, 1863 Battle of Stones River concludes with a late-day counterattack by Rosecrans.

JANUARY 3 Bragg withdraws southward from Murfreesboro.

The New Year brought no cheer to opposing forces in Tennessee, who entered into a prolonged battle along Stones River ❶ on the last day of 1862. Leading that fight for the Union was William Rosecrans, who had occupied Nashville in November after taking charge of the Army of the Cumberland. His opponent, Braxton Bragg, roundly criticized for abandoning Kentucky following the Battle of Perryville, vowed to hold the line with his Army of Tennessee at Murfreesboro ❷, 25 miles southeast of Nashville. Urged on by Lincoln, Rosecrans advanced from Nashville on December 26 with about 40,000 troops, leaving half his army behind to guard the city and his vulnerable supply lines. He would have been outnumbered had not Jefferson Davis sent one of Bragg's divisions off to defend Vicksburg, leaving him with only 35,000 men.

Rejecting the idea of defending the east bank of Stones River as Rosecrans approached from the northwest along the Nashville Pike ❸, Bragg placed his forces astride the river and prepared to attack at dawn on December 31, with the main effort coming on his left from two divisions of Hardee's corps under Major Generals John McCown ❹ and Patrick Cleburne ❺. Rosecrans was planning an attack that same day on Bragg's right, held by Major General John C. Breckinridge's corps ❻. But the Confederates struck first, shattering Brigadier General Richard Johnson's division ❼ and turning the Federal flank. Some Yankees panicked, but Philip Sheridan held firm with his division ❽ until relentless assaults by the hard-driving Cleburne pressed him back toward the turnpike, where Rosecrans rallied troops near his headquarters ❾. Massing infantry and artillery around a cedar grove called the Round Forest, or "Hell's Half Acre," he withstood furious onslaughts reminiscent of Bragg's costly attacks on the Hornet's Nest at Shiloh.

At day's end, Bragg remained confident of victory. "God has granted us a happy New Year," he wired Richmond. But Rosecrans held his ground on New Year's Day, daring Bragg to renew a battle that grew harder for his forces as the Federal line contracted and strengthened. After deliberating overnight, Bragg ordered a reluctant Breckinridge to seize the high ground ❿ east of the river on the afternoon of January 2. As Breckinridge feared, his men paid dearly for that assault, in which they succeeded in driving forces led by Brigadier Generals Horatio van Cleve ⓫ and John M. Palmer ⓬ across the river but then came under devastating cannon fire from massed Union batteries to the west. Late in the day, Federals led by Major General James Negley ⓭ counterattacked, driving the enemy back and fortifying their new line that night ⓮. His hopes dashed, Bragg withdrew the next day, beginning this fateful year on an ominous note for the Confederacy. ■

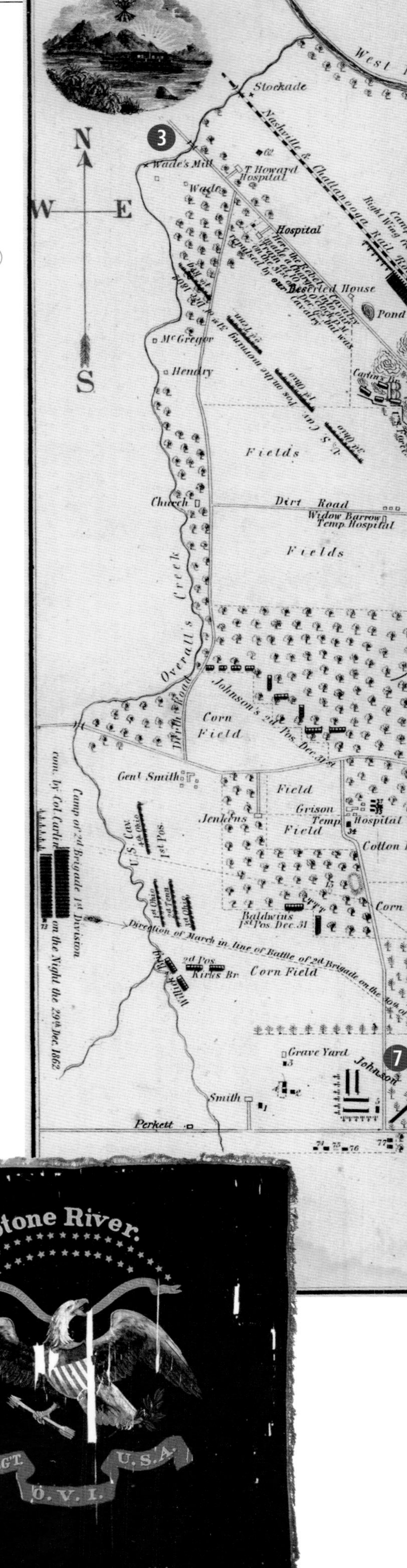

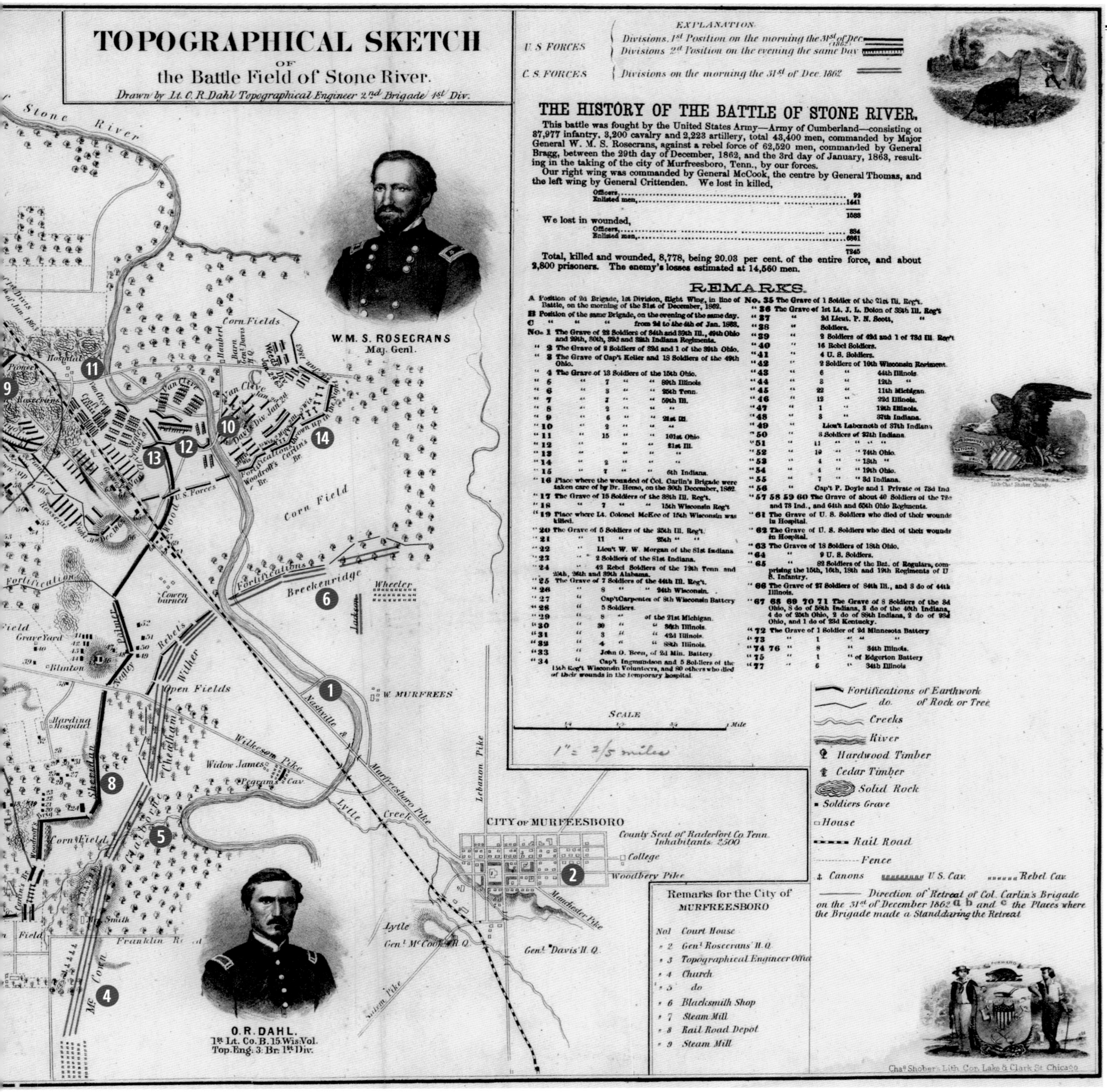

TOPOGRAPHICAL SKETCH
OF
the Battle Field of Stone River.

Drawn by Lt. O. R. Dahl Topographical Engineer 2nd Brigade 1st Div.

EXPLANATION.

U. S FORCES — Divisions. 1st Position on the morning the 31st of Dec. (1862) / Divisions 2d Position on the evening the same Day

C. S. FORCES — Divisions on the morning the 31st of Dec. 1862

THE HISTORY OF THE BATTLE OF STONE RIVER.

This battle was fought by the United States Army—Army of Cumberland—consisting of 37,977 infantry, 3,200 cavalry and 2,223 artillery, total 43,400 men, commanded by Major General W. M. S. Rosecrans, against a rebel force of 62,520 men, commanded by General Bragg, between the 29th day of December, 1862, and the 3rd day of January, 1863, resulting in the taking of the city of Murfreesboro, Tenn., by our forces.

Our right wing was commanded by General McCook, the centre by General Thomas, and the left wing by General Crittenden. We lost in killed,

Officers, ... 92
Enlisted men, ... 1441
1533

We lost in wounded,

Officers, ... 384
Enlisted men, ... 6861
7245

Total, killed and wounded, 8,778, being 20.03 per cent. of the entire force, and about 2,800 prisoners. The enemy's losses estimated at 14,560 men.

REMARKS.

A Position of 2d Brigade, 1st Division, Right Wing, in line of Battle, on the morning of the 31st of December, 1862.
B Position of the same Brigade, on the evening of the same day.
C " " " from 2d to the 4th of Jan. 1863.
No. 1 The Grave of 22 Soldiers of 34th and 39th Ill., 49th Ohio and 29th, 30th, 32d and 39th Indiana Regiments.
" 2 The Grave of 2 Soldiers of 32d and 1 of the 39th Ohio.
" 3 The Grave of Cap't Keller and 13 Soldiers of the 49th Ohio.
" 4 The Grave of 13 Soldiers of the 15th Ohio.
" 5 " 7 " " 89th Illinois
" 6 " 3 " " 25th Tenn.
" 7 " 7 " " 59th Ill.
" 8 " 2 " " "
" 9 " 6 " " 21st Ill.
" 10 " 2 " " "
" 11 " 15 " " 101st Ohio
" 12 " " " 21st Ill.
" 13 " " " "
" 14 " 2 " " "
" 15 " 7 " " 6th Indiana.
" 16 Place where the wounded of Col. Carlin's Brigade were taken care of by Dr. Hemo, on the 30th December, 1862.
" 17 The Grave of 15 Soldiers of the 38th Ill. Reg't.
" 18 " 7 " " 15th Wisconsin Reg't
" 19 Place where Lt. Colonel McKee of 15th Wisconsin was killed.
" 20 The Grave of 5 Soldiers of the 35th Ill. Reg't.
" 21 " 11 " 25th " "
" 22 " Lieu't W. W. Morgan of the 81st Indiana
" 23 " 2 Soldiers of the 81st Indiana.
" 24 " 42 Rebel Soldiers of the 13th Tenn. and 25th, 26th and 39th Alabama.
" 25 The Grave of 7 Soldiers of the 44th Ill. Reg't.
" 26 " 8 " " 24th Wisconsin.
" 27 " Cap't Carpenter of 8th Wisconsin Battery
" 28 " 5 Soldiers.
" 29 " 8 " of the 21st Michigan.
" 30 " 30 " " 36th Illinois.
" 31 " 3 " " 42d Illinois.
" 32 " 4 " " 88th Illinois.
" 33 " John O. Been, of 2d Min. Battery
" 34 " Cap't Ingmundson and 5 Soldiers of the 15th Reg't Wisconsin Volunteers, and 80 others who died of their wounds in the temporary hospital.
No. 35 The Grave of 1 Soldier of the 21st Ill. Reg't.
" 36 The Grave of 1st Lt. J. L. Dolon of 38th Ill. Reg't
" 37 " 2d Lieut. P. N. Scott, "
" 38 " Soldiers.
" 39 " 2 Soldiers of 42d and 1 of 73d Ill. Reg't
" 40 " 16 Rebel Soldiers.
" 41 " 4 U. S. Soldiers.
" 42 " 2 Soldiers of 10th Wisconsin Regiment.
" 43 " 6 " 44th Illinois.
" 44 " 3 " 12th "
" 45 " 22 " 11th Michigan.
" 46 " 12 " 22d Illinois.
" 47 " 1 " 19th Illinois.
" 48 " 3 " 37th Indiana.
" 49 " Lieu't Labernoth of 37th Indiana
" 50 " 3 Soldiers of 37th Indiana.
" 51 " 11 " " " "
" 52 " 10 " " 74th Ohio.
" 53 " 4 " " 13th "
" 54 " 4 " " 19th Ohio.
" 55 " 7 " " 3d Indiana.
" 56 " Cap't P. Doyle and 1 Private of 73d Ind.
" 57 58 59 60 The Grave of about 40 Soldiers of the 72d and 73 Ind., and 64th and 65th Ohio Regiments.
" 61 The Grave of U. S. Soldiers who died of their wounds in Hospital.
" 62 The Grave of U. S. Soldiers who died of their wounds in Hospital.
" 63 The Graves of 18 Soldiers of 18th Ohio.
" 64 " 9 U. S. Soldiers.
" 65 " 82 Soldiers of the Bat. of Regulars, comprising the 15th, 16th, 18th and 19th Regiments of U. S. Infantry.
" 66 The Grave of 27 Soldiers of 84th Ill., and 3 do of 44th Illinois.
" 67 68 69 70 71 The Grave of 8 Soldiers of the 3d Ohio, 8 do of 58th Indiana, 3 do of the 40th Indiana, 4 do of 25th Ohio, 2 do of 88th Indiana, 2 do of 93d Ohio, and 1 do of 23d Kentucky.
" 72 The Grave of 1 Soldier of 2d Minnesota Battery
" 73 " 1 " " "
" 74 76 " 8 " 34th Illinois.
" 75 " 1 " of Edgerton Battery
" 77 " 6 " 34th Illinois

SCALE ¼ ½ ¾ 1 Mile

1" = 2/5 miles

Fortifications of Earthwork
do. of Rock or Tree
Creeks
River
Hardwood Timber
Cedar Timber
Solid Rock
Soldiers Grave
House
Rail Road
Fence
Canons
U. S. Cav.
Rebel Cav.
Direction of Retreat of Col. Carlin's Brigade on the 31st of December 1862 a b and c the Places where the Brigade made a Stand during the Retreat

Remarks for the City of MURFREESBORO

No 1 Court House
" 2 Genl. Rosecrans' H. Q.
" 3 Topographical Engineer Office
" 4 Church
" 5 do
" 6 Blacksmith Shop
" 7 Steam Mill
" 8 Rail Road Depot
" 9 Steam Mill

W. M. S. ROSECRANS
Maj. Genl.

O. R. DAHL.
1st Lt. Co. B. 15 Wis. Vol.
Top. Eng. 3. Br. 1st Div.

CITY OF MURFREESBORO
County Seat of Raderfort Co Tenn. Inhabitants 2500

Chas. Shober's Lith. Cor. Lake & Clark St. Chicago

Rosecrans Regroups A map by Lieutenant Colonel O. R. Dahl of the U.S. Topographical Engineers shows how Rosecrans regrouped after Bragg smashed his right flank at Stones River on December 31. The brigade to which Dahl was attached, led by Colonel William Carlin, was caught in that flank attack at position A and fell back to position B in the new line Rosecrans formed. Late on January 2, Federals counterattacked, and Carlin's brigade crossed Stones River to position C. More than 9,000 men on each side were killed or wounded in the battle, and dozens from some hard-hit regiments were buried together at sites shown here.

Battle Flag After fighting at Stones River, men of the 18th Ohio Volunteer Infantry were allowed to commemorate the battle on their regimental flag.

⓭ **Negley's Counterattack** Federals of Negley's division cross Stones River to pursue retreating Confederates late on the afternoon of January 2.

1863

VICKSBURG

WESTERN THEATER

JULY 26, 1862 David Farragut concludes Union naval assault on Vicksburg and withdraws down the Mississippi River.

DECEMBER 29 Grant's first campaign against Vicksburg ends with Sherman's defeat at Chickasaw Bluffs.

JANUARY 29, 1863 Grant moves his headquarters from Memphis to Young's Point, Louisiana, north of Vicksburg, and tries unsuccessfully to circumvent the city's defenses.

APRIL 16, 1862 Grant launches second campaign against Vicksburg by moving forces downriver to Grand Gulf and then inland to Jackson, Mississippi, to cut off Vicksburg before laying siege to it.

APRIL 29 Battle of Grand Gulf

MAY 14 Battle of Jackson

MAY 16 Battle of Champion's Hill

MAY 18–JULY 4 Siege of Vicksburg

Grant's relentless Vicksburg campaign in 1863 capped a yearlong struggle by Federals to seize that strategic city on the Mississippi ❶. With the fall of New Orleans in April 1862 and the capture of Memphis in June, Vicksburg became the main link between Confederate states to the west and those to the east. With ferries connecting the Vicksburg, Shreveport & Texas Railroad ❷ to the Vicksburg & Jackson Railroad ❸, this hub was "the nailhead that held the South's two halves together," declared Jefferson Davis. Lincoln intended to pry it loose and split the Confederacy.

The first large-scale assault on Vicksburg was made in late June 1862 by David Farragut with a fleet carrying 3,200 troops under Brigadier General Thomas Williams ❹, assigned to dig a canal at a hairpin bend in the river ❺ so that Federal ships could avoid Vicksburg's formidable bluff-top batteries ❻. After bombarding those batteries to no effect, Farragut ran past them and linked up with Flag Officer Charles Davis ❼, whose gunboats had taken Memphis. On July 15, they were surprised by the Confederate ram *Arkansas* ❽, which steamed down the Yazoo River and wreaked havoc. Farragut later withdrew, leaving the canal unfinished. In December 1862, Grant made his first attempt on Vicksburg by advancing along the Mississippi Central Railroad while his trusted corps commander, Major General William T. Sherman, came downriver from Memphis. Grant was blocked when Confederates cut his supply line. Sherman's men landed north of Vicksburg along the Yazoo, where Rebels atop Chickasaw Bluffs ❾ stopped them cold on December 29. After that galling setback, Grant resolved to take Vicksburg in 1863 at all costs. ■

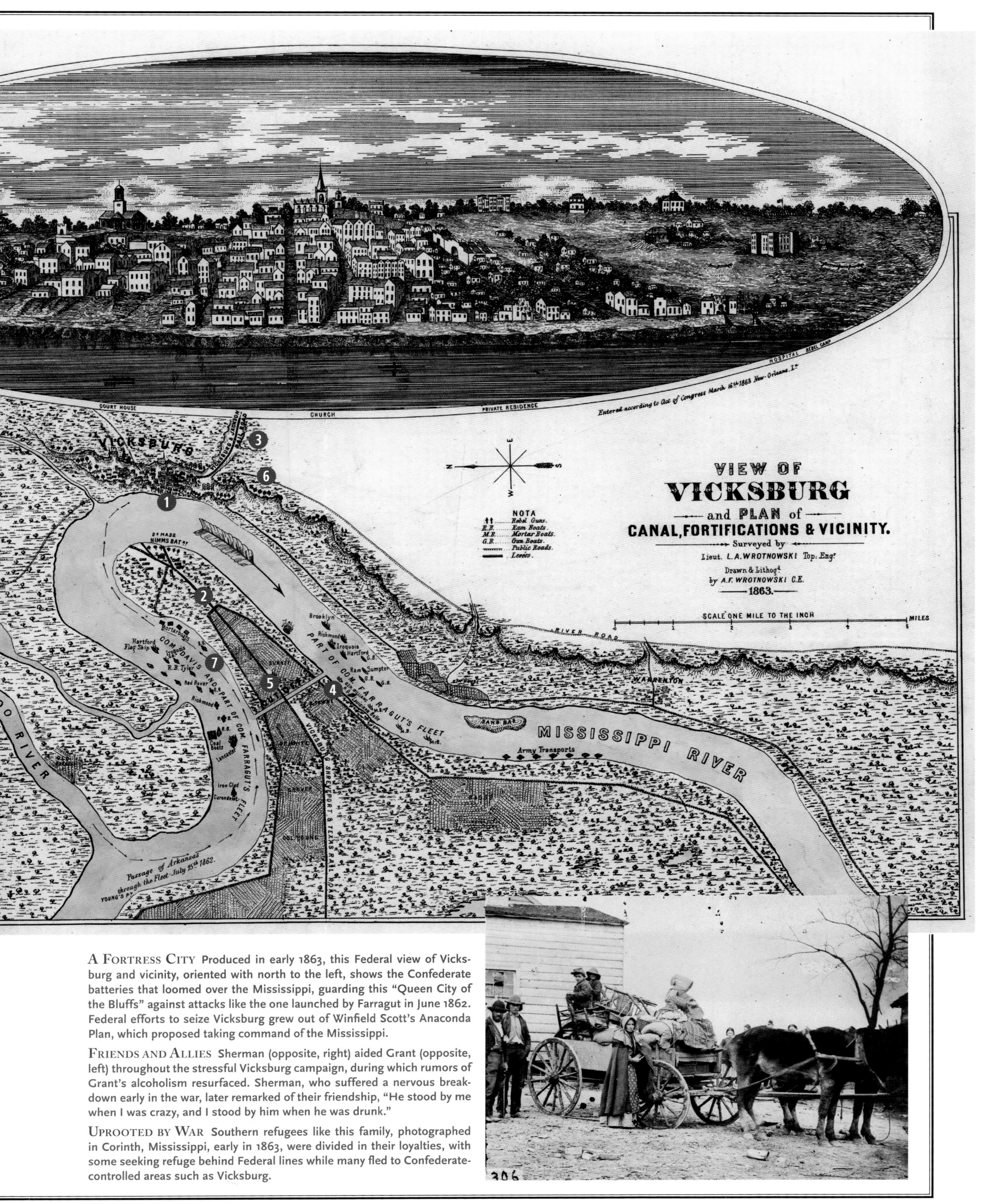

A FORTRESS CITY Produced in early 1863, this Federal view of Vicksburg and vicinity, oriented with north to the left, shows the Confederate batteries that loomed over the Mississippi, guarding this "Queen City of the Bluffs" against attacks like the one launched by Farragut in June 1862. Federal efforts to seize Vicksburg grew out of Winfield Scott's Anaconda Plan, which proposed taking command of the Mississippi.

FRIENDS AND ALLIES Sherman (opposite, right) aided Grant (opposite, left) throughout the stressful Vicksburg campaign, during which rumors of Grant's alcoholism resurfaced. Sherman, who suffered a nervous breakdown early in the war, later remarked of their friendship, "He stood by me when I was crazy, and I stood by him when he was drunk."

UPROOTED BY WAR Southern refugees like this family, photographed in Corinth, Mississippi, early in 1863, were divided in their loyalties, with some seeking refuge behind Federal lines while many fled to Confederate-controlled areas such as Vicksburg.

Grant's Bayou Experiments

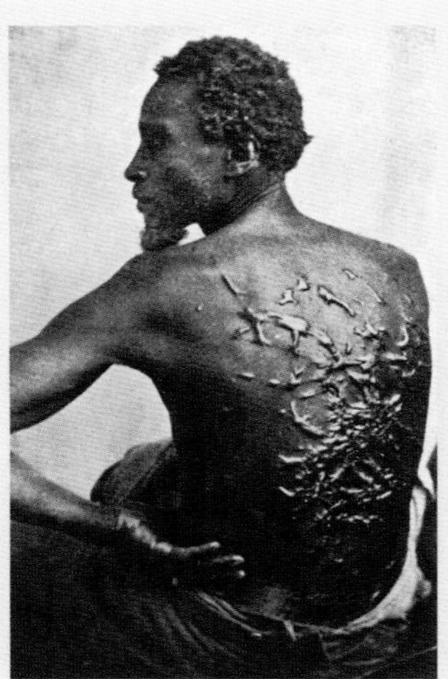

GORDON'S WAR

The impact of Grant's operations on Mississippi and surrounding states was traumatic for some civilians and liberating for others. Many farms and plantations in the region were abandoned as landowners fled the oncoming Yankees and their slaves ran off, seeking freedom behind Union lines. One such fugitive, named Gordon, fled his master in Mississippi in early 1863 and found refuge in Federal-occupied Baton Rouge, Louisiana. Under the terms of Lincoln's Emancipation Proclamation, which went into effect on January 1, he was now free and could volunteer for military service, which he promptly did.

A medical examination revealed harrowing evidence of the abuse he suffered as a slave—welt marks raised by his master's whip, shown in this memorable photograph produced by the team of McPherson & Oliver, based in Baton Rouge. Their haunting image brought Gordon to the attention of *Harper's Weekly*, which ran sketches of him along with views of Grant's siege of Vicksburg in an issue that appeared on July 4, 1863, the day Vicksburg fell. During his escape, the journal reported, Gordon rubbed his body with onions to throw pursuing bloodhounds off the scent. Despite the condition of his back, "furrowed and scarred with the traces of a whipping administered Christmas-day last," he was judged fit to serve the Union and exchanged his ragged civilian clothes for a soldier's uniform.

In late January, Grant moved his headquarters from Memphis to Young's Point, Louisiana ❶, to prepare his Army of the Tennessee for a concerted assault on Vicksburg ❷. Winter rains and flooding all but ruled out an attack before spring, but Grant kept his men busy conducting what he called "experiments" in the surrounding bayous aimed at circumventing Vicksburg's stout defenses along the Mississippi and lower Yazoo Rivers. He assigned Sherman's corps to continue work on the canal begun the previous summer ❸, but Confederates negated that project by extending their batteries below Vicksburg to cover the lower end of the canal ❹ so that it would not offer Federals safe passage. A larger effort to dredge a shipping channel in eastern Louisiana that would bypass a long stretch of the Mississippi above and below Vicksburg proved impractical. Only by taking the city from the east, where it was susceptible to attack, Grant concluded, could he neutralize the big guns along the Mississippi and give Federals command of the river.

One way to reach Vicksburg's vulnerable back door was to land troops along the Yazoo River northeast of Vicksburg, beyond the batteries and obstructions at the lower end of that river ❺. In early February, engineers blew a levee on the Mississippi, enabling transports carrying Union troops to enter Moon Lake ❻ and Yazoo Pass ❼ and begin a circuitous journey to the upper Yazoo River. Confederates anticipated that move, however, and stalled the Federals by sinking ships in the channel at Fort Pemberton ❽, where cannon fire prompted them to reverse course. "We could not go ahead," recalled one Federal. "Suddenly the orders came to turn about and steam as fast as possible to a place of safety." Grant made another try in March by sending a fleet under Admiral David Porter up Steele's Bayou ❾. Porter hoped to reach the Yazoo by way of Rolling Fork and the Sunflower River ❿ but wound up in treacherously narrow channels under enemy fire and backed out. These failed experiments led Grant to take a radically different approach in the spring, confounding his opponents. ■

❸ A Canal to Nowhere Men of Sherman's corps toil on a canal that was left uncompleted at the bend in the Mississippi near Vicksburg. Many of the troops laboring here fell ill, and Sherman dismissed the project as a "pure waste of human effort."

A Maze of Waterways This revealing map, published in Mobile, Alabama, in May 1863, offers abundant information on the backwaters above Vicksburg, which local Confederates knew far better than their opponents. Grant's efforts to find a way around obstacles on the lower Yazoo River—including a Rebel fort on Snyder's Bluff and a "raft" blocking the river below—faltered in this baffling maze of rivers and bayous.

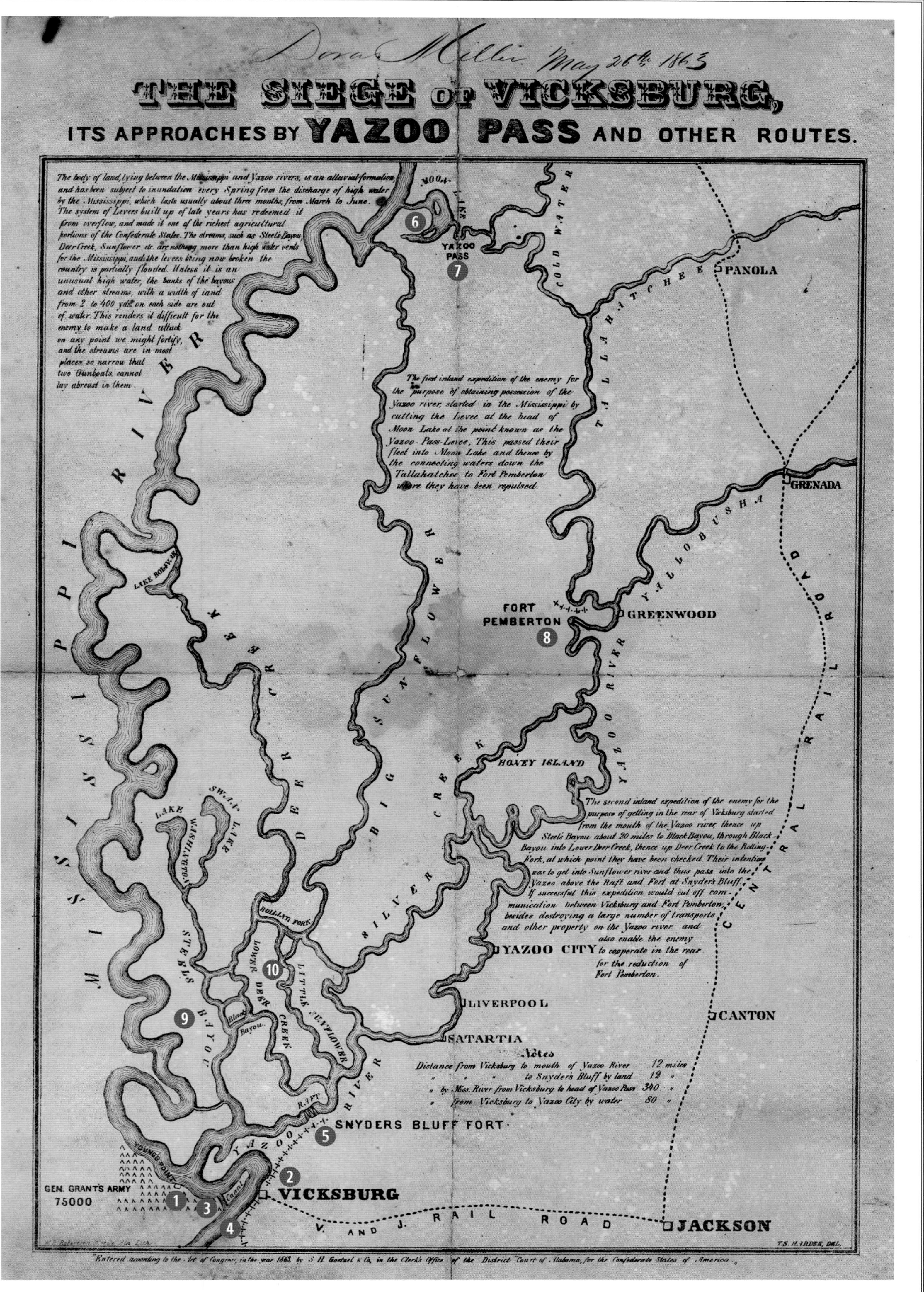
Dora Miller May 26th 1863
THE SIEGE OF VICKSBURG,
ITS APPROACHES BY YAZOO PASS AND OTHER ROUTES.
The body of land, lying between the Mississippi and Yazoo rivers, is an alluvial formation, and has been subject to inundation every Spring from the discharge of high water by the Mississippi, which lasts usually about three months, from March to June. The system of Levees built up of late years has redeemed it from overflow, and made it one of the richest agricultural portions of the Confederate States. The streams, such as Steel's Bayou, Deer Creek, Sunflower etc. are nothing more than high water vents for the Mississippi, and the levees being now broken the country is partially flooded. Unless it is an unusual high water, the banks of the bayous and other streams, with a width of land from 2 to 400 yds. on each side are out of water. This renders it difficult for the enemy to make a land attack on any point we might fortify, and the streams are in most places so narrow that two Gunboats cannot lay abreast in them.
MOON LAKE
YAZOO PASS
COLD WATER
TALLAHATCHEE
PANOLA
MISSISSIPPI RIVER
The first inland expedition of the enemy for the purpose of obtaining possession of the Yazoo river, started in the Mississippi by cutting the Levee at the head of Moon Lake at the point known as the Yazoo Pass Levee. This passed their fleet into Moon Lake and thence by the connecting waters down the Tallahatchee to Fort Pemberton where they have been repulsed.
GRENADA
YALLOBUSHA
LAKE BOLIVAR
FORT PEMBERTON
GREENWOOD
DEER CREEK
BIG SUNFLOWER
YAZOO RIVER
CENTRAL RAIL ROAD
HONEY ISLAND
SILVER CREEK
The second inland expedition of the enemy for the purpose of getting in the rear of Vicksburg started from the mouth of the Yazoo river, thence up Steel's Bayou about 20 miles to Black Bayou, through Black Bayou into Lower Deer Creek, thence up Deer Creek to the Rolling Fork, at which point they have been checked. Their intention was to get into Sunflower river and thus pass into the Yazoo above the Raft and Fort at Snyder's Bluff. If successful this expedition would cut off communication between Vicksburg and Fort Pemberton, besides destroying a large number of transports and other property on the Yazoo river and also enable the enemy to cooperate in the rear for the reduction of Fort Pemberton.
LAKE WASHINGTON
SWAN LAKE
ROLLING FORK
STEELS BAYOU
LOWER DEER CREEK
LITTLE SUNFLOWER
Black Bayou
YAZOO CITY
LIVERPOOL
CANTON
SATARTIA
Notes
Distance from Vicksburg to mouth of Yazoo River 12 miles
" " " to Snyder's Bluff by land 12 "
" by Miss. River from Vicksburg to head of Yazoo Pass 340 "
" from Vicksburg to Yazoo City by water 80 "
RAFT
SNYDERS BLUFF FORT
YAZOO RIVER
YOUNGS POINT
GEN. GRANT'S ARMY 75000
Canal
VICKSBURG
V. AND J. RAIL ROAD
JACKSON
T.S. HARDEE, Del.
Entered according to the Act of Congress, in the year 1863, by S. H. Goetzel & Co, in the Clerk's Office of the District Court of Alabama, for the Confederate States of America.
1
2
3
4
5
6
7
8
9
10

March on Vicksburg

March 29–May 18, 1863

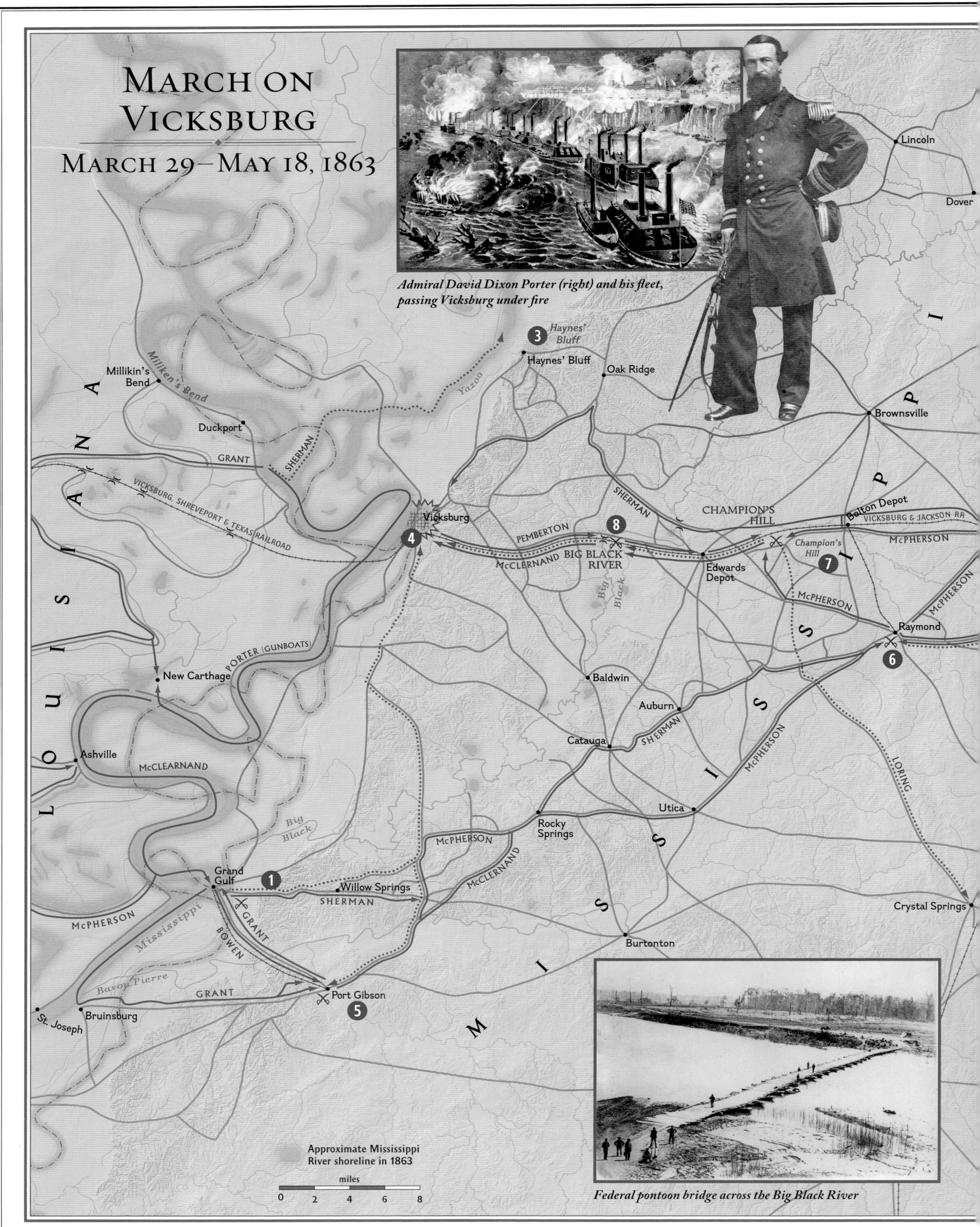

Admiral David Dixon Porter (right) and his fleet, passing Vicksburg under fire

Federal pontoon bridge across the Big Black River

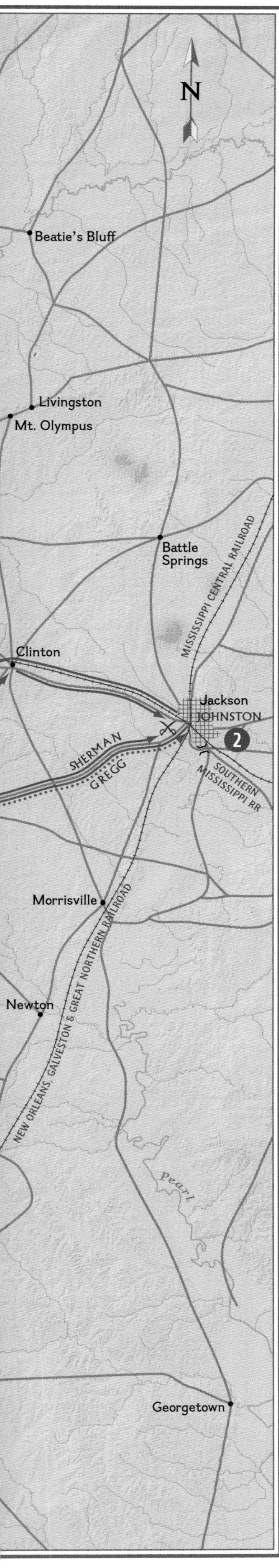

1863 | VICKSBURG

Closing the Trap

Unable to get at Vicksburg from the north, Grant decided in April to move his army south along the west bank of the Mississippi and cross the river near Grand Gulf ❶. From there, he would advance on Jackson ❷, a vital rail junction whose capture would isolate Vicksburg as Grant closed in from the east. Sherman argued against this roundabout approach, which would cut Grant off from his base of supplies and place his forces in jeopardy if Confederates stationed around Vicksburg moved out against them. To keep the city's defenders pinned down, Grant left Sherman's corps behind to stage a diversion at Haynes' Bluff ❸. Porter's fleet swept past Vicksburg's batteries ❹ on the night of April 16 with guns blazing and ferried Grant's troops across the river in late April. Sherman's diversion kept Major General John Pemberton, the Confederate commander in Vicksburg, from shifting troops south to bolster a small force at Port Gibson ❺, which was defeated by Grant on May 1. He then brushed aside Confederates at Raymond ❻ and took Jackson on May 14, driving a wedge between Pemberton and reinforcements assembling there under General Joseph Johnston. Belatedly, Pemberton came out from Vicksburg to challenge the approaching Yankees at Champion's Hill ❼ on May 16. Grant did not have Sherman with him there, but Major General James McPherson carried the day with his corps, forcing Pemberton to retreat to Vicksburg across the Big Black River ❽. He burned the bridge behind him, but Grant would soon span the river with pontoons and lay siege to Vicksburg. After 30 years in service, Pemberton remarked, his career was ending "in disaster and disgrace." ■

John C. Pemberton

Grant's Circuitous Advance As detailed in this National Geographic map, Grant's army reached Vicksburg's vulnerable landward side by sweeping around to the south and east of the city like a snake encircling its prey. Sherman's corps formed the tail, remaining behind to distract Vicksburg's defenders until the rest of the army crossed near Grand Gulf, at which point Sherman followed on the same path, joining Grant's other forces as they laid siege to Vicksburg in May.

ORDER OF BATTLE

UNION FORCES

ARMY OF THE TENNESSEE
Grant | 70,000 men

IX CORPS *Parke*
1ST DIVISION *Welsh*
Brigades Bowman, Leasure
2ND DIVISION *Potter*
Brigades Griffin, Ferrero, Christ

XII CORPS *McClernand*
9TH DIVISION Osterhaus
Brigades Lee, Lindsey
10TH DIVISION *Sixth*
Brigades Burbridge, Landram
12TH DIVISION *Hovey*
Brigades McGinnis, Slack
14TH DIVISION *Carr*
Brigades Benton, Lawler

XV CORPS *Sherman*
1ST DIVISION *Steele*
Brigades Manter, Thayer
2ND DIVISION *Blair*
Brigades G. A. Smith, T. K. Smith, Ewing
3RD DIVISION *Tuttle*
Brigades Buckland, Mower, Matthies

XVI CORPS *Washburn*
1ST DIVISION *W. S. Smith*
Brigades Loomis, Hicks, Cockerill, Sanford
4TH DIVISION *Lauman*
Brigades Pugh, Hall, Bryant

PROVISIONAL DIVISION
Kimball
Brigades Engelmann, Richmond, Montgomery

XVII CORPS *McPherson*
3RD DIVISION Logan
Brigades J. E. Smith, Leggett, Stevenson
6TH DIVISION *McArthur*
Brigades Reid, Ransom, Hall
7TH DIVISION *Quinby*
Brigades Sanborn, Holmes, Boomer
HERRON'S DIVISION
Brigades Van Derveer, Orme

CONFEDERATE FORCES

DEPARTMENT OF MISSISSIPPI & EAST LOUISIANA
Pemberton | 49,000 men

FORNEY'S DIVISION
Brigades Hébert, Moore

SMITH'S DIVISION
Brigades Baldwin, Vaughn, Shoup

LORING'S DIVISION
Brigades Tilghman, Buford, Featherston

STEVENSON'S DIVISION
Brigades Barton, Cumming, S. D. Lee, Reynolds, Waul

BOWEN'S DIVISION
Brigades Cockrell, Green

CONFEDERATE FORCES AT JACKSON, MISSISSIPPI
Johnston | 6,000 men

Brigade Gregg

THE SIEGE OF VICKSBURG

Pemberton's defeat at Champion's Hill stunned civilians in Vicksburg ❶, who watched in dismay as their downtrodden defenders returned. "Wan, hollow-eyed, ragged, footsore, bloody, the men limped along unarmed," one observer wrote. Pemberton still had more than 20,000 troops in Vicksburg, however, and its perimeter had been fortified with earthworks and forts that covered primary avenues of approach. "(Confederate works are shown on the map here in red.) Grant thought the Rebels were so demoralized that he could take the city by storm. But attacks on May 19 by McPherson's 17th Corps ❷ and the 13th Corps ❸ under Major General John McClernand—an inept political protégé of Lincoln's whom Grant later replaced with a thorough professional, Major General Edward O. C. Ord—got nowhere. To the north, troops of Sherman's 15th Corps advanced to Stockade Redan ❹ before being pinned down there by murderous fire. "This is a death struggle," Sherman wrote afterward, "and will be terrible."

Grant tried again on May 22 following a massive bombardment. When the big guns fell silent, one Confederate recalled, "there seemed to spring almost from the bowels of the earth dense masses of Federal troops," advancing with bayonets fixed. Some of the fiercest fighting occurred at the Railroad Redoubt ❺, where troops led by Brigadier General Michael Lawler of McClernand's corps braved searing fire and raised flags on the parapet before being driven back. Assured by McClernand that his men were making headway, Grant kept up the fight, compounding his losses to no avail.

Federals then laid siege to Vicksburg, constructing siege batteries and extending their own trenches (shown in blue) ever closer to enemy lines. With reinforcements from Memphis, Grant's army grew to 70,000 men, enough to deter any attempt by Joseph Johnston to relieve Vicksburg from the east. Cut off by land and by water, where Porter's fleet held sway, troops and civilians in Vicksburg went hungry and were shaken by artillery fire day and night. On June 25, Federals detonated a mine below the Great Redoubt ❻, leaving a gaping crater. Grant's men were unable to break through there, but another explosion on July 1 proved costly for Confederates and reminded Pemberton that his foes were growing stronger as his own resources dwindled. On July 4, he surrendered Vicksburg, leaving the Union in command of the Mississippi everywhere but at Port Hudson, Louisiana, where besieged Confederates gave up when they learned of Vicksburg's fate. "The Father of Waters again goes unvexed to the sea," Lincoln declared triumphantly. ■

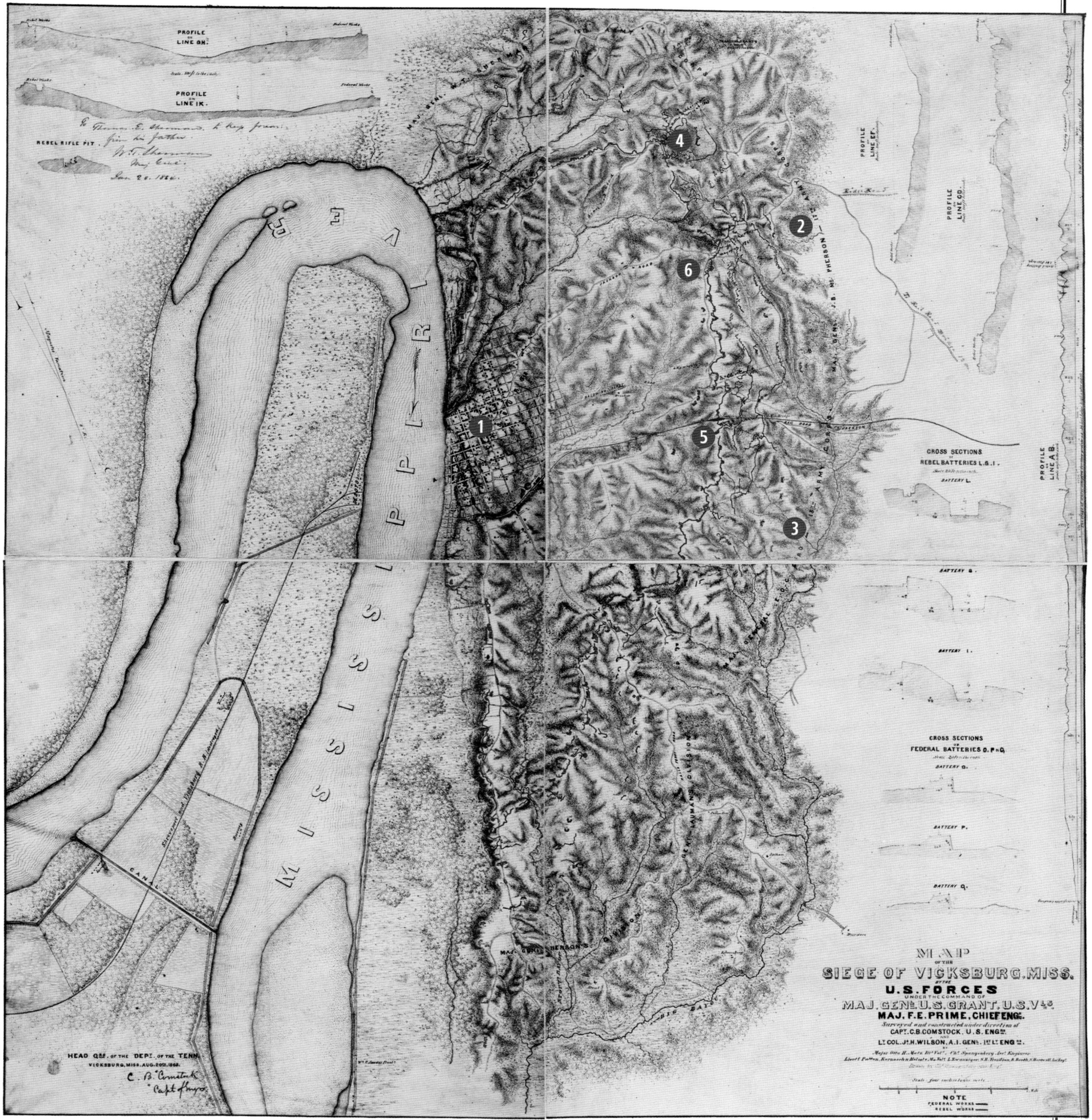
PROFILE ON LINE GH.
PROFILE ON LINE IK.
REBEL RIFLE PIT.
MISSISSIPPI RIVER
1
2
3
4
5
6
CROSS SECTIONS OF REBEL BATTERIES L.G.I.
BATTERY L.
BATTERY G.
BATTERY I.
CROSS SECTIONS OF FEDERAL BATTERIES O.P.&Q.
BATTERY O.
BATTERY P.
BATTERY Q.
PROFILE LINE EF.
PROFILE LINE CD.
PROFILE LINE AB.
CANAL
HEAD QRS. OF THE DEPT. OF THE TENN.
VICKSBURG, MISS. AUG. 20th 1863.
C. B. Comstock
Capt of Engrs.
MAP
OF THE
SIEGE OF VICKSBURG, MISS.
BY THE
U.S. FORCES
UNDER THE COMMAND OF
MAJ. GENL. U.S. GRANT, U.S.VLS.
MAJ. F.E. PRIME, CHIEF ENGR.
Surveyed and constructed under direction of
CAPT. C.B. COMSTOCK, U.S. ENGRS.
AND
LT. COL. JS. H. WILSON, A.I. GENL. 1ST LT. ENGRS.
NOTE
FEDERAL WORKS
REBEL WORKS

1

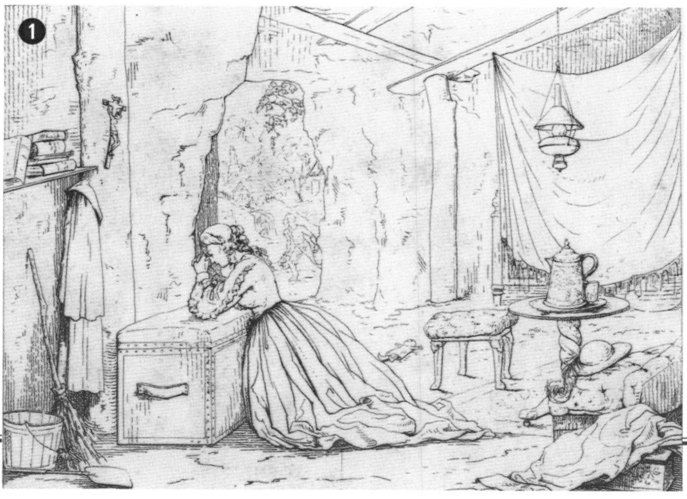

TRENCH WARFARE A map produced by Grant's engineers shows the nine-mile-long line of trenches and redoubts Pemberton's Confederates held for a month and a half as Grant's forces closed in, digging zigzag trenches toward the Confederate works. Within Vicksburg, civilians dug their own fortifications, excavating caves in the hillsides to avoid Federal shells that went astray and exploded in town.

❶ PRAYING FOR DELIVERANCE Sheltered in a cave reinforced with timber to keep it from collapsing, a resident of Vicksburg kneels in prayer during the siege.

❺ REBUFFED AT THE REDOUBT Following their flag-bearer, Federals of the 22nd Iowa Infantry meet with a devastating volley from Confederates defending the Railroad Redoubt on May 22. One Union soldier who witnessed Grant's futile attacks on Vicksburg's well-fortified defenders concluded bleakly, "It was like marching men to their graves in line of battle."

1863

CHANCELLORSVILLE

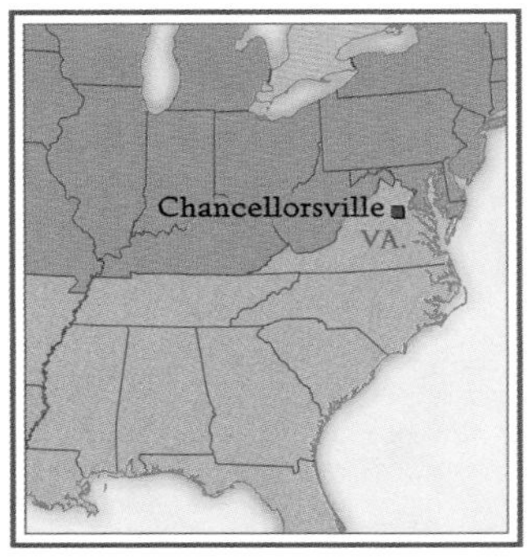

EASTERN THEATER

JANUARY 26, 1863 Joseph Hooker replaces Ambrose Burnside as commander of the Army of the Potomac.

APRIL 27 Hooker launches his flanking movement against Robert E. Lee's Army of Northern Virginia at Fredericksburg.

APRIL 29 Federals cross the Rappahannock below Fredericksburg to hold Lee's army in place while the flanking movement proceeds.

APRIL 30 Lee learns of the threat to his flank near Chancellorsville and sends most of his forces there under Stonewall Jackson.

MAY 1–4 Battle of Chancellorsville

Following the disastrous Battle of Fredericksburg, Fighting Joe Hooker replaced Ambrose Burnside as commander of the Army of the Potomac, encamped east of the Rappahannock below Falmouth ❶, and drew up a promising plan of attack against Lee's forces behind Fredericksburg ❷. With an army twice as large as Lee's, Hooker hoped to put enough pressure on Fredericksburg to keep Confederates in place there while sending most of his forces around Lee's left flank. Lee would have to withdraw southward, Hooker reckoned, or abandon his prepared defenses "and give us battle on our ground, where certain destruction awaits him."

In late April, Hooker sent more than 70,000 men upriver to outflank Lee, with the Fifth, 11th, and 12th Corps under Major Generals George Meade, Oliver Howard, and Henry Slocum crossing at Kelly's Ford ❸ while Major General Darius Couch's Second Corps crossed at U.S. Ford ❹. Meanwhile, the First and Sixth Corps under Major Generals John Reynolds and John Sedgwick crossed on pontoon bridges below Fredericksburg ❺. Major General Daniel Sickles's Third Corps and the First Corps joined the flanking movement later. On April 30, Lee learned of that threat and sent forces under Stonewall Jackson to bolster Major General Richard Anderson's division near Chancellorsville ❻, on the eastern edge of the densely forested Wilderness. Lee was giving battle on what Hooker called "our ground," but Confederates knew this country better than he did. ■

HOOKER AND STAFF Joseph Hooker (second from right), seated with his staff officers, caused controversy before taking command by denouncing his predecessor, Ambrose Burnside.

❺ Bridging the Rappahannock Troops of Reynolds's First Corps cross the Rappahannock south of Fredericksburg on the morning of April 29 to secure the far shore, allowing Federal engineers to lay down pontoon bridges. By afternoon the bridges were completed and Reynolds's men linked up with Sedgwick's Sixth Corps on the south bank.

Hooker's Advance As shown in this National Geographic map, Hooker sent Reynolds and Sedgwick across the river below Fredericksburg to divert Lee's attention from the massive Federal movement. When Lee shifted the bulk of his forces to Chancellorsville on April 30 in response, he left Major General Jubal Early with little more than a division to hold Fredericksburg, but Federals did not attack there until May 3.

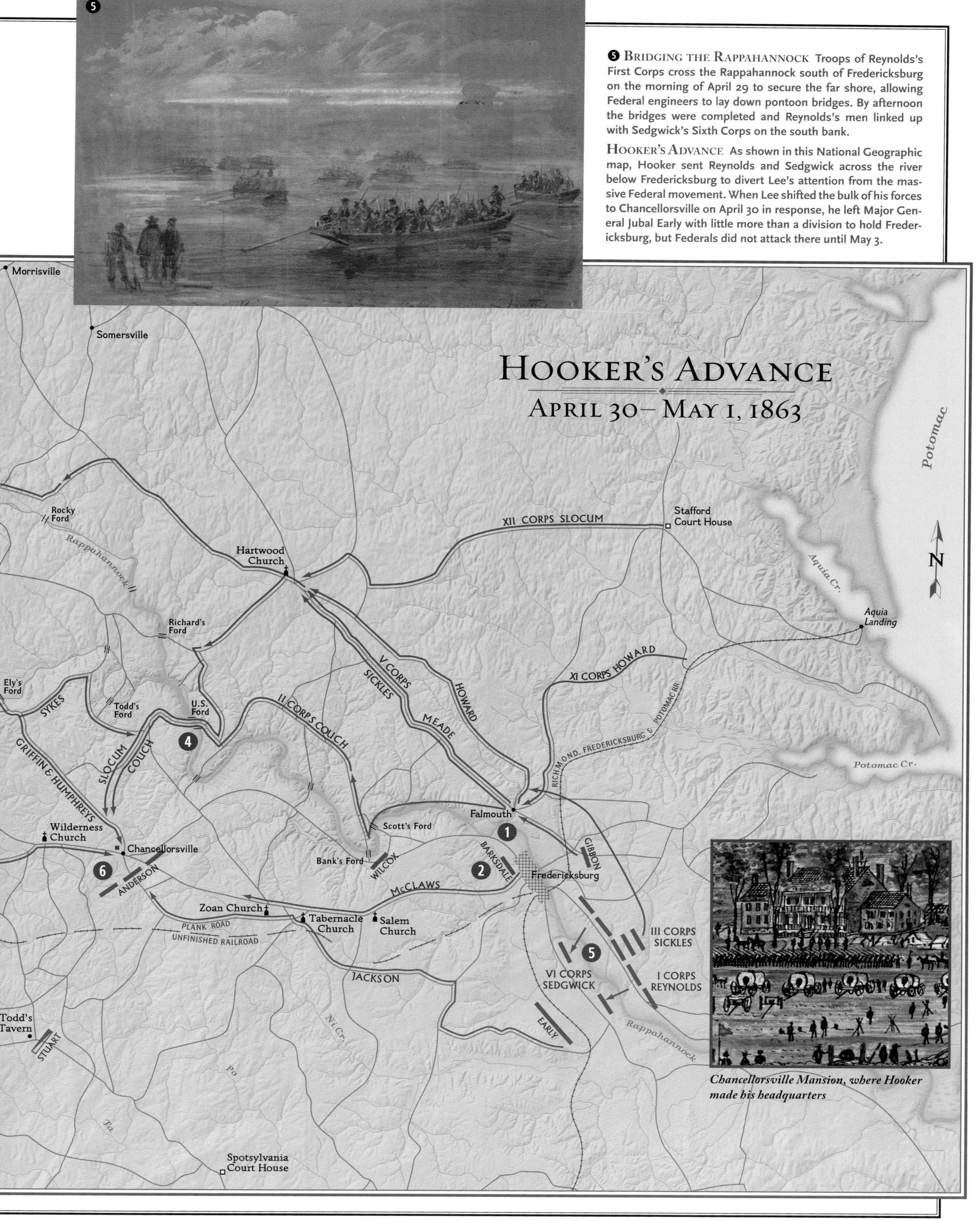

Chancellorsville Mansion, where Hooker made his headquarters

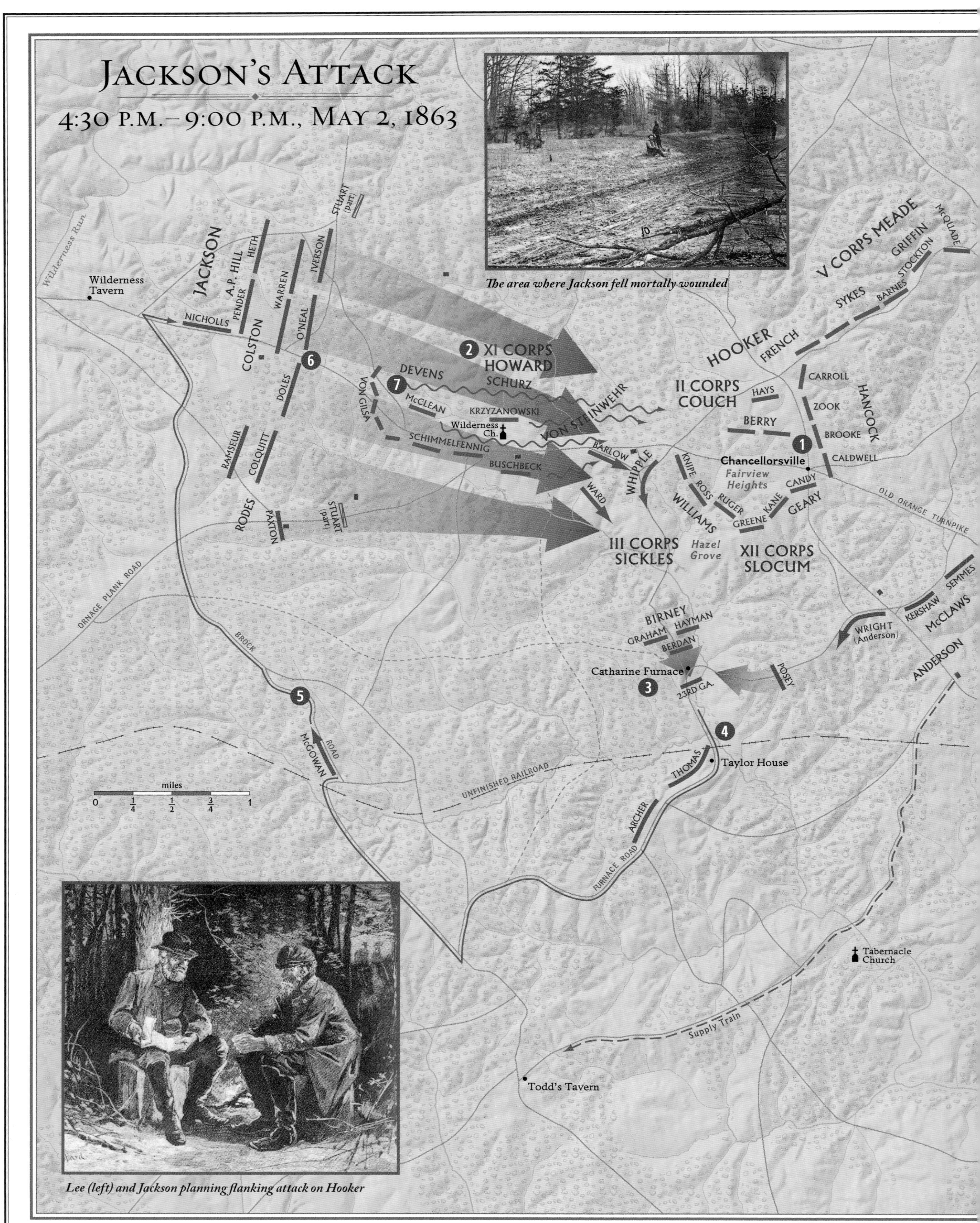

The area where Jackson fell mortally wounded

Lee (left) and Jackson planning flanking attack on Hooker

1863 | CHANCELLORSVILLE

JACKSON STRIKES

On May 1, Federals advancing east toward Fredericksburg came up against strong Confederate opposition, prompting Hooker to halt his advance around the Chancellorsville crossroads ❶. That night, Jackson met with Lee and, using information provided by Jedediah Hotchkiss, proposed to lead some 30,000 troops around Hooker's right flank and launch a surprise attack on Howard's 11th Corps ❷.

On May 2, Federals under Brigadier General David Birney of Sickles's corps clashed at Catharine Furnace ❸ with the tail end of Jackson's column as it turned south down the Furnace Road ❹. Assuming that the Rebels were retreating southward, Hooker and his generals remained complacent as Jackson's men swung north on the Brock Road ❺ undetected and prepared to strike. Although Howard had been warned of a possible flank attack, most of his 11th Corps units were facing south when Jackson's forces came barreling in from the west, led by the division of Brigadier General Robert Rodes ❻. "Forward, men, over friend or foe," shouted Rodes as his troops hit the exposed division of Brigadier General Charles Devens ❼ with a staggering impact. To one Federal, it seemed as if "the whole army had gone to pieces in a panic." The collapse of Howard's corps left Jackson in position to seize Chancellorsville and secure victory. That evening, however, he was accidentally shot by Confederates while reconnoitering and fell critically wounded, losing his arm the next day and his life a week later. ■

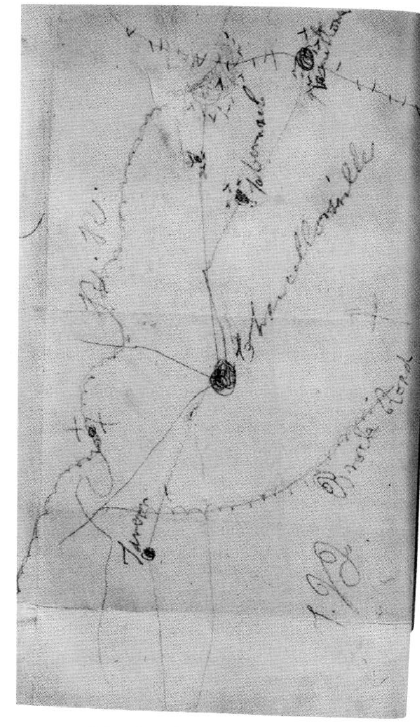

The sketch map Jackson used to plan his flank march

OUTFLANKING HOOKER Stonewall Jackson, whose stated goal as a commander was always to "mystify, mislead and surprise the enemy," did just that on May 2 by outflanking Hooker, as shown here, while Hooker was attempting to outflank Lee. Jeb Stuart's cavalry helped screen Jackson's flanking march, which Sickles detected at Catharine's Furnace but misinterpreted. "I think it is a retreat," he told Hooker.

ORDER OF BATTLE

UNION FORCES

ARMY OF THE POTOMAC
Hooker | 134,000 men

I CORPS *Reynolds*
1ST DIVISION *Wadsworth*
Brigades Phelps, Cutler, Paul, Meredith
2ND DIVISION *Robinson*
Brigades Root, Baxter, Leonard
3RD DIVISION *Doubleday*
Brigades Rowley, Stone

II CORPS *Couch*
1ST DIVISION *Hancock*
Brigades Caldwell, Meagher, Zook, Brooke
2ND DIVISION *Gibbon*
Brigades Sully, Owen, Hall
3RD DIVISION *French*
Brigades Carroll, Hays, MacGregor

III CORPS *Sickles*
1ST DIVISION *Birney*
Brigades Graham, Ward, Hayman
2ND DIVISION *Berry*
Brigades Carr, Revere, Mott
3RD DIVISION *Whipple*
Brigades Franklin, Bowman, Berdan, Von Puttkammer

V CORPS *Meade*
1ST DIVISION *Griffin*
Brigades Barnes, McQuade, Stockton
2ND DIVISION *Sykes*
Brigades Ayres, Burbank, O'Rorke
3RD DIVISION *Humphreys*
Brigades Tyler, Allabach

VI CORPS *Sedgwick*
1ST DIVISION *Brooks*
Brigades Brown, Bartlett, Russell
2ND DIVISION *Howe*
Brigades Grant, Neill
3RD DIVISION *Newton*
Brigades Shaler, Browne, Wheaton, McCarthy

LIGHT DIVISION
Burnham

XI CORPS *Howard*
1ST DIVISION Devens
Brigades Von Gilsa, McLean
2ND DIVISION
Von Steinwehr
Brigades Buschbeck, Barlow
3RD DIVISION *Schurz*
Brigades Schimmelfennig, Krzyzanowski

XII CORPS *Slocum*
1ST DIVISION *Williams*
Brigades Knipe, Ross, Ruger
2ND DIVISION *Geary*
Brigades Candy, Kane, Greene

CAVALRY CORPS *Stoneman*
1ST DIVISION *Pleasonton*
Brigades Davis, Devin
2ND DIVISION *Averell*
Brigades Sargent, McIntosh
3RD DIVISION *Gregg*
Brigades Kilpatrick, Wyndham

CONFEDERATE FORCES

ARMY OF NORTHERN VIRGINIA
Lee | 59,000 men

FIRST CORPS *Lee*
McLAWS'S DIVISION
Brigades Wofford, Semmes, Kershaw, Barksdale
ANDERSON'S DIVISION
Brigades Wilcox, Wright, Mahone, Posey, Perry

SECOND CORPS *Jackson*
HILL'S DIVISION
Brigades Heth, Thomas, McGowan, Archer, Pender
D. H. HILL'S DIVISION
Brigades Rodes, Colquitt, Ramseur, Doles, Iverson
EARLY'S DIVISION
Brigades Gordon, Hoke, Smith, Hays
TRIMBLE'S DIVISION
Brigades Paxton, Jones, Colston, Nicholls

CAVALRY *Stuart*
Brigades Hampton, F. Lee, W. H. F. Lee, Jones

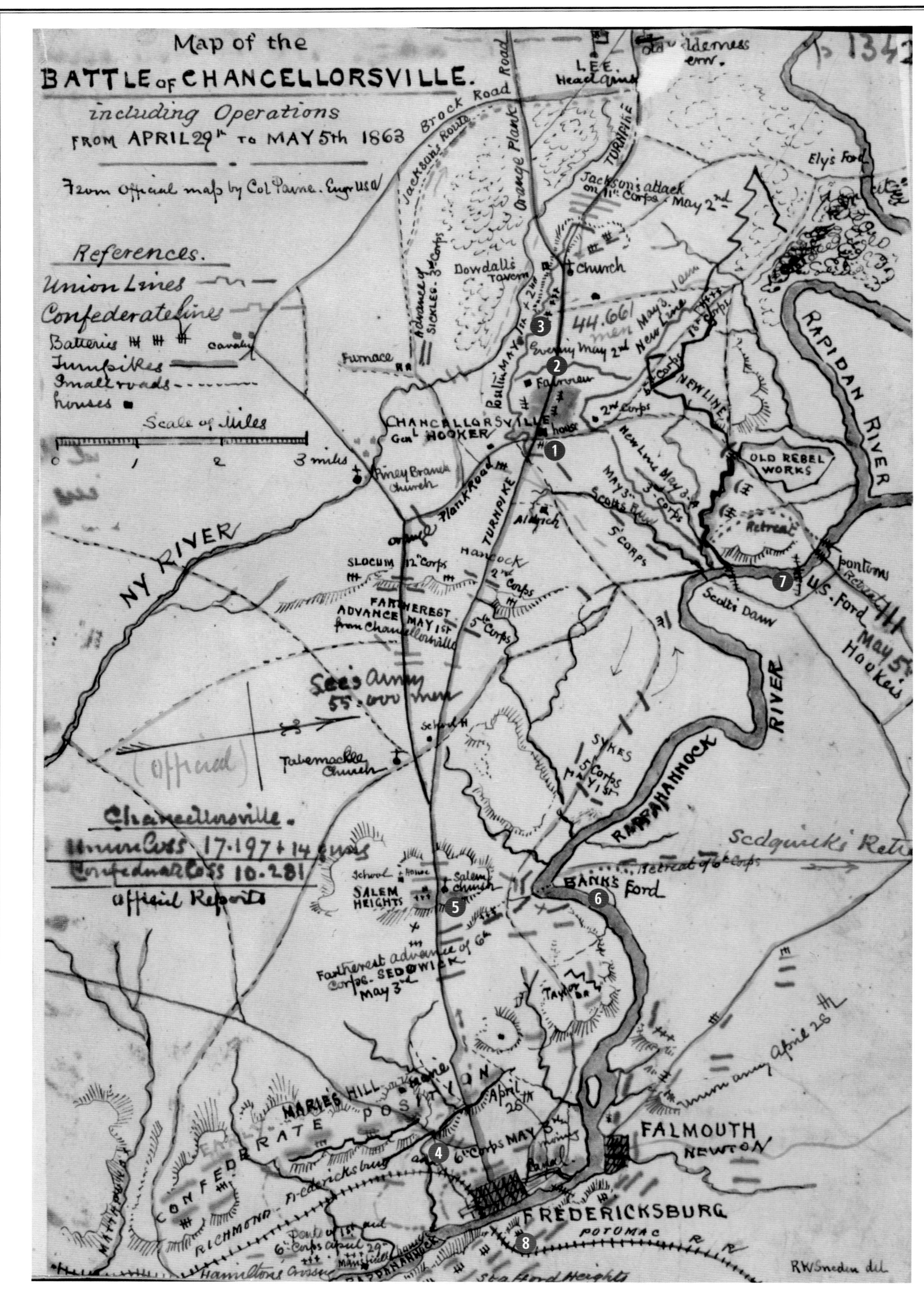

Map of the
BATTLE of CHANCELLORSVILLE.
including Operations
FROM APRIL 29th to MAY 5th 1863
From Official map by Col Paine. Engr USA
References.
Union Lines
Confederate lines
Batteries
cavalry
Turnpikes
Small roads
houses
Scale of Miles
3 miles
LEE. Head Qrs
Brock Road
Orange Plank Road
TURNPIKE
Jackson's Route
Jackson's attack on 11th Corps. May 2nd
Ely's Ford
Dowdall's Tavern
Church
Advance of SICKLES. 3rd Corps
44.661 men May 3.
Evening May 2nd
New Line
Furnace
Fairview
CHANCELLORSVILLE
Genl HOOKER
house
2nd Corps
NEW LINE
RAPIDAN RIVER
OLD REBEL WORKS
Finey Branch Church
Plank Road
TURNPIKE
Aldrich
Scott's Run
5 CORPS
Retreat
pontoons
U.S. Ford
Scott's Dam
May 5th Hooker's
NY RIVER
SLOCUM 12th Corps
Hancock 2nd Corps
FARTHEREST ADVANCE MAY 1ST from Chancellorsville
5th Corps
Lee's Army 55.000 men
School H
Tabernackle Church
(official)
SYKES 5 Corps MAY 1st
RIVER
RAPPAHANNOCK
Chancellorsville.
Union Loss 17.197 + 14 guns
Confederate Loss 10.281
Official Reports
Sedgwick's Retreat
Retreat of 6th Corps
BANK'S Ford
School house
SALEM HEIGHTS
Salem church
Farthereast advance of 6th Corps. SEDGWICK May 3rd
Taylor's
Union army April 28
MARIES HILL
POSITION
April 28
CONFEDERATE
6th Corps MAY 3rd
FALMOUTH
NEWTON
FREDERICKSBURG
RICHMOND Fredericksburg
POTOMAC R R
Hamiltons Crossing
RAPPAHANNOCK
Stafford Heights
RWSneden del

A Knockout Blow to Hooker

Early on May 3, Confederates led by Jeb Stuart, replacing the fallen Jackson, advanced toward Hooker's forces concentrated around Chancellorsville ❶. To consolidate the line held by Sickles's Third Corps across the Orange Turnpike ❷, Hooker withdrew troops and artillery from the high ground at Hazel Grove ❸, which was seized by Brigadier General James Archer's Confederates. That gave Colonel E. Porter Alexander's artillery a fine platform from which to bombard the Federal position. Hooker was knocked unconscious around 9 A.M. when a shell struck his headquarters. He remained dazed for nearly an hour, during which time an appeal for help from Sickles went unheeded and his line crumbled. Hooker then relinquished command temporarily to Darius Couch after instructing him to pull back from Chancellorsville toward the Rappahannock.

That same morning, Sedgwick's Sixth Corps stormed Marye's Heights at Fredericksburg ❹, avenging the Union defeat here in December with a daring bayonet charge that overwhelmed Jubal Early's outnumbered Confederates. Sedgwick had orders to press on to Chancellorsville, but his breakthrough at Fredericksburg came too late to foil Lee, who held Hooker at bay that afternoon and sent the division of Major General Lafayette McLaws to oppose Sedgwick at Salem Church ❺. By committing more troops there on May 4, Lee forced Sedgwick to retreat across the Rappahannock ❻ and took the fight out of Hooker, who ordered a wholesale withdrawal across U.S. Ford ❼ on May 5. "Hooker's day is over," concluded Major General Winfield Scott Hancock, who would soon have ample opportunity to show that Lee was not invincible. ■

❽ GUNS OVER THE RAPPAHANNOCK Federal artillery here on Stafford Heights, across from Fredericksburg on the north bank of the Rappahannock, shielded troops of Sedgwick's corps as they crossed the river and discouraged Confederates from leaving their fortifications and attacking Federals in their bridgehead.

THE BIG PICTURE Robert Knox Sneden's version of a map by Captain William Paine of the U.S. Corps of Engineers, oriented with north to the right, covers the full scope of the Chancellorsville campaign, including the Federal advance across the Rappahannock below Stafford Heights on April 29 and the route followed by Jackson before his flanking attack on Howard's corps on May 2. Hooker suffered over 17,000 casualties in this sprawling struggle and Lee nearly 13,000.

❹ LULL BEFORE THE STORM Men of Sedgwick's corps bivouac near Fredericksburg before advancing on May 3.

1863

GETTYSBURG

EASTERN THEATER

JUNE 3, 1863 Lee launches the campaign that will carry his Army of Northern Virginia into Pennsylvania.

JUNE 9 Battle of Brandy Station (Virginia)

JUNE 24 Lee's forces enter Pennsylvania.

JUNE 25 Jeb Stuart launches cavalry raid from Middleburg, Virginia, and remains out of touch with Lee for the next week.

JUNE 28 George Meade replaces Joseph Hooker as commander of the Army of the Potomac.

JUNE 30 John Buford's Federal cavalry division enters Gettysburg.

JULY 1–3 Battle of Gettysburg

Lee's victory at Chancellorsville came at a steep price and left him determined to abandon his defenses at Fredericksburg ❶ and carry the fight north. "Our loss was severe," he concluded, "and again we had gained not an inch of ground." Following the death of Stonewall Jackson on May 10, Lee welcomed the return of his "old warhorse," Lieutenant General James Longstreet, who had been sent to southeastern Virginia with 20,000 men to shield Richmond and ease the burden of feeding Lee's army. Conferring with Lee, Longstreet agreed that "fruitless victories" like Chancellorsville "were consuming us, and would eventually destroy us." Lee decided to launch another invasion of the North—an advance into Pennsylvania that would allow his hungry, ragged troops to forage at the Union's expense and might result in a fruitful victory that would advance his cause.

Lee launched his campaign on June 3 after reorganizing his army into three corps under Longstreet and Lieutenant Generals A. P. Hill and Richard Ewell, who took charge of Jackson's old corps while Major General Jeb Stuart resumed his duties as Lee's cavalry commander, screening his movements. Hooker tried to smash that screen by ordering his cavalry commander, Major General Alfred Pleasonton, to "disperse and destroy" Stuart's force, leading to the war's largest cavalry battle, waged at Brandy Station ❷ on June 9. Stuart prevailed there and went on to shield Lee's forces as they filed through gaps in the Blue Ridge ❸ into the Shenandoah Valley. Ewell led the way north, seizing Winchester ❹ from Federals in mid-June before passing through Maryland into Pennsylvania, where his corps divided, raiding Carlisle ❺ and threatening York ❻. Hill's corps followed Ewell into Pennsylvania, with Longstreet and Lee bringing up the rear.

On June 25, Stuart embarked on an expedition around the Union army, leaving Lee ill informed on enemy movements as Hooker plodded northward into Maryland east of the mountains. Exasperated at Hooker's slow pace, Lincoln sacked him on June 28 in favor of Major General George Meade, who promptly sent Brigadier General John Buford's cavalry division into Pennsylvania, followed by the First and 11th Corps. On June 30, Buford entered the quiet town of Gettysburg ❼, where a dozen roads converged and two great armies would soon collide. That evening, Lee received a message at Chambersburg ❽ from A. P. Hill at Cashtown ❾, stating that hostile forces were reported in Gettysburg and he would "advance the next morning and discover what was in my front." ■

Lee's men about to ford the Potomac on their way north

Virginia's Champion Lee, shown here in late 1862, invaded Pennsylvania partly to ease the demands of his army on war-torn Virginia and draw Federals away from the state. As the campaign progressed, he saw a chance to fight a "great battle" that might decide the war.

Paths to Gettysburg As shown in this National Geographic map, Lee's forces marched north on separate paths, screened from enemy view by intervening mountains and Stuart's cavalry. But Stuart's absence when battle loomed at Gettysburg left Lee without the officer he called his "eyes and ears."

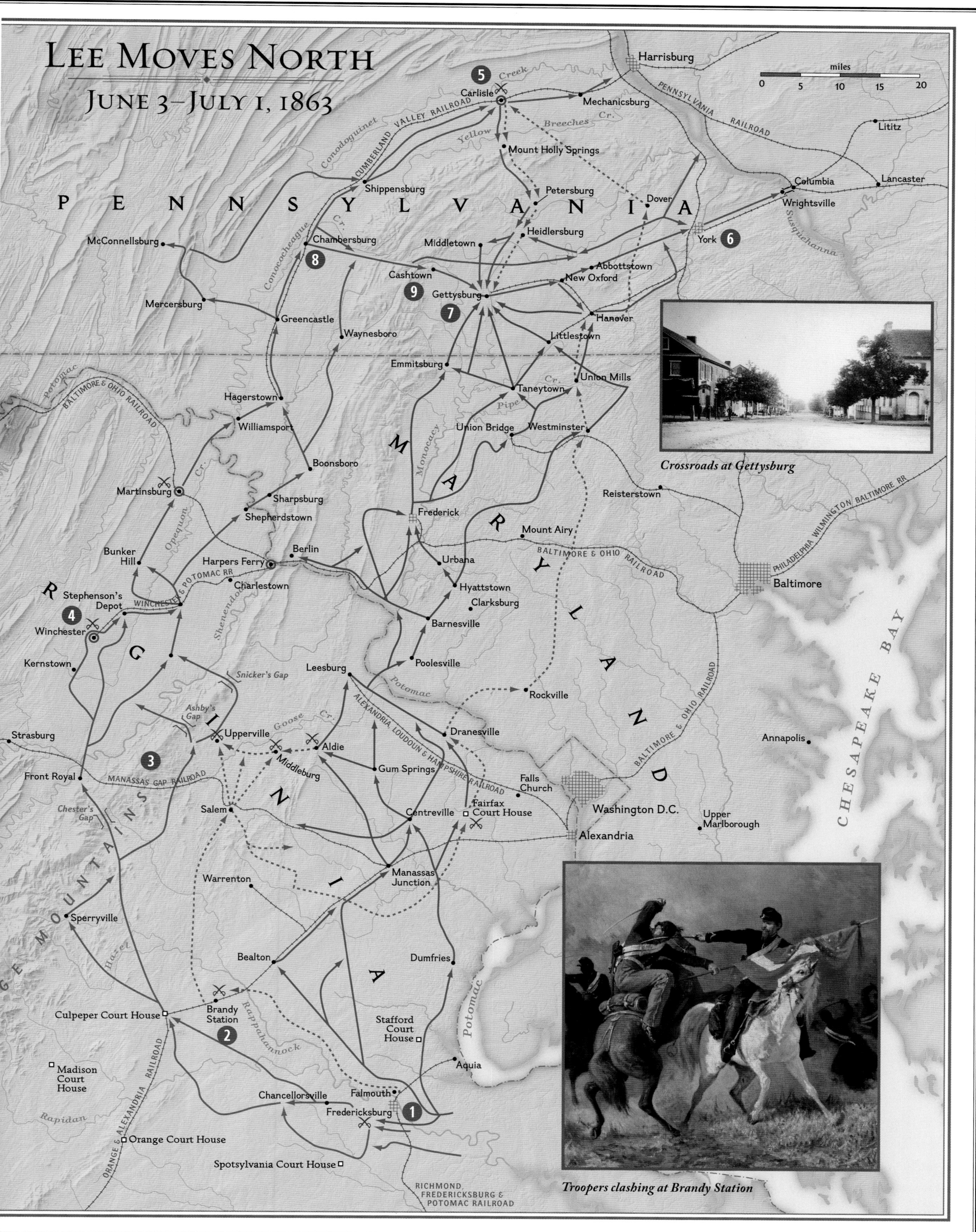

Crossroads at Gettysburg

Troopers clashing at Brandy Station

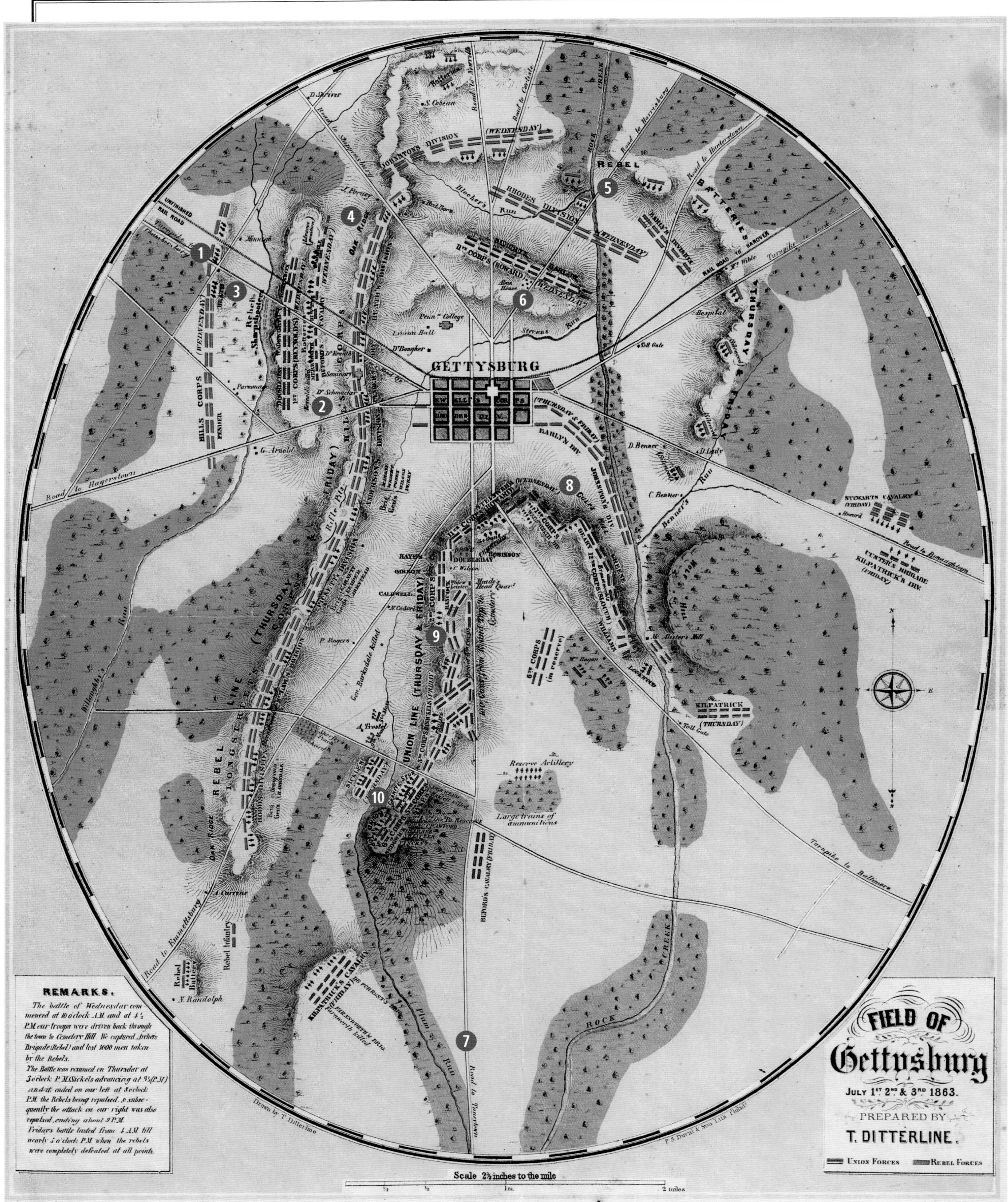

A Fateful Convergence This commercial map published in Philadelphia soon after the battle—waged from Wednesday, July 1, through Friday, July 3—shows the convergence at Gettysburg of Meade's army, which came up from Maryland, and Lee's forces, which came down on various roads north of town. Although largely accurate, this map misplaces Ewell's Confederate divisions on Wednesday. Early's division attacked roughly where Rodes's division is shown here, opposite Howard's 11th Corps. Rodes attacked along the Mummasburg Road, identified here as the road to Shippensburg.

1863 | GETTYSBURG

The Battle Erupts

At dawn on Wednesday, July 1, Confederates of Major General Henry Heth's division, leading the way for A. P. Hill's corps, approached Gettysburg along the Chambersburg Pike ❶. Recognizing the town's significance as a crossroads and lured by reports of stocks of badly needed shoes there, they expected to find Gettysburg lightly defended by militia. Instead they confronted 3,000 dismounted Federal troopers led by Buford, bolstered at mid-morning by the arrival of the First Corps under Major General John Reynolds, who was shot dead as he hurried men into line along McPherson's Ridge ❷. Heth's troops had more than they could handle and fell back toward Herr Ridge, where they were reinforced by another of Hill's divisions, led by Major General William Pender ❸.

George Meade

Lee arrived here from Chambersburg at midday, ahead of Longstreet's corps, to find Ewell's divided corps approaching from the north and east. "I do not wish to bring on a general engagement today," he told Heth. "Longstreet is not up." But it was too late to put out this fire, and he saw an opportunity to annihilate the Federal vanguard at Gettysburg before Meade's entire army got there. Told by Lee to attack as he saw fit, Ewell came in from the north with the division of Robert Rodes, who launched an ill-coordinated assault along Oak Ridge ❹, teeming with Yankees who chewed up one brigade after another. Despite that debacle, Lee gained the upper hand in mid-afternoon by sending Hill's beefed-up forces against the battle-weary First Corps while another of Ewell's divisions, under Jubal Early, swept in from the northeast along the Harrisburg Road ❺ and surprised Oliver Howard's recently arrived 11th Corps ❻. Caught in a vise, the Federals cracked and retreated through Gettysburg to high ground south of town, where Winfield Scott Hancock rode in ahead of his Second Corps and restored order. Hancock recognized that Federals held a stronger position now than when the shooting started. "We can fight here," he wrote Meade, who arrived overnight on the road from Taneytown, Maryland ❼, with the bulk of his army to fill out a line that bent like a fishhook around Culp's Hill ❽ and nearby Cemetery Hill and extended southward along Cemetery Ridge ❾ to Little Round Top ❿. This interior line was two miles shorter than Lee's exterior line, giving Meade a greater density of troops and allowing him to shift them readily from one point to another. The battle that would determine "the fate of our country and our cause," in Meade's words, would be decided here at terrible cost over the next two days. ■

ORDER OF BATTLE

UNION FORCES

ARMY OF THE POTOMAC
Meade | *86,000 men*

I CORPS *Reynolds*
1ST DIVISION *Wadsworth*
Brigades Meredith, Cutler
2ND DIVISION *Robinson*
Brigades Paul, Baxter
3RD DIVISION *Doubleday*
Brigades Biddle, Stone, Stannard

II CORPS *Hancock*
1ST DIVISION *Caldwell*
Brigades Cross, Kelly, Zook, Brooke
2ND DIVISION *Gibbon*
Brigades Harrow, Webb, Hall
3RD DIVISION *Hays*
Brigades Carroll, Smyth, Willard, Hazard

III CORPS *Sickles*
1ST DIVISION *Birney*
Brigades Graham, Ward, DeTrobriand
2ND DIVISION *Humphreys*
Brigades Carr, Brewster, Burling

V CORPS *Sykes*
1ST DIVISION *Barnes*
Brigades Tilton, Sweitzer, Vincent
2ND DIVISION *Ayres*
Brigades Day, Burbank, Weed
3RD DIVISION *Crawford*
Brigades McCandless, Fisher, Martin

VI CORPS *Sedgwick*
1ST DIVISION *Wright*
Brigades Torbert, Bartlett, Russell
2ND DIVISION *Howe*
Brigades Grant, Neill
3RD DIVISION *Newton*
Brigades Shaler, Eustis, Wheaton

XI CORPS *Howard*
1ST DIVISION *Barlow*
Brigades Von Gilsa, Ames
2ND DIVISION *Von Steinwehr*
Brigades Coster, Smith
3RD DIVISION *Schurz*
Brigades Schimmelfennig, Krzyzanowski

XII CORPS *Slocum*
1ST DIVISION *Williams*
Brigades McDougall, Lockwood, Ruger
2ND DIVISION *Geary*
Brigades Candy, Cobham, Greene

CAVALRY CORPS *Pleasonton*
1ST DIVISION *Buford*
Brigades Gamble, Devin, Merritt
2ND DIVISION *Gregg*
Brigades McIntosh, Huey, Gregg
3RD DIVISION *Kilpatrick*
Brigades Farnsworth, Custer

CONFEDERATE FORCES

ARMY OF NORTHERN VIRGINIA
Lee | *75,000 men*

I CORPS *Longstreet*
MCLAWS'S DIVISION
Brigades Kershaw, Barksdale, Semmes, Wofford
PICKETT'S DIVISION
Brigades Garnett, Kemper, Armistead
HOOD'S DIVISION
Brigades Law, Robertson, G. T. Anderson, Benning

II CORPS *Ewell*
EARLY'S DIVISION
Brigades Hays, Smith, Hoke, Gordon
JOHNSON'S DIVISION
Brigades Steuart, Walker, Williams, Jones
RODES'S DIVISION
Brigades Daniel, Doles, Iverson, Ramseur, O'Neal

III CORPS *A. P. Hill*
R. H. ANDERSON'S DIVISION
Brigades Wilcox, Mahone, Wright, Perry, Posey
HETH'S DIVISION
Brigades Pettigrew, Brockenbrough, Archer, Davis
PENDER'S DIVISION
Brigades Perrin, Lane, E. L. Thomas, Scales

CAVALRY *Stuart*
STUART'S DIVISION
Brigades Hampton, Robertson, F. Lee, Jenkins, Jones, W. H. F. Lee
IMBODEN'S COMMAND

DAY TWO: LITTLE ROUND TOP

JOSHUA L. CHAMBERLAIN

Born in Maine in 1828, Chamberlain was given the first name Lawrence for Captain James Lawrence, who uttered the dying words, "Don't give up the ship!" during the War of 1812. That was a fitting motto for the man who later helped stave off defeat for the Union at Gettysburg, but as a student thinking of entering the ministry, he decided to put his middle name first—Joshua, a legendary warrior of Biblical proportions.

In 1862, Chamberlain resigned as professor of rhetoric and oratory at Bowdoin College to serve as lieutenant colonel of the 20th Maine Infantry, taking command of the regiment as its colonel in June 1863. His oratorical training made him a compelling chronicler of the war he experienced. Recalling the desperate battle for Little Round Top, where the 20th Maine held the left flank of Colonel Strong Vincent's brigade—and of Meade's entire army—and refused to give way, Chamberlain wrote eloquently: "The crush of musketry gave way to cuts and thrusts, grapplings and wrestlings. The edge of conflict swayed to and fro, with wild whirlpools and eddies. . . . All around, strange, mingled roar—shouts of defiance, rally, and desperation; and underneath, murmured entreaty and stifled moans; gasping prayers, snatches of Sabbath song, whispers of loved names. . . . How men held on, each one knows—not I."

Early on July 2, Meade bolstered his right flank at Culp's Hill ❶, where he expected an attack, by shifting Brigadier General John Geary's 12th Corps division ❷ there from Little Round Top ❸, which anchored the Federal left wing and offered a commanding perch for artillery. Meade expected Daniel Sickles to extend his Third Corps line southward from Cemetery Ridge ❹ to cover Little Round Top. But Sickles, a headstrong political general from New York, decided instead to advance his line westward from Cemetery Ridge—so low in places that it was barely perceptible—to slightly higher ground around the Peach Orchard ❺. Little Round Top was left undefended as Lee prepared to hit Meade's left hard.

Lee's plan called for two newly arrived divisions of Longstreet's corps under Major Generals John Bell Hood and Lafayette McLaws to mount that attack, supported by Major General Richard Anderson's division of Hill's corps ❻. Longstreet urged Lee to forgo that risky assault or at least postpone it until his trailing division, under Major General George Pickett, arrived from Chambersburg. "I never like to go into battle with one boot off," Longstreet said.

Ordered by Lee to proceed, Longstreet moved slowly, countermarching his troops at one point to avoid detection, and did not unleash Hood's division ❼—slated to launch the attack, which would unfold *en echelon* from right to left—until 4 P.M. By then, Meade had learned of Sickles's blunder and sent his chief engineer, Brigadier General Gouverneur Kemble Warren, to Little Round Top. Finding it undefended, Warren sought help, furnished promptly by Colonel Strong Vincent of the Fifth Corps ❽, who rushed his brigade up the hill before the Rebels got there.

Part of Hood's division advanced through the Devil's Den ❾, below Little Round Top, ousting Sickles's men from that jumble of granite boulders in what a Texan fighting there called "one of the wildest, fiercest struggles of the war." Hood was seriously wounded early on, and Brigadier General Evander Law took charge of the division, leaving no brigade commander to direct the crucial attack on Vincent's men holding Little Round Top. "Hold this ground at all costs!" Vincent told Colonel Joshua Chamberlain, whose 20th Maine Infantry occupied the very end of the Union line. After withstanding repeated assaults by the 15th Alabama Infantry, Chamberlain's men dispersed their foes with a bayonet charge. Heavy fighting continued elsewhere until Brigadier General Stephen Weed came to the aid of the mortally wounded Vincent and secured Little Round Top for the Union at the cost of his own life. ■

❸ GUNS AT THE SUMMIT **Federals of Lieutenant Charles Hazlett's battery fire from Little Round Top after Union forces repulsed Confederates there.**

Attack on Meade's Left A map by Robert Knox Sneden shows the opposing lines on July 2 around the time Hood initiated Lee's attack. Some of Hood's troops reached Little Round Top furtively by way of Round Top, a loftier hill to the south. Others fought their way across Plum Run and through the nearby Devil's Den, grappling with troops led by Brigadier General Hobart Ward, holding the left flank of Sickles's exposed Third Corps. After the attack began, John Sedgwick's trailing Sixth Corps arrived from the south, bolstering Meade's left as fighting spread northward to the Wheat Field and Peach Orchard and Federals on Culp's Hill and Cemetery Hill came under attack by Ewell's corps.

❾ **Lost in the Storm** Killed in the furious fighting on July 2, a Confederate infantryman lies amid boulders near Plum Run below Little Round Top. The rocky terrain here—including the Devil's Den and a more exposed area at the foot of the hill called the Slaughter Pen—offered Hood's men some shelter in the storm of battle but left them fatally vulnerable to shots fired from above.

1863 | GETTYSBURG

Wheat Field & Peach Orchard

While fighting raged on Little Round Top on July 2, the battle spread to the Wheat Field ❶ and vicinity, where Federals of Sickles's beleaguered Third Corps buckled under pressure from brigades led by Colonel George "Tige" Anderson ❷ of Hood's division and Brigadier Generals Paul Semmes ❸ and Joseph Kershaw ❹ of McLaws's division. To hold the line, Meade reinforced Sickles with divisions led by Brigadier Generals James Barnes ❺ and John Caldwell ❻. Barnes went in first but found Kershaw on his flank and pulled his forces back, obstructing Brigadier General Samuel Zook ❼ of Caldwell's advancing division. "If you can't get out of the way," Zook shouted, "lie down and we will march over you." Passing through, Zook's troops entered the Wheat Field alongside the Irish Brigade of Colonel Patrick Kelly ❽, whose devout recruits had just received absolution. A third brigade under Colonel Edward Cross ❾, wearing a black bandana for what he foresaw would be his "last battle," joined in a bloody assault that left Cross and Zook mortally wounded but drove the Rebels into Rose's Woods ❿.

Around 6:30 P.M., the Federals were staggered by another blow, delivered at the Peach Orchard by Brigadier Generals William Barksdale ⓫ and William Wofford ⓬ of McLaws's division. Pouring through the gap left by the collapse of Brigadier General Charles Graham's brigade ⓭, Wofford's Georgians helped drive Federals from the hard-won Wheat Field while Barksdale's Mississippians swung north and routed the remainder of Brigadier General Andrew Humphrey's division along the Emmitsburg Road ⓮. The tide turned, however, when Sickles fell wounded near the Trostle House ⓯ and Meade gave command of this sector to the unflappable Hancock. Once again Hancock restored order, as he did the day before, by rallying retreating units on Cemetery Ridge and bolstering them with reinforcements dispatched by Meade. After sending a brigade led by Colonel George Willard ⓰ to repulse Barksdale in a clash that cost both their lives, Hancock beat back a charge led by Brigadier General Cadmus Wilcox ⓱ of A. P. Hill's division, and Lee's furious attack on Meade's left ended in stalemate. ■

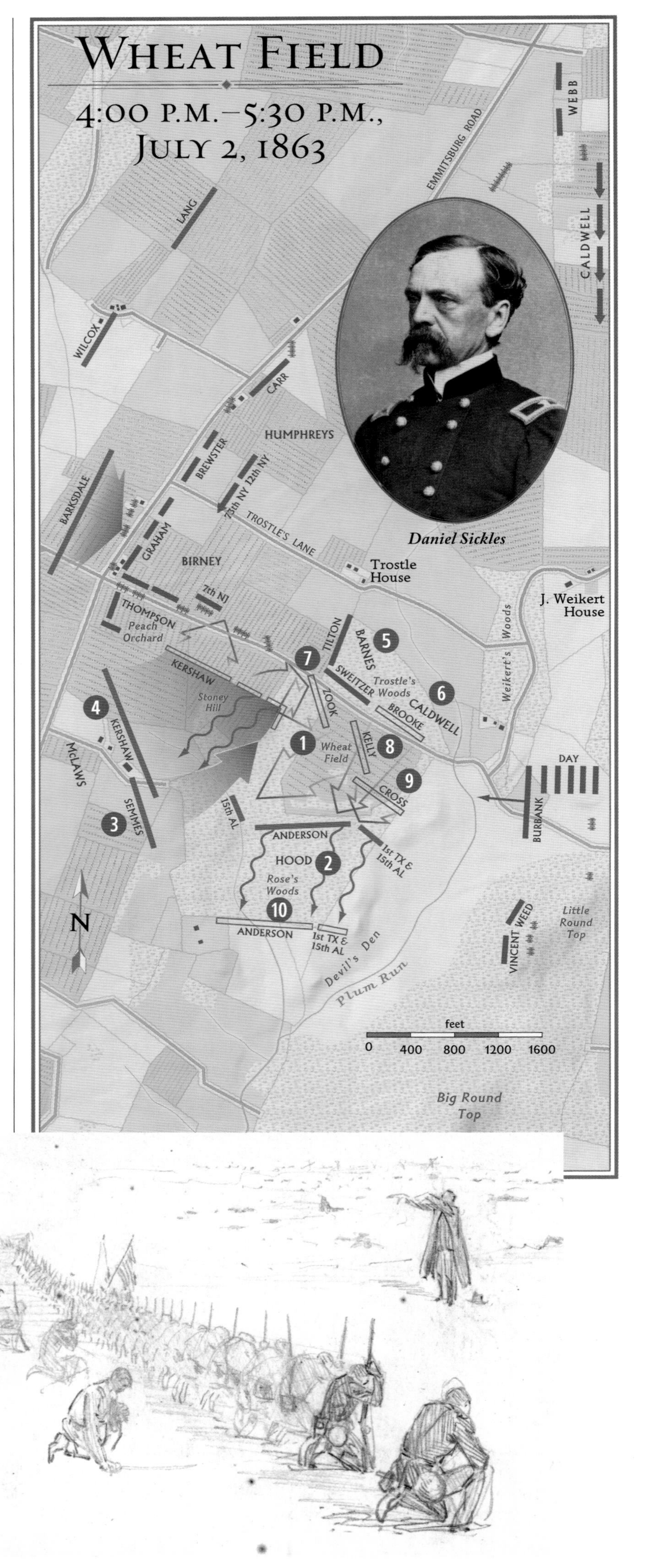

❽

Sickles Besieged As shown in this National Geographic map, Sickles's Third Corps began to crumble when Confederates advancing from the Rose House and Rose's Woods seized the Wheat Field, which changed hands six times during the battle.

❽ Absolution Father William Corby, chaplain of the Irish Brigade, offers the troops absolution before their advance into the Wheat Field. Corby told them there would be no Christian burial for "the soldier who turns his back upon the foe."

McLaws Advances When McLaws hurled the brigades of Barksdale and Wofford into the fray around the Peach Orchard, the Third Corps collapsed, forcing Federals sent earlier to reinforce Sickles to retreat with his battered forces toward Cemetery Ridge, where Hancock shored up the Union line and held firm.

Shattered Soldier Little remained of this dead Confederate after he was gutted by shellfire at Gettysburg.

Lafayette McLaws

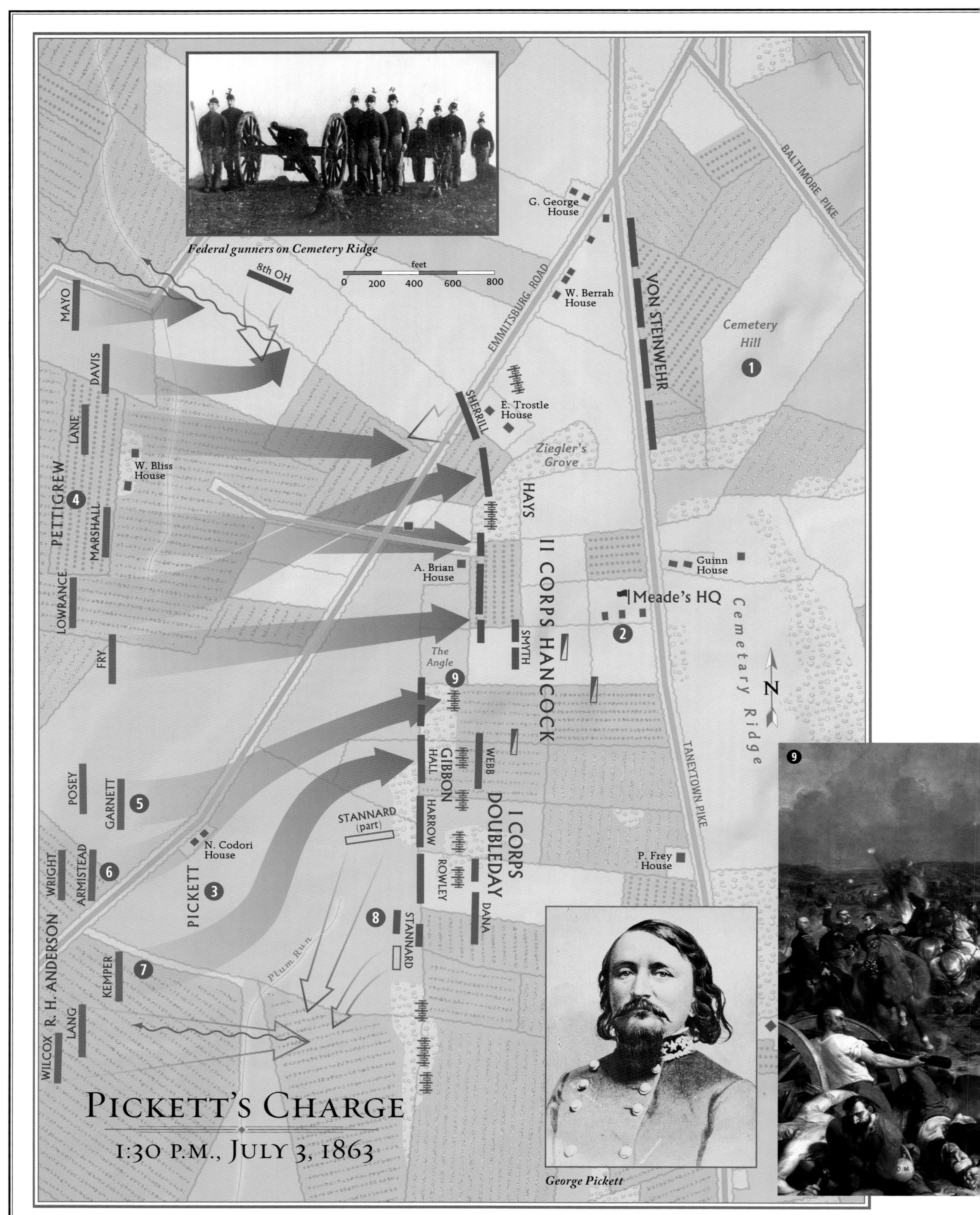

George Pickett

Day Three: Pickett's Charge

After two days of fighting at Gettysburg that brought Confederates to the brink of victory more than once before they were driven back, Lee resolved to try again on July 3. He ruled out another attack on Meade's left, which had been heavily reinforced since Longstreet's division struck there the day before. Prospects for success looked little better on Meade's right, where Confederates of Ewell's division had advanced late on July 2, breaking through at Cemetery Hill ❶ before being repulsed there as they were at Culp's Hill. But further attacks by Ewell might at least prevent Meade from shifting forces from his right to bolster his center, along Cemetery Ridge ❷, where Lee planned a climactic frontal assault, hoping for a decisive breakthrough. That meant advancing across open ground into the teeth of Union defenses—a perilous charge entrusted to George Pickett's fresh division of 6,000 Virginians ❸, with Brigadier General J. Johnston Pettigrew's battle-weary division advancing to their north ❹ and other forces following behind.

Lee's plan went awry early on July 3 when Federals attacked Ewell's forces on Culp's Hill, triggering a battle that ended inconclusively before Pickett was ready to advance. Lee still had hope that a massive artillery bombardment would impair Meade's defenses on Cemetery Ridge. At 1 P.M., Rebel gunners opened up, launching the war's biggest artillery duel. Men were seen "bleeding at both ears from concussion," recalled one soldier, but for all the sound and fury, little damage was done. Confederate gunners overshot their target for the most part while Federal artillerymen limited their counter fire to conserve ammunition for the fighting to come. When the guns fell silent, Longstreet—who had argued against the attack—signaled reluctantly for the infantry to advance. "This is a desperate thing to attempt," said Brigadier General Richard Garnett ❺ of Pickett's division. "It is," replied Brigadier General Lewis Armistead ❻, whose brigade followed in Garnett's path. "But the issue is with the Almighty, and we must leave it in his hands."

To close up with Pettigrew's division to the north, Pickett's men had to march obliquely to their left, which exposed them to deadly flanking fire. Hardest hit were Brigadier General James Kemper's men ❼, who went down in droves when Vermonters led by Brigadier General George Stannard ❽ enveloped their right flank. "Great masses of men seemed to disappear in a moment," wrote Colonel Wheelock Veazey of the 16th Vermont Infantry. All along the line, Confederate ranks crumbled under the searing impact of artillery and infantry fire. Against all odds, Armistead led a few hundred followers over the stone wall at the Angle ❾, where the Federal line jutted forward slightly, but they were soon overpowered in hand-to-hand fighting. As Lee's battered forces withdrew, hopes for the Confederate cause receded with them. ■

LEE'S LAST BID Lee made one last desperate bid at Gettysburg on July 3 by sending some 13,000 men against the center of the Federal line. Pickett's three brigades under Kemper, Armistead, and Garnett formed the strongest component of this advance, known to posterity as Pickett's Charge. Armistead and the small contingent who followed him over the stone wall at the Angle were the only attackers to breach the Federal line here.

❾ **CONFEDERATE HIGH-WATER MARK** Pickett's Charge reaches a furious climax as Federals beat back surging Confederates (right) at the Angle in a painting by Peter Frederick Rothermel, who drew on eyewitness accounts.

THE LAST FULL MEASURE

Like a monstrous storm, the Battle of Gettysburg left carnage and misery in its wake. Each side lost well over 20,000 men killed, wounded, captured, or missing in this tempest—a toll that bore harder on Lee's smaller army and forced him to retreat into Virginia, leaving his dead behind on fields strewn with rotting corpses. "Some with faces bloated and blackened beyond recognition, lay with glassy eyes staring up at the summer sun," recalled Corporal Thomas Marbaker of the 11th New Jersey Infantry. "Hugging the earth like a fog, poisoning every breath," he added, was "the pestilential stench of decaying humanity." Burial parties digging in the hard, rocky soil did not linger over their grim task. "The dead are many, the time is short, so they got but very shallow graves," wrote one soldier who helped dispose of the corpses, "in fact most of them were buried in trenches, dug not over 18 inches deep, and as near where they fell as was possible."

Abraham Lincoln

A few months afterward, remains of the Union dead were moved to a better resting place—the Soldiers' National Cemetery, situated on Cemetery Hill ❶, a local burial ground where Federals of Oliver Howard's 11th Corps had withstood Confederate attacks on July 2. This new cemetery was laid out in a semicircle ❷ and held more than 3,500 bodies. Those whose identities were known were grouped by state, but nearly 1,600 graves were marked unknown. On November 19, 1863, President Lincoln dedicated the cemetery by delivering his Gettysburg Address, urging that "from these honored dead we take increased devotion to the cause for which they gave the last full measure of devotion." ■

BURIED IN HASTE Many Confederates killed at Gettysburg lay in shallow graves like this one until they were reburied decades later in the South.

Field of Honor This bird's-eye view of Gettysburg, showing the position of Federal and Confederate units during the battle, was signed by George Meade, who vouched for its accuracy. Delineated at center are the opposing forces on Cemetery Ridge on July 3, including the Confederate brigades of Armistead and Garnett, both of whom died here.

Tending the Wounded Field hospitals like this one at Gettysburg treated both Federals and those Confederates who were too badly wounded to accompany Lee as he withdrew.

Captured Intact These three men were among more than 5,000 able-bodied Confederates captured at Gettysburg along with 6,800 wounded Rebels.

1863

CHARLESTON

THE BLOCKADE

APRIL 7, 1863 Union ironclad fleet led by Samuel Du Pont withdraws under fire from Charleston Harbor after bombarding Fort Sumter.

JULY 10–18 Federal troops land on Morris Island and launch unsuccessful attacks on Fort Wagner.

AUGUST 21 Federals begin shelling Charleston from Morris Island.

SEPTEMBER 6 Besieged Confederates evacuate Fort Wagner and Battery Gregg after Federal bombardment neutralizes Fort Sumter.

No Southern city was more eagerly targeted by Union forces than Charleston, the Cradle of the Rebellion. "The desire was general to punish that city by all the rigors of war," wrote one Federal. Seizing Charleston would avenge the loss of Fort Sumter ❶ and stop blockade runners from bringing in war supplies here. Confederates fortified their batteries and laid obstructions and submerged mines called torpedoes ❷ to deter enemy warships from entering these hostile waters, guarded by the ironclad rams *Chicora* ❸ and *Palmetto State* ❹.

Those defenses proved too much for Rear Admiral Samuel Du Pont, whose fleet of ironclads ❺ took a beating in a futile attack on Fort Sumter in April. On July 10, Union troops landed on the lower end of Morris Island ❻ and approached Fort Wagner ❼, which if captured would bring Federal siege guns close enough to pound Charleston and the batteries shielding it. The first attack on that fortification, covered in sand that blunted the impact of incoming shells, was crushed the next day. The second attack on July 18 fared no better but brought lasting honor to the 54th Massachusetts Infantry, a regiment of free blacks who went in first, led by Colonel Robert Gould Shaw, a white officer who fell as they reached the parapet. When told that Confederates had buried Shaw in a trench with the many black troops who shared his fate, his father said he could not "wish for him better company."

Rebuffed, Federals laid siege to Fort Wagner and brought their artillery ever closer to Charleston. On the night of August 21, a huge gun dubbed the Swamp Angel ❽ began firing incendiaries into the city, but the blazes caused by that weapon before it burst a short time later only made civilians more determined to resist the Yankees. More effective was the barrage aimed at Fort Sumter by Union gunners on land and at sea. By September, Sumter was in ruins, and Beauregard ordered Fort Wagner and nearby Battery Gregg ❾ evacuated. With Morris Island in hand, Federals stepped up their bombardment of Charleston, but the city held out defiantly. ■

❻ HEAVY ARTILLERY Federal gunners on Morris Island man hulking Parrott rifles that helped reduce Fort Sumter to rubble.

CHARLESTON UNDER THE GUN A map by Robert Knox Sneden shows the formidable defenses—including floating batteries, torpedoes, and wooden obstructions called spiles—that awaited Du Pont when he entered this harbor in April aboard his flagship *New Ironsides* with a fleet of monitors. Federals began to make headway here in August by mounting big guns near Fort Wagner with sufficient range to reach Fort Sumter and Charleston.

SAVING THE FLAG Sergeant William Carney of the 54th Massachusetts holds the flag that he rescued during the regiment's perilous charge on Fort Wagner and carried to the parapet, where he and other survivors were pinned down. Shot in the hip, Carney managed to carry the flag back to Federal lines and was awarded the Medal of Honor.

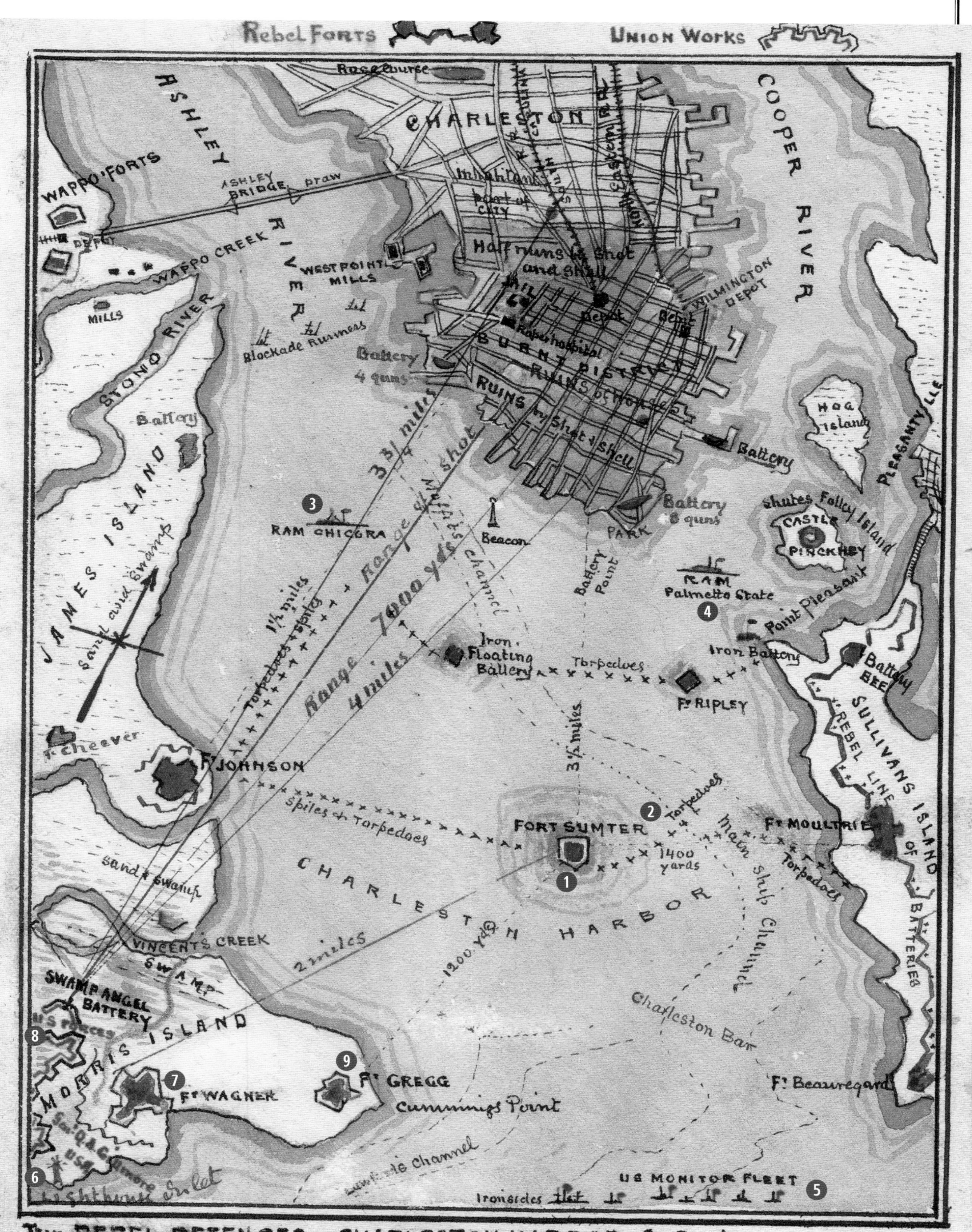
Rebel Forts
Union Works
Race course
CHARLESTON
ASHLEY RIVER
COOPER RIVER
WAPPO FORTS
ASHLEY BRIDGE
Draw
DEPOT
WAPPO CREEK
WEST POINT MILLS
MILLS
STONO RIVER
Blockade Runners
Battery 4 guns
Half ruins by Shot and Shell
JAIL
Depot
WILMINGTON DEPOT
BURNT DISTRICT
RUINS of Houses
RUINS by Shot & Shell
Battery
HOG Island
PLEASANTVILLE
JAMES ISLAND
Battery
Sand and Swamp
3 3/4 miles
Range of Shot
Range 7000 yds
4 miles
1 1/2 miles
Torpedoes & Spiles
RAM CHICORA
Beacon
Battery Point
Battery 8 guns
PARK
Shutes Folley Island
CASTLE PINCKNEY
RAM Palmetto State
Point Pleasant
Iron Floating Battery
Torpedoes
Iron Battery
Battery BEE
Ft RIPLEY
SULLIVANS ISLAND
REBEL LINE OF BATTERIES
Ft cheever
Ft JOHNSON
3 1/2 miles
Spiles & Torpedoes
FORT SUMTER
Torpedoes
1400 yards
main ship channel
Ft MOULTRIE
Torpedoes
CHARLESTON HARBOR
Sand & Swamp
VINCENTS CREEK
SWAMP
SWAMP ANGEL BATTERY
2 miles
1200 yds
US FORCES
MORRIS ISLAND
Charleston Bar
Ft GREGG
Cummings Point
Ft WAGNER
Ft Beauregard
Lighthouse Inlet
Swash Channel
US MONITOR FLEET
Ironsides
THE REBEL DEFENCES of CHARLESTON HARBOR. S. C. August 1863.

1863

CHICKAMAUGA

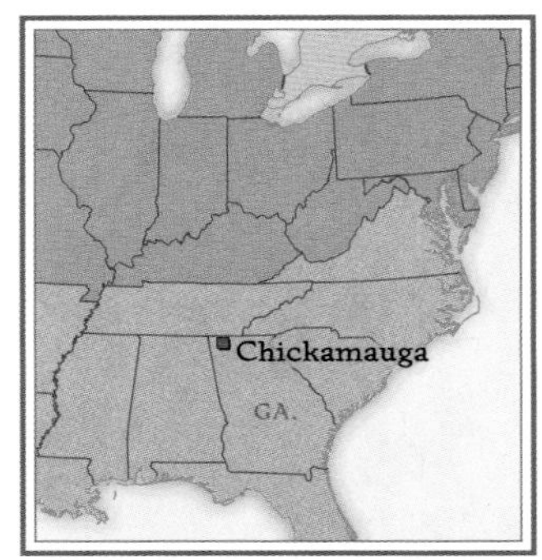

WESTERN THEATER

JUNE 24, 1863 William Rosecrans advances from Murfreesboro with his Army of the Cumberland against Braxton Bragg's Army of Tennessee around Tullahoma.

JUNE 30 Outflanked, Bragg withdraws from Tullahoma to Chattanooga.

AUGUST 21 Federals begin shelling Chattanooga to distract Bragg as Rosecrans sweeps around him to the west.

SEPTEMBER 7 Bragg withdraws southward from Chattanooga into northern Georgia.

SEPTEMBER 19–20 Battle of Chickamauga

In late June, as Grant laid siege to Vicksburg and Lee approached Gettysburg, a third campaign unfolded in Tennessee that received less notice but proved just as significant. Since his victory at Stones River in January, William Rosecrans had remained in Murfreesboro ❶ with his Army of the Cumberland, resisting pressure from Washington to move against Braxton Bragg's Army of Tennessee around Tullahoma ❷, shielded by Confederate troopers led by Major General Joseph Wheeler who menaced Federal supply lines and held Rosecrans back. By June, however, he had a cavalry force nearly as large as Wheeler's and a newly formed brigade of mounted infantry led by Colonel John Wilder and armed with Spencer repeating rifles. On June 24, Rosecrans set his four corps under Major Generals Thomas Crittenden, George Thomas, Alexander McCook, and Gordon Granger against Bragg's two corps led by Lieutenant Generals Leonidas Polk and William Hardee. Preoccupied with threats to his left from Granger at Bellbuckle Gap ❸ and McCook at Liberty Gap ❹, Bragg failed to secure his right, where Thomas sent Wilder's "Lightning Brigade" to seize Hoover's Gap ❺ while Crittenden swept around Bragg's flank, forcing him to fall back to Chattanooga ❻.

Expecting praise, Rosecrans instead received a stern message from Secretary of War Edwin Stanton on July 7: "Lee's army overthrown; Grant victorious. You and your noble army now have the chance to give the finishing blow to the rebellion. Will you neglect the chance?" Relentless pressure from above may have made the usually cautious Rosecrans overeager as he closed in on Chattanooga, a vital railroad junction whose capture would tighten his grip on Tennessee and clear the way for an invasion of Georgia. On August 21, Federals opened fire on Chattanooga from across the Tennessee River ❼. Distracted by that threat to the north, Bragg was once again outflanked by Rosecrans, who sent most of his army across the river to the west near Bridgeport ❽ and forced his foe to abandon Chattanooga without a fight. Urged by Thomas to regroup before advancing into Georgia, Rosecrans instead sent his corps chasing after Bragg's army through gaps in the mountains below Chattanooga. Heavily reinforced, Bragg would soon challenge the overextended Rosecrans along a creek called Chickamauga ❾, a Cherokee name meaning River of Blood. ■

LEADING THE WAY After seizing Chattanooga, Rosecrans was lionized in his home state of Ohio, where this song was dedicated to him. His troops called him "Old Rosy" and admired him for leading from the front.

ROAD TO CHICKAMAUGA As shown in this National Geographic map, Rosecrans methodically outmaneuvered Bragg until his foe withdrew from Chattanooga, luring the Federal commander into a hasty advance through treacherous passes between Lookout Mountain and other steep ridges along the Tennessee-Georgia border.

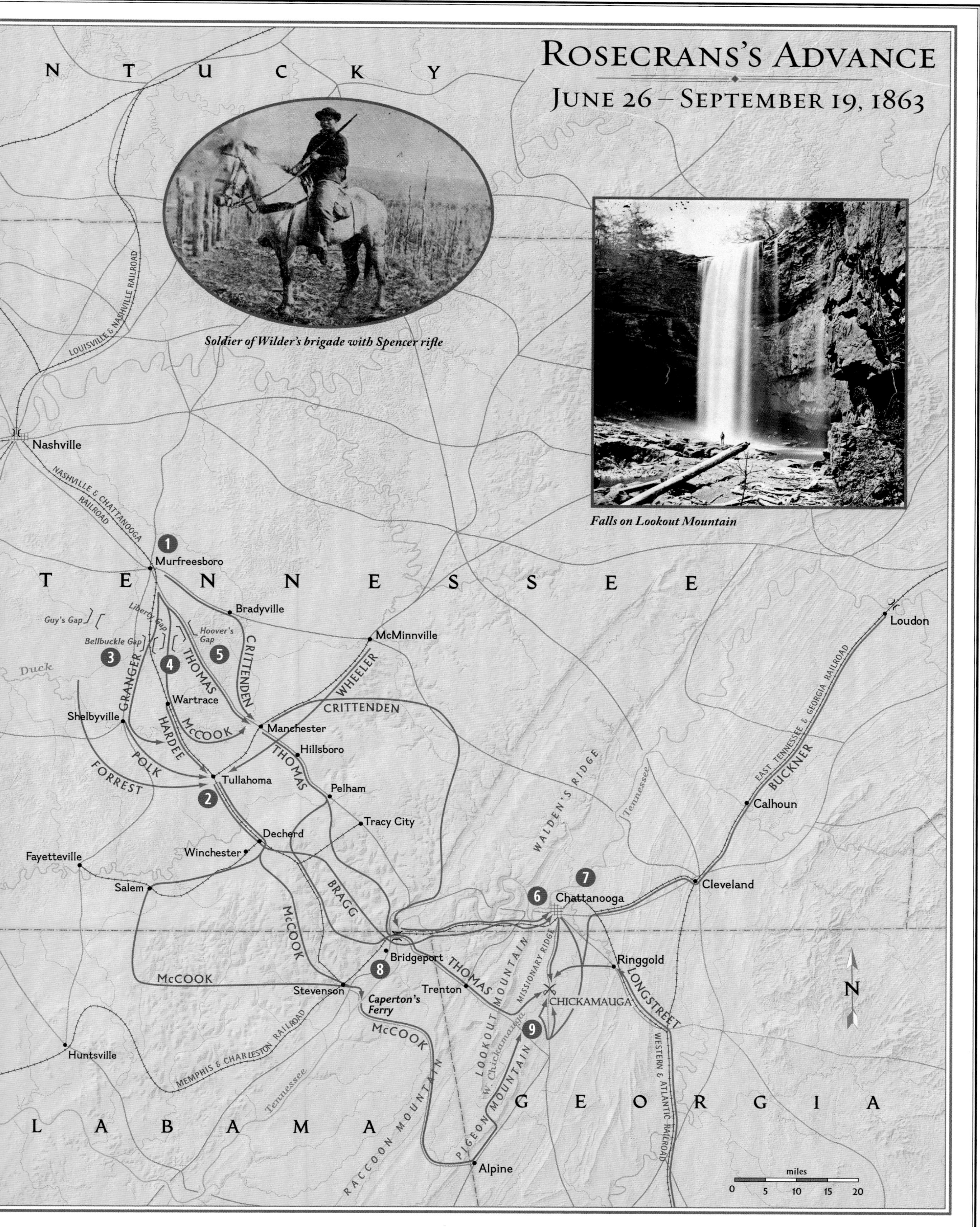

Soldier of Wilder's brigade with Spencer rifle

Falls on Lookout Mountain

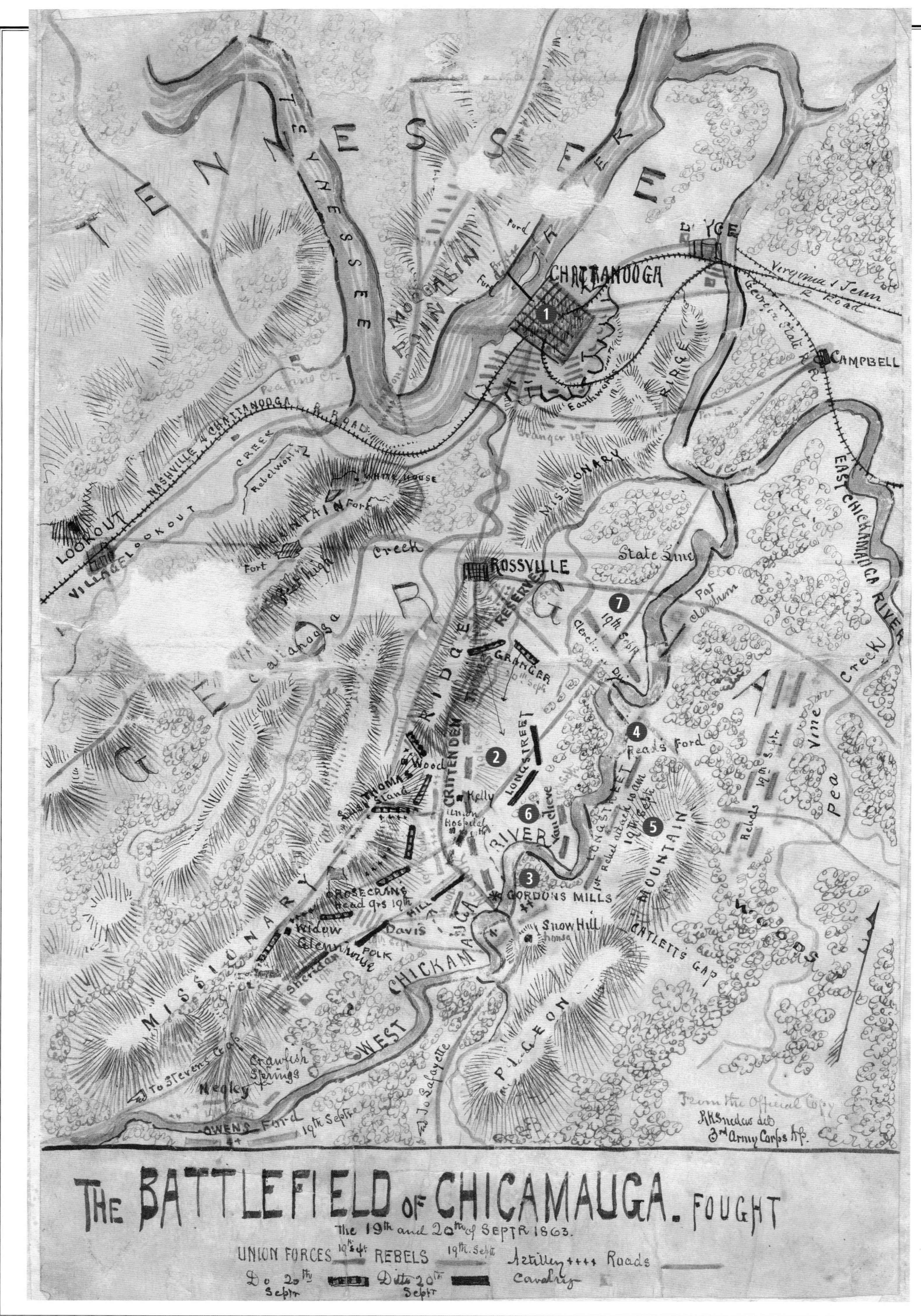
THE BATTLEFIELD OF CHICAMAUGA. FOUGHT
The 19th and 20th of SEPTR 1863.
UNION FORCES 19th Sept REBELS 19th Sept Artillery ++++ Roads
Do 20th Septr Ditto 20th Septr Cavalry
TENNESSEE
TENNESSEE RIVER
CHATTANOOGA
CAMPBELL
Virginia & Tenn R Road
Georgia State R R
NASHVILLE & CHATTANOOGA R ROAD
LOOKOUT MOUNTAIN
LOOKOUT CREEK
LOOKOUT VILLAGE
White House
Rebel works
Earthworks
Ford
MOCCASIN
MISSIONARY RIDGE
ROSSVILLE
State Line
RESERVE
GRANGER
CRITTENDEN
THOMAS
LONGSTREET
Kelly
Wood
Union Hospital
Reeds Ford
Vaucleve
GORDONS MILLS
ROSECRANS Head Qrs 19th
Widow Glenn
Davis
POLK
Sheridan
Snow Hill
CATLETTS GAP
PIGEON MOUNTAIN
WOODS
Pea Vine Creek
EAST CHICKAMAUGA RIVER
WEST CHICKAMAUGA RIVER
Crawfish Springs
To Stevens Gap
To Lafayette
OWENS Ford
Rebels
From the Official Copy
R.K. Sneden
3rd Army Corps

1863 | CHICKAMAUGA

Clash at the River of Blood

By mid-September, Bragg had halted his withdrawal south of Chattanooga ❶ and was gaining strength. Among the reinforcements promised him were 12,000 troops of James Longstreet's corps, coming from Virginia by rail. Bragg would soon have more men at hand than Rosecrans, who had divided his forces in the hope of corralling the Rebels, assuming they would remain on the run. Not until Crittenden's corps ❷ narrowly escaped attack by Bragg's superior forces at Lee and Gordon's Mills ❸ on Chickamauga Creek did Rosecrans realize that reuniting his forces was a "matter of life and death." By September 18, he had his army aligned along the west bank of the creek, where they skirmished with Confederates attempting to cross, but his position remained precarious. Hoping to cave in Rosecrans's left flank and cut his line of retreat to Chattanooga, Bragg sent Confederates across the creek in force overnight, triggering a furious battle that erupted near Reed's Ford ❹ on the morning of September 19. The fighting spread southward that afternoon as the first of Longstreet's men ❺ to arrive, led by John Bell Hood, slammed into Horatio Van Cleve's division ❻ of Crittenden's corps. Patrick Cleburne, known as the Stonewall Jackson of the West, was in position to augment that promising attack, but Bragg instead sent Cleburne's division ❼ against Rosecrans's left in a belated push that lost momentum as night fell. One Union officer likened the wild battle here to "guerrilla warfare on a grand scale." The woods along the aptly named River of Blood were filled with the "ghastly mangled dead and the horribly wounded," a Confederate wrote, and the struggle was far from over. ■

❸ Mill on the Chickamauga The placid fields and forests around Lee and Gordon's Mills, on Chickamauga Creek, became a killing ground in September when forces led by Bragg and Rosecrans collided in one of the bloodiest battles of the war.

A Chaotic Struggle In this map based on official Union Army sources, Robert Knox Sneden attempted to make sense of the chaotic two-day struggle at Chickamauga. Better informed on Federal dispositions there than on enemy movements, he placed most Confederate forces east of Chickamauga Creek on September 19 when in fact many had crossed the night before to the west bank, where the fighting occurred. He correctly identified the stream along which the battle was fought as West Chickamauga Creek, but after the famous battle was fought here other branches of the creek were overlooked and this became known in Civil War annals as the Chickamauga.

Order of Battle

Union Forces

ARMY OF THE CUMBERLAND
Rosecrans | *58,000 men*

XIV CORPS *Thomas*
1ST DIVISION *Baird*
Brigades Scribner, Starkweather, King
2ND DIVISION *Negley*
Brigades Beatty, Stanley, Sirwell
3RD DIVISION *Brannan*
Brigades Connell, Croxton, Van Derveer
4TH DIVISION *Reynolds*
Brigades Wilder, King, Turchin

XX CORPS *A. M. McCook*
1ST DIVISION *Davis*
Brigades Post, Carlin, Heg
2ND DIVISION *R. W. Johnson*
Brigades Willich, Dodge, Baldwin
3RD DIVISION *Sheridan*
Brigades Lytle, Laiboldt, Bradley

XXI CORPS *Crittenden*
1ST DIVISION *Wood*
Brigades G. P. Buell, Wagner, Harker
2ND DIVISION *Palmer*
Brigades Cruft, Hazen, Grose
3RD DIVISION *Van Cleve*
Brigades Beatty, Dick, Barnes

RESERVE CORPS *Granger*
1ST DIVISION *Steedman*
Brigades Whitaker, Mitchell
2ND DIVISION *D. McCook*

CAVALRY CORPS *Mitchell*
1ST DIVISION *E. M. McCook*
Brigades Campbell, Ray, Watkins
2ND DIVISION *Crook*
Brigades Minty, Long

Confederate Forces

ARMY OF TENNESSEE
Bragg | *66,000 men*

RIGHT WING *Polk*
CHEATHAM'S DIVISION
Brigades Jackson, Smith, Maney, Wright, Strahl

HILL'S CORPS *D. H. Hill*
CLEBURNE'S DIVISION
Brigades Wood, Polk, Deshler
BRECKINRIDGE'S DIVISION
Brigades Helm, Adams, Stovall

RESERVE CORPS *Walker*
GIST'S DIVISION
Brigades Colquitt, Ector, Wilson
LIDDELL'S DIVISION
Brigades Govan, Walthall

LEFT WING *Longstreet*
BUCKNER'S CORPS *Buckner*
HINDMAN'S DIVISION
Brigades Anderson, Deas, Manigault
STEWART'S DIVISION
Brigades Johnson, Bate, Brown, Clayton
PRESTON'S DIVISION
Brigades Gracie, Kelly, Trigg

HOOD'S CORPS *Hood*
McLAWS'S DIVISION
Brigades Kershaw, Humphreys, Wofford, Bryan
JOHNSON'S DIVISION
Brigades Fulton, Gregg, McNair
LAW'S DIVISION
Brigades Robertson, Sheffield, Benning

CAVALRY *Wheeler*
WHEELER'S CORPS
Brigades Crews, Harrison
WHARTON'S DIVISION

1863 | CHICKAMAUGA

Federal Fiasco

George Thomas, whose corps held the Federal left at Chickamauga tenaciously against fierce opposition on September 19, expected more of the same when the battle resumed. In a conference that night at Rosecrans's headquarters ❶, Thomas was so weary he dozed off but roused himself when called on and urged his commander to "strengthen the left." Forewarned, Rosecrans responded promptly to fresh attacks by Cleburne's troops ❷ and other Confederates on the morning of September 20 by shifting forces to his embattled left. Brigadier General Thomas Wood, waiting in reserve, was slow to move up with his division when ordered to fill the slot vacated by that redeployment, and Rosecrans lit into him for his "damnable negligence." Later that morning, warned there was a gap in the line, Rosecrans ordered Wood ❸ to close up with Major General John Reynolds's division ❹ "as fast as possible." Wood knew there was no gap. It only appeared that way because Brigadier General John Brannan's intervening division ❺ was concealed amid the trees. But having been blasted earlier by Rosecrans, Wood complied promptly now by marching his division to the left behind Brannan, leaving a quarter-mile-wide hole in the Federal line.

That blunder proved disastrous when the newly arrived Longstreet launched a massive attack, sending several divisions into battle under Hood ❻ just as Wood was making his move. Hood was riding up front—with his left arm, shattered at Gettysburg, in a sling—when a bullet pierced his right leg, which later had to be amputated. Losing Hood did not stop his men from exploiting the yawning gap in the enemy line. "On they came like an angry flood," recalled one Union officer. "Pouring through the opening made by Wood's withdrawal, they struck his last brigade as it was leaving the line. It was slammed back like a door, and shattered."

With his right wing collapsing, Rosecrans retreated with those endangered forces to Chattanooga through McFarland's Gap ❼ while Thomas shielded them from pursuit by making a desperate stand on Snodgrass Hill ❽ and nearby Horseshoe Ridge ❾, where his men clung to the high ground. By late afternoon, they had spent their bullets and were at risk of being outflanked by Major General Thomas Hindman's division ❿ when Reserve Corps commander Gordon Granger came to their rescue with 95,000 rounds of ammunition and 3,900 men of Brigadier General James Steedman's division ⓫. That was enough to hold off the Rebels until nightfall, when Thomas skillfully withdrew his forces, concluding a valiant defense that earned him the title Rock of Chickamauga. ■

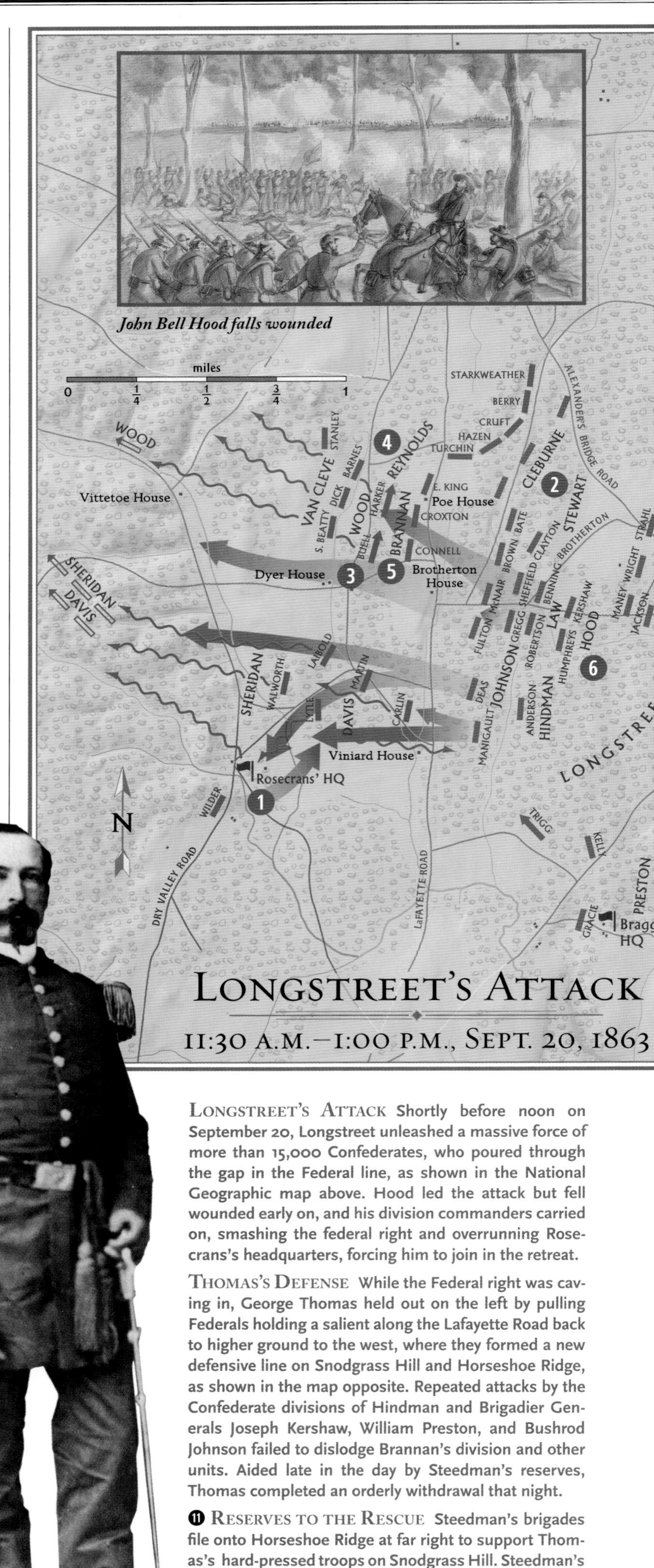

Longstreet's Attack Shortly before noon on September 20, Longstreet unleashed a massive force of more than 15,000 Confederates, who poured through the gap in the Federal line, as shown in the National Geographic map above. Hood led the attack but fell wounded early on, and his division commanders carried on, smashing the federal right and overrunning Rosecrans's headquarters, forcing him to join in the retreat.

Thomas's Defense While the Federal right was caving in, George Thomas held out on the left by pulling Federals holding a salient along the Lafayette Road back to higher ground to the west, where they formed a new defensive line on Snodgrass Hill and Horseshoe Ridge, as shown in the map opposite. Repeated attacks by the Confederate divisions of Hindman and Brigadier Generals Joseph Kershaw, William Preston, and Bushrod Johnson failed to dislodge Brannan's division and other units. Aided late in the day by Steedman's reserves, Thomas completed an orderly withdrawal that night.

⓫ **Reserves to the Rescue** Steedman's brigades file onto Horseshoe Ridge at far right to support Thomas's hard-pressed troops on Snodgrass Hill. Steedman's corps commander, Gordon Granger, deployed these troops after losing touch with Rosecrans and deciding on his own authority to commit the reserves. "I am going to Thomas, orders or no orders!" he declared.

Ruin and Redemption Despite the ruinous consequences for Federals at Chickamauga when he unquestioningly obeyed a misguided order from Rosecrans, Thomas Wood went on to distinguish himself as a commander under Grant and Sherman and win promotion to major general.

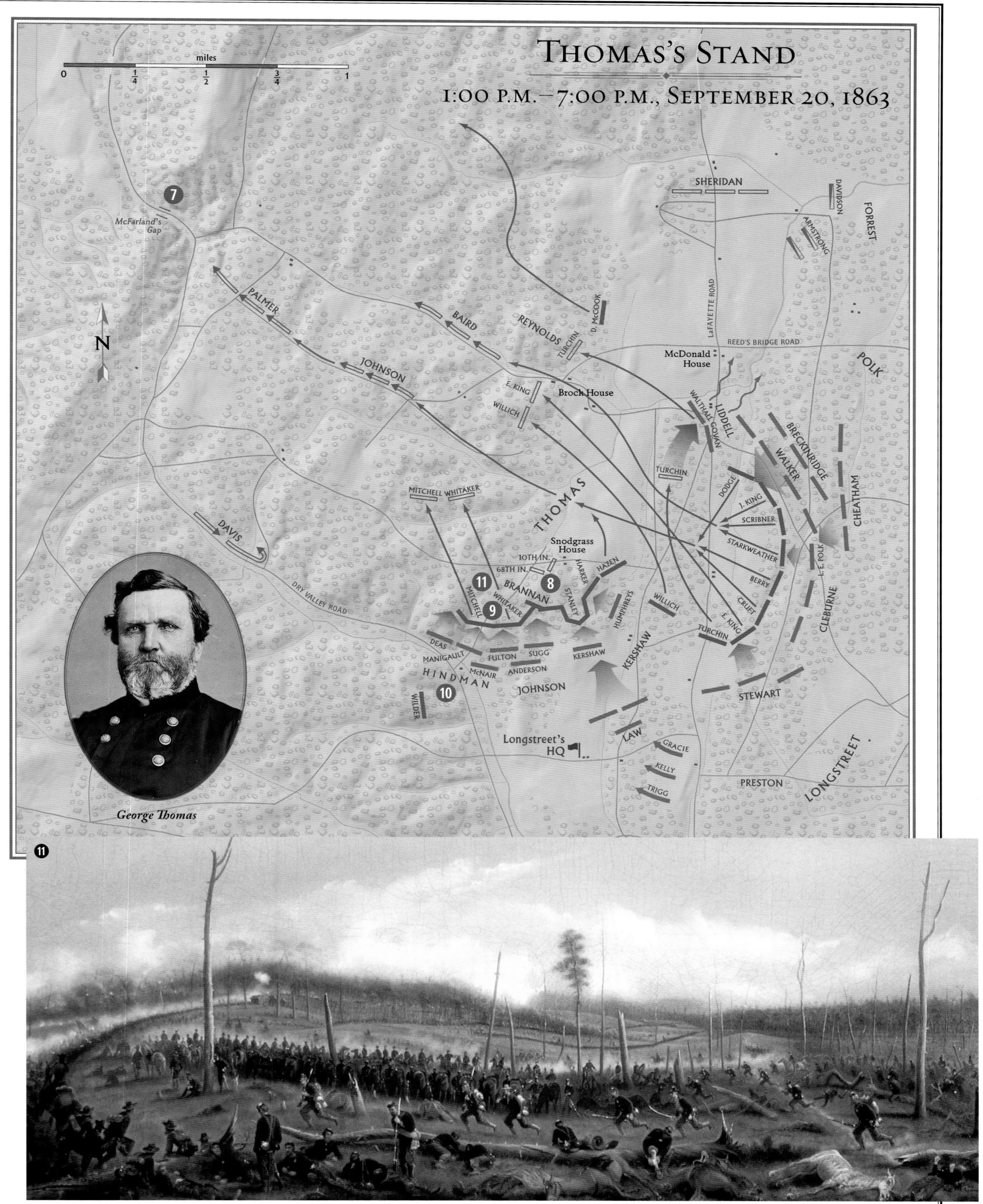

George Thomas

1863

CHATTANOOGA

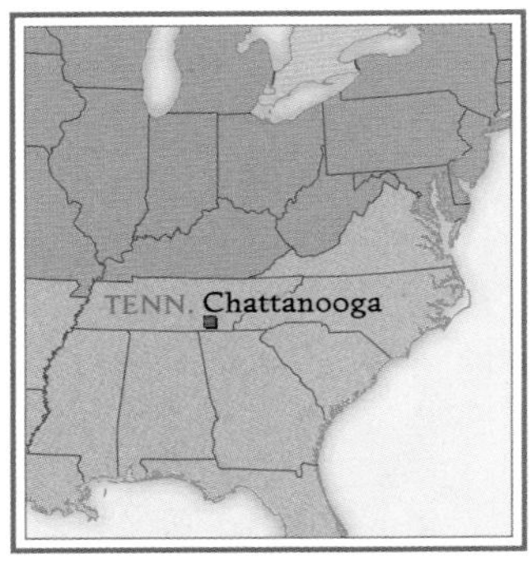

WESTERN THEATER

SEPTEMBER 24, 1863 After retreating to Chattanooga with his army, Rosecrans abandons Lookout Mountain to Bragg's Confederates, who tighten their grip on the town.

SEPTEMBER 30 Confederate cavalry commander Joseph Wheeler begins raiding the precarious Federal supply line to Chattanooga.

OCTOBER 16 Grant takes charge of Federal forces in the region and replaces Rosecrans with George Thomas.

OCTOBER 27 Federals seize Brown's Ferry to open a new supply line to Chattanooga.

NOVEMBER 23–25 Battle of Chattanooga

When Rosecrans reached Chattanooga ❶ after retreating from Chickamauga, a Union officer remarked, "he had the appearance of one broken in spirit." Thanks to George Thomas, his army remained intact, but he had lost 16,000 men in that vicious two-day battle along the River of Blood and seemed dazed by the sudden collapse that left him hemmed in at Chattanooga by Bragg's Confederates. On September 24, against the advice of aides, Rosecrans withdrew forces from Lookout Mountain ❷ and ceded it to Bragg, who placed artillery there overlooking the Tennessee River, halting traffic on the Nashville & Chattanooga Railroad ❸, which Confederates sealed off between here and Bridgeport, Alabama, some 30 miles to the west. Federals now had to haul food and ammunition overland from Stevenson, Alabama, on a circuitous 60-mile route ❹, described by one Federal as the muddiest and steepest "ever crossed by army wagons and mules." Attacks on that line by Rebel cavalry so reduced supplies that hungry soldiers picked up crumbs of food falling from the few wagons that got through.

On October 16, Ulysses Grant took charge of all Federal forces between the Appalachians and the Mississippi and responded to the crisis in Chattanooga by replacing Rosecrans with Thomas, who promised to "hold the town until we starve." Reinforcements were coming to Chattanooga, including 10,000 men from the Army of the Potomac under Joseph Hooker and several divisions from the Army of the Tennessee led by William Sherman. Grant went there himself to oversee operations. Arriving in late October, he found Thomas's chief engineer, Brigadier General William F. Smith, ready with a plan to replace the perilous wagon route with a new and faster "Cracker Line," so-called for the hardtack crackers that made up much of the soldiers' diet. On the night of October 27, 1,500 Federals drifted downriver from Chattanooga and landed in pontoon boats at Brown's Ferry ❺, where they overwhelmed Confederates guarding that crossing and linked up with reinforcements approaching from the west, opening a new supply route that avoided enemy guns on Lookout Mountain. Freight was shipped from the railroad depot at Bridgeport up the Tennessee River to Kelley's Ferry—beyond which navigation was hazardous—and from there by road ❻ to Brown's Ferry, where supply wagons crossed on a pontoon bridge to Moccasin Point ❼ before coming back over the river on another such bridge ❽ at Chattanooga. Up to 30 freight-carloads of goods were unloaded daily at Bridgeport and hauled to Chattanooga along this route, ending the supply crisis there and allowing Grant to move forward with plans to break Bragg's grip on the town.

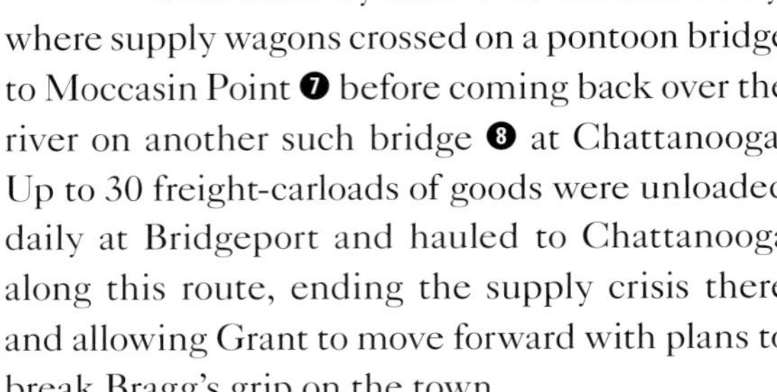

Ulysses Grant

Confederate losses at Chickamauga had been even steeper than Federal casualties. After sending Longstreet and his troops off in early November to challenge Federals who had occupied Knoxville, Tennessee, in September, Bragg had only about 40,000 men left here to hold an eight-mile-long line extending from Lookout Mountain to Missionary Ridge ❾. Lieutenant General Daniel Harvey Hill, a corps commander under Bragg, echoed the opinion of many in the Army of Tennessee when he wrote that Chickamauga became a "barren victory" when Bragg failed to follow up with a quick strike at Chattanooga before Union forces there were reinforced and resupplied. Confederates "fought stoutly to the last," Hill concluded, "but, after Chickamauga, with the sullenness of despair and without the enthusiasm of hope." ■

❶ **FEDERAL CAMP** Union troops stand in a camp in Chattanooga built with planks taken from houses Federals tore down for timber and fuel. Many civilians who did not flee the town lived in shacks that one reporter likened to the "worst tenements in New York City."

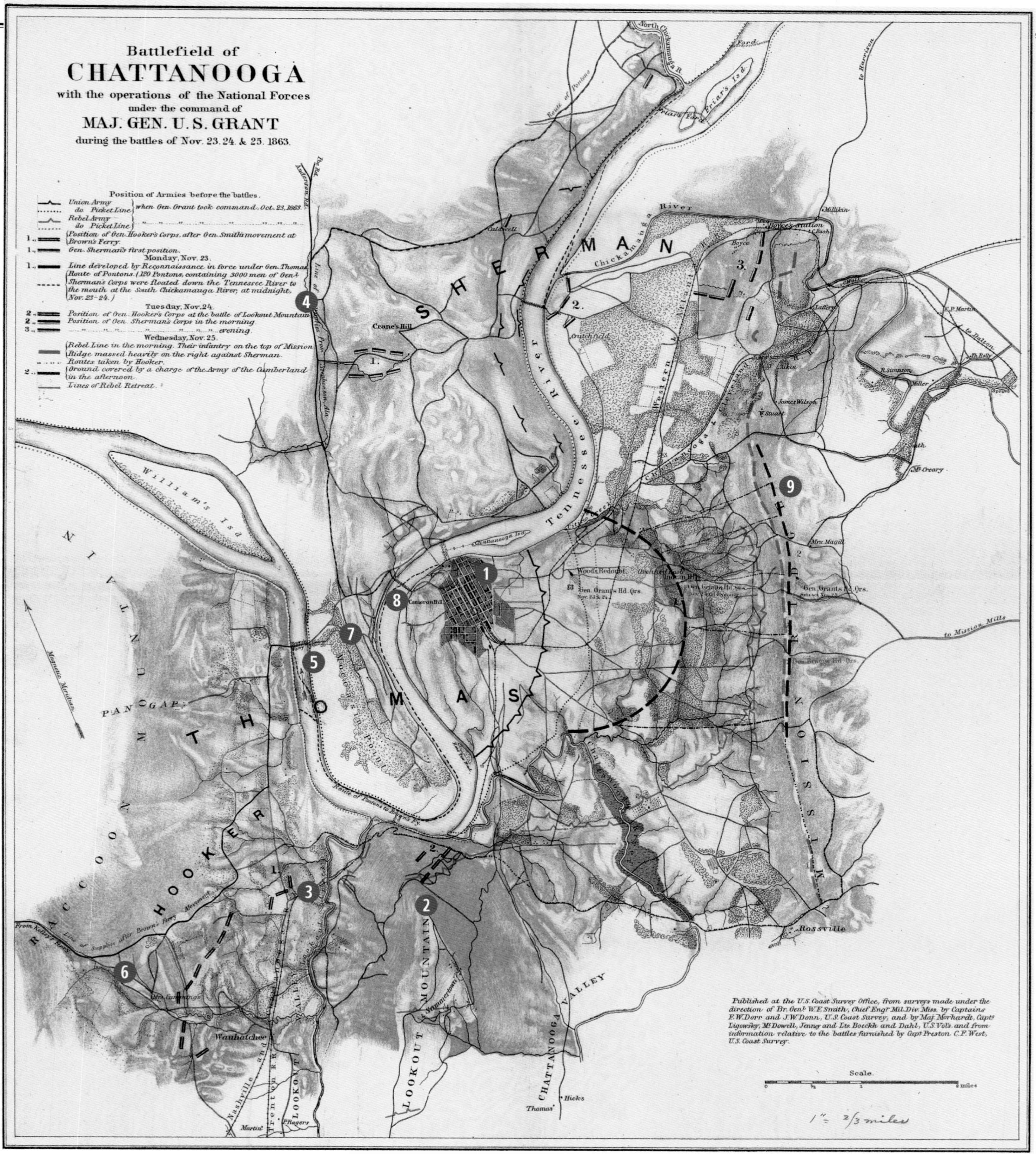

Battlefield of
CHATTANOOGA
with the operations of the National Forces
under the command of
MAJ. GEN. U. S. GRANT
during the battles of Nov. 23. 24. & 25. 1863.

Position of Armies before the battles.

Union Army } when Gen. Grant took command, Oct. 23, 1863.
do Picket Line
Rebel Army } " " " " " " " "
do Picket Line
1 Position of Gen. Hooker's Corps, after Gen. Smith's movement at Brown's Ferry.
1 Gen. Sherman's first position.

Monday, Nov. 23.

1 Line developed by Reconnaissance in force under Gen. Thomas
Route of Pontons. (120 Pontons, containing 3000 men of Gen.l Sherman's Corps were floated down the Tennessee River to the mouth at the South Chickamauga River, at midnight, Nov. 23–24.)

Tuesday, Nov. 24.

2 Position of Gen. Hooker's Corps at the battle of Lookout Mountain
2 Position of Gen. Sherman's Corps in the morning
3 " " " " " " evening.

Wednesday, Nov. 25.

Rebel Line in the morning. Their infantry on the top of Mission Ridge massed heavily on the right against Sherman.
Routes taken by Hooker.
2 Ground covered by a charge of the Army of the Cumberland in the afternoon.
Lines of Rebel Retreat.

Published at the U.S. Coast Survey Office, from surveys made under the direction of Br. Gen.l W. F. Smith, Chief Eng.r Mil. Div. Miss. by Captains F. W. Dorr and J. W. Donn, U.S. Coast Survey, and by Maj. Morhardt, Capt.s Ligowsky, McDowell, Jenney and Lts. Boeckh and Dahl, U.S. Vols. and from information relative to the battles furnished by Capt. Preston C. F. West, U.S. Coast Survey.

Scale.
0 ½ 1 2 miles

1" = 2/3 miles

BREAKING BRAGG'S GRIP A map prepared under the direction of Brigadier General William French Smith, chief engineer of Thomas's Army of the Cumberland, shows how Grant deployed his forces to break the Confederate line extending around the southern perimeter of Chattanooga. Thomas's forces held the town and guarded the supply line from Brown's Ferry while Hooker's troops menaced the Confederate left flank on Lookout Mountain and Sherman's men targeted the right flank on Missionary Ridge.

FREIGHT ON THE CRACKER LINE Loaded with supplies, the steamboat *Chattanooga* docks at Kelley's Ferry, where goods were unloaded and hauled by wagon over the Cracker Line to Grant's forces in Chattanooga.

1863 | CHATTANOOGA

Lookout Mountain and Missionary Ridge

ARTHUR MACARTHUR, JR.

Among those leading the decisive Union charge up Missionary Ridge on November 25 was 18-year-old Lieutenant Arthur MacArthur, Jr., of the 24th Wisconsin Infantry, whose distinguished military record later inspired his son, General Douglas MacArthur, to even greater accomplishments. Just 16 when he volunteered to fight for the Union, Arthur MacArthur obtained a lieutenant's commission with the help of his father, a prominent figure in Milwaukee. Older soldiers in the regiment made fun of the "baby adjutant" but soon learned to respect this precocious leader of men. During the charge up Missionary Ridge, he picked up the regimental flag after the color sergeant fell critically wounded and carried it to the top, yelling "On Wisconsin." As his commander reported afterward, "He was the most distinguished in action on a field where many in the regiment displayed conspicuous gallantry." Awarded the Medal of Honor for his heroics at Chattanooga, he entered the U.S. Army after the war and served as commander of Fort Selden in New Mexico, where his son was born in 1880. "My first memory was the sound of bugles," recalled Douglas MacArthur, who watched in admiration as his father advanced to become military governor of the Philippines and who later followed in his footsteps.

Grant launched his offensive at Chattanooga ❶ on November 23 by ordering Thomas's forces to probe enemy defenses east of town. Thomas took this opportunity to show that troops routed at Chickamauga—including the divisions of Philip Sheridan ❷ and Thomas Wood ❸, whose decision to obey Rosecrans's fateful order triggered the collapse there—still had plenty of fight in them. Brushing aside Confederate pickets, the Federals took Orchard Knob ❹ and pushed their foes back toward Missionary Ridge ❺. That same day, Sherman's troops crossed the Tennessee River northeast of Chattanooga and approached Tunnel Hill ❻, held by Patrick Cleburne's Confederates.

On November 24, the action shifted to the Confederate left flank on Lookout Mountain ❼, where another Union officer who had something to prove—Fighting Joe Hooker ❽, still smarting from his defeat at Chancellorsville—took the initiative. His instructions from Grant were to demonstrate here while Sherman bore down on Bragg's right flank and to take Lookout Mountain only if practicable. Intent on seizing that objective, Hooker sent troops under Brigadier General John Geary ❾ up the steep, fog-shrouded slope that morning while forces led by Brigadier General Peter Osterhaus ❿ advanced around the base of the mountain near the Tennessee River. Geary's men collided with Confederates commanded by Brigadier Edward Walthall ⓫, who called up reinforcements and held out until nightfall, when the Rebels were outflanked by Osterhaus's troops and withdrew.

Early on November 25, Sherman met his match when he clashed at Tunnel Hill with Cleburne, supported by Major General Carter Stevenson's division ⓬. Outnumbered more than two to one and facing Federal fire so intense it formed "a continuous sheet of hissing, flying lead," Cleburne wrote, his troops clung defiantly to the high ground and dashed Sherman's hopes of striking the decisive blow here. That honor went instead to Thomas's forces, who again exceeded Grant's expectations. Ordered to seize rifle pits at the foot of Missionary Ridge, they came under plunging artillery fire there and kept going, surging up the hillside in an impulsive charge that overwhelmed the Confederates and shattered Bragg's line, forcing him to retreat into Georgia. ■

Lookout Mountain

Battle for the Heights Although Confederates held the high ground around Chattanooga, Grant had numerical superiority and pressed Bragg on both flanks, as shown on this National Geographic map. Bragg could not defend against Hooker to his left and Sherman to his right without weakening his center, where Thomas's troops broke through.

Clinging to the Flag Corporal William Montgomery of the 76th Ohio Infantry lost his arm but clung to this bullet-riddled flag in a clash with retreating Confederates at Ringgold, Georgia, on November 27. Bragg's defeat at Chattanooga cost him nearly 1,000 more casualties than the Federals suffered and led him to resign his command.

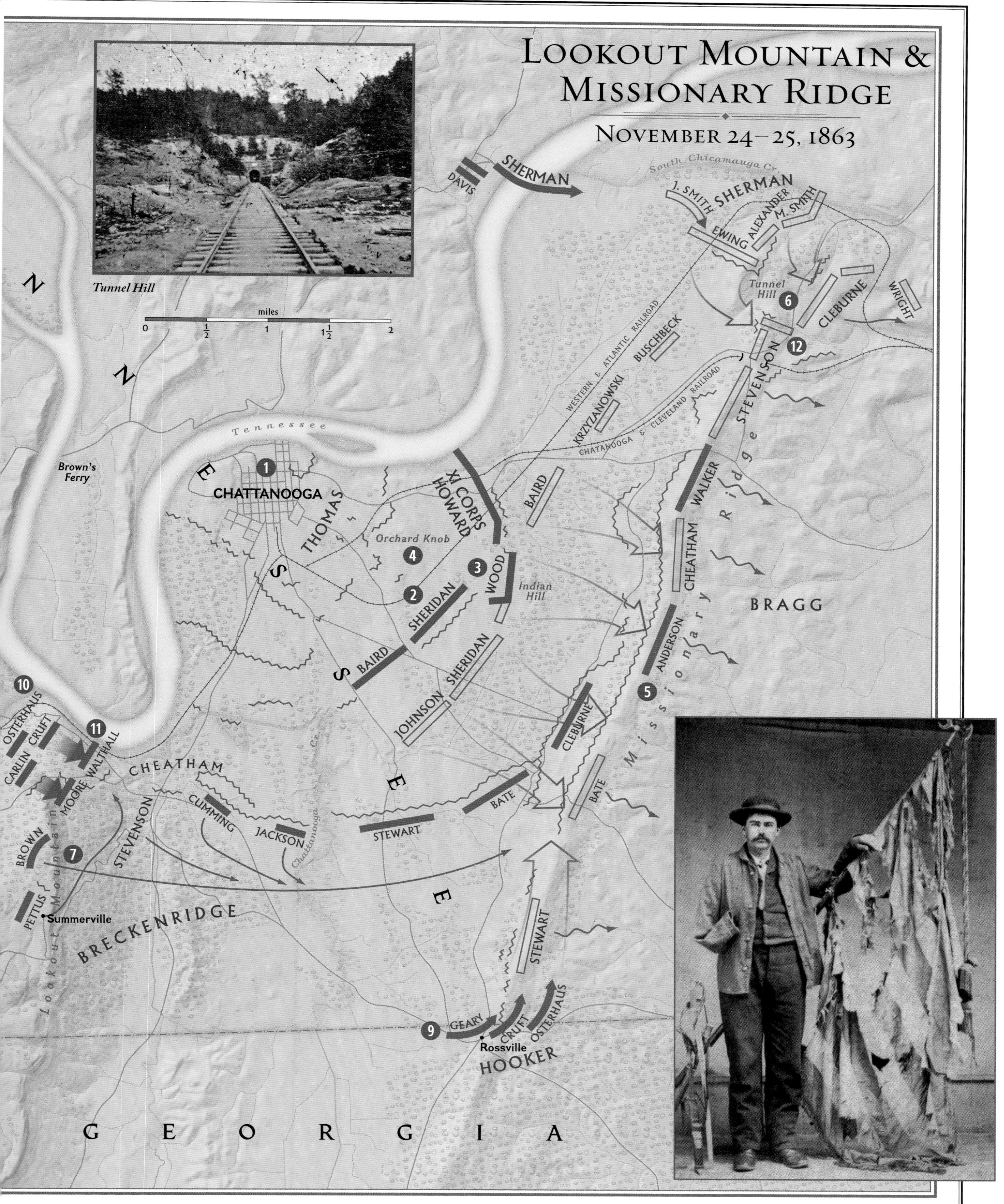

Lookout Mountain & Missionary Ridge
November 24–25, 1863
Tunnel Hill
miles
0
½
1
1½
2
SHERMAN
DAVIS
South Chicamauga Cr.
J. SMITH
SHERMAN
ALEXANDER
M. SMITH
EWING
Tunnel Hill
CLEBURNE
WRIGHT
BUSCHBECK
WESTERN & ATLANTIC RAILROAD
KRZYZANOWSKI
CHATTANOOGA & CLEVELAND RAILROAD
STEVENSON
Tennessee
Brown's Ferry
CHATTANOOGA
THOMAS
XI CORPS HOWARD
BAIRD
WALKER
Ridge
Orchard Knob
WOOD
Indian Hill
CHEATHAM
BRAGG
SHERIDAN
ANDERSON
Missionary
BAIRD
SHERIDAN
JOHNSON
CLEBURNE
OSTERHAUS
CRUFT
CARLIN
WALTHALL
MOORE
CHEATHAM
BATE
BATE
STEVENSON
CUMMING
JACKSON
STEWART
Chattanooga Cr.
BROWN
Lookout Mountain
PETTUS
Summerville
BRECKENRIDGE
STEWART
GEARY
CRUFT
OSTERHAUS
Rossville
HOOKER
TENNESSEE
GEORGIA

1863

KNOXVILLE

WESTERN THEATER

SEPTEMBER 2, 1863 Federals of Ambrose Burnside's Army of the Ohio enter Knoxville, Tennessee, hailed by Unionists there, and take possession for the Union.

NOVEMBER 4 Bragg sends Confederates led by Longstreet from Chattanooga to Knoxville to challenge Burnside.

NOVEMBER 16 Burnside clashes with Longstreet at Campbell's Station before pulling back to Knoxville.

NOVEMBER 29 Federals repulse Longstreet's attack on Fort Sanders, ending his campaign to recapture Knoxville.

Confederates struggling to hold Chattanooga faced a dangerous distraction when Knoxville, a hotbed of Unionist sentiment, fell to Federals led by Major General Ambrose Burnside in early September. That led Jefferson Davis to propose that Bragg send troops there from Chattanooga to regain the town and rebuff its Unionists. Beholden to Davis, who backed him when many officers were urging his dismissal, and eager to be rid of Longstreet, one of his strongest critics, Bragg sent Longstreet off to Knoxville with 10,000 troops whose absence would prove costly when Grant attacked at Chattanooga.

After clashing with Longstreet at Campbell's Station on November 16, Burnside fell back within the defenses of Knoxville, dominated by Fort Sanders (opposite). Late that month, Longstreet decided to attack there despite receiving unconfirmed reports that Confederates had been defeated at Chattanooga, rendering his position at Knoxville untenable. "There is neither safety nor honor in any other course," he concluded. In targeting the fort's northwest bastion ❶, he chose not to use his artillery ❷ but to rely instead on a bayonet charge, hoping to catch Federals off guard. Surprise was lost, however, when his skirmishers left their own rifle pits ❸ on the night of November 28 to seize enemy rifle pits ❹ in advance of the attack. Federal gunners and infantry were ready when Rebels charged at dawn on the next day, stumbling over telegraph wire ❺ strung between tree trunks before descending into a deep ditch ❻ bordering the fort and attempting to climb its steep wall ❼, coated in ice and blood. As one journalist reported, Rebels "struggled up the scarp, and slipping in blood fell back to join their mangled predecessors in the gory mud below." A few determined Confederates scaled the wall and planted battle flags ❽ before being captured, killed, or pushed back. Longstreet soon called off the hopeless attack and withdrew from Knoxville when he learned that Sherman was coming to aid Burnside. This bitter setback for one of the South's most accomplished officers cost him more than 800 casualties, compared to just 13 for Burnside, capping what the *Richmond Examiner* called "the gloomiest year of our struggle." ■

❺ CHARGING THE FORT Crossing a perilous field laced with telegraph wires to trip them, Confederates brave artillery fire and struggle up the ice-slick wall of Fort Sanders on November 29, only to be driven back.

HAILED IN KNOXVILLE Burnside's entry into Knoxville was hailed by Unionists there and touted by the Northern press.

A SOLDIER'S MAP Drawn by John G. Orth, a Union soldier from Ohio, this map of Fort Sanders, oriented with north to the right, details the attack by Longstreet's men, who advanced from the north and west (top).

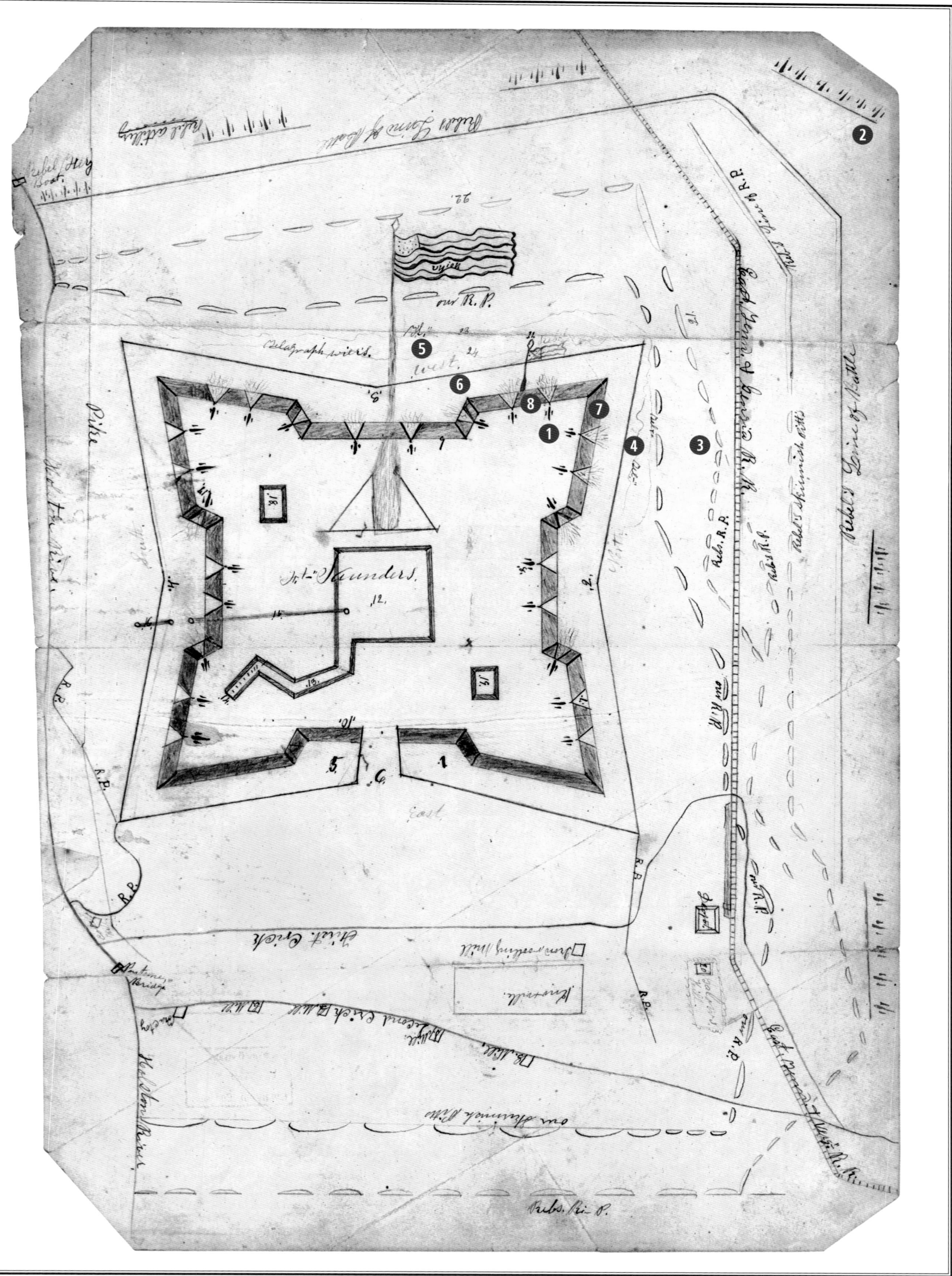

CHAPTER 4

The Landscape of War | 1864

Like Lee's forces, Grant's men fortified their line at Petersburg and created strongpoints like Fort Sedgwick, shown here. Named for General John Sedgwick, killed at Spotsylvania, this forbidding earth-and-timber compound was known to the troops as Fort Hell.

"This army cannot stand a siege. We must end this business on the battlefield, not in a fortified place."

ROBERT E. LEE,
BEFORE THE SIEGE OF PETERSBURG

1864
PATHS TO VICTORY

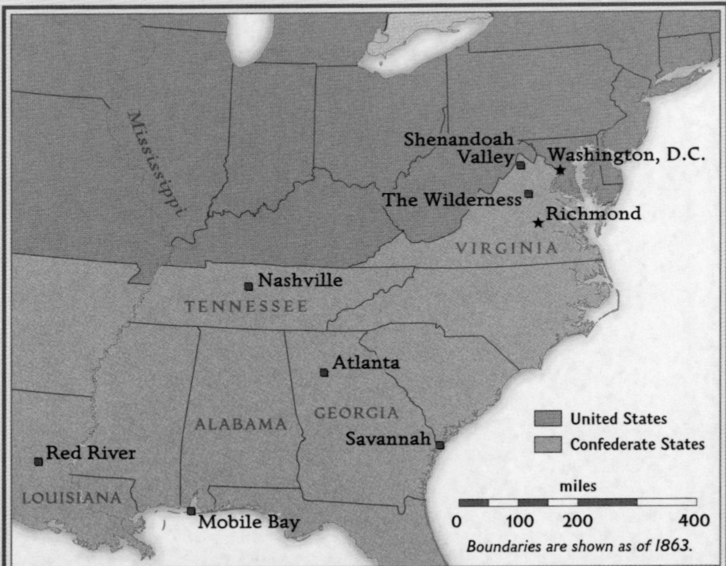

When Ulysses Grant became the Union's general in chief in March 1864, his task was not to carry on the war but to conclude it swiftly and surely by crushing enemy forces. Lincoln had long sought a top commander like Grant who understood what the president called the "awful arithmetic" of this conflict, meaning that if the populous Union pressed its numerical advantage relentlessly on all fronts and endured heavy casualties while exacting a comparable toll from the enemy, Rebel forces would dwindle and the Confederacy would collapse. Simply engaging in a grinding war of attrition, however, would not bring the quick victory Lincoln and Grant hoped for. The Union would have to apply its might shrewdly and flexibly to pin down Confederates on both sides of the Appalachians and sever their supply lines. Dismayed with peripheral efforts like the Red River campaign in Louisiana that diverted Federals, Grant concentrated all available resources against Robert E. Lee's Army of Northern Virginia—which he battled in the Wilderness and later besieged at Petersburg—while William Sherman campaigned tirelessly in Georgia against the other substantial Confederate force, Joseph Johnston's Army of Tennessee.

Although prospects for outright Confederate victory looked dim, Jefferson Davis and his commanders had a more realistic hope—that Northerners would grow weary of the war and reject Lincoln in November in favor of a president willing to end the conflict on terms acceptable to the South. By holding out at Petersburg over the summer and sending Jubal Early off to secure the Shenandoah Valley and threaten Washington, D.C., Lee kept the heat on Lincoln, who fretted that he might "not outlast the rebellion." Not until the presidential campaign began that fall did crucial events in the field, including Sherman's pivotal victory in Atlanta and Philip Sheridan's triumph over Early, lift Lincoln's hopes and dash those of Confederate leaders.

JANUARY–JUNE

Federals and visitor in winter camp in Virginia

January 4, 1864 Jefferson Davis authorizes Robert E. Lee to impress food from civilians, if necessary, to feed his army.

February 1 Abraham Lincoln orders 500,000 men drafted in the North to serve for three years or the duration of the conflict.

February 9 John Schofield named commander of the Union Army of the Ohio, which will join William Sherman's forthcoming Atlanta campaign.

February 17 The experimental Confederate submarine *H. L. Hunley* is lost with its captain and crew after sinking the Federal steam sloop *Housatonic* off Charleston.

February 20 Confederates defeat Federals near Olustee, Florida.

March 1 Federal cavalry commanders Hugh Judson Kilpatrick and Ulric Dahlgren pull back from Richmond, ending their attempted raid on the Confederate capital.

March 9 Ulysses Grant promoted to lieutenant general and given command of all Federal forces.

March 12 Federals led by Nathaniel Banks embark on the Red River campaign with a fleet commanded by David Porter, hoping to ascend the river to Shreveport, Louisiana, and invade Texas.

March 14 Federals capture Fort De Russy on the Red River.

March 17 Grant announces that he will make his headquarters in the field with the Army of the Potomac as it prepares to advance against Lee's Army of Northern Virginia.

JULY–DECEMBER

July 5 Jubal Early crosses into Maryland.

July 8 Lincoln backs constitutional amendment abolishing slavery.

July 9 Battle of Monocacy (Maryland)

July 12 Early repulsed by Federals defending Washington, D.C.

Dockworkers at Alexandria, Virginia

July 17 Joseph Johnston replaced as commander of the Army of Tennessee by John Bell Hood as Sherman's forces approach Atlanta.

July 20 Battle of Peachtree Creek (Georgia)

July 22 Battle of Atlanta (Georgia)

July 28 Battle of Ezra Church (Georgia)

July 30 Battle of the Crater at Petersburg; Confederate cavalry led by John McCausland torch Chambersburg, Pennsylvania.

August 5 Federal fleet commanded by David Farragut enters Mobile Bay between Confederate Forts Morgan and Gaines and defeats a fleet led by Franklin Buchanan.

April 3 Banks leaves Porter's fleet at Grand Ecore, Louisiana, and advances toward Shreveport by road while Confederate forces led by Richard Taylor gather to oppose him.

April 4 Philip Sheridan appointed cavalry commander of the Army of the Potomac.

April 8 Battle of Sabine Crossroads (Louisiana)

Drummer boy, Army of the Potomac

April 9 Battle of Pleasant Hill (Louisiana)

April 12 Confederates led by Nathan Bedford Forrest capture Fort Pillow in Tennessee, held by a racially mixed Federal force, and kill many of the fort's defenders, leading to charges that some who tried to surrender were massacred.

April 21 Banks ends his unsuccessful campaign in Louisiana and retreats with Porter's fleet down the Red River.

April 29 Federals under Franz Sigel march south from Winchester, Virginia, opposed by Confederates led by John Breckinridge.

May 4 Grant launches campaign against Robert E. Lee in Virginia by sending the Army of the Potomac south across the Rapidan River.

May 5–6 Battle of the Wilderness (Virginia)

May 7 William Sherman launches campaign against Joseph Johnston in Georgia.

May 8 Battle of Rocky Face Ridge (Georgia)

Battle flag, 42nd Virginia Infantry, captured at Spotsylvania

May 8–18 Battles at Spotsylvania (Virginia)

May 11 Jeb Stuart mortally wounded in clash with Federal cavalry at Yellow Tavern, Virginia.

May 14–15 Battle of Resaca (Georgia)

May 15 Battle of New Market (Virginia)

May 19 David Hunter replaces Franz Sigel as Federal commander in the Shenandoah Valley.

May 25–28 Battles of New Hope Church, Pickett's Mill, and Dallas (Georgia)

May 31 John Frémont nominated for president by Radical Republicans.

Stereograph of Federal burial during Grant's campaign

June 3 Battle of Cold Harbor (Virginia)

June 8 Abraham Lincoln nominated for president by the National Union Party, a title adopted by Republicans to appeal to Democrats.

June 15 Grant's troops reach Petersburg, Virginia, where Confederates fend off his attacks but soon come under siege.

June 18 David Hunter retreats from Lynchburg, Virginia, after clashing with Jubal Early's Confederates.

June 19 The U.S.S. *Kearsarge* sinks the Confederate commerce raider C.S.S. *Alabama* off Cherbourg, France.

June 27 Battle of Kennesaw Mountain (Georgia)

August 7 Philip Sheridan replaces David Hunter as commander of the Army of the Shenandoah.

August 8 Federal troops on Dauphin Island force surrender of Fort Gaines at the entrance to Mobile Bay.

August 9 Explosives planted by Confederate agents erupt at City Point, Virginia, the supply base for Grant's army at Petersburg, killing 43 people.

August 18 Federals advance at Petersburg, cutting the Weldon Railroad.

August 23 Federals force surrender of Fort Morgan at the entrance to Mobile Bay.

August 31 George McClellan nominated for president by Democrats.

August 31–September 1 Battle of Jonesboro (Georgia)

September 2 Sherman takes Atlanta.

Nathan Bedford Forrest

September 4 Confederate cavalry leader John Hunt Morgan killed by Federal raiders in Greeneville, Tennessee.

September 7 Sherman orders civilians to evacuate Atlanta.

September 19 Battle of Winchester (Virginia)

September 22 Frémont drops out of the presidential race and endorses Lincoln.

September 29 John Bell Hood leads his Army of Tennessee north across the Chattahoochee River to threaten William Sherman's supply line in northern Georgia and draw him away from Atlanta.

October 5 Battle of Allatoona Pass (Georgia)

October 7 The U.S.S. *Wachusetts* forces surrender of the Confederate commerce raider C.S.S. *Florida* off Bahia, Brazil.

October 19 Battle of Cedar Creek (Virginia)

October 23 Federals repulse Confederates at Westport, Missouri, securing their hold on the state.

November 8 Lincoln wins reelection decisively.

November 14 Sherman returns to Atlanta to prepare for his march to the sea after sending troops under Schofield to join George Thomas in Nashville and repel Hood.

November 16 Sherman departs from Atlanta on his devastating march across Georgia to Savannah.

November 22 Sherman's forces repulse a desperate attack by Confederate militiamen at Griswoldville, east of Macon.

November 25 Confederate agents set fires at several locations in New York City but do little damage.

November 29 Hood's Confederates fail to cut off Schofield's Federals at Spring Hill, Tennessee.

November 30 Battle of Franklin (Tennessee)

December 13 Sherman captures Fort McAllister, below Savannah, and links up with Federal fleet.

December 15–16 Battle of Nashville (Tennessee)

December 21 Sherman takes Savannah after Confederates led by William Hardee withdraw to South Carolina.

December 25 Confederates at Fort Fisher, North Carolina, repulse an amphibious assault by Federals.

View from capitol, Nashville 1864

1864

RED RIVER

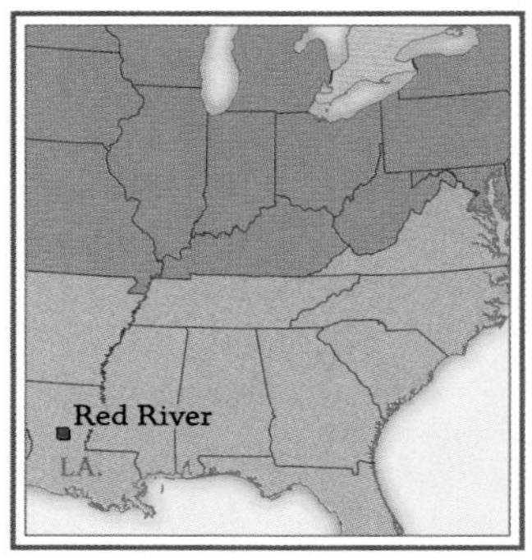

WESTERN THEATER

MARCH 12, 1864 Federals led by Nathaniel Banks embark on the Red River campaign with a fleet commanded by David Porter, hoping to ascend the river to Shreveport, Louisiana, and invade Texas.

APRIL 3 Banks leaves fleet at Grand Ecore, Louisiana, and advances toward Shreveport by road while Confederates led by Richard Taylor prepare to oppose him.

APRIL 8 Battle of Sabine Crossroads (Louisiana)

APRIL 9 Battle of Pleasant Hill (Louisiana)

APRIL 21 Banks ends campaign and retreats with fleet down the Red River.

By taking control of the Mississippi in 1863, the Union did not end the struggle beyond that river. As the war entered its fourth year, Confederates were still fighting for Louisiana and Arkansas and had firm control of Texas. At the risk of diverting Federal forces from crucial campaigns east of the Mississippi, Lincoln and others in Washington urged an invasion of Texas. They hoped to stop European weapons from coming in there through Mexico, seize cotton for foreign exchange and use in Northern textile plants, and discourage Napoleon III of France, who had invaded Mexico in 1861 and installed Maximilian as emperor, from siding with Rebels in the trans-Mississippi West.

Nathaniel Banks

With Confederates guarding the coast closely, Federals tried an inland approach to Texas in early 1864. A fleet commanded by Rear Admiral David Porter would conduct nearly 30,000 troops led by Major General Nathaniel Banks up the Red River to Shreveport, Louisiana ❶, where they would advance into nearby Texas. Launched on March 12, the campaign got off to a promising start when Porter's gunboats pounded Fort De Russy ❷, which fell on March 14 to the Federals, who took 300 Confederates there prisoner. A challenge of a different sort awaited Porter at Alexandria ❸, where the rapids were made especially hazardous by low water. The ironclad *Eastport* ran aground and blocked the channel for three days before the river rose enough to free the vessel and allow most of the Union fleet to squeeze through.

Progress was slow, and Banks had to reach Shreveport by mid-April, when he hoped to be joined by Federals advancing from Little Rock, Arkansas, but would have to send back to Sherman in Georgia some 10,000 troops needed for his forthcoming offensive there. On April 3, Banks left Porter at Grand Ecore ❹, near Natchitoches, and led most of his troops off by road ❺ to Shreveport, figuring that route would prove faster than following the winding Red River upstream with a fleet impeded by low water. The Confederate commander in Louisiana, Major General Richard Taylor, now had a chance to strike Banks while he was unprotected by gunboats.

Lying in wait at Sabine Crossroads ❻ on April 8, Taylor's troops hit the Federals while they were strung out along the road. After losing 20 cannon and 200 supply wagons, Banks regrouped at Pleasant Grove, just south of Sabine Crossroads, and held the Confederates off. He then pulled back overnight to a stronger defensive position at Pleasant Hill ❼, where his men withstood a renewed assault by Taylor's weary troops on April 9 and repulsed them with a late-day counterattack. "Had Banks followed up his success he would have met but feeble opposition to his advance on Shreveport," Taylor wrote afterward. But Banks was shaken by his losses and returned to Grand Ecore, where he found the river level falling and decided to pull out before Porter's fleet was stranded above the Alexandria rapids. Two menacing ledges of rocks there (❽ and ❾), exposed by low water, posed an insurmountable obstacle until a resourceful Federal engineer, Lieutenant Colonel Joseph Bailey, dammed the river with cribs filled with stones (❿ and ⓫), leaving chutes ⓬ through which water surged, raising the level high enough for ships to pass through.

That saved Porter's fleet and gave Banks cover as he retreated to New Orleans. But this costly fiasco left Texas and western Louisiana in Confederate hands and confirmed what Ulysses Grant and others had long suspected: The war would be decided east of the Mississippi. ■

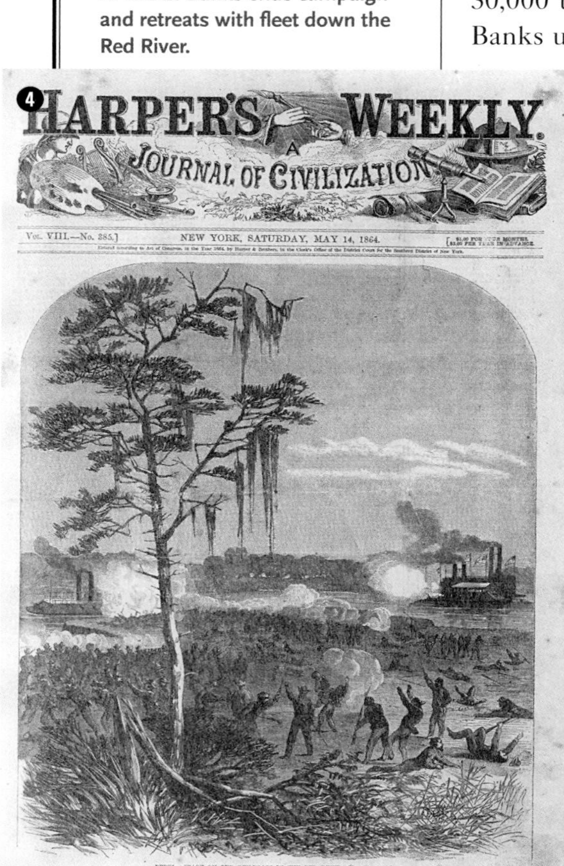
HARPER'S WEEKLY.
A JOURNAL OF CIVILIZATION

Vol. VIII.—No. 385.] NEW YORK, SATURDAY, MAY 14, 1864.

❹ **Attacking the Gunboats** Confederate troops exchange fire with ironclads of Porter's fleet, prowling the Red River near Grand Ecore on April 12, in this cover illustration from *Harper's Weekly*. Porter concluded that the Rebels here "fought with such desperation and courage" that they must have been fortified with "Louisiana rum."

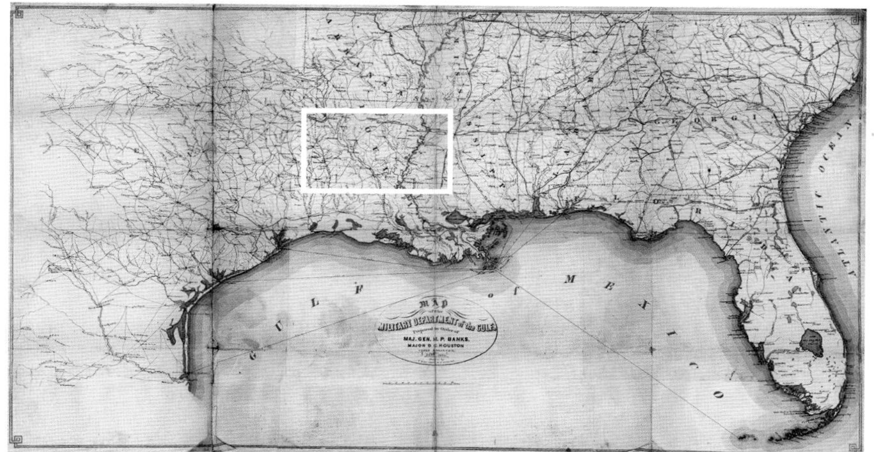

Three Views The map at left, prepared by order of Nathaniel Banks for his department, shows the lower South as a whole, with the area of the Red River campaign outlined in white. As detailed below in a closer view of that area, the amphibious campaign extended from the Union-controlled Mississippi River up the treacherous Red River in Louisiana, where Confederates contested the advance. Hit hard at Sabine Crossroads and Pleasant Hill, the Federals backed out in late April without reaching Shreveport and invading Texas as planned. By the time they returned to Alexandria, Louisiana, in early May, the water level was so low that engineers had to dam the river to create chutes, as shown in the Federal chart at bottom. That allowed Union gunboats and transports to avoid the exposed rocks and continue their ignominious retreat to the Mississippi River.

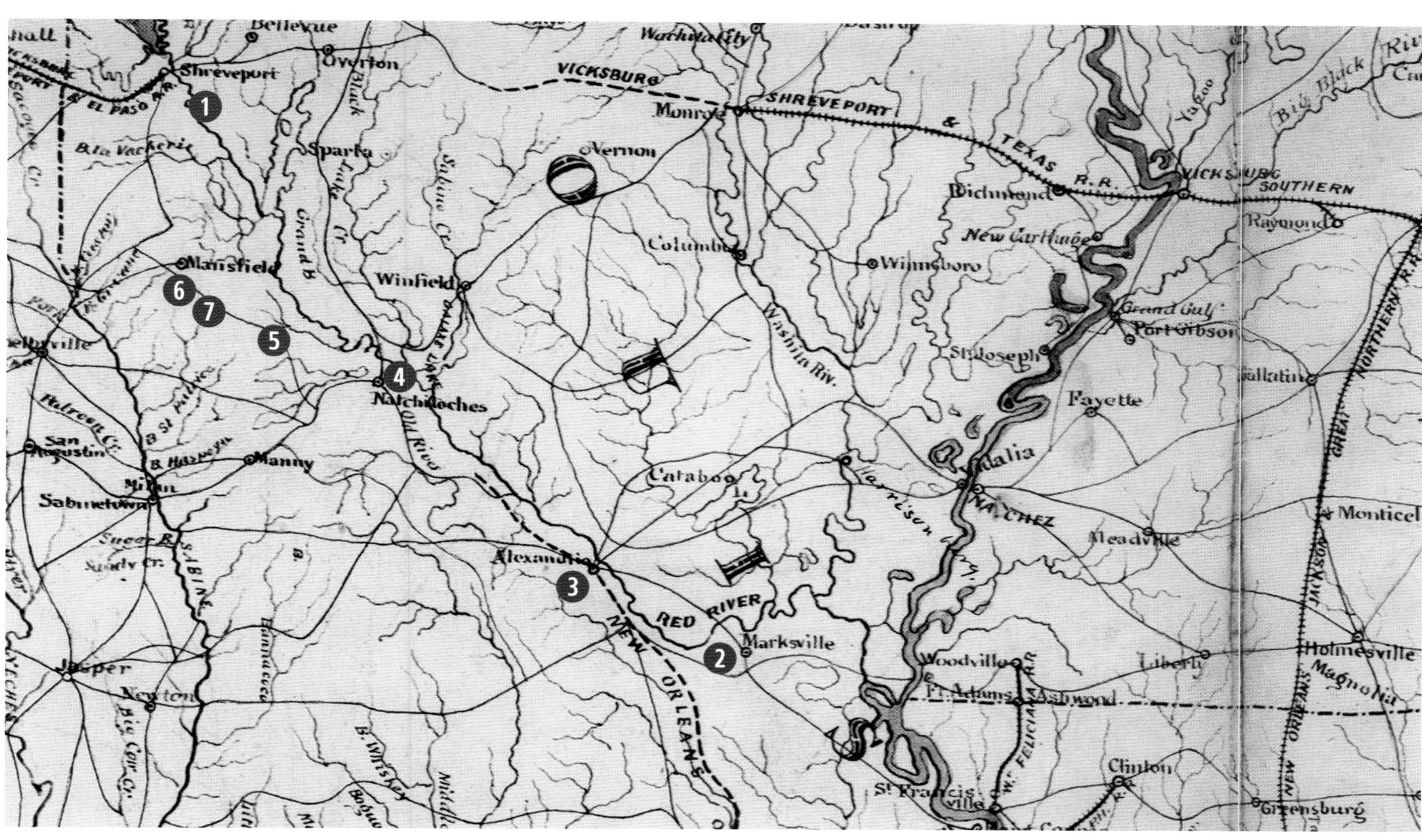

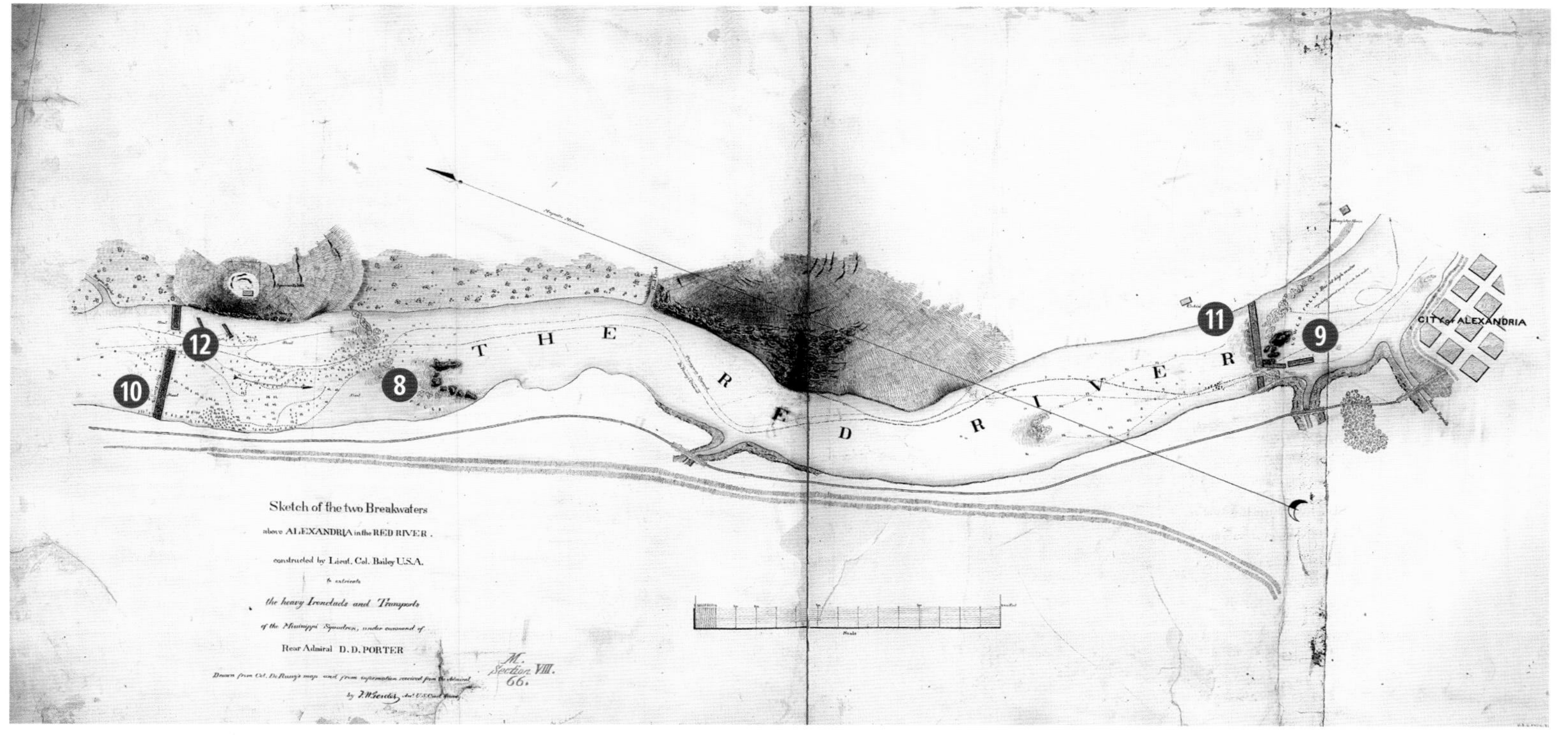

1864

INTO THE WILDERNESS

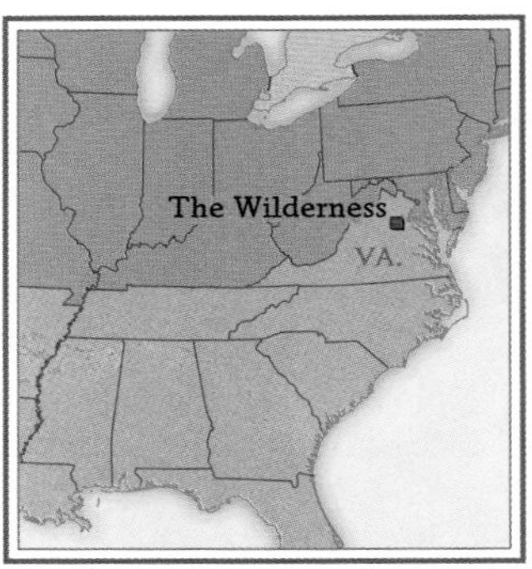

EASTERN THEATER

MARCH 9, 1864 Ulysses Grant promoted to lieutenant general, in command of all Federal forces.

MAY 4 Grant launches campaign against Robert E. Lee.

MAY 5–6 Battle of the Wilderness (Virginia)

MAY 8–18 Battles at Spotsylvania

JUNE 3 Battle of Cold Harbor

JUNE 15 Grant's troops reach Petersburg, Virginia, where Confederates fend off his attacks but soon come under siege.

JULY 30 Battle of the Crater at Petersburg

Promoted to lieutenant general in March and given command of all Federal forces, Grant set out to crush the Confederacy by advancing in overwhelming strength against Lee's Army of Northern Virginia while Sherman took on Joseph Johnston's forces in Georgia. Grant's offensive was not aimed primarily at capturing Richmond ❶ but at shattering Lee's army in the field, which would doom Richmond and leave Jefferson Davis exposed if he tried to flee with his government to a new capital and prolong the war. Grant knew that Lee, defending his own ground tenaciously with some 60,000 men, could be defeated only by a much larger army. By shifting to the front line troops stationed at forts around Washington ❷ or those performing noncombat duties, Grant swelled the Army of the Potomac to nearly 120,000 men and vowed to give the Rebels "no rest from attack."

Lee held a well-fortified line below the Rapidan River near a stream called Mine Run ❸, where George Meade had scrubbed the campaign he launched against the Confederates in late 1863, declaring that he would "sooner sacrifice my commission than my men." He thought he would be ousted as commander of the Army of the Potomac for not making what he considered a suicidal attack on those formidable defenses. But Grant decided to retain Meade, who would take Grant's broad orders and implement them. Grant agreed with Meade that a frontal assault on Lee's defenses would be futile. Instead, he would turn Lee's right flank and force him to abandon his defenses and fight on ground of Grant's choosing. Crossing the Rapidan at Ely's Ford ❹ and Germanna Ford ❺ on May 4, he hoped to make it through the treacherous Wilderness ❻ before his opponent could cut him off. Anticipating that thrust, Lee met Grant there in the Wilderness in a vicious two-day battle that was followed by further bloodbaths at Spotsylvania ❼ and Cold Harbor ❽ before Grant shifted course and laid siege to Lee's army at Petersburg ❾. ■

EMBATTLED VIRGINIA Published in New York in 1864, this commercial map of the hotly contested ground between Washington and Richmond reflects the keen public interest in Grant's campaign against Lee and a growing awareness of Virginia's geography as cartographers focused on the state in greater detail during the war.

❹ CROSSING THE RAPIDAN Federals of Winfield Scott Hancock's Second Corps cross the Rapidan River at Ely's Ford on their way to the Wilderness in a sketch made on the scene for *Harper's Weekly* by artist Alfred Waud.

THE ARMY'S NEW BOSS Grant, pictured here in 1864 after taking charge of the Union Army as a whole, was described by one officer as "stumpy, unmilitary, slouchy." But his men knew he meant business. As one soldier wrote: "We all felt at last that the boss had arrived."

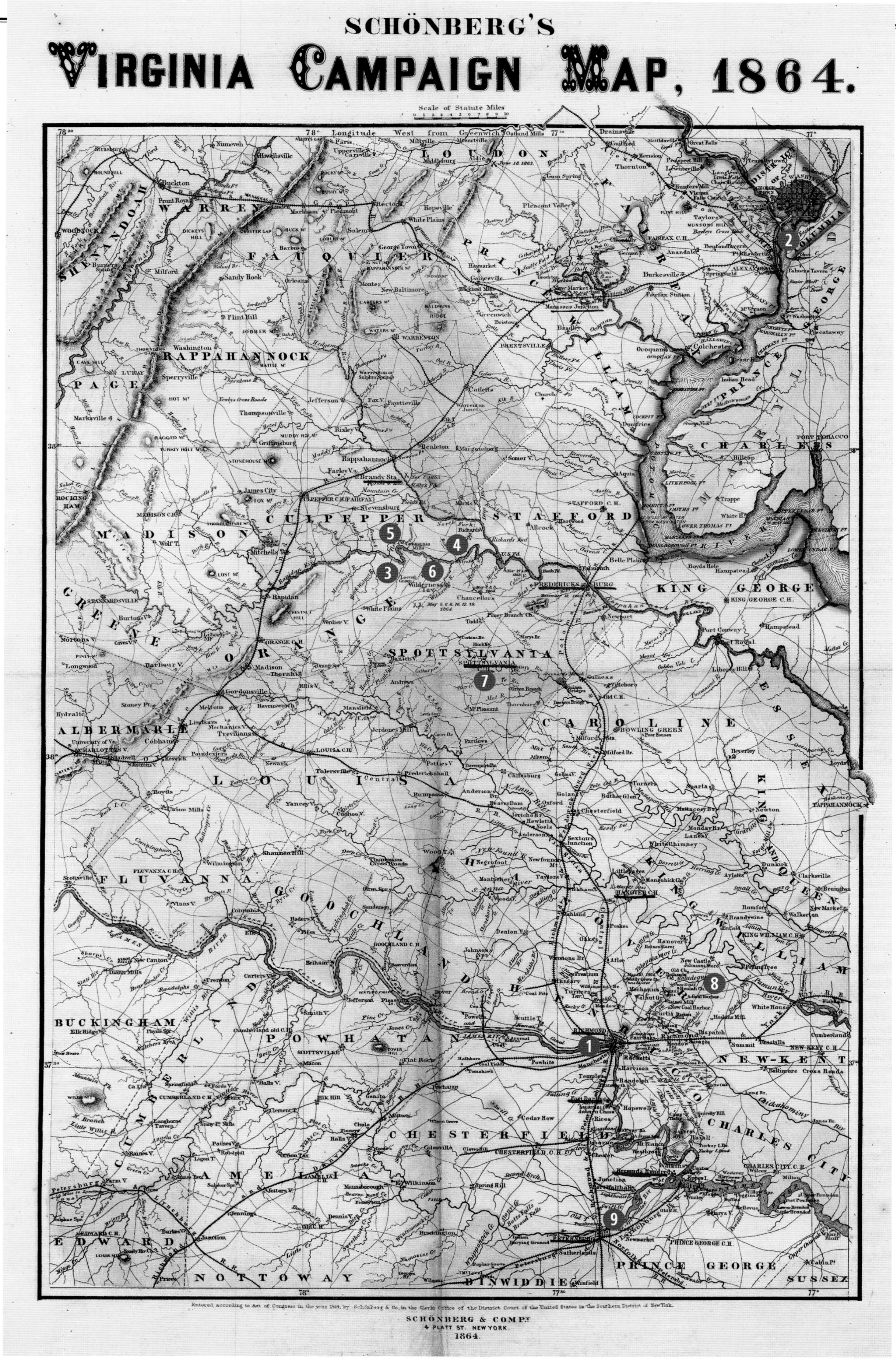

SCHÖNBERG'S

VIRGINIA CAMPAIGN MAP, 1864.

Scale of Statute Miles

Entered according to Act of Congress in the year 1864, by Schönberg & Co., in the Clerks Office of the District Court of the United States in the Southern District of New York.

SCHÖNBERG & COMPY
4 PLATT ST. NEW YORK.
1864.

ACROSS THE RAPIDAN

When Lee learned on May 4 that Grant's forces were crossing the Rapidan, he set forces in motion to intercept them. Closest to the Federals was Richard Ewell's Second Corps, which marched eastward along the Orange Turnpike ❶. Any chance Grant had of eluding Ewell and flanking Lee was lost when Meade halted the troops to allow their supply wagons to catch up. Federals spent an eerie night in the Wilderness, where the skeletons of men hastily buried after the Battle of Chancellorsville lay exposed and bitter memories of that defeat haunted the army's veterans.

Skeletons in the Wilderness

Grant's response when told Rebels were approaching was defiant. "If any opportunity presents itself for pitching in to a part of Lee's army, do so," he instructed Meade, who ordered Major General Gouverneur Warren's Fifth Corps to pivot westward and advance against the enemy on May 5. "The jungle through which we now had to struggle was almost impassable," recalled Lieutenant Sartell Prentice of the 12th U. S. Infantry, groping forward north of the turnpike with Brigadier General Romeyn Ayres's brigade of Warren's corps. As Prentice and company neared a clearing called Saunders Field ❷, where the enemy waited on the far side, an oppressive silence descended over this "dismal Wilderness, in which a bird had scarce heart to peep."

Shortly after noon that silence was broken as cheering Zouaves of the 140th New York Infantry led the way for Ayres across Saunders Field. Staggered by a terrific volley from Confederates led by Brigadier General George Steuart ❸, the Zouaves were soon forced back with others in their brigade when Steuart counterattacked. South of the turnpike, meanwhile, Federals launched a furious assault that claimed the life of Confederate Brigadier General John Marshall Jones ❹ and punctured Ewell's line. Ewell turned to Brigadier General John B. Gordon, whose Georgians were just coming up. "The fate of the day depends upon you, sir," he told Gordon, who replied at the top of his voice so that his troops could hear: "These men will save it, sir." Then Gordon threw them into the breach below the turnpike ❺. "With a deafening yell that must have been heard miles away, that glorious brigade rushed upon the hitherto advancing enemy," he wrote, and shattered the Union phalanx "into fragments." Fierce fighting continued here and to the south, along the Orange Plank Road, where Confederates of A. P. Hill's Third Corps collided with Federals of Sedgwick's Sixth Corps and Hancock's Second Corps. But neither side could knock out the other in this brutal "slugging match," as one Confederate put it, which ceased "only when exhaustion and night commanded a rest." ■

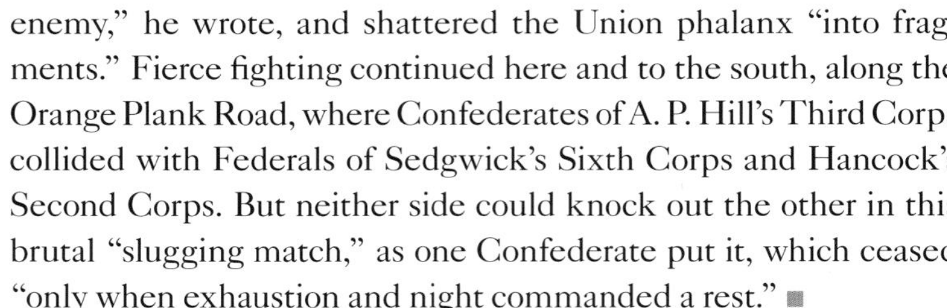

ORDER OF BATTLE

UNION FORCES

ARMY OF THE POTOMAC
Meade | *118,000 men*

II CORPS *Hancock*
1ST DIVISION *Barlow*
Brigades Miles, Smyth, Frank, Brooke
2ND DIVISION *Gibbon*
Brigades Webb, Owen, Carroll
3RD DIVISION *Birney*
Brigades Ward, Hays
4TH DIVISION *Mott*
Brigades McAllister, Brewster

V CORPS *Warren*
1ST DIVISION *Griffin*
Brigades Ayres, Sweitzer, Bartlett
2ND DIVISION *Robinson*
Brigades Leonard, Baxter, Denison
3RD DIVISION *Crawford*
Brigades McCandless, Fisher
4TH DIVISION *Wadsworth*
Brigades Cutler, Rice, Stone

VI CORPS *Sedgwick*
1ST DIVISION Wright
Brigades Brown, Upton, Russell, Shaler
2ND DIVISION *Getty*
Brigades Wheaton, Grant, Neil, Eustis
3RD DIVISION Ricketts
Brigades Morris, Seymour

IX CORPS *Burnside*
1ST DIVISION *Stevenson*
Brigades Carruth, Leasure
2ND DIVISION *Potter*
Brigades Bliss, Griffin
3RD DIVISION *Willcox*
Brigades Hartranft, Christ
4TH DIVISION *Ferrero*
Brigades Sigfried, Thomas

CAVALRY CORPS *Sheridan*
1ST DIVISION *Torbert*
Brigades Custer, Devin, Merritt
2ND DIVISION *D. M. Gregg*
Brigades Davies, J. I. Gregg
3RD DIVISION *Wilson*
Brigades Bryan, Chapman

CONFEDERATE FORCES

ARMY OF NORTHERN VIRGINIA
Lee | *61,000 men*

1ST CORPS *Longstreet*
KERSHAW'S DIVISION
Brigades Henagan, Wofford, Humphreys, Bryan
FIELD'S DIVISION
Brigades Jenkins, Law, G. T. Anderson, Gregg, Benning

2ND CORPS *Ewell*
EARLY'S DIVISION
Brigades Hays, Pegram, Gordon
JOHNSON'S DIVISION
Brigades J. A. Walker, Jones, Steuart, Stafford
RODES'S DIVISION
Brigades Daniel, Doles, Ramseur, Battle, R. D. Johnston

3RD CORPS *A. P. Hill*
R. H. ANDERSON'S DIVISION
Brigades Perrin, Harris, Mahone, Wright, Perry
HETH'S DIVISION
Brigades Davis, Cooke, Kirkland, H. H. Walker, Archer
WILCOX'S DIVISION
Brigades Lane, Scales, McGowan, Thomas

CAVALRY CORPS *Stuart*
HAMPTON'S DIVISION
Brigades Young, Rosser, Butler
F. LEE'S DIVISION
Brigades Lomax, Wickham
W. H. F. LEE'S DIVISION
Brigades Chambliss, Gordon

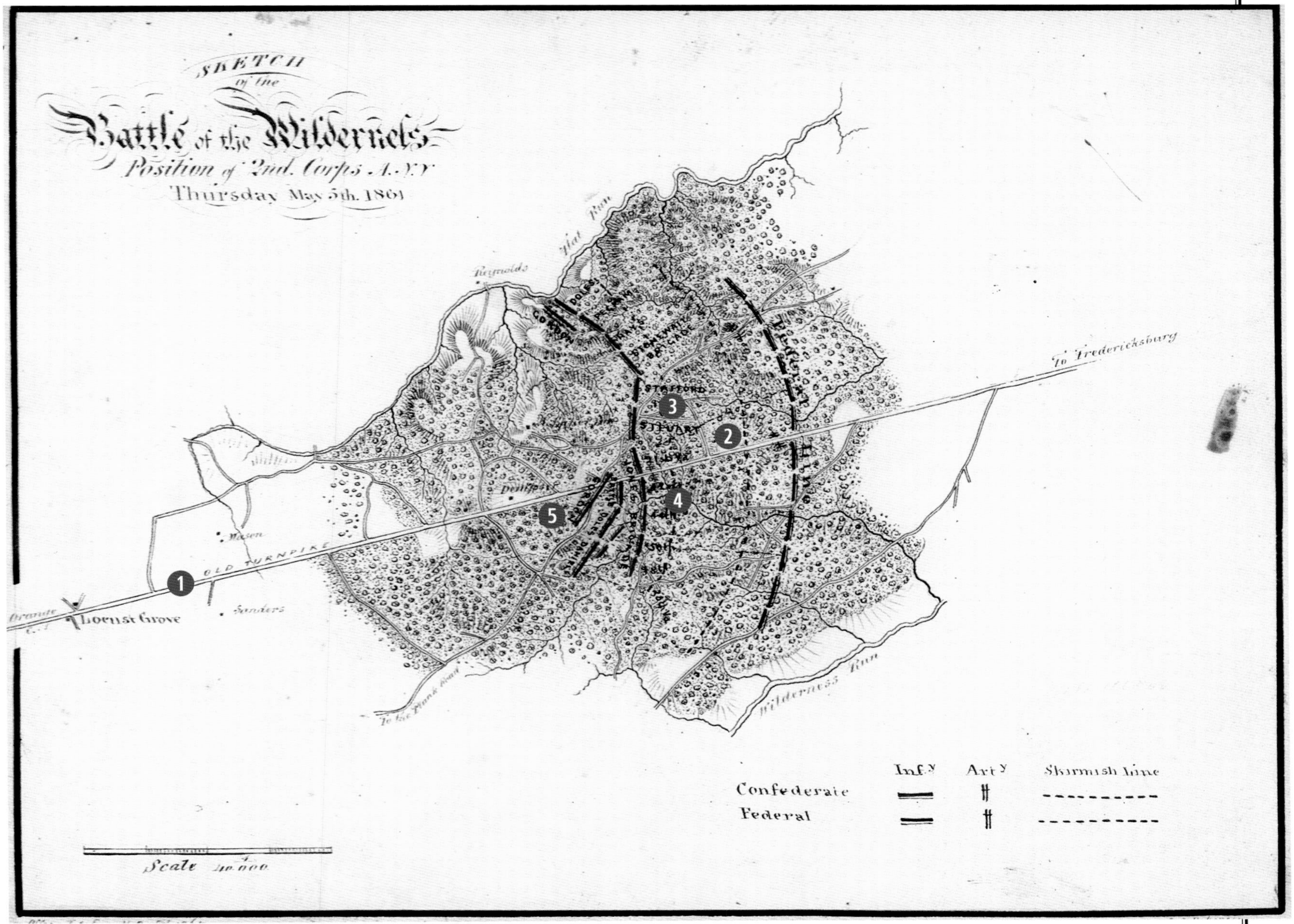

COLLISION ON THE TURNPIKE This map by Jedediah Hotchkiss, produced to accompany official Confederate reports of the battle, shows his fine eye for topographical detail and his thorough grasp of the situation of Ewell's Second Corps when it clashed with advancing Federals along the Orange Turnpike on May 5. After serving under Stonewall Jackson, Hotchkiss remained on the staff of his successor, Ewell, through the Wilderness campaign.

NO TIME TO REST Hard-marching Federals dry laundry on their bayonets during Grant's relentless advance against Lee, which left them little time for personal chores.

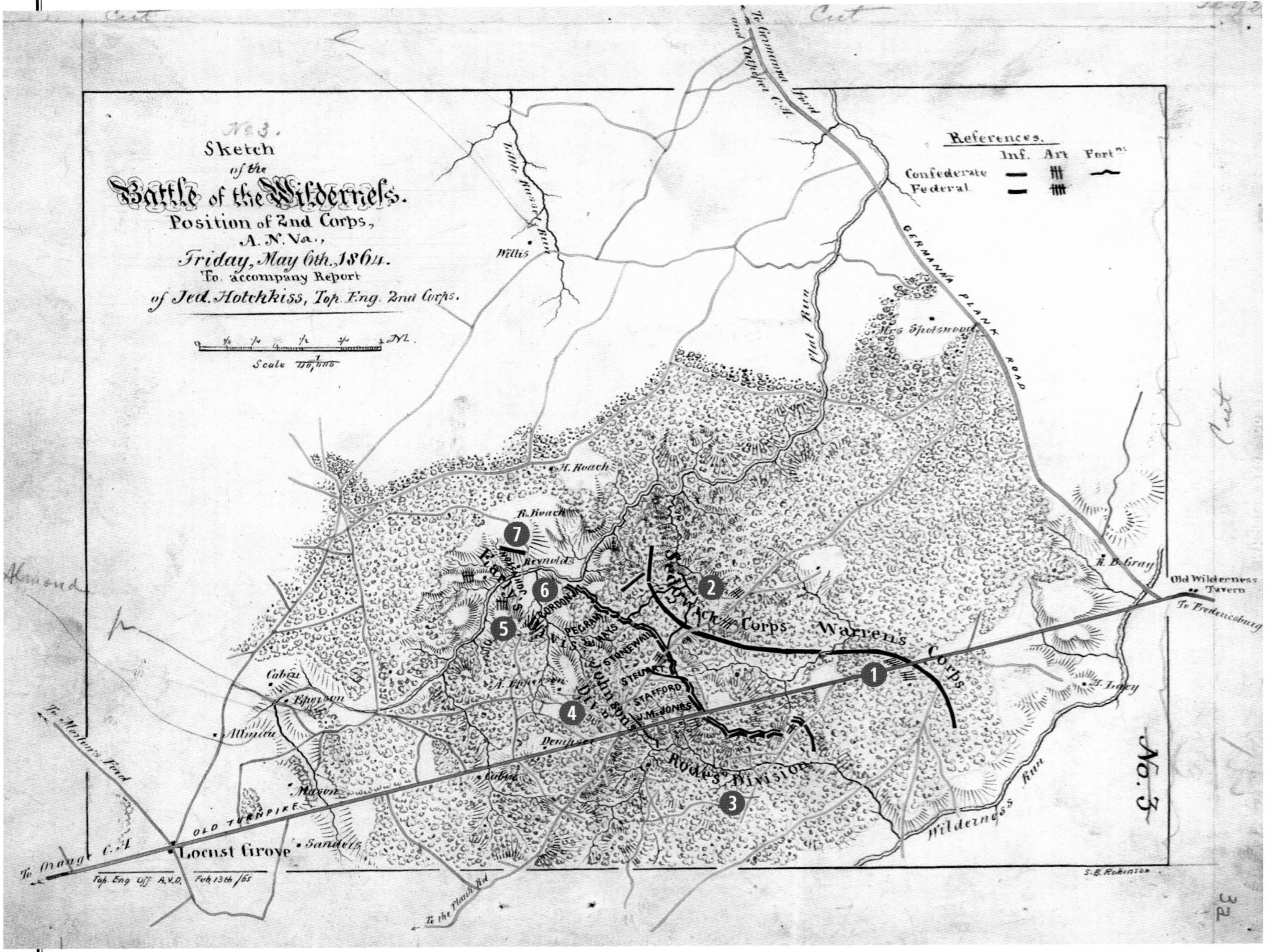
No. 3.
Sketch
of the
Battle of the Wilderness.
Position of 2nd Corps,
A. N. Va.,
Friday, May 6th, 1864.
To accompany Report
of Jed. Hotchkiss, Top. Eng. 2nd Corps.
Scale
References.
Inf. Art Fortns
Confederate
Federal
To Germanna Ford
GERMANNA PLANK ROAD
Willis
Mrs Spotswood
H. Roach
R. Roach
Reynolds
Sedgwick's Corps
Warren's Corps
Old Wilderness Tavern
To Fredericksburg
R. B. Gray
J. Lacy
Early's Division
Johnson's Div.
Rodes' Division
GORDON
PEGRAM
HAYS
STONEWALL
STEUART
STAFFORD
J.M. JONES
Cabell
Almond
Alliniau
Mason
Dempsey
Locust Grove
Sanders
OLD TURNPIKE
To Orange C. H.
Wilderness Run
To the Plank Rd
Top. Eng. Off. A.N.V. Feb. 13th /65
S. E. Robinson
No. 3
1
2
3
4
5
6
7

A Stormy Front Hotchkiss's map for the second day of fighting along the Orange Turnpike shows the opposing sides in much the same position as on the first day, aligned on a front that remained stationary as the thunderous battle progressed. Ewell had an opportunity to break the stalemate by flanking Sedgwick's corps, but that advance came too late on May 6 to alter the outcome.

Ordeal by Fire A picture taken after the Battle of the Wilderness shows Confederate trenches amid trees charred by fire that swept the woods during the fighting.

Salvaged from the Flames Union troops use a blanket suspended from their interlocked muskets to rescue a wounded man from the flaming Wilderness.

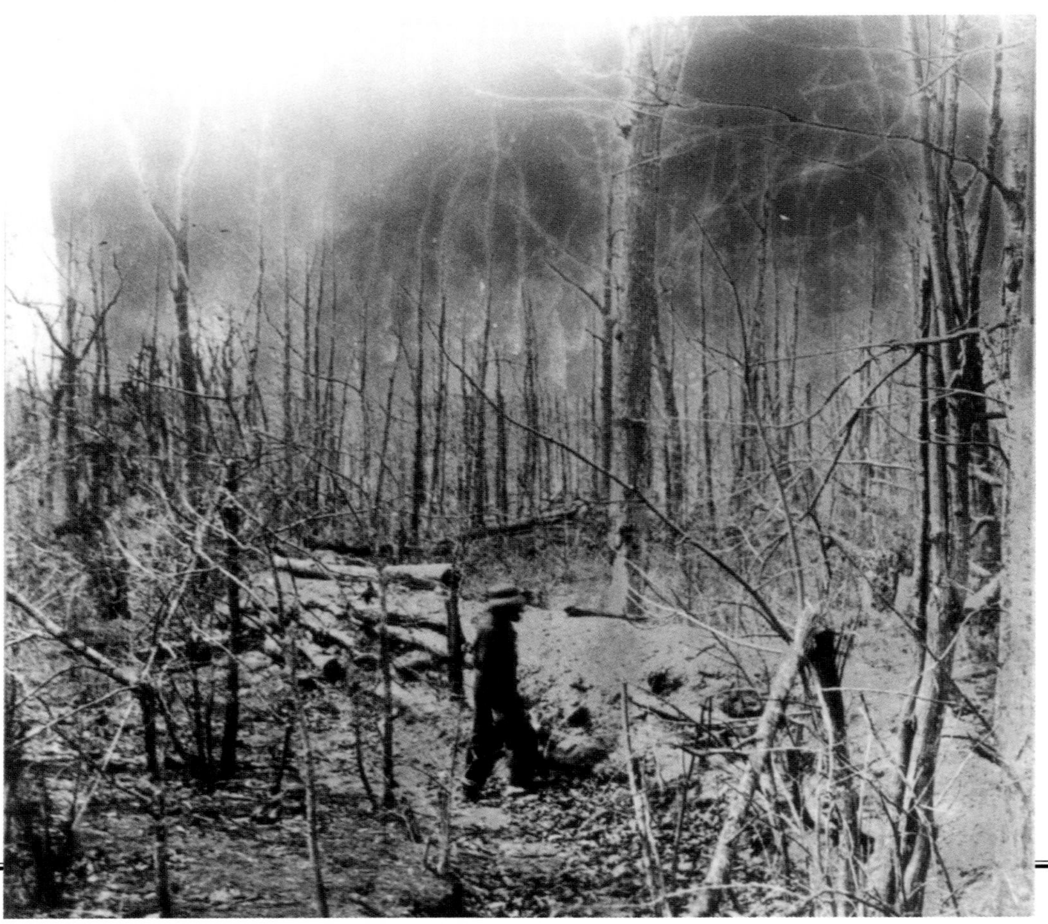

The Burning Woods

The horror of battle did not end when night fell on the Wilderness on May 5. Blazes sparked by gunfire flared up, burning wounded men to death. "The air was hazy and pungent with the smoke," recalled Lieutenant Abner Small of the 16th Maine Infantry, part of Warren's Fifth Corps, which remained astride the Orange Turnpike overnight ❶. "We couldn't see the wounded and dying," Small added, but their "cries we heard all too clearly."

At daybreak on May 6, Warren's forces and John Sedgwick's Sixth Corps ❷ renewed the attack on Ewell's Second Corps. Ewell had been hard-pressed the day before when his men were still coming up, but he now had all three divisions firmly in place under Major Generals Robert Rodes ❸, Edward Johnson ❹, and Jubal Early ❺. With the Federal attack stalled, John Gordon, whose brigade had saved the day for Ewell on May 5, saw from his position on the far left ❻ that his line overlapped the Union line and asked permission to strike Sedgwick's exposed right flank. Ewell would not agree until reconnaissance confirmed Gordon's report and eased concerns that Ambrose Burnside's Ninth Corps was lurking behind Sedgwick. In fact, Grant's aim was to hold Ewell in check here while Burnside supported the big Federal push to the south, led by Hancock's Second Corps, which slammed into A. P. Hill's Third Corps. Hancock surged forward until James Longstreet weighed in with his First Corps and rolled up the overextended Yankees "like a wet blanket," in Hancock's words. When Longstreet was shot accidentally by Confederates, his counterattack faltered and Lee turned to Ewell, who unleashed Gordon's forces and those of Brigadier General Robert Johnston ❼ around 6 P.M. Enveloping Sedgwick's right flank, they captured two brigade commanders and several hundred troops before darkness and mounting Federal resistance brought them to a halt, ending the two-day battle with the two sides deadlocked. ■

Those Left Standing These nine were all who remained of the 86 men in Company I of the 57th Massachusetts after the Wilderness campaign.

1864 | INTO THE WILDERNESS

Spotsylvania

Grant's losses in the fiery Battle of the Wilderness amounted to over 17,000 men, exceeding Lee's casualties there by more than 50 percent. Many expected Grant to give way like earlier Federal commanders after taking such punishment, but he vowed there would be "no turning back." Late on May 7, he sent his forces marching southward along the Brock Road ❶ toward Spotsylvania Court House ❷, hoping to seize that crossroads and slip between Lee and Richmond. Lee responded by sending Jeb Stuart's cavalry to delay the advancing Federals at Todd's Tavern, which allowed Confederate infantry to reach Spotsylvania on back roads in advance of Grant's forces.

Striking quickly at Confederates who were frantically fortifying their position, Grant followed a jab at Lee's left wing along the Po River ❸—where Confederates fell back on May 9 before rallying with the help of reinforcements—with a hard blow to Lee's center on May 10 at a salient called the Mule Shoe ❹, where Ewell's corps waited behind barricades of earth and timber. Charging with bayonets fixed, some 5,000 Yankees led by Colonel Emory Upton bore down on Brigadier General George Doles ❺ and his startled Georgians. "Like a resistless wave, the column poured over the works," wrote Upton. But his bold advance went unsupported and receded like a spent wave as night fell.

Spotsylvania Court House

Encouraged by Upton's initial success, Grant sent 20,000 men against the Mule Shoe at dawn on May 12, hoping to pierce the heart of Lee's defenses and shatter his army. Caught in that terrific storm was Stonewall Jackson's old brigade ❻, led by Brigadier General James Walker, whose division commander, Edward Johnson, was one of many Confederates captured as Federals gouged what looked to be a fatal hole in their line. Once again, however, John Gordon helped stave off defeat, as he did on May 5, by throwing troops into that breach ❼ and holding back the enemy while Lee formed a new defensive line at the base of the salient ❽ and sealed off the Mule Shoe. After this massive Federal attack failed, one officer observed, wounded men lay buried amid piles of dead, "struggling to extricate themselves from their horrid entombment." ■

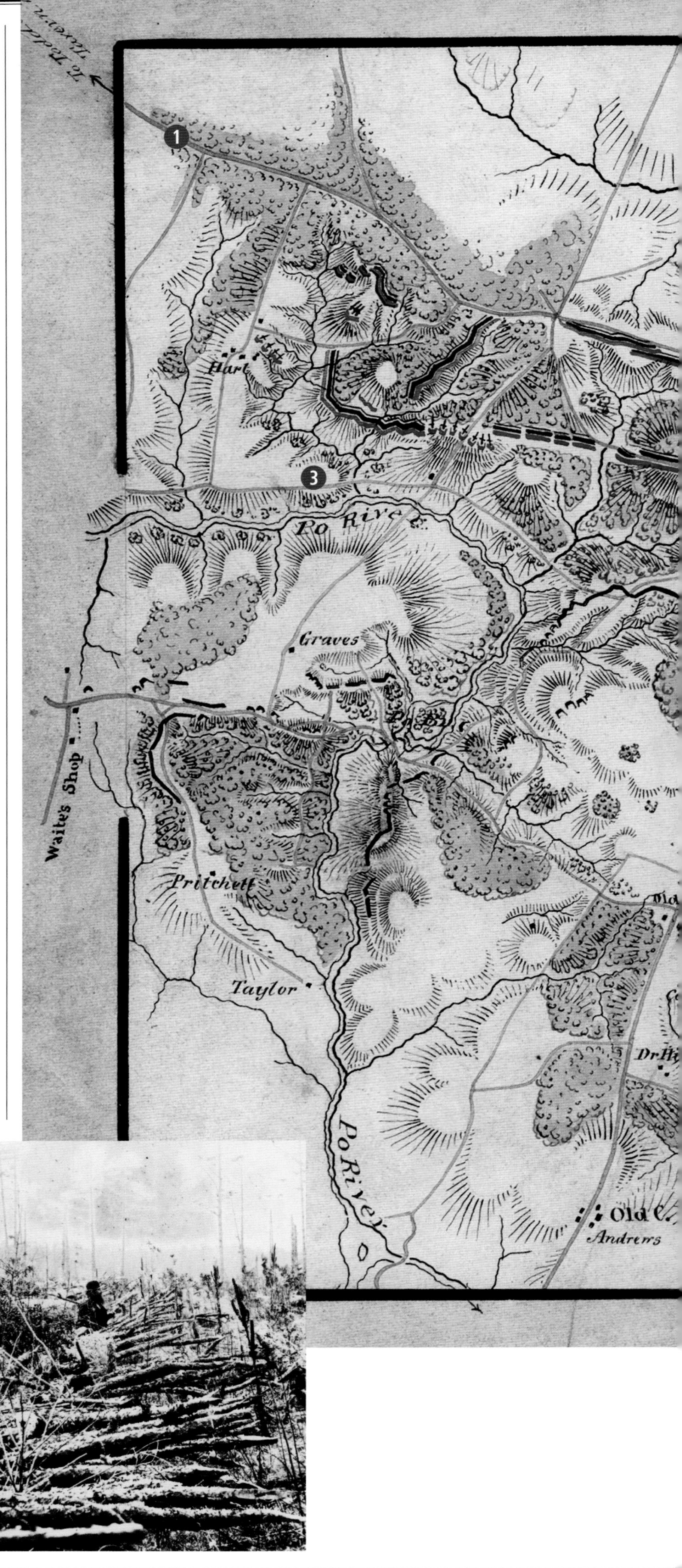

A Forbidding Obstacle Confederates at Spotsylvania formed this defensive barrier, known as an abatis, by felling trees and aligning them so that their sharpened points faced the enemy.

Defending the Mule Shoe This map of the Spotsylvania battlefield by Hotchkiss, like those he drew to document the fighting in the Wilderness, focuses on Ewell's Second Corps, which held the Mule Shoe and repulsed fierce attacks here on May 10 and 12. "Even Grant thought it useless to knock our heads against a brick wall," wrote Meade after those bitter setbacks. "We shall now try to maneuver again, so as to draw the enemy out of his stronghold."

One of Many This Confederate was one of many soldiers killed in the battles around Spotsylvania, where Lee suffered nearly 10,000 casualties and Grant's losses were even higher.

Descent to Cold Harbor

Deadlocked at Spotsylvania ❶, Grant resumed his southward advance around Lee's eastern flank on May 21. Hancock's Second Corps ❷ led the way, trying to lure Lee into attacking rashly, but he did not take the bait. His army no longer had great offensive capacity, and he had recently lost his vaunted cavalry leader, Jeb Stuart, mortally wounded at Yellow Tavern ❸ on May 11 in a clash with Philip Sheridan's troopers. Lee responded with due caution to Grant's maneuver by moving south to shield Hanover Junction ❹, which linked Richmond ❺ by rail with the Shenandoah Valley. Major General Richard Anderson's First Corps—formerly under Longstreet, wounded in the Wilderness—and Ewell's Second Corps reached the North Anna River ❻ by a shorter interior line while the Federals followed longer exterior lines in three columns.

Crossing that river in advance of Grant's troops, Confederates formed a strong defensive line below the south bank. A. P. Hill's Third Corps joined them there before Federals reached the north bank on May 23 and began crossing, with Hancock on the left, Burnside's Ninth Corps ❼ in the center, and the Fifth and Sixth Corps ❽ under Warren and Major General Horatio Wright—replacing John Sedgwick, killed by a sharpshooter at Spotsylvania—on the right. Lee was hoping to attack Grant's forces when they had the river to their backs but fell ill and missed that chance. After probing Confederate defenses and meeting with sharp resistance, Grant concluded that "a direct attack would cause a slaughter of our men that even success would not justify." He consoled himself with the thought that Lee's army was whipped because it would not do battle "outside of entrenchments." But even if Lee had to remain on the defensive, he could still inflict such heavy losses on Grant that he and Lincoln, who was up for reelection, would lose public support.

When Grant tried again to slip around the enemy to the southeast, Lee pulled back to Cold Harbor ❾. Grant hoped to strike before the Rebels were well-entrenched. But it took him two days to assemble forces for a dawn attack on June 3, which proved disastrous. Five Federals fell for every Confederate lost at Cold Harbor, bringing Grant's casualties for the campaign to more than 50,000. One Union officer wrote privately that his men had been "foolishly and wantonly sacrificed," and Navy Secretary Gideon Welles noted that people in Washington were now calling Grant "a butcher." ■

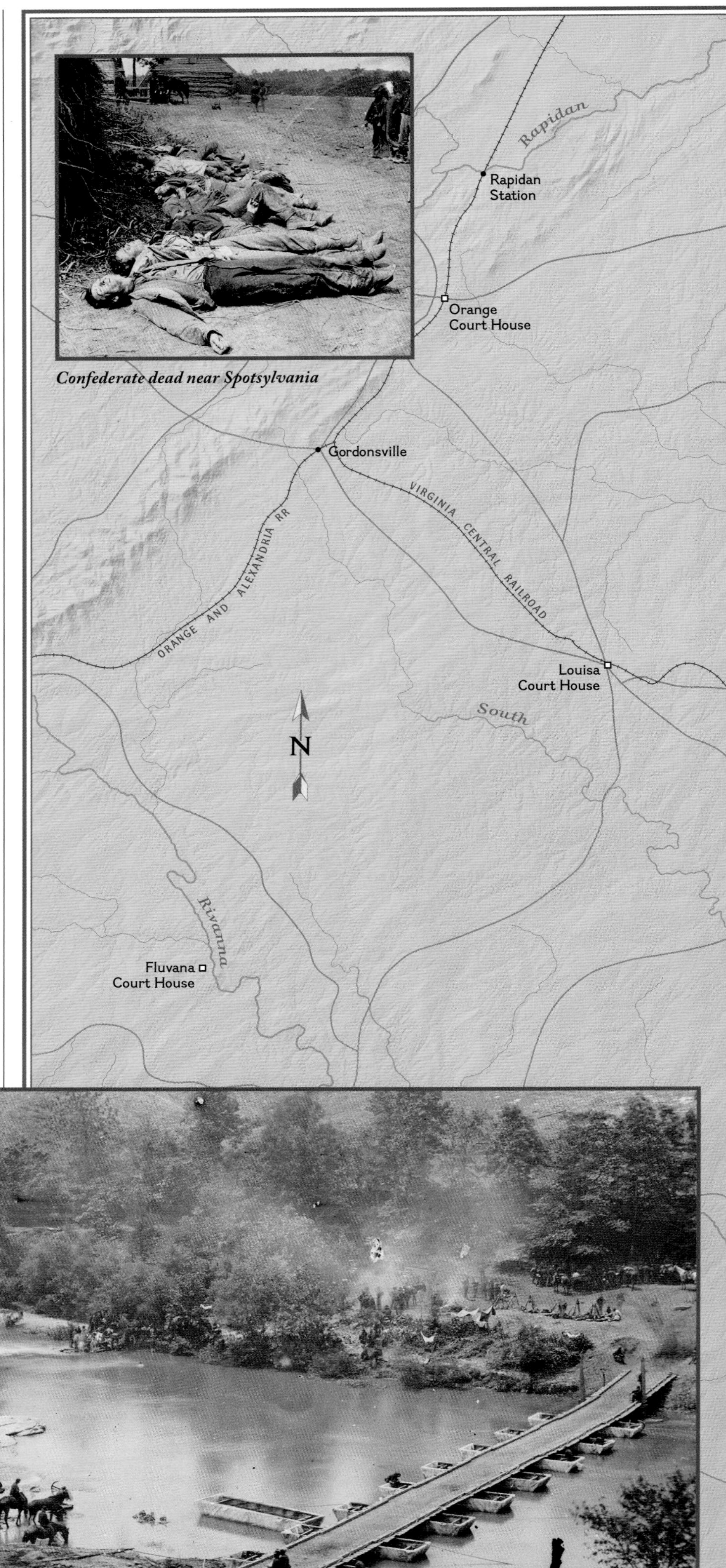

Confederate dead near Spotsylvania

Parallel Paths Grant and Lee matched each other step for step as their armies descended to Cold Harbor along the paths shown in this map. Major General William F. Smith's corps, detached from Benjamin Butler's army on the Peninsula, reinforced Grant at Cold Harbor but did not alter the outcome there.

❻ **Across the North Anna** Federals of Warren's Fifth Corps crossed the North Anna River on this pontoon bridge at Jericho Mill on May 23—and went scurrying back across to the north bank (background) when rebuffed by A. P. Hill's Third Corps.

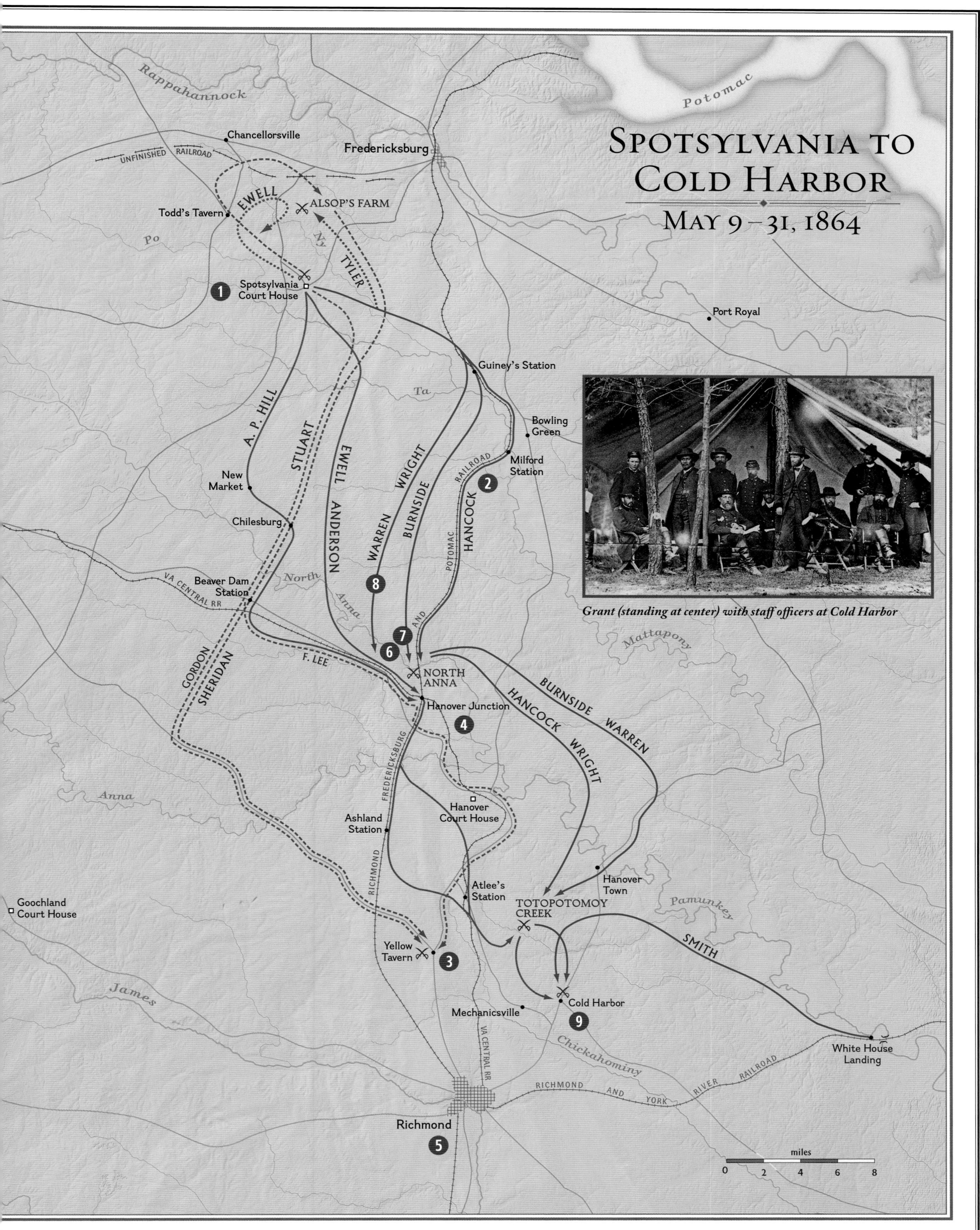

Grant (standing at center) with staff officers at Cold Harbor

THE THRUST TO PETERSBURG

P. G. T. BEAUREGARD

The military career of Pierre Gustave Toutant Beauregard stood in marked contrast to that of Ulysses Grant, whose forces he fended off at Petersburg in June 1864. Unlike Grant, who rose from obscurity to fame during the war, Beauregard, a Louisianan of French ancestry, began the conflict as the South's most acclaimed general, hailed for capturing Fort Sumter, but gradually fell into disfavor. Having graduated second in his class at West Point in 1838, he was likened to Napoleon for his impressive appearance and command of military theory, but that was no guarantee of success in the field. "Oh, that I had the genius of a Napoleon," he wrote before the First Battle of Bull Run, "to be more worthy of our cause." He might not have won that battle without the aid of Joseph Johnston, who hurried troops there and helped counter a blistering Federal attack that left Beauregard shaken. At Shiloh a year later, he was faulted for not pressing his attack on Grant and finishing him off. Relieved a few months later, Beauregard took charge of the defenses of Charleston, frustrating Federal attempts to seize that city before thwarting Grant at Petersburg. As he demonstrated there, his great talent was not for bold Napoleonic strokes but for the gritty task of preparing defenses and holding out stubbornly against superior numbers.

Grant was at his best when things were at their worst. His calamitous assault at Cold Harbor, referred to as "Grant's slaughter pen," would have devastated a less-confident commander. But as Sherman told Grant, the "chief characteristic of your nature is the simple faith in success you have always manifested." Time and again—at Fort Donelson, Shiloh, Vicksburg, and Chattanooga—he had shrugged off setbacks and prevailed. Within days of his debacle at Cold Harbor, he salvaged his campaign by shifting course so abruptly that even Lee, who had matched his every move, was caught by surprise.

While Lee guarded against an assault on Richmond ❶, Grant planned to descend instead on Petersburg ❷, a hub through which supplies from the south reached Richmond and its defenders on the Weldon Railroad ❸. His Federals would be at great risk if Lee detected his movement and attacked while they were crossing the James River ❹. So Grant made a feint toward Richmond and sent Sheridan on a diversionary cavalry raid to the west, tearing up tracks used to haul supplies between the Shenandoah Valley and the capital. Confederate cavalry went after Sheridan, and Lee lost sight of Grant. He surmised on June 14 that Grant was "preparing to move south of the James River," but remained unsure of his whereabouts until June 17, by which time the entire Federal army had crossed on a pontoon bridge over the James below its confluence with the Appomattox River ❺.

Grant now had a secure supply line, for Federals controlled the James River up to City Point ❻, a Union base that he linked to Petersburg by repairing the City Point Railroad ❼. His bold thrust also relieved pressure on Benjamin Butler, pinned down at Bermuda Hundred ❽ with 30,000 Federals by a smaller Confederate force led by P. G. T. Beauregard, who now had to withdraw to Petersburg to shield that city. Beauregard dashed Grant's hopes of seizing Petersburg before Lee's forces arrived there and began strengthening their fortifications ❾. But as Lee declared earlier in the campaign, "This army cannot stand a siege." With his troops hemmed in at Petersburg by a much larger and better-supplied army, he now faced a prolonged siege that threatened to grind down his forces until surrender was his only option. ■

1. City Point.—2. Bermuda Hundred.—3. City Point Railroad.—4, 4. Appomat
13. Deep Bottom.—14. Canal at Dutch Gap.—15. Farrar's Island.—16. Reb
O, Norfolk Railroad.

❷ HUB ON THE APPOMATTOX **Located on the Appomattox River, lined with tobacco warehouses and cotton mills like those shown here, Petersburg was Virginia's second largest city and a rail hub vital to the defense of Richmond.**

❾ DIGGING DEEP **Confederates fortified their line at Petersburg by digging deep, wide trenches such as these, reinforced with log embankments called revetments, enabling troops to move readily to areas that came under attack.**

❼ SERVING THE DICTATOR Federal gunners attend a monstrous mortar called the Dictator, used during the siege of Petersburg. Transported along the tracks of the City Point Railroad and a military railway nearby, the 12-inch mortar could hurl a 200-pound shell more than two miles.

PATHS TO PETERSBURG Published in the North after Grant's forces descended on Petersburg, this bird's-eye view of the area, looking westward, shows the rivers and railroads that proved crucial to the outcome as Federals secured their own supply lines and cut off those feeding Richmond and its defenders. The numbers superimposed on this map refer to places mentioned in the text; the numbers within the map refer to places identified in the key at bottom.

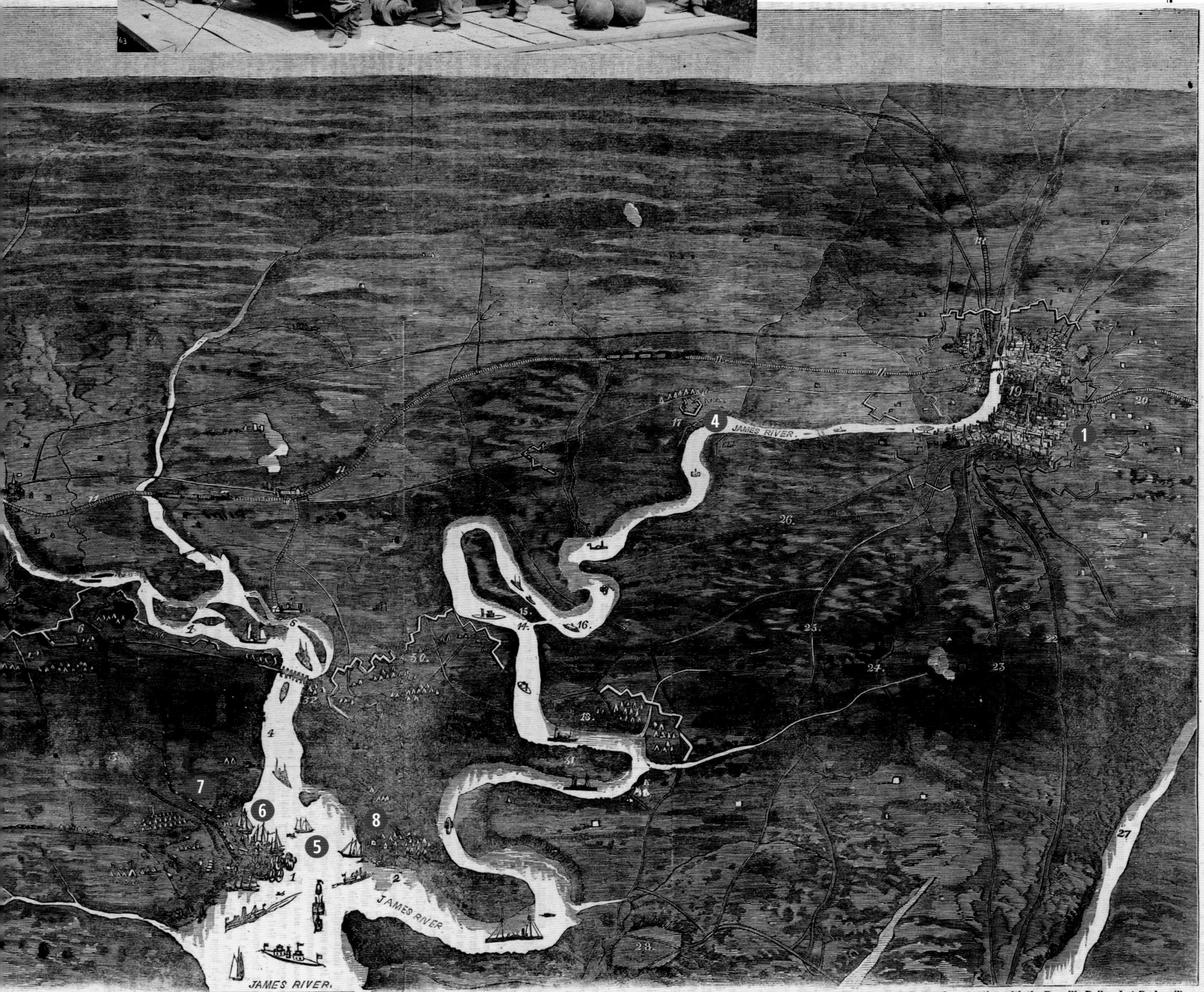

JAMES RIVER

JAMES RIVER

JAMES RIVER.

ver.—5. Port Walthal.—6, 6, 6, 6, 6, 6. Union lines.—7, 7, 7. Rebel lines.—8. Petersburg.—9. Reams Station.—10. Weldon Railroad.—11, 11, 11, 11. Richmond and Petersburg Railroad.—12, Lynchburg Railroad, connecting with the Danville Railroad at Burkesville.—
-boats above this point.—17. Fort Darling.—18. Danville Railroad.—19. Richmond.—20. Richmond and Fredericksburg Railroad.—22, 23, 24, 25, 26. Roads leading out of Richmond.—27. The Chickahominy.—28. Malvern Hill.—30. Butler's lines.—31. Jones's Neck.—

ISOMETRIC VIEW OF GENERAL GRANT'S VIRGINIA CAMPAIGN.—[SEE FIRST PAGE.]

HW 1864

1864 | INTO THE WILDERNESS

Explosion at Petersburg

Despite outnumbering Lee two to one at Petersburg, Grant had little chance of breaking through his formidable defenses until his poorly supplied army was gradually worn down by hunger, disease, and losses to artillery and sniper fire. For now, Lee felt secure enough to send some troops north of the James River to shield Richmond after dispatching others in mid-June under Jubal Early to defend the Shenandoah Valley. With Lee's forces spread thin, Grant approved a proposal by Lieutenant Colonel Henry Pleasants of the 48th Pennsylvania Infantry. In late June, coal miners in his regiment began digging a 500-foot tunnel ❶ from Federal lines to beneath an enemy salient called Fort Elliott ❷ for its commander, Brigadier General Stephen Elliott. By stuffing magazines ❸ at the end of the tunnel with four tons of gunpowder, they hoped to "blow that damned fort out of existence," as Pleasants put it, leaving a gaping hole through which troops of Burnside's Ninth Corps would pour.

Shortly before dawn on July 30, the mine blew, killing nearly 300 Confederates and leaving a crater ❹ 30 feet deep and twice as wide. Chosen by lot to lead the Federal attack was the division of Brigadier General James Ledlie ❺, who took shelter in a bombproof and fortified himself with rum. Instead of advancing rapidly and overpowering Elliott's dazed brigade ❻, Ledlie's men stumbled into the Crater and the rubble-filled trenches on either side and became trapped there when Confederates rallied. By the time black troops of Brigadier General Edward Ferrero's division ❼ joined the attack, Confederate Major General William Mahone had brought up two brigades, with Brigadier General David Weisiger's Virginians ❽ reinforcing Eliott's right while Brigadier General Ambrose Wright's Georgians ❾ shored up his left. Federals tried to advance beyond the Crater as ordered by Ferrero, who stayed in the bombproof with Ledlie, but they were forced back into the pit, described by one witness as "a seething cauldron of struggling, dying men." Some were killed while trying to surrender to Rebels who showed no mercy to black troops or white soldiers fighting alongside them. Grant called it the "saddest affair I have ever witnessed in this war." But he resolved to keep up the pressure on Lee's army here until it cracked. ■

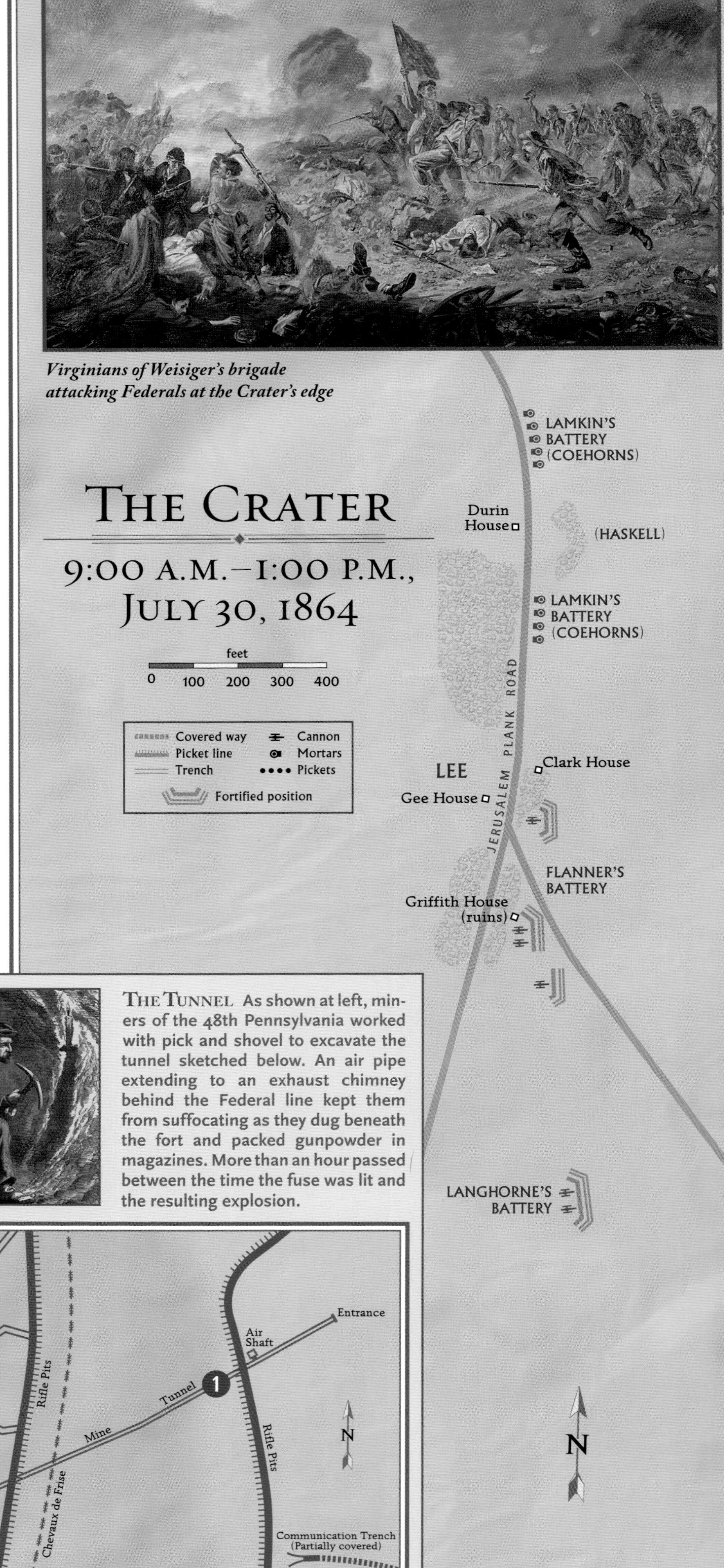

Virginians of Weisiger's brigade attacking Federals at the Crater's edge

The Tunnel As shown at left, miners of the 48th Pennsylvania worked with pick and shovel to excavate the tunnel sketched below. An air pipe extending to an exhaust chimney behind the Federal line kept them from suffocating as they dug beneath the fort and packed gunpowder in magazines. More than an hour passed between the time the fuse was lit and the resulting explosion.

Lost Opportunity The blast that gouged the Crater, shown at the center of this National Geographic map, gave Federals a chance to break through at Petersburg. But troops attacking on either side of the Crater were stopped cold, while those advancing into the gap were ill served by their commanders and sacrificed to no end.

MACON'S BATTERY
36th N.C.
ELLETT & LETCHER'S BATTERIES
WRIGHT'S BATTERY
35th
JOHNSON
Picket Line
Poo Creek
DUNCAN
CARR (XVIII CORPS)
2nd ME. ART
ORD XVIII CORPS
McAFEE
Covered Way
25th N.C.
HASKELL (COEHORNS)
64th GA.
48th GA.
WRIGHT
22nd GA.
ELLIOTT
25th S.C.
3rd GA.
12th VA.
17th S.C.
49th N.C.
MAHONE
2nd N.Y. M.R.
97th PA.
76th PA.
47th N.Y.
COAN
36th MASS. (Bliss)
48th N.Y.
169th N.Y.
9th ME.
4th N.H.
13th IND.
TURNER (X CORPS)
3rd N.Y.
117 th N.Y.
112th N.Y.
142nd N.Y.
CURTIS
BELL
51st N.Y. (Bliss)
3rd MD. Bn.
POTTER
SIGFRIED
7th R.I. Eng.
STEWART
STEDMAN
FAIRCHILD
19th N.Y. ART. (COEHORNS)
1st CONN. H.A. (MORTARS)
AMES (XVIII CORPS)
STEVENS
BURNSIDE IX CORPS
BURNHAM (XVIII CORPS)
NORFOLK & PETERSBURG RAILROAD
WEISIGER
61st N.C. (Hoke)
17th S.C.
16th VA.
61st VA.
41st VA.
6th VA.
4th R.I. (Bliss)
179th N.Y.
MARSHALL
GRIFFIN
4th R.I. (Bliss)
2nd PA. H.A.
BARTLETT
45th PA.
BLISS
58th Mass.
(Wilcox)
30th U.S.C.T.
39th U.S.C.T.
43rd U.S.C.T.
27th U.S.C.T.
23rd U.S.C.T.
31st U.S.C.T.
29th U.S.C.T.
THOMAS
HENRY
7th ME. ART.
22nd S.C. (Elliott)
LEDLIE
14th N.Y. H.A.
HARTRANFT
FERRERO
19th U.S.C.T.
2nd PA. (PROV.) H.A.
59th VA.
26th VA.
28th U.S.C.T.
Taylor House (ruins)
1st CONN. H.A.
DAVIDSON'S BATTERY (1 Gun)
1st MICH.
2nd MICH.
WILLCOX
HUMPHREY
20th MICH.
60th OHIO
46th OHIO
2nd PA. (PROV.) H.A.
(Elliott) 23rd S.C.
JOHNSON
GOODE
46th VA.
50th PA.
24th N.Y.
Covered Way
BAXTER ROAD
DAVIDSON'S BATTERY
Picket Line
Picket Line
CULLEN (Burnham)
34th VA.

1864

SHENANDOAH VALLEY

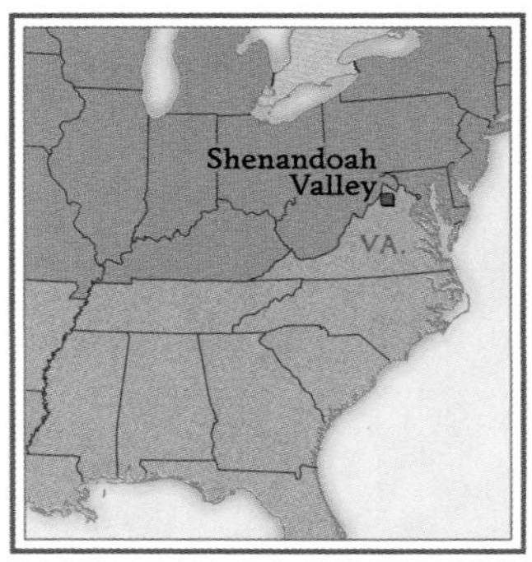

EASTERN THEATER

APRIL 29, 1864 Federals led by Franz Sigel march south from Winchester, Virginia, opposed by Rebels led by John Breckinridge.

MAY 15 Battle of New Market (Virginia)

MAY 19 David Hunter replaces Sigel as Federal commander in the Shenandoah Valley.

JUNE 18 Hunter retreats from Lynchburg, Virginia, after clashing with Jubal Early.

JULY 5 Early crosses into Maryland.

JULY 9 Battle of Monocacy (Maryland)

JULY 12 Early repulsed by Federals defending Washington, D.C.

AUGUST 7 Philip Sheridan replaces Hunter.

SEPTEMBER 19 Battle of Winchester (Virginia)

OCTOBER 19 Battle of Cedar Creek (Virginia)

While Grant and Lee faced off in eastern Virginia, a related struggle unfolded in the Shenandoah Valley to the west. Grant's plan there was for Major General Franz Sigel to link up in May at Staunton ❶ with Brigadier General George Crook, advancing from West Virginia. Together, Sigel and his subordinate Crook would command around 15,000 Federal troops and several thousand cavalrymen—enough to discourage Confederates in the Valley from moving north and threatening Washington, D.C., while Grant's army was advancing southward. Beyond that, Grant hoped Sigel would disrupt the flow of supplies from the bountiful valley to Lee's army and pose enough of a threat to Richmond to prevent Lee from focusing all his attention and resources on Grant.

That was too much to ask of Sigel, a political general from St. Louis who owed his command to his ability to persuade many of his fellow German-Americans to fight for the Union. Opposing him was a Confederate officer with stronger credentials in both the political and military arenas, Major General John Breckinridge, a former U.S. vice president and corps commander under Bragg in Tennessee. Breckinridge was short on troops, but he was aided by keen cavalry officers who knew this country by heart, among them Lieutenant Colonel John Mosby, a native of the Shenandoah Valley whose Rangers—partisans who had been a thorn in the side of Union forces here—captured Sigel's supply train in early May.

John Mosby

Distracted, Sigel and Crook did not link up as planned, and Breckinridge swung into action. Calling up cadets at VMI in Lexington ❷ to bolster his forces, he marched north from Staunton and challenged Sigel at New Market ❸ on May 15. With the outcome there in doubt, he committed the cadets, some as young as 15. "Put the boys in," Breckinridge said, "and may God forgive me for the order." Fighting like veterans, they helped him secure victory.

Grant then replaced Sigel with Major General David Hunter, a stern Unionist from Virginia who ordered that when fired on by partisans, his troops should burn "every rebel house within five miles." His fiery reprisals and the threat his Army of the Shenandoah posed to Lynchburg ❹ and the Virginia & Tennessee Railroad ❺ compelled Lee to send his Second Corps—led now by Jubal Early—westward in mid-June. Hard fighting had reduced Early's corps to a mere 8,000 men. But Hunter thought it was far stronger than that and more than he could handle. When challenged by Early at Lynchburg, he pulled out on June 18 and retreated into West Virginia. That left the door open for Early, who marched to Staunton, moved north on the Valley Turnpike ❻ to Winchester ❼, and crossed the Potomac ❽ into Maryland, where his forces advanced to the outskirts of Washington ❾. ■

EARLY'S CAMPAIGN Two maps by Jedediah Hotchkiss, who accompanied the Second Corps under Early, show in red the paths his forces followed from June 13 to 27 (top) and from June 27 to July 22 (bottom). Departing from Gaines's Mill, near Cold Harbor, Early's forces marched to Charlottesville and moved by train to Lynchburg, where they drove Hunter's Federals away on June 18. Reconstituted as the Army of the Valley District, they then entered the Shenandoah Valley and headed north, reaching Staunton by June 27. From there, they invaded Maryland, doing battle at Monocacy and reaching the fortified perimeter of Washington before turning back (dotted lines).

❻ WHERE ARMIES TROD Wide, straight, and firm, the Valley Turnpike was the highway of choice for opposing forces here.

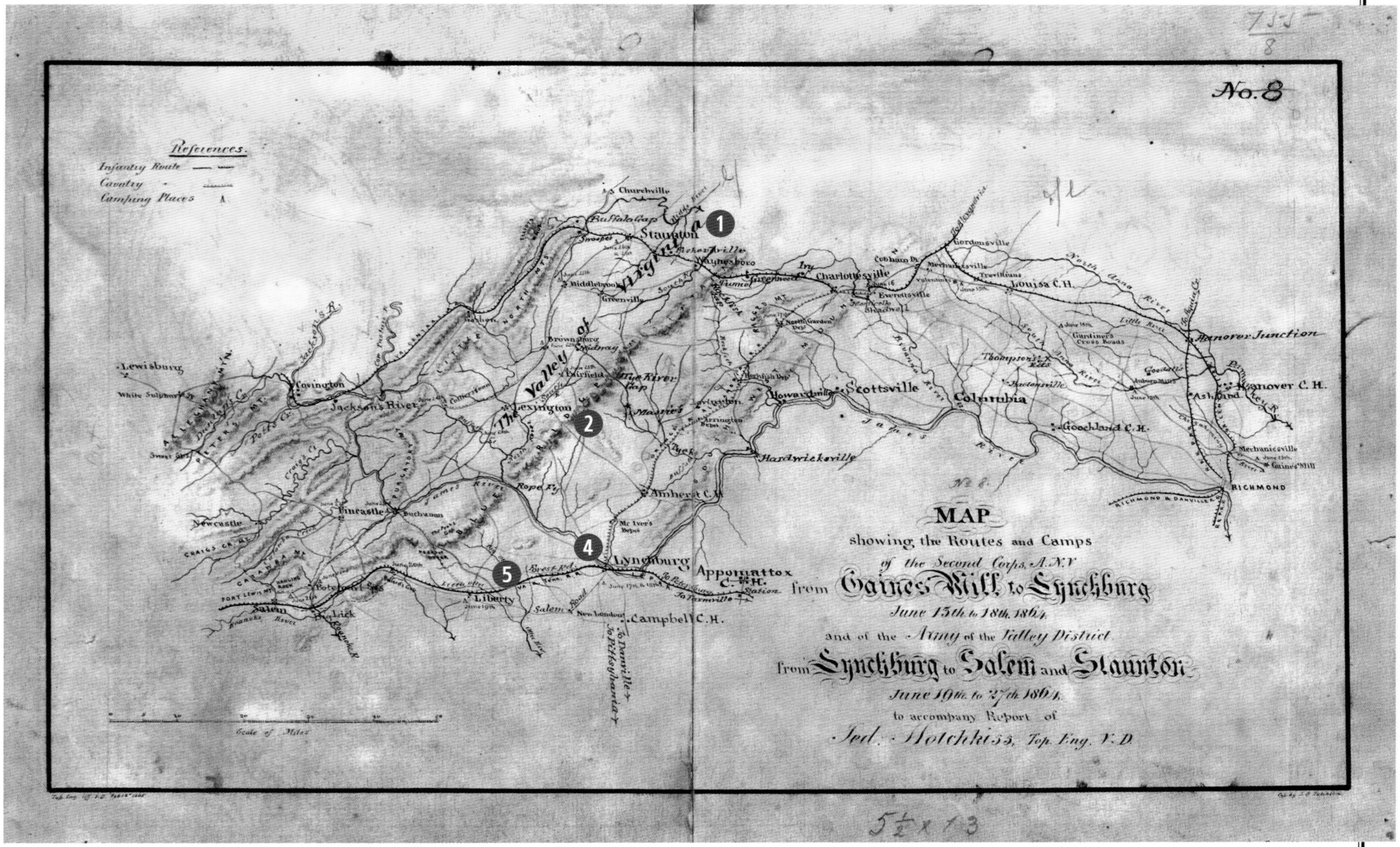
No. 8
References.
Infantry Route
Cavalry
Camping Places
Staunton
Waynesboro
Charlottesville
Gordonsville
Louisa C.H.
Hanover Junction
Hanover C.H.
Lexington
Covington
Lewisburg
Jacksons River
Scottsville
Columbia
Howardsville
Amherst C.H.
Lynchburg
Appomattox C.H.
Liberty
Salem
Campbell C.H.
Richmond
MAP
showing the Routes and Camps
of the Second Corps, A.N.V.
from Gaines' Mill to Lynchburg
June 13th to 18th 1864
and of the Army of the Valley District
from Lynchburg to Salem and Staunton
June 19th to 27th 1864
to accompany Report of
Jed. Hotchkiss, Top. Eng. V.D.
Scale of Miles
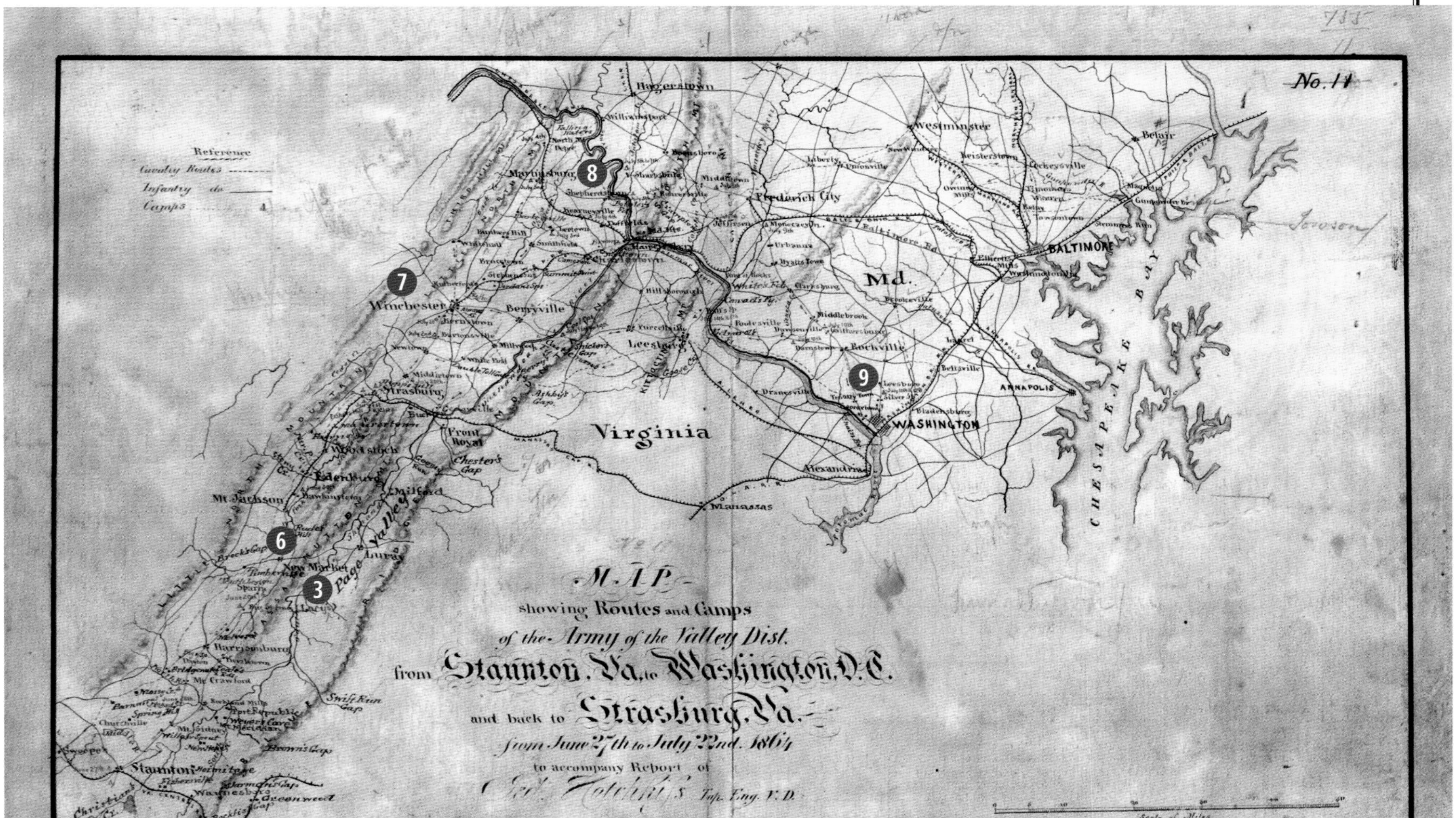
No. 11
Reference
Cavalry Routes
Infantry do
Camps
Hagerstown
Westminster
Martinsburg
Frederick City
Winchester
Berryville
Leesburg
Md.
Baltimore
Annapolis
Washington
Alexandria
Manassas
Virginia
Front Royal
Strasburg
Woodstock
Edenburg
Mt Jackson
New Market
Luray
Page Valley
Harrisonburg
Staunton
Waynesboro
Chesapeake Bay
MAP
showing Routes and Camps
of the Army of the Valley Dist.
from Staunton, Va. to Washington, D.C.
and back to Strasburg, Va.
from June 27th to July 22nd 1864
to accompany Report of
Jed. Hotchkiss Top. Eng. V.D.
Scale of Miles

Advance on Washington

JUBAL EARLY

Like many of his fellow Virginians, Jubal Early—born along the Blue Ridge in 1816—was initially reluctant to leave the Union but took offense when Federals bore down hard on his state, and he defied the Yankees to the bitter end. A West Point graduate who served in the Seminole and Mexican Wars and became a successful attorney, Early argued strongly against secession when Virginia delegates met to debate that step in 1861. Once the die was cast and Union forces intruded on his homeland, however, he took up the Rebel cause with a vengeance and struck fear into the hearts of Unionists by invading their territory twice under Lee in 1862 and 1863 and again as an army commander in his own right in 1864. His operational principle during those campaigns was that Yankees who were scourging the South deserved a good whipping in return. While sweeping through Pennsylvania before the Battle of Gettysburg, he burned down the Caledonia Iron Works, owned by Congressman Thaddeus Stevens, a Radical Republican whom he blamed for urging that Southerners be subjected to "the most vindictive measures of confiscation and devastation." Lee called the cantankerous Early his "bad old man" and tolerated his severe war measures as an antidote to injurious enemy policies. Unlike Lee, "Old Jube" refused to yield when defeated in Virginia and went off to Texas to prolong the struggle against a Union he once honored but now deplored.

When Jubal Early invaded Maryland on July 5 and advanced on Washington, D.C. ❶, his aims were both military and political. With only 14,000 troops and cavalrymen under his command, he could not capture and hold Washington. But he could relieve pressure on Lee at Petersburg by drawing Federals northward to defend their capital. And if they failed to arrive in time, he could sack Washington and so embarrass Lincoln that he might lose in November to a candidate willing to come to terms with the Rebels. Early could also make Unionists pay for the damage done by their troops in the Shenandoah Valley and elsewhere—wreckage so extensive that one Confederate officer, Major Henry Kyd Douglas, felt that "vengeance ought not to be left entirely to the Lord." Entering Frederick, Maryland, on July 9, Early threatened to burn the town if he was not paid $200,000 in reparations. That ultimatum was met, but his cavalry commander, Brigadier General John McCausland, torched Chambersburg, Pennsylvania, later in the month when his ransom demand was refused there.

Early achieved one of his objectives when Grant reduced his forces at Petersburg by sending Horatio Wright's Sixth Corps to defend Washington. But Early's chances of entering the capital before those reinforcements arrived faded when Federals led by Major General Lew Wallace waged a hard battle against him along the Monocacy River, east of Frederick, on July 9 before retreating. Early did not reach the fortified perimeter of Washington until July 11 ❷ and found it swarming with defenders. The Sixth Corps ❸ had just arrived in force to bolster the Eighth Corps ❹. And troops of the 19th Corps, sailing from Louisiana, had disembarked and were marching out Seventh Street ❺ to Fort Stevens ❻, the northernmost link in Washington's defensive chain. Lincoln went there himself on July 12 to watch as Federals led by Brigadier General Frank Wheaton ❼ clashed with the Rebels. Unable to puncture Washington's armor, Early withdrew. ■

Burned Out Residents stand amid the charred ruins of Chambersburg, Pennsylvania, burned by Confederate cavalry on July 30 during a raid ordered by Early after he withdrew from Washington.

❻ Fort Stevens Normally a quiet outpost where men like these gunners drilled for a war that seemed far away, Fort Stevens was at the front line when Federals clashed with Early's forces on July 12. Lincoln stood on the parapet watching the battle, one witness noted, until Sixth Corps commander Wright "peremptorily represented to him the needless risk he was taking."

WASHINGTON UNDER THE GUN A map by Robert Knox Sneden shows the daunting defenses that awaited Early's weary forces when they reached the outskirts of Washington on July 11. His army, which had been reduced to 12,000 men, needed time to prepare for battle and faced opposition that was mounting by the hour as reinforcements poured into Washington, swelling Federal forces here from less than 10,000 that morning to 20,000 by July 12. "I had, therefore, reluctantly to give up all hopes of capturing Washington," Early concluded, "after I had arrived in sight of the dome of the Capitol."

THE BATTLE OF WINCHESTER

PHILIP SHERIDAN

When Grant chose 33-year-old Philip Sheridan to command Federal forces in the Shenandoah Valley, he passed over many older candidates with finer records in the prewar U.S. Army. But Grant judged officers not by their standing at West Point or their exploits in Mexico but by their achievements in this conflict, a harsher test than anything Americans had faced before. In that sense, Sheridan—proven under fire at Stones River, Chickamauga, and Chattanooga and glowing with combative energy that one subordinate likened to "an electric shock"—was much like his fellow Ohioans Grant and Sherman, who vaulted past their elders in the Union Army by fighting Confederates relentlessly in remote areas where combatants did not always play by polite rules. As early as 1862, Grant was arguing that Southerners would not be defeated until they were deprived of "everything that could be used to support or supply armies" and that protecting their property would only prolong the conflict. In waging total war against the Confederacy, he was aided mightily by Sheridan and Sherman and backed firmly by Lincoln, who saw this as a desperate struggle that could not be won by the tender-hearted. The same tribute Lincoln paid Grant could have been extended to Sheridan as he punished Early's army and laid waste to the Shenandoah Valley: "I can't spare this man. He fights."

Following Early's advance on Washington, D.C., Grant resolved to crush his army and strip bare the Shenandoah Valley, depriving Confederates of its sustenance. He assigned that task to Philip Sheridan, his keen young cavalry chief who had earlier commanded infantry and was thus well prepared for campaigning in this rugged country where success depended on coordinating troop movements with mounted operations. Sheridan had instructions from Grant to draw from the Valley and its inhabitants "all provisions, forage and stock wanted for the use of your command. Such as cannot be consumed, destroy."

Sheridan receiving battle report

Taking charge in August of a refurbished Army of the Shenandoah, which grew to more than twice the size of Early's army, Sheridan moved his troops cautiously until he learned that part of Early's forces had been recalled by Lee to Petersburg. Grant met with Sheridan in mid-September to propose an attack but found him ready with a plan to challenge Early at Winchester ❶ and told him simply, "Go in." Crossing Opequan Creek ❷ before dawn on September 19, the Sixth Corps ❸ advanced against Early's right and came under heavy fire from artillery on high ground ❹. Sheridan's line ❺ buckled when Confederates counterattacked, but he had deep reserves and brought them to bear. To the north, cavalry led by Brigadier Generals William Averell and Wesley Merritt ❻ forced Rebels on Early's left flank at Stephenson's Depot ❼ back toward Winchester. George Crook's Eighth Corps ❽ then moved up and joined the cavalry in hammering that retracted flank ❾ until it caved in. "Crook and Averell are on their left and rear," Sheridan shouted. "We've got 'em bagged, by God!" Unhinged, Confederates fled through Winchester. Many escaped as night fell, but nearly 2,000 were captured. Early's casualties were proportionally higher than Sheridan's, amounting to roughly one-fourth of his army. ■

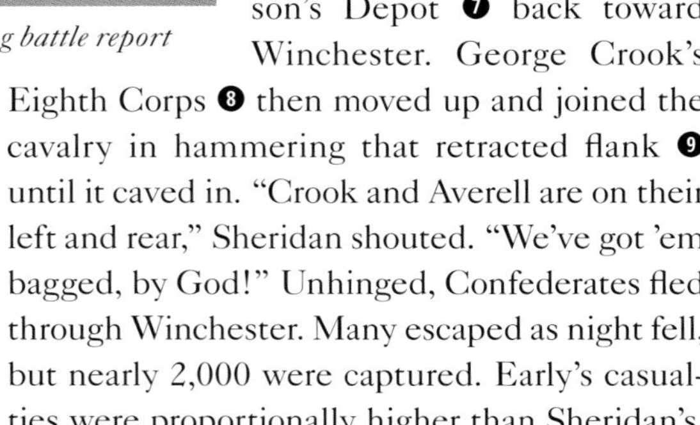

❸ ADVANCE OF THE SIXTH CORPS Carrying the Stars and Stripes and a banner emblazoned with a Greek cross, their corps insignia, men of the Sixth Corps advance into battle at Winchester in this sketch by Alfred Waud.

SHERIDAN BREAKS THROUGH Sneden drew this rough map of the Battle of Winchester, based on Federal reports. He misidentified the Sixth Corps commander as John Sedgwick, who had been killed at Spotsylvania and replaced by Horatio Wright. And he did not have enough information to identify Confederate commanders here, among them a seasoned officer Early could ill afford to lose—Brigadier General Robert Rodes, mortally wounded by a shell fragment.

PLAN OF THE BATTLE OF WINCHESTER, Va.
Fought September 19th 1864.
Union Army under SHERIDAN - Losses - 697 Killed 3983 wounded - and 338 Captured or missing - Total 5.018 - Rebel Army under EARLY lost, including the missing or prisoners 3-611.
NORTH MT
Apple Pie Ridge
MERRITT Cavalry
2 PM Sept 19
RAIL ROAD
Stephenson's DEPOT
TURNPIKE
POTOMAC
Red Bud
WINCHESTER
OLD FORT
MILROY'S FORTS
Signal STATION
Red Bud Creek
CROOK
11½ am
Mill
Ford
WINCHESTER
Abraham's Mill
SHERIDAN
SEDGWICK 6th CORPS
Greenwood Church
MILLTOWN
Mill
TURNPIKE
OPEQUAN CREEK
PLEASANT VALLEY MILL
Kernstown
Reference
Union Army
Rebel Army
Cavalry
Sneden del
1
2
3
4
5
6
7
8
9

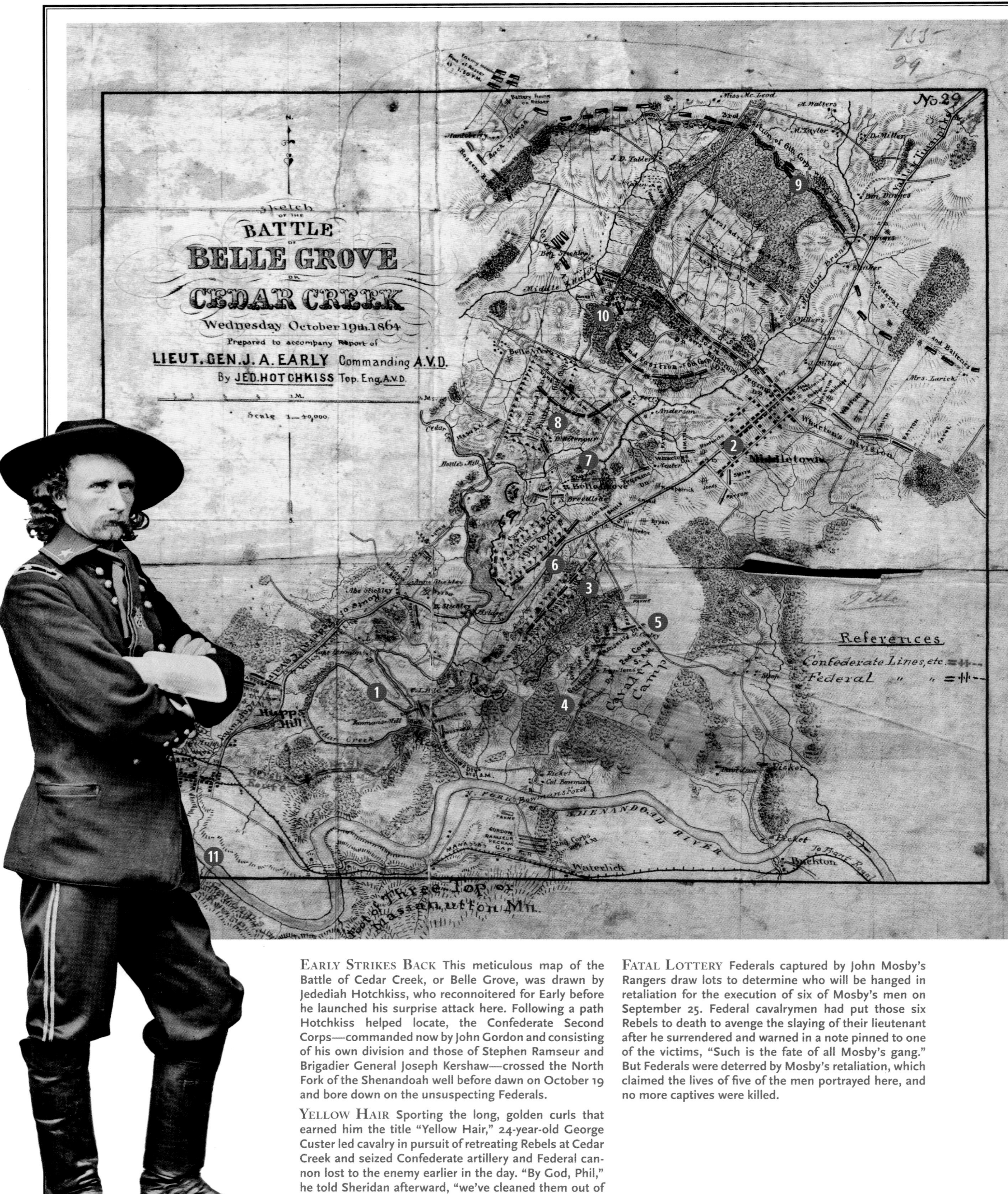

EARLY STRIKES BACK This meticulous map of the Battle of Cedar Creek, or Belle Grove, was drawn by Jedediah Hotchkiss, who reconnoitered for Early before he launched his surprise attack here. Following a path Hotchkiss helped locate, the Confederate Second Corps—commanded now by John Gordon and consisting of his own division and those of Stephen Ramseur and Brigadier General Joseph Kershaw—crossed the North Fork of the Shenandoah well before dawn on October 19 and bore down on the unsuspecting Federals.

YELLOW HAIR Sporting the long, golden curls that earned him the title "Yellow Hair," 24-year-old George Custer led cavalry in pursuit of retreating Rebels at Cedar Creek and seized Confederate artillery and Federal cannon lost to the enemy earlier in the day. "By God, Phil," he told Sheridan afterward, "we've cleaned them out of their guns and got ours back."

FATAL LOTTERY Federals captured by John Mosby's Rangers draw lots to determine who will be hanged in retaliation for the execution of six of Mosby's men on September 25. Federal cavalrymen had put those six Rebels to death to avenge the slaying of their lieutenant after he surrendered and warned in a note pinned to one of the victims, "Such is the fate of all Mosby's gang." But Federals were deterred by Mosby's retaliation, which claimed the lives of five of the men portrayed here, and no more captives were killed.

THE BATTLE OF CEDAR CREEK

Following his victory at Winchester, Sheridan pursued Early southward, defeating him again at Fisher's Hill on September 22 and taking more captives. Then he began torching farms in a systematic rampage known as "the Burning." By Sheridan's reckoning, his men destroyed 2,000 barns and killed or confiscated 50,000 cattle, horses, and other livestock. Fulfilling a threat issued by his predecessor, David Hunter, Sheridan responded to an ambush that claimed the life of a Federal officer by burning every house within five miles of the spot. But he did not go unchallenged. John Mosby goaded him by hanging several Federal captives after six of Mosby's Rangers were seized and executed. And Early posed a renewed threat when he was reinforced by Lee and went after Sheridan.

Shortly before dawn on October 19, while Sheridan was 15 miles away at Winchester on his way back from a war conference in Washington, Early's forces surprised the Federals in their encampment along Cedar Creek ❶ near Middletown ❷. First to feel that staggering blow was the Eighth Corps ❸, routed so swiftly by the divisions of Major Generals John Gordon ❹ and Stephen Ramseur ❺ that Yankees "fled in their night clothes," one Confederate recalled, "without their guns, hats or shoes." Federals of the 19th Corps ❻, camped near Belle Grove plantation ❼, tried to stem the Rebel tide but were pushed back into the camp of the Sixth Corps ❽, where Horatio Wright, commanding in Sheridan's absence, put up a hard fight before retreating to a line north of Middletown ❾. Meanwhile, Sheridan had learned of the attack and was galloping to the scene on his horse Rienzi. A midday pause in the fighting—ordered by Early to regain control of his hungry troops, who were looting the well-stocked Federal camps—enabled Sheridan to rally his forces and launch a counterattack. Cavalry led by Brigadier General George Armstrong Custer turned Early's left flank, and the hard-pressed Rebel line ❿ gave way. Spurred on by Sheridan, his men chased their foes back across the North Fork of the Shenandoah River ⓫, ending this last Confederate bid to regain command of the Shenandoah Valley, draw Federals away from Petersburg, and help sustain Lee's besieged army. ■

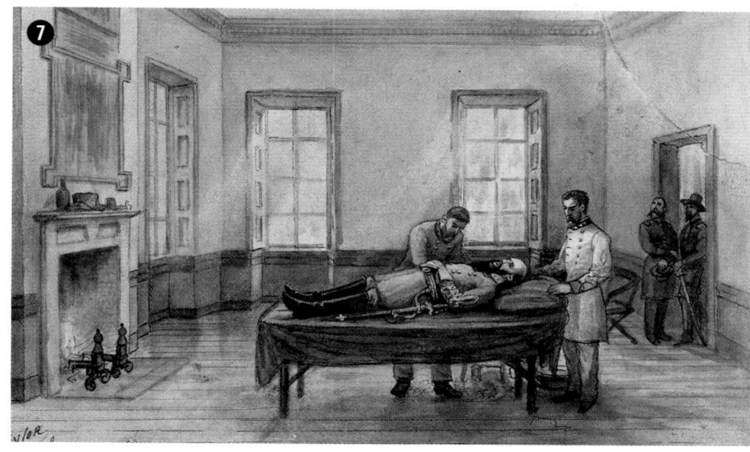

❼ RAMSEUR'S DEATHBED **Twenty-seven-year-old General Stephen Ramseur, mortally wounded during the Federal counterattack at Cedar Creek, lies near death at Belle Grove plantation after being captured. Among those who visited him before he died was an acquaintance of his at West Point, George Armstrong Custer.**

1864

SINKING THE ALABAMA

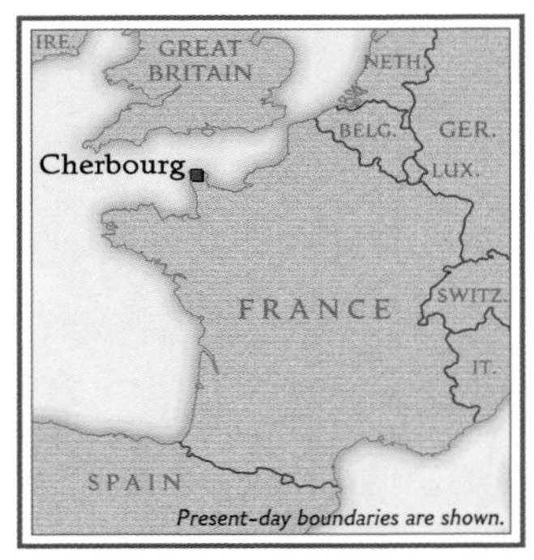

THE BLOCKADE

AUGUST 24, 1862 Captain Raphael Semmes takes command of the newly commissioned Confederate commerce raider *Alabama.*

JUNE 10, 1864 The *Alabama* seeks harbor in Cherbourg, France, for repairs.

JUNE 14 Captain John Wilson, commanding the U.S.S. *Kearsarge,* reaches Cherbourg in pursuit of the *Alabama.*

JUNE 19 Battle between the *Alabama* and the *Kearsarge* off Cherbourg.

The long run of the Confederate commerce raider C.S.S. *Alabama* and its notorious captain, Raphael Semmes, ended in a spectacular battle with the warship U.S.S. *Kearsarge* off Cherbourg, France ❶, in June 1864. Assigned to seize Union merchant ships and inflict on the Northern economy "the greatest injury in the shortest time," Semmes had taken command of the *Alabama*—a steam sloop-of-war built in Liverpool, England, expressly for this purpose—in August 1862. To skirt Great Britain's neutrality laws, the ship left Liverpool unarmed, bound for the Azores, where it took on eight guns, including a pivoting, 110-pounder Blakely rifle that overawed the merchantmen Semmes preyed on. Semmes went on to capture 65 ships, most of which he destroyed after removing their crew and passengers. He also sank the warship U.S.S. *Hatteras* and eluded pursuit by the U.S. Navy until he entered Cherbourg Harbor on June 10, 1864, hoping to repair the run-down *Alabama.* Word of his arrival reached American officials in Paris, and the *Kearsarge* was ordered to Cherbourg, arriving there from the Dutch coast on June 14.

Semmes had no hope of eluding the *Kearsarge*—which was in far better condition than the *Alabama*—and no intention of yielding without a fight. He sent a message to Captain John Winslow, promising to meet his ship soon in battle and adding defiantly, "I beg she will not depart before I am ready to go out." Winslow, of course, was not going anywhere before he finished this business with Semmes. Around 9:30 A.M. on June 19, the *Alabama* raised anchor ❷ and was escorted by a French frigate into international waters, three miles off shore. The *Kearsarge* ❸, better-armed and better-manned, was waiting seven miles from the harbor so that the *Alabama* could not easily withdraw under duress to neutral French waters. Semmes fired the first shot from a distance of a mile, then the two vessels began cruising in a circle ❹, roughly a half mile apart, exchanging shots as the current nudged them westward toward the harbor entrance. Gradually, the circle tightened until the *Kearsarge* was only a quarter mile from the *Alabama* ❺ and doing fearful damage. Around 12:15, with dozens of his men dead or wounded and his ship foundering, Semmes lowered his colors. Winslow sent lifeboats and allowed the British vessel *Deerhound* ❻ to aid the stricken crew. Rescued by its sympathetic captain and taken to England, Semmes later returned to the South, where he was promoted to rear admiral. ■

MAN OF WAR **Raphael Semmes, shown here aboard the *Alabama* beside its imposing Blakely rifle, was denounced by Northerners as a pirate. But commerce raiding had long been part of war and was similar in its methods and objectives to the Federal blockade, which did far more damage to the South economically than Semmes and others preying on Union merchantmen did to the North.**

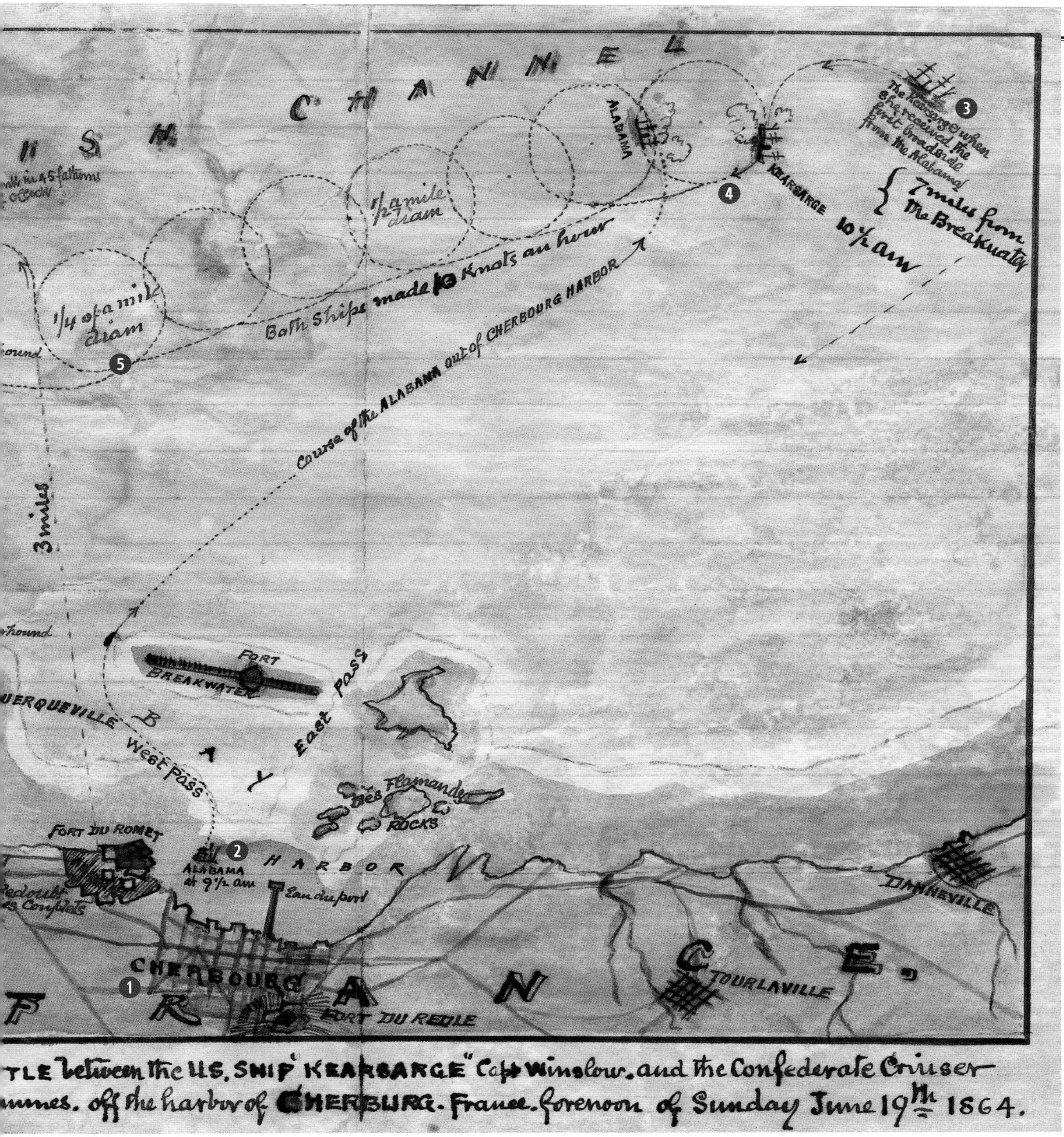

TLE between the U.S. SHIP "KEARSARGE" Capt Winslow. and the Confederate Cruiser
mmes. off the harbor of CHERBURG. France. forenoon of Sunday June 19th 1864.

DECISION AT CHERBOURG Drawing on official documents, Robert Knox Sneden composed this authoritative map of the battle between the *Alabama* and the *Kearsarge* outside Cherbourg Harbor on June 19, noting the exact time at which the *Alabama* went down: 12:24 P.M. The battle was heralded well in advance, and crowds gathered along the shore to watch it.

ALABAMA IN ACTION Shown at full sail, the *Alabama* targets a merchant ship in 1862 shortly after entering service as a Confederate commerce raider.

1864

MOBILE BAY

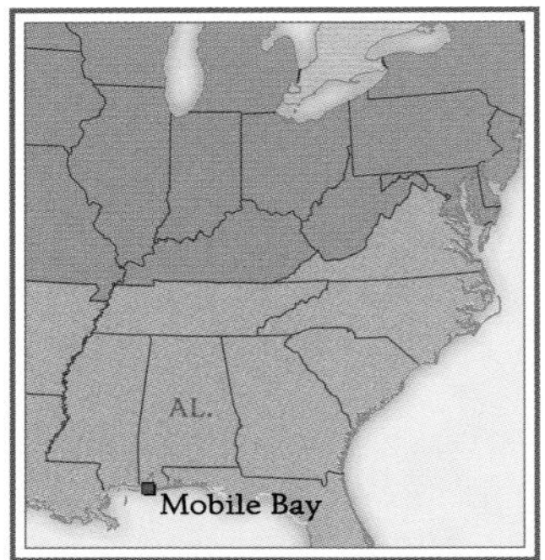

THE BLOCKADE

AUGUST 5, 1864 Federal fleet commanded by David Farragut enters Mobile Bay between Confederate Forts Morgan and Gaines and defeats a fleet led by Franklin Buchanan.

AUGUST 8 Federal troops on Dauphin Island force surrender of Fort Gaines.

AUGUST 23 Federals on Mobile Point force surrender of Fort Morgan.

Mobile, Alabama, was one of the few Southern ports that Federals had not sealed off by 1864. Blockade runners continued to slip in and out of Mobile Bay in defiance of Admiral David Farragut's West Gulf Blockading Squadron. And a new threat had recently appeared at the entrance to the bay, flanked by the Confederate strongholds Fort Morgan ❶ and Fort Gaines ❷—the ironclad ram *Tennessee* ❸, supported by three gunboats. These were daunting obstacles for Farragut as he made plans to seize this fine harbor and isolate Mobile. Sunken pilings in the channel ❹ and torpedoes ❺, or submerged mines, left his vessels only a narrow opening, which lay directly beneath the menacing guns of Fort Morgan.

Farragut in the rigging

At dawn on August 5, Farragut's fleet of four monitors and seven big wooden ships, each with a smaller gunboat lashed to its side, ran past Fort Morgan with guns blazing. The monitors were supposed to hug the shore, but the *Tecumseh* ❻ strayed into the minefield, hit a torpedo, and went down, alarming the captain of the leading wooden ship, *Brooklyn* ❼, who was hesitant to proceed. "Torpedoes ahead!" he signaled Farragut, who was lashed to the rigging of his flagship *Hartford* ❽ so that he could see beyond the billowing gun smoke. "Damn the torpedoes!" he shouted. "Full speed ahead!" Passing the *Brooklyn*, his flagship entered the minefield, striking defective torpedoes that failed to detonate. Once his big ships made it through, they cut free the gunboats, which helped capture the Confederate gunboat *Selma* ❾, disable the *Gaines* ❿, and chase away the *Morgan* ⓫. Admiral Franklin Buchanan aboard the *Tennessee* carried on the fight alone until a shot disabled the ironclad's rudder, forcing the wounded Buchanan to raise the white flag ⓬ and surrender Mobile Bay to Farragut. ■

❻ INTO THE MINEFIELD **After striking a torpedo, the Federal monitor *Tecumseh* capsizes as Farragut's wooden ships prepare to pass through the minefield near Fort Morgan and battle the Confederate ironclad ram Tennessee and its trailing gunboats.**

TAKING MOBILE BAY **A chart prepared for Farragut afterward shows the positions of his vessels as they approached the entrance to the bay (yellow), with the *Brooklyn* in the lead; as they passed Fort Morgan (red), with Farragut's *Hartford* in the lead; and as they did battle in the bay (blue) with Buchanan's fleet. As shown in the inset, the ram *Tennessee* was itself rammed by several Federal ships before Buchanan surrendered.**

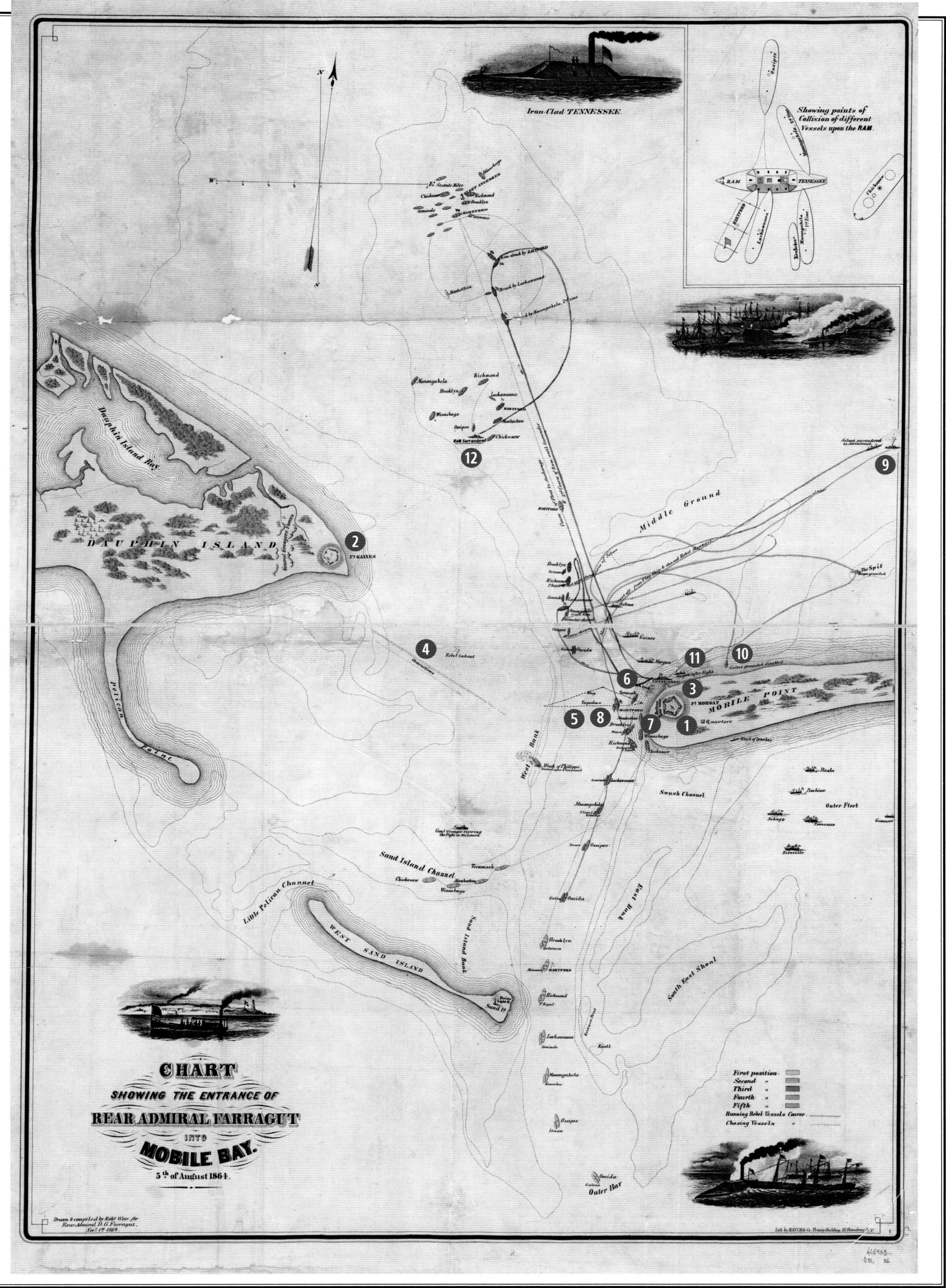
Iron-Clad TENNESSEE.
Showing points of Collision of different Vessels upon the RAM.
DAUPHIN ISLAND
Dauphin Island Bay
Ft. GAINES
Pelican Point
Middle Ground
The Spit
Ft. MORGAN
MOBILE POINT
Quarters
Swash Channel
Outer Fleet
Sand Island Channel
Little Pelican Channel
WEST SAND ISLAND
Sand Island Bank
East Bank
South East Shoal
Outer Bar
First position
Second
Third
Fourth
Fifth
Running Rebel Vessels Course
Chasing Vessels
CHART
SHOWING THE ENTRANCE OF
REAR ADMIRAL FARRAGUT
INTO
MOBILE BAY.
5th of August 1864.
Drawn & compiled by Robt. Weir, for Rear Admiral D. G. Farragut, Nov. 1st 1864.
1
2
3
4
5
6
7
8
9
10
11
12

1864

CAMPAIGN FOR ATLANTA

WESTERN THEATER

MAY 7, 1864 William Sherman launches campaign against Joseph Johnston in Georgia.

MAY 8 Battle of Rocky Face Ridge (Georgia)

MAY 14–15 Battle of Resaca

MAY 25–28 Battles of New Hope Church, Pickett's Mill, and Dallas

JUNE 27 Battle of Kennesaw Mountain

JULY 17 Johnston replaced as commander of the Army of Tennessee by John Bell Hood as Sherman's forces approach Atlanta.

JULY 20 Battle of Peachtree Creek

JULY 22 Battle of Atlanta

SEPTEMBER 2 Sherman takes Atlanta.

Sherman's offensive in Georgia was timed to coincide with Grant's campaign in Virginia and to prevent Confederates from shifting forces from one theater to another. For too long, Federal armies on either side of the Appalachians had operated "like a balky team, no two pulling together," as Grant observed. Now he and Sherman would work in tandem, pressing southward simultaneously against the main Confederate forces standing between the Union and victory—Lee's Army of Northern Virginia and Joseph Johnston's Army of Tennessee. Sherman's orders were "to move against Johnston's army, to break it up, and to get into the interior of the enemy's country as far as you can, inflicting all the damage you can against their war resources."

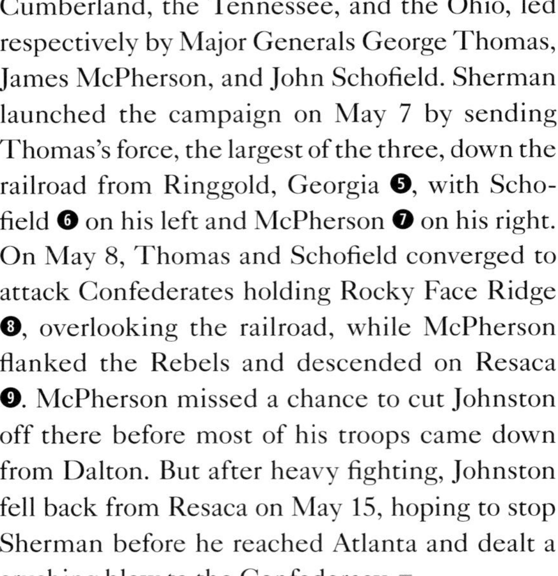
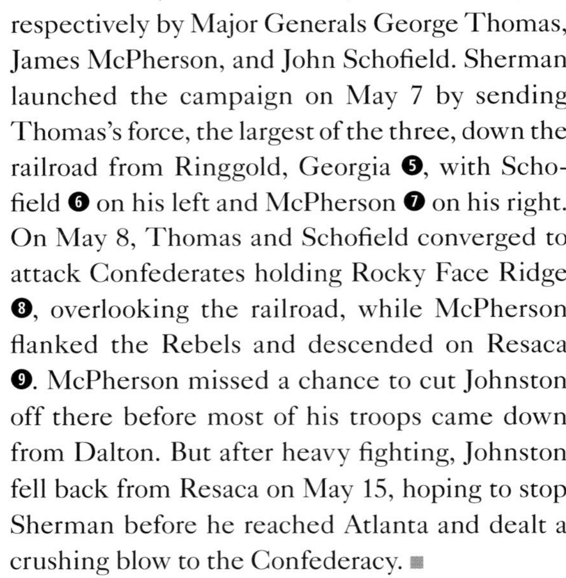

William Sherman

Breaking up Johnston's army would not be easy. Since replacing Braxton Bragg after his defeat at Chattanooga ❶, Johnston had rehabilitated his forces at Dalton, Georgia ❷. As one Confederate recalled, "He was loved, respected, admired; yea, almost worshiped by his troops." Although his army was barely half the size of Sherman's 100,000-man force, he would soon receive reinforcements from Alabama under Lieutenant General Leonidas Polk, who would serve as one of Johnston's three corps commanders along with Lieutenant Generals William Hardee and John Bell Hood. Cool and cautious, Johnston would use much the same tactics in Georgia as he had against McClellan in Virginia in 1862, withdrawing when hard-pressed and conserving his assets until he had his opponent at a disadvantage. The mountainous terrain of northern Georgia suited his defensive purposes, and he would carefully guard the Western & Atlantic Railroad ❸, his fragile supply line from Atlanta ❹.

If Sherman could not smash Johnston's army, he intended to force it to abandon Atlanta, a vital rail junction, arsenal, and manufacturing center whose war resources he would then destroy. To achieve that objective, Sherman had under his command the Armies of the Cumberland, the Tennessee, and the Ohio, led respectively by Major Generals George Thomas, James McPherson, and John Schofield. Sherman launched the campaign on May 7 by sending Thomas's force, the largest of the three, down the railroad from Ringgold, Georgia ❺, with Schofield ❻ on his left and McPherson ❼ on his right. On May 8, Thomas and Schofield converged to attack Confederates holding Rocky Face Ridge ❽, overlooking the railroad, while McPherson flanked the Rebels and descended on Resaca ❾. McPherson missed a chance to cut Johnston off there before most of his troops came down from Dalton. But after heavy fighting, Johnston fell back from Resaca on May 15, hoping to stop Sherman before he reached Atlanta and dealt a crushing blow to the Confederacy. ■

SHERMAN'S SUPPLY LINE **Federals camped in the foreground guard a railroad bridge in Tennessee to protect Sherman's supply line between Nashville and Chattanooga. Sherman left thousands of troops behind in Tennessee to fend off Confederate raiders while he advanced into Georgia and tried to cut Johnston's supply line.**

THE ROAD TO ATLANTA **A Federal map of the Atlanta campaign signed by Brigadier General Charles Ewing, Sherman's brother-in-law and a member of his staff, traces the paths followed by Sherman's three subordinate army commanders—Thomas, Schofield, and McPherson. Shown in red here are Confederate positions and battle sites, including Rocky Face Ridge, Resaca, New Hope Church, Kennesaw Mountain, and Atlanta.**

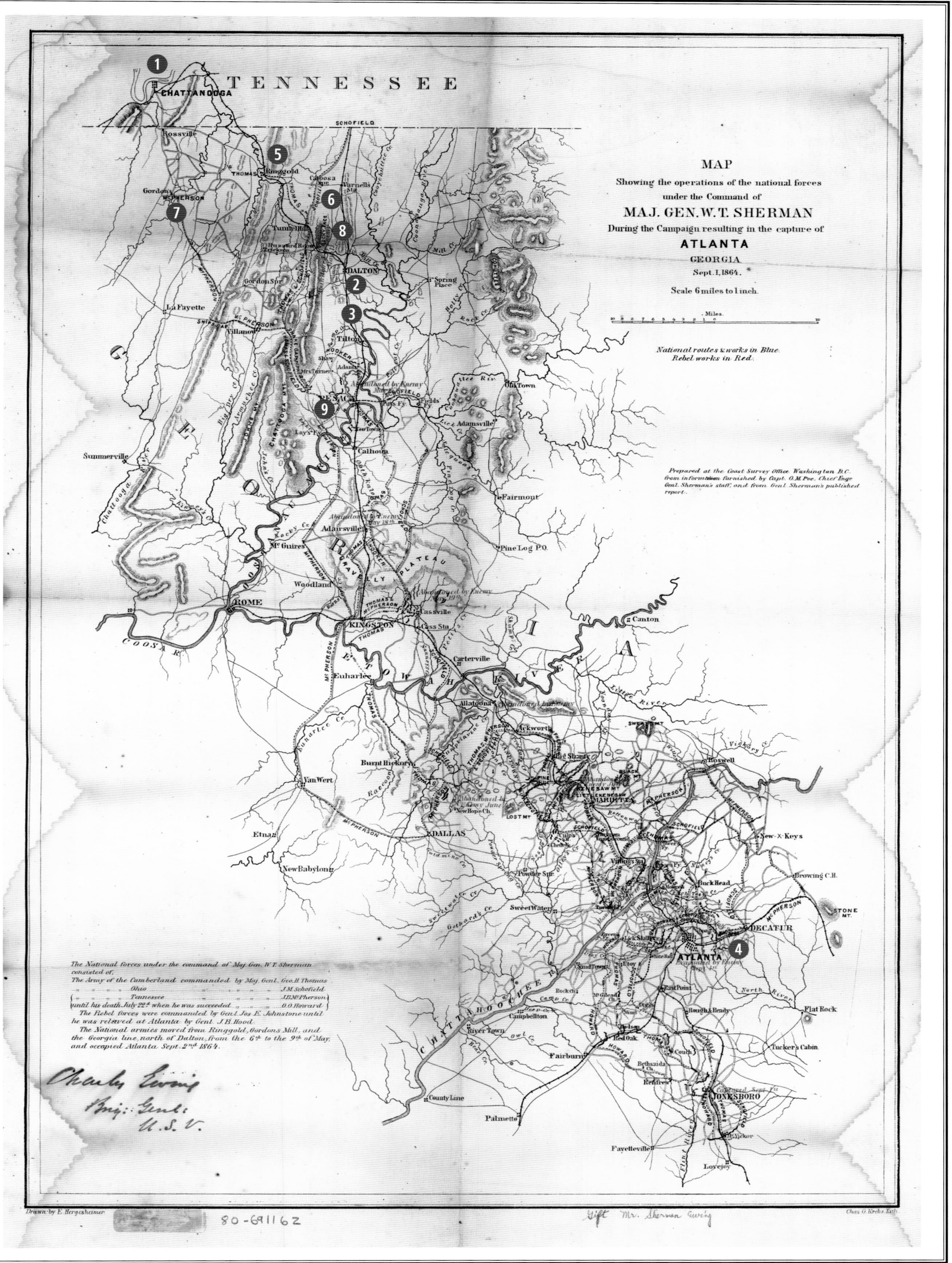
MAP
Showing the operations of the national forces
under the Command of
MAJ. GEN. W.T. SHERMAN
During the Campaign resulting in the capture of
ATLANTA
GEORGIA
Sept. 1, 1864.
Scale 6 miles to 1 inch.
Miles.
National routes & works in Blue.
Rebel works in Red.
Prepared at the Coast Survey Office Washington D.C. from information furnished by Capt. O.M. Poe, Chief Engr Genl. Sherman's staff, and from Genl. Sherman's published report.
The National forces under the command of Maj. Gen. W.T. Sherman consisted of,
The Army of the Cumberland commanded by Maj. Genl. Geo. H. Thomas
" " " " Ohio " " " " J.M. Schofield
" " " " Tennessee " " " " J.B. McPherson
until his death July 22d when he was succeeded " " " O.O. Howard
The Rebel forces were commanded by Genl. Jos E. Johnstone until he was relieved at Atlanta by Genl. J.B. Hood.
The National armies moved from Ringgold, Gordons Mill, and the Georgia line, north of Dalton, from the 6th to the 9th of May, and occupied Atlanta Sept. 2nd 1864.
Drawn by E. Hergesheimer
Chas. G. Krebs, Lith.
TENNESSEE
GEORGIA
CHATTANOOGA
SCHOFIELD
Rossville
Ringgold
THOMAS
Gordons
McPHERSON
Tunnel Hill
DALTON
Spring Place
La Fayette
Villanow
Tilton
Resaca
Calhoun
Summerville
Adairsville
Fairmount
Pine Log P.O.
Mc Guires
Woodland
ROME
KINGSTON
Cassville
Cass Sta.
Carterville
COOSA R.
Euharlee
ETOWAH RIVER
Allatoona
Ackworth
Canton
Big Shanty
Burnt Hickory
Van Wert
MARIETTA
LOST MT.
DALLAS
Etna
New Babylon
Powder Spr.
Sweet Water
Roswell
New-X-Keys
Buck Head
Browing C.H.
STONE MT.
DECATUR
ATLANTA
East Point
Rough & Ready
Flat Rock
Campbellton
River Town
Fairburn
Tucker's Cabin
CHATTAHOOCHEE R.
County Line
JONESBORO
Palmetto
Fayetteville
Lovejoy
HOWARD
1
2
3
4
5
6
7
8
9
80-691162

STOPPED AT NEW HOPE CHURCH

Sherman's aim as he descended on Atlanta was to fight "cautiously, persistently, and to the best advantage." That meant avoiding costly frontal attacks, when possible, and relying on flanking movements like the one he tried at Resaca. Sherman marveled at Johnston's "lynx-eyed watchfulness" in guarding his flanks, as shown in late May when he anticipated Sherman's move around fortified Allatoona Pass on the Western & Atlantic Railroad and sidestepped to New Hope Church ❶, where his troops raised breastworks reaching to the town of Dallas ❷.

On May 25, Sherman ordered Joseph Hooker's 20th Corps ❸, leading the way for Thomas's army, to test those defenses. "Hundreds of men surged right up to the breastworks and died there," recalled one Federal after that futile assault at New Hope Church, repulsed by Major General Alexander Stewart's division ❹ of Hood's corps. On May 26, Sherman sent Oliver Howard's Fourth Corps ❺ to turn Johnston's right flank. Once again, Johnston anticipated him by shifting divisions led by Thomas Hindman ❻ and Patrick Cleburne ❼ eastward to Pickett's Mill ❽. Howard, groping through tangled woods, could not see where their line ended. "I am now turning the enemy's right flank, I think," he mistakenly reported. His ill-fated troops came up against entrenched infantry and were themselves hit in the flank by Brigadier General John Kelly's dismounted cavalry ❾. Routed twice in two days, Sherman wanted out of this "Hell Hole." But Johnston tried to snare him by sending Hardee's corps ❿ against McPherson's army ⓫ at Dallas on May 28. This time, Confederates charged entrenched Federals and got the worst of it. Unable to pin Sherman down, Johnston shadowed him as he shifted back to the railroad, below Allatoona. ■

ALLATOONA PASS **Sherman's flanking march around Allatoona Pass—guarded by a Confederate fort atop the hill at left—was blocked by Johnston at New Hope Church.**

ORDER OF BATTLE

UNION FORCES
Sherman | *100,000 men*

ARMY OF THE CUMBERLAND *Thomas*

IV CORPS *Howard*
1ST DIVISION *Stanley*
Brigades Cruft, Whitaker, Grose
2ND DIVISION *Newton*
Brigades F. Sherman, Wagner, Harker
3RD DIVISION *Wood*
Brigades Willich, Hazen, Beatty

XIV CORPS *Palmer*
1ST DIVISION *Johnson*
Brigades Carlin, King, Scribner
2ND DIVISION *Davis*
Brigades Morgan, Mitchell, D. McCook
3RD DIVISION *Baird*
Brigades Turchin, Van Derveer, Este

XX CORPS *Hooker*
1ST DIVISION *A. Williams*
Brigades Knipe, Ruger, Robinson
2ND DIVISION *Geary*
Brigades Candy, Buschbeck, Ireland
3RD DIVISION *Butterfield*
Brigades Ward, Coburn, J. Wood

Reserve Brigade Burke

CAVALRY CORPS *Elliott*
1ST DIVISION *E. M. McCook*
Brigades Dorr, La Grange, Watkins
2ND DIVISION *Garrard*
Brigades Minty, Long, Wilder
3RD DIVISION *Kilpatrick*
Brigades Klein, Smith, Murray

ARMY OF THE TENNESSEE *McPherson*

XV CORPS *Logan*
1ST DIVISION *Osterhaus*
Brigades Woods, Williamson, Wangelin
2ND DIVISION *M. L. Smith*
Brigades G. A. Smith, Lightburn
3RD DIVISION *Smith*
Brigades Alexander, Raum, Matthies
4TH DIVISION *Harrow*
Brigades Williams, Walcutt, Oliver

XVI CORPS (LEFT WING) *Dodge*
2ND DIVISION *Sweeny*
Brigades Rice, Burke, Bane
4TH DIVISION *Veatch*
Brigades Fuller, Sprague, Howe

XVII CORPS *Blair*
3RD DIVISION *Legett*
Brigades Force, Scott, Malloy
4TH DIVISION *Gresham*
Brigades Potts, Logan, Hall

ARMY OF THE OHIO (XXIII CORPS) *Schofield*

1ST DIVISION *Hovey*
Brigades Barter, McQuiston
2ND DIVISION *Judah*
Brigades McLean, Hascall, Strickland
3RD DIVISION *Cox*
Brigades Reilly, Manson, McLean
Dismounted Brigade Crittenden
CAVALRY *Stoneman*
Brigades Garrard, Biddle, Capron
Independent Brigade Holeman

CONFEDERATE FORCES
ARMY OF TENNESSEE
Johnston | *60,000 men*

HARDEE'S CORPS
CHEATHAM'S DIVISION
Brigades Maney, Strahl, Wright, Vaughan
CLEBURNE'S DIVISION
Brigades Polk, Govan, Lowrey, Granbury
BATE'S DIVISION
Brigades Tyler, Lewis, Finley
WALKER'S DIVISION
Brigades Mercer, Gist, J. K. Jackson, Stevens

HOOD'S CORPS
HINDMAN'S DIVISION
Brigades Deas, Tucker, Manigault, Walthall
STEVENSON'S DIVISION
Brigades Brown, Reynolds, Cumming, Pettus
STEWART'S DIVISION
Brigades Stovall, Gibson, Clayton, Baker

POLK'S CORPS
LORING'S DIVISION
Brigades Featherston, Adams, Scott
FRENCH'S DIVISION
Brigades Ector, Sears, Cockrell
WALTHALL'S DIVISION
Brigades Reynolds, Quarles, Cantey

CAVALRY CORPS *Wheeler*
MARTIN'S DIVISION
Brigades Morgan, Iverson
KELLY'S DIVISION
Brigades Allen, Dibrell, Hannon
HUMES'S DIVISION
Brigades J. T. Wheeler, Harrison, Grigsby
JACKSON'S DIVISION
Brigades Armstrong, Ross, Ferguson

Deadlock at Dallas As shown in this National Geographic map, Rebels on Johnston's right shattered attacks by Hooker's corps at New Hope Church on May 25 and Howard's corps at Pickett's Mill on May 26. Johnston's subsequent attack on Sherman's right at Dallas on May 28 fared no better, producing a deadlock.

❶ **Forbidding Breastworks** Confederates firing from behind solid breastworks like these at New Hope Church, made of earth reinforced with logs, repulsed Sherman's troops on May 25.

KENNESAW MOUNTAIN

LEONIDAS POLK

The death of 58-year-old Leonidas Polk atop Pine Mountain on June 14 came as a severe blow to Southern troops and civilians alike. "Every private soldier loved him," wrote Sam Watkins, who served as a private in the Army of Tennessee while Polk was a corps commander. "Second to Stonewall Jackson, his loss was the greatest the South ever sustained." As a general, Polk lacked the drive and daring that distinguished Jackson. But as the Confederacy's "Fighting Bishop," he played an inspirational role, serving in Robert E. Lee's words as "a model for all that was soldierly, gentlemanly, and honorable."

After graduating from West Point in 1827, Polk answered a higher calling and entered the Virginia Theological Seminary, much to the dismay of his father, who when asked where his son was stationed answered gruffly, "Stationed? Why, he's over there in Alexandria at the Seminary!" After three decades as an Episcopal priest and bishop, however, he took up the sword as a Confederate general while remaining a clergyman and performing services that included the baptism of fellow corps commander John Bell Hood in May 1864. His son, Lieutenant William Polk, was on his staff and described his last moments atop Pine Mountain: "Folding his arms across his breast, he stood intently gazing on the scene below. While he thus stood, a cannon-shot crashed through his breast, and opening a wide door, let free that indomitable spirit."

Returning to the Western & Atlantic Railroad at Ackworth ❶ in early June, Sherman found Confederates blocking his way south. The enemy line, which crossed the railroad below Big Shanty ❷ and extended westward to Pine Mountain ❸ and Lost Mountain ❹, was backed by entrenched artillery on imposing Kennesaw Mountain ❺. "Kennesaw is the key to the whole country," wrote Sherman, who could not get past Marietta ❻ to Atlanta until he knocked Rebels off that perch.

On June 14, Sherman approached Pine Mountain from the north and noticed grey-clad officers surveying the field from its bare crest. Unaware that Joseph Johnston, William Hardee, and Leonidas Polk were among that party, he ordered artillery to fire on them. The opening shot prompted Johnston and Hardee to seek cover, but Polk lingered in the open and was struck dead. "We killed Bishop Polk yesterday," Sherman informed Washington on June 15, "and have made good progress today."

Johnston soon fell back to a shorter and more formidable line extending southward from Kennesaw and Little Kennesaw Mountain ❼ to the Powder Springs Road ❽, where John Bell Hood challenged Federals as they approached the Confederate left flank at Kolb's farm on June 22. Hood's attack proved costly, and Johnston stayed on the defensive thereafter, daring Sherman to risk a frontal assault. Frustrated by Johnston's success in countering his flanking moves, Sherman prepared to do just that.

On June 27, troops of Major General John Logan's 15th Corps, part of McPherson's army, struggled up Little Kennesaw Mountain under heavy fire from Confederates led by Major General Samuel French of Polk's old corps. Logan's men were beaten back before they reached the Rebel breastworks, leaving the hillside strewn with dead and wounded. To the south, below the Dallas Road ❾, 8,000 men of Thomas's army formed what one officer called a "human battering ram" to smash through Hardee's well-fortified corps but were themselves battered and pinned down. "It was almost sure death to take your face out of the dust," one Federal recalled. By midday, Sherman had lost nearly 3,000 men without making a dent in the enemy line. But his attacks served a purpose by distracting the Confederates and allowing Schofield's army to begin edging around to their south. Soon Johnston was flanked and forced to pull back, abandoning Marietta and bringing Sherman a step closer to Atlanta. ■

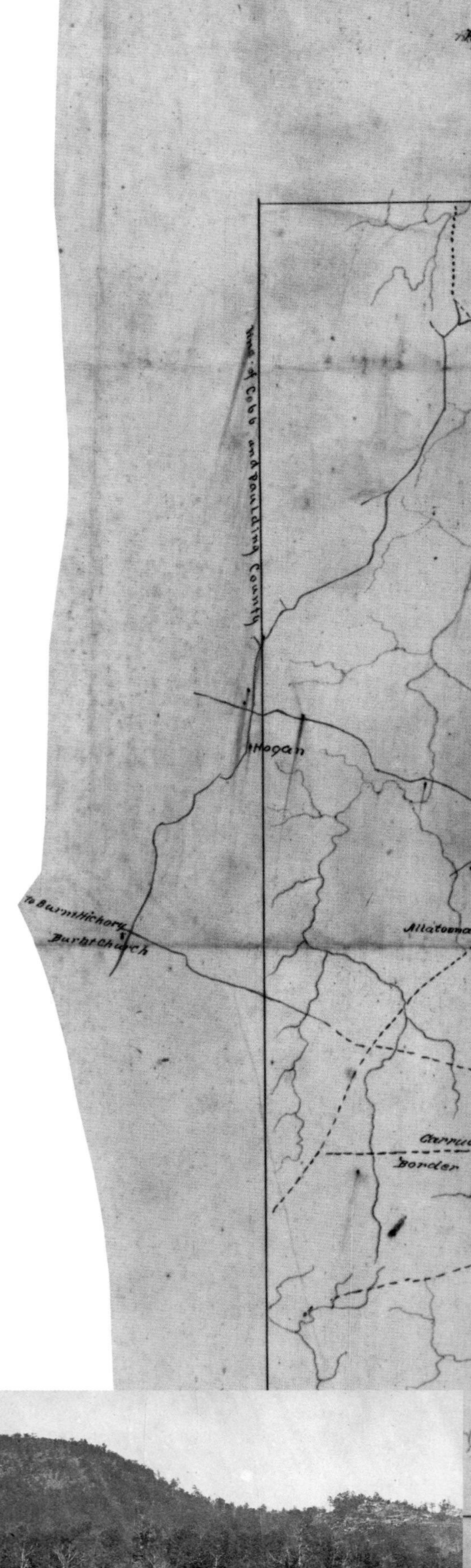

❺ EARTHWORKS BELOW KENNESAW **Sherman's forces dug these earthworks below Kennesaw and Little Kennesaw Mountain (right) in case Johnston attacked but left their trenches to assault fortified Confederates on the heights on June 27.**

SHERMAN'S PATH **A reconnaissance map prepared by Sherman's topographical engineers as his troops closed in on Confederates defending Kennesaw Mountain and environs shows Federal works and roads drawn from observation (solid lines) or from information (dotted lines) provided by fugitive slaves or other sources.**

❸ POLK'S DEATH **An artist's sketch shows Johnston and Hardee taking cover atop Pine Mountain as Polk reels from the impact of a shell, which killed him instantly.**

❺

Compiled from Surveys made by the Top'l Engrs of the Dept. of the Cumb.
Dept. and Army of the Tennesse
23rd Army Corps
Under the direction of
at Head Quarters Dept. Cumb
True Meridian
Rail Road
Union Works
Common Road
Roads from Information
ACWORTH
Shiloh Church
BIG SHANTY
Davenport
Durham
Wesson
Peters
Proctors Cr.
Allatoona Cr.
Newton
Adams
Collins
Golgotha
PINE HILL
Cheatham
KENESAW MOUNTAIN
Tannery
MARIETTA
LOST MT.
Powell
Bradford
Darby
Ballinger
Wallace
Mud Cr.
Gartrell
Clay
D. Dobbs
Anderson's Steam Mill
(Thomas)
1
2
3
4
5
6
7
8
9

1864 | CAMPAIGN FOR ATLANTA

Battles for Atlanta

Sherman drew within reach of Atlanta on July 8 when his enterprising subordinate, John Schofield, again flanked Johnston's entrenched forces and crossed the Chattahoochee River. Johnston then pulled back below Peachtree Creek ❶, just five miles from the city. Pressed by Jefferson Davis, who wanted Atlanta vigorously defended, Johnston said he would have to remain on the defensive until an opportunity arose "to fight to advantage." On July 17, he was replaced by the aggressive Hood. "He'll hit you like hell," Schofield warned Sherman, "now, before you know it."

Hood soon took the offensive, hoping to catch Thomas's army as it crossed Peachtree Creek on July 20. His attack there did not begin until most of Thomas's troops were across the creek, however, and faltered late in the day when he sent Patrick Cleburne's redoubtable division off to deal with McPherson's army, approaching Atlanta from the east. On July 21, McPherson clashed with Cleburne and took Bald Hill ❷, from which Federal artillery could bombard the city. That led to the furious Battle of Atlanta on July 22, during which McPherson died while trying to shore up his left flank ❸ against Hardee's surging corps. John Logan took his place and rallied the troops, crying, "McPherson and revenge, boys!" By evening, Federals had restored their line ❹ and inflicted more casualties on Hood in three days than Johnston had suffered in ten weeks.

Sherman then began shelling Atlanta and wheeling around the city in a counterclockwise direction to sever its arteries. After repulsing an assault at Ezra Church ❺ on July 29, his troops cut the Atlanta & West Point Railroad ❻ below East Point ❼. On September 1, they pinched off the city's last lifeline, the Macon & Western Railroad ❽, by capturing Jonesboro. That night, Hood pulled out of Atlanta, and Sherman marched in on September 2. ■

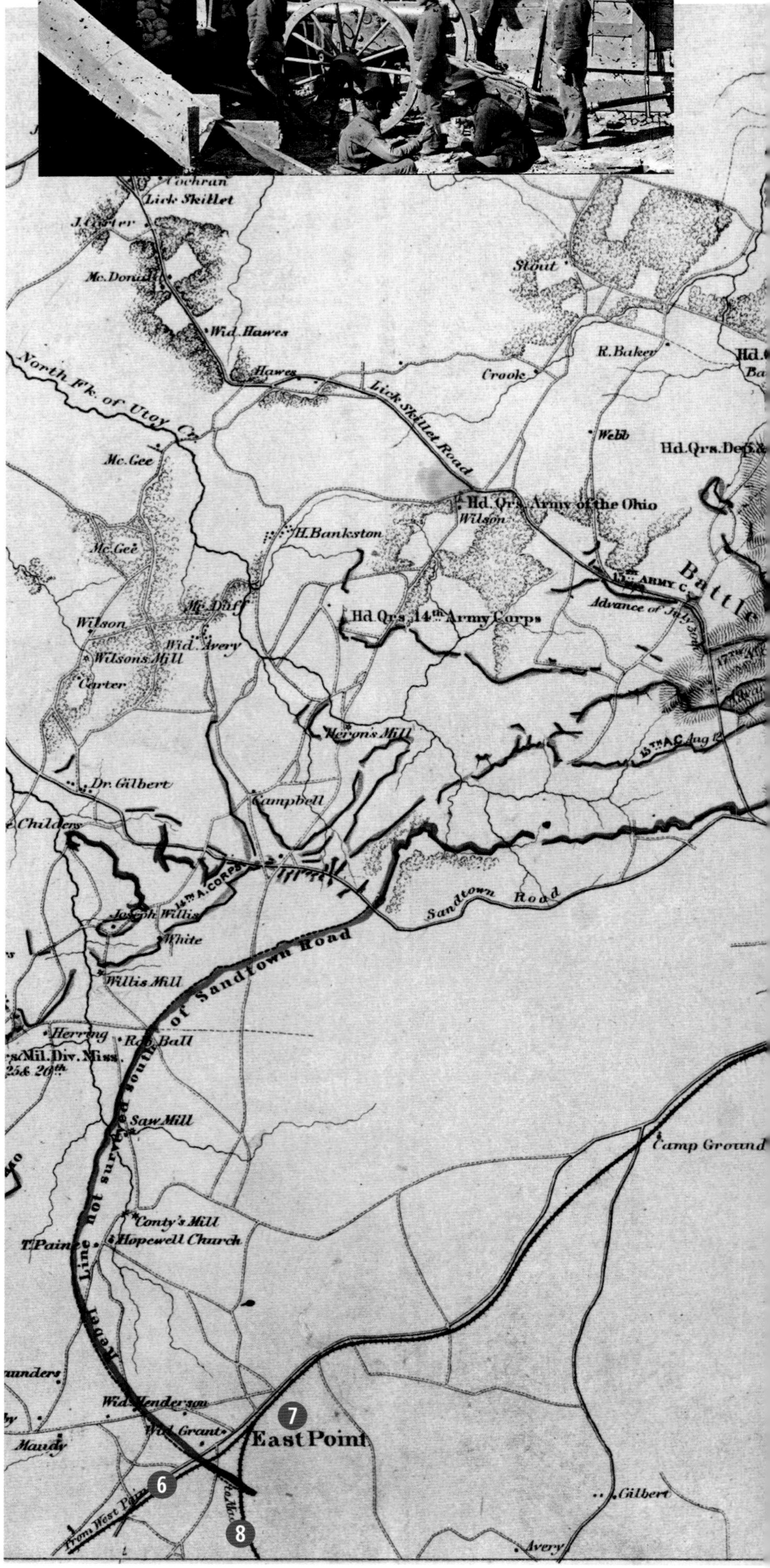

Atlanta's Defenses Spiked logs called chevaux-de-frise and a palisade shield a Confederate redoubt on Atlanta's strongly fortified perimeter.

Sherman Closes In This map by Orlando Poe, chief engineer for Sherman, shows how he overcame Atlanta's fortifications (red) by fighting battles on the outskirts, cutting supply lines, and hemming in the city's defenders. Union lines (blue) were so close to Atlanta's defenses that the two overlap in places here.

CAPTURED FORT Federals occupy a fort on Atlanta's outskirts that fell without a fight when Sherman cut off the city and its defenders.

RIDING HIGH Sherman, shown here in the saddle after occupying Atlanta, made no effort to soften the impact of his bruising campaign on civilians. "War is cruelty," he once remarked. "There is no use trying to reform it; the crueler it is, the sooner it will be over."

1864

THE ELECTION OF 1864

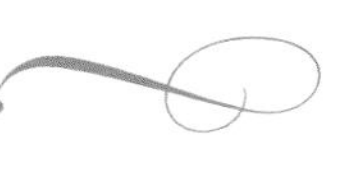

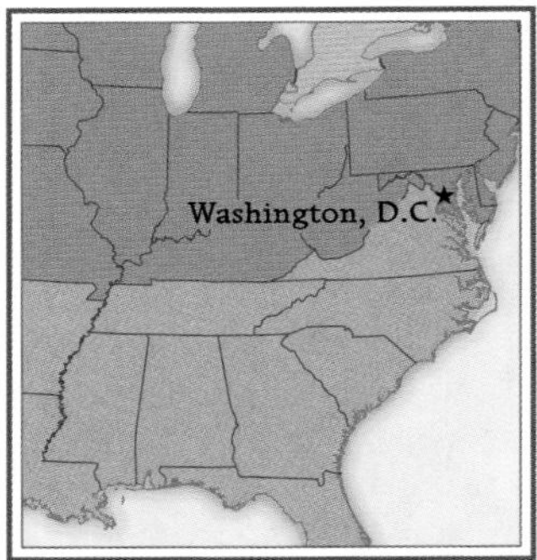

POLITICS & POWER

MAY 31, 1864 John Frémont nominated for president by Radical Republicans.

JUNE 8 Abraham Lincoln nominated for president by the National Union Party, a title adopted by Republicans to appeal to Democrats.

AUGUST 31 George McClellan nominated for president by Democrats.

SEPTEMBER 22 Frémont drops out of the race and endorses Lincoln.

NOVEMBER 8 Lincoln wins reelection decisively.

When Abraham Lincoln learned that Sherman had taken Atlanta, he proclaimed a national day of thanksgiving. Lincoln himself had much to be thankful for, after a demoralizing summer in which Confederates reached the outskirts of Washington. "People are getting tired of the war," remarked Lincoln's old friend David Davis of Illinois in early August. "Some of them can't see a ray of light." More than a few Republicans hoped that Lincoln, nominated in June, would yield to a stronger candidate. "Mr. Lincoln is already beaten," wrote editor Horace Greeley to the mayor of New York. "We must have another ticket to save us from utter overthrow."

Sherman's triumph transformed the political landscape by restoring faith in Lincoln's war effort and undermining Peace Democrats, who sought a negotiated end to the conflict. At the party's convention in Chicago in late August, Peace Democrats passed a platform urging that "immediate efforts be made for cessation of hostilities." But the nominee in Chicago—George McClellan, former Union general-in-chief—sided with War Democrats by ruling out negotiations unless the rebellious states agreed to return to the Union. McClellan did not make the abolition of slavery in the South a condition for peace, and that became the core issue in his race against Lincoln, who was committed to ending slavery. By choosing Andrew Johnson, a War Democrat from Tennessee, as his running mate, however, Lincoln distanced himself from Radical Republicans, who favored stringent policies toward the defeated South. Their choice for president was John Frémont, but on September 22 Frémont dropped out and endorsed Lincoln. With victory on the battlefield seemingly within reach, Northerners were less inclined to favor McClellan's call for "compromise and conciliation." Union soldiers backed Lincoln heavily in November, when he won 55 percent of the popular vote and swept every state in the Union except Kentucky, Delaware, and McClellan's home ground, New Jersey. ■

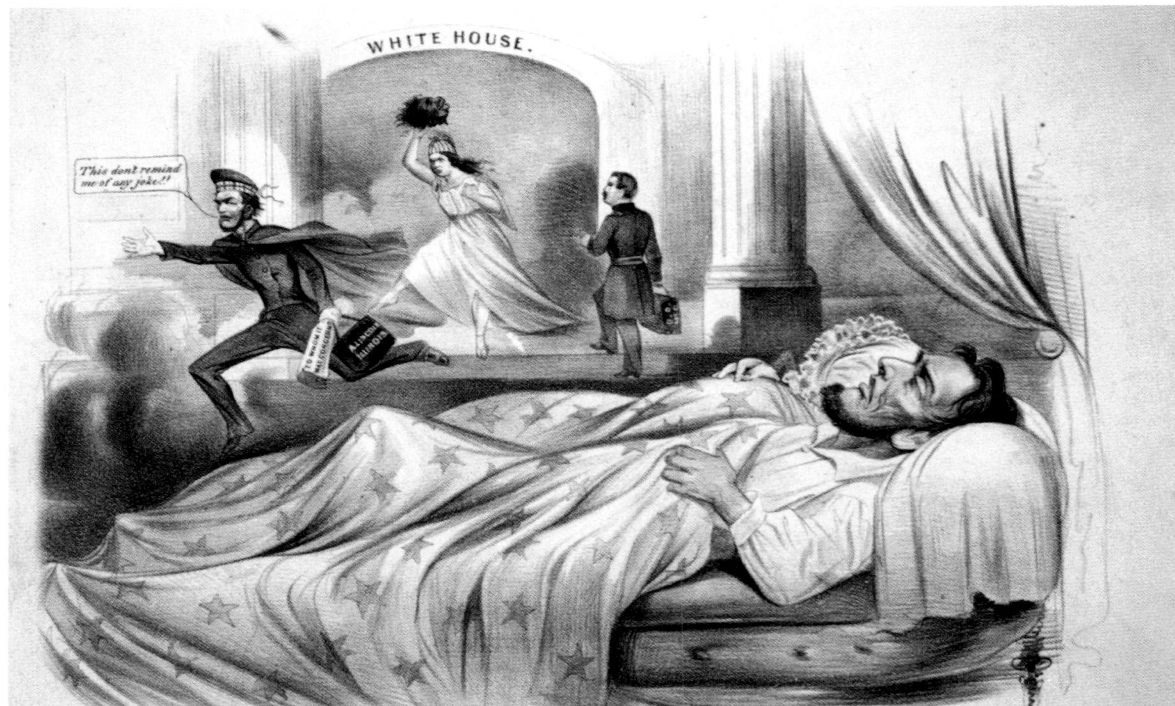

LINCOLN'S NIGHTMARE **A political cartoon published in 1864 portrays Lincoln's worst nightmare—losing the White House to his Democratic opponent, George McClellan, whom he had dismissed as commander of the Army of the Potomac in 1862.**

CHARTING THE RACE **This 1864 presidential primer includes a map showing a large area in yellow that was once Confederate or neutral but was now claimed by Federals. Those military gains boosted Lincoln, who ran on a platform opposing "compromise with rebels." McClellan—whose running mate, Congressman George Pendleton of Ohio, was a prominent Peace Democrat—implicitly criticized Lincoln's stand against slavery by stating that preserving the Union was the sole object for which the war "should have been conducted."**

PRESIDENTIAL CAMPAIGN, 1864
CANDIDATES FOR PRESIDENT AND VICE-PRESIDENT OF UNITED STATES.
ELECTION, TUESDAY, NOVEMBER 8, 1864.
ABRAHAM LINCOLN, OF ILLINOIS.
GEORGE B. McCLELLAN, OF NEW JERSEY.
ANDREW JOHNSON, OF TENNESSEE.
GEORGE H. PENDLETON, OF OHIO.
UNION PLATFORM.
DEMOCRATIC PLATFORM.
ABRAHAM LINCOLN.
GEO. BRINTON McCLELLAN.
ANDREW JOHNSON.
GEORGE H. PENDLETON.
Lincoln's Letter of Acceptance.
McClellan's Letter of Acceptance.
MAP showing Loyal States in GREEN, what the Rebels still hold in RED, and what the Union Soldiers have wrested from them in YELLOW.
UNITED STATES.
GULF OF MEXICO
Popular Vote for President.
SHRINKAGE OF THE REBELLION.
ELECTORAL COLLEGE.
NATIONAL UNION EXECUTIVE COMMITTEE.
NATIONAL DEMOCRATIC EXECUTIVE COMMITTEE.
JOHN ADAMS.
THOMAS JEFFERSON.
JAMES MADISON.
JAMES MONROE.
JOHN TYLER.
JAMES K. POLK.
ZACHARY TAYLOR.
MILLARD FILLMORE.
FRANKLIN PIERCE.
JAMES BUCHANAN.
JOHN QUINCY ADAMS.
ANDREW JACKSON.
MARTIN VAN BUREN.
W. H. HARRISON.
Published by H. H. LLOYD & CO., 21 John Street, New York.
B. B. RUSSELL, 515 Washington Street, Boston.
R. R. LANDON, 88 Lake Street, Chicago.

1864

TENNESSEE CAMPAIGN

WESTERN THEATER

SEPTEMBER 29, 1864 John Bell Hood leads his Army of Tennessee north across the Chattahoochee River to threaten William Sherman's supply line.

OCTOBER 5 Battle of Allatoona Pass (Georgia)

NOVEMBER 14 Sherman returns to Atlanta to prepare for his march to the sea after sending troops under John Schofield to join George Thomas in Nashville.

NOVEMBER 30 Battle of Franklin (Tennessee)

DECEMBER 15–16 Battle of Nashville

After being driven from Atlanta ❶, John Bell Hood moved north in late September to menace the Western & Atlantic Railroad ❷, which served now as Sherman's supply line. His goal was to "draw Sherman back into the mountains, then beat him in battle." That was a lot to ask of the battered Army of Tennessee, reduced to 40,000 men, half Sherman's number. Pursuing Hood, Sherman sent troops under Brigadier General John Corse ahead to hold Allatoona Pass ❸, where they repulsed an attack on October 5. Rebuffed a week later at Resaca ❹, Hood avoided a showdown with Sherman and cut through Alabama to Tennessee, where he planned to link up with cavalry led by Major General Nathan Bedford Forrest and reclaim that state for the Confederacy.

Sherman pursued his foe to Gaylesville ❺, but his huge force and heavy supply wagons could not keep up with Hood's smaller, quicker army. "My business is down south," concluded Sherman, who returned to Atlanta to lead troops across Georgia to the sea after sending nearly 30,000 men under John Schofield to reinforce George Thomas at Nashville ❻ and reckon with Hood. Reaching Pulaski ❼ by rail, Schofield was nearly cut off by Hood at Spring Hill ❽ before making a stand at Franklin ❾. "I do not like the looks of this fight," corps commander Benjamin Cheatham told Hood when they found Federals entrenched there on November 30. Hood attacked nonetheless and lost 7,000 men—among them Patrick Cleburne, one of six Confederate generals killed in desperate assaults that failed to stop Schofield's forces from joining Thomas in Nashville. ■

❸ CHARGE AT ALLATOONA John Corse, standing atop the hill with his sword raised, urges on his Federals as they beat back Confederates at Allatoona Pass.

ROAD TO NASHVILLE As shown in this National Geographic map, Sherman pursued Hood to the Alabama border. He then left the defense of Tennessee to Thomas and Schofield and returned to Atlanta to march to the sea. Hood, advancing with three corps led by Major Generals Benjamin Cheatham, Stephen D. Lee, and Alexander Stewart, made ruinous attacks on Schofield at Franklin and further reduced his forces at Nashville by sending Forrest off to take Murfreesboro.

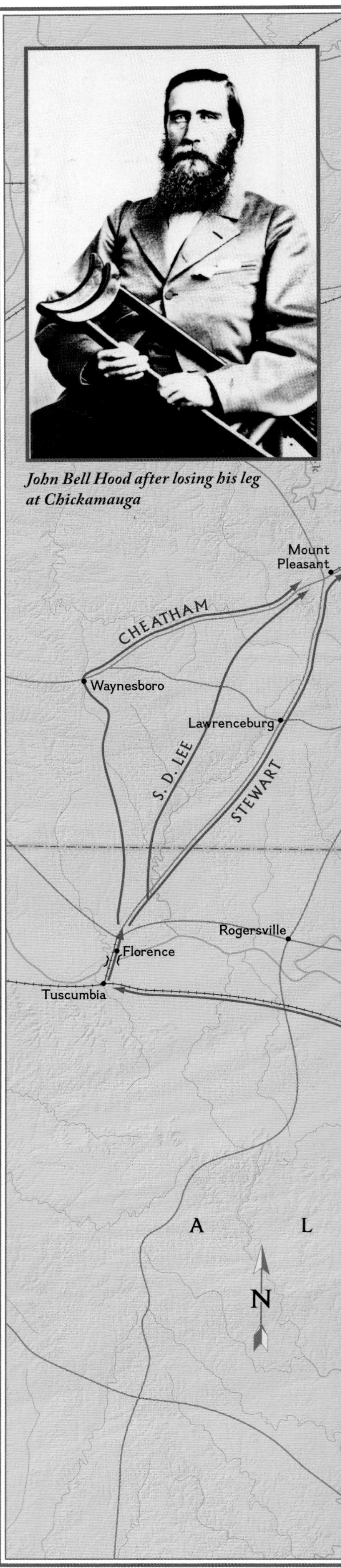

John Bell Hood after losing his leg at Chickamauga

Hood's Tennessee Campaign

September 29 – December 16, 1864

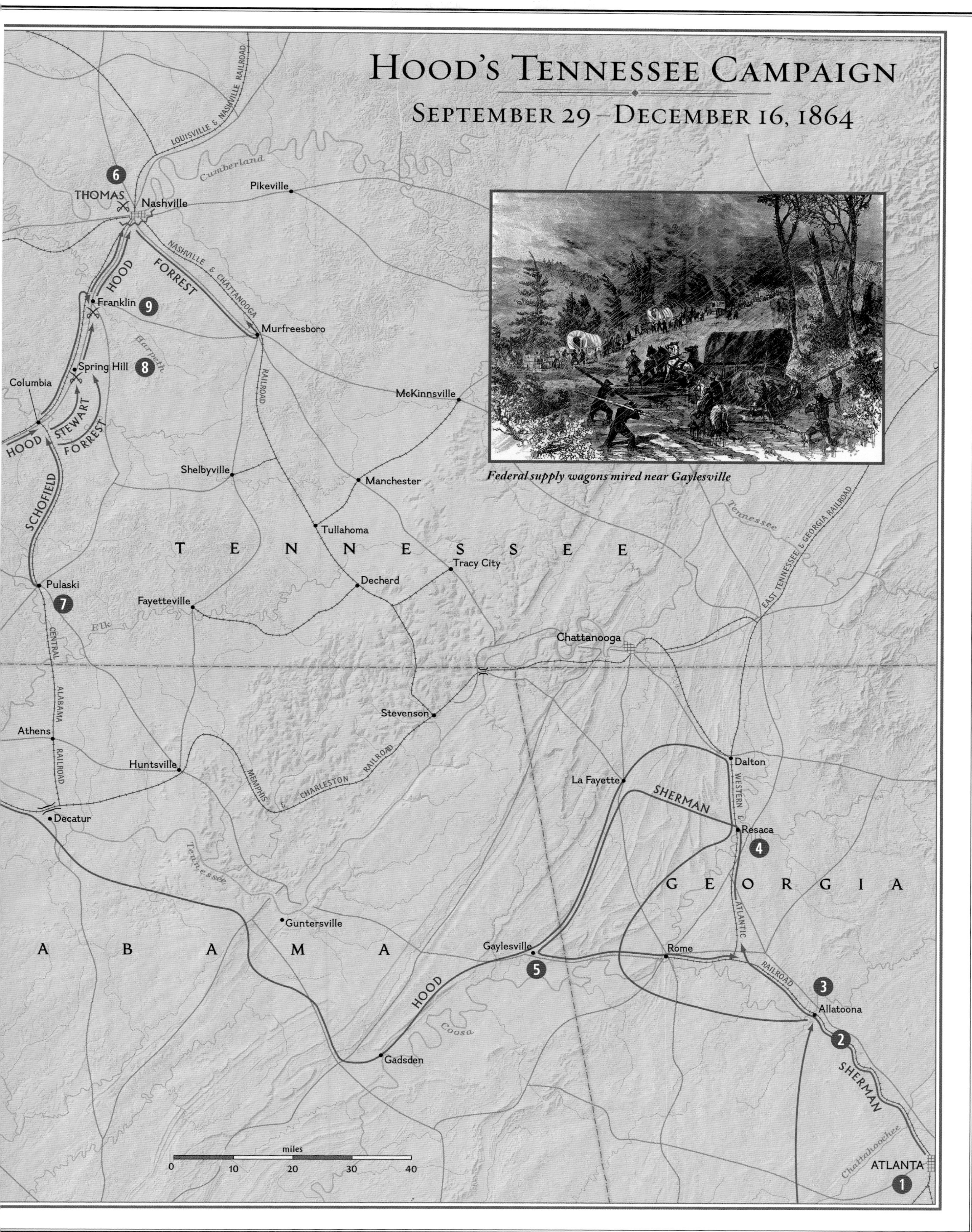

Federal supply wagons mired near Gaylesville

1864 | TENNESSEE CAMPAIGN

THE BATTLE OF NASHVILLE

Hood's army was near the breaking point. He had only 25,000 men left and lacked the confidence of his troops, who admired his courage in the face of crippling battle wounds but dreaded his reckless combativeness. At Franklin, one Confederate wrote, Hood had sent his troops "into a slaughter pen to be shot down like animals." His prospects looked no better at Nashville ❶, where Thomas, reinforced by Schofield, had more than 50,000 men holding a fortified line below town ❷. Hood dug in a few miles away ❸, hoping to lure his foe into a rash assault, which he would then counter.

Never one to act rashly, Thomas resisted pressure from Washington to attack Hood in early December, when the ground was icy, and waited until the weather improved. Then on December 15, his forces bore down like an avalanche, sweeping around Hood's left flank, where Brigadier General Thomas Wood's Fourth Corps ❹ and Major General Andrew Jackson Smith's 16th Corps ❺ surged across the Hillsboro Pike ❻. Retreating southward, Hood formed a new line from Overton Hill ❼ to Shy's Hill ❽. On December 16, Thomas prodded Hood's right before pounding his left flank on Shy's Hill, where Schofield ❾ and Smith ❿ converged from the west and north. A daring bayonet charge launched by Brigadier General John McArthur of Smith's corps opened a gap that proved fatal for Hood's army, which lost this climactic battle for Tennessee and broke up, with its remnants joining other forces later in the Carolinas in a last-ditch effort to save the Confederacy. ■

❽ **TAKING SHY'S HILL** Minnesotans of John McArthur's division charge Confederates on Shy's Hill, a name conferred after the battle in honor of Lieutenant Colonel William Shy, commander of the 37th Tennessee Infantry, who died resisting the furious Federal assault here.

HOOD'S LAST STAND This Union map, oriented with north to the left, uses color-coding to chart the progress of Federal forces at Nashville, keyed at upper right. This decisive defeat cost Hood more than 6,000 casualties, twice as many as Thomas suffered, and left him devastated. A soldier saw him pulling at his hair with his one good hand "and crying like his heart would break."

39th Cong. 1st Sess.–Report of the Chief Engineer U.S.A.

LEGEND

Thursday Dec. 15th

Gen. Steedman attacks Enemy's advanced position on their right as a demonstration. Wilson's Cavalry makes a wide detour to attain the Enemy's left and rear.

Gen. A.J. Smith moves forward 'en echalon' to strike the Rebel left in conjunction with cavalry movement.

Gen. T.J. Wood. holding to his intrenched line at X connects with Gen. Smith on his right.

The Intrenchments and Forts from the pivot point X to the Cumberland River at Reservoir Hill are held mostly by new troops.

Gen. Schofield's Corps is in reserve.

Gen. Steedman's demonstration is successful. Gen. Johnson's Cavalry on the extreme right drives the Rebel Gen. Chalmer's Cavalry on the Charlotte Pike. Gen. Wood carries Montgomery Hill 'A' and N. at 10 O'clock. Gen. Smith and Hatch's Cavalry seize the rebel position's 'a' and 'b' at 2 O'clock. Gen. Schofield then moves rapidly to the right of Gen. Smith.

The whole Line sweeps forward. Gen. Wood's Corps forcing the Enemy's position's at O. P. and Q. while Gens. Smith and Schofield and the dismounted Cavalry press back the Rebel left a mile into the Hills.

Darkness ends the conflict which results in the capture of 30 guns and 2000 prisoners and in forcing the Enemy's strong defensive Line from left to right.

Gen. Hood (comdr. Rebel Army) after the loss of much time commenced moving troops rapidly from his right to his left and intrenched the Hill's in rear of his first position: these movements and night saved his Army from rout.

Friday Dec 16th

Gen. Wood's Corps pushes the Enemy's advanced line back across the Franklin pike into his intrenchments on the Overton Hills. Gen. Smith connecting with Wood and Schofield presses the Enemy very closely. The first attack upon the Overton Hill's is forced back.

Gen. Wilson's Cavalry under Gen's Hatch and Croxton makes a detour to the Granny White pike and attack's the Enemy's left and rear vigorously. Gen. Smith assails and carries the key point 'd' at 4.15 P.M.

This success is followed by the advance of the whole line to the extreme left and results in the capture of the Rebel intrenchments 25 gun's and 3000 prisoners.

The Enemy is routed at all points.

Note

The Elevations along the line of Fortifications are expressed in feet.

Cumberland River

Capitol ❶

NASHVILLE

Gunboat

Surveyed and drawn under the direction of
Gen: Tower
by M. Peseux

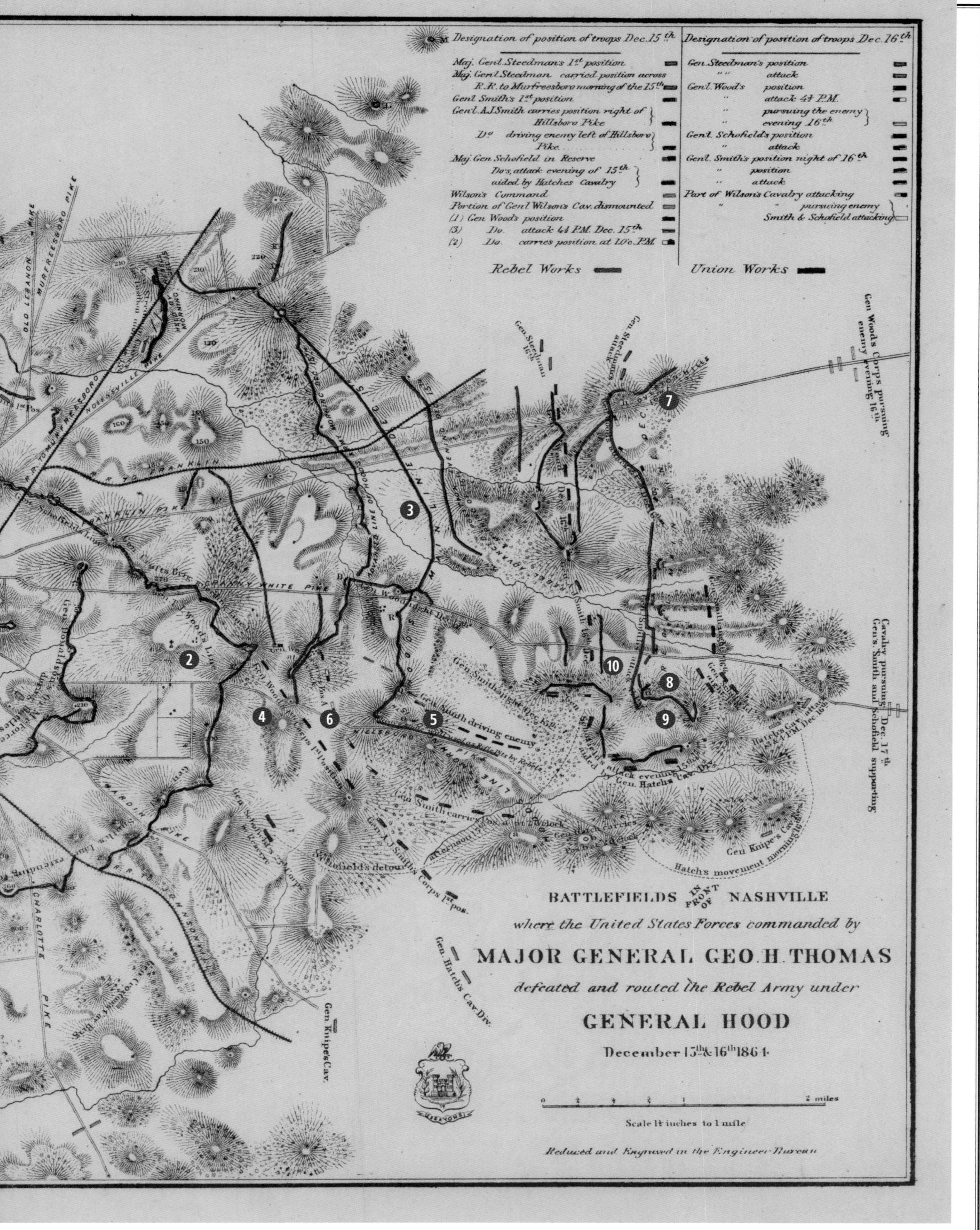

Designation of position of troops Dec. 15th
Maj. Genl. Steedman's 1st position
Maj. Genl. Steedman carried position across R.R. to Murfreesboro morning of the 15th
Genl. Smith's 1st position
Genl. A.J. Smith carries position right of Hillsboro Pike
Do driving enemy left of Hillsboro Pike
Maj. Gen. Schofield in Reserve
Do's attack evening of 15th aided by Hatches Cavalry
Wilson's Command
Portion of Genl. Wilson's Cav. dismounted
(1) Gen Wood's position
(3) Do. attack 4½ P.M. Dec. 15th
(2) Do. carries position at 1 O'c. P.M.
Designation of position of troops Dec. 16th
Gen. Steedman's position
" " attack
Genl. Wood's position
" attack 4½ P.M.
" pursuing the enemy
" evening 16th
Genl. Schofield's position
" attack
Genl. Smith's position night of 16th
" position
" attack
Part of Wilson's Cavalry attacking
" " pursuing enemy
Smith & Schofield attacking
Rebel Works
Union Works
MURFREESBORO PIKE
OLD LEBANON PIKE
NOLENSVILLE PIKE
R.R. TO FRANKLIN
FRANKLIN PIKE
GRANNY WHITE PIKE
HILLSBORO PIKE
HARDIN PIKE
CHARLOTTE PIKE
R.R. TO JOHNSONVILLE
Gen Woods Corps pursuing enemy evening 16th
Cavalry pursuing Dec. 17th Gen's Smith and Schofield supporting
Gen. Smith driving enemy
Gen Knipe's Cav.
Hatch's movement morning 15th
Schofield's detour
Gen. A.J. Smith's Corps 1st pos.
Gen. Hatch's Cav. Div.
Gen Knipes Cav.
2
3
4
5
6
7
8
9
10
BATTLEFIELDS IN FRONT OF NASHVILLE
where the United States Forces commanded by
MAJOR GENERAL GEO. H. THOMAS
defeated and routed the Rebel Army under
GENERAL HOOD
December 15th & 16th 1864
2 miles
Scale 1½ inches to 1 mile
Reduced and Engraved in the Engineer Bureau

1864

SHERMAN'S MARCH

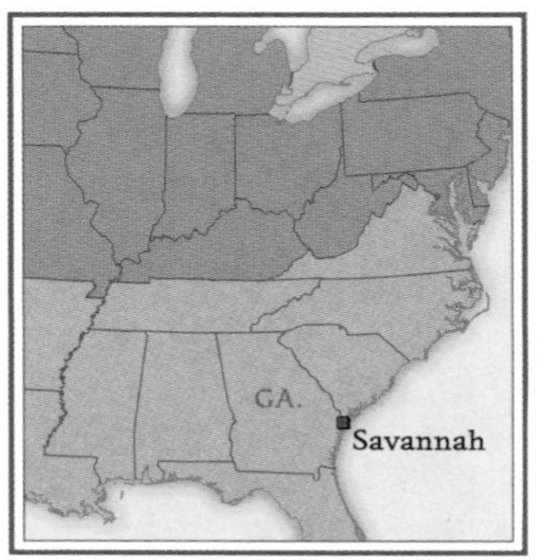

EASTERN THEATER

NOVEMBER 16, 1864 Sherman departs from Atlanta on his devastating march to the sea at Savannah.

NOVEMBER 22 Sherman's forces repulse a desperate attack by Confederate militiamen at Griswoldville, east of Macon.

DECEMBER 13 Sherman captures Fort McAllister, below Savannah, and links up with Federal fleet.

DECEMBER 21 Sherman takes Savannah.

Sherman's plan to leave some forces behind to deal with Hood and march the rest from Atlanta ❶ to Savannah ❷ on the Georgia coast was so daring that even Grant, a great risk-taker, initially opposed it. Dispense with Hood first, Grant urged, then "you can go where you please with impunity." But Sherman had taken Hood's measure and thought Thomas could handle him. If Sherman was wrong, he risked prolonging the war. But if he was right, he would hasten the Confederacy's collapse.

Sherman and son Thomas

"I can make this march, and make Georgia howl!" Sherman promised Grant. Having gained approval, he set out from Atlanta on November 16 after demolishing the city's defenses and rail network and torching its factories. As in most campaigns, his forces progressed on parallel paths, with Major General Henry Slocum commanding the left wing ❸, consisting of the 14th and 20th Corps, and Major General Oliver Howard leading the right wing ❹, made up of the 15th and 17th Corps. This avoided the risk Sherman might face if attacked while strung out on a single path and allowed his troops to forage more widely. It also allowed them to cut a wider swath of destruction as they burned farms and tore up railroad tracks. Although harried by Confederate cavalry led by Joseph Wheeler, they faced only sporadic opposition from organized infantry. At Griswoldville ❺ on November 22, 3,000 Georgia militiamen, many of them underage or elderly, made a brave but futile attack on Federals, of whom a large number were armed with repeating rifles. "I hope we never have to shoot at such men again," said one Yankee after his brigade gunned down the young and the old. By month's end, Sherman's forces had seized the state capital of Milledgeville ❻ and were approaching Savannah. Slocum's wing came down from the north ❼ while Howard's wing, advancing along the Ogeechee River ❽, swung south of town and targeted Fort McAllister ❾, on which the fate of Savannah rested. ■

MAYHEM IN GEORGIA **In this composite view of Sherman's march, slaves seeking freedom follow his army as Federals forage for livestock, wreck a bridge, and destroy telegraph lines and railroad tracks, which they mangled beyond repair by heating the rails and twisting them into loops called "Sherman's neckties."**

MARCH TO THE SEA **This map of Sherman's march was drawn by Robert Knox Sneden, who was being held as a prisoner of war at Andersonville (lower left) when Sherman reached Atlanta in August and was later moved to prison camps in Millen and Savannah.**

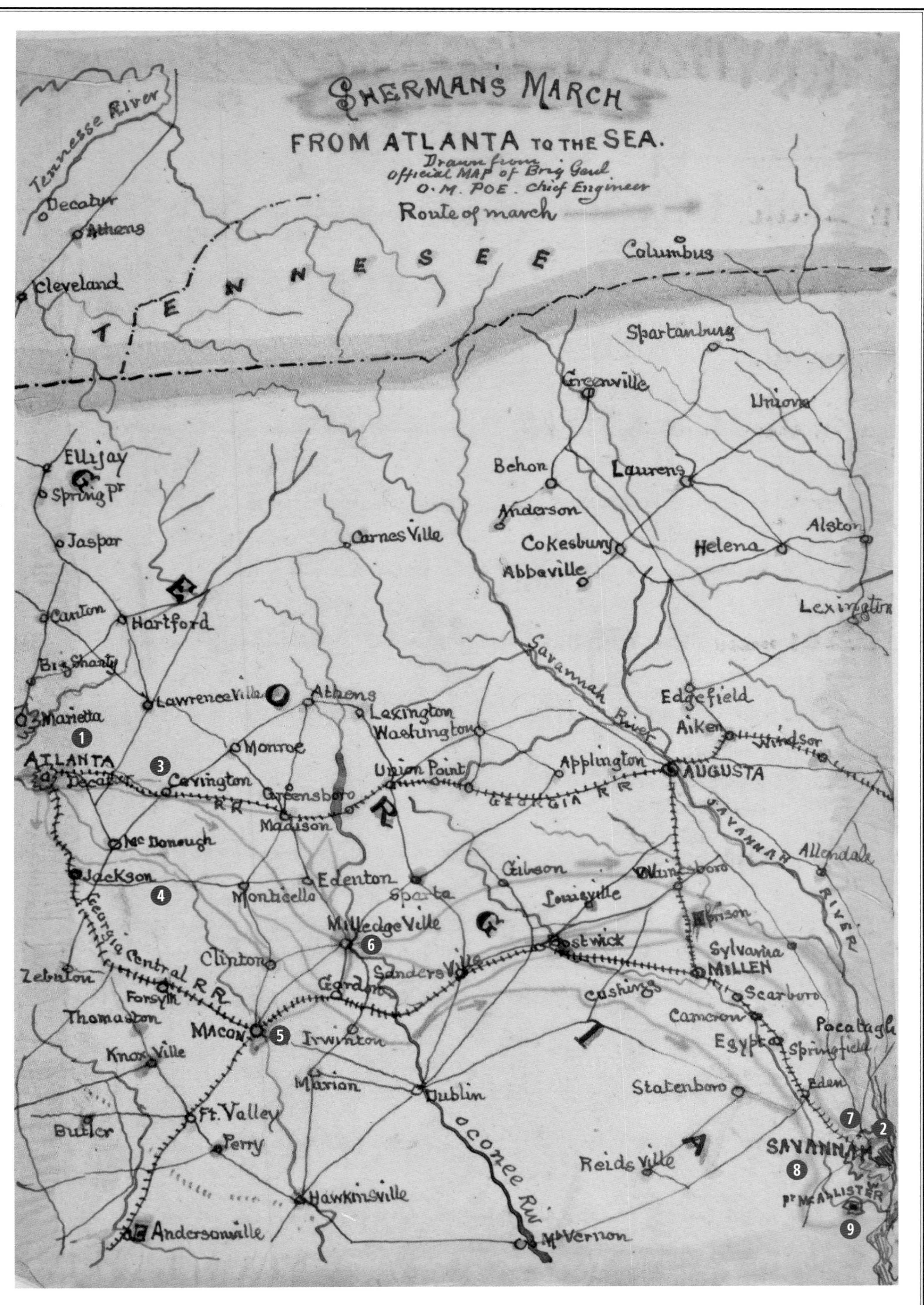
SHERMAN'S MARCH
FROM ATLANTA TO THE SEA.
Drawn from Official MAP of Brig Genl O. M. POE. Chief Engineer
Route of march
Tennessee River
Decatur
Athens
Cleveland
TENNESSEE
Columbus
Spartanburg
Greenville
Union
Ellijay
Spring Pr
Jasper
Belton
Laurens
Anderson
Cokesbury
Helena
Alston
Abbeville
Carnes Ville
Canton
Hartford
Lexington
Big Shanty
Marietta
Lawrence Ville
Athens
Lexington
Washington
Savannah River
Edgefield
Aiken
Windsor
Monroe
ATLANTA
Decatur
Covington
Greensboro
Union Point
Applington
AUGUSTA
GEORGIA RR
Madison
Mc Donough
Jackson
Edenton
Monticello
Sparta
Gibson
Louisville
Waynesboro
Allendale
Milledge Ville
Clinton
Sanders Ville
Sylvania
MILLEN
Georgia Central R R
Zebulon
Forsyth
Thomaston
MACON
Irwinton
Cushings
Scarboro
Cameron
Egypt
Springfield
Pocataligo
Knox Ville
Marion
Dublin
Statenboro
Eden
Ft. Valley
Butler
Perry
Oconee Riv
Reids Ville
SAVANNAH
Ft McALLISTER
Hawkinsville
Andersonville
Mt Vernon
1
2
3
4
5
6
7
8
9

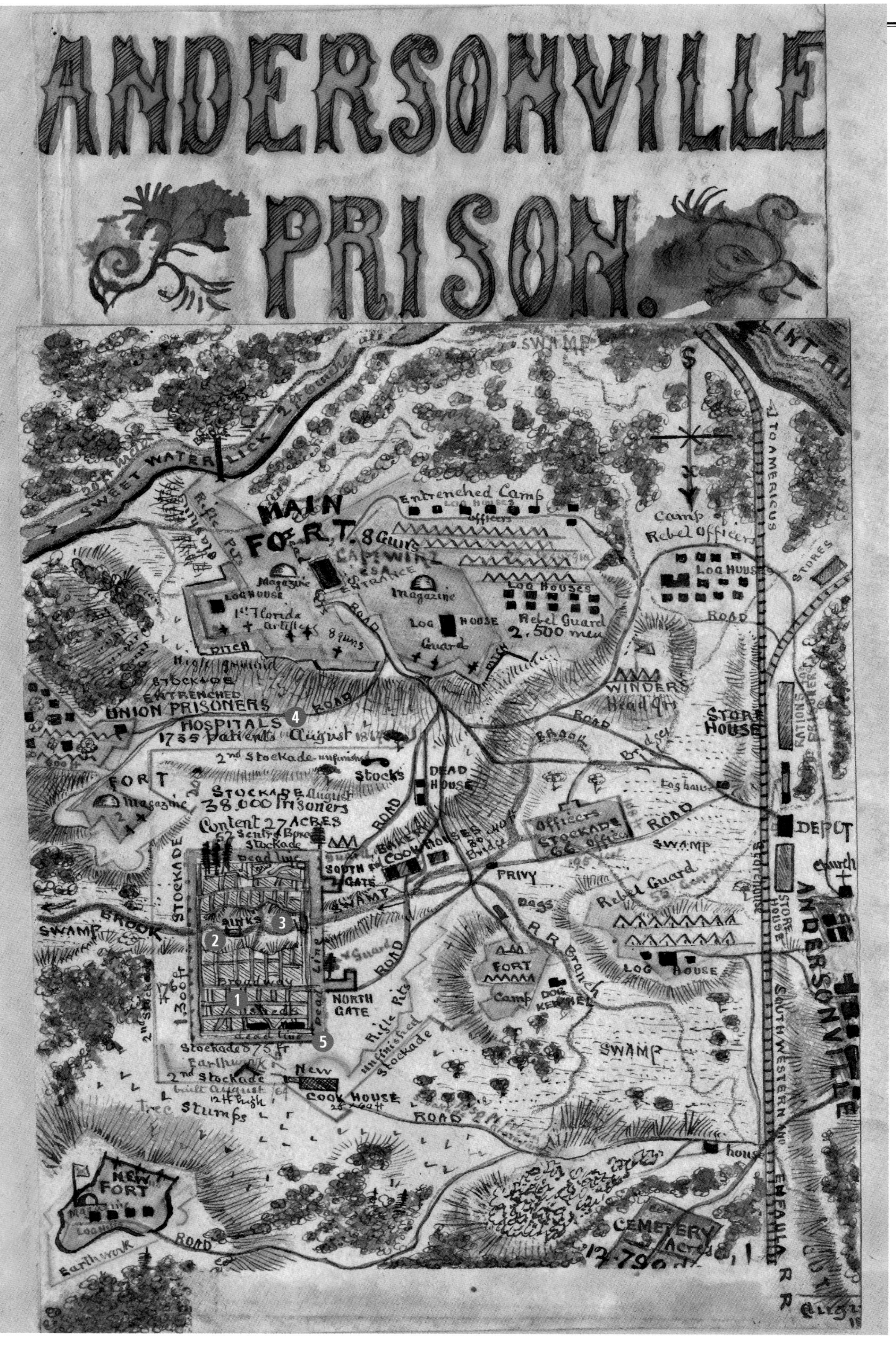
ANDERSONVILLE
PRISON.
SWAMP
SWEET WATER LICK
MAIN
FORT
8 Guns
CAPT WIRZ
CSA
ENTRANCE
Magazine
LOG HOUSE
1st Florida artillery
8 guns
DITCH
ROAD
Entrenched Camp
LOG HOUSES
officers
Log Houses
LOG HOUSE
Guard
Rebel Guard
2,500 men
Camp of
Rebel Officers
LOG HOUSES
STORES
TO AMERICUS
STOCKADE
ENTRENCHED
UNION PRISONERS
HOSPITALS
1735 patients August 1864
WINDERS
Head Qrs
STORE
HOUSE
RATIONS
BROOK
Bridges
Log house
2nd Stockade-unfinished
Stocks
DEAD
HOUSE
FORT
Magazine
STOCKADE August
38,000 Prisoners
Content 27 ACRES
Dead line
Officers
STOCKADE
DEPOT
Church
BAKERY
COOK HOUSES
SOUTH GATE
PRIVY
SWAMP
Bridge
Rebel Guard
BROOK
SWAMP
SINKS
STORE HOUSE
ANDERSONVILLE
Dogs
R R Branch
FORT
Camp
DOG KENNEL
LOG HOUSE
Broadway
Sheds
dead line
NORTH
GATE
Rifle Pits
unfinished
Stockade
SWAMP
Stockade 7 5 Ft
2nd Stockade
built August 64
12 ft high
New
COOK HOUSE
Tree Stumps
ROAD
SOUTHWESTERN
house
NEW
FORT
ROAD
Earthwork
CEMETERY
Acres
EUFAULA R R
R R

PRISONERS OF WAR

Sherman's menacing presence in Georgia proved beneficial for more than 30,000 Federal prisoners of war penned up at Andersonville. To prevent Sherman from freeing them, most inmates there were transferred to other places of detention. That did not end their ordeal, for with few exceptions the prison camps established by Confederate as well as Federal authorities were wretched and disease-ridden. But none was deadlier than Andersonville, described by inmate Robert Knox Sneden, who drew the map opposite, as a "charnel house," where corpses piled up at a rate of more than 1,000 a month.

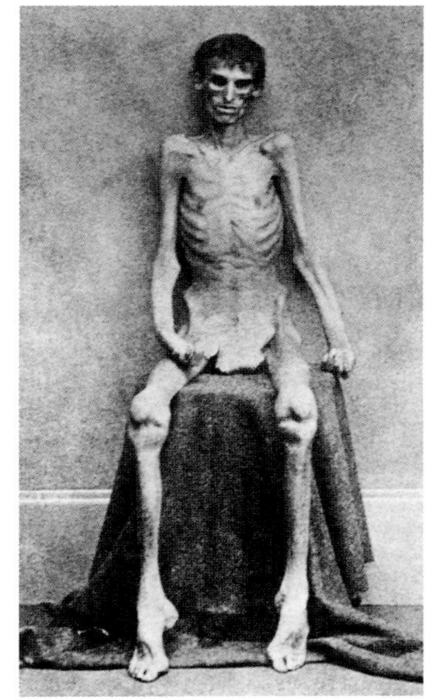

Built by slaves in January 1864 to house 10,000 prisoners, the stockade ❶ at Andersonville was expanded from 17 to 27 acres as the population swelled. But conditions for the captives, sheltered in crude tents of their own making, grew increasingly cramped, debilitating, and dangerous as prison gangs formed. Food was scarce across the war-ravaged South, and rations here were woefully inadequate. "All the meat had turned blue, green, yellow, and black," Sneden wrote. "Hundreds kept on eating it however, despite the maggots, and in three or four hours were seized with cramps and violent diarrhea which kept them running to the sinks all night." Those sinks ❷, or latrines, overflowed into a sluggish stream ❸ from which inmates drew their drinking water. Disease and malnutrition caused men to waste away, and few improved when sent to what Sneden called "the pest house known as the hospital," located nearby ❹. Guards had orders to fire on any man who crossed the "dead line" ❺, a wooden railing near the wall of the stockade. Men shot there while prying wood from the dead line for campfires were sometimes left for days to rot alongside bodies dragged from the tents, Sneden observed. The stench was "worse than any battlefield," he noted, and some bodies were "so decomposed as to have to be shovelled into the dead wagon!"

Inmates who survived confinement here railed against Andersonville's harsh commandant, Captain Henry Wirz, who was tried by a U.S. military court after the war and executed. Defeated Confederates had no such recourse against those who oversaw dreadful Union prison camps like Fort Delaware, which was so filthy, one inmate wrote, "a respectable hog would have tuned up his nose in disgust at it." Nearly 26,000 Confederates and 30,000 Federals died during the war in such shameful conditions. ■

WASTING AWAY This emaciated Federal soldier, ravaged by dysentery, was released from a Confederate camp as a part of a medical exchange between the two sides.

HELL ON EARTH Sneden's map of Andersonville—a place he remembered as "hell on earth"—shows facilities surrounding the stockade, including a kennel for guard dogs, a fort with rifle pits and artillery to deter uprisings by prisoners or attempts to free them, and the headquarters of Brigadier General John Winder, who had wide responsibility for Confederate prison camps.

❷ DEADLY CONFINES A telling photograph of Andersonville taken in 1864 shows prisoners at the latrine that fouled the water supply in this dangerously overcrowded compound.

SURRENDER OF SAVANNAH

Approaching Savannah ❶ in early December, Sherman encountered the strongest opposition he had faced since leaving Atlanta. Savannah's defenders, commanded by William Hardee, numbered only about 10,000 but were shielded by fortifications north of town ❷. To the south, the Savannah River was closed to Federal ships, which were waiting offshore to supply Sherman. If his men took Fort McAllister ❸, however, he could link up with the U.S. Navy there.

On December 13, Sherman watched anxiously as troops under Brigadier General William Hazen stormed the fort, advancing across ground sown with land mines. Rebel guns were "belching forth dense clouds of smoke, which soon enveloped our assaulting lines," wrote Sherman, who remained unsure of the outcome until he saw Hazen's men raising their flags atop the parapet. "I've got Savannah!" Sherman cried, confident that a secure naval supply line would give him all he needed to overpower the city's defenders. Hardee reached the same conclusion and withdrew with his forces across the Savannah River to South Carolina ❹ on the night of December 20 on a pontoon bridge, which he destroyed behind him. Sherman took possession the next day, offering Savannah's capture "as a Christmas gift" to President Lincoln. ■

❸

❸ DISARMING THE FORT Federals remove artillery shells and land mines in wheelbarrows from captured Fort McAllister. Unearthing the mines was a hazardous task assigned by Sherman to Confederate prisoners.

APPROACHES TO SAVANNAH This map was based partly on information obtained in Savannah by cartographer Sneden, who was released into the custody of a surgeon there in late 1864 after taking an oath not to escape. As indicated, Fort Pulaski and other points at the mouth of the Savannah River were under Union control by then, but the capture of Fort McAllister linked Federal land and naval forces and sealed Savannah's fate.

❶

❶ PARADING IN TRIUMPH Mounted at left ahead of his aides, Sherman reviews his troops in Savannah before advancing into the Carolinas.

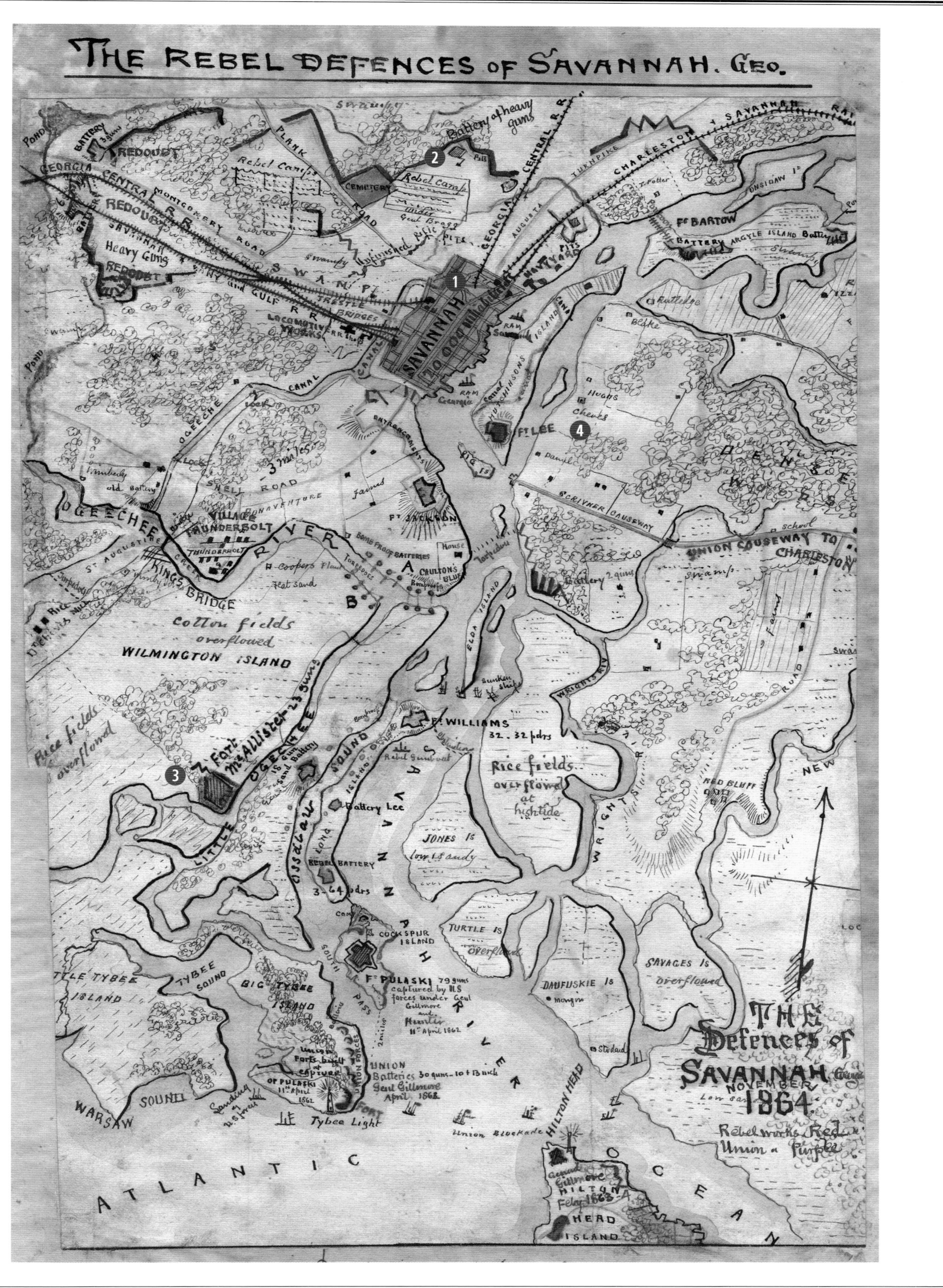
THE REBEL DEFENCES OF SAVANNAH. GEO.
1
2
3
4
SAVANNAH
Ft. LEE
Fort McAllister 23 guns
Ft. WILLIAMS
Ft PULASKI 79 guns
WILMINGTON ISLAND
TYBEE SOUND
BIG TYBEE ISLAND
Tybee Light
ATLANTIC OCEAN
HILTON HEAD ISLAND
Union Blockade
The Defences of Savannah November 1864
Rebel works Red
Union " Purple

CHAPTER 5

Tightening the Noose | 1865

"Lincoln had too much of the milk of human kindness to deal with these damned rebels. Now they will be dealt with according to their deserts."

SENATOR BENJAMIN WADE OF OHIO
AFTER LINCOLN'S ASSASSINATION

At Washington's Old Penitentiary on July 7, 1865, troops preside over the execution of four people convicted in military court of conspiring with John Wilkes Booth to assassinate Lincoln and other Union leaders. Hanged were George Atzerodt, who was supposed to kill Vice President Andrew Johnson but backed out; Lewis Powell, who wounded Secretary of State William Seward; David Herold, who guided Powell to Seward's home and fled with Booth, who was slain by pursuing Federals; and Mary Surratt (far left), the mother of escaped conspirator John Surratt and owner of a boardinghouse where the plotters met. "Mrs. Surratt is innocent," Powell said on the scaffold. "She doesn't deserve to die with the rest of us."

1865
THE FINAL ACT

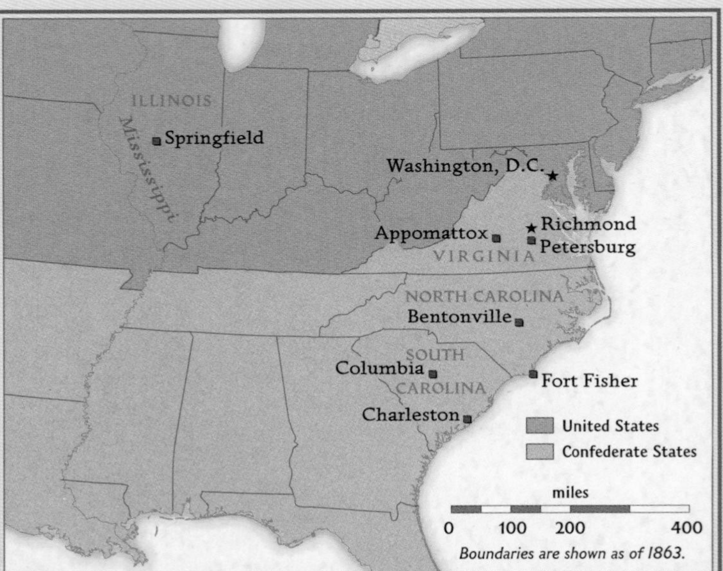

The Confederacy was in such desperate straits by January 1865 that leaders on both sides wondered if further bloodshed could be avoided through a negotiated settlement that might allow the South to yield without surrendering outright. In a letter to Jefferson Davis, Lincoln expressed a willingness to explore the possibility "of securing peace to the people of our one common country." Davis responded by sending Vice President Alexander Stephens and other commissioners to seek an accord between "the two countries." That fundamental disagreement over whether the Confederacy would have to give up its identity to reconcile with the Union doomed the talks that followed. Meeting with Lincoln and Secretary of State William Seward on the steamer *River Queen* at Hampton Roads on February 3, the Confederate commissioners learned that the U.S. Congress had just passed the Thirteenth Amendment, prohibiting slavery. Lincoln would not compromise on that issue and would not offer Rebels peace unless they submitted to the Union and its laws, raising the threat that their leaders might be charged with treason.

When the commissioners returned to Richmond without a deal, Davis vowed to make the Union "petition us for peace, on our terms." But he no longer had enough troops in the field to back up his defiant words. The very survival of Richmond as the Confederate capital depended on Lee's dwindling army, which could not hold out much longer at Petersburg against Grant's huge force. Meanwhile, Sherman's hard-marching troops had left Savannah and were blazing a fiery trail northward through the Carolinas. Effectively, Lee's surrender at Appomattox Court House on April 9 brought the war to a conclusion, but it did not end the drama. Lincoln's assassination just days later marked the start of a momentous epilogue that would last far longer than the action preceding it—a struggle to reconstruct the defeated South and reunite a divided nation.

1865 (TO APPOMATTOX)

January 4, 1865 Federal troops led by Alfred Terry embark in transports from Virginia to assault Fort Fisher on the North Carolina coast and seal off Wilmington.

January 7 Benjamin Butler replaced as commander of the Federal Army of the James by E. O. C. Ord.

January 13 Federal fleet led by David Porter bombards Fort Fisher while Terry's troops come ashore to the north; John Bell Hood resigns as commander of the Army of Tennessee, whose remnants will join other Confederate forces in the Carolinas.

January 15 Federals storm Fort Fisher, which surrenders that night.

January 18 Lincoln sends letter to Jefferson Davis inviting talks aimed at "securing peace to the people of our one common country."

January 21 Sherman leaves Savannah to advance northward through the Carolinas.

Union leaders who won peace

AFTERMATH (ASSASSINATION TO RECONSTRUCTION)

April 14, 1865 Lincoln shot at Ford's Theater in Washington by Confederate sympathizer John Wilkes Booth.

April 15 Lincoln dies at 7:22 A.M.; Andrew Johnson sworn in as president.

April 17 Joseph Johnston and William Sherman meet to discuss an armistice.

April 26 Booth shot dead in Virginia while resisting arrest by Federals; Johnston surrenders his forces to Sherman.

May 4 Lincoln buried in Springfield, Illinois, after his funeral train draws millions of mourners; Richard Taylor surrenders Confederate forces in Alabama and Mississippi.

May 10 Jefferson Davis seized by Federals in Georgia and imprisoned.

May 23–24 Union forces march in victory parade in Washington.

May 29 Johnson agrees to pardon most Confederates on condition of their taking an oath of allegiance.

June 2 Edmund Kirby Smith surrenders Confederate forces west of the Mississippi.

June 23 Johnson ends the Union blockade of Southern ports.

July 7 Four people found guilty by a military tribunal of conspiring with Booth—George Atzerodt, David Herold, Lewis Powell, and Mary Surratt—executed in Washington.

Hat worn by Lincoln on the night of his assassination

January 24 Grant, who had suspended prisoner exchanges with the Confederates, agrees to resume them.

January 28 Jefferson Davis appoints Vice President Alexander Stephens and two other commissioners to engage in peace talks with Federal authorities.

January 31 U.S. Congress passes the Thirteenth Amendment, abolishing slavery; Davis appoints Lee general-in-chief of Confederate forces after being urged by the Confederate Senate to relinquish that responsibility.

February 3 Lincoln and Secretary of State Seward meet with Confederate commissioners at Hampton Roads in talks that fail to produce a peace agreement.

February 5 Federal cavalrymen torch Barnwell, South Carolina, during Sherman's march.

February 17 Sherman's troops occupy Columbia, South Carolina; Confederates abandon Charleston, South Carolina.

February 22 Wilmington, North Carolina, seized by Union forces after Confederates led by Braxton Bragg withdraw.

February 25 Joseph Johnston takes charge of Confederate forces in South Carolina opposing Sherman's advance.

Dead Confederate at Fort Mahone, Petersburg

March 2 Remnants of Jubal Early's army dispersed at Waynesboro in the Shenandoah Valley by Federal cavalry under Sheridan, who will soon join Grant at Petersburg.

March 3 Lincoln orders Grant to have no discussion with Lee unless it concerns the surrender of Lee's army, adding that Grant was "not to decide, discuss, or confer upon any political question."

March 4 Lincoln delivers his Second Inaugural Address, promising to act "with malice toward none" and "bind up the nation's wounds."

March 6 Johnston's responsibilities as Confederate commander are extended to North Carolina, where he will attempt to unite his own forces and bring them to bear against part of Sherman's divided army before it comes together at Goldsboro.

March 8–10 Battle of Kinston (North Carolina)

March 13 Davis signs measure authorizing the enlistment of slaves as Confederate soldiers; none of those recruited will see action before the war ends.

March 16 Battle of Averasborough (North Carolina)

March 19–21 Battle of Bentonville (North Carolina)

March 25 Grant's troops repulse a Confederate assault on their lines at Fort Stedman at Petersburg, Virginia.

March 31–April 1 Battle of Five Forks (Virginia)

April 2 Grant breaks through at Petersburg, forcing Confederates to abandon that city and nearby Richmond overnight.

April 3 Federal troops occupy Richmond.

April 6 Battle of Sayler's Creek (Virginia)

April 9 Lee surrenders to Grant at Appomattox Court House.

Former slaves, freed when Richmond fell

Jefferson Davis, imprisoned at Fort Monroe

September 14 Representatives of Cherokee, Creek, and other Indian tribes divided by the Civil War pledge loyalty to the United States at Fort Smith, Arkansas.

November 10 Captain Henry Wirz, commandant at Andersonville prison, executed after being convicted by a military tribunal of "murder in violation of the laws and customs of war."

December 4 Republican-dominated Congress challenges Democrat Andrew Johnson's Reconstruction plan by refusing to recognize Southern states reorganized under his terms and launching its own Radical Reconstruction program.

December 13 Thirteenth Amendment ratified.

June 1866 Congress passes Fourteenth Amendment, defining all people born in the United States as citizens and thus giving blacks the same constitutional rights as whites.

July 1866 Congress passes Freedman's Bureau Act, extending the life of the Freedman's Bureau, established during the Civil War to aid and protect former slaves who gained freedom.

March 1867 Congress passes first Reconstruction Act, dividing the former Confederacy into five military districts and setting requirements for states there seeking readmission to the Union, including ratifying the Fourteenth Amendment.

May 1867 Jefferson Davis released from prison after being held without trial.

March 1868 Johnson impeached by the House of Representatives after clashing with Congress over Reconstruction.

May 1868 Johnson acquitted in the Senate.

July 1868 Fourteenth Amendment ratified.

November 1868 Republican Ulysses Grant elected president.

February 1869 Congress passes Fifteenth Amendment, forbidding the denial of voting rights on the basis of race.

March 1870 Fifteenth Amendment ratified.

April 1871 Congress passes the second Ku Klux Klan Act, giving Grant broad powers, including the use of troops, to protect the civil rights of blacks.

November 1872 Grant reelected president.

Remains of Union soldiers near Gaines's Mill, unearthed at war's end for reburial

November 1874 Voters deal a setback to Republican Reconstruction efforts as Democrats win a majority in both houses of Congress and increase the number of Southern state governments under their control.

November 1876 Presidential race between Republican Rutherford B. Hayes and Democrat Samuel Tilden, supported by white Southerners opposed to Reconstruction, ends in a deadlock.

February 1877 Reconstruction ends as Hayes breaks deadlock and wins election by promising concessions to Democrats, including removing the last federal troops from the South.

1865

FORT FISHER

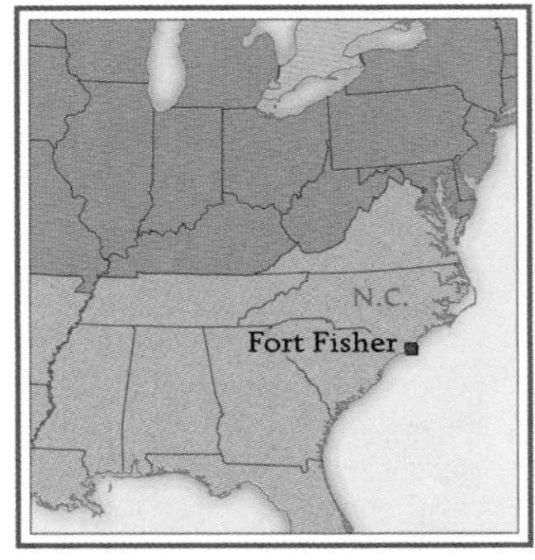

THE BLOCKADE

DECEMBER 25, 1864 Federal attack repulsed by Confederates at Fort Fisher, guarding the mouth of the Cape Fear River below Wilmington, North Carolina.

JANUARY 13, 1865 Federal fleet led by David Porter renews assault on Fort Fisher by bombarding its defenders while troops led by Alfred Terry come ashore to the north.

JANUARY 15 Federals storm Fort Fisher, which surrenders that night.

FEBRUARY 22 Wilmington seized by Union forces.

Federals had sealed off all major Confederate ports by 1865 except Wilmington, North Carolina, where blockade runners continued to bring in weapons, ammunition, and clothing from abroad to sustain Lee's army at Petersburg. Efforts to halt that traffic were thwarted by imposing Fort Fisher ❶, guarding the mouth of the Cape Fear River ❷ below Wilmington. By holding off Federal warships and shielding blockade runners, Fort Fisher kept open "the last gateway between the Confederate States and the outside world," wrote Colonel William Lamb, the fort's commander. Fort Anderson ❸ and other strongholds bolstered Rebel defenses here, but if Fort Fisher fell they too would succumb and Wilmington would be throttled.

Battery at Fort Fisher

After failing to take Fisher in late December 1864, Federals returned a few weeks later with transports carrying 8,000 troops led by Major General Alfred Terry, met by 60 vessels of the North Atlantic Blockading Squadron commanded by Rear Admiral David Porter aboard his flagship *Brooklyn* ❹. On January 13, Porter's warships drew within 1,000 yards and bombarded the fort, whose gunners were short of ammunition and returned fire fitfully. Mounds of sand shielding the fort's walls did not prevent 200 of the fort's 1,800 defenders from being killed or wounded by incoming shells over the next two days. Meanwhile, Terry's troops landed above the fort and raised a breastwork facing north ❺ in case Confederates came down the road from Wilmington ❻. On January 15, 2,000 sailors and Marines landed and stormed Fisher's northeast salient ❼. Their assault was repulsed but served to distract Confederates from the larger threat posed by Terry's troops, who braved fire from enemy gunboats ❽ in the Cape Fear River and overran a battery at the fort's northwest corner ❾. Fort Fisher fell that night, and Wilmington was abandoned to Union forces in February. ■

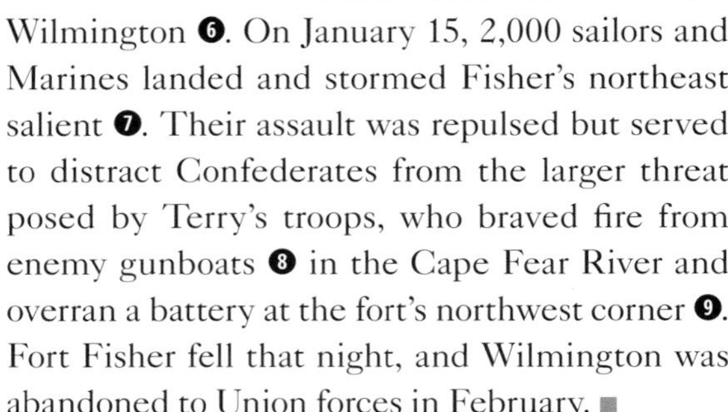

❼ STORMING THE FORT Confederates open fire on Marines and sailors armed with pistols and cutlasses as they break through a palisade and storm Fort Fisher's northeast salient. Porter urged that Navy men take part in the attack, but they had no experience fighting on land and were soon routed, leaving the capture of the fort to Terry's troops.

CLOSING THE GATE A map derived by Robert Knox Sneden from a survey by by the U.S. Corps of Engineers shows how the combined operations of Porter and Terry closed the Confederacy's last gateway to the outside world. Roughly half of Terry's troops—including Colonel Newton Curtis's brigade of Brigadier General Adelbert Ames's division—joined the attack.

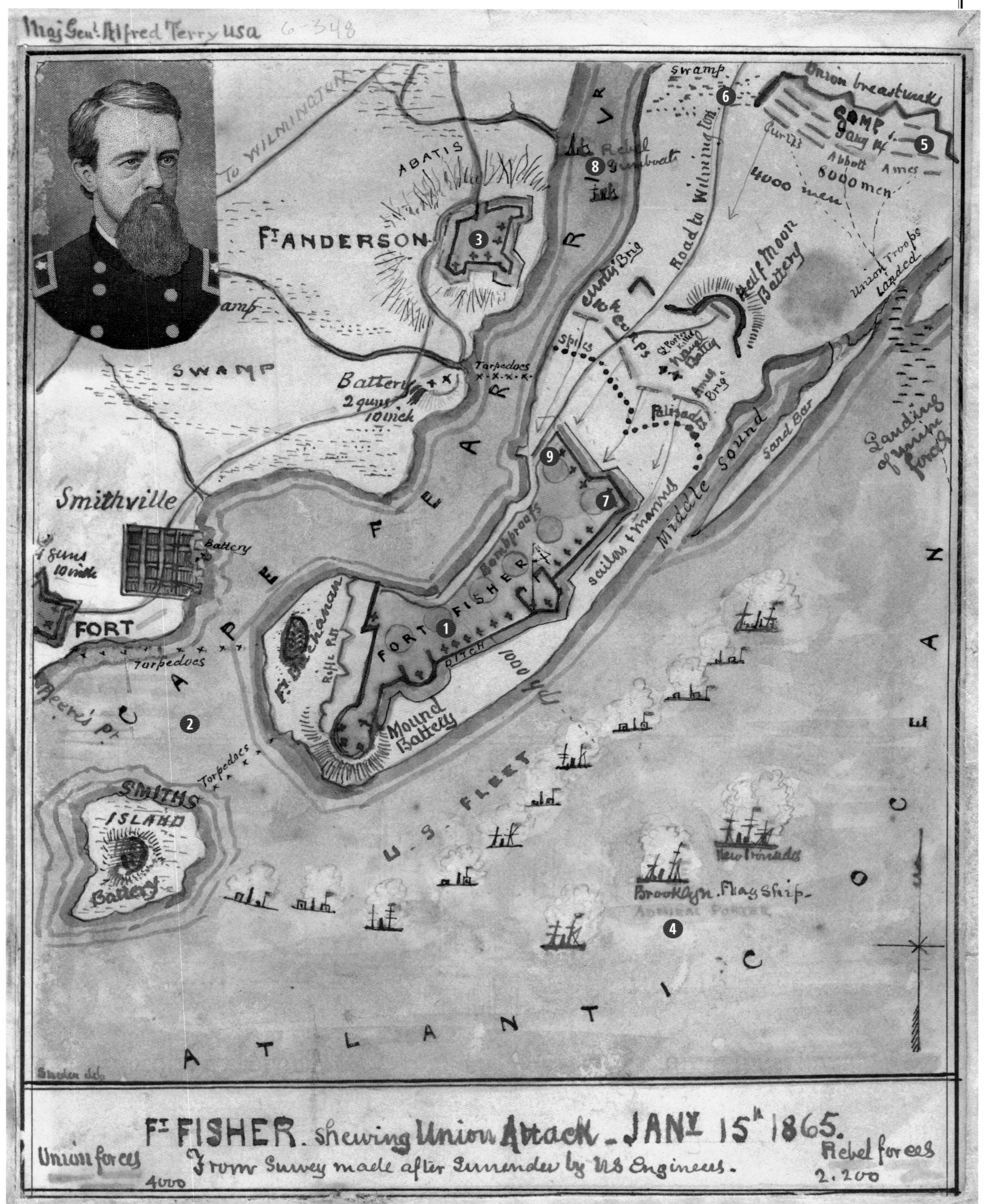
Maj Genl. Alfred Terry USA
Ft. FISHER. shewing Union Attack _ JANY 15th 1865.
From Survey made after Surrender by US Engineers.
Union forces 4000
Rebel forces 2.200
Ft. ANDERSON
Smithville
FORT FISHER
Mound Battery
Half Moon Battery
SMITHS ISLAND Battery
U. S. FLEET
Brooklyn. Flag Ship
New Ironsides
CAPE FEAR R
ATLANTIC OCEAN
Middle Sound
Sand Bar
Road to Wilmington
TO WILMINGTON
SWAMP
ABATIS
Torpedoes
Union breastworks
Union Troops Landed
8000 men
4000 men
Palisades
Rebel Gunboat
Landing of union forces
Battery 2 guns 10 inch
1
2
3
4
5
6
7
8
9

CONQUERING THE CAROLINAS

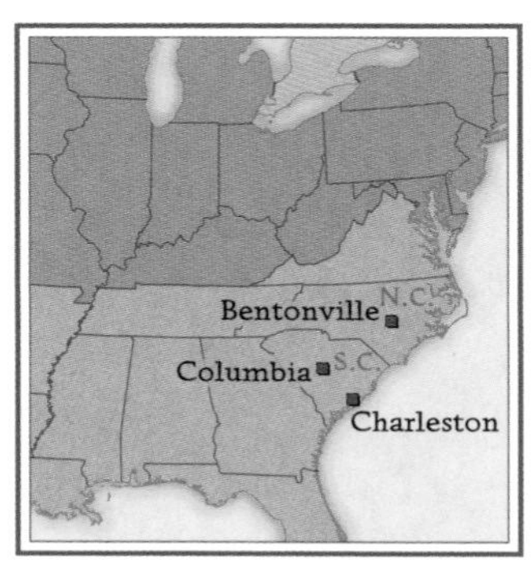

EASTERN THEATER

JANUARY 21, 1865 Sherman leaves Savannah to advance northward through the Carolinas.

FEBRUARY 5 Federal cavalry torches Barnwell, South Carolina.

FEBRUARY 17 Sherman's troops occupy Columbia, South Carolina; Confederates abandon Charleston, South Carolina, to the Federals.

MARCH 8–10 Battle of Kinston (North Carolina)

MARCH 16 Battle of Averasborough (North Carolina)

MARCH 19–21 Battle of Bentonville (North Carolina)

After taking Savannah ❶, Sherman received welcome news from Grant, who dropped the idea of bringing Sherman's forces by boat up the coast to Petersburg and approved his plan to march north and scourge the Carolinas as he had Georgia. Trusting in Sherman's instincts had served Grant well as general in chief, and conquering the Carolinas would further constrict the Confederacy.

Sherman left Savannah by boat on January 21, heading for Beaufort ❷ with the 17th Corps, which joined the 15th Corps near Pocotaligo ❸ to form the army's right wing, under Oliver Howard. Meanwhile, Henry Slocum's left wing, consisting of the 14th and 20th Corps, was slogging through swamps and burning the property of South Carolinians, blamed by Unionists for launching the rebellion. "If we don't purify South Carolina," wrote one Federal, "it will be because we can't get a light." Preceding Slocum's troops were cavalry led by Brigadier General Hugh Judson Kilpatrick, who made sure his men had plenty of matches. Entering Barnwell ❹ on February 5, they torched it so thoroughly that troops marching through afterward called it Burnwell. Hardest hit was Columbia ❺, the state capital, where fire destroyed much of the city after Sherman's two wings converged there on February 17. Residents blamed unruly Federals, while Sherman said that Rebels had sparked the blaze by igniting cotton to deny it to the Yankees. On the same day Columbia fell, Charleston ❻ was abandoned by Confederates, who were now at risk of being cut off by Sherman's advance.

Entering North Carolina in March, Sherman worried that his old foe Joseph Johnston, commanding Rebel forces there, would attack before his two wings linked up at Goldsboro ❼ with John Schofield's 23rd Corps, coming from Wilmington ❽. To prevent Sherman's forces from consolidating, Confederates clashed with Schofield's men at Kinston ❾ on March 8 and Slocum's troops at Averasborough ❿ on March 16 before hitting Slocum at Bentonville ⓫ with everything they had. ■

❻ SUMTER IN RUINS Although reduced to rubble by Federal artillery fire, Fort Sumter was held tenaciously by a 300-man Confederate garrison until Charleston was abandoned on February 17.

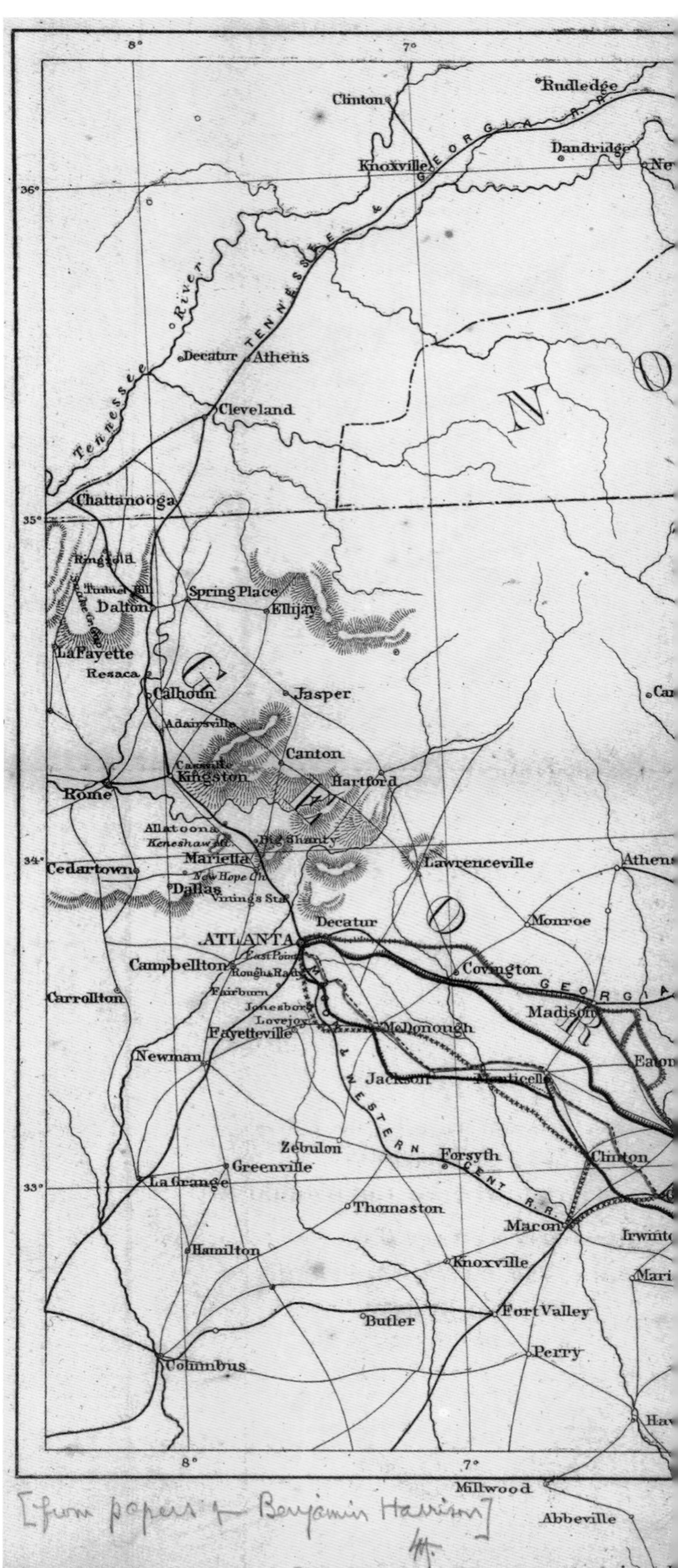

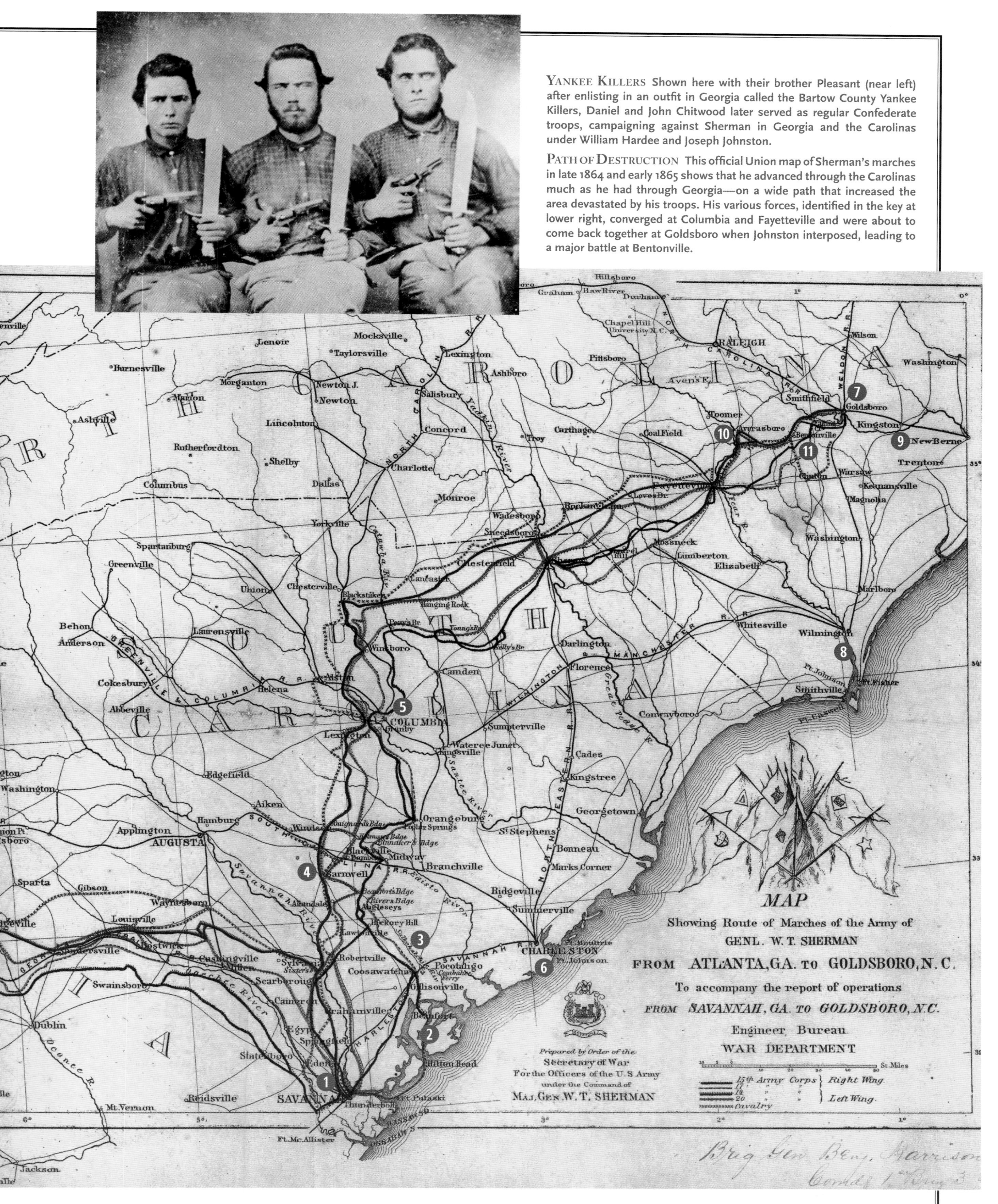

Yankee Killers Shown here with their brother Pleasant (near left) after enlisting in an outfit in Georgia called the Bartow County Yankee Killers, Daniel and John Chitwood later served as regular Confederate troops, campaigning against Sherman in Georgia and the Carolinas under William Hardee and Joseph Johnston.

Path of Destruction This official Union map of Sherman's marches in late 1864 and early 1865 shows that he advanced through the Carolinas much as he had through Georgia—on a wide path that increased the area devastated by his troops. His various forces, identified in the key at lower right, converged at Columbia and Fayetteville and were about to come back together at Goldsboro when Johnston interposed, leading to a major battle at Bentonville.

THE BATTLE OF BENTONVILLE

WILLIAM HARDEE

Bentonville was a bitter defeat for Joseph Johnston's weary, depleted forces. But for his trusted corps commander, Lieutenant General William Hardee, it was something more—a devastating personal loss. Born in Georgia in 1815, Hardee was one of the South's most accomplished officers. A former commandant at West Point, he wrote a textbook on tactics that served as a bible for cadets who would later fight on opposing sides during the Civil War. Known as "Old Reliable," he did not hesitate to lecture superiors if he felt their plans were tactically deficient. "Don't scatter your forces," he admonished Braxton Bragg before the Battle of Perryville in 1862. "There is one rule in our profession that should never be forgotten—it is to throw the masses of your troops on the fractions of the enemy." By 1865, however, the Confederacy no longer had masses of troops, and Hardee had to bend the rules. The best he and Johnston could do at Bentonville was to attack while their numbers were roughly equal to the enemy's fraction. And numbers did not tell the whole story, for many of their Confederates were older or younger than would have been deemed acceptable earlier in the war. Hardee reluctantly allowed his only son, 16-year-old Willie, to enlist in Johnston's army shortly before the battle began. On March 21, the boy was mortally wounded at Bentonville resisting the Federal flank attack that prompted Johnston to withdraw.

Joseph Johnston had only about 20,000 Confederates under his command in North Carolina, including the remnants of the Army of Tennessee and troops withdrawn from Savannah by William Hardee and from Wilmington by Braxton Bragg. Sherman would have nearly 70,000 troops when he linked up with John Schofield's corps at Goldsboro. Johnston's one chance was to throw all his forces against part of the opposing army before it coalesced. On March 18, his cavalry commander, Lieutenant General Wade Hampton, found a good spot south of Bentonville from which to challenge Sherman's left wing, led by Henry Slocum, and held off Slocum long enough there for Johnston to align his troops across the road to Goldsboro ❶. Bragg held Johnston's left ❷, while 4,000 troops of the once-mighty Army of Tennessee held Johnston's right above the road ❸. Last to come up was the division of Brigadier General William Taliaferro ❹ and other elements of Hardee's corps, which Johnston moved to the center of the line on March 19 as he attacked the exposed 14th Corps divisions of Brigadier Generals William Carlin and James Morgan.

Carlin's three brigades—led by Lieutenant Colonel David Miles ❺ and Brigadier Generals George Buell ❻ and Harrison Hobart ❼—were overwhelmed by the Confederate onslaught and fell back in disarray. On the Federal right, Morgan's three brigades—led by Brigadier Generals William Vandever ❽, John Mitchell ❾, and Benjamin Fearing ❿—held fast against Bragg's oncoming troops but were flanked by other Rebel troops advancing above the road. Fearing's men pivoted to face the road ⓫, while Mitchell and Vandever's beleaguered troops leaped over their breastworks to battle Confederates to their rear ⓬. Morgan's resilient division eventually fought its way out of this predicament and lined up with Brigadier General James Robinson's troops ⓭ and other elements of the 20th Corps to hold off the attackers.

The following day, troops from Sherman's right wing poured in to reinforce his embattled left wing, and Johnston's position grew increasingly precarious. On March 21, after staving off a flank attack by Major General Joseph Mower's division of the 17th Corps, he withdrew, having lost 2,600 men at Bentonville. "Sherman's course cannot be hindered by the small force I have," he wrote Lee. "I can do no more than annoy him." After consolidating his forces at Goldsboro, Sherman was so secure that he was able to attend a war conference in late March at City Point, Virginia, where Lincoln and his top commanders discussed how to finish off the Confederacy. ■

WAR CONFERENCE **Lincoln confers with Sherman, Grant, and Porter aboard the steamboat *River Queen*, anchored in the James River at City Point on March 28. Lincoln's "earnest desire," wrote Sherman, was "to end the war speedily, without more bloodshed or devastation."**

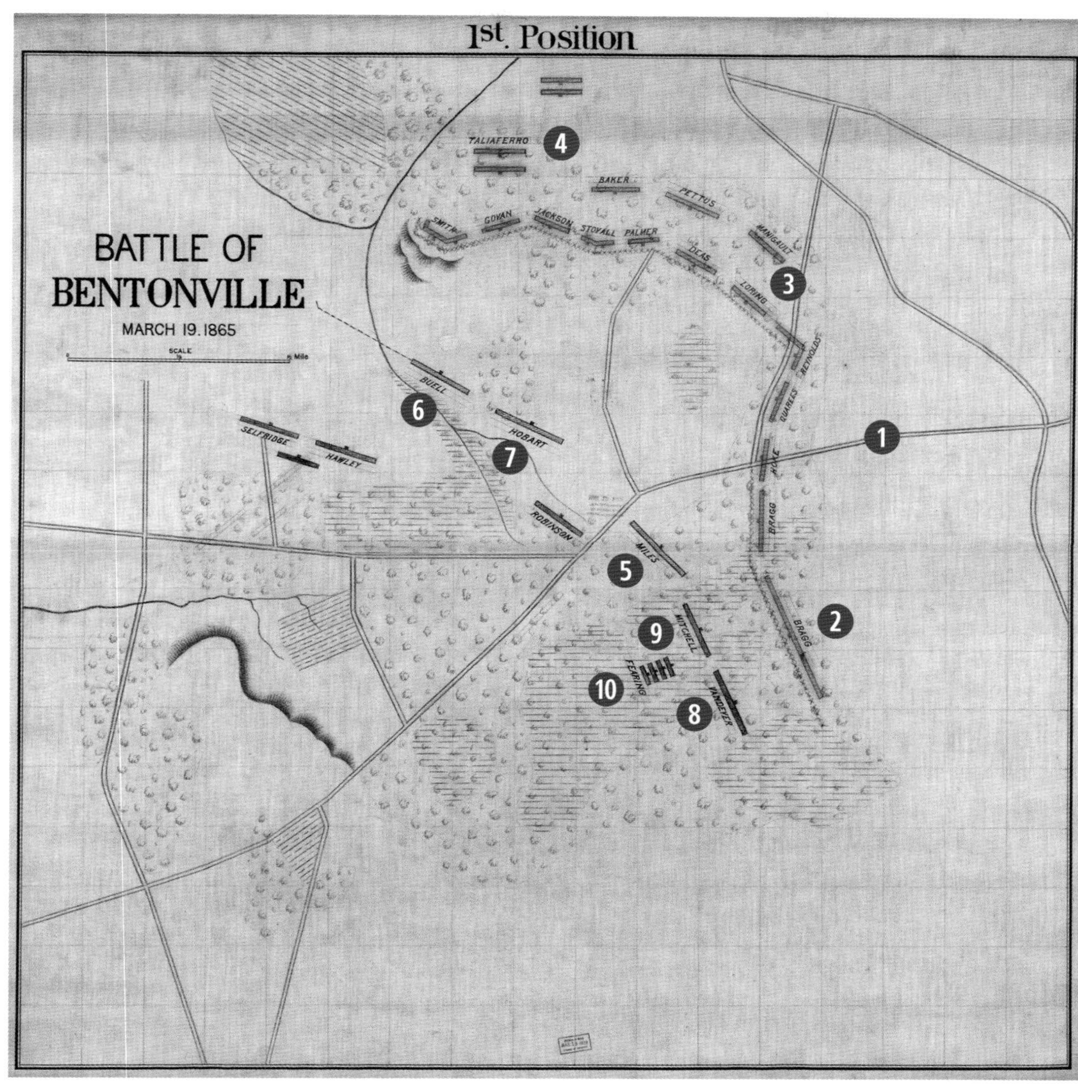

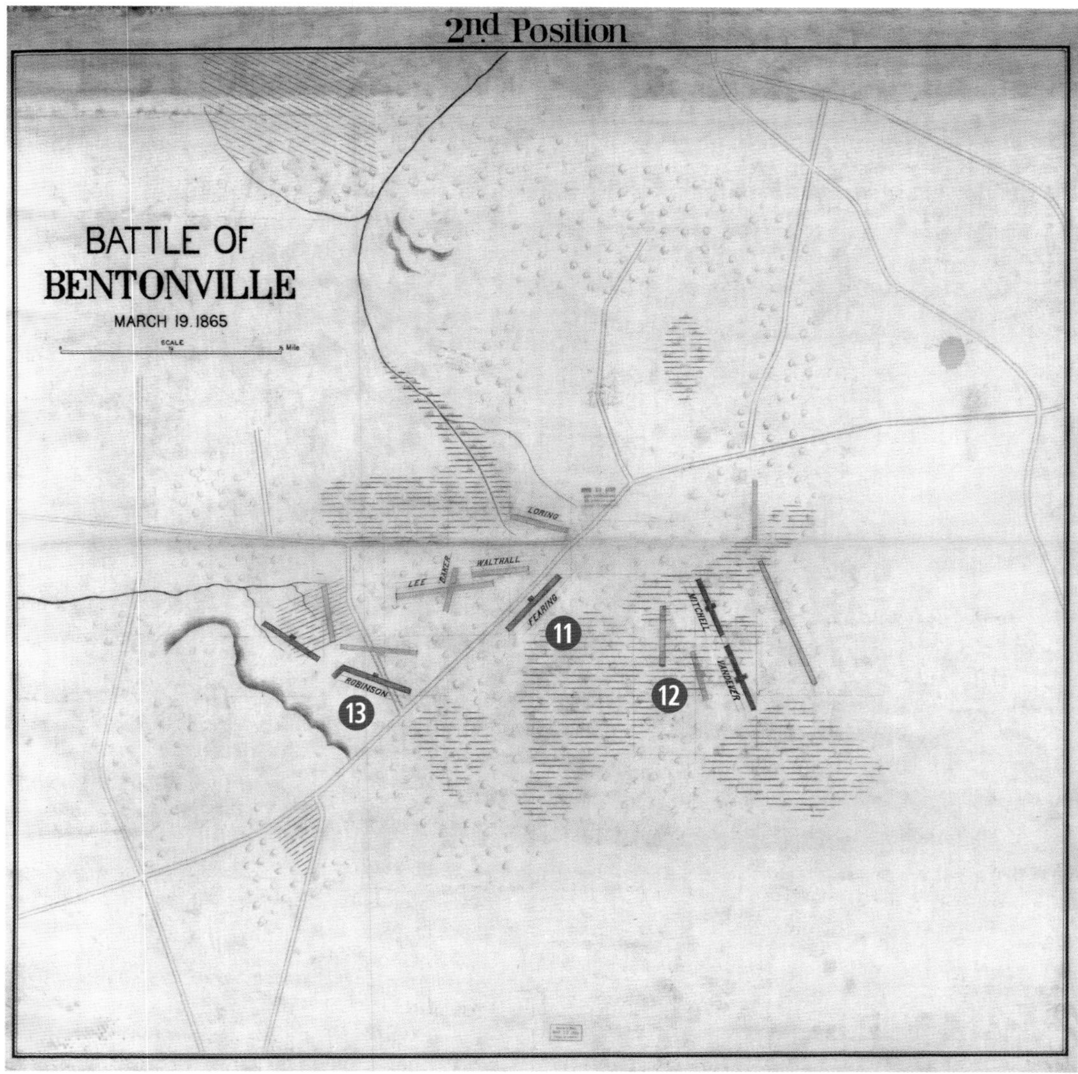

"Sherman's course cannot be hindered by the small force I have. I can do no more than annoy him."

Joseph Johnson
after the Battle of Bentonville

First Position A map drawn after the battle shows the approximate positions of Federal and Confederate units around the time the struggle began at Bentonville on the afternoon of March 19. Major General Robert Hoke's division, shown astride the road to Goldsboro, was under Bragg's command. The Confederate line above the road included troops under such seasoned commanders of the old Army of Tennessee as Brigadier General Daniel Govan and Major General William Loring. But Rebel ranks had been ravaged by casualties, famine, disease, and desertion. Johnston's forces attacked with spirit but lacked the strength to sustain their drive when the Federals rallied.

Second Position This map shows the critical moment in the battle, when Carlin's Federal division above the road had been routed and Morgan's division below the road was in desperate straits. "If Morgan's troops can stand this, all is right," said Brigadier General Jefferson C. Davis, the 14th Corps commander. "If not, all is lost. There is no reserve." Davis was unaware that troops of the 20th Corps were hurrying into line above the road to the rear of Morgan's division, which made a fighting retreat to link up with those Federals.

1865

THE LAST BATTLES

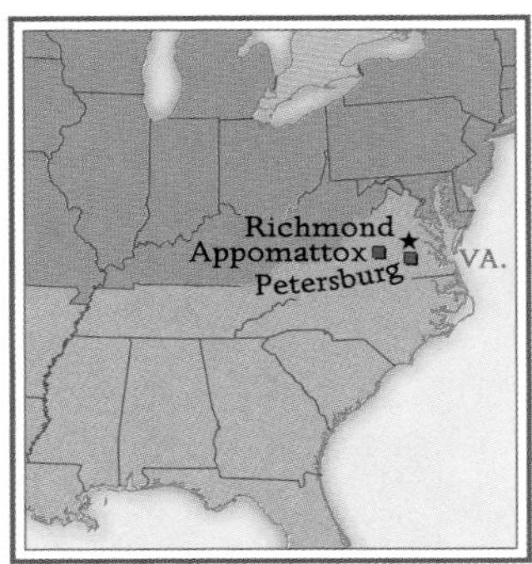

EASTERN THEATER

MARCH 25, 1865 Grant's troops repulse a Confederate assault on Fort Stedman at Petersburg, Virginia, and prepare to attack Lee's forces there.

MARCH 31–APRIL 1 Battle of Five Forks (Virginia)

APRIL 2 Grant breaks through at Petersburg, forcing Confederates to abandon that city and nearby Richmond overnight.

APRIL 6 Battle of Sayler's Creek (Virginia)

APRIL 9 Lee surrenders to Grant at Appomattox Court House.

Lee's desperate situation at Petersburg ❶ in March 1865 was symptomatic of the plight of the Confederacy as a whole. For four years, Union forces had blockaded the South, severed its supply lines, and crippled its economy, resulting in severe shortages of food and other essentials, rampant inflation, and growing unrest. Many Confederates deserted in the waning months of the war to protect their families as conditions deteriorated. Rebel forces had been "worn out and killed out and starved out," one officer remarked, and those who remained could not hold out much longer.

Lee's army was the Confederacy's last hope, but it too was wearing down under the pressure applied by Grant's much-larger and better-supplied force. Like the Federal blockade, Grant's investment, or siege, of Petersburg did not cut off the Confederates entirely. Lee could still communicate by road and rail with Richmond ❷. And Grant's line below Petersburg stopped just short of the Southside Railroad ❸, which Lee could use to withdraw to North Carolina and link up with Joseph Johnston's remaining forces. But any movement by Lee away from Richmond would doom the Confederate capital, and Jefferson Davis would not allow that. At Davis's urging, Lee resolved to attack the Federals at Petersburg before his army, which now had only about 40,000 men fit for duty south of the James River, was further depleted.

Lee entrusted the attack to Major General John Gordon, a hero of the Wilderness campaign who had recently been promoted to corps commander. Shortly before dawn on March 25, Gordon's troops stormed Fort Stedman ❹, hacking away at the log barricades shielding that strongpoint and surging over the parapet. After capturing the fort and adjacent batteries, however, they found themselves trapped in the works, much as Union troops had been during the Battle of the Crater and other attacks on Confederate fortifications here. By afternoon, Federals had closed the breach and were pounding the penned-up Rebels, who suffered 4,000 casualties before retreating. Grant, who was away at City Point that morning welcoming Lincoln, described the battle as "a little rumpus up the line" and was so confident of the outcome that he went ahead with plans to review troops with the president that afternoon. This was Lee's last gasp, concluded Grant, who prepared an attack of his own to cut the Southside Railroad and ensure that his vulnerable opponent did not slip away. ■

NAVAL MIGHT **Union steamers like these near City Point gave Grant a secure maritime supply line and kept Confederate warships bottled up near Richmond.**

WINTER CAMP **Cavalrymen from New York relax at their well-constructed winter camp near Petersburg in early 1865. Not many in Grant's army lived as comfortably as this during the siege, but they fared far better than Lee's starving troops.**

GRANT'S REWARDING INVESTMENT **This map made by Robert Knox Sneden shows Grant's siege line in purple extending around Petersburg below the Appomattox River. The lines left open to Lee brought him little food or other supplies over the winter of 1864–1865. Grant's investment paid dividends as spring approached when Lee's depleted army lost the capacity to defend its lines (red), leading to the capture on April 2 of Fort Mahone and other Confederate strongpoints and the abandonment of Petersburg.**

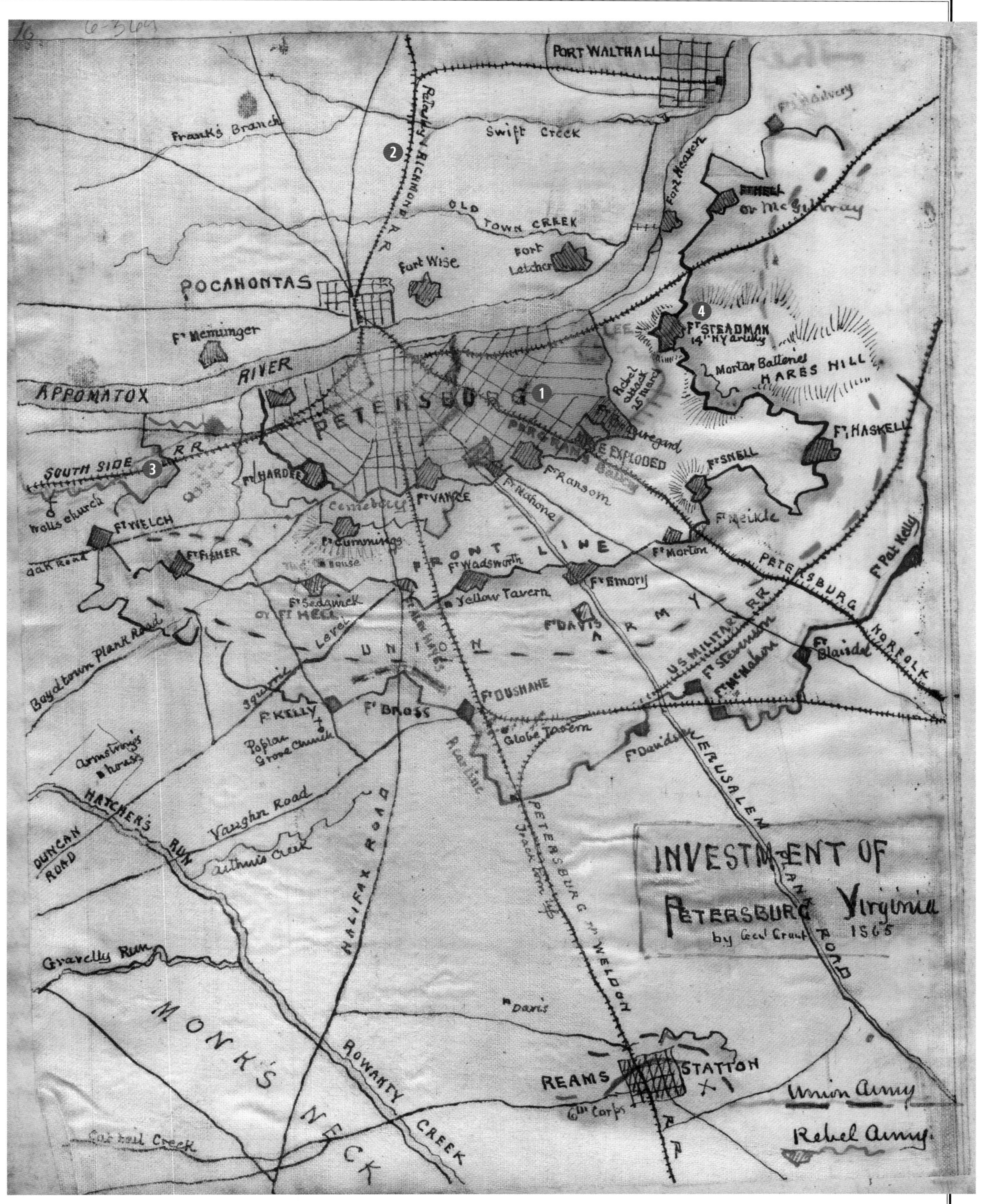
PORT WALTHALL
Frank's Branch
Swift Creek
Petersburg & Richmond R.R.
OLD TOWN CREEK
Fort Wise
Fort Letcher
POCAHONTAS
Ft Steadman
14th NY arty
Mortar Batteries
HARES HILL
Ft Memminger
RIVER
APPOMATOX
PETERSBURG
MINE EXPLODED
Ft Haskell
SOUTH SIDE R.R.
Ft Hardee
Ft Ransom
Ft Vance
Cemetery
Ft Mahone
FT WELCH
Ft Cummings
FRONT LINE
Ft Morton
PETERSBURG NORFOLK
Ft Pat Kelly
Oak Road
FT FISHER
Ft Wadsworth
Yellow Tavern
Ft Emory
Ft Sedgwick
or Ft Hell
Ft Davis
UNION ARMY
US MILITARY RR
Ft Stevenson
Ft McMahon
Boydtown Plank Road
Ft Dushane
Ft Kelly
Ft Bross
Poplar Grove Church
Globe Tavern
JERUSALEM PLANK ROAD
HATCHER'S RUN
Vaughn Road
DUNCAN ROAD
HALIFAX ROAD
PETERSBURG & WELDON
INVESTMENT OF
PETERSBURG Virginia
by Genl Grant
Gravelly Run
MONK'S NECK
Davis
ROWANTY CREEK
REAMS STATION
6th Corps
Union Army
Rebel Army
1
2
3
4

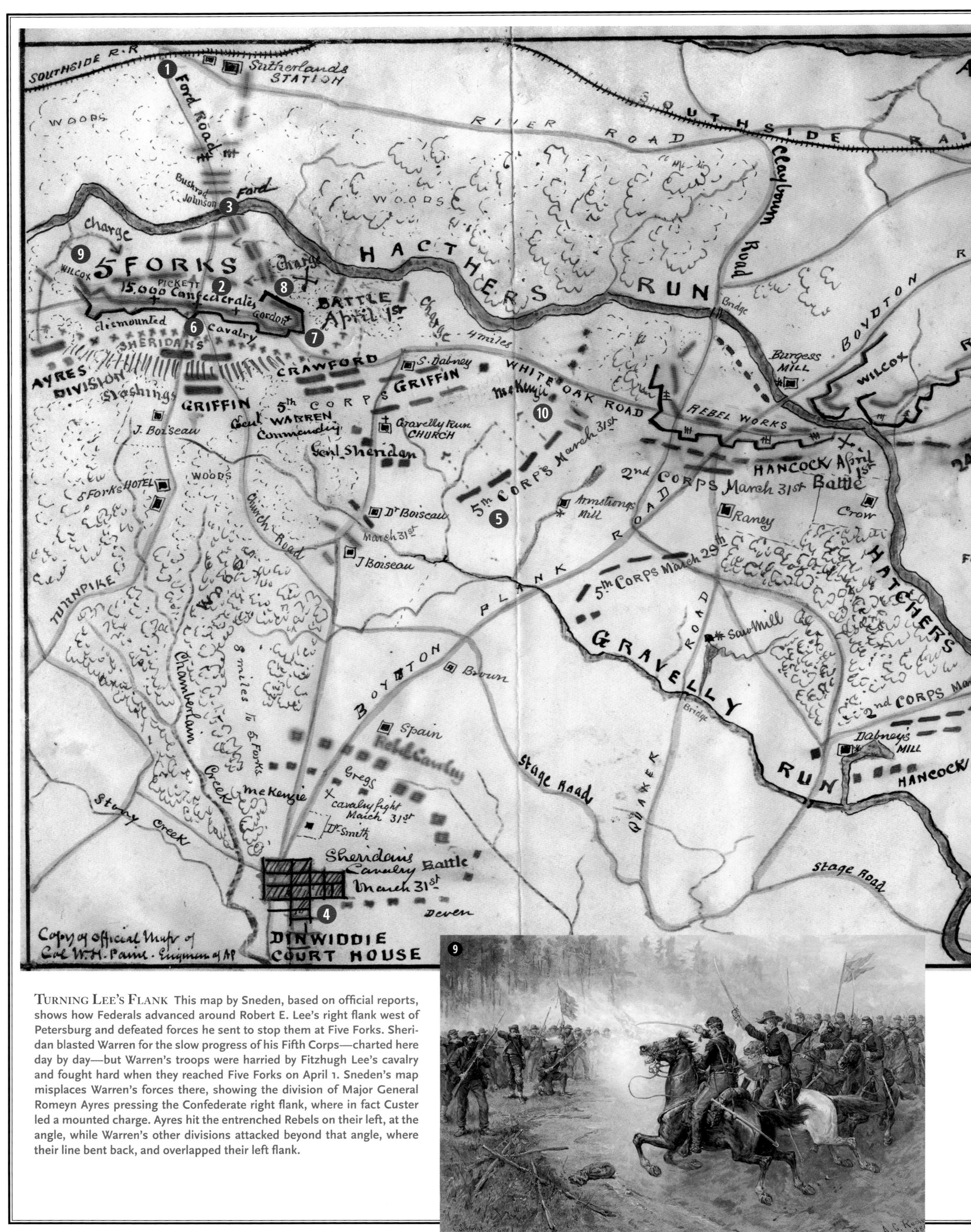

Turning Lee's Flank This map by Sneden, based on official reports, shows how Federals advanced around Robert E. Lee's right flank west of Petersburg and defeated forces he sent to stop them at Five Forks. Sheridan blasted Warren for the slow progress of his Fifth Corps—charted here day by day—but Warren's troops were harried by Fitzhugh Lee's cavalry and fought hard when they reached Five Forks on April 1. Sneden's map misplaces Warren's forces there, showing the division of Major General Romeyn Ayres pressing the Confederate right flank, where in fact Custer led a mounted charge. Ayres hit the entrenched Rebels on their left, at the angle, while Warren's other divisions attacked beyond that angle, where their line bent back, and overlapped their left flank.

❾ Cavalry Charge Troopers of Custer's cavalry division, part of Sheridan's force, charge Virginians on the Confederate right flank at Five Forks. Most of Sheridan's troopers fought dismounted against entrenched Rebels here, but charges on horseback by Custer's mounted brigades proved effective against disorganized Confederate infantry during the final stages of the battle.

Rivals in the Saddle Fitzhugh Lee (near right) performed well as Robert E. Lee's cavalry chief in the days leading up to the showdown at Five Forks on April 1. But his embarrassing absence when Federals attacked there late that afternoon proved costly, and his forces were bested by Sheridan's aggressive young cavalry commanders, including Ranald Mackenzie (far right). Like Sheridan, Mackenzie went on to lead U.S. cavalry against defiant Indians in the West after the Civil War.

1865 | THE LAST BATTLES

Five Forks

Returning from the Shenandoah Valley to resume his duties as cavalry chief, Philip Sheridan told Grant on March 30 that he was ready to "strike tomorrow and go to smashing things!" Supported by the Second and Fifth Corps, Sheridan would turn Lee's right flank to the west and sever the Southside Railroad ❶, drawing Confederates away from Petersburg before Grant attacked there. Lee had to defend the railroad because he depended on it for supplies and would have great difficulty sustaining his army if he withdrew by any other route. He sent cavalry commanded by his nephew, Major General Fitzhugh Lee, and infantry led by Major General George Pickett to the crossroads of Five Forks ❷, where they dug in to prevent Federals from fording nearby Hatcher's Run ❸ and cutting the tracks.

On March 31, Pickett advanced with cavalry to challenge Sheridan at Dinwiddie Court House ❹ but fell back to Five Forks after sharp clashes to avoid being caught between Sheridan and Gouverneur Warren's slowly advancing Fifth Corps ❺. Blaming Warren for failing to cut Pickett off, Sheridan rode to Five Forks in a fury on April 1 and paced up and down there "like a caged tiger," as one officer put it, waiting for Warren to arrive. With no enemy infantry in sight, Pickett and Fitzhugh Lee went off to a shad bake that afternoon hosted by a fellow officer north of Hatcher's Run. They should have realized they were facing a commander who never gave opponents a break. Instead of waiting until the next day to attack when the Fifth Corps showed up around 4 P.M., Sheridan rushed into battle, advancing head on with dismounted cavalry ❻ while the infantry attacked the entrenched Confederates on their left flank where their line angled back ❼. Major General Samuel Crawford's division cut their line of retreat ❽ before Pickett and Lee returned, and cavalry charges by George Custer ❾ and Brigadier General Ranald Mackenzie ❿ sealed their fate. Thousands of Rebels were captured in this debacle, remembered as the Waterloo of the Confederacy. ■

No. 12.
Region
embraced in the Operations
of the Armies against
RICHMOND and PETERSBURG.
Engraved at the Engineer Bureau, War Dep.
1865.
AUTHORITIES. North of James & Appomattox from Photograph Map
Captured from the Enemy
South of Do. from Surveys of Col. N. Michler
CORPS OF ENGINEERS.
APPOMATTOX RIVER
JAMES RIVER
PAMUNKEY RIVER
CHICKAHOMINY RIVER
Chesterfield C.H.
City Point
Five Forks
Dinwiddie C.H.
Prince George C.H.
Union Works
Rebel Works
Bowen & Co. lith. Philada.
1
2
3
4
5
6
7
8

1865 | THE LAST BATTLES

THE FALL OF RICHMOND

Grant followed Sheridan's smashing victory at Five Forks ❶ by launching an all-out attack at Petersburg ❷ before dawn on April 2. Robert E. Lee had lost nearly one-fourth of his able-bodied men in the past week, and his line (shown in blue on the map opposite, which reverses the color scheme of most Civil War maps) was stretched to the breaking point. Yet his troops fought fiercely at strongpoints like Fort Mahone ❸ and Fort Gregg ❹, which was wreathed in gun smoke "like the crater of a volcano," one Confederate wrote. A Union officer, Colonel Rufus Lincoln, was awed by the determination shown on both sides there: "Cheer after cheer rent the air—the Rebels fighting with the desperation of madmen, and shouting to each other, 'Never surrender! Never surrender!'"

Here and elsewhere along the line, die-hard Rebels lost the fight but bought time for Lee to organize a withdrawal. He could not follow the Southside Railroad ❺, which had been severed by Sheridan's forces, and retreating to Richmond ❻ was out of the question. For if Lee's troops managed to reach the capital without being cut off by Grant's surging army, they would soon be surrounded and the populace would be caught in their death struggle. His only hope was to withdraw westward, hold off pursuing Federals, and try to link up with Joseph Johnston in southwestern Virginia or North Carolina.

Lee informed Jefferson Davis on April 2 that he was about to abandon Petersburg. That would allow Federals to take Richmond from the south, where its defenses were minimal compared with the fortifications to the north and east ❼. "I advise that all preparations be made for leaving Richmond tonight," Lee wrote. Davis and his cabinet fled the capital that evening on the Richmond & Danville Railroad ❽ and continued on from Danville, Virginia, to Greensboro, North Carolina, which served briefly as the seat of the collapsing Confederacy. As the last troops departed Richmond overnight after blowing up warships of the James River squadron and torching public buildings and warehouses, order collapsed and fires raged unchecked. For Confederate loyalists there, it was a nightmare. But for blacks in Richmond, there was joy amid the rubble when black troops marched in on April 3 to take possession. As one Union officer wrote, "From the colored population of Richmond we received such a reception as could only come from a people who were returning thanks for the deliverance of their race." ■

"Cheer after cheer rent the air— the Rebels fighting with the desperation of madmen, and shouting to each other, 'Never surrender! Never surrender!'"

UNION COLONEL RUFUS LINCOLN
AT FORT GREGG

❸ LAST TO FALL **Killed at Fort Mahone on April 2 as Federals broke through, this Confederate was among the last to fall in the long, painful siege of Petersburg.**

❻ RICHMOND IN RUINS **Men stand amid the ruins of Richmond after Confederates abandoned their capital on the night of April 2, destroying supplies by kindling fires, which spread rapidly.**

CAPITAL DISTRICT **This distinctive Union map of the crucial area between Petersburg and Richmond, which shows Confederate fortifications in blue and Federal fortifications in red, was based in part on a captured Confederate map reproduced photographically, one of several methods used to copy maps during the war.**

PURSUIT TO APPOMATTOX

To preserve his army after withdrawing from Petersburg, Lee had to reach a rail depot where his famished forces could receive shipments of food and gather strength. Lee aimed for Amelia Courthouse ❶, on the Richmond & Danville Railroad ❷, where most of his forces arrived by April 4. But he found that no food had been shipped there by rail from Richmond before it fell. Meanwhile, Federals were advancing rapidly on paths to his south and cutting other lines of supply or escape he might use. Grant's left wing, including the Ninth Corps, was pressing westward from Sutherland's Depot ❸ along the Southside Railroad ❹ toward Burkeville Junction ❺, where they would sever the Richmond & Danville Railroad and continue on to Rice's Station ❻. His right wing—led by Sheridan's cavalry, followed by the bulk of the Army of the Potomac—had repulsed Confederate cavalry at Namozine Church ❼ on April 3 and would reach Rice's Station ahead of the Ninth Corps, seeking to prevent Lee from using that stretch of the Southside Railroad as his lifeline.

With his army starving, Lee had to march in that direction and risk battle with superior Federal forces. At Sayler's Creek ❽ on April 6, Sheridan's cavalry and Horatio Wright's Sixth Corps caught troops led by Lieutenant Generals Richard Ewell and Richard Anderson in a vise and stripped Lee of nearly 8,000 men, most of them captured. He continued westward with his diminished forces, fighting rear-guard actions at Farmville ❾ and Cumberland Church ❿, sustained by the knowledge that provisions awaited them at Appomattox Station ⓫. But when Sheridan got there first on April 8, seized those supplies, and cut Lee's avenue of retreat, surrender was inevitable. "There is nothing left me but to go and see General Grant," Lee told his aides, "and I had rather die a thousand deaths." ■

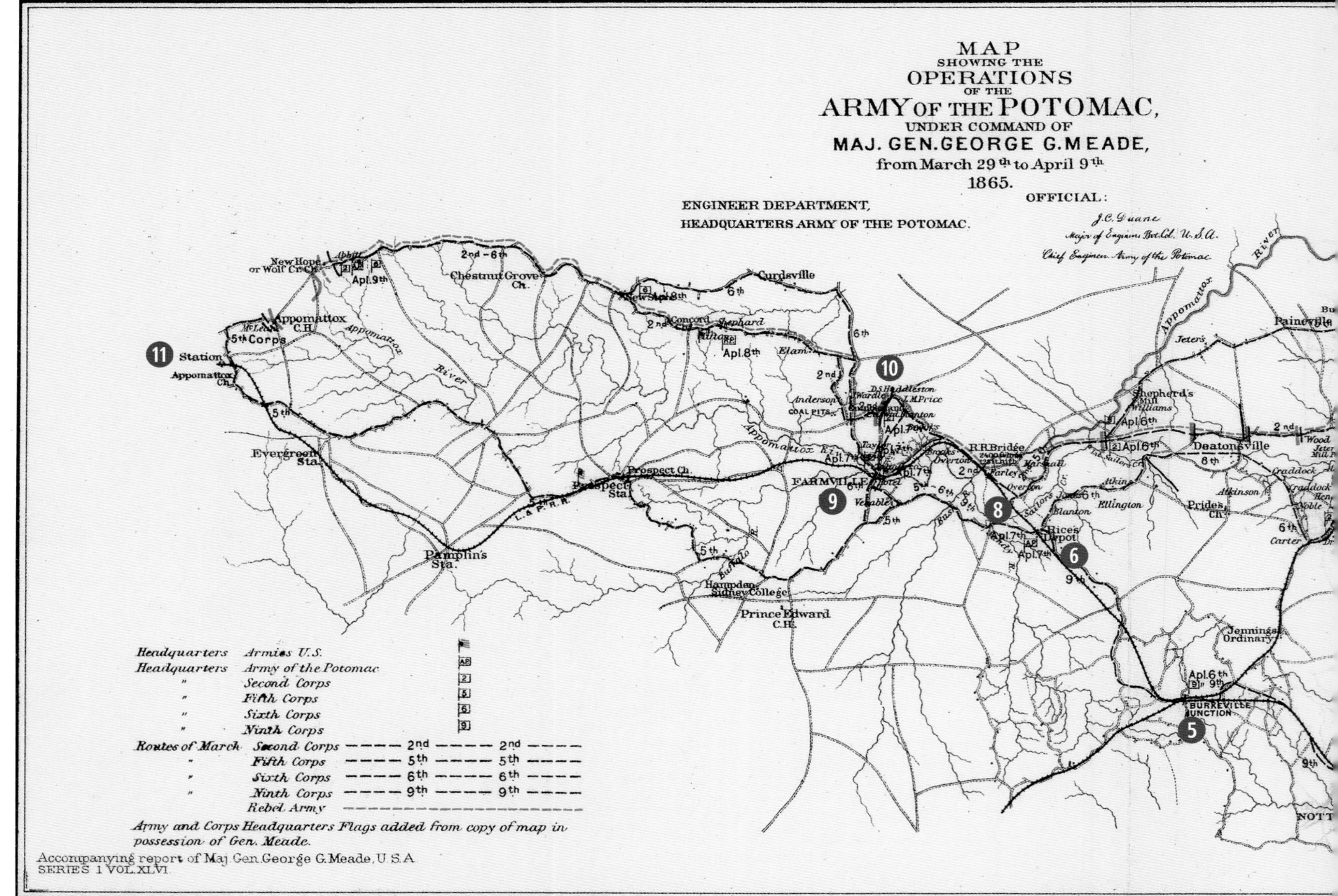

A RELENTLESS PURSUIT **As detailed in a map showing the routes of various elements of the Army of the Potomac, the pursuit of Lee conformed to the plan Grant, Sheridan, and Sherman had been following relentlessly. By cutting the enemy's lines and depriving him of supplies, mobility, and manpower, they drew him into desperate battles that exhausted his strength and forced him to disband or surrender.**

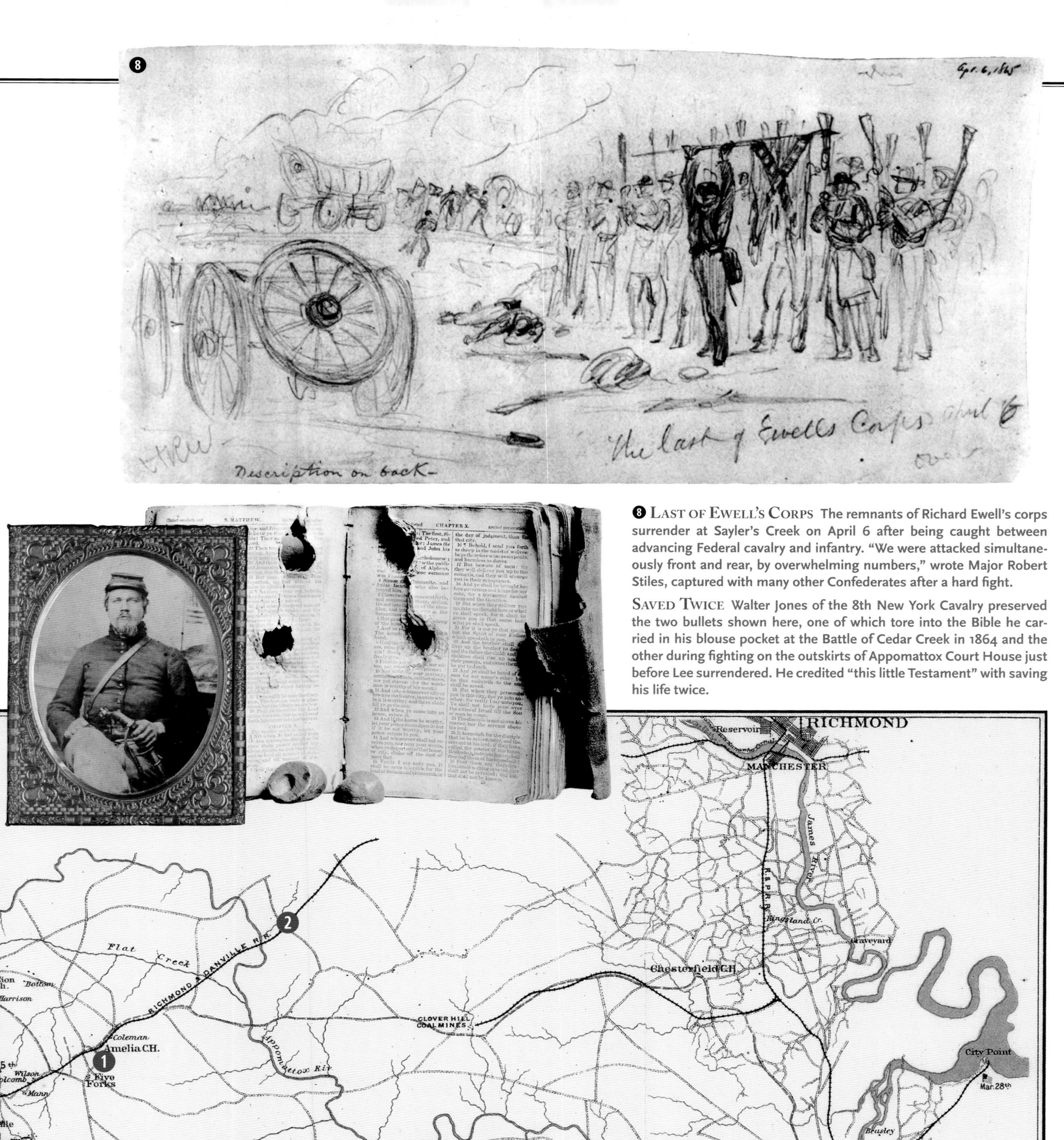

8 LAST OF EWELL'S CORPS The remnants of Richard Ewell's corps surrender at Sayler's Creek on April 6 after being caught between advancing Federal cavalry and infantry. "We were attacked simultaneously front and rear, by overwhelming numbers," wrote Major Robert Stiles, captured with many other Confederates after a hard fight.

SAVED TWICE Walter Jones of the 8th New York Cavalry preserved the two bullets shown here, one of which tore into the Bible he carried in his blouse pocket at the Battle of Cedar Creek in 1864 and the other during fighting on the outskirts of Appomattox Court House just before Lee surrendered. He credited "this little Testament" with saving his life twice.

MAP OF APPOMATTOX COURT HOUSE AND VICINITY.

Showing the relative positions of the Confederate and Federal Armies at the time of General R. E. LEE'S Surrender, April 9th 1865.

Lee's Head-Quarters.

Historical Notes.

On Sunday, the 2d of April 1865, General Lee was holding at Petersburg a semi-circular line south of the Appomattox River, with his left resting on the river, and his right on the South Side Rail Road, fifteen miles from the city. The Federals were pressing his whole line. Sheridan with his cavalry on the right. To save his right flank, General Lee telegraphed to Richmond, that during the night be would fall back to the north side of the river, and ordered that Richmond be evacuated simultaneously.

On the morning of the 3d the retreat commenced in earnest, General Grant hurrying up to get possession of Burkesville—the junction of the South Side and Danville Railroad—in hopes of cutting off General Lee from Danville or Lynchburg. On the 5th a portion of the Federal forces occupied Burkesville, Sheridan with his cavalry being in advance at Jetersville on the Danville Railroad. General Lee at Amelia C. H., 6 miles north of Sheridan's advance. In this situation General Sheridan telegraphed:—"I feel confident of capturing the entire Army of Northern Virginia, if we exert ourselves. I see no escape for Lee." On the evening of the 6th some heavy fighting took place between the Federal advance and Lee's retreating column. Sheridan again telegraphed: "If the thing is pressed I think Lee will surrender." Lee continued to press for Lynchburg—his men probably anticipating the result, daily leaving him by thousands,—until on the morning of the fated 9th of April, 1865, he confronted the overwhelming forces of Gen. Grant with a little less than 8,000 muskets.

The position of the Confederate army was briefly this: occupying the narrow strip of land between the South Side Railroad and the James River; the only road on which it was possible to retreat, was that marked Lynchburg road on the map. Sheridan with his cavalry having struck the railroad at Appomattox Station, obtaining possession of the Lynchburg road, thus effectually cutting off Lee's retreat. Gen. Lee now had the choice of either cutting his way directly through the Federal forces, or immediate surrender. In view of the immense disparity of forces between the ranks of the half starved Confederates and the overwhelming army of General Grant, he chose the letter alternative.

Generals Lee and Grant met at the house of Wilmer McLane, Esq., and after a brief interview, at 3½ o'clock p. m.

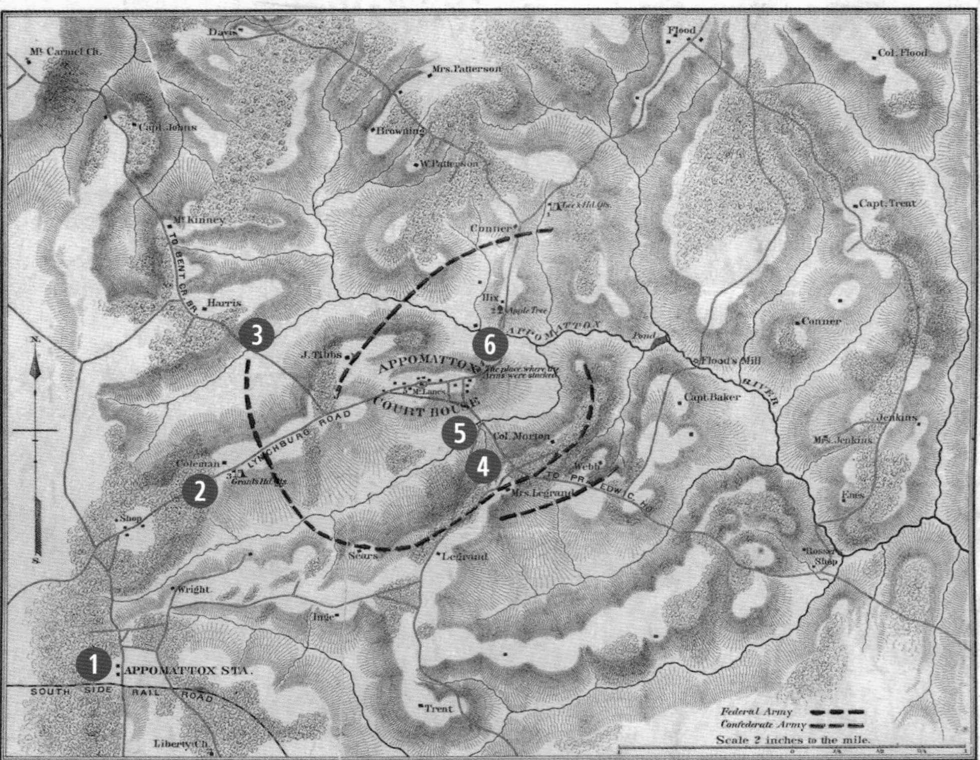

Grant's Head-Quarters.

on the 9th of April 1865, the Articles of Capitulation were signed by General Lee. While negotiations were being conducted by the two Commanders-in-Chief, the General officers of either army were mingling socially together in the streets of Appomattox C. H., and drinking mutual healths. Gens. Ord, Sheridan, Gibbon, Michie and others of the Federals, Gens. Longstreet, Heath, Gordon and others, of the Confederates.

At 4 o'clock p. m. the announcement of Lee's surrender was made to Grant's army. The wildest enthusiasm immediately broke forth, and all seemed mad with joy.

As the great Confederate General rode past his gallant little band from his interview with Gen. Grant, whole lines of battle rushed to the beloved old chief, and breaking ranks, each struggled with the other to wring him by the hand. With tears rolling down his cheeks, General Lee could only say, "Men, we have fought through the war together. I have done the best that I could for you."

On the morning of the 12th April the Army of Northern Virginia marched by divisions to a point near Appomattox Court House, and stacked arms and accoutrements. Maj. Gen. Gibbon representing the United States authorities.

On the afternoon of the 12th, with an escort of Federal cavalry as a guard of honor, attended by a portion of his staff, General Lee returned to Richmond.

Thus quietly passed from the theater of the most desperate war of modern times the renowned Commander of the Army of Northern Virginia, and the remnants of that once invincible army were quietly wending their way to their long forsaken homes.

LIST OF ENGRAVINGS.

Gen. Lee's Head-Quarters near Conner's House.—Position marked by a flag and No. 1 on the map.

View of Appomattox Court House.

General Grant's Head-Quarters near Coleman's House.—Position marked by a flag and No. 3 on the map.

Place where the arms were stacked. The exact spot is marked No. 4 on the map. In this picture may be seen the famous apple tree, (position marked with a tree and No. 2 on the map,) near Hix's house, where the first meeting between the Commanders was generally, but incorrectly, supposed to have taken place.

McLane's House, in the village of Appomattox Court House, where the articles of capitulation were signed. The signing took place in the front room, on the right of the door, entering from the porch.

McLane's House.

GEN. LEE'S FAREWELL TO HIS ARMY.

HEAD-QUARTERS ARMY NORTHERN VIRGINIA,
APRIL 10TH, 1865.

After four years of arduous service, marked by unsurpassed courage and fortitude, the Army of Northern Virginia has been compelled to yield to overwhelming numbers and resources.

I need not tell the survivors of so many hard-fought battles, who have remained steadfast to the last, that I have consented to this result from no distrust of them; but feeling that valor and devotion could accomplish nothing that could compensate for the loss that would have attended the continuation of the contest, I have determined to avoid the useless sacrifice of those whose past services have endeared them to their countrymen.

By the terms of agreement, officers and men can return to their homes and remain there until exchanged.

You will take with you the satisfaction that proceeds from the consciousness of duty faithfully performed; and I earnestly pray that a merciful God will extend to you His blessing and protection.

With an unceasing admiration of your constancy and devotion to your country, and a grateful remembrance of your kind and generous consideration of myself, I bid you an affectionate farewell.

R. E. LEE, *General.*

Appomattox Court House.

LITH. by A. HOEN & CO. Baltimore.

Place where the Arms were Stacked.

198 Entered according to act of Congress, in the year 1866, by Henderson & Co. in the Clerk's office of the District Court of Maryland.

WHERE HOSTILITIES ENDED Published in Maryland in 1866, this map of Appomattox Court House and environs is accompanied by text extolling Lee, the "great Confederate General," and his "gallant little band." Such sentiments were stronger in border states like Maryland than in the North as a whole, but Lee gained credit among Unionists by accepting defeat and urging reconciliation.

4 PEACE OVERTURE Confederate Captain Robert Sims, bearing a flag of truce, steadies his rearing horse as he presents General Gordon's request for a suspension of hostilities to Custer (center), who rejected the overture. "We are behind your army now," he declared, "and it is at our mercy."

SURRENDER AT APPOMATTOX

Defiant to the last, Confederates battled their foes around Appomattox Court House even as Lee prepared to meet there with Grant on April 9 to work out terms of surrender. Urged by Lincoln to be lenient toward Rebels who yielded, Grant did not seek Lee's unconditional surrender and was prepared to offer generous conditions. But until an agreement was reached by the two commanders, their forces were still at war. Sheridan's cavalrymen had seized Appomattox Station ❶ the day before, depriving Lee of food his troops desperately needed, and were holding the Lynchburg Road ❷. But Federal infantry had not yet arrived in force, and Sheridan was vulnerable on his left flank. Just hours before Lee went to discuss surrender, his last effective corps, led by John Gordon, attacked along the Bent Creek Road ❸, supported by Fitzhugh Lee's cavalry.

For a while, it looked as if the Confederates might break out of the bind they were in at Appomattox. But Federals of Major General E. O. C. Ord's Army of the James, who had just arrived at the station, moved up to bolster Sheridan's embattled left and close off the Bent Creek Road while Custer's cavalry division advanced from the east ❹, trapping Gordon's forces. When an envoy from Gordon requested a suspension of hostilities, Custer replied grandly: "We will listen to no terms but unconditional surrender." Fortunately, the matter rested not with the posturing Custer but with his superior, Ulysses Grant, who promptly agreed when Robert E. Lee wrote requesting a cessation of hostilities.

That afternoon, the two commanders met in Appomattox at the home of merchant Wilmer McLean ❺, who had moved here from Manassas in 1862 to avoid the fighting there. When Grant sat down with Lee at the McLean house, his elation at finally defeating his resilient opponent ebbed away, leaving him "sad and depressed," he wrote later. "I felt like anything rather than rejoicing at the downfall of a foe who had fought so long and valiantly." To ease the strain, Grant engaged in small talk until Lee asked pointedly "upon what terms you would receive the surrender of my army." His men would be paroled, Grant responded, and officers would be allowed to keep their side arms and troopers their horses. All would then "return to their homes," the agreement stated, "not to be disturbed by United States authority so long as they observe their paroles and the laws in force where they reside."

After the two men signed, Grant arranged for rations to be sent to Lee's forces. On April 12, the Army of Northern Virginia assembled for the last time and stacked its arms ❻ in token of surrender. With Lee and his stalwarts no longer at war, Confederate forces elsewhere had little reason to keep fighting. ■

❺ SIGNING OFF **Lee signs the articles of surrender at the McLean house in Appomattox Court House as Grant and his generals look on.**

1865

AFTERMATH

POLITICS & POWER

APRIL 14, 1865 Lincoln shot by John Wilkes Booth.

APRIL 15 Lincoln dies; Andrew Johnson sworn in as president.

APRIL 17 Johnston and Sherman meet to discuss an armistice.

APRIL 26 Booth shot dead in Virginia while resisting arrest.

MAY 4 Lincoln buried in Springfield, Illinois.

MAY 10 Jefferson Davis seized by Federals in Georgia.

MAY 23–24 Union forces march in Grand Review in Washington.

JUNE 2 Edmund Kirby Smith surrenders Confederate forces west of the Mississippi.

Despite Lee's surrender, Jefferson Davis hoped to keep up the fight. On April 12 he met at Greensboro, North Carolina, with Generals P. G. T. Beauregard and Joseph Johnston, who had just abandoned Raleigh to Sherman's vastly superior army. When asked by Davis what he thought of prolonging the struggle, Johnston was forthright: "My views are, sir, that our people are tired of war, feel themselves whipped, and will not fight." His forces were disbanding of their own accord, he added, and he could "retain no man beyond the by-road or cowpath that leads to his house."

Beauregard agreed that further resistance was futile, and Davis reluctantly authorized Johnston to make arrangements with Sherman "to terminate the existing war." When the opposing commanders met at Durham Station on April 17, Sherman stunned Johnston by informing him that President Lincoln had been assassinated. Johnston called the deadly attack by John Wilkes Booth at Ford's Theater ❶ a "disgrace" and hoped that Sherman did not hold the Confederate government responsible. Surprisingly for an officer who had wreaked havoc across the South, Sherman proposed a broad and lenient settlement that included an armistice with all Confederate armies and a provision restoring rebellious state governments to the Union once legislators and officials took oaths of loyalty. Sherman's offer exceeded his authority, however, and was rejected by his superiors in Washington. In the end, Johnston and other Confederate commanders surrendered on the same terms Lee did, leaving the South's political fate to be thrashed out later. Jefferson Davis was captured by Federals in Georgia on May 10 as he attempted to reach General Edmund Kirby Smith, his top commander west of the Mississippi, whose surrender on June 2 brought an end to organized Confederate resistance.

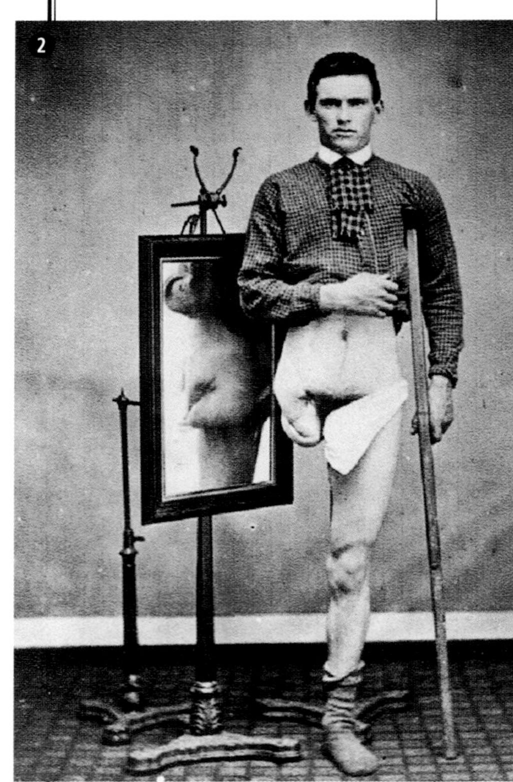

❷ AMPUTEE This man was one of nearly 30,000 Union soldiers who underwent amputations during the war after being wounded in battle. The picture was taken by Dr. Reed Brockway Bontecou, a Federal surgeon and director of Washington's Harewood Army Hospital, who documented war wounds to aid in the training of physicians.

SURRAT. BOOTH. HAROLD.

War Department, Washington, April 20, 1865,

$100,000 REWARD!

THE MURDERER

Of our late beloved President, Abraham Lincoln,

IS STILL AT LARGE.

$50,000 REWARD

Will be paid by this Department for his apprehension, in addition to any reward offered by Municipal Authorities or State Executives.

$25,000 REWARD

Will be paid for the apprehension of JOHN H. SURRATT, one of Booth's Accomplices.

$25,000 REWARD

Will be paid for the apprehension of David C. Harold, another of Booth's accomplices.

LIBERAL REWARDS will be paid for any information that shall conduce to the arrest of either of the above-named criminals, or their accomplices.

All persons harboring or secreting the said persons, or either of them, or aiding or assisting their concealment or escape, will be treated as accomplices in the murder of the President and the attempted assassination of the Secretary of State, and shall be subject to trial before a Military Commission and the punishment of DEATH.

Let the stain of innocent blood be removed from the land by the arrest and punishment of the murderers.

All good citizens are exhorted to aid public justice on this occasion. Every man should consider his own conscience charged with this solemn duty, and rest neither night nor day until it be accomplished.

EDWIN M. STANTON, Secretary of War.

DESCRIPTIONS.—BOOTH is Five Feet 7 or 8 inches high, slender build, high forehead, black hair, black eyes, and wears a heavy black moustache.

JOHN H. SURRAT is about 5 feet, 9 inches. Hair rather thin and dark; eyes rather light; no beard. Would weigh 145 or 150 pounds. Complexion rather pale and clear, with color in his cheeks. Wore light clothes of fine quality. Shoulders square; cheek bones rather prominent; chin narrow; ears projecting at the top; forehead rather low and square, but broad. Parts his hair on the right side; neck rather long. His lips are firmly set. A slim man.

DAVID C. HAROLD is five feet six inches high, hair dark, eyes dark, eyebrows rather heavy, full face, nose short, hand short and fleshy, feet small, instep high, round bodied, naturally quick and active, slightly closes his eyes when looking at a person.

NOTICE.—In addition to the above, State and other authorities have offered rewards amounting to almost one hundred thousand dollars, making an aggregate of about TWO HUNDRED THOUSAND DOLLARS.

For Northerners, Lincoln's death left millions grieving for the late president and for loved ones lost in the war. More than 360,000 Federals and 260,000 Confederates had perished, and others had been maimed for life and were recuperating at military hospitals like Harewood Army Hospital ❷ in Washington. Some of the Union's walking wounded later joined in a stirring ceremony that officially ended the nation's period of mourning—a triumphal Grand Review in the capital, where the Army of the Potomac marched down Pennsylvania Avenue ❸ on May 23, followed by Sherman's forces on May 24. Having been roundly criticized for offering overgenerous terms to the Rebels, Sherman felt vindicated when his troops—a "ragged, dirty, and sassy" lot, by his own account—were hailed as conquerors in the capital. "Felt kind of queer to get such a welcome," wrote one Union soldier who had marched for months under Sherman through hostile country. "Makes us feel like the war is over." ■

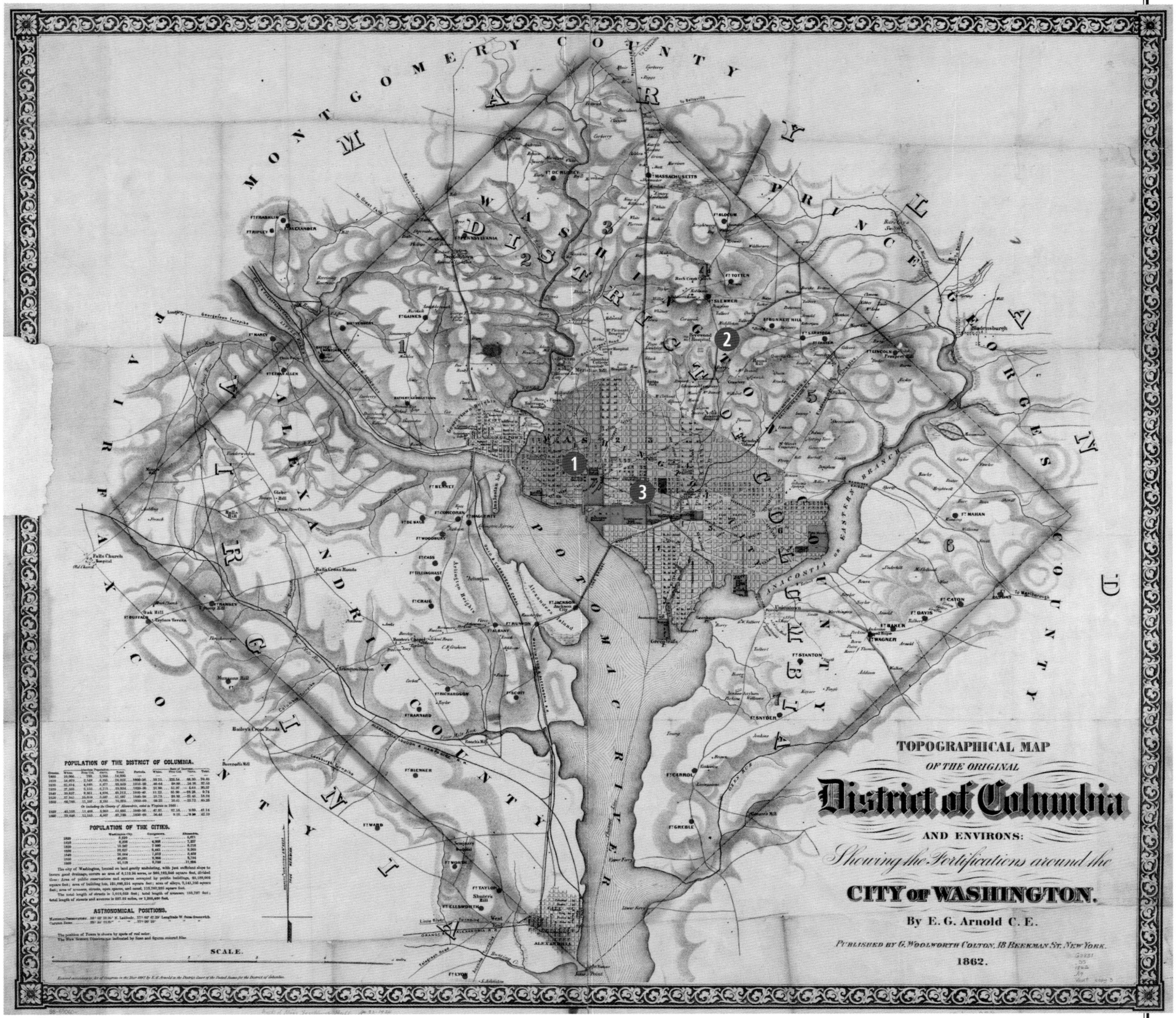

TOPOGRAPHICAL MAP
OF THE ORIGINAL
District of Columbia
AND ENVIRONS:
Showing the Fortifications around the
CITY OF WASHINGTON.
By E. G. Arnold C. E.
Published by G. Woolworth Colton, 18 Beekman St. New York.
1862.

A FORTRESS CITY An 1862 map of the District of Columbia shows the complex of forts (red) that shielded the Union's capital from attack. The ring of fortresses would expand dramatically by the war's end. Alexandria County, which included Arlington Heights, was part of the original district but was restored to Virginia in 1846 and remained part of that state when the Federal occupation of Alexandria launched in 1861 came to an end. Congress abolished slavery in the District of Columbia in April 1862, before Lincoln's Emancipation Proclamation, and many slaves fled here from the South during the war seeking freedom.

WANTED FOR MURDER A poster distributed by the War Department offers hefty rewards for information leading to the arrest of Booth, Lincoln's assassin, and two of his accomplices, John Surratt and David Herold. The conspirators also planned to kill other Union leaders, including Secretary of State William Seward, who was attacked at home and injured along with several members of his household.

❸ VICTORY MARCH The Army of the Potomac parades triumphantly down Pennsylvania Avenue in Washington on May 23. This procession was polished compared with that of Sherman's forces the following day, who were trailed down the avenue by camp followers, including black refugees who joined Sherman's march to escape slavery.

ASSASSINATION OF LINCOLN

Four days before he died, Abraham Lincoln addressed a festive crowd outside the White House celebrating the surrender of Lee's army at Appomattox. Instead of offering a victory speech, Lincoln spoke of the struggle that lay ahead—reconstructing a war-torn nation. He did not insist that Southern states grant full civil rights to blacks as a condition for rejoining the Union, he told the crowd, but he believed that some blacks, including those serving as soldiers, deserved the vote. Standing on the White House lawn that evening as Lincoln concluded his remarks was John Wilkes Booth, who turned to fellow conspirator Lewis Powell and said intently, "That is the last speech he will ever make."

Born in Maryland, Booth was an actor and Confederate sympathizer who waited until all was lost to strike a terrible blow for his cause. On the night of April 14, Booth entered the president's box at Ford's Theater ❶, shot him in the head, and leaped to the stage below, breaking an ankle in the process. He managed to get away on horseback to the Navy Yard Bridge ❷, where he met accomplice David Herold, who had guided Lewis Powell that same evening to the home of Secretary of State William Seward. Knifed by Powell—who was caught and later executed—Seward survived. Lincoln never regained consciousness and died the next morning.

Lincoln's last portrait

Crossing the bridge into Maryland, Booth and Herold rode to Surrattsville ❸, where they picked up a carbine and field glasses at a tavern owned by Mary Surratt, the mother of conspirator John Surratt who was herself charged with conspiracy and executed. Before dawn on April 15, they reached the home of Dr. Samuel Mudd ❹, who set Booth's broken bone and later went to prison for aiding him. That afternoon, the pair continued to the farm of Oswell Swann ❺, whom they paid to guide them across Zekiah Swamp to the home of Confederate sympathizer Samuel Cox ❻. After hiding out near Cox's place for several days, they were guided by Confederate agent Thomas Jones to his home ❼ before crossing the Potomac River ❽ by rowboat on the night of April 20. In Virginia they hurried from one house to another, receiving food or lodging. Then on April 24, a former Confederate soldier they met while crossing the Rappahannock River ❾ by ferry guided them to the farm of sympathizer Richard Garrett ❿. Cornered there by Union cavalry on April 26, Herold surrendered and later died on the gallows. Booth resisted and was shot dead, uttering these last words: "Useless, useless." ■

❶ FATAL SHOT Pointing his derringer, John Wilkes Booth fires a single, fatal shot at Lincoln at Ford's Theater. Major Henry Rathbone, seated at right beside his wife and Mary Todd Lincoln, then grappled with Booth, who cut him with a knife before leaping to the stage below.

FLIGHT FROM JUSTICE This National Geographic map traces the flight of Booth and Herold from Washington, D.C., through Maryland to the Garrett home in Virginia, where they were caught on April 26. The fugitives followed a route used by Confederate agents and known to Federal authorities.

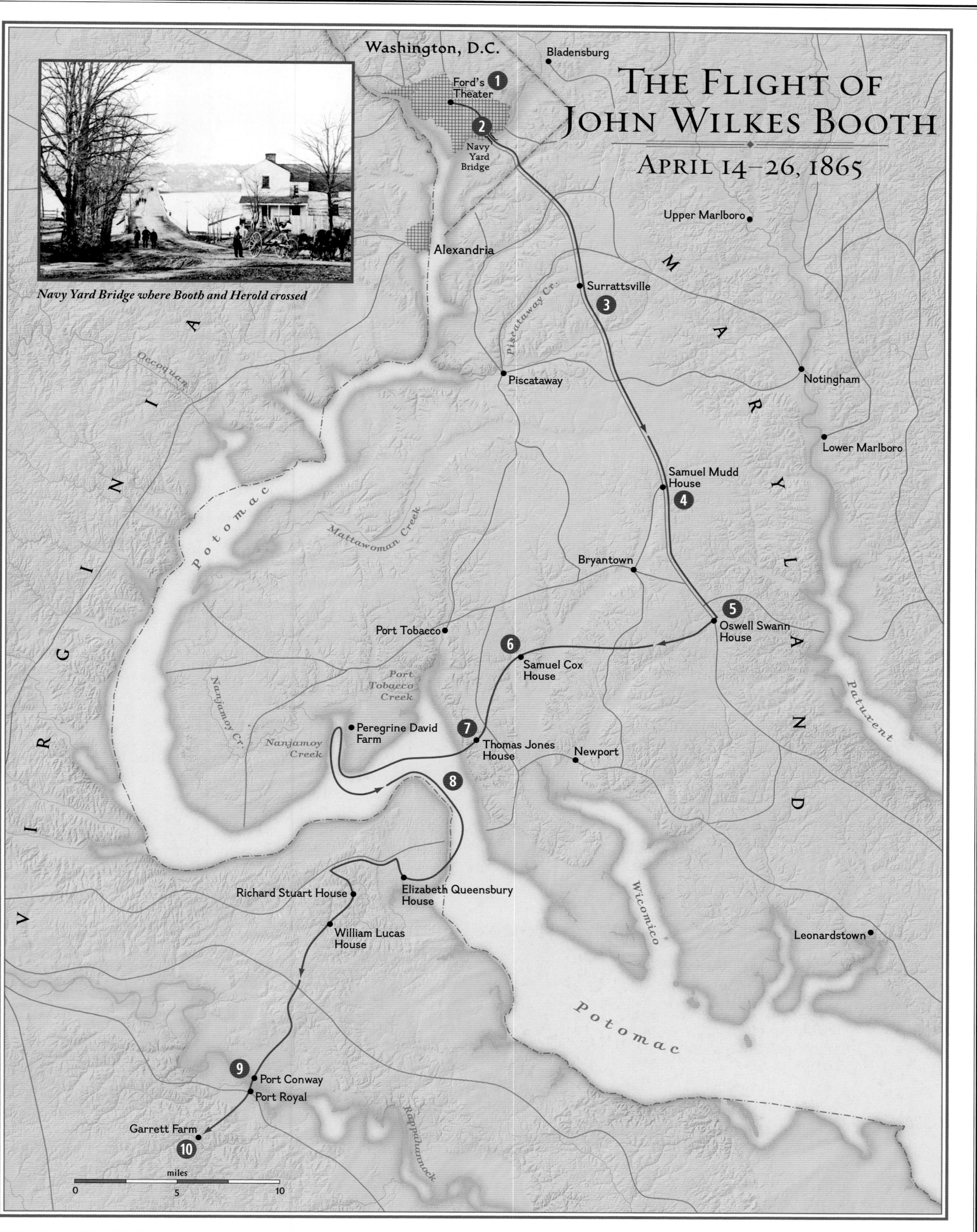

Navy Yard Bridge where Booth and Herold crossed

Lincoln's Long Ride Home

The deadly blow struck at Lincoln was an act of revenge meant to divide and demoralize the Union. But it united Northerners as never before in a massive outpouring of grief and showed how deeply Lincoln had touched and transformed this country. Fittingly, his body would return home now by rail to Springfield, Illinois ❶, for burial, following a route close to that he had taken eastward in 1861 for his inauguration. Before that long ride began, he lay in state at the Capitol in Washington ❷, where wounded soldiers from the city's hospitals, some on crutches, were the first of 25,000 mourners to pass by.

Then on April 21 a funeral train consisting of a burial car for Lincoln's coffin and that of his beloved son Willie—who had died of fever in 1862 and would soon be reinterred beside his father—and coaches carrying Mary Todd Lincoln, sons Tad and Robert, and friends from Illinois left the depot in Washington for Baltimore ❸. Four years earlier, on his way to take office, Lincoln had passed through Baltimore in disguise to avoid attack by proslavery ruffians. Now some 10,000 mourners filed by his open coffin there in three hours before the train continued on to Harrisburg ❹, where an estimated 40,000 turned out to hail the departed chief whose troops had saved Pennsylvania in 1863 and hallowed their ground.

In the days ahead, crowds honoring the president's memory grew to epic proportions, exceeding 300,000 in Philadelphia ❺, by one reckoning, and a half million in New York City ❻, where draft rioters had cursed Lincoln after the Battle of Gettysburg and attacked blacks in the streets. Now by order of Secretary of War Edwin Stanton, who wanted no "discrimination respecting color" in these observances, troops stood by to ensure that blacks marching at the end of a massive procession from City Hall to the railroad depot went unharmed. As the funeral train continued through Albany ❼ and Buffalo ❽ to Cleveland ❾, Columbus ❿, and Indianapolis ⓫, people living in towns too small to warrant a stop stood holding bouquets or lit bonfires at night as it passed by.

Nothing surpassed the heartfelt farewell to Lincoln in Illinois. Mourners thronged the Cook County courthouse in Chicago ⓬ to pay their respects before the train continued on through Joliet ⓭, where 12,000 gathered at midnight. "Come Home," read signs along the tracks addressed to Lincoln in spirit. On May 3 he finally did, reaching Springfield and passing in cortege through a sea of humanity the next day to Oak Ridge Cemetery, where he and Willie came to rest together. ■

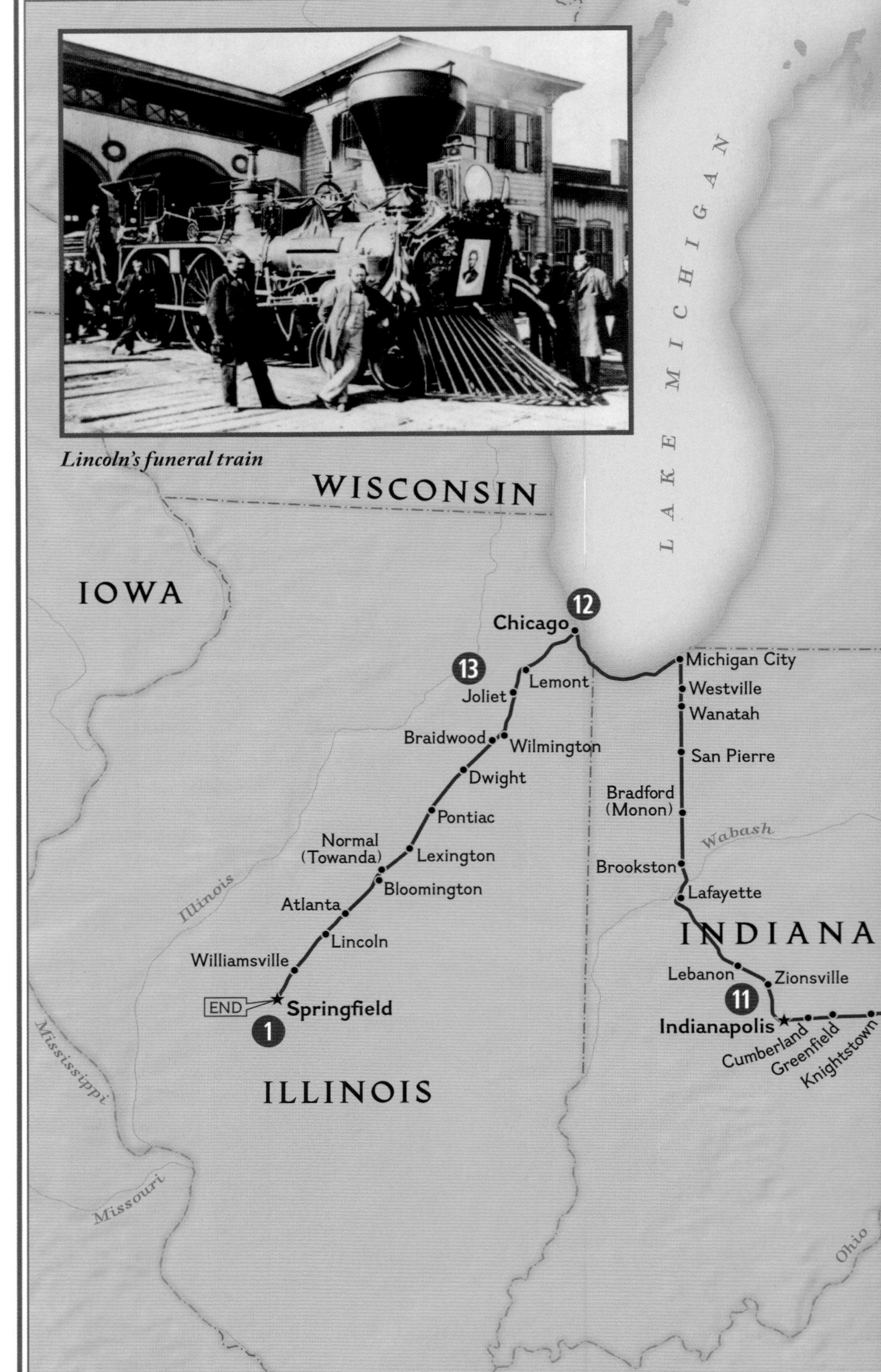

Lincoln's funeral train

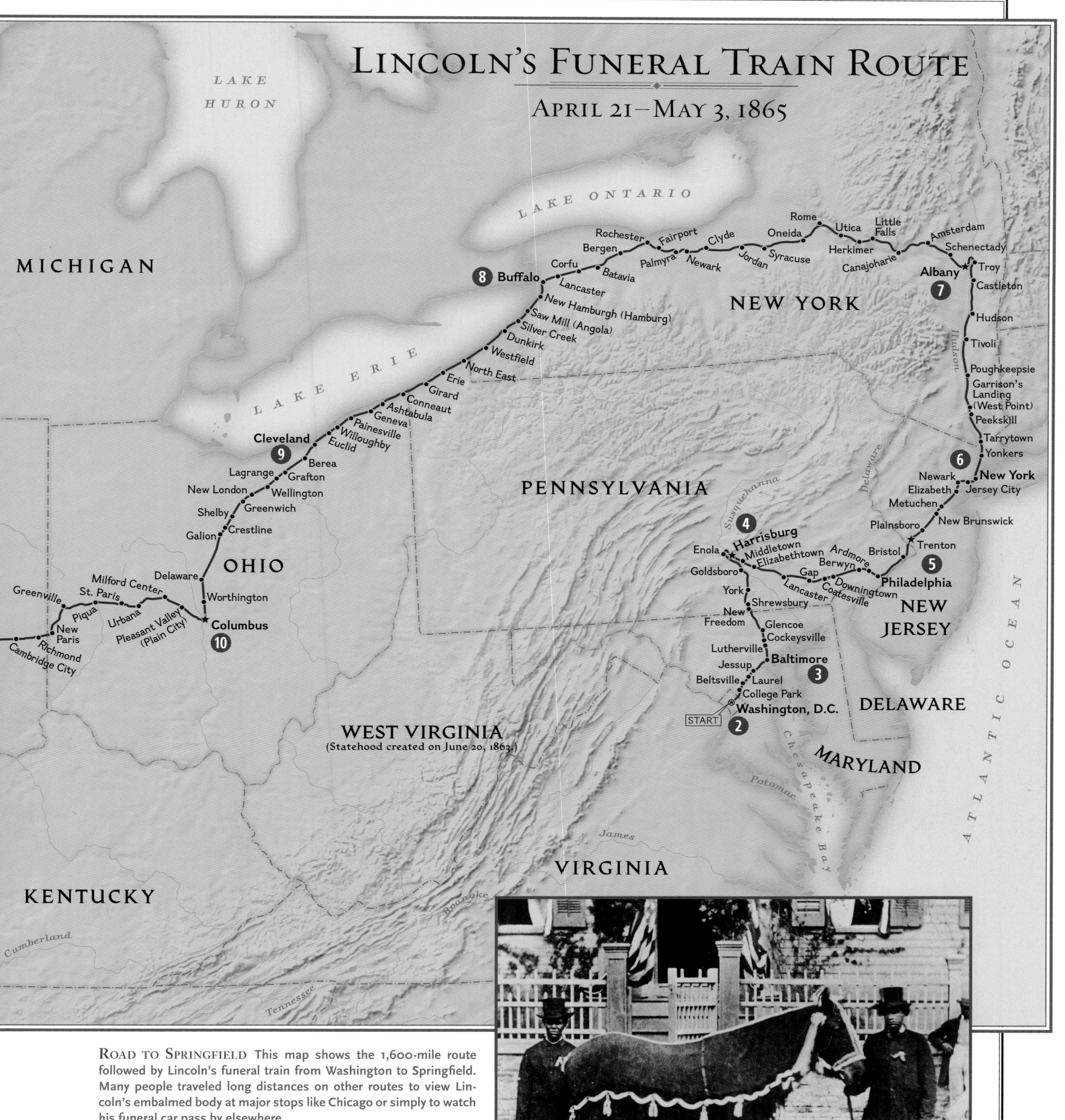

ROAD TO SPRINGFIELD This map shows the 1,600-mile route followed by Lincoln's funeral train from Washington to Springfield. Many people traveled long distances on other routes to view Lincoln's embalmed body at major stops like Chicago or simply to watch his funeral car pass by elsewhere.

⓬ HONORED IN ILLINOIS Mourners pack the streets in Chicago on May 1 as Lincoln's hearse reaches the Cook County courthouse, where he lay in state.

❶ OLD BOB Lincoln's horse, Old Bob—conducted by Reverend Henry Brown (standing behind the horse at near right), a minister long acquainted with the president—followed his hearse in Springfield to Oak Ridge Cemetery, where he was buried on May 4.

Reconstruction

Reconstructing the defeated South and reuniting the nation took 12 years as leaders wrestled with the issue of granting rights to freedmen—freed slaves—and restoring rights to former Rebels. Lincoln was pondering that issue in his last days and bequeathed it to his successor, Andrew Johnson, a Democrat from Tennessee who had opposed secession. Johnson's Reconstruction plan required Southern states to ratify the Thirteenth Amendment, prohibiting slavery, but it did not call for blacks to vote or hold office. "White men alone must manage the South," he declared.

Opposing Johnson were Radical Republicans, who believed that only by granting blacks civil rights and remaking the South could they achieve what Lincoln at Gettysburg called "a new birth of freedom." This served their political interest, for freedmen would support their party at the polls. But Radicals like Congressman Thaddeus Stevens of Pennsylvania held strong convictions. They wanted to see Rebels punished and blacks who had backed the Union—and provided it with nearly 200,000 troops—rewarded. They were appalled when Johnson allowed Southern states to form new governments at conventions dominated by ex-Confederates, resulting in the election of representatives like Alexander Stephens, who had declared slavery the "natural and normal condition" of blacks as Jefferson Davis's vice president. The new state governments passed "Black Codes," severely restricting the rights of freedmen.

Carpetbag

In December 1865, the Republican-dominated Congress refused to recognize the state governments organized under Johnson's plan or seat their representatives. Congress initiated Radical Reconstruction by passing sweeping legislation over the veto of Johnson, who was impeached by his congressional foes in 1868 but acquitted. Tennessee was readmitted to the Union in 1866, but other Southern states were divided by Congress into five military districts, where only black men and those white men who had not taken part in the rebellion or had applied for amnesty were allowed to vote for delegates to new state conventions. States seeking readmission to the Union had to ratify the Fourteenth Amendment—which defined all those born in the United States as citizens regardless of race—and the Fifteenth Amendment, stating that no one could be denied the right to vote because of race "or previous condition of servitude."

Johnson's Accusers **After impeaching Andrew Johnson, the House named these congressmen, including Radical Republicans Benjamin Butler (far left) and Thaddeus Stevens (cane in hand), to prosecute him. Moderate Republicans in the Senate voted with Democrats to acquit Johnson.**

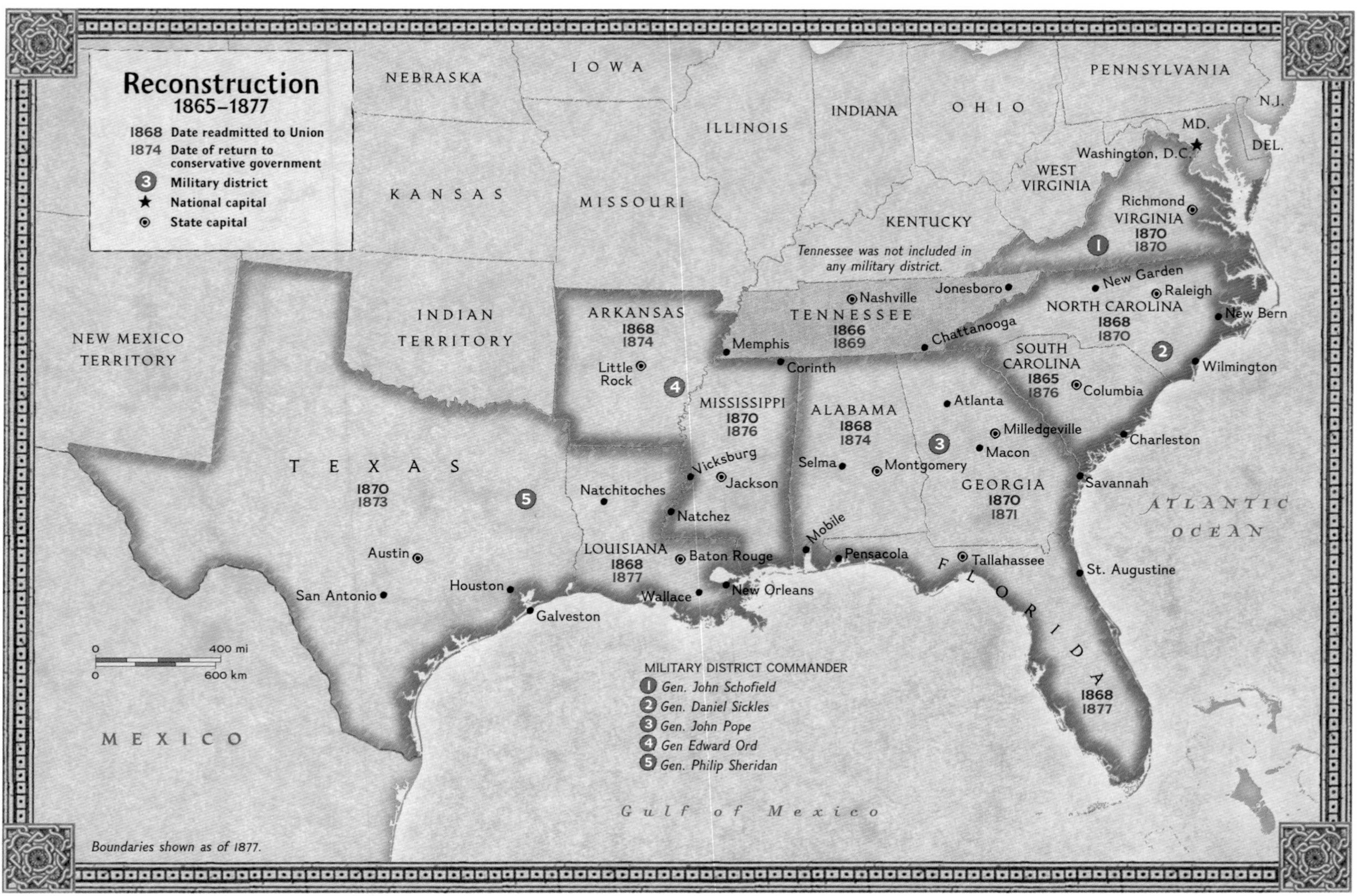

Out from Under Congress divided the South into the five military districts numbered on this National Geographic map. States within these districts remained under military occupation, commanded by the generals listed, until readmitted to the Union. As conservative white Democrats regained control of those states, the civil rights of blacks were drastically curtailed.

Posing as Klansmen Officers wear hoods and gowns seized in Alabama in 1868 during a crackdown on the Ku Klux Klan.

By 1870, states placed under military rule had rejoined the Union on those terms. Most ex-Confederates could now vote, but many whites deeply resented the new political system, which resulted in the election of 17 blacks to the U.S. Congress during Reconstruction. That number was impressive, but blacks in the South were in fact underrepresented in Washington and in state governments, which slipped from the hands of Republican reformers and returned to conservative rule under white Democrats called Redeemers. That was partly the result of terror tactics by the Ku Klux Klan and other secret societies that discouraged blacks from voting and Republican candidates from seeking their votes.

Ulysses Grant, elected president in 1868, sent federal troops into the South to crack down on the Klan. But his authority as a reformer was later undermined by corruption within his Republican administration and among some Republican Reconstruction officials, caricatured as carpetbaggers, or intruders from the North with bag in hand. Not many white men in the North cared deeply about defending the right of black men to vote—or granting that right to women. In 1877, Republican Rutherford B. Hayes, like Grant a former Union general, won a hotly disputed election by compromising with Democrats and removing the last federal troops from the South. Reconstruction was over, and this nation conceived in liberty would have to wait several generations for a new birth of freedom. ■

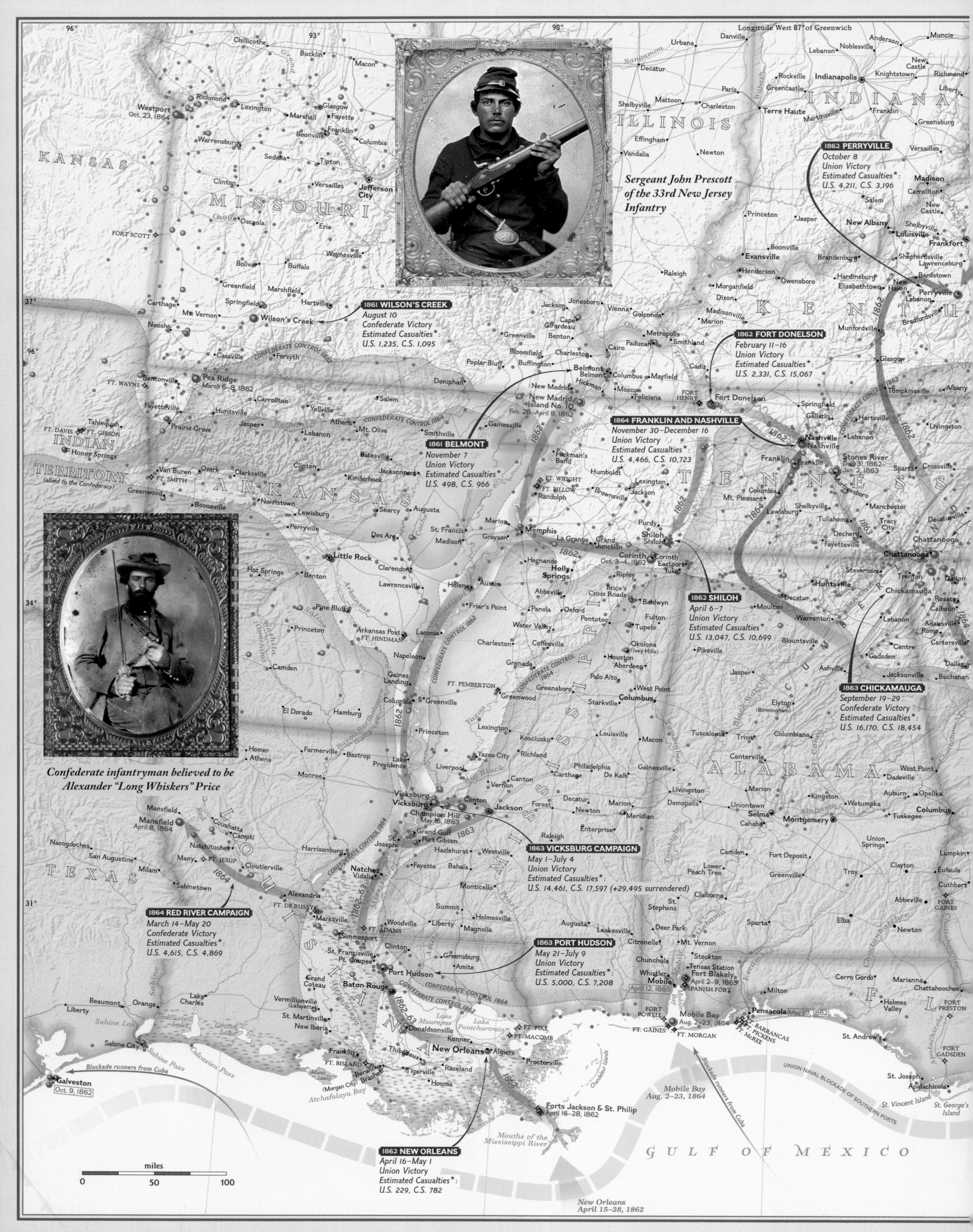

Sergeant John Prescott of the 33rd New Jersey Infantry

Confederate infantryman believed to be Alexander "Long Whiskers" Price

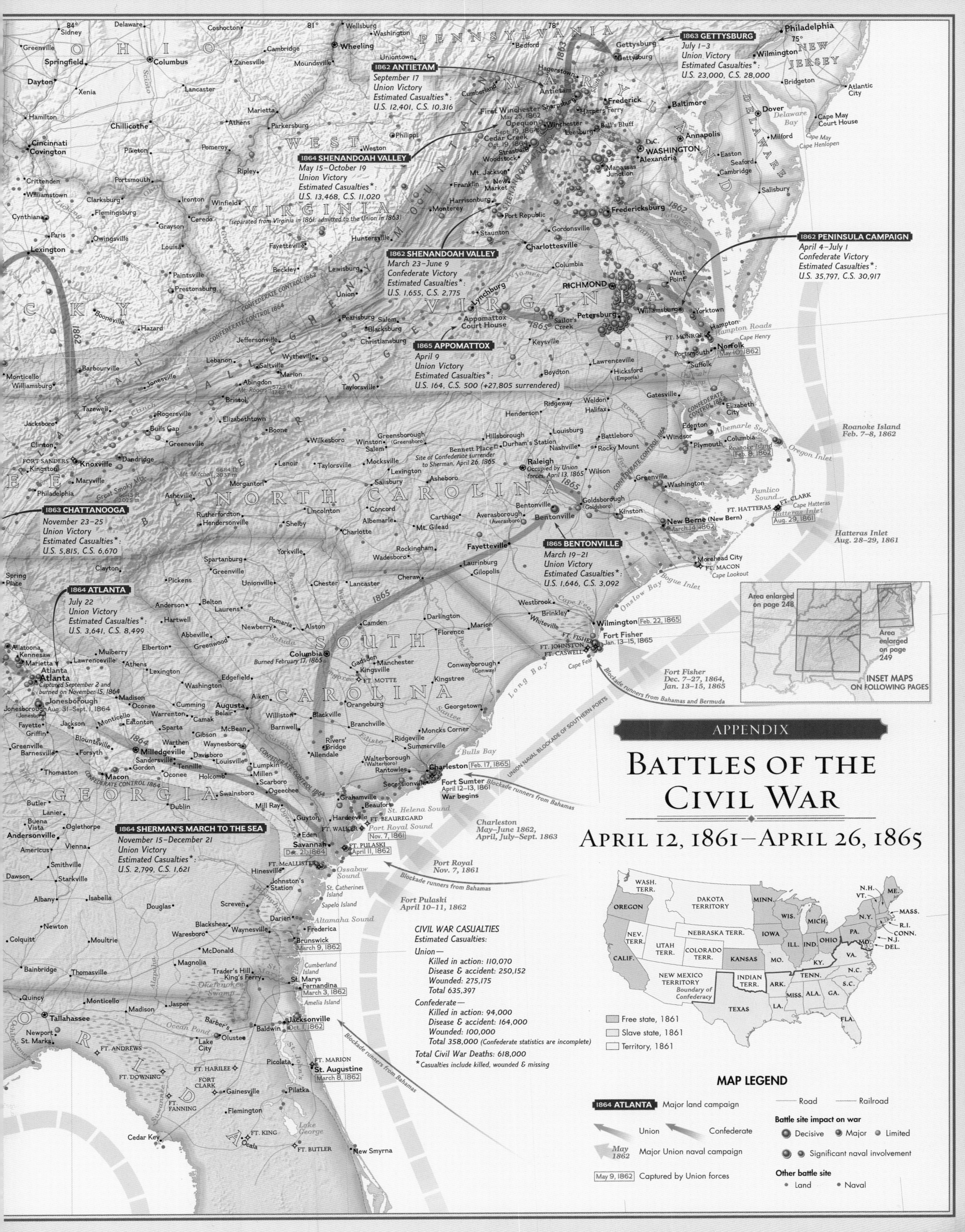
APPENDIX
BATTLES OF THE CIVIL WAR
APRIL 12, 1861–APRIL 26, 1865
1863 GETTYSBURG
July 1–3
Union Victory
Estimated Casualties*:
U.S. 23,000, C.S. 28,000
1862 ANTIETAM
September 17
Union Victory
Estimated Casualties*:
U.S. 12,401, C.S. 10,316
1864 SHENANDOAH VALLEY
May 15–October 19
Union Victory
Estimated Casualties*:
U.S. 13,468, C.S. 11,020
1862 SHENANDOAH VALLEY
March 23–June 9
Confederate Victory
Estimated Casualties*:
U.S. 1,655, C.S. 2,775
1862 PENINSULA CAMPAIGN
April 4–July 1
Confederate Victory
Estimated Casualties*:
U.S. 35,797, C.S. 30,917
1865 APPOMATTOX
April 9
Union Victory
Estimated Casualties*:
U.S. 164, C.S. 500 (+27,805 surrendered)
1863 CHATTANOOGA
November 23–25
Union Victory
Estimated Casualties*:
U.S. 5,815, C.S. 6,670
1865 BENTONVILLE
March 19–21
Union Victory
Estimated Casualties*:
U.S. 1,646, C.S. 3,092
1864 ATLANTA
July 22
Union Victory
Estimated Casualties*:
U.S. 3,641, C.S. 8,499
1864 SHERMAN'S MARCH TO THE SEA
November 15–December 21
Union Victory
Estimated Casualties*:
U.S. 2,799, C.S. 1,621
Roanoke Island
Feb. 7–8, 1862
Hatteras Inlet
Aug. 28–29, 1861
Fort Fisher
Dec. 7–27, 1864,
Jan. 13–15, 1865
Charleston
May–June 1862,
April, July–Sept. 1863
Port Royal
Nov. 7, 1861
Fort Pulaski
April 10–11, 1862
Fort Sumter
April 12–13, 1861
War begins
Blockade runners from Bahamas and Bermuda
Blockade runners from Bahamas
UNION NAVAL BLOCKADE OF SOUTHERN PORTS
Raleigh
Occupied by Union forces, April 13, 1865
Bennett Place
Site of Confederate surrender to Sherman, April 26, 1865
Columbia
Burned February 17, 1865
Atlanta
Captured September 2 and burned on November 15, 1864
Norfolk May 10, 1862
Wilmington Feb. 22, 1865
Fort Fisher Jan. 13–15, 1865
Charleston Feb. 17, 1865
Savannah Dec. 21, 1864
FT. PULASKI April 11, 1862
Port Royal Sound Nov. 7, 1861
Brunswick March 9, 1862
Fernandina March 3, 1862
Jacksonville Oct. 1, 1862
St. Augustine March 8, 1862
New Berne (New Bern) March 14, 1862
Roanoke Island Feb. 8, 1862
Hatteras Inlet Aug. 29, 1861
PENNSYLVANIA
MARYLAND
DELAWARE
NEW JERSEY
OHIO
WEST VIRGINIA
(separated from Virginia in 1861, admitted to the Union in 1863)
VIRGINIA
KENTUCKY
TENNESSEE
NORTH CAROLINA
SOUTH CAROLINA
GEORGIA
FLORIDA
ALLEGHENY MOUNTAINS
BLUE RIDGE
CONFEDERATE CONTROL 1862
CONFEDERATE CONTROL 1864
CONFEDERATE CONTROL 1863
Philadelphia
Gettysburg
Wilmington
Bridgeton
Atlantic City
Dover
Cape May Court House
Milford
Cape May
Cape Henlopen
Frederick
Baltimore
Harpers Ferry
Hagerstown
Sharpsburg
Antietam
First Winchester May 25, 1862
Opequon Sept. 19, 1864
Cedar Creek Oct. 19, 1864
Winchester
Leesburg
Ball's Bluff
Annapolis
WASHINGTON D.C.
Alexandria
Manassas Junction
Fredericksburg
Strasburg
Woodstock
Mt. Jackson
New Market
Harrisonburg
Port Republic
Staunton
Charlottesville
Gordonsville
Columbia
RICHMOND
Lynchburg
Appomattox Court House
Sailor's Creek
Petersburg
Williamsburg
Yorktown
West Point
Hampton
Hampton Roads
FT. MONROE
Cape Henry
Portsmouth
Suffolk
Keysville
Lawrenceville
Hicksford (Emporia)
Boydton
Wheeling
Washington
Wellsburg
Uniontown
Bedford
Cumberland
Moundsville
Cambridge
Zanesville
Columbus
Springfield
Dayton
Xenia
Sidney
Greenville
Delaware
Coshocton
Lancaster
Marietta
Parkersburg
Athens
Chillicothe
Hamilton
Cincinnati
Covington
Piketon
Pomeroy
Philippi
Weston
Ripley
Portsmouth
Crittenden
Williamstown
Clarksburg
Flemingsburg
Ironton
Winfield
Ceredo
Grayson
Cynthiana
Paris
Owingsville
Louisa
Lexington
Fayetteville
Huntersville
Beckley
Lewisburg
Paintsville
Prestonsburg
Union
Franklin
Monterey
Booneville
Hazard
Pearisburg
Salem
Blacksburg
Christiansburg
Jeffersonville
Wytheville
Saltville
Marion
Abingdon
Mt. Rogers 5729 ft 1746 m
Lebanon
Barbourville
Jonesville
Monticello
Williamsburg
Taylorsville
Bristol
Tazewell
Rogersville
Elizabethtown
Jacksboro
Bulls Gap
Boone
Greeneville
Clinton
FORT SANDERS
Kingston
Knoxville
Dandridge
Maryville
Philadelphia
Great Smoky Mts. 6643 ft 2025 m
Mt. Mitchell 6684 ft 2037 m
Asheville
Morganton
Lenoir
Wilkesboro
Taylorsville
Winston Salem
Greensborough (Greensboro)
Mocksville
Lexington
Salisbury
Asheboro
Hillsborough
Durham's Station
Ridgeway
Henderson
Louisburg
Weldon
Halifax
Nashville
Battleboro
Rocky Mount
Wilson
Goldsborough (Goldsboro)
Kinston
Greenville
Washington
Plymouth
Windsor
Edenton
Elizabeth City
Gatesville
Columbia
Oregon Inlet
Albemarle Snd.
Pamlico Sound
FT. HATTERAS
FT. CLARK
Cape Hatteras
Morehead City
FT. MACON
Cape Lookout
Beaufort
Bogue Inlet
Onslow Bay
Cape Fear
Bentonville
Averasborough (Averasboro)
Carthage
Mt. Gilead
Fayetteville
Rockingham
Wadesboro
Laurinburg
Gilopolis
Cheraw
Lincolnton
Concord
Albemarle
Charlotte
Shelby
Rutherfordton
Hendersonville
Yorkville
Spartanburg
Greenville
Unionville
Chester
Lancaster
Pickens
Anderson
Belton
Laurens
Hartwell
Abbeville
Greenwood
Newberry
Pomaria
Alston
Camden
Darlington
Florence
Marion
Westbrook
Brinkley
Whiteville
Wilmington
FT. FISHER
FT. JOHNSTON
FT. CASWELL
Long Bay
Conwayborough (Conway)
Kingstree
Gadsden
Manchester
Kingsville
FT. MOTTE
Georgetown
Santee
Monks Corner
Bulls Bay
Orangeburg
Branchville
Edgefield
Aiken
Augusta
Belair
Williston
Blackville
Barnwell
Ridgeville
Summerville
Rivers' Bridge
Allendale
Walterborough (Walterboro)
Rantowles
Secessionville
Grahamville
Beaufort
St. Helena Sound
FT. BEAUREGARD
Hardeeville
FT. WALKER
Guyton
Eden
FT. McALLISTER
Hinesville
Ossabaw Sound
Johnston's Station
St. Catherines Island
Sapelo Island
Darien
Altamaha Sound
Frederica
Brunswick
Cumberland Island
St. Marys
Amelia Island
Kingsland
Allatoona
Kennesaw
Marietta
Lawrenceville
Atlanta
Mulberry
Elberton
Athens
Lexington
Washington
Jonesborough (Jonesboro)
Jonesborough Aug. 31–Sept. 1, 1864
Fayette
Griffin
Jackson
Monticello
Eatonton
Madison
Oconee
Warrenton
Camak
Cumming
Sparta
Gibson
McBean
Waynesboro
Warthen
Milledgeville
Sandersville
Davisboro
Louisville
Gordon
Tennille
Macon
Oconee
Holcomb
Lumpkin
Millen
Scarboro
Ogeechee
Swainsboro
Dublin
Mill Ray
Greenville
Barnesville
Forsyth
Thomaston
Butler
Lanier
Buena Vista
Oglethorpe
Andersonville
Americus
Vienna
Smithville
Dawson
Starkville
Albany
Isabella
Douglas
Screven
Blackshear
Waresboro
Waynesville
Newton
Colquitt
Moultrie
McDonald
Magnolia
Trader's Hill
King's Ferry
Okefenokee Swamp
Bainbridge
Thomasville
Quincy
Monticello
Madison
Jasper
Tallahassee
Newport
St. Marks
Barber's
Ocean Pond
Olustee
Lake City
Baldwin
Jacksonville
Picolata
FT. MARION
St. Augustine
FT. ANDREWS
FT. HARILEE
FT. DOWNING
FORT CLARK
Gainesville
FT. FANNING
Palatka
Flemington
Lake George
FT. KING
Ocala
FT. BUTLER
Cedar Key
New Smyrna
Spring Place
Clayton
Area enlarged on page 248
Area enlarged on page 249
INSET MAPS ON FOLLOWING PAGES
WASH. TERR.
OREGON
DAKOTA TERRITORY
MINN.
WIS.
MICH.
N.Y.
VT.
N.H.
ME.
MASS.
R.I.
CONN.
N.J.
DEL.
MD.
PA.
OHIO
IND.
ILL.
IOWA
NEBRASKA TERR.
NEV. TERR.
UTAH TERR.
COLORADO TERR.
KANSAS
MO.
KY.
VA.
CALIF.
NEW MEXICO TERRITORY
INDIAN TERR.
TENN.
N.C.
S.C.
ARK.
MISS.
ALA.
GA.
LA.
TEXAS
FLA.
Boundary of Confederacy
Free state, 1861
Slave state, 1861
Territory, 1861
CIVIL WAR CASUALTIES
Estimated Casualties:
Union—
Killed in action: 110,070
Disease & accident: 250,152
Wounded: 275,175
Total 635,397
Confederate—
Killed in action: 94,000
Disease & accident: 164,000
Wounded: 100,000
Total 358,000 (Confederate statistics are incomplete)
Total Civil War Deaths: 618,000
*Casualties include killed, wounded & missing
MAP LEGEND
1864 ATLANTA Major land campaign
Union
Confederate
May 1862 Major Union naval campaign
May 9, 1862 Captured by Union forces
Road
Railroad
Battle site impact on war
Decisive
Major
Limited
Significant naval involvement
Other battle site
Land
Naval

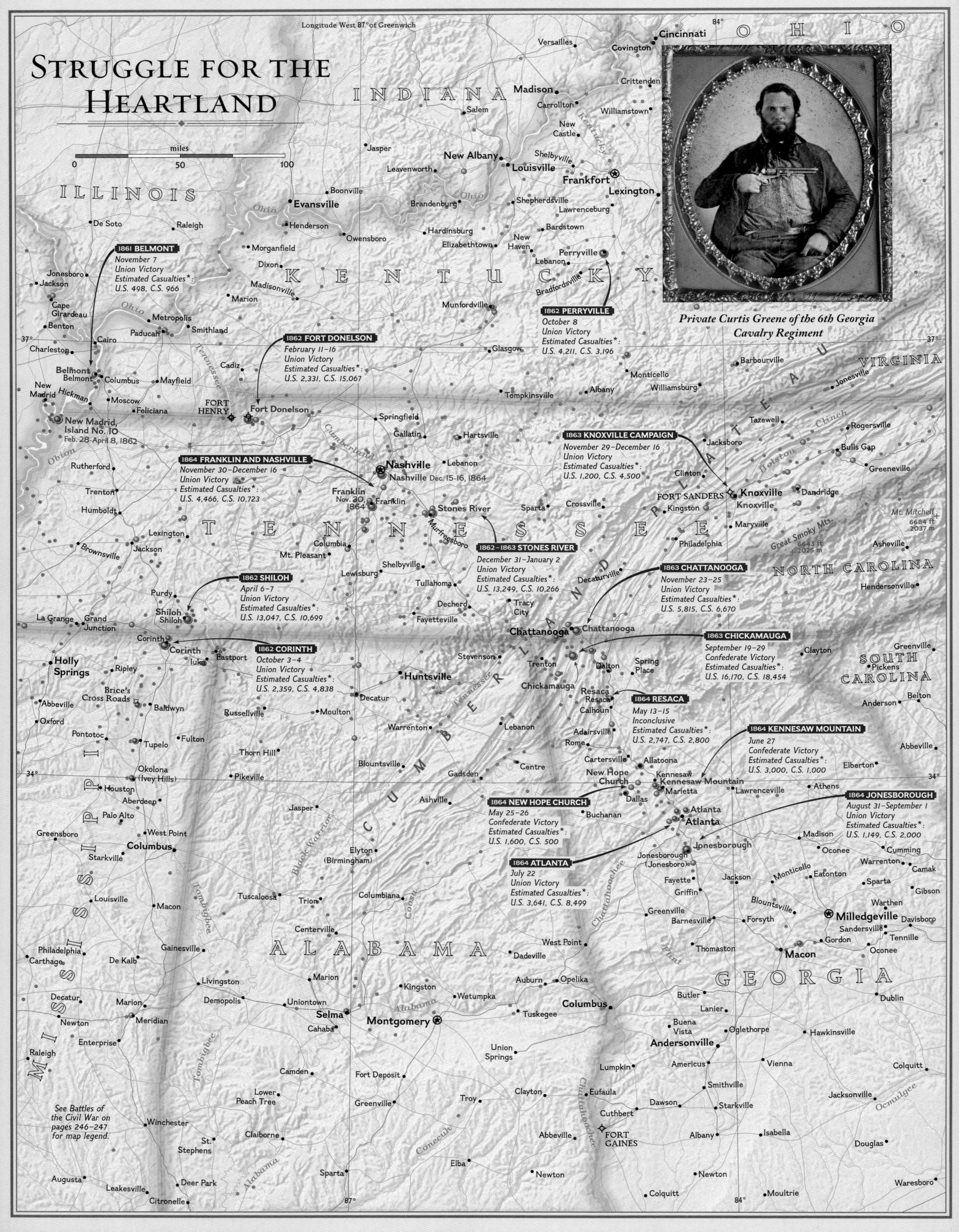

STRUGGLE FOR THE HEARTLAND
miles
0
50
100
Longitude West 87° of Greenwich
84°
87°
37°
34°
ILLINOIS
INDIANA
OHIO
KENTUCKY
TENNESSEE
VIRGINIA
NORTH CAROLINA
SOUTH CAROLINA
GEORGIA
ALABAMA
MISSISSIPPI
CUMBERLAND PLATEAU
1861 BELMONT
November 7
Union Victory
Estimated Casualties*:
U.S. 498, C.S. 966
1862 FORT DONELSON
February 11–16
Union Victory
Estimated Casualties*:
U.S. 2,331, C.S. 15,067
1862 PERRYVILLE
October 8
Union Victory
Estimated Casualties*:
U.S. 4,211, C.S. 3,196
1864 FRANKLIN AND NASHVILLE
November 30–December 16
Union Victory
Estimated Casualties*:
U.S. 4,466, C.S. 10,723
1863 KNOXVILLE CAMPAIGN
November 29–December 16
Union Victory
Estimated Casualties*:
U.S. 1,200, C.S. 4,500
1862–1863 STONES RIVER
December 31–January 2
Union Victory
Estimated Casualties*:
U.S. 13,249, C.S. 10,266
1862 SHILOH
April 6–7
Union Victory
Estimated Casualties*:
U.S. 13,047, C.S. 10,699
1863 CHATTANOOGA
November 23–25
Union Victory
Estimated Casualties*:
U.S. 5,815, C.S. 6,670
1862 CORINTH
October 3–4
Union Victory
Estimated Casualties*:
U.S. 2,359, C.S. 4,838
1863 CHICKAMAUGA
September 19–29
Confederate Victory
Estimated Casualties*:
U.S. 16,170, C.S. 18,454
1864 RESACA
May 13–15
Inconclusive
Estimated Casualties*:
U.S. 2,747, C.S. 2,800
1864 KENNESAW MOUNTAIN
June 27
Confederate Victory
Estimated Casualties*:
U.S. 3,000, C.S. 1,000
1864 NEW HOPE CHURCH
May 25–26
Confederate Victory
Estimated Casualties*:
U.S. 1,600, C.S. 500
1864 JONESBOROUGH
August 31–September 1
Union Victory
Estimated Casualties*:
U.S. 1,149, C.S. 2,000
1864 ATLANTA
July 22
Union Victory
Estimated Casualties*:
U.S. 3,641, C.S. 8,499
New Madrid, Island No. 10
Feb. 28–April 8, 1862
Nashville Dec. 15–16, 1864
Franklin Nov. 30, 1864
FORT HENRY
Fort Donelson
FORT SANDERS
FORT GAINES
Mt. Mitchell 6684 ft 2037 m
Great Smoky Mts. 6643 ft 2025 m
Cincinnati
Covington
Versailles
Madison
Carrollton
Crittenden
Williamstown
New Castle
Salem
Jasper
New Albany
Louisville
Leavenworth
Shelbyville
Frankfort
Lexington
Boonville
Evansville
Brandenburg
Shepherdsville
Lawrenceburg
De Soto
Raleigh
Henderson
Owensboro
Hardinsburg
Bardstown
Elizabethtown
New Haven
Lebanon
Perryville
Morganfield
Dixon
Madisonville
Marion
Bradfordsville
Jonesboro
Jackson
Cape Girardeau
Benton
Metropolis
Smithland
Paducah
Munfordville
Cairo
Charleston
Glasgow
Cadiz
Mayfield
Columbus
Belmont
Monticello
Barbourville
Williamsburg
Jonesville
New Madrid
Hickman
Moscow
Feliciana
Tompkinsville
Albany
Springfield
Gallatin
Hartsville
Tazewell
Rogersville
Jacksboro
Bulls Gap
Greeneville
Rutherford
Lebanon
Nashville
Clinton
Knoxville
Dandridge
Trenton
Humboldt
Franklin
Stones River
Murfreesboro
Sparta
Crossville
Kingston
Maryville
Lexington
Jackson
Brownsville
Columbia
Mt. Pleasant
Philadelphia
Asheville
Shelbyville
Lewisburg
Tullahoma
Decatur ville
Hendersonville
Purdy
Shiloh
Decherd
Tracy City
La Grange
Grand Junction
Fayetteville
Chattanooga
Corinth
Iuka
Eastport
Stevenson
Trenton
Dalton
Spring Place
Clayton
Greenville
Holly Springs
Ripley
Huntsville
Chickamauga
Resaca
Calhoun
Pickens
Belton
Brice's Cross Roads
Baldwyn
Decatur
Anderson
Abbeville
Oxford
Russellville
Moulton
Warrenton
Lebanon
Adairsville
Pontotoc
Tupelo
Fulton
Rome
Abbeville
Thorn Hill
Cartersville
Allatoona
Elberton
Okolona (Ivey Hills)
Pikeville
Blountsville
Gadsden
Centre
New Hope Church
Kennesaw
Kennesaw Mountain
Marietta
Lawrenceville
Athens
Houston
Aberdeen
Ashville
Dallas
Palo Alto
Jasper
Buchanan
Atlanta
West Point
Greensboro
Columbus
Madison
Starkville
Elyton (Birmingham)
Jonesborough
Jonesborough (Jonesboro)
Oconee
Cumming
Warrenton
Camak
Fayette
Jackson
Monticello
Eatonton
Sparta
Gibson
Griffin
Louisville
Macon
Tuscaloosa
Trion
Columbiana
Warthen
Milledgeville
Davisboro
Blountsville
Greenville
Barnesville
Forsyth
Sandersville
Tennille
Centerville
Gordon
Philadelphia
Gainesville
Carthage
De Kalb
West Point
Dadeville
Thomaston
Macon
Oconee
Auburn
Opelika
Livingston
Marion
Kingston
Decatur
Marion
Demopolis
Uniontown
Wetumpka
Columbus
Butler
Dublin
Newton
Meridian
Selma
Cahaba
Montgomery
Tuskegee
Lanier
Buena Vista
Oglethorpe
Hawkinsville
Enterprise
Andersonville
Raleigh
Union Springs
Americus
Vienna
Lumpkin
Colquitt
Camden
Fort Deposit
Smithville
Lower Peach Tree
Troy
Clayton
Eufaula
Jacksonville
Greenville
Dawson
Starkville
Cuthbert
Winchester
St. Stephens
Claiborne
Abbeville
Albany
Isabella
Douglas
Elba
Augusta
Deer Park
Sparta
Newton
Newton
Leakesville
Citronelle
Colquitt
Moultrie
Waresboro
Ohio
Tennessee
Cumberland
Obion
Kentucky
Clinch
Holston
Tennessee
Black Warrior
Tombigbee
Coosa
Chattahoochee
Flint
Alabama
Conecuh
Ocmulgee
Private Curtis Greene of the 6th Georgia Cavalry Regiment
See Battles of the Civil War on pages 246–247 for map legend.

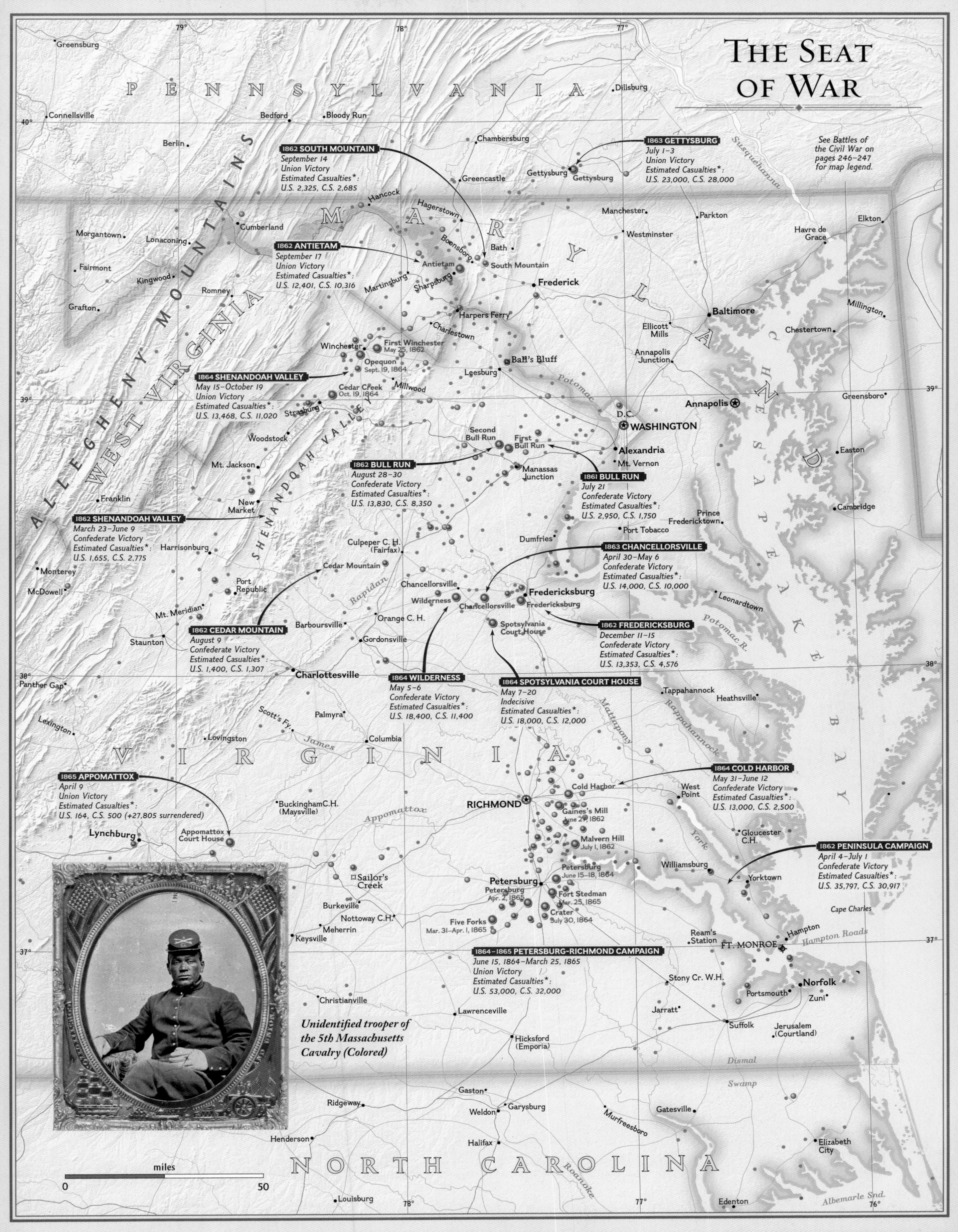

Unidentified trooper of the 5th Massachusetts Cavalry (Colored)

ILLUSTRATION CREDITS

ABBREVIATION KEY
FMTW: *Frank and Marie-Therese Wood Print Collection, Alexandria, VA*
LC: *Library of Congress, Prints and Photographs Division*
LCGM: *Library of Congress, Geography and Maps Division*
MOLLUS-MASS: *Military Order of the Loyal Legion of the United States-Massachusetts*
MOC: *Museum of the Confederacy, Richmond, VA*
NARA: *National Archives and Records Administration*
USAMHI: *United States Army Military History Institute*
VHS: *Virginia Historical Society, Richmond, VA*

FRONT MATTER 1, Kansas State Historical Society; 2-3, LC-DIG-CWPB-04753; 4 (UP LE), NARA; 4 (UP RT), LC-USZ62-66616; 5 (UP LE), LC-B8184-7964-A; 5 (UP CTR), LC-DIG-cwpb-01334; 5 (UP RT), LC-DIG-cwpbh-04230; 8 (LE), LCGM, CA000001; 8 (RT), LCGM, CA000018; 9 (LO), Photo by Neil Kagan/Courtesy of the Winchester-Frederick County Historical Society/Stonewall Jackson's Headquarters Museum Collection; 9 (UP), Jedediah Hotchkiss Papers, Stewart Bell Jr. Archives Room, Handley Regional Library, Winchester, VA; 10, Courtesy MOLLUS-MASS and USAMHI; 11 (UP), LCGM, CWS00013A; 12, LC-DIG-cwpb-00124; 13 (UP), MOC; 13 (LO LE), MOC; 13 (LO RT), LCGM, CW0642000; 14 (UP), LCGM, CW0012700; 14 (LO), LCGM, PM009504; 15, VHS.

CHAPTER 1 16-17, NARA; 18 (UP LE), LC-USZC4-2439; 18 (UP RT), LC-USZC4-6189; 18 (LO), MOC; 19 (LE), Kansas State Historical Society; 19 (UP RT), New York Historical Society, neg. #1574; 19 (LO CTR), MOC; 19 (UP CTR), National Park Service, Historic Graphic Collection, Harpers Ferry Center; 19 (LO RT), NARA; 20, Courtesy MOLLUS-MASS and USAMHI; 20-21, LCGM, CW0014100; 21 (LO), The Historic New Orleans Collection; 22 (LO LE), Robin Stanford; 22-23, LCGM, CW0013200; 22 (LO CTR), 22 (LO CTR), Harvard University, Peabody Museum, 35-5-10/53043; 22 (LO RT), Harvard University, Peabody Museum, 35-5-10/53048; 23 (LO LE), Harvard University, Peabody Museum, 35-5-10/53037; 23 (LO RT), Harvard University, Peabody Museum, 35-5-10/53040; 24 (UP LE), NARA; 24 (UP RT), LC-USZ62-39380; 24 (LO), Louisiana State Museum; 25 (LO), Getty Images; 25 (UP), NG Maps; 26 (UP), LC; 26 (LO), LC-USZ62-14834; 27 (LO), Chicago Historical Society; 28 (LO), Boston Atheneum; 28-29, LCGM, CW0024000; 29 (LO), LC-USZ62-5962; 30, VHS; 31 (UP), NARA; 31 (LO), LC-USZC4-528; 32 (UP), LC-DIG-ppmsca-08357; 32 (LO), Cook Collection, Valentine Richmond History Center; 32-33, LCGM, CW0014900; 33 (LO), Courtesy of Picture History; 34 (LO), LC-USZ62-40070; 34-35, LCGM, CW0011000; 35 (LO), NARA; 36, LCGM, CW0544000; 37 (UP), LC-USZC4-5371; 37 (LO), LC-USZC4-5178; 38 (LO), LC-DIG-cwpb-06588; 39 (UP LE), NARA; 39 (UP RT), LC-DIG-cwpb-05378; 39 (LO), LC-USZ62-3131; 40 (UP), Courtesy of the Stonewall Jackson Collection, Stonewall Jackson Foundation, Lexington, VA; 40-41, LCGM, CW0566000; 41 (LO LE), LC-DIG-cwpb-00964; 41 (LO RT), LC-DIG-cwpb-00953; 42, Western Reserve Historical Society; 42-43, The Library of Virginia; 43 (UP LE), LC-USZ62-90934; 43 (UP RT), LC-DIG-cwpb-06714; 44 (LO), LC-USZC2-3134; 44-45, LCGM, CW0368A00.

CHAPTER 2 46-47, LC-USZ62-66616; 48 (UP), Courtesy Vicksburg National Military Park; 48 (LO), MOC; 49 (UP LE), MOC; 49 (UP RT), LC-DIG-cwpb-00193; 49 (LO LE), LC-DIG-cwpb-04339; 49 (LO RT), NARA; 50, LC-USZC2-1985; 50-51, LCGM, CW0023500; 52, Courtesy MOLLUS-MASS and USAMHI; 52 (LO), LC-USZ62-76968; 52-53 (UP), LCGM, CW0412000; 53 (LO), LC-USZ62-133797; 54 (UP LE), LC-USZ62-3580; 54 (UP RT), State Historical Society of Missouri, Columbia, #021000; 55, LC-USZ62-36385; 56 (UP), LC-USZC4-1910; 56 (LO LE), LC-USZ62-59432; 56 (LO RT), LC-USZ62-59433; 56-57, LCGM, CW0436000; 57 (LO), LC-USZ62-6204; 58 (LO), LC-DIG-cwpbh-03121; 58-59, LCGM, CW0037000; 59 (LO), Courtesy MOLLUS-MASS and USAMHI; 60 (LO), VHS; 60 (UP), VHS; 61 (UP), LC-USZC4-7170; 61 (LO), VHS; 62 (UP), LC-DIG-cwpb-05369; 62 (LO), LC-USZ62-3450; 63 (LE), LCGM, CW0317120; 63 (RT), LCGM, CW0317100; 64 (UP), LC-DIG-cwpbh-04058; 64 (LO), LC-USZC2-3065; 64-65, LCGM, CW0559000; 65 (LO), LC-DIG-cwpb-01061; 66, Chicago Historical Society; 66-67, LCGM, CW0001700; 68 (LO), MOC; 69 (LO), Fredericksburg and Spotsylvania National Military Park; 69 (UP), MOC; 70, Greenville County Museum of Art; 71, LCGM, CWH00089; 72 (UP), LC-USZ61-164; 72 (LO), LC-USZC4-10797; 73, LCGM, CWH00090; 74, LC-USZC4-5108; 75 (UP RT), MOC; 75 (LO), LC-USZC4-5106; 75, LCGM, CWH00096; 76 (LO), LC-DIG-cwpb-05665; 76-77, LCGM, CW0003000; 77 (LO), NARA; 78 (LO), LC-DIG-cwpb-01001; 79 (LO), LC-DIG-cwpb-01005; 79 (UP), LC-DIG-cwpb-01580; 80 (UP LE), LC-USZ6-928; 80 (CTR), NASM Smithsonian Institution; 80-81, VHS; 82, LC-DIG-cwpb-04402; 83, LC-DIG-cwpb-00159; 84 (LO), Courtesy MOLLUS-MASS and USAMHI; 84-85, FMTW; 85, LC-DIG-cwpb-07546; 86, LC-DIG-cwpb-04402; 86-87, LCGM, CW0621000; 88, VHS; 89 (LO), LC-DIG-cwpbh-03387; 89 (UP RT), LC-USZC4-5820; 90 (LO), LC-DIG-cwpb-00260; 90 (UP), LC-DIG-cwpb-06341; 91, VHS; 92 (UP), LC-USZ62-57508; 92 (LO), LC-DIG-cwpb-00220; 93 (LO), VHS; 93 (UP), VHS; 94, VHS; 95, Valentine Richmond History Center; 96-97, VHS; 96 (LO), LC-DIG-cwpb-00237; 97 (LO), LC-DIG-cwpb-04017; 97 (UP), LC-USZ62-55424; 98 (LO), LC-USZC2-3813; 98 (UP), LC-DIG-cwpb-00262; 99 (LO), LC-DIG-cwpb-04106; 99 (UP), LC-USZ62-65332; 100-101, VHS; 100 (LO), LC-DIG-pga-01231; 101, Courtesy MOLLUS-MASS and USAMHI; 102, Collection of Michael J. McAfee; 103, LCGM, CW0253000; 104 (UP), FMTW; 105 (LO LE), LC-DIG-cwpb-01097; 105 (UP RT), LC-DIG-cwpbh-00839; 106 (LO), LC-DIG-cwpb-01099; 106 (UP), NARA; 107 (UP), LC-DIG-ppmsca-07751; 107 (LO), LC-DIG-cwpb-07081; 108, NARA; 109 (UP LE), LC-USZ62-79752; 109 (UP RT), LC-DIG-cwpb-00664; 110 (LO), LC-DIG-cwpb-01131; 111 (UP LE), LC-DIG-cwpb-01109; 111 (CTR), LC-DIG-cwpb-01085; 112 (UP), Chicago Historical Society; 112 (LO), LC-DIG-cwpb-01436; 113 (LO), LCGM, CW0267000; 114 (LO), LC-USZ62-80740; 115 (UP RT), LC-USZC4-7984; 115 (CTR), The Library of Virginia; 115 (LO), LC-USZ62-13178; 116 (LO), LC-USZC4-9829; 116-117 (UP), LCGM, PM009560; 117 (UP), LC-DIG-cwpb-01318; 118 (UP LE), C. Paul Loane Collection; 118 (LO LE), MOC; 118 (LO RT), Courtesy MOLLUS-MASS and USAMHI; 118-119, VHS; 119 (LO), FMTW.

CHAPTER 3 120-121, LC-B8184-7964-A; 122 (UP), Courtesy of West Point Museum, United States Military Academy, West Point, NY; 122 (LO), FMTW; 123 (UP LE), Old Court House Museum Collection, Vicksburg, Mississippi; 123 (UP CTR), NARA; 123 (UP RT), Fredericksburg and Spotsylvania National Military Park; 123 (LO LE), Chicago Historical Society; 123 (LO RT), C. Paul Loane Collection; 124 (LO), Ohio Historical Society; 124-125 (LO), LCGM, CW0442000; 125 (LO), LC-USZ62-12777; 126 (LO), LC-DIG-cwpb-06577; 126-127, LCGM, CW0294000; 127 (LO), LC-DIG-cwpb-00943; 128 (UP), LC; 128 (LO), FMTW; 129 (LO), LCGM, CW0280000; 130 (UP LE), Courtesy MOLLUS-MASS and USAMHI; 130 (UP RT), LC-USZC2-1917; 130 (LO), LC-B8184-10195; 131 (UP RT), LC-USZ62-130838; 132, LC-USZC2-499; 133 (UP), LCGM, CWS00120; 133 (LO), LC-USZ62-100070; 134 (LO), Courtesy MOLLUS-MASS and USAMHI; 135 (UP LE), LC-USZC4-13347; 135 (UP RT), VHS; 136 (LO), LC-USZ62-72090; 136 (UP), Courtesy MOLLUS-MASS and USAMHI; 137 (UP), Fredericksburg and Spotsylvania National Military Park; 138, VHS; 139 (UP), Courtesy USAMHI; 139 (LO), Western Reserve Historical Society; 140, Stratford Hall; 141 (UP), Courtesy Gettysburg National Military Park; 141 (CTR), Chicago Historical Society; 141 (LO), Wadsworth Atheneum Museum of Art, Hartford, CT, The Ella Gallup Sumner and Mory Catin Sumner Collection Fund; 142, LCGM, CW331000; 143, LC-DIG-cwpb-05008; 144 (UP), LC-DIG-cwpbh-03163; 144 (LO), LC-USZC4-976; 145, VHS; 145 (LO), LC-DIG-cwpb-00836; 146 (UP), LC-DIG-ppmsca-08355; 146 (LO), LC Manuscript Division, Papers of Charles Wellington Reed, Volume 3, "Absolution in Wheat Field"; 147 (UP), LC-DIG-cwpb-00911; 147 (LO), LC-DIG-cwpb-07548; 148 (LO), LC-DIG-cwpb-07523; 148 (UP), LC-USZ62-76426; 148-149, State Museum of Pennsylvania, Pennsylvania Historical and Museum Commission; 150 (UP LE), LC-USZ62-13016; 150 (LO), LC-DIG-cwpb-00844; 150-151, LCGM, CW0322000; 150 (UP RT), Kenan Research Center at the Atlanta History Center; 151 (UP RT), LC-DIG-cwpb-01450; 152 (LO LE), Courtesy USAMHI; 152 (LO RT), LC-DIG-cwpb-04734; 153, VHS; 154 (LO), Clements Library, University of Michigan; 155 (UP LE), C. Paul Loane Collection; 155 (UP RT), LC-DIG-cwpb-03433; 156, VHS; 157, NARA; 158 (LO), LC-USZ62-77938; 158 (UP), info + Harvard College Library; 159 (CTR), LC-DIG-cwpbh-03123; 159 (LO), Courtesy of the National Museum of the U.S. Army, Army Art Collection; 160 (LO), Medford Historical Society/CORBIS; 160 (UP), LC-USZ62-90928; 161, LCGM, CW0403000; 161 (LO), Minnesota Historical Society; 162 (UP), Wisconsin Historical Society, ID#4502; 162 (LO), Richard F. Carlile Collection; 163 (UP), Courtesy MOLLUS-MASS and USAMHI; 163 (LO), CORBIS; 164 (LO LE), FMTW; 164 (LO RT), FMTW; 165, LCGM, CW042600.

CHAPTER 4 166-167, LC-B8171-1084; 168 (UP), LC-DIG-CWPB-04066; 168 (LO), NARA; 169 (UP LE), LC-USZ62-79244; 169 (CTR), MOC; 169 (UP RT), Western Reserve Historical Society; 169 (LO LE), Bettmann/CORBIS; 169 (LO RT), LC-DIG-cwpb-02068; 170 (UP), LC-DIG-ppmsca-08366; 170 (LO), LC-USZ62-117668; 171 (UP), LCGM, CWS00003; 171 (LO), LCGM, CW0241000; 172 (LO LE), LC-DIG-cwpb-04407; 172 (LO RT), LC-USZC4-5983; 173, LCGM, CW0498000; 174, Courtesy MOLLUS-MASS and USAMHI; 175 (UP), LCGM, CA00005; 175 (LO), LC-USZC4-5996; 176 (UP), CA000008; 176 (LO), LC-USZ62-53684; 177 (UP), CORBIS; 177 (LO), LC-USZC4-1308; 178 (UP LE), LC-DIG-cwpb-04406; 178-179, LCGM, CA00009; 178 (LO), LC-USZ62-53692; 179 (LO), LC-DIG-cwpb-01187; 180 (LO), LC-DIG-cwpb-01199; 180 (UP), LC-USZ62-104044; 181 (CTR), LC-DIG-cwpb-03543; 182 (UP LE), LC-DIG-cwpb-05517; 182 (UP RT), LC-DIG-cwpb-02790; 182 (LO), LC-DIG-cwpb-03714; 182-183, LCGM, CW0488400; 183 (UP), LC-DIG-cwpb-03851; 184 (UP), FMTW; 184 (LO), Courtesy of the Petersburg Museums, City of Petersburg, VA; 186 (LO), Courtesy MOLLUS-MASS and USAMHI; 186 (UP), LC-DIG-cwpbh-03240; 187 (UP), LCGM, CA000013; 187 (LO), LCGM, CA000016; 188 (UP LE), Cook Collection, Valentine Richmond History Center; 188 (UP RT), Historical Society of Pennsylvania; 188 (LO), LC-DIG-cwpb-04232; 189, VHS; 190 (UP LE), LC-DIG-cwpbh-01010; 190 (CTR), LC-USZC4-5789; 190 (LO), LC-USZC4-5793; 191, VHS; 192 (LE), LC-DIG-cwpbh-03110; 192, LCGM, CA000034; 193, Western Reserve Historical Society; 194 (LO), United States Naval Historical Center; 194-195, VHS; 195 (LO), LC-USZC4-11456; 196 (LO), LC-USZC4-781; 196 (UP), LC-DIG-pga-02396; 197, LCGM, CW0110000; 198 (UP), LC-DIG-cwpb-07136; 198 (UP), NARA; 199, LCGM, CW0128000; 200, LC-B8184-10159; 201 (UP), LC-DIG-cwpb-07052; 201 (LO), Medford Historical Society Collection/CORBIS; 202 (UP), LC-USZ62-79794; 202 (LO), NARA; 202-203, LCGM, CWS00085; 203 (RT), LC-DIG-ppmsca-17648; 204 (LO LE), NARA; 204 (UP), LC-DIG-cwpb-03400; 204-205, LCGM, CWS00040; 205 (UP RT), LC-DIG-cwpb-03628; 206, LC-USZC2-1913; 207, LCGM, CW0049A00; 208 (LO), LC-USZC2-497; 208 (UP RT), Chicago Historical Society; 209 (UP RT), FMTW; 210, Minnesota Historical Society; 210-211, LCGM, CW1012000; 212 (UP), Fairfield Heritage Association/Sherman House Museum; 212 (LO), LC-DIG-ppmsca-09326; 213, VHS; 214, VHS; 215 (UP), Bettmann/CORBIS; 215 (LO), NARA; 216 (UP), LC-DIG-cwpb-03159; 216 (LO), LC-DIG-ppmsca-09919; 217, VHS.

CHAPTER 5 218-219, LC-B817-7798; 220 (UP), LC-DIG-cwpb-07620; 220 (LO), NMAH Smithsonian Institution; 221 (LO LE), LC-USZC4-1157; 221 (LO RT), LC-DIG-cwpb-04324; 221 (UP RT), LC-DIG-cwpb-00468; 221 (UP LE), LCGM, CW02566; 222 (UP), LC-DIG-cwpb-04367; 222 (LO), Courtesy Beverly R. Robinson Collection/U.S. Naval Academy Museum; 223, VHS; 224 (LO), LC-USZ62-116996; 224-225, LCGM, CW0090000; 225 (UP), Courtesy Georgia Archives, Vanishing Georgia Collection, #gor517; 226 (UP), LC-USZ62-14973; 227 (UP), LCGM, CW030900; 227 (LO), LCGM, CW030900; 228 (LO), LC-DIG-cwpb-03713; 228 (UP), LC-DIG-cwpb-02061; 229, VHS; 230-231 (UP), VHS; 230 (LO), LC-DIG-PGA-02695; 231 (LO LE), Cook Collection, Valentine Richmond History Center; 231 (LO RT), LC-USZ62-77935; 232, LCGM, CW0644000; 233 (UP), LC-DIG-cwpb-02548; 233 (LO), LC-USZC4-4593; 234-235, The Library of Virginia; 235 (UP), LC-USZ62-14654; 235 (CTR), LC-DIG-ppmsca-09873; 236 (UP), LCGM, CW0524000; 236 (LO), LC-USZCN4-262; 237 (LO), NGS Image Collection; 238 (LO), LC-PPMSCA10106; 238 (UP), LC-USZC4-5341; 239 (UP), LCGM, CW0674002; 239 (LO), LC-DIG-cwpb-02941; 240 (LO), FMTW; 240 (UP), LC-USZ62-8812; 241 (UP), NARA; 242 (UP), LC-USZ62-11964; 242 (LO), Chicago Historical Society; 243 (LO), Abraham Lincoln Presidential Library & Museum; 244 (LO), LC-USZ62-31933; 244 (UP), Children's Museum of Indianapolis, photography by Wendy Kaveny; 245 (UP), NG Maps; 245 (LO), Rutherford B. Hayes Presidential Center.

APPENDIX AND ENDPAPERS 246 (LO LE), David Wynn Vaughan Collection; 246 (UP RT), C. Paul Loane Collection; 248, David Wynn Vaughan Collection; 249, C. Paul Loane Collection. Endsheets, LCGM, CW0003000.

ADDITIONAL READING

Alexander, Edward P. *Fighting for the Confederacy: The Personal Recollections of General Edward Porter*, ed. Gary W. Gallagher. University of North Carolina Press, 1989.

Beers, Henry P. "A History of the U.S. Topographical Engineers, 1813–1863." *The Military Engineer* 34 (June 1942): 287–91; (July 1942): 348–52.

Blackford, William W. *War Years with Jeb Stuart*. Charles Scribner's Sons, 1945.

Blaisdell, Bob, ed. *The Civil War: A Book of Quotations*. Dover Publications, 2004.

Boatner, Mark M. *The Civil War Dictionary*. David McKay, 1959.

Bosse, David. *Civil War Newspaper Maps: A Historical Atlas*. The Johns Hopkins University Press, 1993.

Boutin, Bernard L. *Civil War Maps in the National Archives*. General Services Administration, 1964.

Civil War Preservation Trust. *Civil War Sites: The Official Guide to the Civil War Discovery Trail*. Globe Pequot, 2007.

Coombe, Jack D. *Gunfire Around the Gulf: The Last Major Naval Campaigns of the Civil War*. Bantam Books, 1999.

Culpepper, Marilyn Mayer. *Trials and Triumphs: Women of the American Civil War*. Michigan State University Press, 1991.

Davis, George B. *Battle at Bull Run: A History of the First Major Campaign of the Civil War*. Doubleday, 1977.

Esposito, Vincent J., ed. *The West Point Atlas of American Wars: 1689–1900*. Praeger, 1959.

Ferrell, Claudine L. *Reconstruction*. Greenwood Press, 2003.

Freeman, Douglas Southall. *Lee's Lieutenants* Scribner, 1998.

Foote, Shelby, and the Editors of Time-Life Books. *The Civil War: A Narrative*. 14 vols. Time-Life Books, 1998–2000.

Gallagher, Gary W. *The Confederate War*. Harvard University Press, 1999.

Griess, Thomas E., ed. *Atlas for the American Civil War*. The West Point Military History Series. Square One Publishers, 2002.

Harsh, Joseph L. *Confederate Tide Rising: Robert E. Lee and the Making of Southern Strategy, 1861–1862*. Kent State University Press, 1998.

Hotchkiss, Jedediah. *Make Me a Map of the Valley: The Civil War Journal of Stonewall Jackson's Topographer*, ed. Archie P. McDonald. Southern Methodist University Press, 1973.

Johnson, Robert Underwood, and Clarence Clough Buell, eds. *Battles and Leaders of the Civil War*. 4 vols. Thomas Yoseloff, 1958.

Kagan, Neil, ed. *Great Photographs of the Civil War*. Oxmoor House, 2003.

Kagan, Neil, and Stephen Hyslop. *Eyewitness to the Civil War: The Complete History from Secession to Reconstruction*. National Geographic, 2006.

Katcher, Philip. *The Civil War Source Book*. Facts on File, 1982.

Keegan, John. *The Military Geography of the American Civil War*. Gettysburg College, 1997.

Long, E. B., with Barbara Long. *The Civil War Day by Day: An Almanac 1861–1865*. Doubleday, 1971.

McElfresh, Earl B. *A Civil War Watercolor Map Series*. McElfresh Map Co., 1994.

McElfresh, Earl B. *Maps and Mapmakers of the Civil War*. Harry N. Abrams, 1999.

McPherson, James M. *The Battle Cry of Freedom*. Ballantine Books, 1989.

McPherson, James M. *Ordeal by Fire: Civil War and Reconstruction*. Alfred Knopf, 1982.

National Archives and Record Service. *A Guide to the Civil War Maps in the National Archives*. Smithsonian Institution Press, 1986.

Nelson, Christopher, and Brian Pohanka. *Mapping the Civil War: Featuring Rare Maps from the Library of Congress*. Library of Congress Classics Series. Starwood Publishing, 1992.

Phillips, David. *Maps of the Civil War: The Roads They Took*. Friedman/Fairfax Publishers, 1998.

Reps, John W. *Bird's Eye Views: Historic Lithographs of North American Cities*. Princeton Architectural Press, 1998.

Robinson, Arthur H., et al. *Elements of Cartography*. Wiley, 1995.

Roper, Peter W. *Jedediah Hotchkiss: Rebel Mapmaker and Virginia Businessman*. White Mane Publishing, 1992.

Sears, Stephen W. *George B. McClellan: The Young Napoleon*. Ticknor & Fields, 1988.

Sears, Stephen W. *Gettysburg*. Houghton Mifflin, 2003.

Sears, Stephen W. *Landscape Turned Red: The Battle of Antietam*. Houghton Mifflin, 1983.

Sears, Stephen W. *To the Gates of Richmond: The Peninsula Campaign*. Houghton Mifflin, 1992.

Smith, Jean Edward. *Grant*. Simon & Schuster, 2001.

Sneden, Robert Knox. *Eye of the Storm: A Civil War Odyssey*, ed. Charles F. Bryan, Jr., and Nelson D. Lankford. Touchstone, 2000.

Southern Historical Society. *Southern Historical Society Papers*. CD-ROM ed. Guild Press/Oliver Computing, 2001.

Stephenson, Richard W. *An Annotated List of Maps and Atlases in the Library of Congress*. Library of Congress, 1989.

Time-Life. *The Civil War*. 28 vols. Time-Life Books, 1983–1987.

Time-Life. *Echoes of Glory: Illustrated Atlas of the Civil War*. Time-Life Books, 1991.

Time-Life. *Voices of the Civil War*. 18 vols. Time-Life Books, 1998–2000.

Trudeau, Noah Andre. *Out of the Storm: The End of the Civil War: April–June 1865*. Little, Brown, 1993.

Tucker, Spencer. *A Short History of the Civil War at Sea*. SR Books, 2005.

United States Naval War Records Office. *The Civil War CD-ROM: Official Records of the Union and Confederate Navies in the War of the Rebellion*. CD-ROM ed. Guild Press/Oliver Computing, 2001.

United States War Department. *The War of the Rebellion: A Compilation of the Official Records of the Union and Confederate Armies*. Government Printing Office, 1880. Reprint, National Historical Society, 1971.

Wagner, Margaret E., Gary W. Gallagher, and Paul Finkelman, eds. *The Library of Congress Civil War Desk Reference*. Simon & Schuster, 2002.

White, Harry Kidder, ed. *Official Records of the Union and Confederate Navies in the War of the Rebellion*. U.S. Government Printing Office, 1922. Reprint, The National Historical Society, 1987.

Woodworth, Steven E., and Kenneth J. Winkle. *The Oxford Atlas of the Civil War*. Oxford University Press, 2004.

Wraight, A. Joseph. *The Coast and Geodetic Survey, 1807–1957: 150 Years of History*. United States Government Printing Office, 1957.

CONTRIBUTORS

Neil Kagan, editor, heads Kagan & Associates, Inc., a firm specializing in innovative illustrated books. Over his 30-year career the former Time-Life Books executive was the guiding spirit behind numerous book series, including the award-winning *Voices of the Civil War* and *Our American Century*. Recently he edited *Great Battles of the Civil War*, *Great Photographs of the Civil War*, and for National Geographic the best-selling *Concise History of the World* and *Eyewitness to the Civil War*.

Stephen G. Hyslop, author, has written books on American and world history, including *Bound for Santa Fe: The Road to New Mexico and the American Conquest, 1806–1848* and for National Geographic *Eyewitness to the Civil War* and *Almanac of World History* (with Patricia S. Daniels). He served as a writer and editor for many volumes on the Civil War and the American West. His articles have appeared in *American History* and the *History Channel Magazine*, and his work has taken him to historical sites and battlefields throughout the country.

Harris J. Andrews is a military historian and consultant specializing in the American Civil War. He has extensive experience researching historical and topographical data to prepare Civil War maps for numerous publications and has contributed to numerous Civil War projects, including *Echoes of Glory* and *Voices of the Civil War*. He was a contributing editor to National Geographic's *Fields of Honor: Pivotal Battles of the Civil War* by Edwin C. Bearss, *From the Front: The Story of War* by Michael S. Sweeney, and *Eyewitness to the Civil War*.

INDEX

Boldface indicates illustrations.

Abolition 206, 220, 239, 244
Agassiz, Louis 22
Alabama **245**
  map 11
Alabama, C.S.S. 194, **194,** 195, **195**
Alexander, E. Porter 139
Alexandria, La. 170, 171
Alexandria, Va. **14,** 32, 76, **168,** 239
  map 76–77
Allatoona Pass, Ga. 200, **200,** 208, **208**
Amelia Courthouse, Va. 234
Ames, Adelbert 222
Anaconda Plan 34, 58, 127
  map 34–35
Anderson, George 106, 146
Anderson, Richard H. 106, 134, 144, 180, 234
Anderson, Robert 31
Andersonville Prison, Ga. 15, 213, 215, **215**
  map 214
Antietam, Battle of (1862) 48, **49,** 62, **98–111**
  maps 98–99, 103–107, 110–111
Appomattox Court House, Appomattox, Va. 220, 235, 237, **237**
  map 236
Appomattox River, Va. 182
Appomattox Station, Va. 234, 237
Archer, James 108, 118, 139
Arizona 29
Arkansas 48, 170
Arkansas (Confederate ram) 126
Armistead, Lewis 89, 149, 151
Ashby, Turner 72, **72,** 74, **75,** 80
Ashby's Harbor, N.C. 62, **62,** 63
Atlanta, Ga. 11, 20, 168, 198–205, **204,** 212
  maps 199, 204–205
Atzerodt, George **218–219**
Averasborough, Battle of (1865) 224
Averell, William 190
Ayres, Romeyn 174, 231
Bachmann, John 14
  maps by 50–51, 66–67, 76–77, 86–87
Bailey, Joseph 170
Baldwin, James **123**
Baltimore, Md. 32, 242
Banks, Nathaniel **170**
  Cedar Mountain 90, 92, **92**
  Red River 170
  Red River map 171
  Shenandoah Valley 68
Barksdale, William 146
Barnes, James 146
Barnwell, S.C. 224
Barton, Clara 108, **108**
Bartow, Francis 40
Baton Rouge, La. 128
Beaufort, S.C. **22,** 224
Beauregard, P. G.T.
  assessment of war 238
  Bermuda Hundred 182
  Bull Run 38, 39, 40, 182
  Charleston 152, 182
  Corinth 112
  military command 114
  Petersburg 182
  portrait **39,** 182, **182**
  Shiloh 56, 182
Bee, Barnard 40
Bell, John 26, 27
Belmont, Battle of (1861) 42
  map 42–43
Benjamin, Judah P. 28
Benning, Henry 108
Bentonville, Battle of (1865) 224, 225, 226, 227
  maps 227
Big Bethel, Battle of (1861) 37, **37**
Birney, David 137
Black soldiers **123,** 128, 152, 184, 233, 240
Blockades
  in Anaconda Plan 34, 35
  Atlantic Coast 37, 44, 58, 222
  blockade-runners 35, 58, 222
  Gulf Coast 58, **59,** 196
Bontecou, Reed Brockway 238
Booth, John Wilkes **218–219,** 219, **238–241**
Boswell, James K. 8, 13
Bragg, Braxton
  Bentonville 226, 227
  Chattanooga 154, 162, 198
  Chickamauga Creek 157
  commanders 186
  Kentucky campaign 48, 114
  Knoxville 164
  Lookout Mountain 160
  military command 114
  Perryville 114, 115, 124, 226
  Shiloh 56
  Stones River 122, 124, 125
  Tullahoma 154
  Vicksburg 124
Branch, Lawrence O'Brien 108
Brandy Station, Battle of (1863) 140, **141**
Brannan, John 158
Breckinridge, John C. 26, 27, 55, 124, 186
Bridgeport, Ala. 154, 160
Brooklyn (ship) 196, 222
Brooks, Preston **19**
Brown, Henry **243**
Brown, John 24
Buchanan, Franklin 196
Buckner, Simon 52
Budd's Ferry, Va. **60,** 61
Buell, Don Carlos 55, 56, **57,** 114, **114,** 115
Buell, George 226
Buford, John 140, 143
Bull Run, First Battle of (1861) 32, 38, 39, 40, 79, 182
  maps 38–39, 40–41
Bull Run, Second Battle of (1862) 90–97, **95**
  maps 94, 96–97
Burnside, Ambrose
  Antietam 62, 98, 102, 108
  Cold Harbor 180
  Falmouth 116
  Fredericksburg 62, 116, 117, 118, 119, 122
  Hatteras Inlet 62
  Knoxville 164, **164**
  military command 62, 116, 122, 134
  Mud March 122, **122**
  North Carolina 62, **62**
  North Carolina map 63
  Petersburg 184
  portrait 62, **62**
  Rappahannock River 116
  Richmond 116
  Roanoke Island 58
  Warrenton **117**
  Wilderness 177
Burnside Bridge, Md. 62, 102, 106, 108, **108–109**
  map 108–109
Butler, Benjamin 37, 66, 180, 182, **244**
Cairo, Ill. 42, 50
  map 50–51
Caldwell, John 146
Carlin, William 125, 226, 227
Carney, William **152**
Carter, Robert 121
Casey, Silas 80
Cedar Creek, Battle of (1864) 193, **193,** 235
  map 192
Cedar Mountain, Battle of (1862) 90, 92, **92, 93**
  map 93
Chamberlain, Joshua L. 144, **144**
Chambersburg, Pa. 110, 140, 188, **188**
Chambliss, John R. **13**
Champion's Hill, Battle of (1863) 131, 132
Chancellorsville, Battle of (1863) 8, 122, 134–139, **135,** 174, **174**
  maps 134–138
Chantilly, Battle of (1862) 80, 98
Charleston, S.C.
  blockade 44
  calls for secession 24
  Confederate defenses 182
  harbor 30
  maps 30, 153
  population 20
  Union attacks **10,** 152
  Union control 224
Charlottesville, Va. 186
Chattanooga, Tenn. 154, 158, **160–162,** 164, 182, 190
  maps 161, 162–163
Cheatham, Benjamin 208
Cherbourg, Fance 194, **195**
  map 195
Cherokee Indians 48
Chew, Robert 72
Chicago, Ill. 242, **242**
Chickahominy River, Va. 79, 80, 82, 85, 86, **86–87**
Chickamauga, Battle of (1863) 154–160, **159,** 162, 190
  maps 154–155, 156, 158, 159
Chicora (ironclad) 152
Chitwood brothers **225**
City Point, Va. 182, 226, **226,** 228
Civil rights 240, 244
Cleburne, Patrick
  Atlanta 204
  Chattanooga 162
  Chickamauga 157, 158
  death 208
  Franklin 208
  Pickett's Mill 200
  Shiloh 55
  Stones River 124
Cobb, Thomas 118, **118**
Cockpit Point, Va. 58, 61
Coffin, Levi 24
Cold Harbor, Battle of (1864) 172, 180, **180, 181,** 182, **221**
  map 180–181
Colquitt, Alfred 106
Colton, Joseph H. 9
Columbia, S.C. 224, 225
Columbus, Ky. 50
Confederate States of America
  capital **28,** 32, 233
  condition of troops 102
  currency **48**
  economy 228
  flags **16–17, 19, 169**
  food shortages 228
  formation 18
  map 28–29
  map deficit 13–14
  military advantages 18
  spies 38, **39**
Conrad's Ferry, Va. **61**
Cooke, John Esten 85
Cooke, Philip St. George 85
Corby, William **146**
Corinth, Miss. 52, 112, **112, 127**
  map 113
Corse, John 208, **208**
Cotton 22, 34
Couch, Darius 80, 134, 139
Cox, Jacob 101, 116
Cox, Samuel 240
Crater, Battle of the (1864) 184, **184**
  map 184–185
Crawford, Samuel 92, 106, 231
Creek Indians 48
Crittenden, Thomas J. 114, 115, 154, 157
Crook, George 186, 190
Cross, Edward 146
Cross Keys, Battle of (1862) 68, 74
Crozet, Claudius 9
Culpeper, Va. 90, 92, 110
Cumberland Landing, Va. **46–47,** 78, **79**
Cumberland River, Ky.-Tenn. 50, 52
Curtis, Newton 222
Custer, George Armstrong 192, **192,** 193, **230,** 231, **236,** 237
Dahl, O. R.
  map by 124–125
Dallas, Battle of (1864) 200, 201
  map 201
Davis, Charles 126
Davis, David 206
Davis, Jefferson **28**
  Atlanta 204
  call for privateers 34
  commanders 79, 114
  determination 28
  Fort Sumter 28, 108
  imprisonment **221,** 238
  inauguration **28**
  Knoxville 164
  military skills 29
  peace talks 220
  Richmond 228, 233
  strategy 168
  Vicksburg 124, 126
Davis, Jefferson C. 227
Davis, Varina **28,** 29
Dawes, Rufus 105
Deep Bottom, Va. 13
Deerhound (ship) 194
Democratic Party 206
Devens, Charles 137
Doles, George 178
Donn, John W. 12
Dorr, F. W. 12
Doubleday, Abner 105
Douglas, Henry Kyd 92, 188
Douglas, Stephen 26, **26,** 27
Douglass, Frederick 24, **24**
Douglass, Marcellus 105
Du Pont, Samuel 44, 152
Dunker Church, Md. 105, 106, **106**
Duryée, Abram 105
Early, Jubal
  Antietam 106
  Cedar Creek 192, 193
  Chancellorsville 135
  Fisher's Hill 193
  Gettysburg 142, 143
  Marye's Heights 139
  Maryland advance 186, 188
  Monocacy 188
  Petersburg 190
  portrait 188, **188**
  Shenandoah Valley 168, 184, 186, 193
  Texas battles 188
  Washington, D.C. 186, 188, 189
  Wilderness 177
  Winchester 190
Eastport, U.S.S. 170
Elections 26, 206
  map 27, 207
Elizabeth City, N.C. 58
Elliott, Stephen 184
Ellsworth, Elmer 32, **32**
Eltham's Landing, Va. 79
Emancipation Proclamation 48, 110, 128
Emerson, Ralph Waldo 48
Evans, Nathan 40
Ewell, Richard
  Cedar Mountain 92
  Cold Harbor 180
  Cross Keys 74
  Gettysburg 142, 143, 145, 149
  Pennsylvania 140
  Sayler's Creek 234, **235**
  Shenandoah Valley 68
  Spotsylvania 178, 179
  Wilderness 174, 175, 176, 177
Ewing, Charles 199
Fair Oaks Station, Va. 80, 82
Fairchild, Harrison 108
Farragut, David **58, 220**
  map 66–67
  Mobile Bay 196, **196**
  New Orleans 58, 66, **66**
  Vicksburg 126, 127
Fayetteville, N.C. 225
Fearing, Benjamin 226
Ferrero, Edward 108, 184
Five Civilized Tribes 48
Five Forks, Battle of (1865) **230,** 231
  map 230–231
Floyd, John 52
Foote, Andrew 50, 52
Ford's Theater, Washington, D.C. 238, 240, **240**
Forrest, Nathan Bedford 114, **169,** 208
Fort Anderson, N.C. 222
Fort Bartow, N.C. 62, 63
Fort De Russy, La. 170
Fort Delaware, Del. 215
Fort Donelson, Tenn. 50, 52, **53,** 182
  maps 50–51, 52–53
Fort Fisher, N.C. 222, **222**
  map 223
Fort Gaines, Ala. 196
Fort Gregg, Va. 233
Fort Henry, Tenn. 50, **50,** 52
  map 50–51, 52–53
Fort Jackson, La. 66, **66**
Fort Johnson, S.C. 31
Fort Mahone, Va. **221,** 228, 233, **233**
Fort McAllister, Ga. 212, 216, **216**
Fort Monroe, Va. **36**
  Jefferson Davis's imprisonment **221**
  maps 36, 76–77
  Richmond advance 76, 78, 79
  Union forces 32, 37, 58
Fort Morgan, Ala. 196
Fort Pickens, Fla. **35**
Fort Pulaski, Ga. 216
Fort Sanders, Tenn. 164, **164**
  map 165
Fort Sedgwick, Va. **166–167**
Fort St. Philip, La. 66, **66**
Fort Stedman, Va. 228
Fort Stevens, Washington, D.C. 188, **188**
Fort Sumter, Charleston, S.C.
  Confederate forces **16–17,** 28, 31, **31,** 108, 182
  map 30
  in ruins **224**
  Union forces **19,** 152, **152**
Foster, John
  maps by 63

Franklin, Battle of (1864) 208, 210
Franklin, William 79, 98, 101, 106, 118
Frederick, Md. 98, **99,** 101, 188
Fredericksburg, Battle of (1862)
map 118–119
Fredericksburg, Va.
Battle of (1862) 48, **49,** 62, **116–120,** 122, **122**
Confederate defenses 134, 135, 140
Union troops 116, 139
Freedmen **221,** 240, 242, 244, 245
Frémont, John 42, 68, 74, **74,** 206
French, Samuel 202
French, William 106, 118
Front Royal, Va. 68
Gaines (ship) 196
Gaines's Mill, Va. 82, 86, **86–87,** 186
map 86–87
Galena (ironclad) **89**
Garland, Samuel 101
Garnett, Richard 72, 149, 151
Garrett, Richard 240
Gaylesville, Ala. 208, **209**
Geary, John 144, 162
Georgia
Confederate defenses 198
maps 11, 224–225
Union troops 168, 170, 212, **212**
Gettysburg, Battle of (1863) **120–123, 140–151**
maps 140–142, 145–147, 150–151
Gettysburg Address 150
Gibbon, John 101, 105
Gillmore, Quincy Adams **10**
Gilmer, Jeremy F. 14
Glendale, Battle of (1862) 82, 86, 89
Goldsborough, Louis 58, 62
Goldsborough, N.C. 224, 225, 226
Gordon (former slave) 128, **128**
Gordon, John B.
Antietam 106
Appomattox **236,** 237
Cedar Creek 192, 193
Fort Stedman 228
Spotsylvania 178
Wilderness 174, 177
Gosport Navy Yard, Va. 32, 37, 58, 64
Govan, Daniel 227
Graham, Charles 146
Grand Review, Washington, D.C. 238, **239**
Granger, Gordon 154, 158, **159**
Grant, Ulysses S. **43, 52, 126, 160, 220**
alcoholism 127
Belmont 42
Cairo 42, 50
campaign against Lee 172–185, **182–183**
Chattanooga 160, 161, 162, 164, 182
chief engineer 10, 53
Cold Harbor 172, 180, **181,** 182
commanders 160, 186, 190
Corinth 112
criticism of 90, 180
Fort Donelson 50, 52, 182
Fort Henry 50, **50**
headquarters 128
ironclads **48,** 50
Lee's surrender 234, 237, **237**
map of Tennessee campaign 50–51
maritime supply line **228**
Memphis 128
military command 112, 168, 172, **172**
Mississippi River 128
perseverance 42, 182
Petersburg **166–167,** 168, 172, 182, 184, 188, 220, 228, 231, 233
physical description 172
Pittsburg Landing 50
presidency 245
press coverage **52**
realism 122
relationship with Meade 172
relationship with Sherman 127, 182, 212, 224
Shenandoah Valley 186, 190
Shiloh 48, 50, 52, 56, **56,** 90, 182
Spotsylvania 172, 178, 179
strategy 42, 190, 198
Tennessee River 50
unconditional surrender 52
Vicksburg 122, 126–133, 182
Virginia campaign 172–185, **182–183**
war conference **226,** 228
Washington, D.C. 188
Wilderness 168, 172, 174, 177, 178
Young's Point 128
Greeley, Horace 34, 206
Greene, George 106
Greenhow, Rose O'Neal 38, **39**
Greensboro, N.C. 233, 238
Gregg, Maxcy 95, 108, 118
Griswoldville, Ga. 212
Grover, Cuvier 95
Hall, Edward S. 14
Halleck, Henry 52, 112, 114
Hammond, James 20
Hampton, Wade 226
Hampton Roads, Va. 37, 58, 64, **64,** 65, 220
map 64–65
Hancock, Winfield Scott 118, 139, 143, 146, 174, 177, 180
Hanover Court House, Va. 79, 85
Hardtack **123**
Hardee, William
Atlanta 204
Bentonville 226
Dallas 200
Georgia defenses 198
Kennesaw Mountain 202
Perryville 114
Polk's death **203**
portrait 226, **226**
Savannah 216
Shiloh 55
Stones River 124
troops **225**
Tullahoma 154
Hardee, Willie 226
Harland, Edward 108
Harpers Ferry, W.Va.
Confederate control 32, 98, 101, 102
John Brown's raid 24
ruined bridge **99**
Union troops 32, 38, 110
Harpers Ferry Road, Md. 102, 108
Harrisburg, Pa. 242
Harrisonburg, Va. 68, 72, 74
Harrison's Landing, Va. 82, 86, 89
Hartford (ship) 196, **197**
Hatcher's Run, Va. 231
Hatteras, U.S.S. 194
Hatteras Inlet, N.C. 44, 58, 62, 63
Hayes, Rutherford B. **100,** 101, 245
Hays, Harry 105
Hazen, William 216
Hazlett, Charles **144**
Heintzelman, Samuel 79, 80, 90, 91, 95
Henry, Judith 40
Herold, David **218–219, 238,** 239, 240, **241**
Heth, Henry 143
Hill, Ambrose Powell **108**
Antietam 98, 102, 108
Cedar Mountain 92
Cold Harbor 180, **180**
Gettysburg 140, 143, 144, 146
Seven Days' Battles 82
Wilderness 174, 177
Hill, Daniel Harvey 80, 82, 89, 101, 106, 160
Hill, Nicodemus 105
Hindman, Thomas 158, 200
Hobart, Harrison 226
Hoke, Robert 227
Holmes, Theophilus 38
Hood, John Bell **208**
Antietam 105, 106
Atlanta 204
baptism 202
Bull Run 97
Chickamauga 157, 158, **158,** 208
Eltham's Landing 79
Franklin 208, 210
Georgia forces 198, 208
Gettysburg 144, 145, 146
Kennesaw Mountain 202
Nashville 210
Resaca 208
Tennessee campaign 208, 212
Hooker, Joseph **105**
Antietam 102, 105, 106
Brandy Station 140
Bull Run 95
Chancellorsville 122, 135, **135,** 137, 139
Chattanooga 160, 161, 162
deliberation 140
denouncement of Burnside 134
Fredericksburg 119, 134
military command 122, 134, **134,** 140
New Hope Church 200, 201
Peninsula campaign 105
Potomac River 61
Seven Pines 80
Hot-air balloons **80**
Hotchkiss, Jedediah **9**
admiration for Turner Ashby 72
background 70
Cedar Creek 192
Chancellorsville 8, 137
friends 8, 13
mapmaking 8, **9,** 10, 15, 68, 70
maps by 71, 73, 75, 175, 176, 178–179, 187, 192
Shenandoah Valley 68
sketchbook **8**
Howard, Oliver
Carolina campaign 224
Chancellorsville 134, 137
Gettysburg 142, 143, 150
march to the sea 212
Pickett's Mill 200, 201
Huger, Benjamin 80, 82
Humphrey, Andrew 146
Hunter, David 40, 186, 193
Hurlbut, Stephen 55
Indian Territory, U.S. 29
Intrepid (hot-air balloon) **80**
Ives, Joseph 82
Jackson, James 32, 114
Jackson, Miss. 131
Jackson, Thomas J. "Stonewall" **40, 69, 123**
Antietam 98, 101, 105
Bull Run 40, 95, 97
Cedar Mountain 90, 92
Chancellorsville 8, 13, 122, 134, **136,** 137
Cross Keys 68
Culpeper 90
death 8, 13, 122, **136,** 137
forage cap **68**
Fredericksburg 118
Gaines's Mill 86
Harpers Ferry 101, 102
Kernstown 68, 72
leadership 70, 72, 92, 202
Manassas Junction 90, **90,** 95
mapmaker 8, **9**
maps 68–69, 71, 137
Marye's Heights 116
McDowell 68
Mechanicsville 86
Port Republic 68, 74
replacement 139, 140
Richmond 68, 72, 85
Seven Days' Battles 82
Shenandoah Valley 8, 68, 70, **70**
troop losses 75
James River, Va.
Confederate forces 79, 184, 233
maritime traffic 37, 58
Union forces 78, 79, 86, 89, **89,** 182, **226, 228**
Jefferson, Thomas 20
Johnson, Andrew 206, 219, 244, **244**
Johnson, Bushrod 158
Johnson, Edward 177, 178
Johnson, Richard 124
Johnston, Albert Sidney 50, 52, 55, **55,** 56, 200
Johnston, Joseph **79**
Atlanta 204
Bentonville 225, 226, 227
Bull Run 38, 40, 79, 182
compared to McClellan 79
Dallas 201
Georgia defenses 168, 172, 198, 204
Kennesaw Mountain 202
Manassas Junction 76
New Hope Church 200, 201
North Carolina defenses 224, 226
Pickett's Mill 200
Polk's death **203**
Raleigh 238
Resaca 200
Richmond 78
Seven Pines 79, 80
surrender 238
troops **225**
Vicksburg 131, 132
Williamsburg 79
Yorktown **225**
Johnston, Robert 177
Joliet, Ill. 242
Jones, Marcellus 174
Jones, Thomas 240
Jones, Walter **235**
Kansas **19,** 26
Kansas-Nebraska Act (1854) 26
Kearny, Philip 80, **80,** 95
Kearsarge, U.S.S. 194, **195**
map of battle 195
Kelly, John 200
Kelly, Patrick 146
Kemper, James 149
Kennesaw Mountain, Battle of (1864) 11, 202, **202**
map 199, 202–203
Kentucky 48, 53
map 50–51
Kernstown, Battle of (1862) 68, 72, **72**
map 73
Kershaw, Joseph 146, 158, 192
Keyes, Samuel 79, 80
Kilpatrick, Hugh Judson 224
Kinston, Battle of (1865) 224
Knoxville, Tenn. 160, 164, **164**
Ku Klux Klan 245, **245**
Lamb, William 222
Lane, James 118
Law, Evander 144
Lawler, Michael 132
Lawrence, James 144
Ledlie, James 184
Lee, Fitzhugh 231, **231,** 237
Lee, Robert E. **82, 140**
Antietam 48, 62, 98, 101, 102, 103, 106, 108, 110
Bull Run 90, 95, 97
Chancellorsville 122, 134, **136,** 137, 139, 140
Chantilly 98
Cold Harbor 172, 180
condition of troops 102
Culpeper Court House 116
Fredericksburg 118, 119, 134, 140
Gaines's Mill 86
Gettysburg 122, 140, 142–146, 149, 150, 151
Grant's campaign against 172–185, **182–183**
leadership style 85, 92
Lynchburg 186
Malvern Hill 89
map of northern Virginia campaign 91
Marye's Heights 116
Maryland advance 48, 98, **98,** 110, 114, 188
Mechanicsville 86
military command 82
Mine Run 172
opinion of McClellan 82
opinion of Pope 90
opinion of Polk 202
Pennsylvania advance 140, 188
Petersburg 168, 172, 182, 184, 190, 220, 228, 231, 233
public opinion of 82, 236
relationship with Early 188
Richmond 68, 79, 82, 86, 182
Sayler's Creek 234
Sharpsburg 98
Shenandoah Valley 186, 193
South Mountain 100, 101, 102
Spotsylvania 172, 178, 179
supply line 231
surrender 220, 234, 237, **237**
Wilderness 168, 172, 174, 177, 178
Lee, Stephen D. 208
Letcher, John 32
Lexington (gunboat) 42, 56, **57**
Libby Prison, Richmond, Va. 15
Lincoln, Abraham
abolitionism 206
Antietam **49**
assassination 219, 220, 238, 239, **240**
debates with Douglas 26
election (1860) 18, 26, 27, **27**
election (1864) 168, 188, 206, **206**
Emancipation Proclamation 48, 110, 128
Fort Sumter 31
frustration with commanders 89, 110, 114
funeral train 242
funeral train map 242–243
Gettysburg Address 150
hat **220**
"house divided" speech 18

INDEX

inauguration 28
Manassas Junction 38, 76
and McClellan 76, 89, 110, **110**
naval blockade 34
offering position to Lee 82
peace talks 220
political cartoon **26, 206**
portraits **18,** 26, **26, 150, 220, 240**
prewar concessions to South 28
public opinion of 180
Reconstruction 240, 244
relationship with Ellsworth 32
replacement of Buell 114
replacement of Burnside 122
replacement of Frémont 42
replacement of Hooker 140
replacement of McClellan 62, 110, 116
replacement of Pope 98
respect for fighting men 64
strategy 168, 190
terms of surrender for Confederacy 237
Texas invasion 170
thanksgiving day proclamation 206
Vicksburg 126, 132
war conference 226, **226,** 228
Washington, D.C. 68, 74, 188
Lincoln, Mary Todd 18, **18, 240,** 242
Lincoln, Robert 242
Lincoln, Rufus 233
Lincoln, Tad 242
Lincoln, Willie 242
Lloyd, James T. 14
Logan, John 202, 204
Longstreet, James **97**
Antietam 98
Blue Ridge Mountains 110
Bull Run 40, 95, 97
Chickamauga 157, 158
Culpeper 90, 110
Fort Sanders 164
Fredericksburg 118
Gettysburg 143, 144, 149
Knoxville 160, 164
Manassas Junction 90
Marye's Heights 116, 118
Pennsylvania advance 140
Seven Days' Battles 82
Seven Pines 80
South Mountain 101
Wilderness 177, 180
Williamsburg 79
Lookout Mountain, Ala.-Ga.-Tenn. 154, **155,** 160, 161, 162, **162**
Loring, William 227
Louisiana 170
Louisiana, C.S.S. 66
Lowe, Thaddeus **80**
Lucas, Fielding 9
Lynchburg, Va. 186
Lynchburg Road, Va. 237
MacArthur, Arthur, Jr. 162, **162**
MacArthur, Douglas 162
Mackenzie, Ranald 231, **231**
Magnus, Charles 14
Magruder, John B. 76, 79, 82, 86, 89
Mahone, William 184
Malvern Hill, Battle of (1862) 82, 86, 89, **89**
map 88
Manassas, C.S.S. 66
Manassas Junction, Va. 76, **90,** 95
see also Bull Run
Mansfield, Joseph 106, **106–107**
Mapmaking 9–14, 233
instruments **9, 12**
Maps
Anaconda Plan 34–35
Andersonville Prison 215
Antietam 98–99, 103–111
Appomattox Court House 236
Army of the Potomac operations 234–235
Atlanta 199, 204–205
Belmont 42–43
Bentonville 227
Booth's escape route 241
Bull Run (First) 38–39, 40–41
Bull Run (Second) 94, 96–97
Cedar Creek 192
Cedar Mountain 93
Chancellorsville 134–138
Charleston 30, 153
Chattanooga 161, 162–163
Cherbourg, France 195
Chickamauga 154–155, 156, 158, 159
Cold Harbor 180–181
Corinth 113
Dallas 201
elections 27, 207
Five Forks 230–231
Fort Donelson 52–53
Fort Fisher 223
Fort Henry 52–53
Fort Monroe 36
Fort Sanders 165
Fredericksburg 118–119
Gaines's Mill 86–87
Georgia 202–203, 224–225
Gettysburg 140–142, 145–148, 150–151
Hampton Roads 64–65
Kennesaw Mountain 202–203
Kentucky 50–51
Kernstown 73
Lincoln's funeral train 242–243
Malvern Hill 88
Manassas Junction 38–39, 40–41, 94, 96–97
march to the sea 213
McClellan's campaigns 76–79
Nashville 210–211
New Hope Church 201
North Carolina 63, 224–225
Peninsula campaign 76–79
Perryville 114
Petersburg 182–183, 184–185, 229, 232
Pickett's Mill 201
Port Republic 75
Port Royal Sound 44–45
Potomac River 60
railroads 20–21
Reconstruction 245
Red River 171
Richmond 32–33, 76–77, 232
Savannah 217
secession 28–29
Seven Days' Battles 83
Seven Pines 80–81
Shenandoah Valley 68–69, 71, 187
Sherman's campaigns 202–205, 213, 224–225
Shiloh 54–55, 56–57
slavery 22–23
South (region) 58–59, 171
South Carolina 224–225
South Mountain 100–101
Spotsylvania 178–179
Stones River 124–125
Stuart's mission 84–85
Tennessee 50–51, 208–209
Underground Railroad 25
Vicksburg 126–127, 129, 130–131, 133
Virginia 32–33, 91, 173
Washington, D.C. 32–33, 189, 239
Wilderness 175, 176
Winchester 190
Yazoo River 129
Marbaker, Thomas 150
March to the sea (1864) 208, 212
map 213
Marye's Heights, Va. 116, 118, 139
Maryland 9, 32, 48, 98, 186, 188
Maximilian, Emperor (Mexico) 170
McArthur, John 210, **210**
McCausland, John 188
McClellan, Ellen **76**
McClellan, George **76**
Alexandria 61
Antietam 48, 62, 102, 103, 105, 106, 108, 110
balloon reconnaissance **80**
deliberations 42, 79, 102
division commanders 80, 89
Fort Monroe 61, 79
Frederick 98, **99**
Gaines's Mill 86
Harrison's Landing 86, 89
and Lincoln 76, 89, 110, **110**
Malvern Hill 89, **89**
military command 62, 98, 110, 116
Oak Grove 86
opinion of Lee 82
opposition to Emancipation Proclamation 110
Peninsula campaign **12, 83,** 105
Potomac River 61, 110
presidential nomination 206
Richmond 47, 48, 58, 62, 68, 74
Richmond maps 76–77, 78–79
Seven Days' Battles 86
Sharpsburg 110, **110**
South Mountain 100, 101
supply lines 78, 85, 86
topographers **12**
McClernand, John 55, 56, 132
McCook, Alexander 154
McCown, John 124
McDowell, Battle of (1862) 68
McDowell, Irvin **39**
Bull Run (First) 38, 39, 40
Bull Run (Second) 95
Port Republic 74
replacement 42
Shenandoah Valley 68
Washington, D.C. 76
McLaws, Lafayette 106, 139, 144, 146, **147**
McLean, Wilmer 237, **237**
McPherson, James B. **201**
Atlanta 204
Champion's Hill 131
Dallas 200
death 204
as engineer 10
Georgia campaign 198
Kennesaw Mountain 202
map by 52–53
Vicksburg 131, 132
McRae, D. K. 106
Meade, George **143**
Antietam 105
Chancellorsville 134
as engineer 10
Fredericksburg 118
Gettysburg 142–146, 149, 151
military command 140, 172
Mine Run 172
relationship with Grant 172
South Mountain 101
Spotsylvania 179
Wilderness 174
Mechanicsville, Battle of (1862) 82, 86
Memphis, Tenn. 20, 112, 126, 128
Merrimack, U.S.S. 58, 61, 64
Merritt, Wesley 190
Mexican War 20, 80
Mexico, Gulf of 58, **59,** 196
Miles, David 226
Milledgeville, Ga. 212
Missionary Ridge, Tenn. 160, 161, 162
Mississippi River and Valley, U.S.
Anaconda Plan 58, 127
blockades 34, 35
canal-building efforts **128**
map of Farragut's path 66–67
Union forces 50, 66, 132
Vicksburg campaign 122, 128
Missouri 20, 24
Missouri Compromise 20
Mitchell, John 226
Mitchell, Samuel
maps by 40–41
Mobile, Ala. 20
Mobile Bay, Ala. 196
map 197
Monitor, U.S.S. 58, 64, **64,** 65, **65,** 79
Monocacy, Battle of (1864) 186, 188
Montgomery, Ala. **28**
Montgomery, William **163**
Mooney, Thomas **38**
Morgan (ship) 196
Morgan, John Hunt 114, 226, 227
Morris Island, S.C. **10,** 152, **152**
Mosby, John 186, **186,** 192, 193, **193**
Mower, Joseph 226
Mud March (1863) 122, **122**
Mudd, Samuel 240
Murray, George **123**
Napoleon III, Emperor (France) 170
Nashville, Tenn. 20, 50, 52, 124, **169,** 208, 210, **210**
map 210–211
Nashville & Chattanooga Railroad 160
Negley, James 124, **125**
New Bern, N.C. 58, 62
New Hope Church, Battle of (1864) 200, 201, **201**
map 199, 201
New Ironsides (ironclad) 153
New Market, Battle of (1864) 186
New Mexico 29, 48
New Orleans, La. 20, 21, **21,** 58, 66, 126
map 66–67
New York, N.Y. 20, **20,** 21, **122,** 242
Norfolk, Va. 37, 58, 64, 79
North (region), U.S. 20, 21, 236
North Anna River, Va. 180, **180**
North Carolina 62, 221, 224–227
maps 63, 224–225
Oak Grove, Va. 82, 86
Orange Turnpike, Va. 139, 174, 175, 176, 177
Ord, Edward O. C. 132, 237
Orth, John G.
maps by 165
Osterhaus, Peter 162
Paducah, Ky. 50
Paine, William 139
Palmer, John M. 124
Pamlico Sound, N.C. 44, 58, 62, 63
Pamunkey River, Va. 78, 79, 85
map 84–85
Patterson, Robert 38
Peace talks 221
Pemberton, John C. 131, **131,** 132, 133
Pender, William 143
Pendleton, George 206
Peninsula campaign (1862) **12,** 76–89, **80, 83,** 105
maps 76–77, 78–79
Perryville, Battle of (1862) 114, 115, **115,** 226
map 114
Petersburg, Va.
Confederate forces 182, **182,** 190, 222, 228
Crater, Battle of the 184, **184**
maps 182–185, 229, 232
population 20
siege 172, 182, 220, 228, **233**
Union forces **166–167,** 168, **228,** 231, 233
weapons **183**
Pettigrew, J. Johnston 149
Philadelphia, Pa. 242
Pickens, Francis 31
Pickett, George 144, **148,** 149, 231
Pickett's Mill, Battle of (1864) 200, 201
map 201
Pillow, Gideon 52
Pinkerton, Allan 76
Pirates 194
Pittsburg Landing, Tenn. 50, 55, 56, **56, 57**
Pleasant Hill, Battle of (1864) 170, 171
Pleasants, Henry 184
Pleasonton, Alfred 140
Pocahontas, U.S.S. **59**
Poe, Orlando
map by 204
Polk, Leonidas
background 42
Belmont 42
death 202, **203**
Georgia defenses 198
Kennesaw Mountain 202
Perryville 114
Pine Mountain 202
portrait **43,** 202, **202**
Shiloh 55
Tullahoma 154
Polk, William 202
Pope, John 90, **90,** 92, 95, 97, 98
map of Virginia campaign 91
Port Hudson, La. 132
Port Republic, Battle of (1862) 68, 74
map 75
Port Royal Sound, S.C. 44, **44,** 58
map 44–45
Porter, David Dixon **130, 220**
Fort Fisher 222, **222**
New Orleans 66
Potomac Flotilla 61
Red River 170, **170**
Vicksburg 128, **130,** 131, 132
war conference **226**
Porter, Fitz-John 86, 90, 95, 97
Potomac River, U.S.
Booth's crossing 240
Confederate forces 61, **61,** 98, **98,** 102, 110, **140,** 186
maps 60, 76–77
Union forces 33, 58, 61, **61,** 76, 110
Powell, Lewis **218–219,** 240
Prentice, Sartell 174
Prentiss, William 55, 56, **56**
Preston, William 158
Price, Sterling 112, 114
Prisoners of war 15, **75, 151,** 190, 213, 215, **215**
Pulaski, Tenn. 208
Radical Republicans 206, 244, **244**
Railroads 9, 20, 21
map 20–21
Raleigh, N.C. 238
Ramseur, Stephen 192, 193, **193**

Ransoms 188
Rapidan River, Va. 32, 172, **172,** 174
Rappahannock River, Va.
Booth's crossing 240
difficulty of crossing 32
Union forces 76, 90, **116,** 118, 134, **135,** 139, **139**
Rathbone, Henry **240**
Reconstruction 240, 244–245
map 245
Red River campaign, La. (1864) 168, 170, **170**
map 171
Reno, Jesse 97, 101
Republican Party 26, 206, 244, **244**
Resaca, Ga. 198, 200, 208
map 199
Reynolds, John 134, 135, **135,** 143, 158
Richardson, Israel 106, **107**
Richmond, Va.
call for attacks on 34
Confederate capital 32, 172
Confederate forces (1862) 68, 79, 82, 86
Confederate forces (1863) 140
Confederate forces (1864) 13, 184
Confederate forces (1865) 220, 228, 233, **233,** 234
freedmen **221,** 233
James River access route 37
maps 13, 32–33, 76–77, 78–79, 232
population 20
railroads 180, 182
Union forces (1862) 47, 48, 58, 68, 76–77, 79, 116
Ricketts, James 40, 105
Ringgold, Ga. 162, 198
River Queen (steamboat) 220, **226**
Roanoke Island, N.C. 58, 62, **62,** 63
Robinson, James 226
Rocky Face Ridge, Battle of (1864) 198
map 199
Rodes, Robert 101, 137, 142, 143, 177, 191
Rodman, Isaac 108
Rosecrans, William
Chattanooga 154, 158, 160
Chickamauga 157, 158, 162
Corinth 112
deliberation 154
Lookout Mountain 160
military command 114, 160
Nashville 124
popularity **154**
Stones River 124, 125
Tullahoma 154
Ruffin, Edmund 31, **31**
Sabine Crossroads, Battle of (1864) 170, 171
Savage's Station, Battle of (1862) 82, 86, **86**
Savannah, Ga. 20, 44, 212, 213, 216, **216**
map 217
Sayler's Creek, Battle of (1865) 234, **235**
Schell, Frank 105
Schofield, John
Atlanta 204
Carolina campaign 224, 226
Franklin 208
Georgia campaign 198
Kennesaw Mountain 202
Kinston 224
Nashville 208, 210
Scott, Dred 26
Scott, Winfield 34, **34,** 37, 58, 127
Secession
calls for 24
map 28–29
Northern sympathizers 32
reasons for 18, 20, 22, 28
by state 26, 28
Sedgwick, John
Antietam 106
Chancellorsville 134, 135, **139**
death 166, 180, 191
Gettysburg 145
Marye's Heights 139
Spotsylvania 166, 180
Wilderness 174, 176, 177
Selma (gunboat) 196
Semmes, Paul 146
Semmes, Raphael 194, **194**
Seven Days' Battles (1862) 82, 86, 89
map 83
Seven Pines, Battle of (1862) **49,** 79, 80
map 80–81
Seward, William 219, 220, 239, 240
Sharpsburg, Md. 98, **98,** 101, 102, 108, 110, **110**
Shaw, Robert Gould 152
Shenandoah River, Va. 74, **74,** 168, 192, 193
Shenandoah Valley, Va.
campaign (1862) 68–75, **70**
campaign (1864) 168, 186–193
Confederate forces 8, 98, 102, 110, 140, 184
maps 68–69, 71, 187
rail link to Richmond 180, 182
Sheridan, Philip
Appomattox 237
Cedar Creek 192, 193
Chattanooga 162, 190
Chickamauga 162, 190
cutting Southside Railroad 233
execution of captives 192, 193
Fisher's Hill 193
Five Forks **230,** 231
military command 231
Namozine Church 234
Perryville 114
portrait 190, **190, 220**
Rice's Station 234
Sayler's Creek 234
Shenandoah Valley 168, 182, 190
Stones River 124, 190
total war philosophy 190, 193
Winchester **190**
Yellow Tavern 180
Sherman, Thomas **212**
Sherman, William T. **126, 198, 220**
armistice talks 238
Atlanta 11, 168, 200, 204, **205,** 206
atlas **11**
Bull Run 40
Carolina campaign 220, 224–227, 238
Chattanooga 160, 161, 162
Chickasaw Bluffs 126
coordinated military campaigns 198
Corinth 112
Dallas 200, 201
Georgia campaign 168, 170, 172, 198–205
Kennesaw Mountain 202
Knoxville 164
maps of campaigns 202–203, 213, 224–225
march to the sea 208, **212,** 212–217
nervous breakdown 127
New Hope Church 200, 201
Pickett's Mill 200
realism 122
relationship with Ewing 199
relationship with Grant 127, 182, 212
Resaca 200
Savannah 216, **216**
Shiloh 55, 56
with son **212**
supply line **198,** 208
total war philosophy 190, 205
Vicksburg 126, 128, **128,** 131, 132
victory parade 238, 239
war conference 226, **226**
Shields, James 68, 72, 74
Shiloh, Battle of (1862) 48, **50–57,** 182
maps 54–55, 56–57
Shreveport, La. 170, 171
Shy, William 210
Sickles, Daniel **146**
Chancellorsville 134, 137, 139
Gettysburg 144, 145, 146
Potomac River security 61, **61**
Sigel, Franz **97,** 186
Sims, Robert **236**
Slavery 18, 28, 220, 244
map 22–23
Slaves
as contraband 37, **37,** 78, **79**
daily life **18, 22–23**
fugitive slaves 24, **25,** 28
population 22
rebellions 28, 34
treatment 22, **22,** 24, **24, 128**
and Union Army 62
Slocum, Henry 134, 212, 224, 226
Small, Abner 177
Smith, Andrew Jackson 210
Smith, Charles Ferguson 52, **52,** 114
Smith, Edmund Kirby 40, 114, 238
Smith, Gustavus 80
Smith, W. S. 115
Smith, William F. 160, 161, 180
Sneden, Robert Knox
diary 15, **15**
maps by 15, 30, 60, 80–81, 88, 91, 93, 94, 100–101, 118–119, 138, 145, 153, 156, 189, 191, 195, 213, 214, 223, 229, 230–231
Potomac River 61
as prisoner of war 15, 213, 215, 216
sketches by **93**
Snodgrass Hill, Ga. 158
map 159
South (region), U.S. 20, 21, 28, 58–59, 127, 171
South Carolina
map of Sherman's campaign 224–225
secession 20, 24, 26, 28
Sherman's campaign 221, 224–227
South Mountain, Battle of (1862) 98, **100,** 101, 102
map 100–101
Southside Railroad 228, 231, 233, 234
Spotsylvania, Battles of (1864) 166, **169,** 172, **178–180,** 191
map 178–179
Springfield, Ill. 242, 243
Stannard, George 149
Stanton, Edwin 154, 242
Starke, William 105, **105**
Starkweather, John 114, **115**
Steedman, James 158, **159**
Stephens, Alexander 220, 244
Steuart, George 174
Stevens, Thaddeus 188, **244**
Stevenson, Ala. 160
Stevenson, Carter 162
Stewart, Alexander 200, 201, 208
Stiles, Robert **235**
Stone Bridge, Va. 40, **41,** 96
Stone House, Va. 40, **41**
Stones River, Battle of (1862-1863) 122, 124, **124,** 125, **125,** 190
map 124–125
Stuart, James Ewell Brown **85**
Antietam 103
Brandy Station 140
Bull Run 97
Catlett's Station 90
Chancellorsville 137, 139
Gettysburg 140
Pennsylvania advance 110, 140
reconnaissance map 84–85
reconnaissance mission 82, 85
Spotsylvania 178
Yellow Tavern 180
Sumner, Charles **19**
Sumner, Edwin "Bull" 79, 80, 98, 106
Supreme Court, U.S. 26
Surratt, John 219, **238,** 239, 240
Surratt, Mary **218–219,** 240
Surrattsville, Md. 240
Swann, Oswell 240
Taliaferro, William 226
Taylor, Richard 170
Tecumseh (monitor) 196
Tennessee
campaign (1864) 208–211
maps 50–51, 208–209
readmission to the Union 244
Tennessee, C.S.S. 196, **197**
Tennessee River, U.S. 50, 55, 56, **56,** 154, 160, 162
Terry, Alfred 222, **222**
Texas 48, 170, 171
Thom, George
map by 56–57
Thomas, George **159, 220**
Atlanta 204
Chattanooga 160, 161, 162
Chickamauga 158
Georgia campaign 198
map by 115
Nashville 208, 210
New Hope Church 200
Tennessee campaign 212
Tullahoma 154
Toombs, Robert 108
Traubel, M. H. 14
Tubman, Harriet 24, **25**
Tullahoma, Tenn. 154
Tyler (gunboat) 42, 56, **57**
Tyler, Daniel 40
Underground Railroad 24
map 25
United States
call for volunteers 32, 38
map 28–29
military advantages 18
naval superiority 34
Upton, Emory 178
U.S. Colored Infantry **123**
U.S. Constitution 18, 28, 220, 244
Valley Turnpike, Va. 68, 71, 72, 186, **186**
Van Brunt, Henry 64
Van Cleve, Horatio 115, 124, 157
Van Dorn, Earl 112, **112,** 114
Vandever, William 226
Veazey, Wheelock 149
Vicksburg, Miss. 122, 124, **126–133**
maps 126–127, 129–131, 133
Vincent, Strong 144
Virginia
breakaway of West Virginia 29
Confederate volunteers **32**
divided loyalties 85
mapmaking 9, 14
maps 32–33, 91, 173
secession 32, 188
Virginia, C.S.S. 58, 64, **64,** 65
Virginia Central Railroad 68, 79, 85
Von Buchholtz, Ludwig 9
Voting rights 240, 244, 245
Wabash, U.S.S. **44**
Walker, James 178
Walker, John 106
Wallace, Lew 188
Wallace, W. H. L. 55
Walthall, Edward 162
Ward, Hobart 145
Warren, Gouverneur
Bull Run 96, 97
Cold Harbor 180, **180**
Five Forks 231
Gettysburg 144
Wilderness 174, 177
Warrenton, Va. 110, **117**
Warrenton Turnpike, Va. 38, 40, 95, 96, **96,** 97
Washington, D.C.
abolition 239
Confederate threats 186, 188
defenses **33,** 76, 172, 188, 239
hospitals 238
maps 32–33, 189, 239
victory parade 238, **239**
Watkins, Sam 202
Waud, Alfred
sketches by 15, **37, 61, 72, 89, 98, 172, 190**
Weed, Stephen 144
Weisiger, David 184, **184**
Welles, Gideon 180
West Point, Va. 79
West Virginia 29
Western & Atlantic Railroad 198, 200, 202, 208
Wheat, Roberdeau 40
Wheaton, Frank 188
Wheeler, Joseph 154, 212
White House Landing, Va. 78, **84,** 85
Wilcox, Cadmus 146
Wilder, John 154, **155**
The Wilderness, Va. 8, 32, 134, 168, 172, **172, 174–178,** 180
maps 175, 176
Willard, George 146
Willcox, Orlando 108
Williams, Alpheus 106
Williams, Thomas 126
Williamsburg, Battle of (1862) 79, 80
Wilmington, N.C. 222, 224
Winchester, Va. 38, 68, 79, 110, 140, 186, 190, **190**
map 190
Winder, Charles Sydney 92, **92**
Winder, John 215
Winslow, John 194
Wirz, Henry 215
Wofford, William 146
Wood, Thomas 115, 158, **158,** 162, 210
Woodstock, Va. **75**
Worden, John 64, **64**
Wright, Ambrose 184
Wright, Horatio 180, 188, 191, 193, 234
Yazoo River, Miss. 126, 128, 129
York River, Va. 78, 79
Yorktown, Va. **12,** 76, 78, **78,** 79, **79**
Zook, Samuel 116, 146

LYNCHBURG
LEXINGTON
STAUNTON
COVINGTON
APPOMATTOX C.H.
CUMBERLAND C.H.
MANCHESTER
RICHMOND
PETERSBURG
JAMES R.
NEW KENT C.H.
CHARLES CITY C.H.
WAVERLY
PRINCE GEORGE C.H.
WEST POINT
WILLIAMSBURGH
YORK R.
YORKTOWN
GLOUCESTER C.H.
GLOUCESTER
SALUDA
URBANNA
SUFFOLK
SMITHFIELD
BACON CASTLE
JAMES RIVER
NANSEMOND R.
WARWICK C.H.
BIG BETHEL
HAMPTON
NEWPORT NEWS PT
HAMPTON ROADS
CRANEY I.
TANNERS PT
SEWALLS POINT
DISMAL
DRUMMONDS LAKE
SWAMP
VIRGINIA CITY
PORTSMOUTH
FT NORFOLK
NAVY YARD
NORFOLK
RIP RAPS
OLD PT COMFORT
FT MONROE
MOBJACK BAY
MATHEWS C.H.
CHESAPEAKE BA
PRINCESS ANNE C.H.
LONDON BR.
BACK B.
C. CHARLES
FISHERMANS I.
CAPEVILLE
EASTVILLE
BROAD WATER
ATLANTIC OCEAN